ness, Arts

HOW TO cheat IN Adobe Animate CC

The art of design and animation

HOW TO cheat IN Adobe Animate CC

The art of design and animation

Myra Ferguson • Chris Georgenes

CRC Press
Taylor & Francis Group
Boca Raton London New York

CRC Press is an imprint of the
Taylor & Francis Group, an **informa** business
A FOCAL PRESS BOOK

CRC Press
Taylor & Francis Group
6000 Broken Sound Parkway NW, Suite 300
Boca Raton, FL 33487-2742

Printed on acid-free paper

International Standard Book Number-13: 978-1-4987-9738-2 (Paperback)
978-1-138-70713-9 (Hardback)

Visit the Taylor & Francis Web site at
http://www.taylorandfrancis.com

and the CRC Press Web site at
http://www.crcpress.com

Printed and bound in the United States of America by Sheridan

Contents

Foreword

Creativity really reaches its apex when it involves as many senses as possible—everything from visuals to animation to interactivity, which is what has drawn myself, and longtime friend and Adobe Community Professional Myra Ferguson to Adobe Animate CC. No other app really gives users the flexibility to create to their hearts' content. You can create whatever you want. Add some animation to capture eyeballs. And then add some interactivity to take things to really blow minds. It really is where all the fun happens.

It's fun to see how the software has evolved, starting out as Flash and now becoming more robust but so easy to work with as you will find out. It has evolved with the times from publishing to the SWF format to now being platform agnostic—HTML, SWF, SVG, WebGL, to name a few. What other app has that flexibility? You want to create and add some animation? Done. You want some interactivity? Done. You want to publish to HTML and SWF? Done. You want it to make you a sandwich? It can't because it's software.

I'm really excited for you to dive into this book because not only is the subject fantastic, it's authored by one of the kindest, smartest, and most genuine people you'll meet. I've known Myra for over a decade since she's been an integral part of the Adobe Community, and we've worked together at a number of events and speaking engagements. This book attests to her knowledge, and I want to attest to her personally as being a quality individual who just makes you feel good after being around her. So I hope this book fills your brain with knowledge and feels like a warm hug from Myra. Because both are really what makes life wonderful. Creativity and hugs!

Now go create!

Paul Trani
Senior Creative Cloud Evangelist
Adobe Systems Inc.

Acknowledgments

I especially want to thank Chris Georgenes. Without him, I wouldn't have had the opportunity to work on this book. He's a talented animator, an inspiring mentor, and a great friend.

Special Thanks to

Scott Ferguson for being a wonderful husband. Thank you for believing in me, for all your help and support, and for all times we laughed so hard that we cried.

Thomas Ferguson for being an amazing son. I'm so proud of you. Your energy and excitement are contagious.

Ruth Ferguson, my mother-in-law, who is one of the most stylish women I know and whose boundless encouragement means the world to me.

Roger Osborn whose frequent calls to check on me and this book got me to the finish line.

I'd Also Like to Thank

The Boulder Valley Adobe User Group for welcoming previews of material for this book at our meetings.

The Adobe Community, especially Tricia Lawrence who has helped me on numerous occasions and encourages me to think creatively.

Ajay Shukla and the rest of the Adobe Animate Team for bringing new life to an awesome program.

Sean Connelly and Jessica Vega from Focal Press for helping make this book a reality.

Thomas Benner and Carlotta Eaton for giving me your feedback.

Anissa Thompson for helping review materials and for providing guidance while I navigated this bumpy road.

Monarch High School Marching Band and Director, Chuck Stephen, whose band direction has provided much artistic inspiration.

Gentry Middle School teacher, Caitlin Cunningham, for your captivating STEM projects.

Thank You for Your Friendship and Encouragement

Paul Trani, Deke McClelland, Colleen Wheeler, Barb Binder, Melissa Piccone, James Williamson, JP Revel, Mark and Sheila Spangler, and Elizabeth Danekind.

About Using This Book: A Cheat Sheet for You

Why Cheat?

Honestly, I'm not all that comfortable with the word "cheat," but pretty much everything around us can be used in some way either for good or for evil. In the case of cheating, the evil side should be pretty obvious. But there are actually good types of cheating: video game cheats that give you special abilities or open up other places for you to explore, cheating death, cheating on your diet (however results may vary), the adorable Homestar Runner character known as The Cheat, or what is probably the most applicable—the cheat sheet. I remember in college being allowed to make cheat sheets for quizzes and exams. It was a single page that we were allowed to completely fill with notes to use during a test. Preparing the sheets was part of studying. The process of learning how to cheat in Adobe Animate CC is similar. By checking out the cheats, you will actually learn more about the program and discover techniques and workflows that help to make you more efficient at producing your work.

The Passing of the Torch

So much has happened since the last edition of *How to Cheat in Adobe Flash*. For starters, Adobe renamed the application to Animate and reinvigorated it with a ton of new features. But this book series itself has also gone through a change. You might have noticed an additional name on the cover. That's me. I'm Myra. Flash, now Animate, has been a huge part of my career, and I'm truly honored to be entrusted with bringing you new ideas and examples for using it.

I met the series author, Chris Georgenes, at a function for Adobe Community Leaders at Adobe MAX several years ago, and we have been friends ever since. I helped tech edit his book *Pushing Pixels* (Georgenes 2013) and have been his tech editor on the last two editions of *How to Cheat in Adobe Flash*. Now we're switching roles—I'm writing and updating content, and he's tech editing for me. Oh, and in his newly found spare time, he's finally living his dream as a drummer.

Using this Book

This book is set up the same way as before with a double-spread to make it easier for you to keep it open and work through step-by-step. Although the exercises are divided by topic and to some extent increase in complexity, they illustrate individual, self-contained techniques. So you could work your way through this book from the beginning to the end, but you can also jump around anywhere in this book to grab a technique that solves a specific problem for you.

Previous examples have been reviewed and updated or replaced. I've created new ones to demonstrate recently added features and current trends. As an Adobe User Group Manager, I regularly prepare presentations with samples to illustrate how new features work and to demonstrate techniques. I'm using a similar approach to create exercises for you. Like Chris, I'm also wrapping up each chapter with an Interlude to share some of my experiences and insights.

Terminology

Even though the name has changed, the basic features that were found in Flash continue to be used in Animate. You'll create objects, convert them into either Graphic or Movie Clip symbols, and put instances of them on the Stage where they will appear as keyframes in the Timeline. If you are familiar with those terms and the basics of Animate, then you'll be able to understand the terminology used in this book.

Download Example Files

You can find files for the examples in this book that are indicated by the download icon in a downloadable zip file at www.crcpress.com/How-to-Cheat-Adobe-Animate-CC/Ferguson-Georgenes/p/book/9781498797382. Some exercises start from scratch, so you won't need a start file for those. Otherwise the zip file includes a START and FINISH version to help.

Beyond this Book

If you have any questions about this book, post your questions to www.facebook.com/htcianimate. You're welcome to post your designs and animations here, too.

Follow Me on Twitter

You can also reach me on Twitter @myraferguson. I usually tweet about interesting projects, Adobe-related topics, and various digital media events.

Reference

Georgenes, Chris. Pushing pixels: secret weapons for the modern animator. New York: Focal Press, Taylor & Francis Group, 2013.

Introduction

I usually refer to myself as a Multimedia Designer/Developer for lack of a better title. Maybe I'm also an Interdisciplinary Digital Media Artist/Animator, Interactive Consultant, and Author. Can you see the problem? It gets a little wordy trying to describe all of the different roles I have. It might be better to say that I'm more of a high-level digital media generalist. Whatever the designation, my background not only includes animation but also interactive software, video, motion graphics, eLearning, advertising, web design, and graphic design. It's my hope that this wide range of previous experience translates into examples that provide you with inspiration and solutions for whatever your role or project is.

Following in the tradition of the *How to Cheat* series, I'm writing with the understanding that you have some basic knowledge of how Animate works with regard to the various parts of the interface, how the Timeline works, and what Movie Clip and Graphic symbols are. If you need the basics, the Help docs are a great source of information. Adobe offers a number of free videos to get you started on their website at helpx.adobe.com/animate.html. I'd also recommend checking out your local Adobe User Group to learn more and connect with other users who are learning just like you. Find the Adobe User Group nearest to you at www.adobe.com/communities/user-groups.html. I'd also recommend making use of the Adobe Forums at forums.adobe.com to find FAQs, search for answers, and post your own questions.

If you're having trouble figuring out a technique, you can tweet your question to me @htcianimate or ask me on Facebook at www.facebook.com/htcianimate.

I hope you enjoy this book, and I can't wait to see what it may help or inspire you to create.

An
Adobe Creative Cloud
Animate CC
2017 Release
© 1993-2016 Adobe Systems Incorporated and its licensors. All Rights Reserved. See the legal notices in the about box.
Artwork by Daniele De Nigris
See About screen for details
Initializing Fonts...

■ Rewritten, renamed, and now released, Adobe Animate CC offers tons of new tools and output options for animators, designers, and interactive developers. Animate CC has everything you loved about Flash Professional and more, and it keeps getting better. Find a renewed sense of creativity with Animate CC.

1 What's New in Animate CC

A CLOSER LOOK AT ADOBE ANIMATE CC REVEALS SO MUCH more than just a name change from Flash Professional. The release of Animate CC in February 2016 delivered a smorgasbord of new drawing tools, improvements to existing tools, integration with the Creative Cloud, and a cornucopia of output options. The frequent updates through the Creative Cloud also served up some goodies since *How to Cheat in Adobe Flash CC®* was written, and Adobe keeps bringing out more. As the Animate team continues to produce, this list just keeps growing. So let's highlight some of the most significant additions and dig in!

Vector Art Brushes

SIMILAR TO Art Brushes in Illustrator, the new vector art brushes in Animate open up a world of creativity by applying a vector shape to a path. Use them to access specific shapes to be applied to a custom stroke, to re-create the appearance of various mediums, to generate banners or dividers, or to imagine your own creative uses.

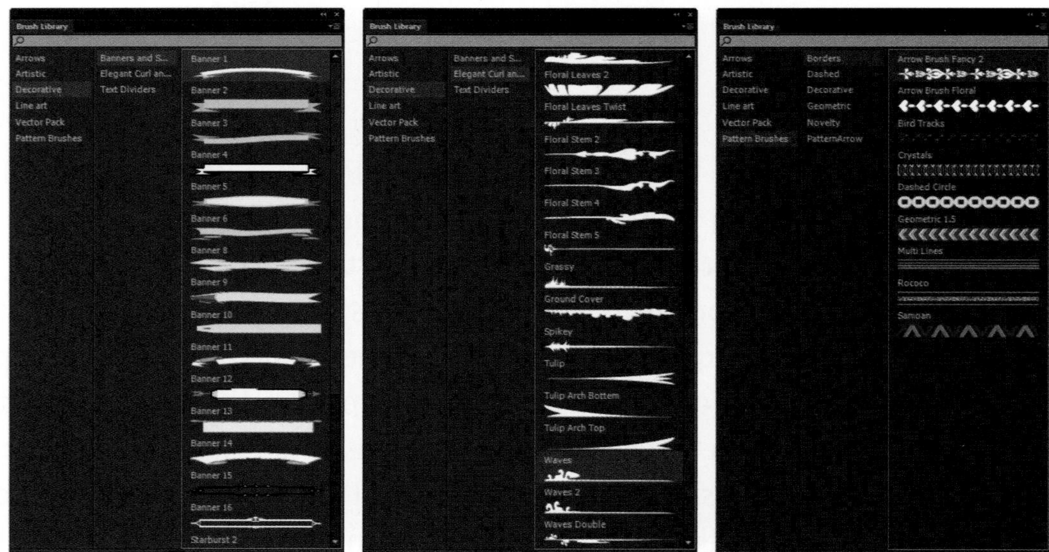

1 Animate comes with several styles of vector art brushes ready for use that include arrows, simulated artistic mediums, banners, and all sorts of shapes and patterns.

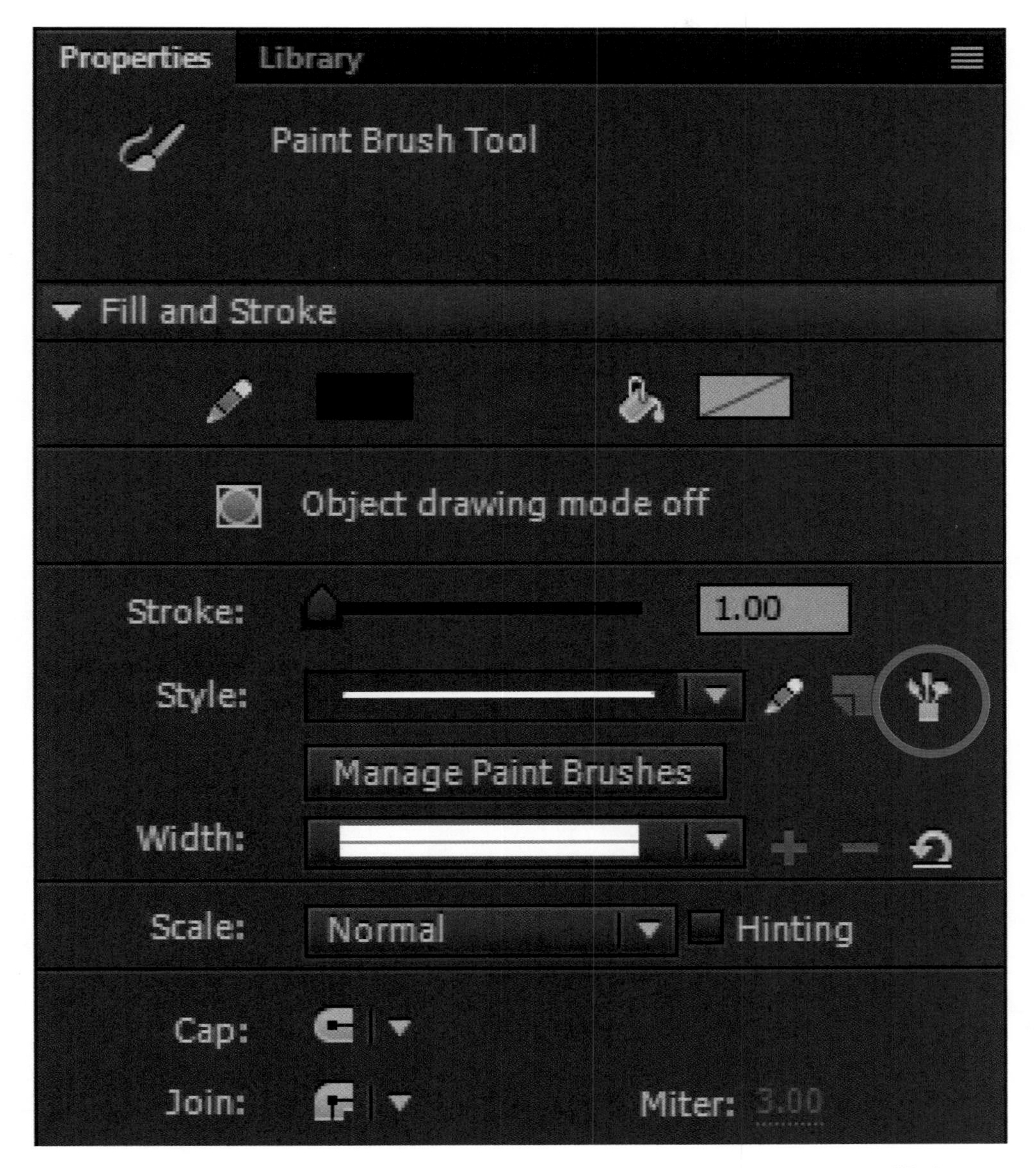

2 The vector brushes are available with any tool that draws a stroke with the exception of the Pencil Tool Shift Y. A handy way to remember is to look for the Brush Library button in the Property panel. It will be active only for these tools.

Vector Art Brushes (cont.)

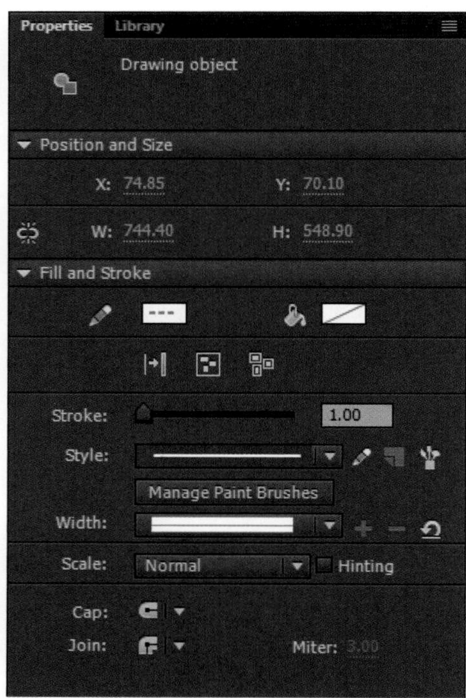

3 Even though the brushes aren't initially available with the Pencil Tool, you can modify a stroke after drawing it. Select one or more strokes with the Selection Tool, click the Brush Library button to open that panel, and choose a style to apply a vector art brush to your selection. Adjust the width of the stroke as needed in the Properties panel.

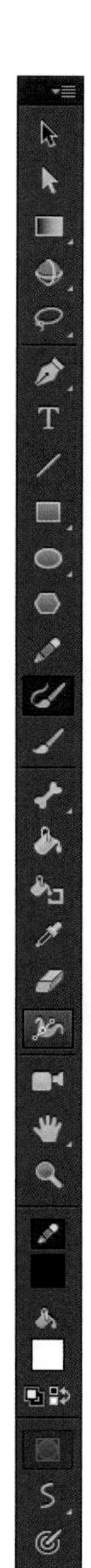

4 If you want to draw with the vector art brushes, use the new Paint Brush Tool Y.

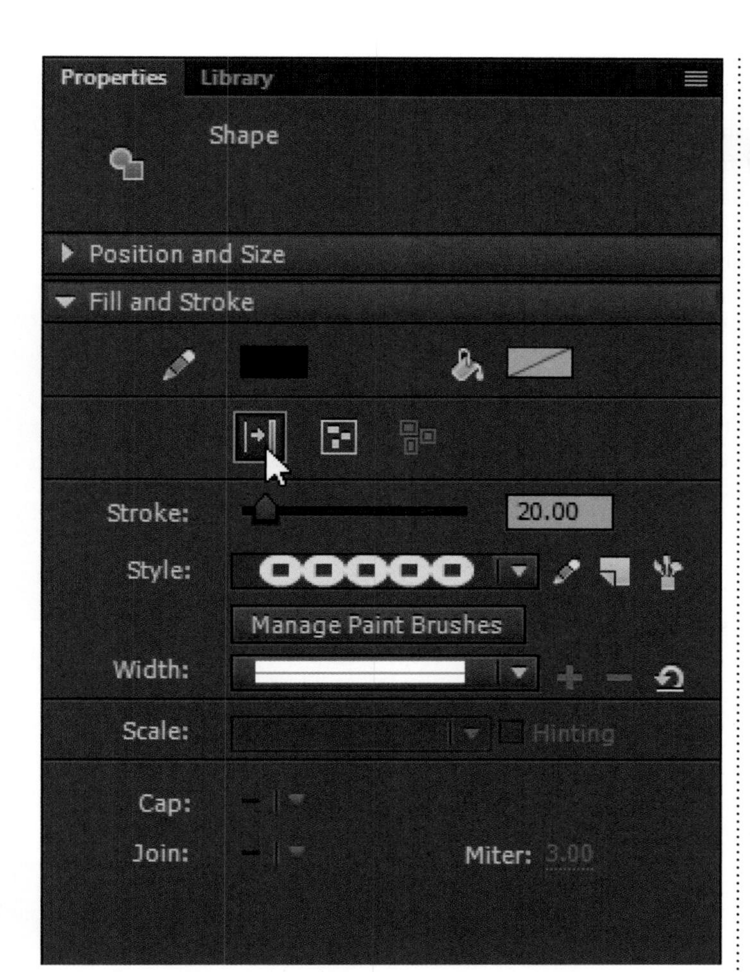

5 Whatever tool you choose to apply your vector art brush and whichever brush you apply, consider using Expand to Fill. It converts your editable stroke to a fill, which can no longer be changed through the style drop-down menu, but you'll see a noticeable improvement in performance.

HOT TIP

If you don't find the right brush, make your own! At first, the only way to make a brush was to use Adobe Capture for iOS or Android. Now you can create your own brush within Animate. Design the shape(s) you want for your brush, right-click, and select Create Paint Brush. Make it either an Art Brush or a Pattern Brush. Choose a tool that can enable the Brush Library button in the Properties panel. The Manage Paint Brushes button will become enabled, too. Click it to open the Manage Document Paint Brushes dialog, select the brush you want to save, and click Save To Brush Library. Animate adds it to the Brush Library under My Brushes and the name of the FLA from which it was saved. Your brush will be displayed with a preview of its style.

SHORTCUTS
MAC WIN BOTH

360° Rotatable Canvas

THE DRAWING TOOLS IN Animate make it a go-to app for artists, especially those who use it for hand-drawing with a Wacom tablet. One adjustment that was previously needed when going from a traditional drawing medium to digital was a way to rotate the canvas to compensate for the angle of the artist's hand. Now Animate CC offers a 360° rotatable canvas.

1 Click the Rotation Tool (H) which is grouped with the Hand Tool (H) in Tools.

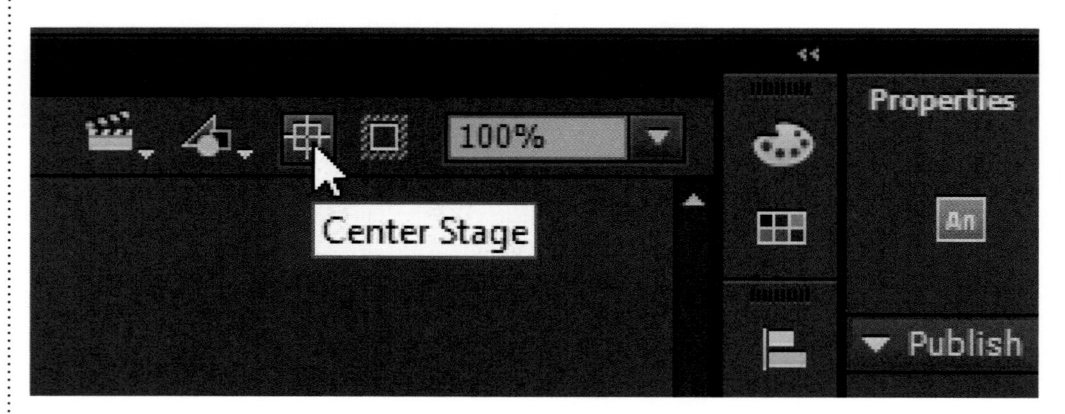

4 To return the Stage to its default orientation, click the Center Stage Button in the upper right of the document window or double-click the Rotation Tool in the Tools panel.

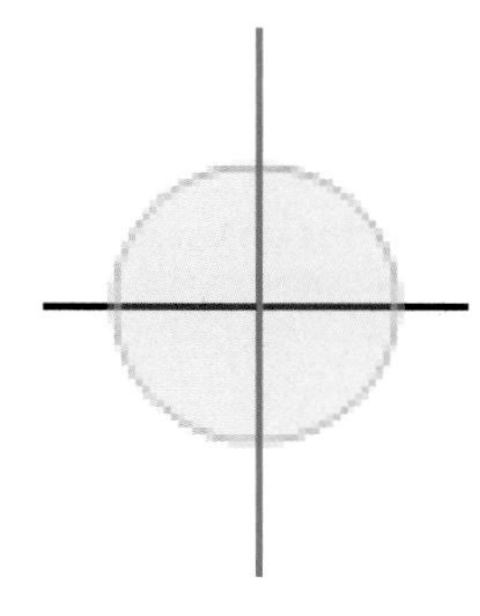

2 A large gray circle with a red vertical and black horizontal crosshairs appears in the center of the Stage, and the cursor changes to a smaller crosshair icon.

3 Drag the cursor left or right to rotate the Stage from its center, or click on a different location on the Stage to change the pivot point. The red line updates, indicating the degree of rotation.

HOT TIP

Use Shift + Space bar to temporarily access the Rotation Tool while any other tool is selected.

Improved Drawing Tools

HOLY MOLY, A WHOLE lot is happening with brushes in Animate CC! To start, there are improvements to the accuracy of rendering your drawing, the brand new Paint Brush Tool, new types of strokes to apply as either Pattern Brushes or Art Brushes (vector art brushes), the Width Tool for creating variable widths at any point on a stroke, custom stroke profiles, and new brush sizes.

The Brush B and the new Paint Brush Y both make drawing better and faster now. What you draw is now more accurately reflected without unintended stroke width issues. Curve fitting has also been improved. For the Paint Brush Tool, if you'd like to adjust the curve settings go to Edit > Preferences... > Drawing > Shape Recognition and use the drop-down menu.

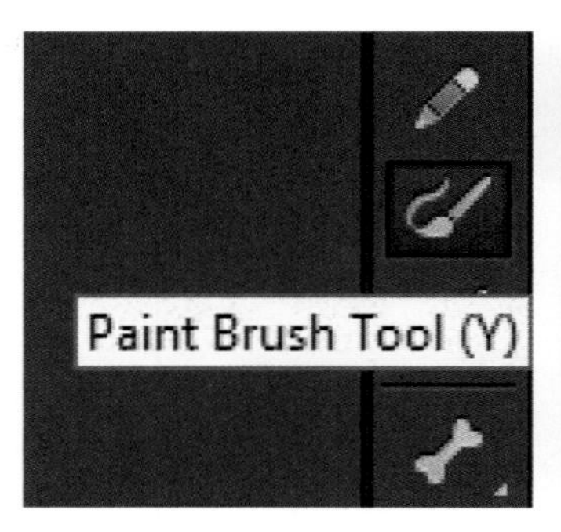

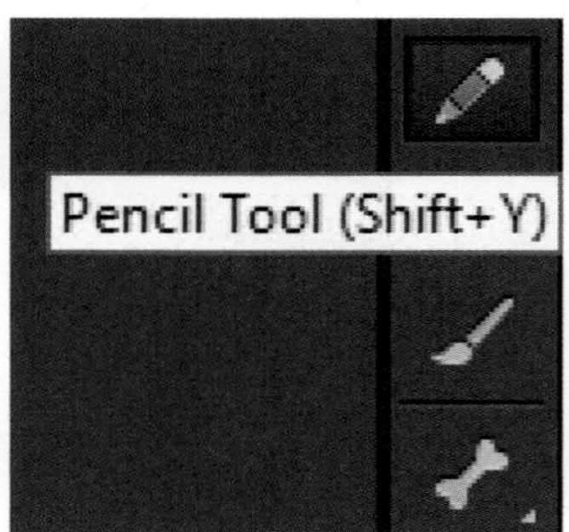

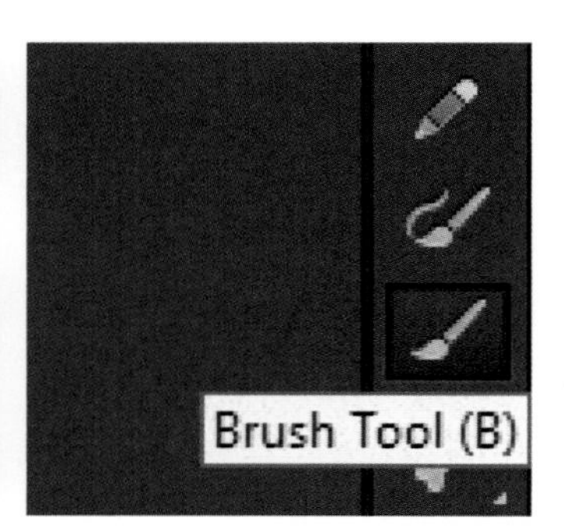

1 The Paint Brush Tool Shift Y lets you draw with strokes similar to the Pencil Tool Y or strokes that can be set to automatically convert to fill a bit like the Brush Tool B. (See Vector Art Brushes for more details on how these work with strokes.)

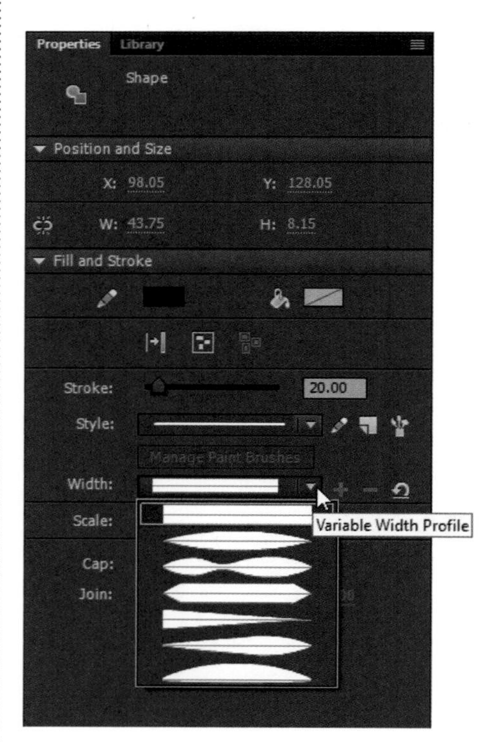

5 There are several width presets available in the Properties panel.

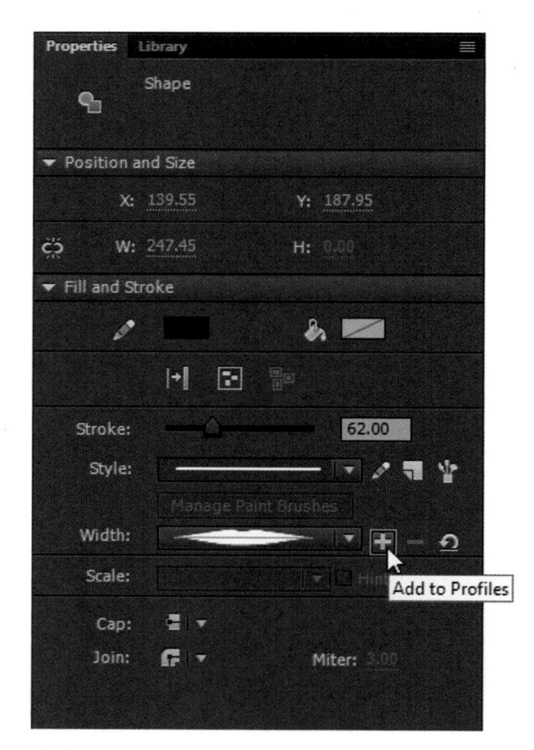

6 If you create a stroke with width settings you'll reuse, select it and click the + button next to the width preview.

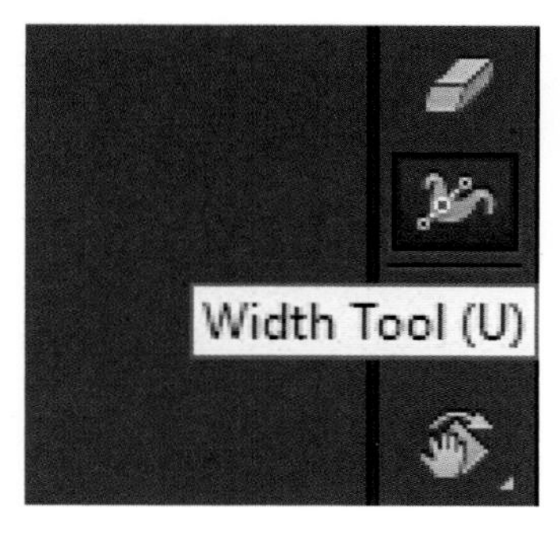

2 The Width Tool U slipped in as a feature just before Flash Professional became Animate. It's just like the Width Tool in Illustrator.

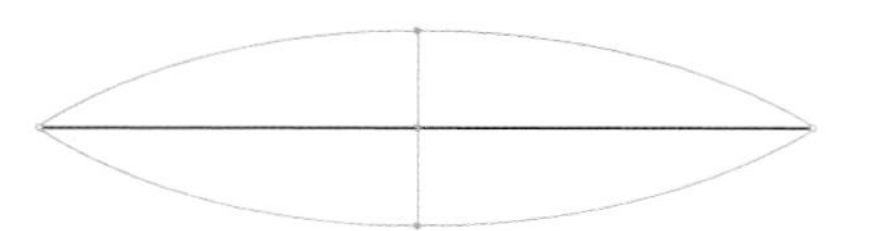

3 Draw a stroke. Select the Width Tool U. Click on the stroke and drag out how far you'd like to make the width.

4 You can add multiple points, move the points, or ⌥ alt Shift + drag to adjust the width on just one side.

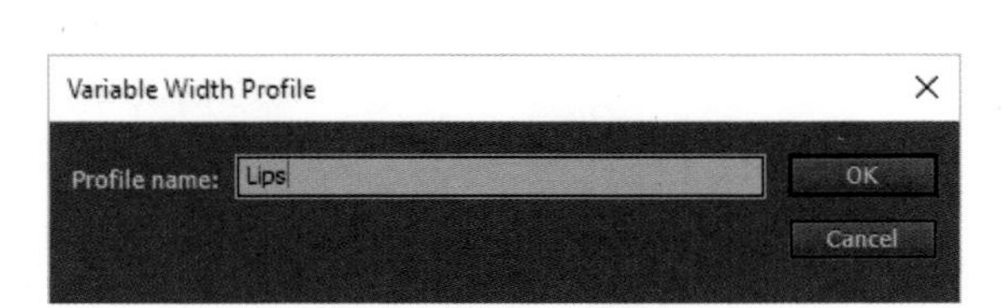

7 Give it a name and apply it anytime.

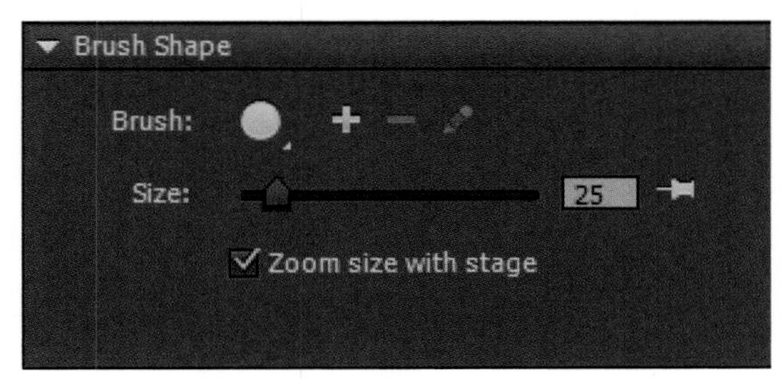

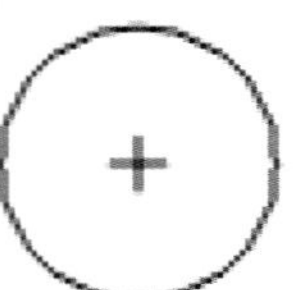

8 As of the August 2016 release, Animate offers more brush sizes. Set your brush to anywhere from 1 to 200 pixels and get a live preview as an outline while you adjust the Size slider. Animate's Brush uses sticky settings, so you can switch tools and come right back to your Brush with the shape and size that you set.

HOT TIP

Animate your width settings by using Shape Tweens. It works great for mouth shapes. If you don't get the results you're expecting, try converting your strokes to fills. If your shape is still not tweening how you would expect, apply shape hints.

Colored Onion Skinning

IF YOU DO A LOT of animating, Onion Skin is one of those indispensable features. Turn it on from the Timeline to see all the frames you select with diminishing transparency as they occur further from the currently selected frame. You know what would make it even better? Color coding your past, current, and future frames. Done. Colored Onion Skinning is available now in Animate CC.

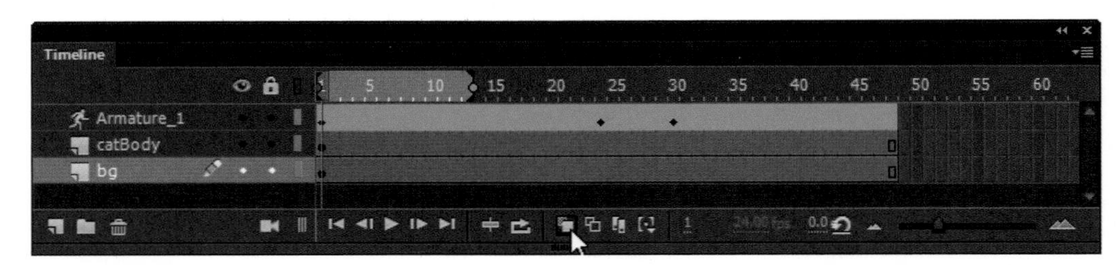

1 In the Timeline, select Onion Skin ⌥ alt Shift O. The Start Onion Skin and End Onion Skin markers appear at the top of the Timeline. To toggle Onion Skin off, click the Onion Skin button or use the keyboard shortcut again.

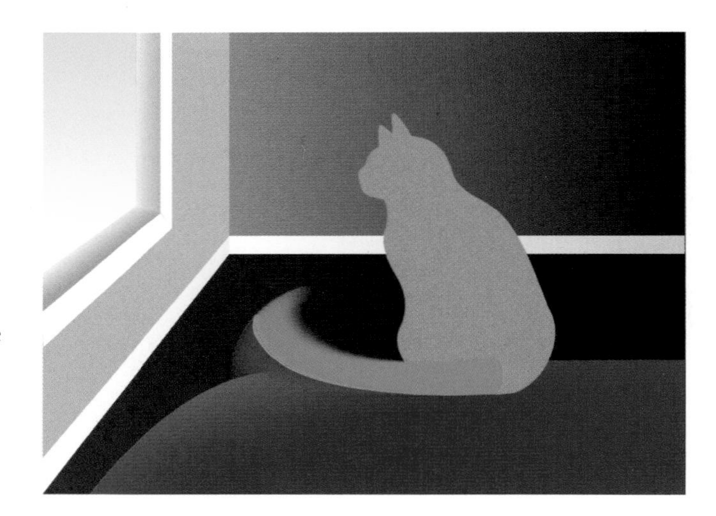

3 The Onion Skin of the selected frames are displayed on the Stage with the colors corresponding to the previous and next frames. As you move the playhead, the span follows showing the same number of frames before and/or after as what you initially set.

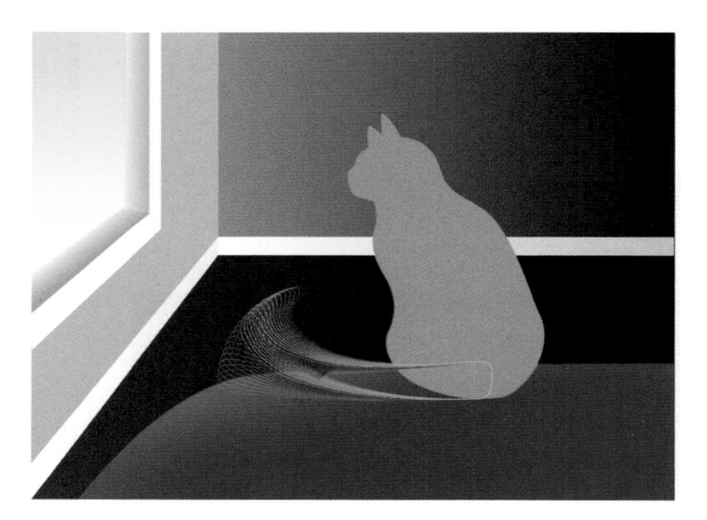

5 The same colors are applied to Onion Skin Outlines.

VECTOR ILLUSTRATION: MYRA FERGUSON

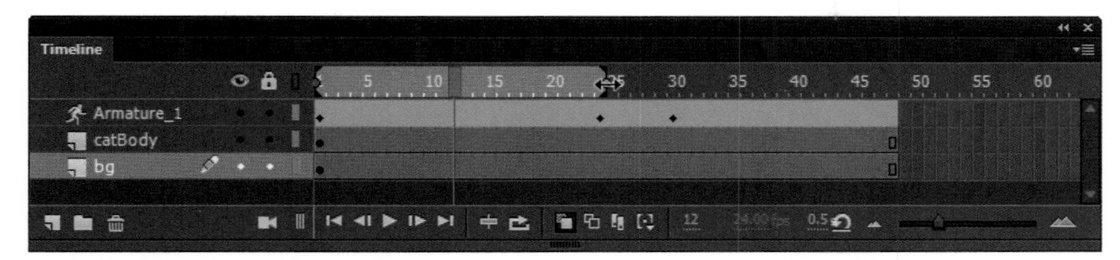

2 Move the playhead and drag the markers to enclose a span of however many frames you want to view before and after the current frame. The Onion Skin markers look just like the Edit Multiple Frames markers but display a sample of the color for the past and future frames on the brackets.

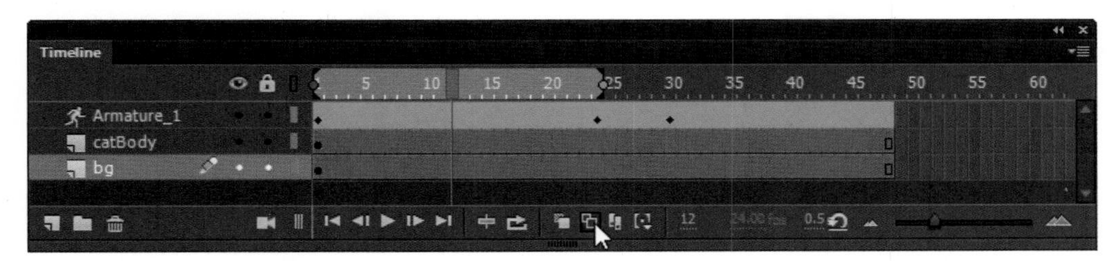

4 Sometimes it helps to be able to see through the shape being animated. In that case, use Onion Skin Outline. The button for it is to the right of Onion Skin.

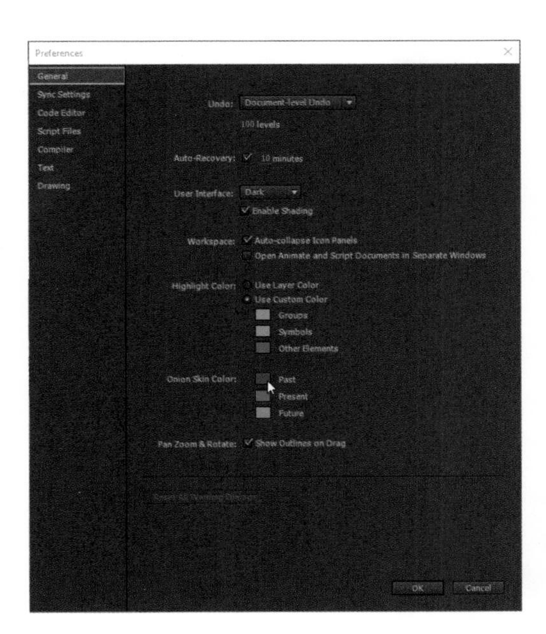

6 You can change the colors used for Onion Skin by going to Edit > Preferences… > General to whatever you like or set them to black or gray if you'd like them to resemble the previous settings.

HOT TIP

Onion Skin doesn't have to show an equal number of frames before and after the playhead. In fact, you could eliminate all future frames so that your current frame is on top of the stack or eliminate all past frames so that your current frame is on the bottom.

Creative Cloud Libraries

CC LIBRARIES IN Animate keep getting better. In Animate CC, you can add and/or retrieve Brushes, Colors, Color Themes, Animations (which include both FLAs and Symbols), and Graphics. CC Libraries makes it easy to organize and access assets you've created for use in Animate.

1 Click CC Libraries if it's docked in a panel group or go to Window > CC Libraries to open your CC Libraries.

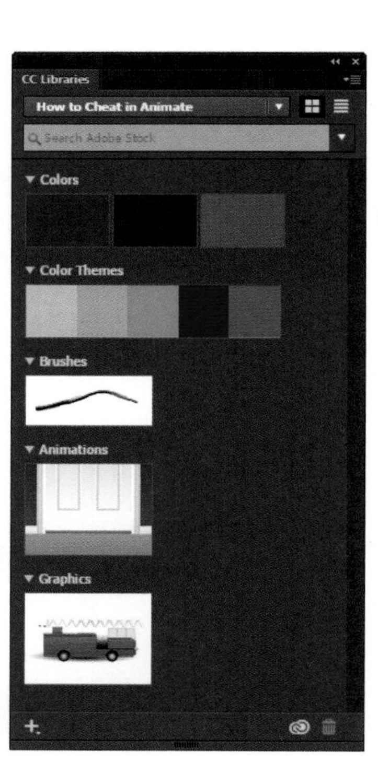

2 Brushes, Colors, Color Themes, and Graphics are all asset types that can be created in other applications, saved to your Creative Cloud Library, and brought into your Animate CC document.

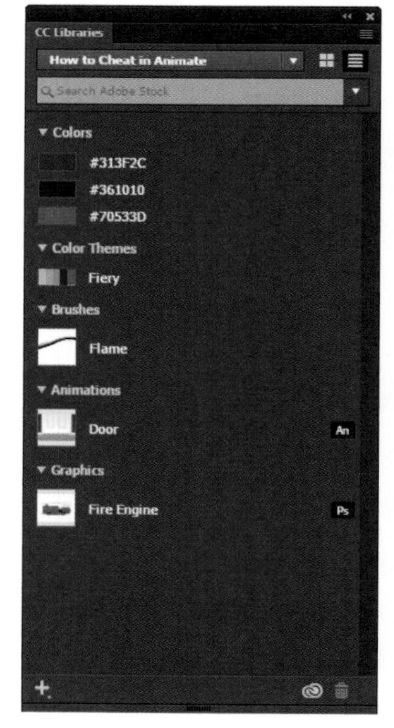

5 To distinguish between a FLA and a symbol, set your view to List. Under Animations, the files will be identified as AN for animate documents and SYM for symbols.

3 Symbols and FLAs can be saved from Animate to your CC Libraries. To add a Symbol, select it, click on the Add Content button on the CC Libraries panel, make sure Add Symbol to Library is checked, and click Add.

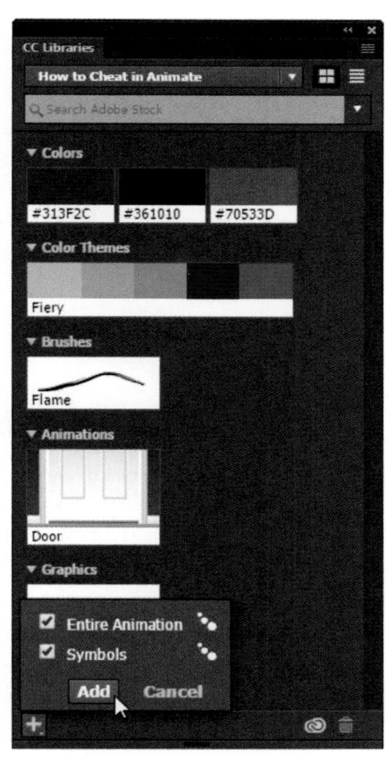

4 It doesn't matter if you have anything selected if you want to add the FLA to your CC Libraries. The document just needs to be open otherwise the Add Content button won't be available.

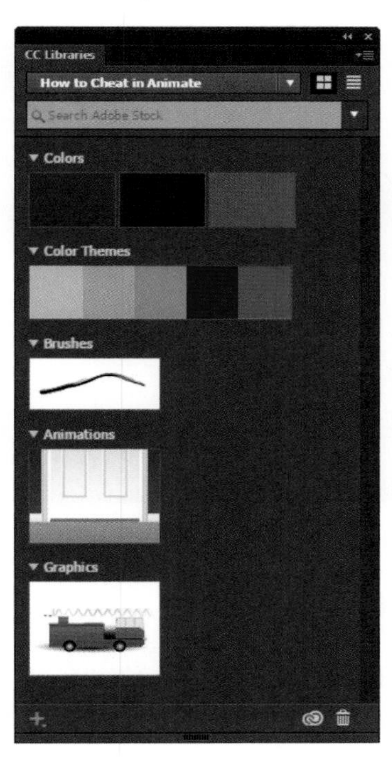

6 Right-click and select Open New Document. The entire Animate document opens with all layers intact and all assets named properly in the Library.

7 To add colors from Animate, create a shape with the desired fill and/or stroke color. Select the shape and click the Add Content button. If the shape's Fill and Stroke Color are both selected, you can add both or either color to your CC Library.

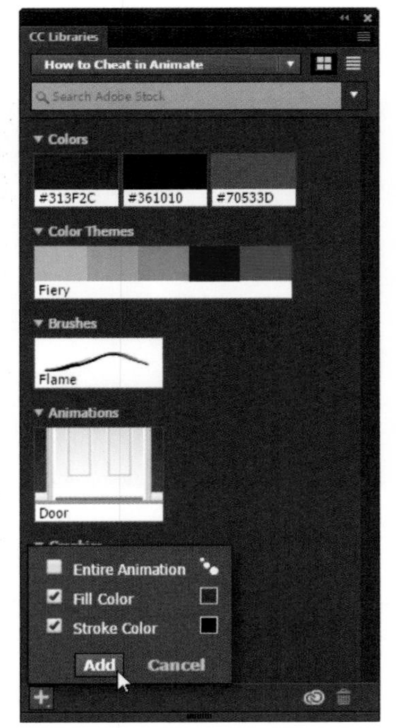

HOT TIP

Use CC Libraries to organize and share assets. You can create CC Libraries that contain frequently used assets or files and share them with your team. To let your team work with the assets which would include editing, moving, or deleting, click the fly-out menu on the CC Libraries panel and select Collaborate… to open a browser window where you can invite collaborators by entering their email. Set the permissions to "Can edit." If you're looking for a way to let a client review assets or files where they can view and comment but not make any edits or downloads, you'll also click the fly-out menu and select Collaborate… but set the permissions to "Can view." If you want to make a file publicly available, click the fly-out menu and select "Share Link…" which also opens a browser window. From there you'll get a link that you can share. Anyone with the link will be able to view the library. You have the option of making the assets downloadable or not, and you can remove the public link at any time.

Tagged Swatches

YOU'RE PROBABLY FAMILIAR WITH SWATCHES. SELECT A COLOR or a gradient and in the Swatches panel click the Create a new Swatch button or from the Color panel click the Add to Swatches button. Animate saves your color or gradient as a Swatch in your document, so you can select that color anytime. Admittedly, that's pretty handy especially if you have a complex gradient with lots of stops. But what if you've applied that color to multiple objects (not just one symbol) and would like to change that color everywhere at the same time? Now you can with Tagged Swatches.

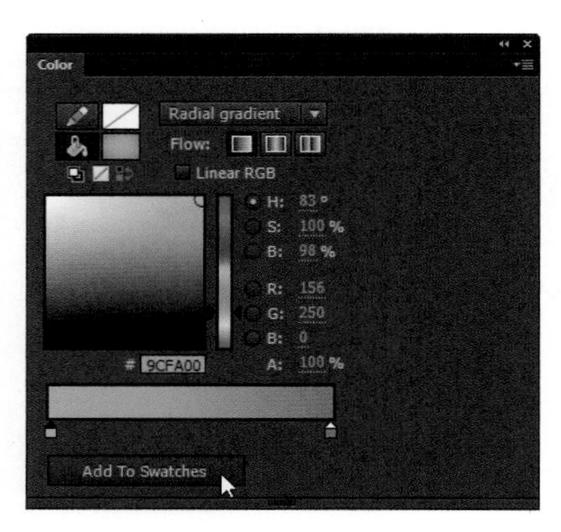

1 Start by setting or sampling a color then creating a Swatch. To create a Swatch either click Add to Swatches from the Color panel or click the Create a new Swatch button in the Swatch panel.

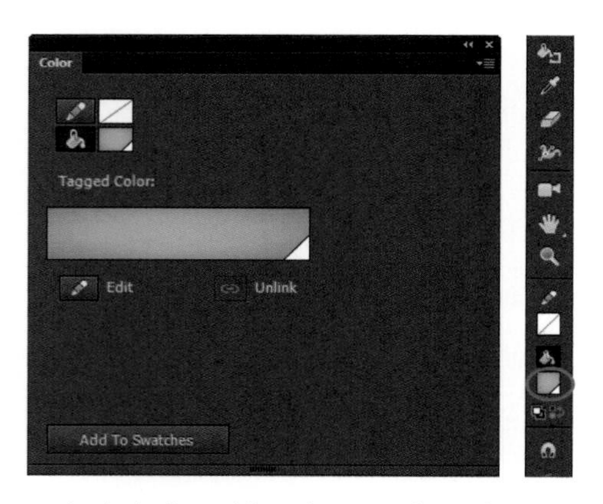

5 Apply the Tagged Swatch to your shapes. It appears as the same color as your regular Swatch, but notice it has a white triangle in the lower right corner. That icon indicates the color selected is a Tagged Swatch and appears wherever your color selection is shown.

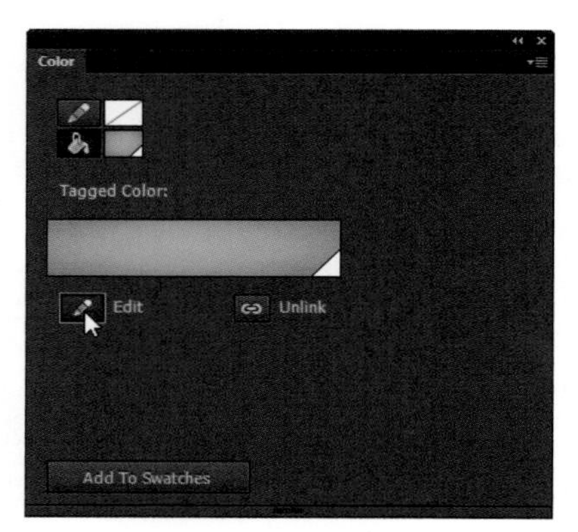

6 Now update the Tagged Swatch. You don't have to select any of the shapes—just the Tagged Swatch. Editing a Tagged Swatch is done in the Tagged Color Definition dialog as opposed to the Color panel. If you double-click the Tagged Swatch from the Swatches panel, the Tagged Color Definition dialog opens automatically. But you can still get to it through the Color panel by clicking the Edit button.

VECTOR ILLUSTRATION: MYRA FERGUSON

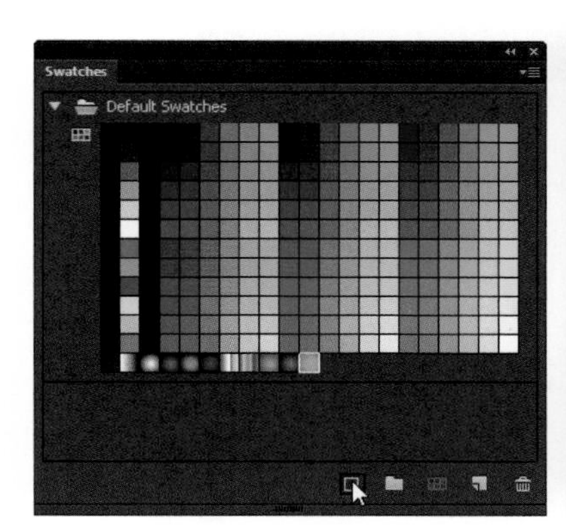

2 To make a Tagged Swatch you'll need to convert the regular Swatch by clicking the Convert to Tagged Swatch button on the bottom left of the Swatches panel.

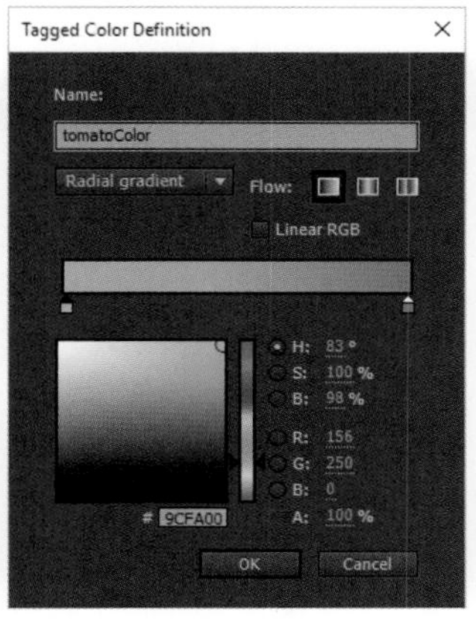

3 Name your color in the Tagged Color Definition dialog and click OK.

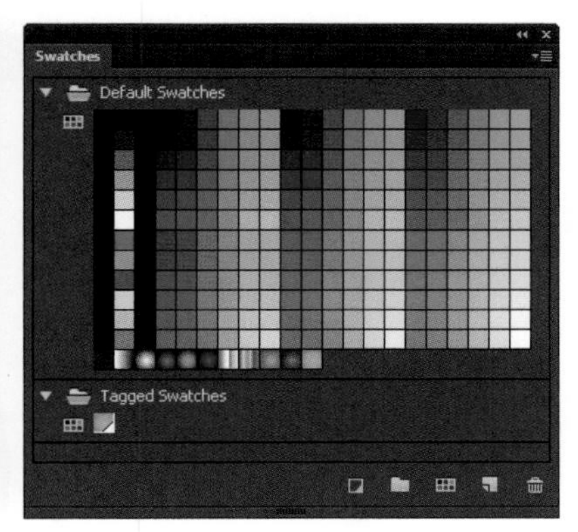

4 After it's saved, it'll appear in the Tagged Swatches folder in the Swatches panel.

7 Immediately after you edit the Tagged Swatch, all objects linked to that color will be updated with the new color. It doesn't even matter if they are Symbols or not.

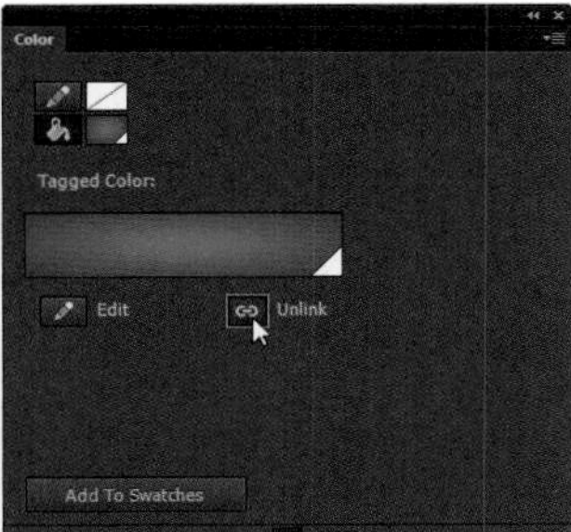

8 If there's a shape you'd like to keep as the Tagged Swatch color but not update with the other objects, you can unlink it. Select the shape, then in the Color panel click the Unlink button.

9 Now it'll just behave like a regular color or gradient has been applied; however, next time you edit the Tagged Swatch only those shapes linked to the Tagged Swatch get updated.

HOT TIP

CC Libraries in Animate only support retrieving and adding colors but not tagged swatches. However, if you want to make a tagged swatch available through a CC Library, add them to a FLA and add that FLA to your library. You wouldn't need to keep anything else in the FLA—no keyframes, no symbols, no layers. If you do want to remove everything but the colors, right-click on the FLA in your CC Library and select Edit and delete the extras. If you want to bypass the CC Libraries and use your Tagged Swatch in another Animate document, you can copy a shape with the Tagged Swatch applied and paste it into another FLA.

The Bone Tool

BONES ARE BACK! You may recall that the Bone Tool was removed when the application was rewritten for the update to Flash CC. As the tool proved to be a popular feature, it has made its way back. Bones are a metaphor for how inverse kinematics (IK) works. Think of a skeleton and how bones define mobility based on where joints are and what they connect. Additional constraints like enabling or constraining rotation or movement can make animation with bones more convincing.

When you use bones, you create an armature, or underlying structure, that doesn't get seen when published. There are two types of armatures that you can create—one based on a shape and the other based on multiple symbol instances.

1 Use a shaped-based armature to control distortion and movement of a single shape. Start by drawing a shape.

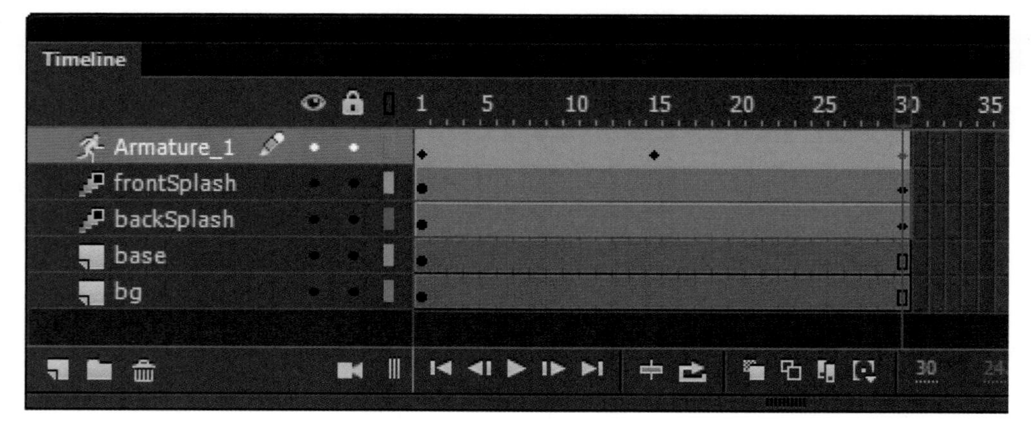

3 Create poses at different frames on the Armature layer to automatically set keyframes much like you would with the Motion model.

POURING A GLASS OF WATER: VECTOR ILLUSTRATION: MYRA FERGUSON | EXTENDING PUNCHING GLOVE: VECTOR ILLUSTRATION: MYRA FERGUSON

2 With the shape selected, apply bones to the shape.

4 Use a symbol-based armature for more complex subjects. Make sure all the parts you want to connect are separated into individual Movie Clip symbol instances. Each bone can attach one instance to another, but it cannot have multiple connections within the one instance.

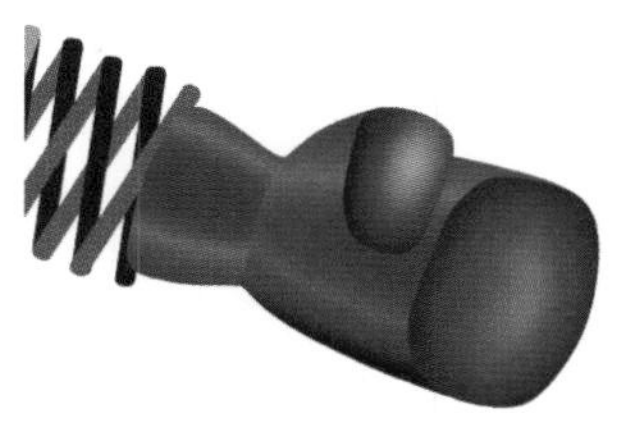

5 Creating poses at different frames on the Armature layer with the symbol-based armature works the same way as it does for the shape-based armature.

HOT TIP

While bones are usually used for humans, animals, or other personified characters, the cheat here is that they can be used to set poses for so much more, like anything that could benefit from some movement or inanimate objects like mechanical gadgets that have hierarchical relationships related to movement.

Advanced PSD Import Options

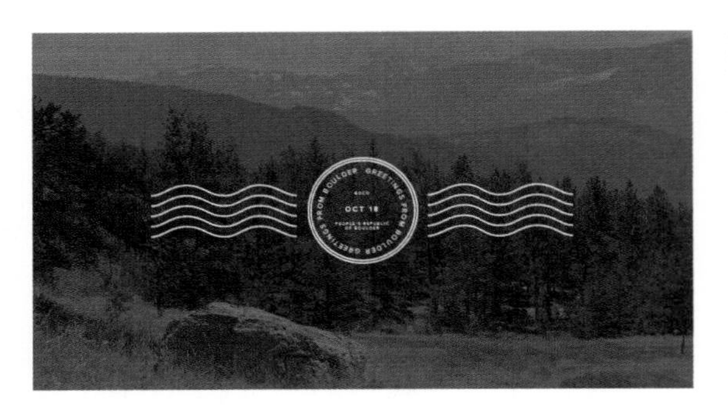

IT'S SO GOOD TO SEE THAT LAYER THUMBNAILS are back in the PSD Importer! Previously the Photoshop importer let you see and select one or more layers. Then the importer changed. There were a bunch of helpful options, but you couldn't see your layers anymore. Thankfully, it has changed again. Now you get all the import options, and you can see your layers.

1 In Animate, go to File > Import > Import to Stage… ⌘ ctrl R, navigate to your PSD, and open. The PSD Importer opens with the Advanced Options. Let's start at the top. If you have layer comps in your PSD, select the one you want to use.

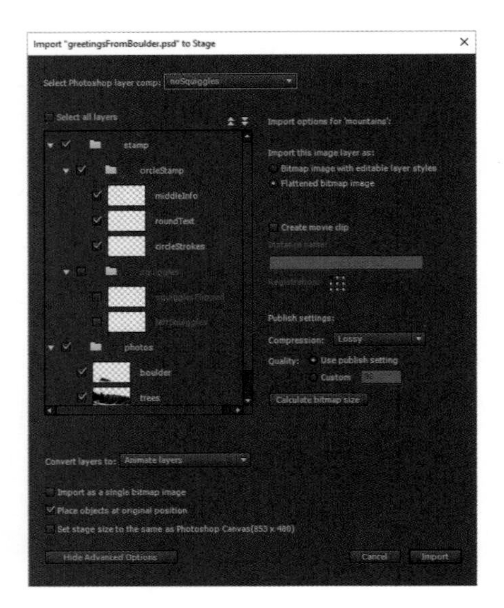

4 Select options for importing individual layers if you want to keep shapes or text editable. Otherwise the default is to import them as a flattened bitmap image.

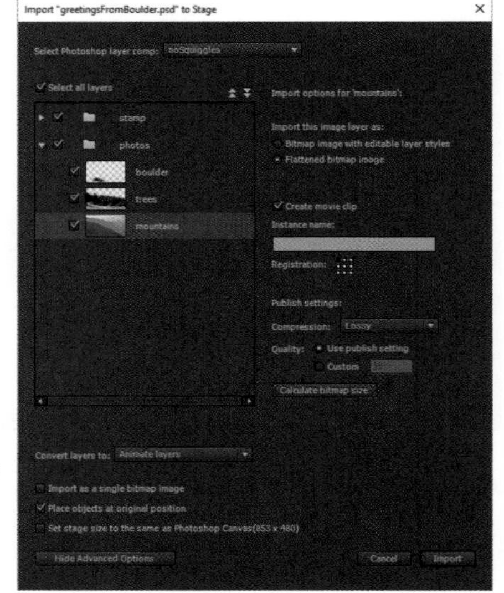

PHOTO: MYRA FERGUSON

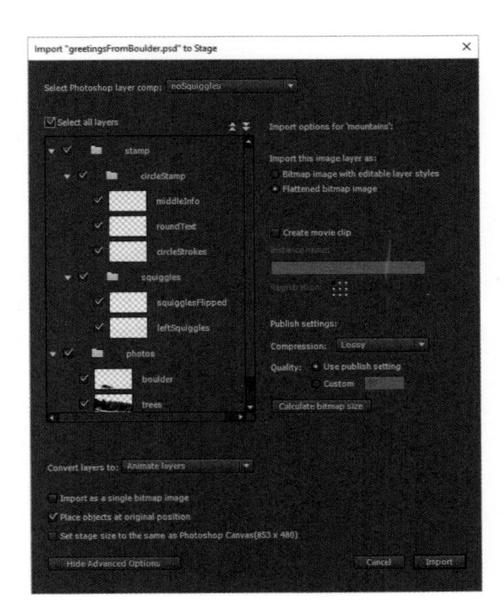

2 All the layers in your PSD will appear below. If there was a layer in your file or layer comp that wasn't turned on, it still appears in the list but remains unselected. You can select any of the layers. If you want to select them all, check Select all layers.

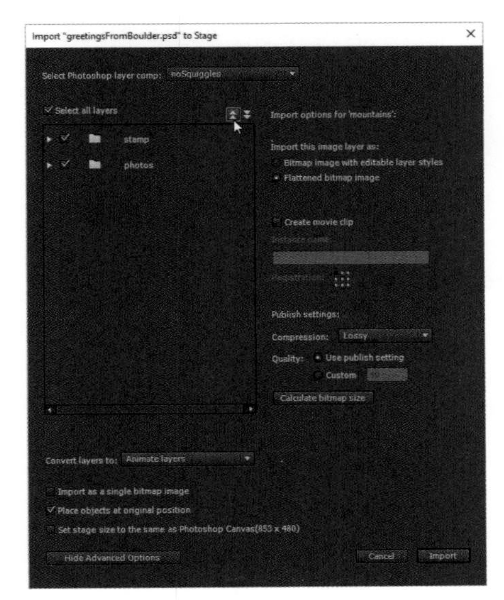

3 Sometimes, Photoshop files can get a little unruly with multiple artboards and groups full of layers, which can make navigating complicated. With the double up or double down arrows, collapse or expand all the layers at once.

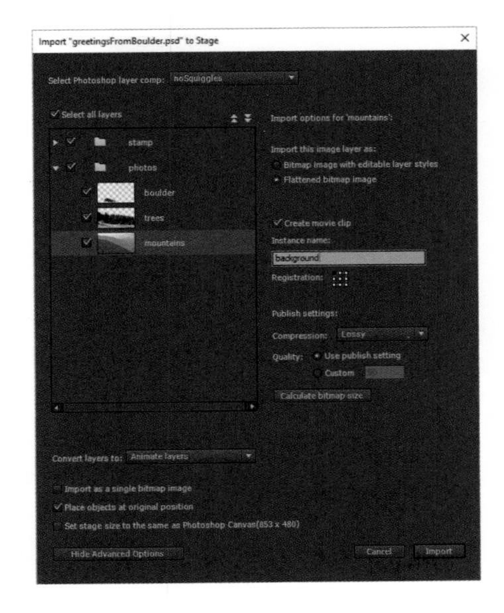

5 You have the time-saving option of selecting Create movie clip, entering an instance name, and setting registration. Animate automatically names your symbol whatever your layer was called.

Advanced PSD Import Options (cont.)

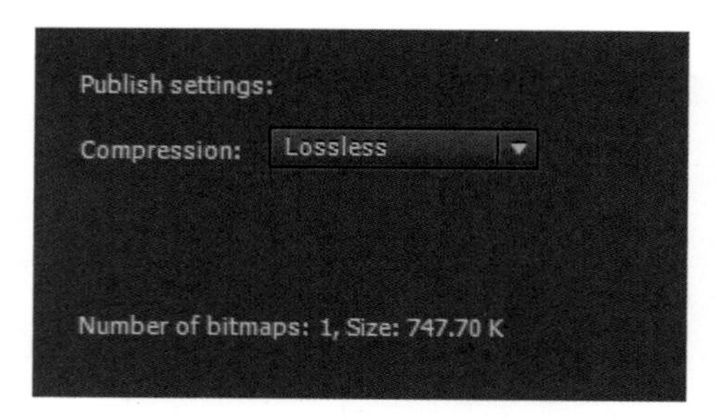

6 For your bitmaps, you have the option of setting the Compression. If you choose Lossless, your image is not compressed. It will look great, but the file size will be large.

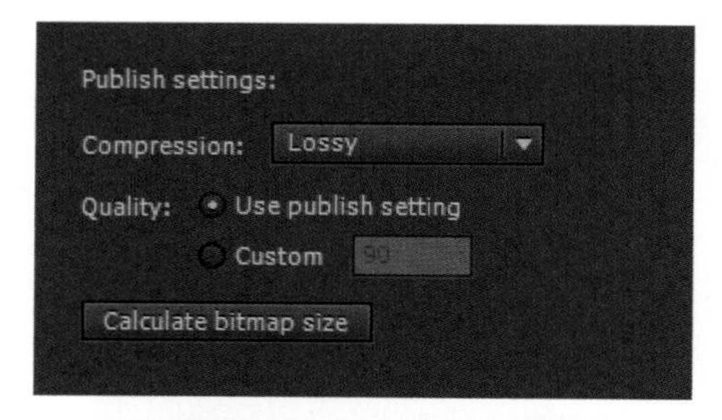

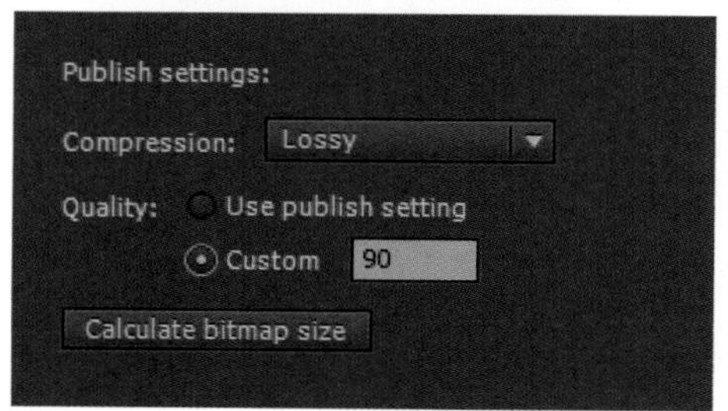

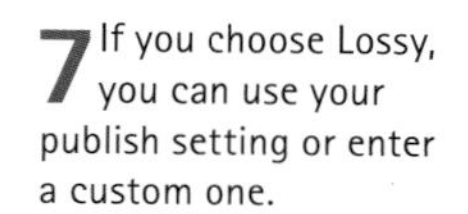

7 If you choose Lossy, you can use your publish setting or enter a custom one.

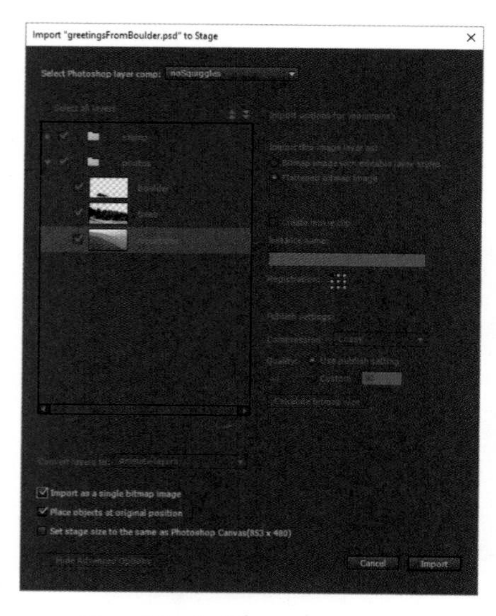

10 You might decide you really just want all of your selected Photoshop layers to turn into one flattened image. If so, select Import as a single bitmap image. That selection turns off all of your other options with the exception of matching your Stage size to your PSD.

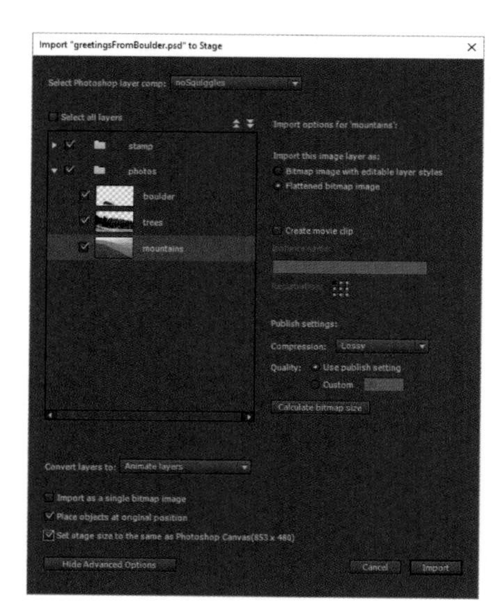

11 Place objects at original position is selected by default. It's a great option if your layers are already placed where you want them in the PSD. And if your Stage size doesn't match your PSD, you can select the last option on the left to adjust it so that it does.

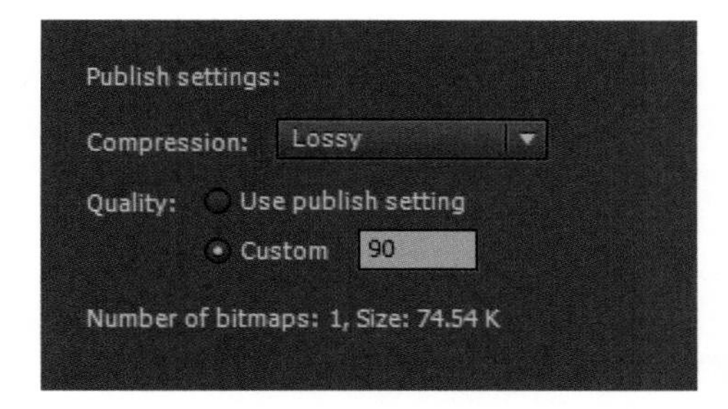

8 The Calculate bitmap size button lets you know what your new file size is based on the compression you choose.

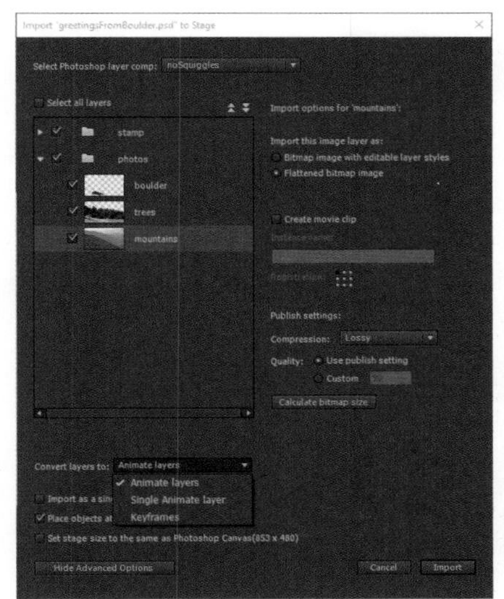

9 Below the list of layers is the Convert layers options drop-down menu. You can set your Photoshop layers to Animate layers, a Single Animate layer, or Keyframes.

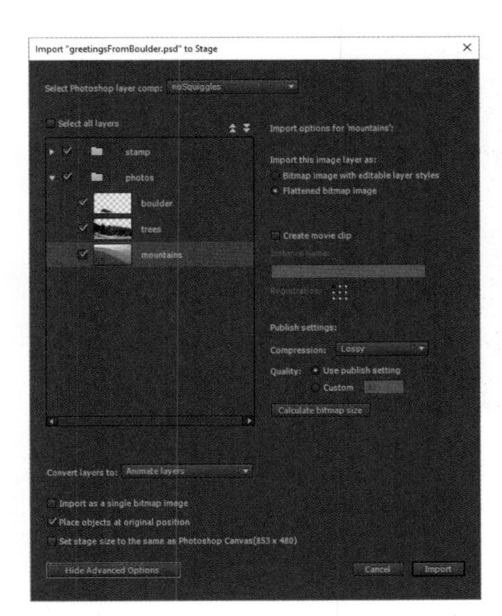

12 If these options are overwhelming, you can select the Hide Advanced Options button at the bottom left.

HOT TIP

If you add a layer mask in Photoshop and bring that layer into Animate, Animate recognizes the alpha channel and applies the transparency to your image.

Advanced AI Import Options

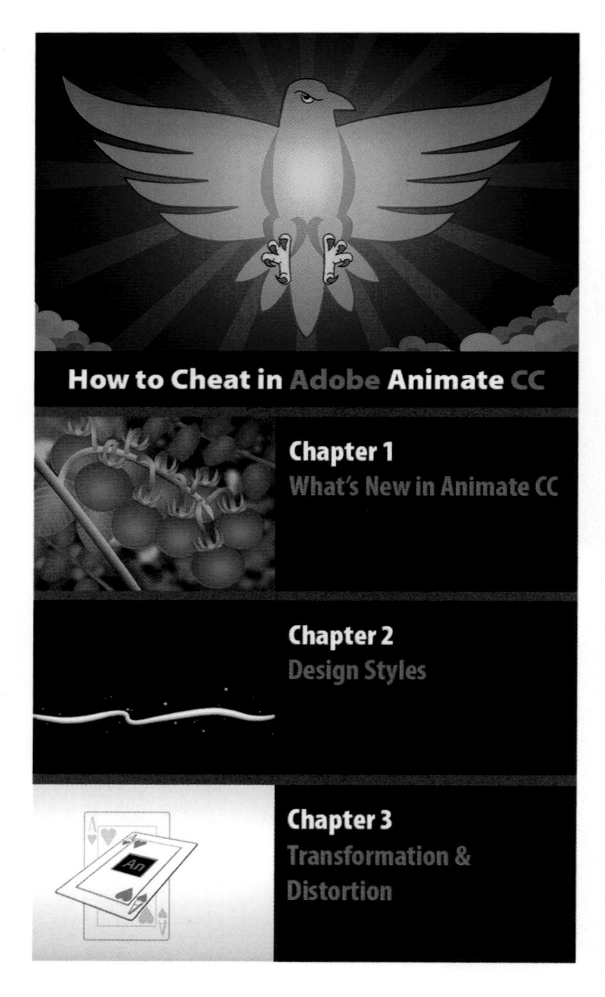

PROTOTYPE MOCK-UP: MYRA FERGUSON

ANIMATE CC NOW PROVIDES ADVANCED options for importing your Illustrator artwork, so you have more control over preserving editability, RGB color, and effects. Some effects may not have a method of being preserved in which case Animate's AI Importer alerts you.

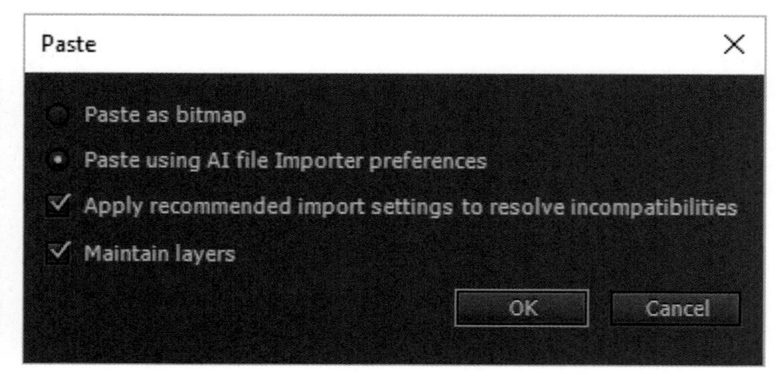

1 You don't even have to use import to bring in your artwork. You can copy and paste it from Illustrator with a few options. Of course, you can make it a bitmap, but the default copy setting is to Paste using AI file Importer preferences, Apply recommended import settings to resolve incompatibilities, and Maintain layers.

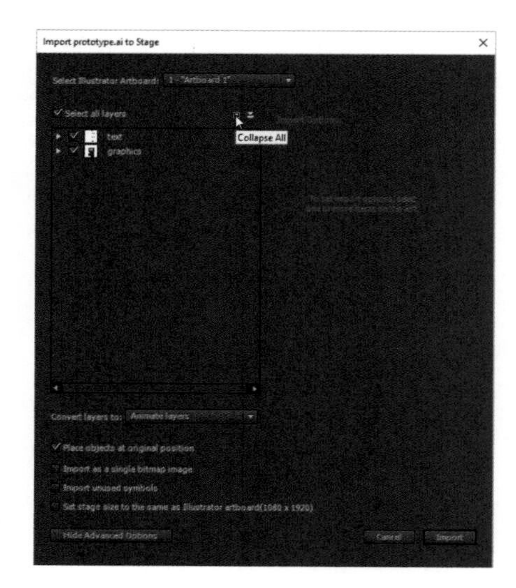

4 The layers from that artboard or your file (if there's just one artboard) are displayed with thumbnails in the dialog. You can select any or all of the layers. Use the Collapse All or Expand All arrows to help navigate the file's layers and groups.

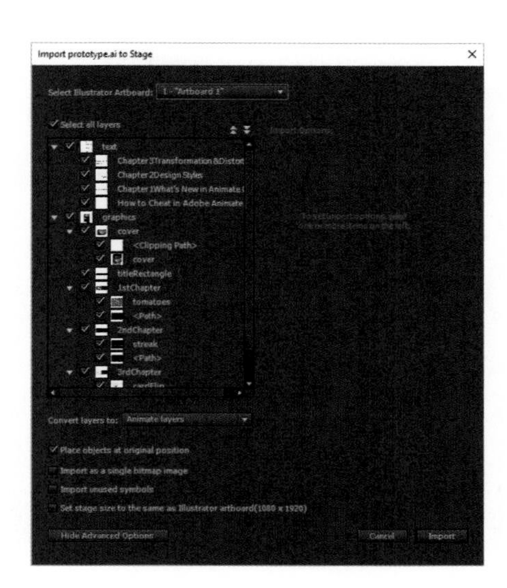

2 When you use either the File > Import to Stage... or File > Import to Library command, the Import AI dialog gives you multiple options much like the advanced PSD Importer.

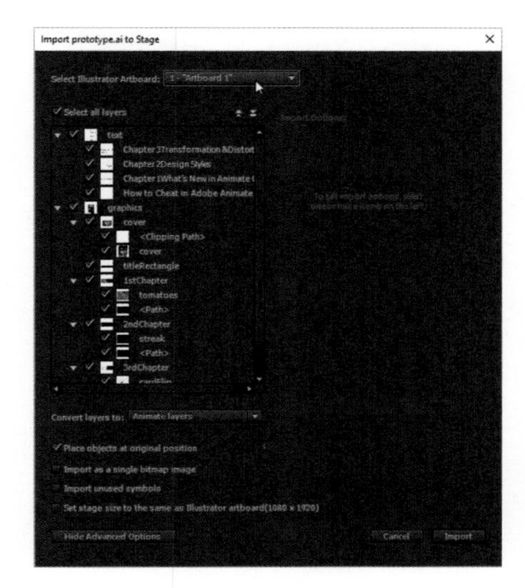

3 First, if your file has multiple artboards, use the drop-down menu to select one.

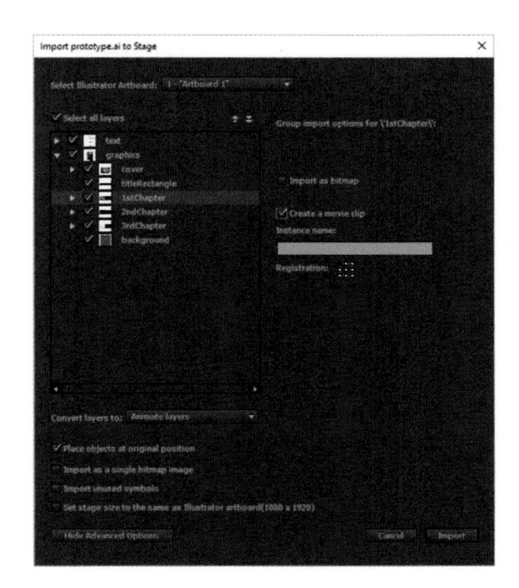

5 Like the PSD Importer, you can import your layers as individual bitmaps and/or create a Movie Clip from your selection. If you create a Movie Clip, Animate automatically names it based on your layer name. You can enter an instance name, but it's not necessary.

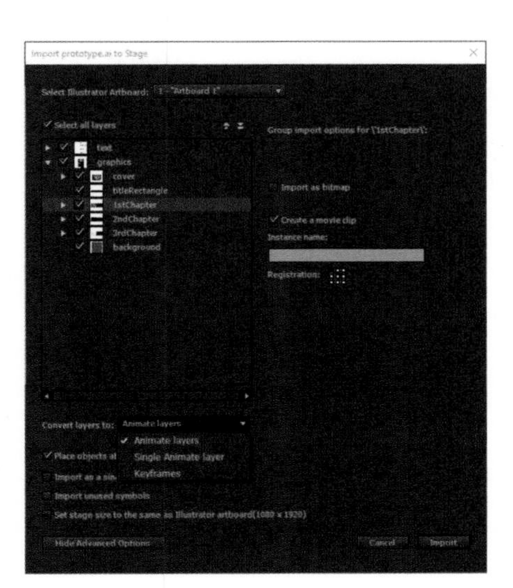

6 You can also choose to convert your Illustrator layers to Animate layers, a Single Animate layer, or Keyframes. By default, Place objects at original position is selected to keep all your content where it was placed in relation to your other layers in the artwork.

HOT TIP

If your Illustrator file's color mode is set to CMYK, convert it to RGB and make any necessary color adjustments before import to get the closest results.

SHORTCUTS
MAC WIN BOTH

Advanced AI Import Options (cont.)

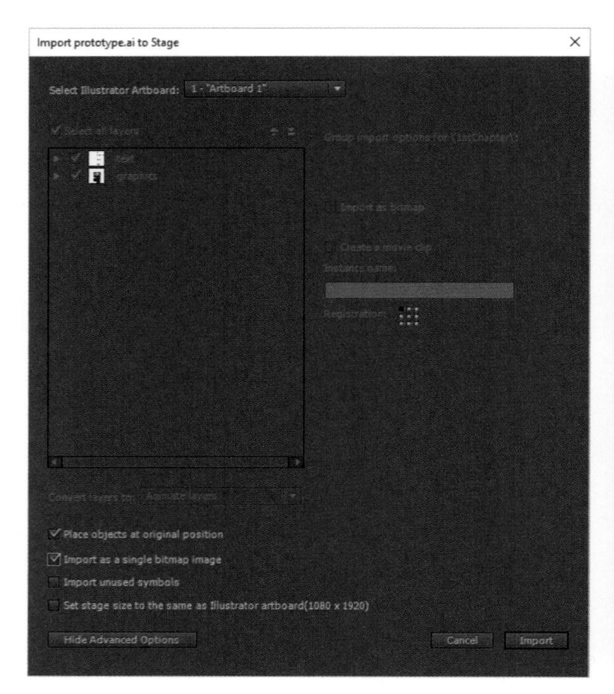

7 At the bottom of the dialog, you can import the entire selection as a single bitmap image.

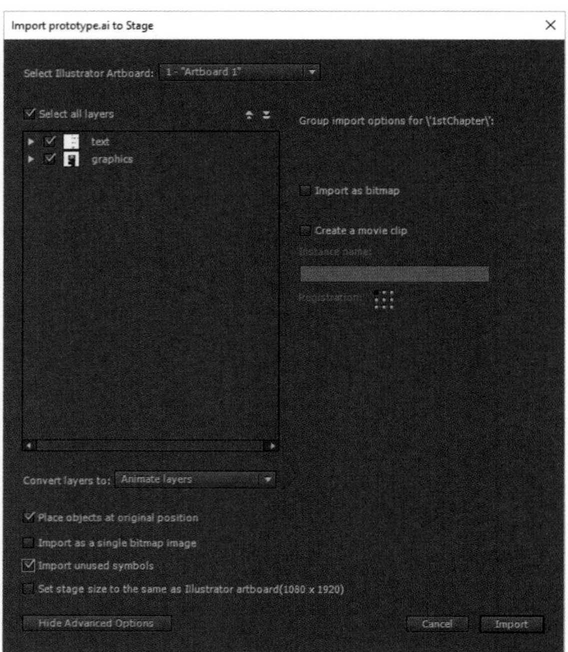

8 If you Import unused symbols, they won't show up on the Stage but are made available to you in your Animate Library.

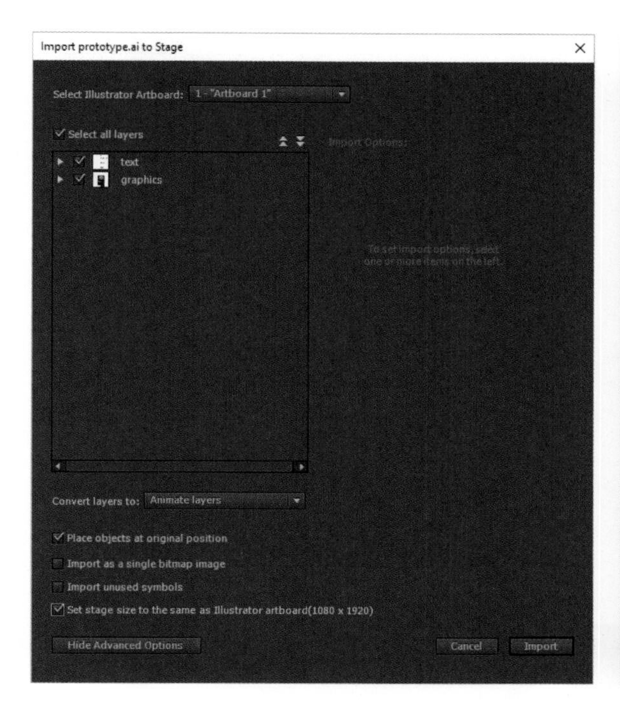

9 If your Stage size doesn't match the size of your Illustrator file, you can select Set stage size to the same as Illustrator artboard to adjust it. Animate lets you know what that size is.

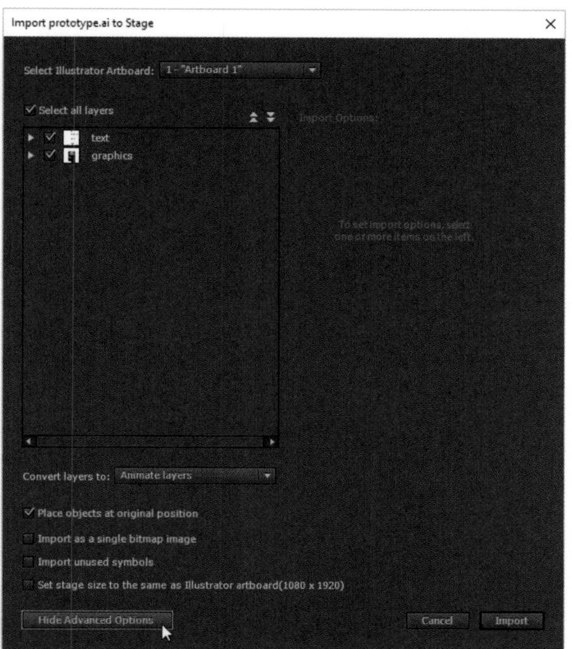

10 And if you want to simplify the options in the importer, click the Hide Advanced Options button. You can always switch back by clicking the Show Advanced Option button.

Vector Art Brush Editing Options

AS IF vector art brushes weren't amazing enough, Adobe added editing options!

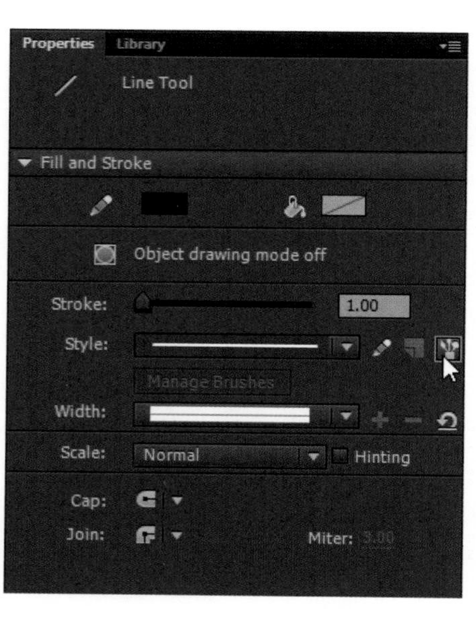

1 With a tool selected that creates strokes (Line Tool N, Rectangle Tool R, Oval Tool O, PolyStar Tool, Paint Brush Tool Y, or Ink Bottle Tool S), open the Brush Library either by going to Window > Brush Library or clicking the Brush Library button in the Fill and Stroke section of the Properties panel.

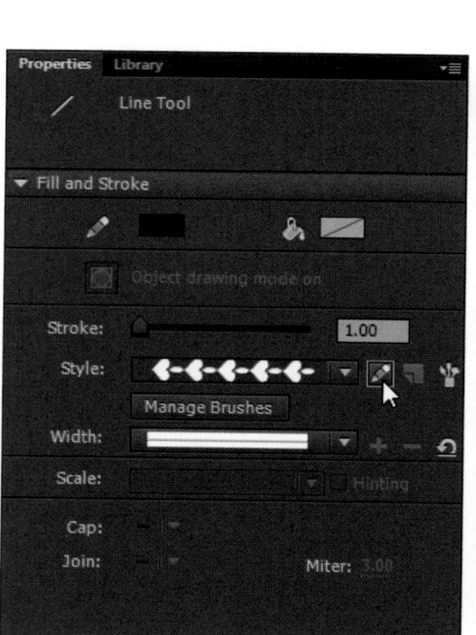

3 While the style is selected, click the Edit stroke style button to open the Paint Brush Options dialog.

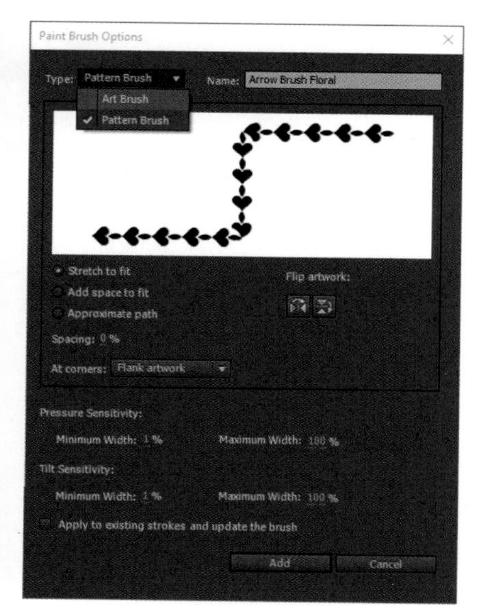

4 The current style attributes such as Type, Name, fitting, spacing, corner treatment, Pressure Sensitivity, and Tilt Sensitivity are displayed in the dialog. From the Type drop-down menu, you can switch between the Art Brush and Pattern Brush.

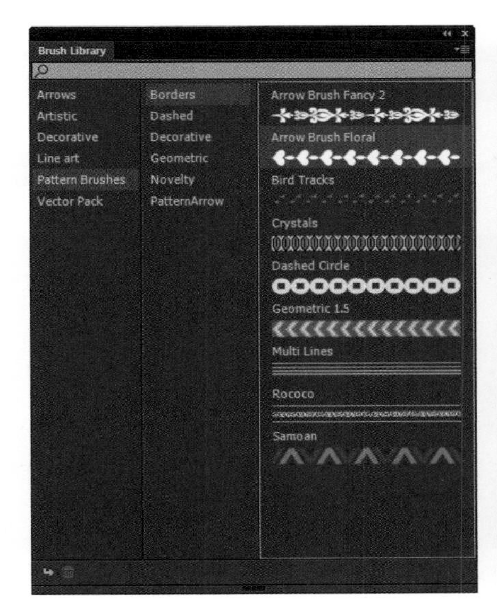

2 Double-click any stroke from the library to add it to your document.

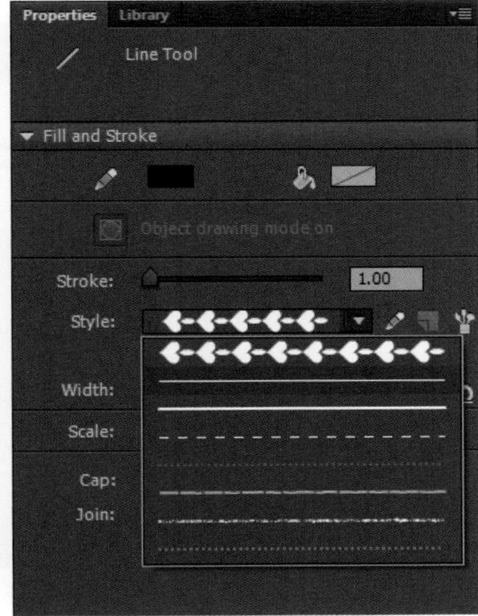

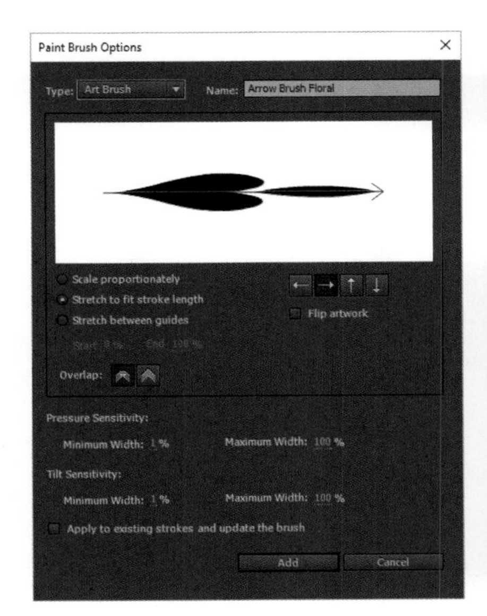

5 By default, the Art Brush is set to Stretch to fit stroke length.

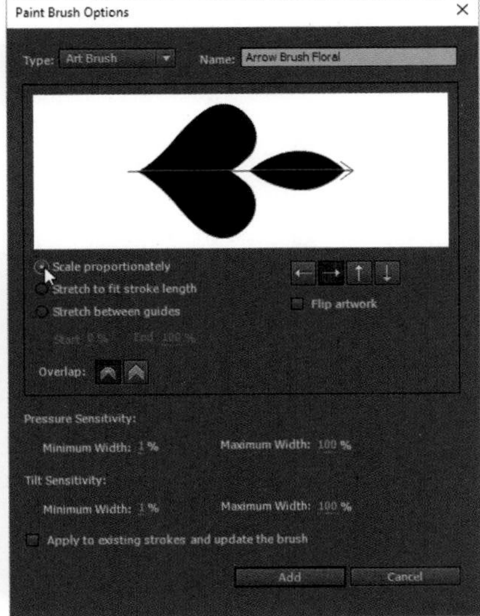

6 For the Art Brush, scaling can be set so that it is proportional to the stroke which fits a proportional version of the artwork to the stroke.

Vector Art Brush Editing Options (cont.)

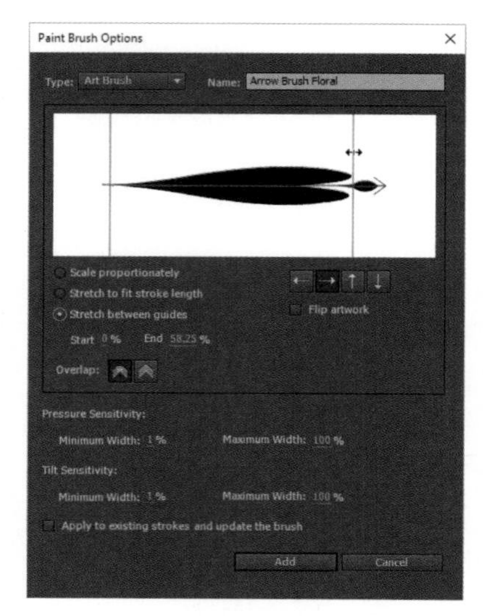

7 An Art Brush with the setting Stretch between guides keeps the artwork outside of the guides proportional while stretching the artwork between the guides along the stroke. Adjust the guides so that the parts you don't want distorted are outside of the guides.

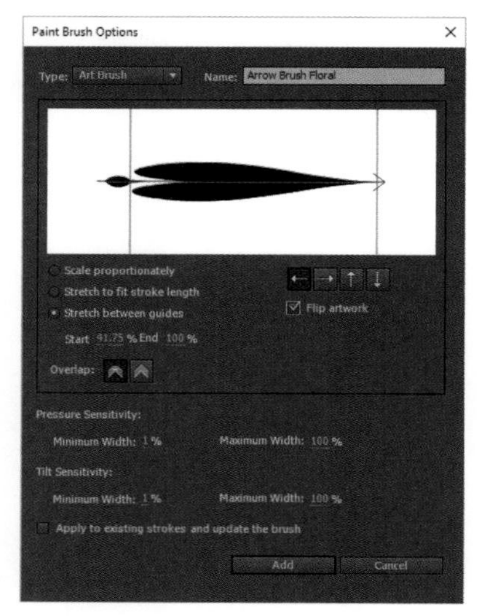

8 You can use the arrows and the Flip artwork option in order to orient the artwork within the guides.

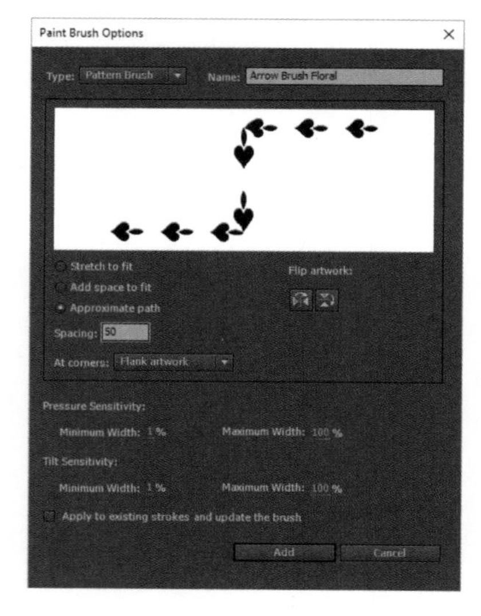

11 Likewise, spacing lets you add more space between each instance of the artwork along the stroke.

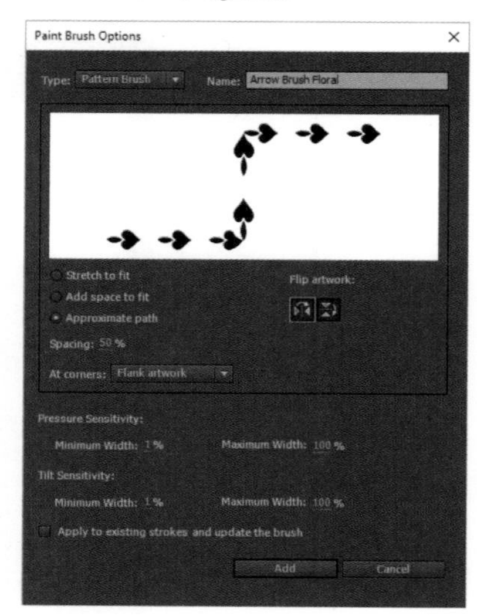

12 You can flip the artwork for the Pattern Brush to control the direction of the artwork along the stroke.

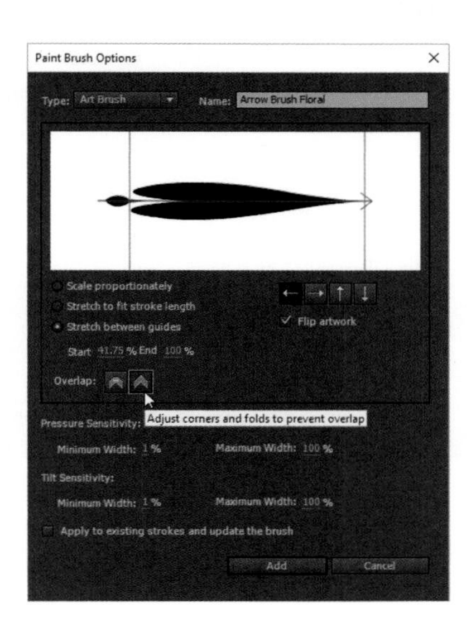

9 Set the Overlap for the Art Brush to indicate how corners should be treated.

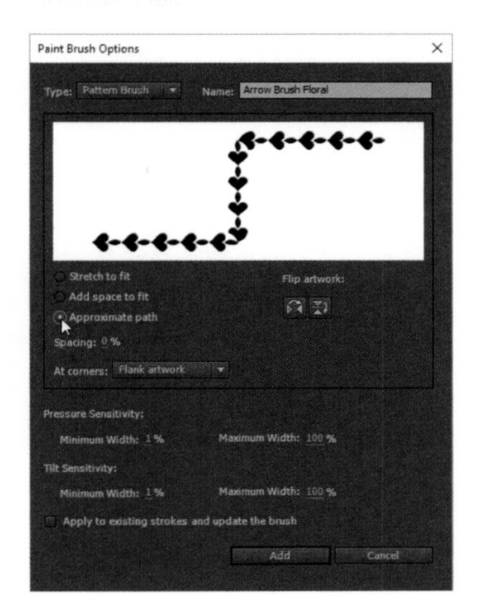

10 The Pattern Brush applies multiple instances along a stroke. The fitting options allow you to control the spacing of the multiple instances along the stroke.

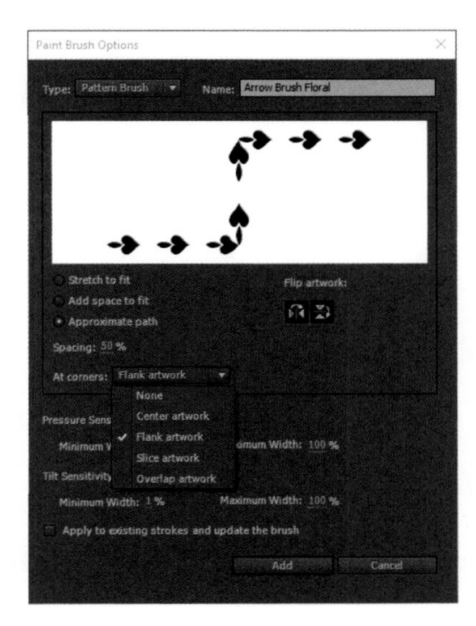

13 The Pattern Brush has more options for handling corners than the Art Brush. The options in the drop-down menu include the following: None, which leaves the corners blank; Center artwork, which splits the top of the instance with the bottom of the preceding one diagonally through the center; Flank artwork, which also splits the corner; Slice artwork, which cuts the previous and next instances through the center of the corner; and Overlap, which overlaps the previous and next instances at the corner.

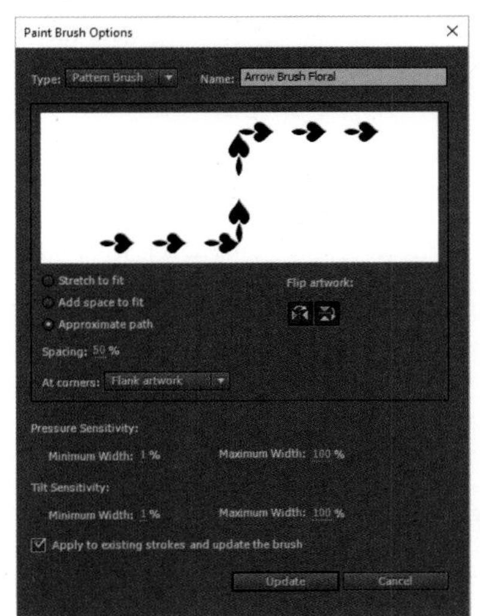

14 For both brush types, Pressure and Tilt Sensitivity are set from 1% to 100% by default. And if you want to apply your new settings to any strokes you made with the brush before editing it, select Apply to existing strokes and update the brush. If not, leave it unselected, and when you click Add, Animate adds it to your document.

HOT TIP

Also new to Animate is the Manage Brushes button on the Properties panel. Click it to open the Manage Document Brushes dialog. It lists all the varieties of new brush edits that you made in the document. You can delete any of the brushes. Animate shows you an alert if you try to delete a brush that is currently being used in the document to explain why it's not being deleted. If you want to save your edited brush to the Brush Library, select it and click Save to Brush Library. It will appear in the category named My Brushes.

The Lightning Round

AS TIME runs out at the end of some game shows, there is often a switch to a lightning round. Think of that idea while we blaze through these updates which undoubtedly are going to be worth a lot to us.

1 Layer Transparency is one of those quick workflow improvements that make tasks like using a sketch as a guide to create artwork easier. Shift-click the layer on the Show or Hide Layer column to turn that to 50% of its opacity. Shift-click again to toggle it back to 100%.

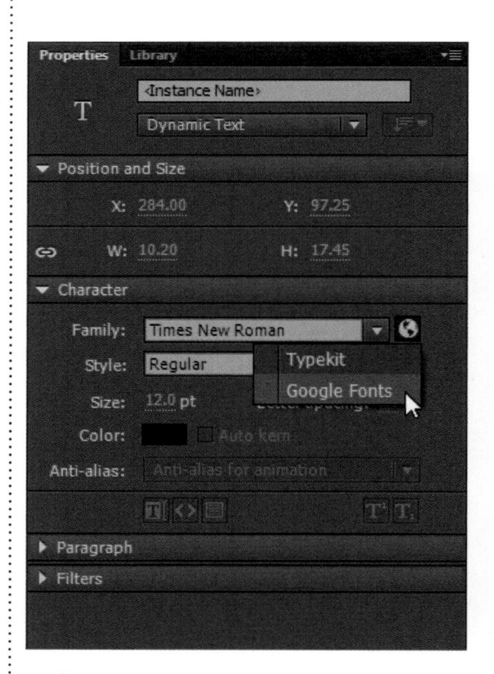

3 Google Font support for HTML5 Canvas lets you select from free open-source fonts served by Google for a faster and more aesthetically pleasing experience. In your HTML5 Canvas document, set your text field to Dynamic, click on the Add Web fonts button, and select Google Fonts.

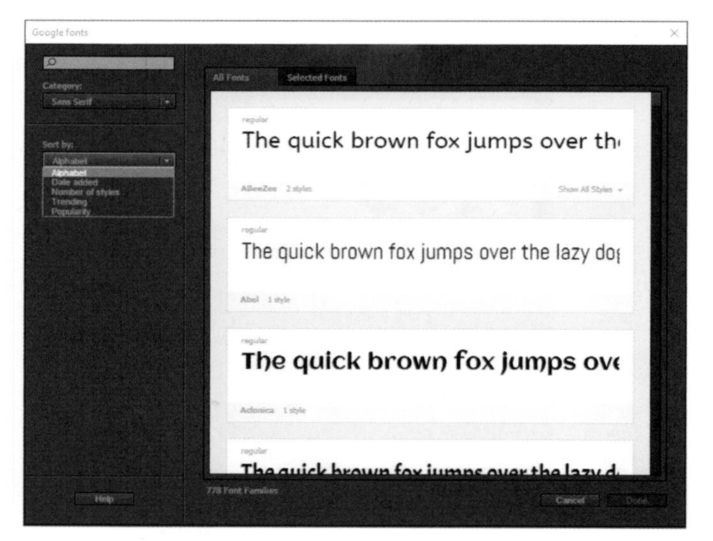

4 From the Google Fonts dialog, you can search through available fonts, make your selection, and have your font(s) added to your document.

VECTOR ILLUSTRATIONS: MYRA FERGUSON

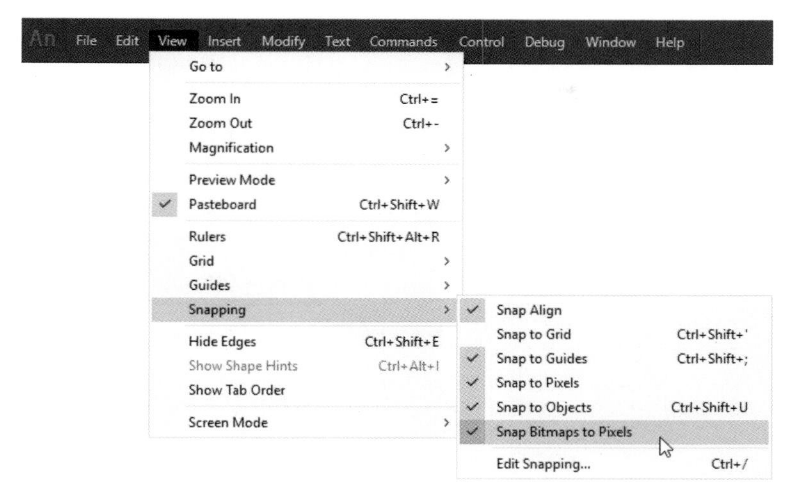

2 Bitmap Snapping is an option under View > Snapping that snaps any placed bitmap to the nearest pixel, which translates into placing it at a location on the *X* or *Y* axis at an integer. Without Bitmap Snapping turned on, a bitmap could be placed at a fractional location, which makes it blurry when published.

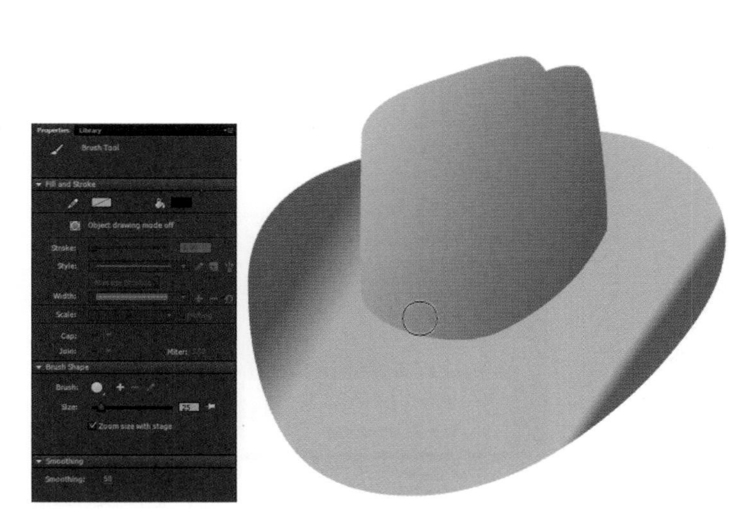

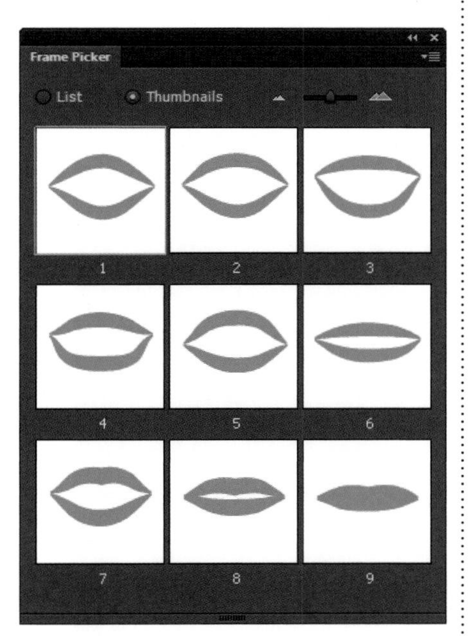

5 New brush sizes are among one of the most recent updates. You now can select a brush from 1 to 200 pixels and see a live preview as you change sizes. Both the brush and eraser show their outlines, so you can see what area you'll be affecting underneath. Brush settings are sticky, so Animate remembers what brush you last used.

6 The Frame Picker is a panel you can launch from the Properties panel when you're working with a Graphic symbol. It's especially useful when animating. Instead of entering a number for a single frame, use the previews as either a List with small thumbnails or larger Thumbnails to find which frame to use. Click the thumbnail to set your frame.

The Lightning Round (cont.)

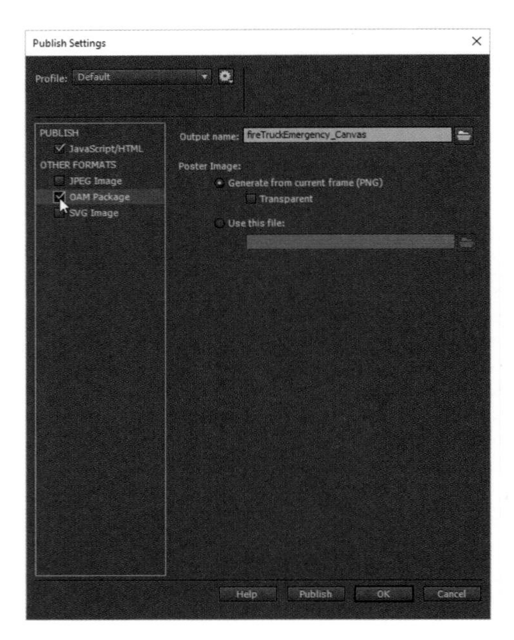

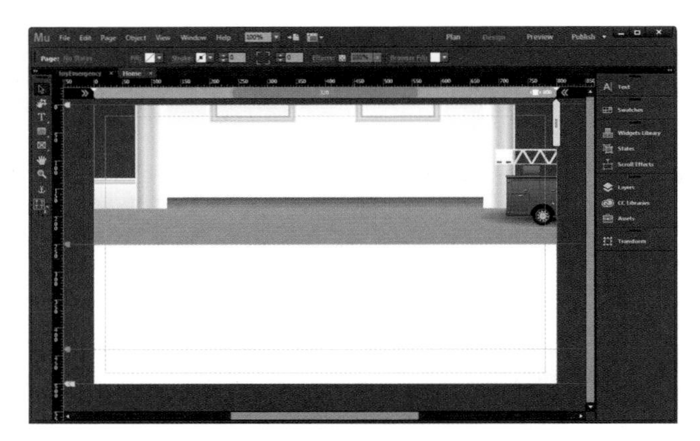

7 OAM publishing support has been added for AS3, WebGL, and HTML5 Canvas documents. What's OAM? For the curious, it stands for OpenAjax Metadata. What it does is package your animation so that it can be placed into web layouts for Dreamweaver, Muse, and InDesign. Select OAM Package in your Publish Settings and Publish.

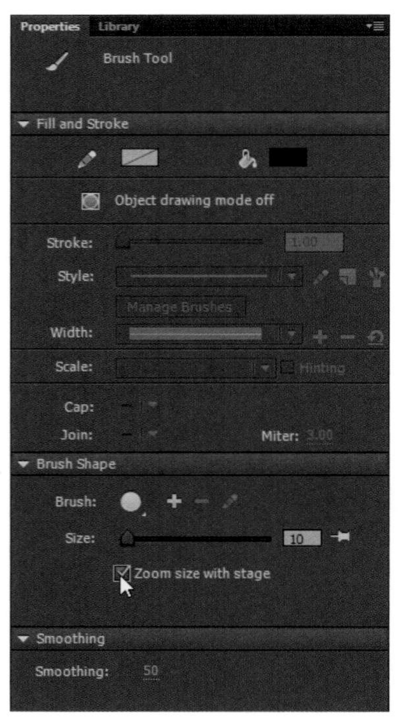

9 Brush scaling with Stage zoom also just barely predated the name change. It's a handy option that lets you choose if you want your brush to zoom with the Stage or not.

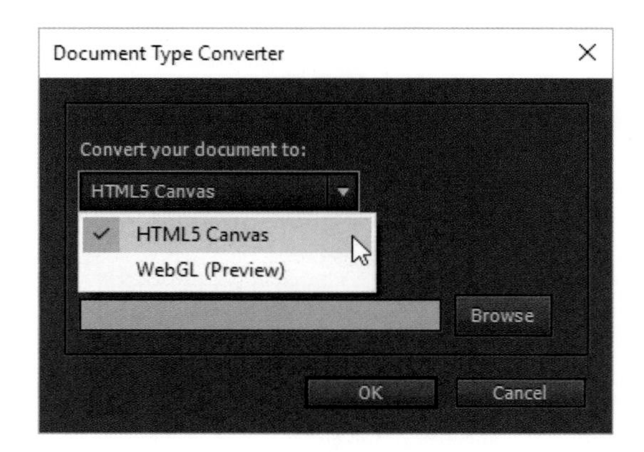

10 Last but certainly not least, the Universal document type converter lets you turn your FLA into another document type like HTML5 Canvas or WebGL, so you can work on your document using Animate's toolset for those document types.

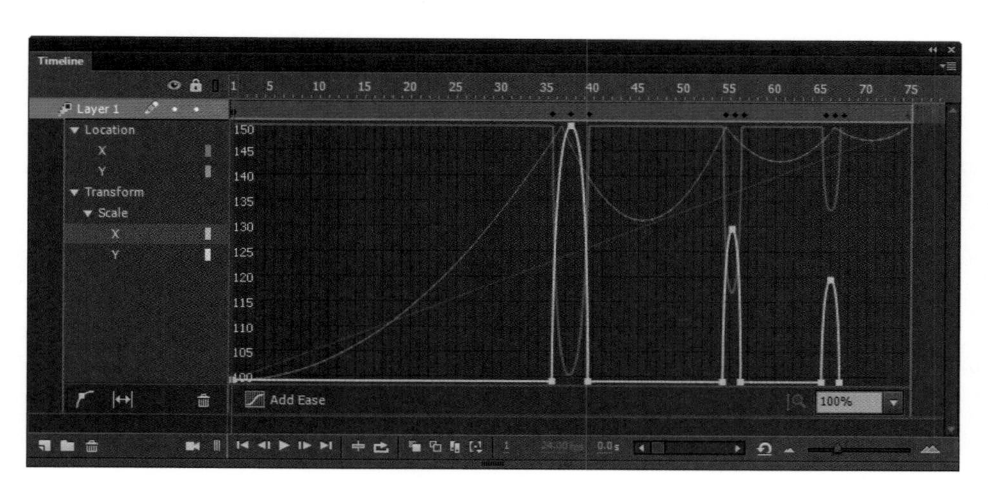

8 The Improved Motion Editor was an update that was released just before Animate's name change. Right-click on a Motion Tween and select Refine Tween or double-click on the Motion Tween span to open the Editor. Select a property to access its curve to edit it.

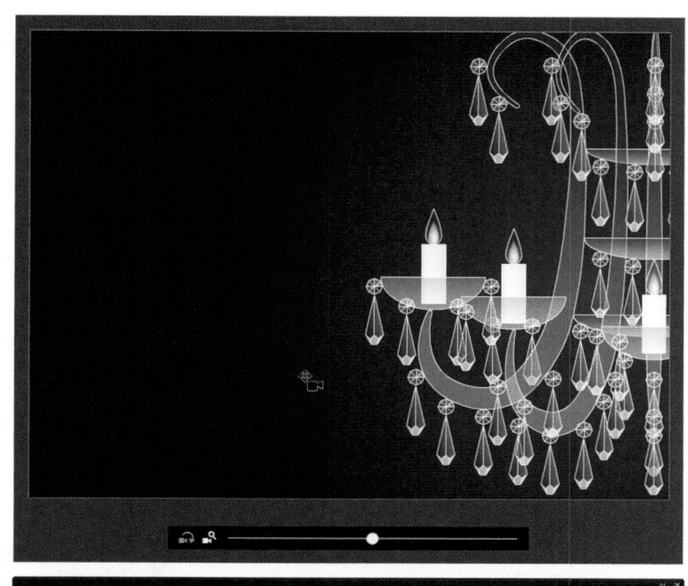

11 The camera in Animate is a virtual camera that lets you pan, zoom, change a focal point, rotate, and add tints or filters. The camera makes animated camera moves and cuts much simpler by affecting just the one camera layer.

HOT TIP

Among Animate's new features was a grab bag labeled "Other enhancements" that are worth checking out. These improvements include faster saving, Auto-recovery improvements, organizing imported GIFs in the Library, searching Library by linkage name, Edit > Invert Selection, pasting and overwriting frames, Reset timeline zoom to the default level, Pinscript, faster performance on Windows, and Stage clipping.

And That's Not All....

I HATE TO SOUND LIKE A TV INFOMERCIAL, BUT SHORT OF A FAST SCROLLING LIST OF NEW FEATURES AND UPDATES WITH a voice-over that's so sped up that it's unintelligible, it's practically impossible to keep up with the mountain of features the Animate Team has been releasing. Below you'll find a list of notable updates that I haven't even mentioned yet. I'll leave it up to you to read it really fast in your best TV voice.

Easier audio syncing

Multiplatform support

4K+ video export

Custom resolution export

Import H.264 videos with audio

Export bitmaps as sprite sheet for HTML5 Canvas

Improved audio workflows

Panel locking

Code snippet support for WebGL

Enhancement in Custom Platform Support SDK

Integration of latest Flash Player and AIR SDK

Integration of latest CreateJS libraries

TypeScript definition file for WebGL runtime API

Turbocharged Performance on Windows platform

Center Stage options for Canvas Publishing

Responsive Scaling options for Canvas Publishing

Preloader options for Canvas Publishing

Option to Publish Canvas assets to root folder

JSAPI support to import and export HTML templates for Canvas documents

Latest Flash Player and AIR SDK integration

New publish profile format (.apr)

Changes to zoom in timeline

Enhancements to Onion Skin markers

Custom ease and ease presets

Export texture atlas

Packaging, distributing, and installing HTML5 custom components

Additional language support

Custom time stamp URL option

In-app toast notifications for help with specific features

Automatic creation of keyframes using the Frame Picker

Mute and poster properties support for HTML5 video component

Support for Typekit Market Place fonts

Improved sketching with the Brush Tool

Pasteboard color as an infinite canvas

There's no sign of the team slowing down with the new features anytime soon. So you can always find out what's in the latest release as well as previous releases by visiting the Adobe Animate Features page on the Adobe website at www.adobe.com/products/animate/features.html.

Turning over a New Leaf

LOW POLY PUMPKIN: VECTOR ILLUSTRATION: MYRA FERGUSON

FALL IS MY FAVORITE SEASON. I LOVE THE COLORS OF FALL, AND THE COOL, CRISP AIR means sweater weather is upon us. It's the beginning of a new school year with new school clothes and supplies or just good sales if you're out of school and not shopping for kiddos. It's also when the fall television season begins. It's exciting. It's new. You can feel the energy and all the potential. I absolutely love it! Even though Animate was introduced in February of 2016, the team keeps generating updates that make it feel like Animate is in this new season with this same vibrance.

Did you see all the new features in Chapter 1? The best part is the Animate team keeps bestowing on us fabulous surprises. What's encouraging is all the support for Animate from Adobe—not just in terms of what the team is doing, but in support for the users. Adobe MAX sold out of many of its Animate labs, so they kept adding more.

The interest keeps growing and with good reason. If you used Flash before, you know the tools let you realize just about any idea you can conceive. And now with such a new lease on life, it couldn't be a better time to see what's been added and updated. Renaming the application to Animate represents this transformation with new tools, improved performance, updated features, and several new output options.

What I'm most thrilled to see is what users like you make with Animate. Summer break is over. Let's get to work and make this our most creative year!

■ No two snowflakes are exactly alike, and the same can be said for artists and designers. A good drawing program will allow this individuality to be expressed without limitation.

2 Design Styles

ANIMATE'S DRAWING TOOLS NOT ONLY MAKE GETTING started easy, but they also allow for designing with greater complexity as you become more proficient. With new features being added regularly through your Creative Cloud subscription, there are even more ways to create. Let's take a look at the fundamentals of designing in Animate, some new tools to enjoy, and some techniques for creating popular effects along the way.

Drawing with Basic Shapes

IF YOU PLAYED WITH LEGO BUILDING blocks as a kid, you may find this drawing style familiar (or at least intuitive). You'll use several basic shapes and then connect them together. This technique requires breaking down each body part of the character into basic building blocks using the Rectangle and Oval Tools. It's a fast and efficient way to simplify the character into manageable sections while achieving a very professional cartoon style.

Here, we will use shapes to cut into other shapes. We'll cut holes out of objects as well as alter the edges of shapes. Of course these techniques can be applied to background elements as well.

The key here is using simple shapes to build complex images suitable for animating with Animate, which we will get to in later chapters.

1 Here is my original pencil sketch that I have scanned and saved as a JPG file. I prefer to start with pencil on paper, because I simply like the feel of this medium and the results are always a little more, shall we say, artistic.

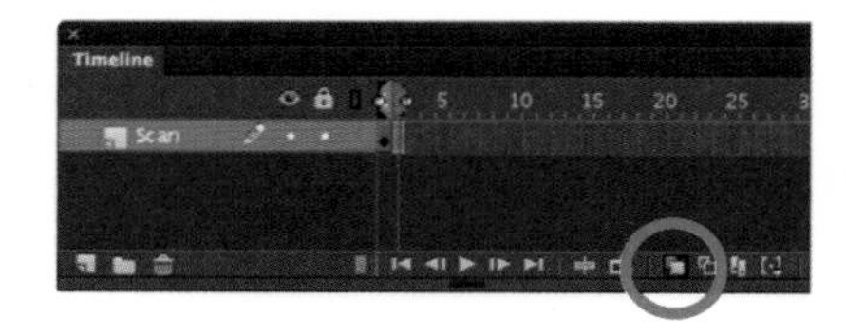

2 After importing the scanned image, insert a blank keyframe on frame 2 and turn on Onion Skin. Onion Skinning allows you to trace the image in a new frame while using the original image as a reference.

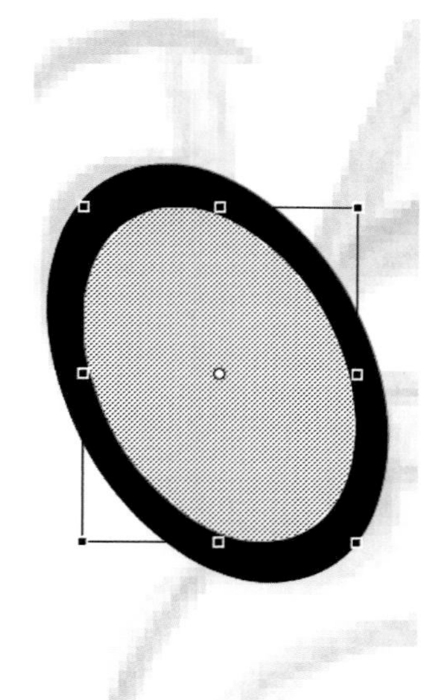

6 To achieve the black outline, select the shape, copy it using ⌘ ctrl C, and paste it in place using ⌘ ctrl Shift V. While it's still selected, select a different color from the Mixer panel and scale it about 80% smaller.

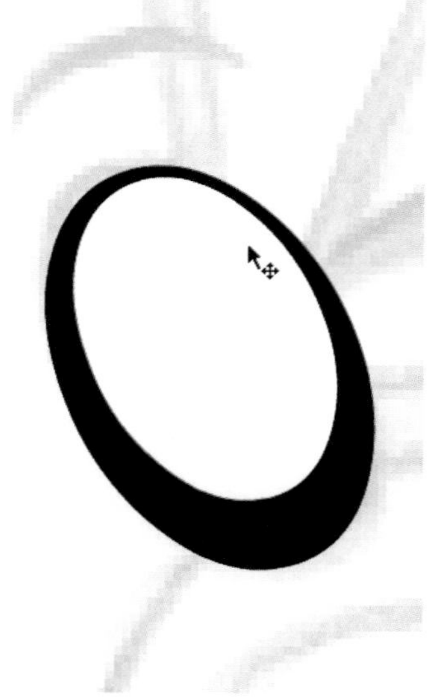

7 The original shape is still present underneath your new shape. The trick is to position the new shape off-center from the original to achieve an outline with a varied weight.

3 Using the Oval Tool O and Rectangle Tool R allows you to quickly achieve the basic forms of the character. The Selection Tool V is great for pushing and pulling these basic fills into custom shapes based on the sketch.

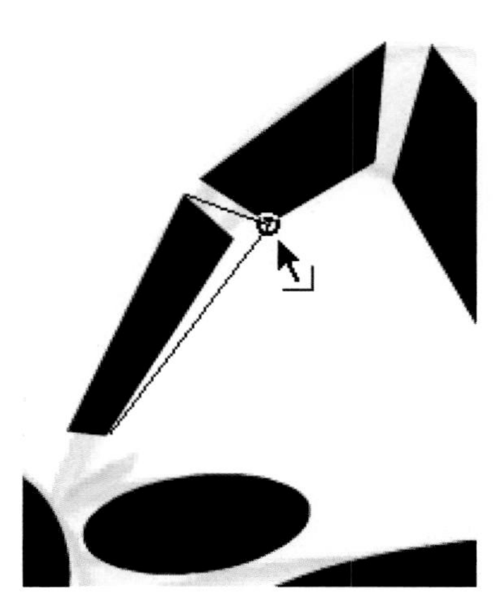

4 Turn on the Snap option (magnet icon) and drag corners to each other, so they snap together. This process is not unlike those Lego building blocks you played with when you were a kid.

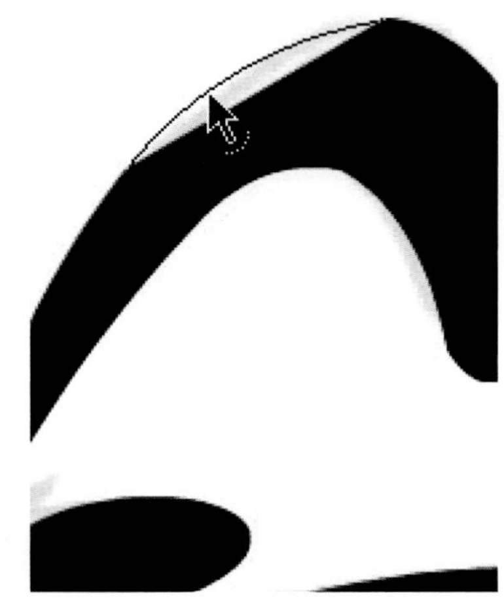

5 Next, click and drag the sides of your shapes to push and pull them into curves. This process is fun as your character really starts to take shape.

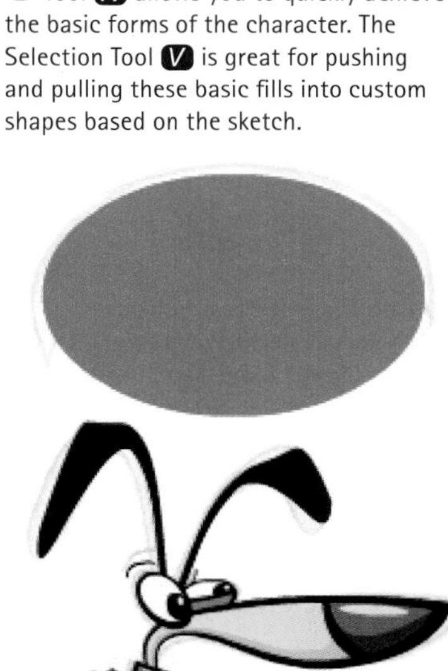

8 The parachute uses a slightly different technique I like to call "cutting in." Let's start with the Oval Tool O for the parachute's basic shape.

9 You can cut into this shape using different colored shapes such as this blue oval. Position it over the area you want to cut into, deselect it, select it, and hit the Delete key Delete.

10 Once your shape is the way you want it, you can use the Ink Bottle Tool S to quickly add an outline to it.

HOT TIP

As you complete individual sections of your character, cut and paste them into new layers and lock them. Putting them on separate layers will prevent them from being inadvertently edited. Better yet, convert them to symbols while you're at it.

Geometric and Organic Shapes

DESIGNING WITH BASIC SHAPES IS NOT limited to characters. For most Animate projects, I start with primitive shapes for all objects including props and backgrounds. At their most basic level, my designs start with simple ovals or rectangles, and from there I build upon these shapes to create relatively complex images. What I love about working with vectors is the ability to push and pull them into anything I want as if they were made of clay.

VECTOR ILLUSTRATION: CHRIS GEORGENES

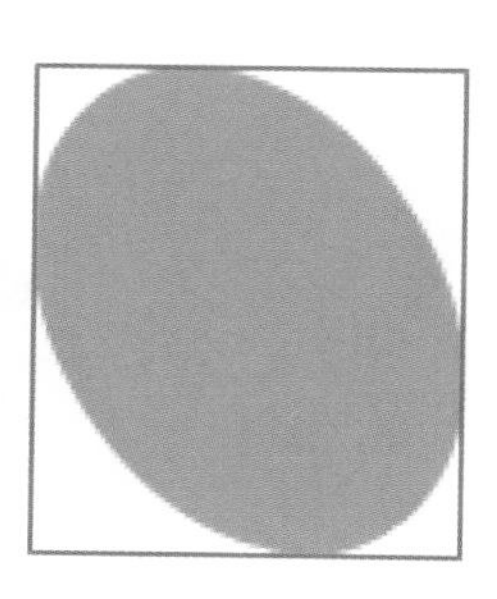
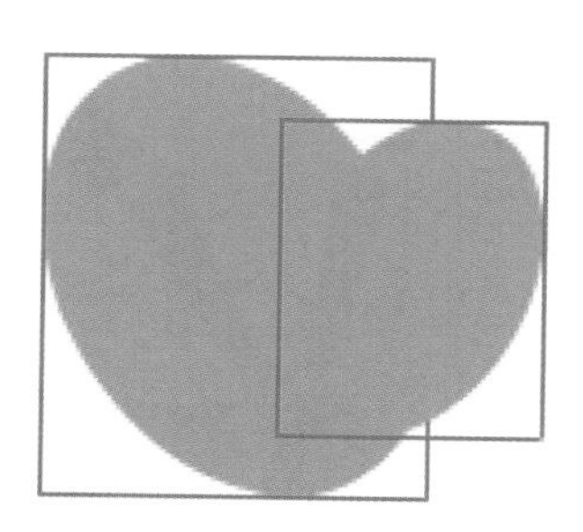

1 To suggest a fully mature tree with a plumage of leaves, you don't actually have to draw each individual leaf. Since the design style is targeted at young children, it's valid to keep the level of detail to a minimum. Select the Oval Tool (O) and your desired fill color and create an oval shape. Next rotate it or skew to position it at an angle. Copy and paste it and scale it to add more leaves. Rotate and position the new oval as shown above. There's no wrong decision at this stage as it is entirely up to you as to how much variation you want your tree to have.

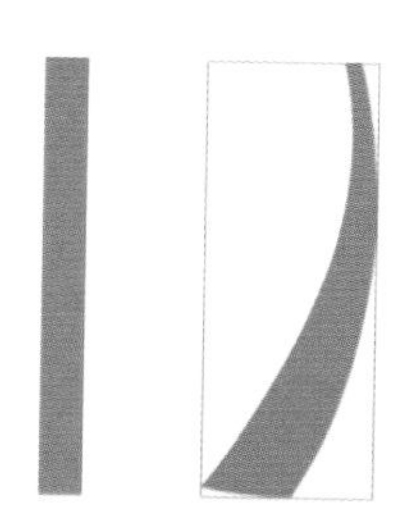

3 The trunk of the tree is designed in a similar fashion. Create a basic rectangle using the Rectangle Tool (R) and use the Selection Tool (V) to push and pull the sides and corners to give the trunk a slight curve and taper. Each branch is a duplicate of the tree trunk shape. Hold down (⌥/alt) and then click and drag the trunk to create as many duplicates of it as you want. Scale, skew, rotate, and position each duplicate shape so that they resemble tree branches.

5 With Snap to Objects on, drag a corner point to another corner point until they snap together. Snapping to an object makes it easy to merge different shapes together accurately. To complete the front side of the birdhouse, create another square and drag the top two corner points to the bottom two corner points of the triangle with the Selection Tool (V) until they snap together. Skew the shape with the Distort Tool (subselection of the Free Transform Tool (Q)) to suggest perspective.

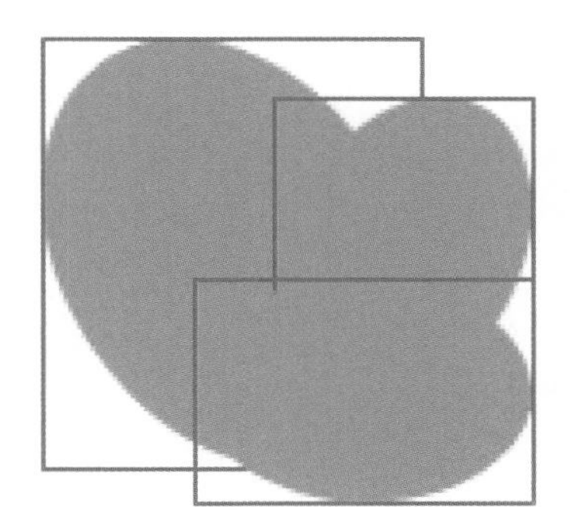

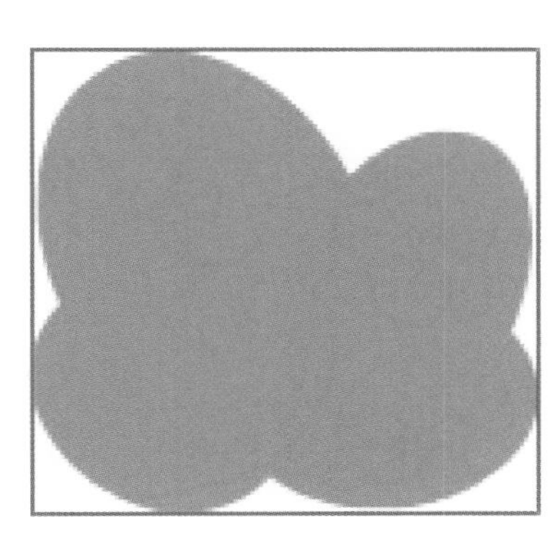

2 Repeat the previous step by copying and pasting the same oval to suggest a larger plumage of leaves. Scale, skew, and rotate the shape and position it off-center from the original oval. The objective here is to create a nonsymmetrical organic shape to suggest the imperfections that are found in nature. Remember, nothing in nature is perfectly horizontal, vertical, round, or square, which is why there's no wrong way to position these. As you can see I used a total of four ovals to complete my plumage of leaves. I could have used more or less, but I felt this was just the right amount. Feel free to experiment with the number of shapes and variations for your tree. At this stage, I couldn't help but add a little bit of texture to suggest some volume using the Brush Tool B and a subtle yellow color.

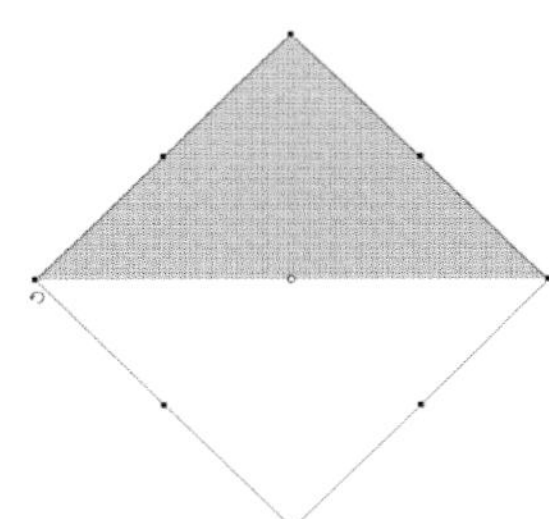

4 The birdhouse is also built using simple shapes. The key here is to turn on the Snap to Objects feature represented by the magnet icon in the toolbar when you select the Rectangle Tool R. Create a perfect square by dragging with the Rectangle Tool while holding down the Shift key. Using the Subselection Tool A, select one of the corner points and press the Delete key. The square is now a triangle. Rotate the triangle using the Free Transform Tool Q. Hold down the Shift key to constrain the rotation to 45° increments. Rotate the triangle until the bottom side is flat and the top side is pointed.

6 The remaining additional shapes for the birdhouse are also (you guessed it) simple rectangles and ovals. Keeping the Snap option turned on, drag corner points to each other to join shapes and as Object Drawings you can also overlap shapes to complete the image.

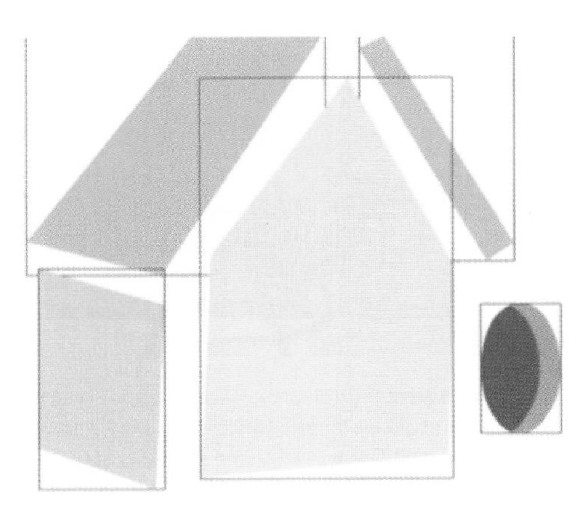

HOT TIP

As you can see each shape has a bounding box around it because Object Drawing Mode J was turned on at the time the objects were drawn. Object Drawing Mode allows you to overlap objects without merging them together.

The Brush Tool

THE BRUSH TOOL IS PROBABLY THE most versatile of all the drawing tools especially when combined with a pressure-sensitive tablet.

Drawing with the Brush Tool is essentially drawing with shapes. It's the tool that feels the most natural due to the support of pressure sensitivity and tilt features.

Wacom makes a series of popular tablets that work great with Animate. They can work in conjunction with your existing mouse or replace your mouse completely. Many digital designers use a tablet with any number of graphics editors including Adobe Photoshop and Adobe Illustrator. Deciding to use the Brush Tool is really a matter of style and preference. For this character, I wanted to achieve a loose, hand-drawn feel, so the Brush was a perfect choice.

1 The first adjustment you will want to make when using the Brush Tool (B) will be the amount of smoothing you want applied. This option appears as a hot text slider in the Properties panel when the Brush Tool is selected. The right amount of smoothing to use depends on personal preference. The higher the number, the smoother the line (and vice versa). For this character, we'll choose a low amount of smoothing to maintain an organic quality to the line work.

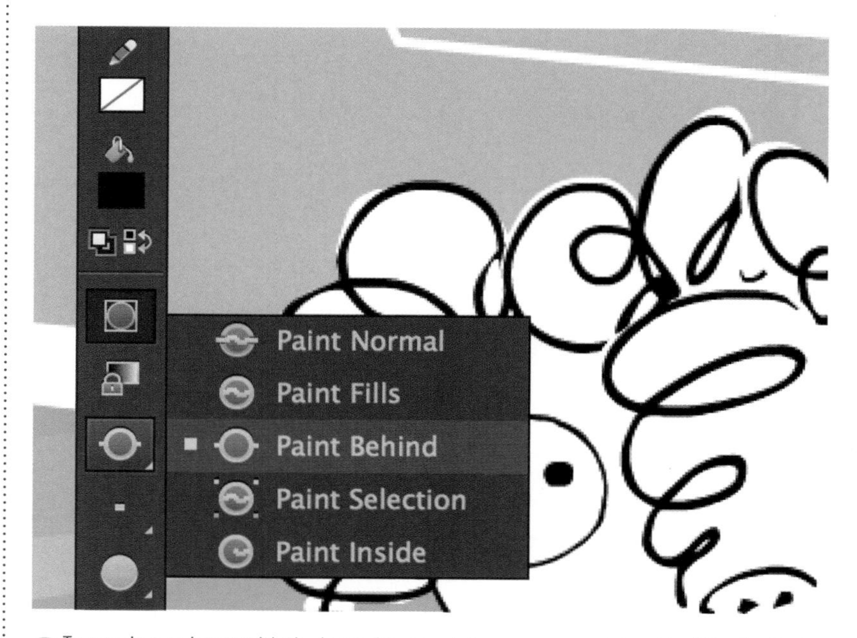

3 To remain consistent with the loose drawing style, you may want to add a fill color that bleeds outside of the outlines a little. There are several ways to achieve this effect by painting on a new layer below the outline art or setting the brush to "Paint Behind" and painting on the same layer.

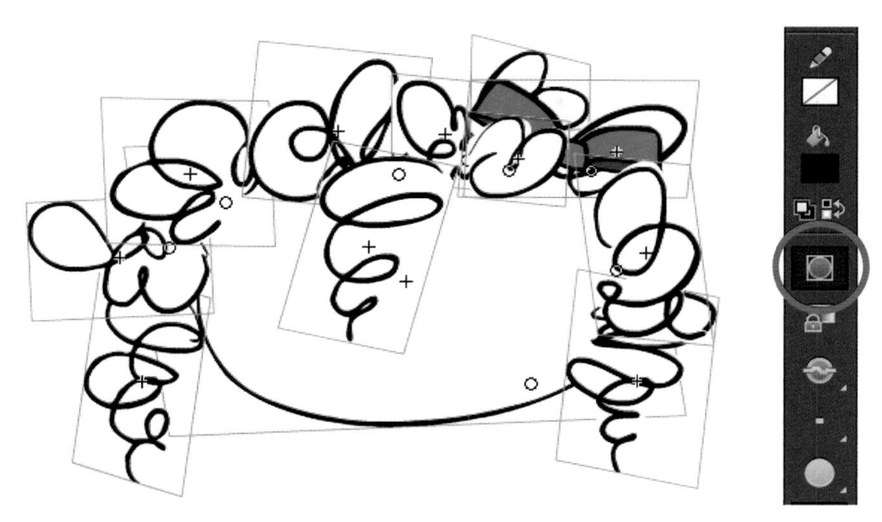

2 Always design your characters with the intended purpose in mind: animation. Form follows function, and the animation style can often dictate how a character is designed. If you're a perfectionist like me, you'll want the hair to look as much like individual curls as possible. To make their movement more realistic avoid designing the hair as one large flat object. Instead, draw individual sections of curls to keep them as separate objects, so they can be moved independently of each other. Turn on Object Drawing Mode J (subselection of the Brush Tool). Object Drawing Mode allows you to draw shapes as separate objects. These objects can be drawn over each other without them being merged together. You can select each Object Drawing with the Selection Tool V and then convert each one to a symbol.

4 The final result represents the loose hand-drawn style we were after. The line quality feels natural and reflects the imperfections the human hand is capable of. We are not trying to achieve a slick design style here but rather to convey a looser line quality representative of hand-drawn artwork. This style lends itself well to a child character as the integrity of the line is similar to how a real child would draw.

HOT TIP

Experiment with different Stage magnifications when drawing. I prefer to draw on a larger scale and with the Stage magnified about 400%. Even when the option Zoom size with Stage is checked in the Brush Shape section of the Properties panel, which retains the brush size regardless of the magnification, the result is typically a smoother line quality.

The Brush Tool (cont.)

IN ITS DEFAULT MODE, THE BRUSH TOOL—along with a graphics tablet that supports pressure sensitivity—is great for drawing shapes with a varied width. The success of the Brush Tool may be due to its simplicity, but that doesn't mean you can't achieve sophisticated results when using it. The Brush Tool provides several options that affect how the paint is applied, and with a little ingenuity you can dictate how the Brush works based on your needs and workflow. This example shows my use of the Paint Selection setting for the Brush, allowing it to paint within the confines of a selected fill color only.

1 The character sketch was created using Procreate, a powerful drawing app for the Apple iPad. I used a drawing stylus instead of my finger because of its accuracy.

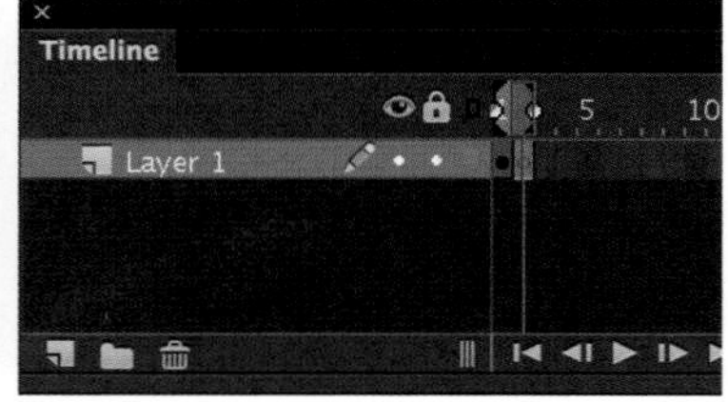

2 After importing the scanned image, I inserted a blank keyframe on frame 2 and turned on Onion Skin. I began tracing the image in a new frame while using the original image as a reference.

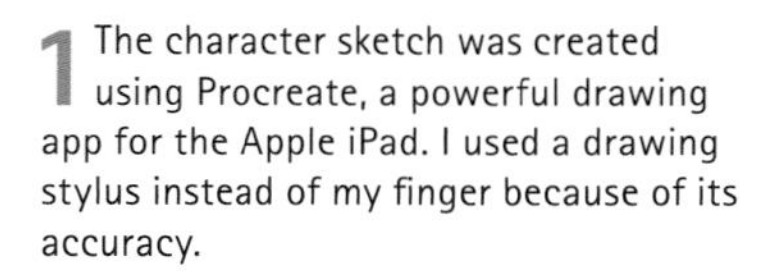

6 Paint anywhere inside the selected fill color without destroying any other part of the drawing. The shapes made with this Brush Tool setting will be limited to the selected area only.

7 The Paint Selection setting is perfect for adding lines to suggest strands of hair. I also used this same technique for adding the shadows around the character's eyes.

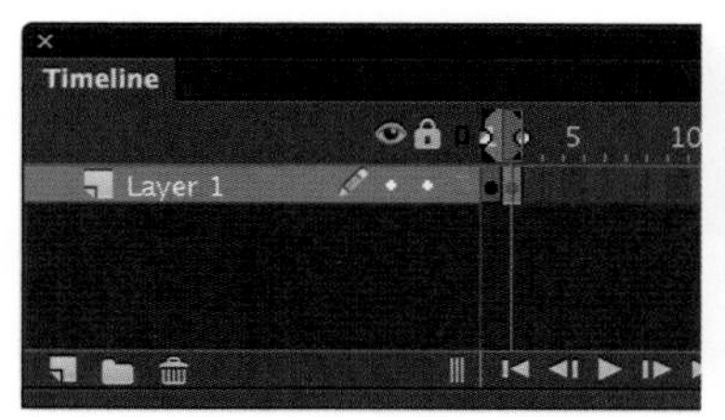

3 I traced the character using the Brush Tool B. Typically I have the Brush Tool smoothness setting at a value between 60 and 75, which can be adjusted in the Smoothing section of the Properties panel while the Brush Tool is selected.

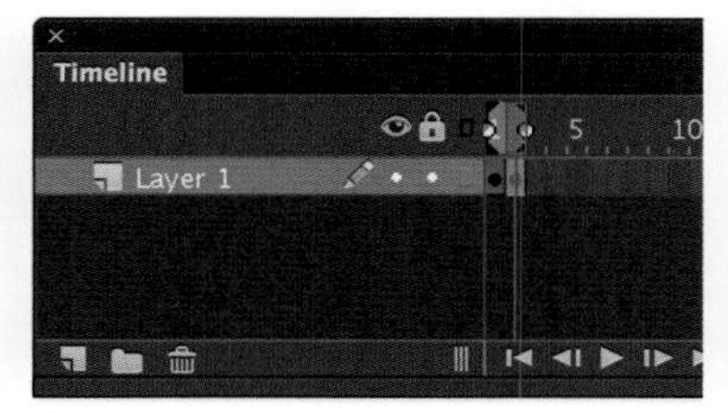

4 With the character outline complete, it's time to mix a color for his skin tone and fill the head using the Paint Bucket Tool K.

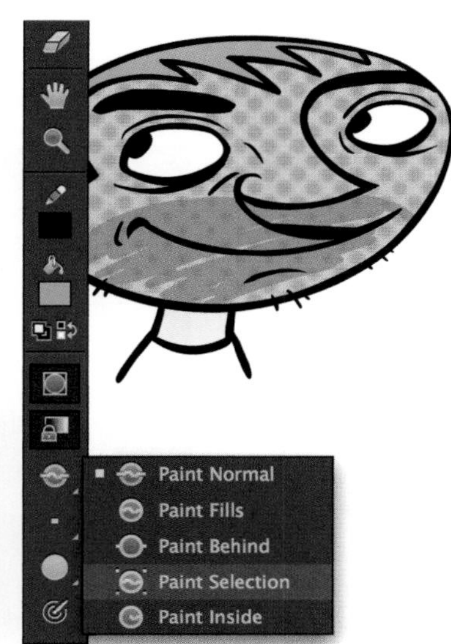

5 Select the fill color using the Selection Tool V. To add some shading to the character, mix a darker value of the skin tone and then select the Paint Selection option from the Brush Tool subselection menu.

8 The Smoothing value was set to 72 for this drawing, meaning Animate smoothed the shapes created with the Brush Tool just enough to remove most of my natural imperfections of drawing by hand. For a more natural-looking drawing, adjust the Smoothness to a lower numerical value.

9 Here's a version of the same character drawn with a Smoothing value of 0. The difference in line quality is subtle, but if you look closely it's quite noticeable how imperfect the overall image is. With no smoothing applied, the drawing can take on a completely different look and feel.

HOT TIP

You can apply smoothing after a shape has been drawn with the Brush Tool. Select the shape with the Selection Tool and click Smooth at the bottom of the Tools panel. Alternately you can click Straighten to straighten the edges of the selected shape.

SHORTCUTS
MAC WIN BOTH

Vector Art Brush: Artistic Brushes

THE NEW VECTOR ART BRUSHES open up a lot of creative possibilities especially with the wide range of styles including Arrows, Artistic, Decorative, Line art, Vector Pack, and Pattern Brushes. The Artistic brushes are vector versions of mediums representing an array of techniques, but these brushes can be used for more than merely what they simulate. Be creative! We're going to apply a mix of them to text to create the impression of chalkboard sign art.

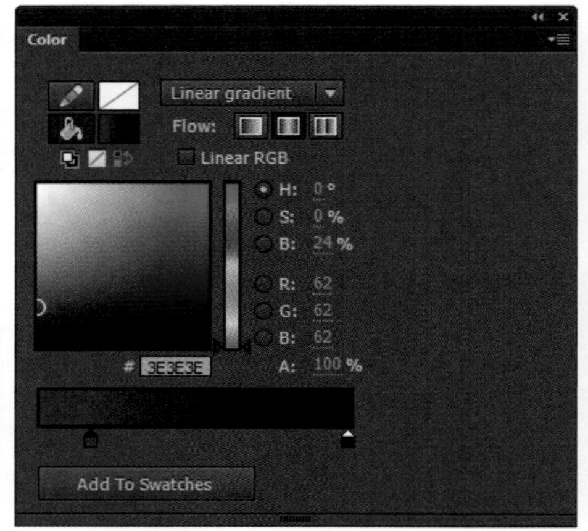

1 Start with a background that looks like a chalkboard with some faded chalk dust left after erasing an earlier message. On an 800 × 600 pixels. Stage, make a rectangle of the same size. Open the Color panel and set the fill to a linear gradient using dark gray and black. Move the dark gray stop inward for the gray to occupy more of the space. Set the Flow to Reflect color.

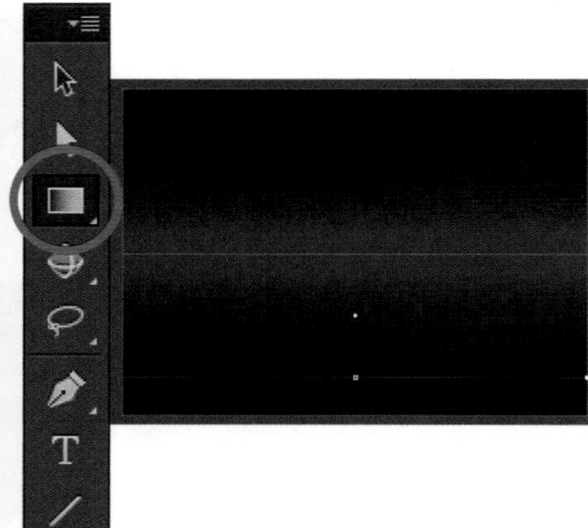

2 Use the Gradient Transform Tool (F) to rotate the gradient making it horizontal and scaled so that the next repeated reflection starts to show. Position the gradient from the middle to near the bottom edge where the main gray band should be nearly centered vertically.

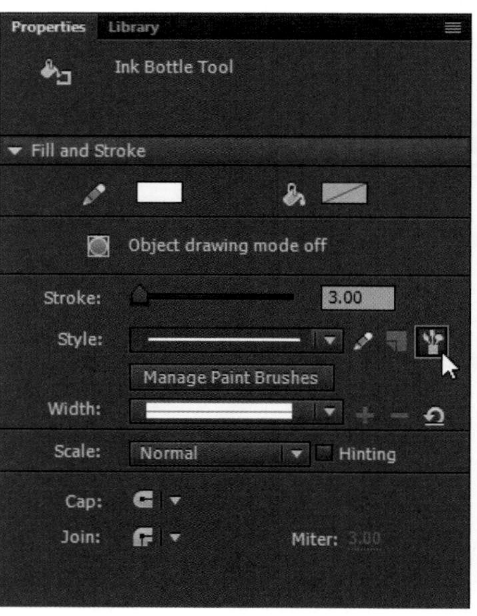

6 Click the Brush Library button to open the Brush Library.

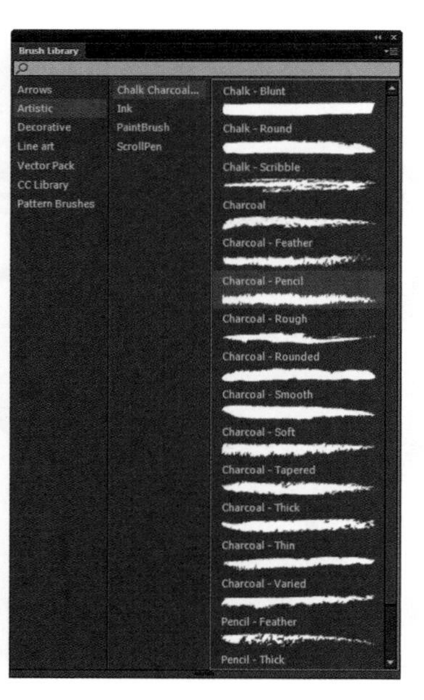

7 In the Brush Library, go to Artistic > Chalk Charcoal Pencil and double-click Charcoal - Pencil to add it to our document's stroke styles.

VECTOR ILLUSTRATION: MYRA FERGUSON

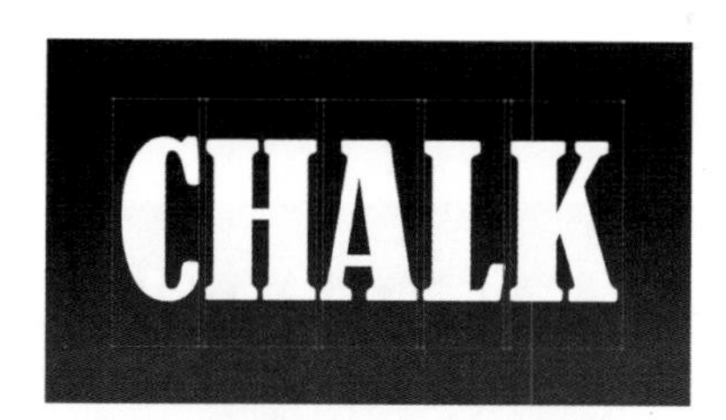

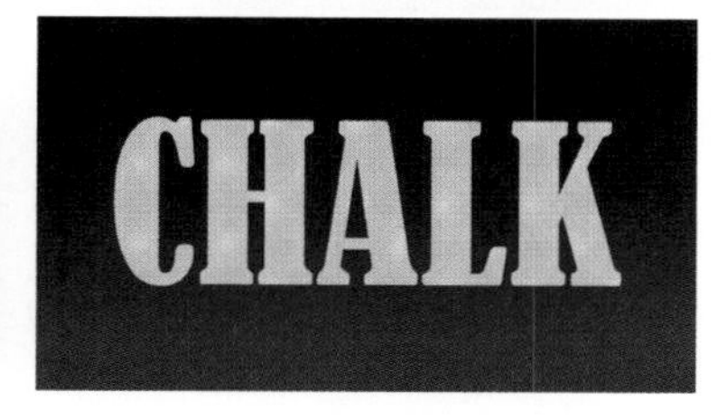

3 Lock the background layer and type "CHALK" on a new layer. I used Bernard MT Condensed at 145 pt. in white.

4 Break the text apart ⌘/ctrl B twice which first makes the editable word a collection of editable text boxes containing the individual letters and then turns all the letters into shapes, which are no longer editable as text.

5 Currently the text has no stroke, so set up what to apply. Select the Ink Bottle Tool S, which contextually opens the Fill and Stroke settings in the Properties panel.

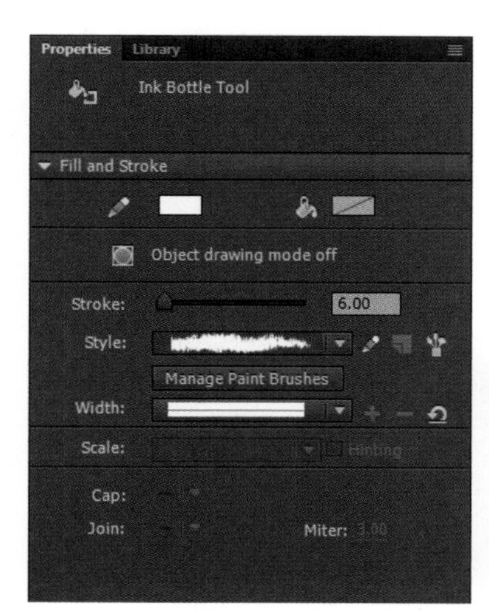

8 Set the stroke color to white and the Stroke height to 6 pt.

9 With the Ink Bottle Tool S still selected, click on all the letters including inside the "A."

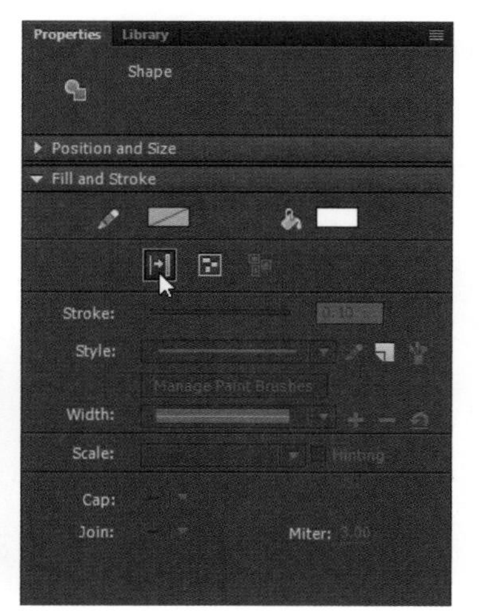

10 Select all and click the Expand to fill button. If you don't change the stroke to a fill, you can still edit it. However, you'll notice remarkably sluggish performance.

HOT TIP

Find a wide range of fonts on Typekit for a variety of projects. If you're a subscriber to the Creative Cloud (all apps and most single app memberships) or to the standalone Typekit plan, you get access to their library. Even Creative Cloud free trials get access to a limited sampling of fonts. Access to Typekit isn't integrated into Animate for desktop fonts, but you can still use them in your animations and select and sync them through the Typekit website.

Vector Art Brush: Artistic Brushes (cont.)

11 On a new layer, type "Effects" a little larger below that. I used Typekit's Kari Pro Regular at 200 pt. in white. Repeat the process to break apart the letters and apply the stroke.

12 Lock the other layers and on a new layer, type "Animate CC" in Bernhard MT Condensed at 72 pt. in white.

13 Break it apart, deselect, and add a white 2 pt. stroke with the Ink Bottle Tool S. Make sure to apply the stroke inside the "A," "a," and "e."

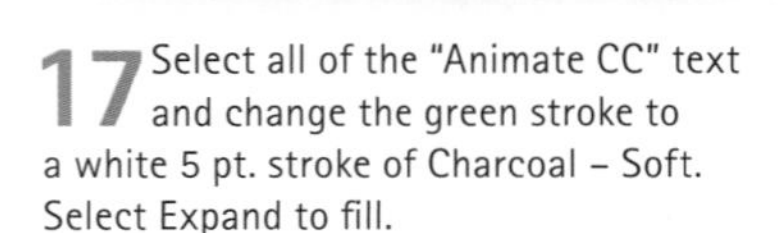

17 Select all of the "Animate CC" text and change the green stroke to a white 5 pt. stroke of Charcoal – Soft. Select Expand to fill.

18 Add another layer for the text "in." I used Kari Pro at 36 pt. in white. Rotate it and skew it to angle it up as you read it from left to right.

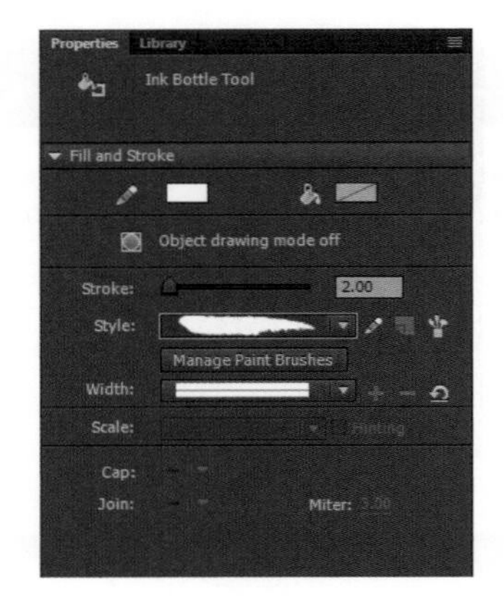

19 Apply a 2 pt. white stroke with the Ink Bottle Tool S with the Charcoal - Smooth brush.

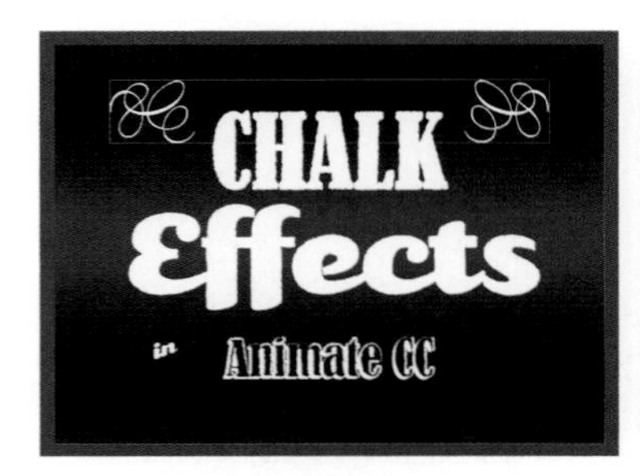

23 Use ⌥ alt Shift + drag to copy and Shift + move to add a copy of the flourish over to the other side while keeping them aligned vertically. Group ⌘ ctrl G and center align.

24 Copy the flourish on the right and paste it on a new layer. Scale it down to fit under the "in." With the Lasso Tool L select the end to delete it, and use the Move Tool V to drag out a point to continue the curlicue.

25 Lock all layers and set all but the Background to outlines. On a new layer called "line and dots," make a 6 pt. white line and a 6 pt. white circle with no stroke above "CHALK."

14 Group it ⌘ ctrl G, Copy it ⌘ ctrl C, and Paste in Place ⌘ ctrl Shift V. Nudge the copy down and over to the left 3 pixel. Ungroup ⌘ ctrl Shift G and while it's still selected click on Expand to Fill in the Properties panel. Double-click on the grouped copy to edit it in isolation.

15 Temporarily change the colors of the stroke and fill. I used red for the fill and bright green for the stroke.

16 Ungroup the red and green copy and deselect. Select all the red fills and delete.

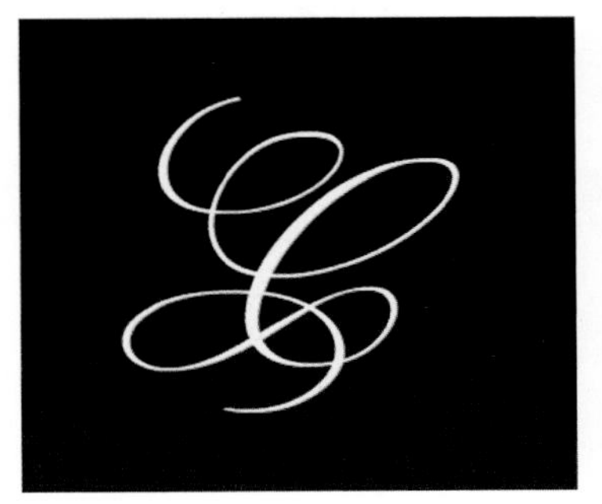

20 Add flourishes. You can draw your own or modify a font that uses them. I'm using the letter "C" in 90 pt. Monsieur La Doulaise in white. Make sure the text box is large enough to display the entire flourish.

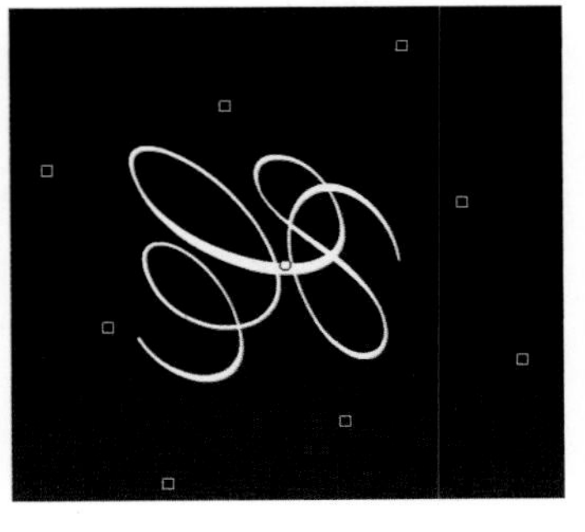

21 Rotate it so that it doesn't look like a letter.

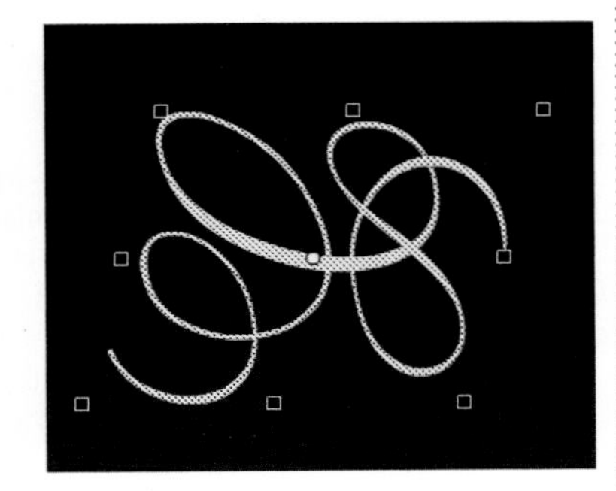

22 Break it apart and skew it to continue to modify it.

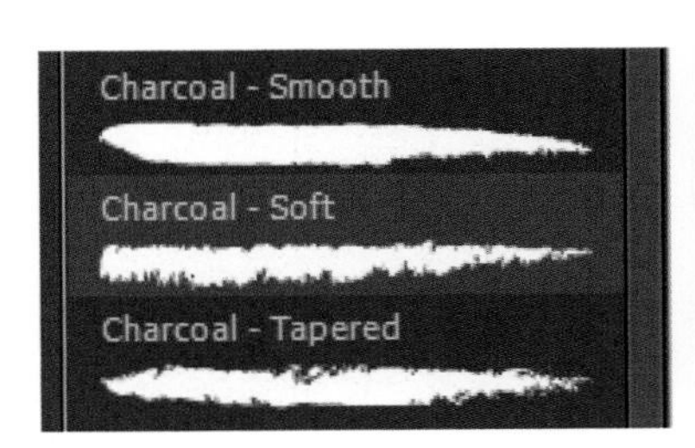

26 With the Move Tool V select the line and click Expand to fill. Select the keyframe to highlight both the line and circle. Set the Ink Bottle Tool S to 2 pt. Charcoal – Soft and apply to the line and the circle. Select both again and click Expand to Fill. Select the circle and Convert to Symbol F8.

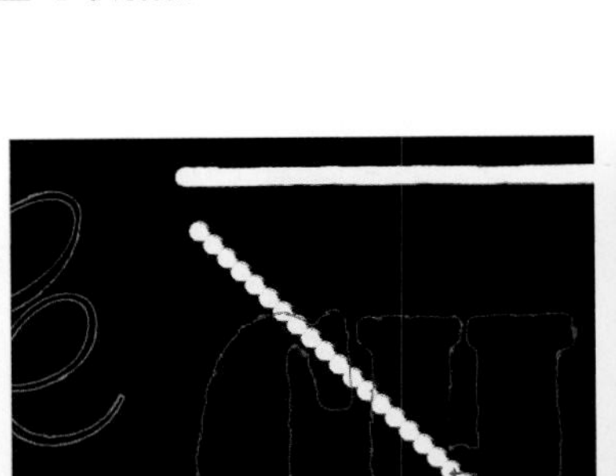

27 Duplicate ⌘ ctrl D the circle instance 19 times. Select the last circle and the line and Align Right. Select the first circle and the line and Align Left. Select the keyframe to select all and deselect the line by Shift + clicking on it. Align all the tops of the circles. Distribute left edge of the circles and group ⌘ ctrl G.

28 Select Align to Stage and center the group of circles. Add the line to the selection by Shift + clicking on it. To copy the circles and the line, ⌥ alt Shift + drag and place them at the bottom below "Animate CC." With the bottom line and circle group selected, right-click to Transform > Flip Vertical.

HOT TIP

If you draw your own flourishes, you can use the new 360° rotatable canvas to draw with a tablet and stylus at a more natural angle. Access the Rotation Tool H as an option embedded with the Hand Tool H or rotate the canvas at any time by holding down Shift + the spacebar and controlling the amount of rotation with the cursor. Return to the original orientation by clicking the Center Stage button on the right above the Stage.

Vector Art Brush: Pattern Brushes

ZENTANGLES ARE becoming a popular art form. What started as a doodling technique for relaxation has blossomed into its own style. It has branched out in various formats from its folksy origin into organized shapes and even more sophisticated patterned fills for complex drawings. If you're a purist in the art form, there are guidelines to follow. But we're cheating, remember? So let's take a look at a technique for simulating this style with the new vector art brushes.

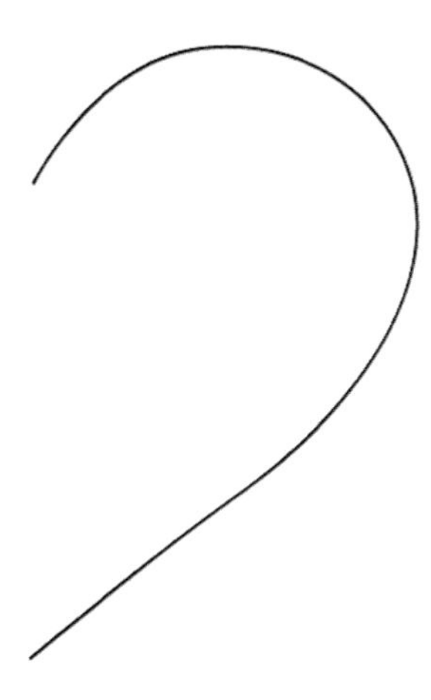

1 Start by drawing half of a heart shape with the Paint Brush Tool Y with a stroke of any color. The color won't matter because this heart will become a mask.

2 Make sure the beginning and end points align horizontally. Select it and click Smooth as much as needed to smooth it out.

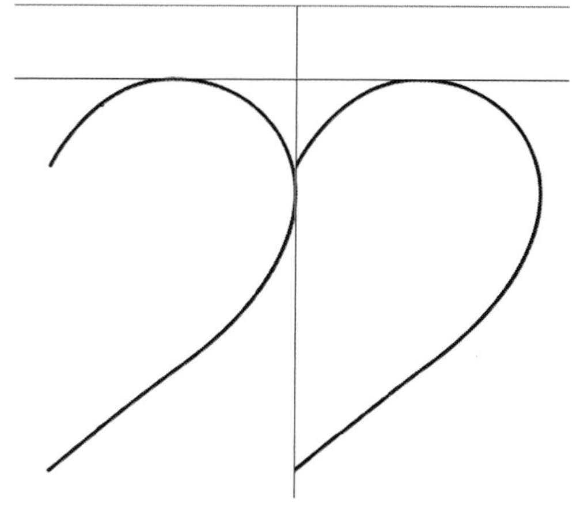

3 Use ⌥ alt + drag to duplicate the half heart. Use smart guides to align the new half with no space between the two.

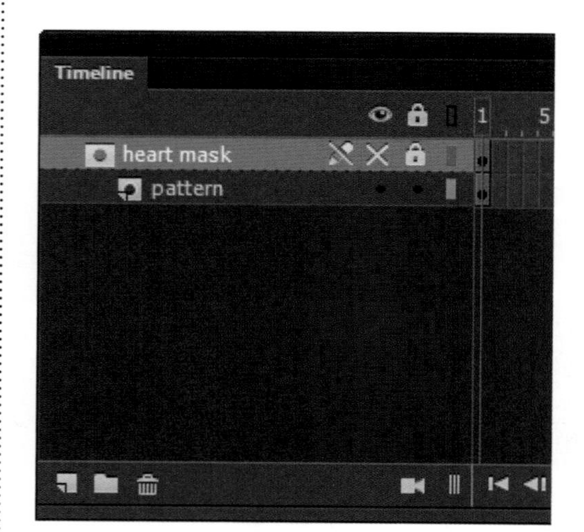

6 Lock and hide the heart mask layer and create a new layer called "pattern." Move the new layer under the mask so that it becomes indented.

7 Make a vertical line with a 1 pt. stroke set to a solid stroke style and duplicate ⌘ ctrl D the line six times. Align them to each other and distribute them evenly.

VECTOR ILLUSTRATION: MYRA FERGUSON

4 Right-click and select Transform > Flip Horizontal. Center horizontally and nudge down to allow space for type.

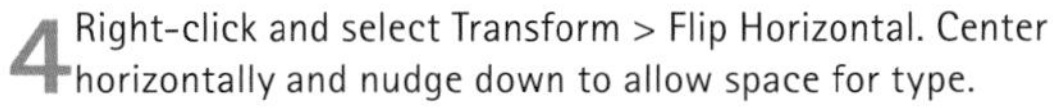

5 Use the Paint Bucket Tool (K) to fill the heart with any color. Double-click to select the shape and the stroke. Right-click and select Mask. Label the layer "heart mask."

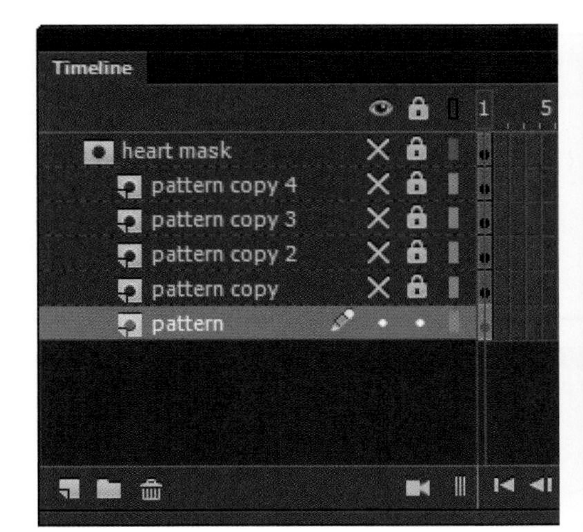

8 Select the pattern layer, right-click, and duplicate the layer until there are five total pattern layers. Hide and lock all but the first pattern layer.

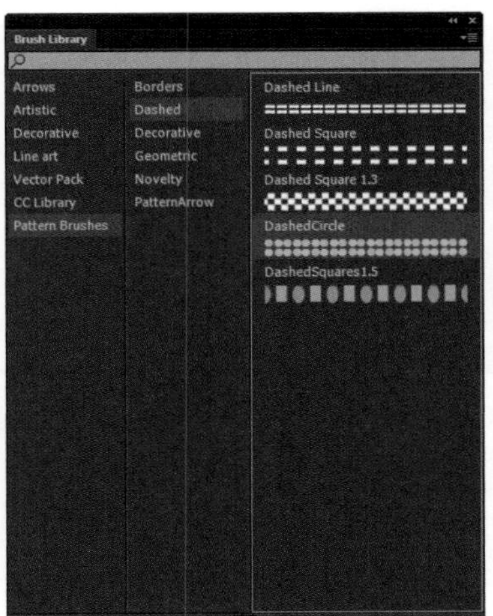

9 Select all the lines on the layer. Open the Brush Library (Window > Brush Library) or click the button next to Style in the Fill and Stroke section of the Properties panel. Select Pattern Brushes > Dashed and double-click on DashedCircle.

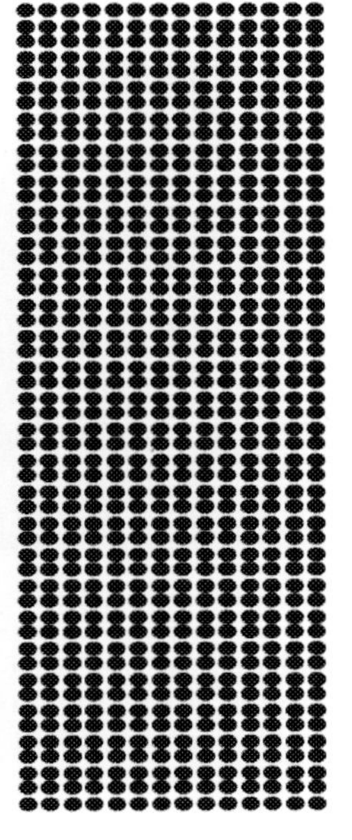

10 Change the Stroke height to 20 pt. in the Properties panel and click the Expand to fill button. Select all and change the fill to black.

Vector Art Brush: Pattern Brushes (cont.)

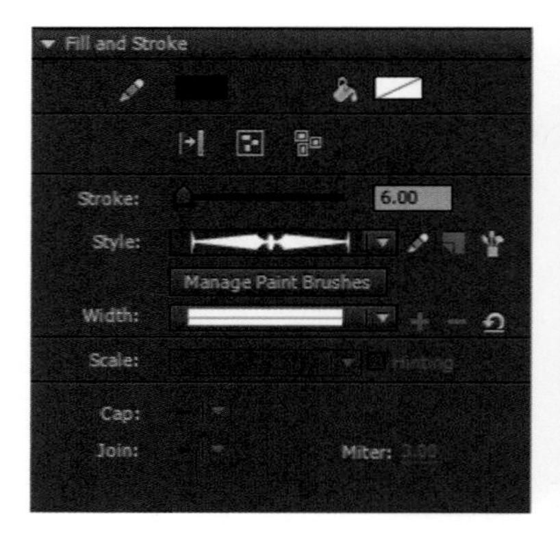

11 Hide and lock that layer and select the lines on the next pattern layer. Select Pattern Brushes > Decorative > Ornaments with a Stroke height of 6 pt.

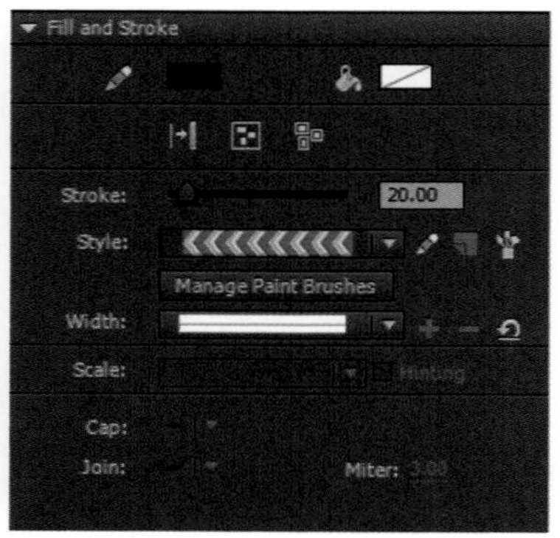

12 Hide and lock that layer and select the lines on the next pattern layer. Select the multicolored Geometric 1.5 brush from Pattern Brushes > Borders and set the stroke height to 20. Nudge the lines with the arrow keys leaving no space between them.

13 Select all the lines and Expand to fill. Select all the green triangles and zigzags and change the fill to black. While the selection is still active, go to Edit > Invert Selection to select all the coral and beige parts. Change those fills to white.

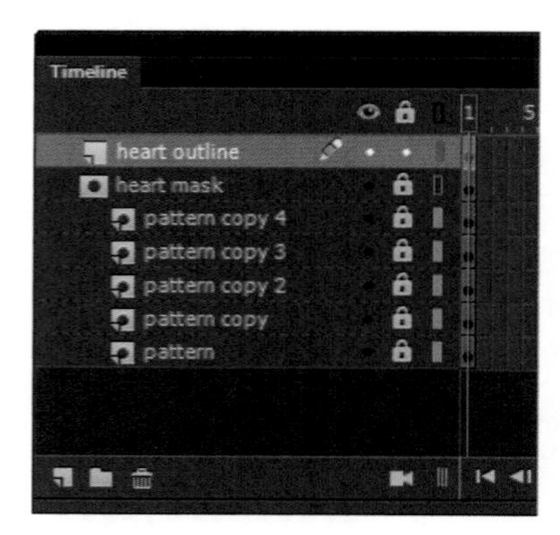

17 Unlock the heart mask. Right-click on it and select Duplicate Layers. Lock the original mask. Right-click on the copy to toggle off Mask. Rename the layer "heart outline." Select the fill and delete it.

18 Select the Width Tool U and click and drag on the widest part of the heart.

19 Do the same on the opposite side. Turn on Rulers ⌘ ⌥ ctrl alt Shift R and drag a horizontal rule down to line up the width adjustments.

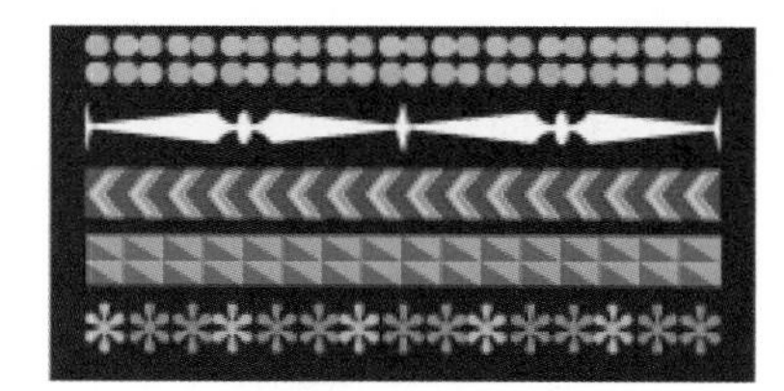

14 Use the same process to assign a pattern to the lines on each of the remaining layers. Adjust stroke width, spacing, and color as needed to make a black-and-white pattern that stands out. (I used all Pattern Brushes: Geometric > Geometric at 25 pt. with the red changed to black and the orange changed to white, and Novelty > Flowers at 20 pt. with the color changed to black.)

15 Show all the layers but keep them all locked. On the heart mask, toggle Show Layer as Outline to see the shape of the heart with the patterns visible through it. Unlock one pattern at a time and arrange them to fill the width of the heart. Use the Free Transform Tool Q to scale as needed to fill the blank spaces.

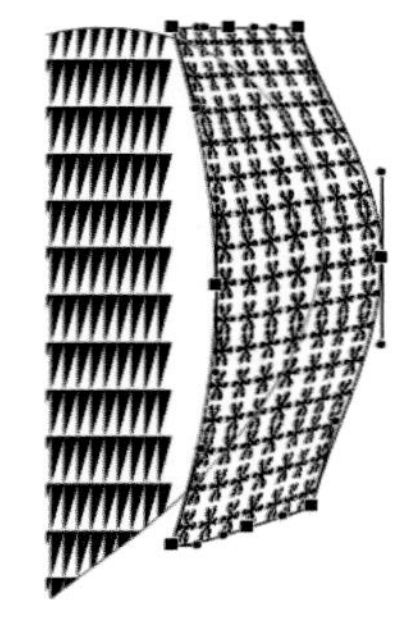

16 You could leave the patterns as rectangles of fills, but if you want to make it feel more hand-drawn then unlock a layer at a time, right-click, and select Transform > Envelope. Adjust the handles and anchors to bend each pattern to curve and fit together.

20 Use the Width Tool U again on the bottom point to make it narrow. Lock the heart outline layer.

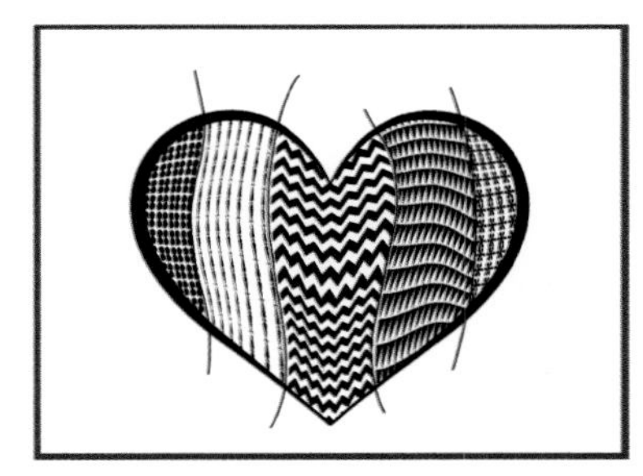

21 Show all the layers as outlines and make a new layer called "divider." Use the Paint Brush Tool Y to draw curved strokes between the sections.

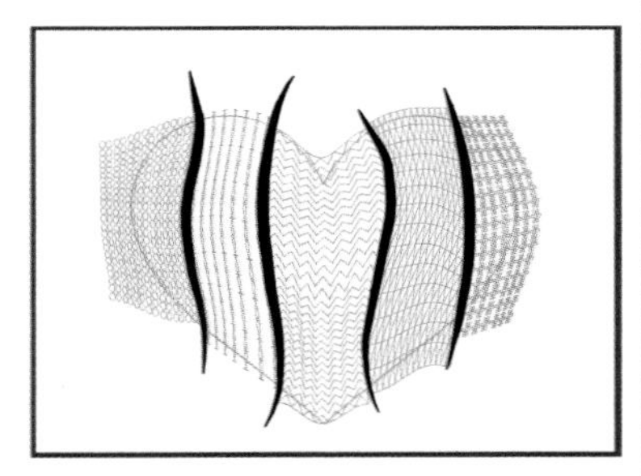

22 Use the Width Tool U on the divider strokes. Move this layer under the heart mask to hide the edges.

23 If the heart needs to be resized, unlock the layers and scale while holding the Shift key to keep it centered. Add text.

HOT TIP

Create your own pattern brushes with Adobe Capture on iOS or Android. Take a picture or use an image from your Creative Cloud files, your previous photos, or Adobe Stock. Crop, edit, and save it. Set it as an Illustrator Brush, so it's compatible with Animate. In Animate, open CC Libraries and navigate to the library that contains your brush. Click the brush from the CC Library to add it to the Brush Library. It'll show up in the CC Library group of brushes in the subgroup named for the Library that contains your brush.

Mixing Colors

INSTEAD OF HAVING TO choose between HSB or RGB in the Color panel, we have both color models displayed simultaneously, and all color values are accurately controlled using hot text sliders.

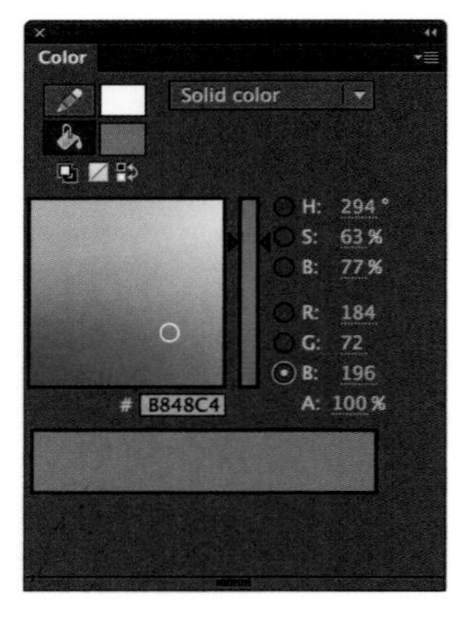

Mixing colors in Animate is easy and accurate. The creative folks over at Big Pink asked me to create an animation for children between 2 and 5 years of age. Because of the target audience, I wanted the animation to have a soft yet inviting color palette.

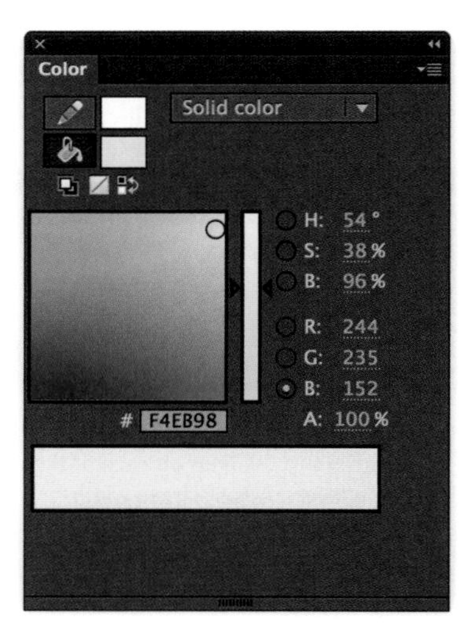

1 My typical workflow when mixing colors is to click and drag within the gradient window in order to select the approximate color I'm after. Once I have this color selected, I like to use the hot text sliders to fine-tune my color selection. Hue and saturation can play an important role in the design process, and for this particular background image I wanted to keep the colors muted to avoid overpowering the characters that were added later on. As you can see here, the main color of the house has a very low level of saturation but enough brightness to maintain a good level of clarity.

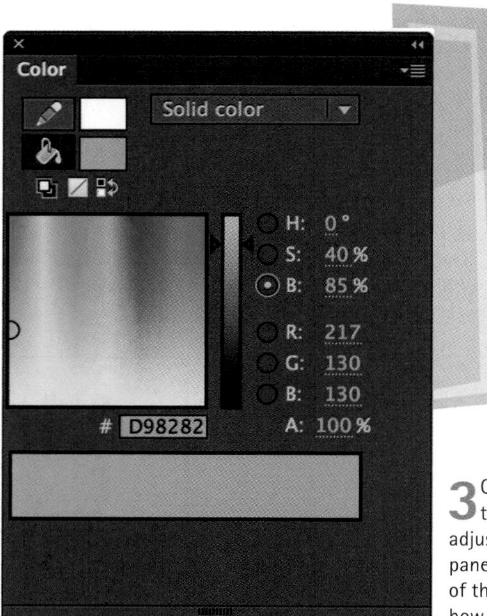

3 Once I had the overall pink color selected, mixing the darker shade of pink required a simple brightness adjustment. The large color swatch at the bottom of the Color panel will split to reveal the current color being mixed on top of the original color. This split provides a visual reference for how the new color will contrast against the original color.

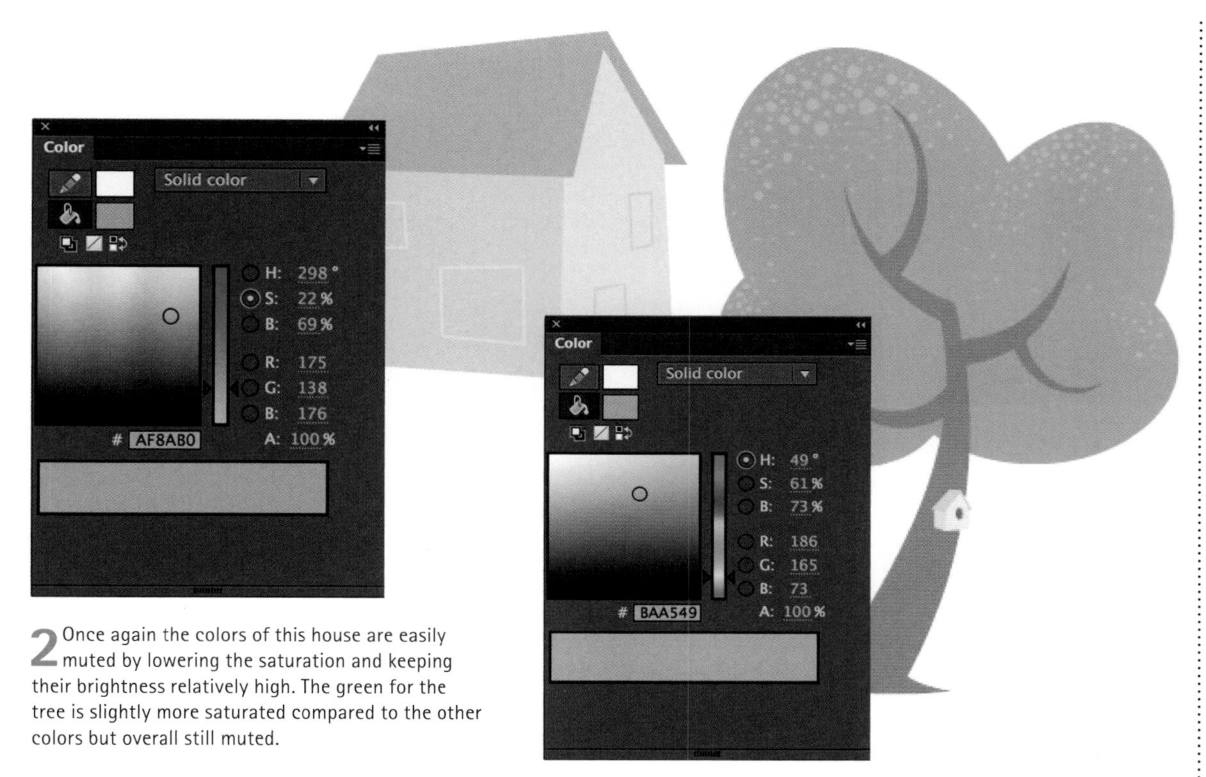

2 Once again the colors of this house are easily muted by lowering the saturation and keeping their brightness relatively high. The green for the tree is slightly more saturated compared to the other colors but overall still muted.

HOT TIP

You can use the Animate Color panel to pick any color from anywhere on your screen—even outside of Animate! Just click on the fill color swatch to activate the color picker and then click on the area of your screen that contains the color you desire.

Advanced Color Effect

THE ADVANCED COLOR EFFECT separately adjusts the alpha, red, green, and blue values of the instance of a symbol. It can be used in a variety of ways to suggest the tone of your graphic design or the mood of an entire animated scene. Let's take a look at how to adjust the color values of a symbol using the RGB hot text sliders. In the Color Effect section of the Properties panel, change the style mode to Advanced.

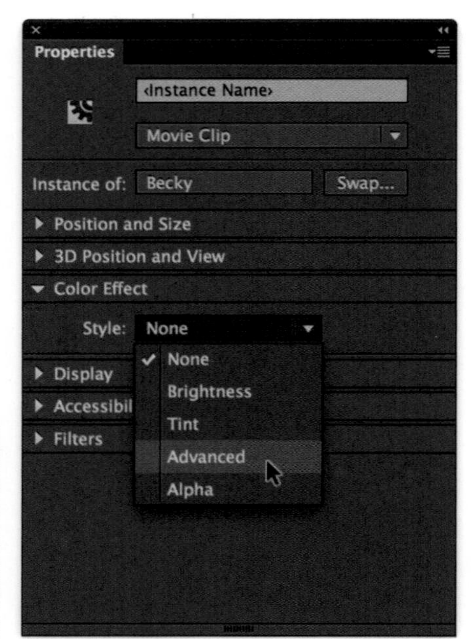

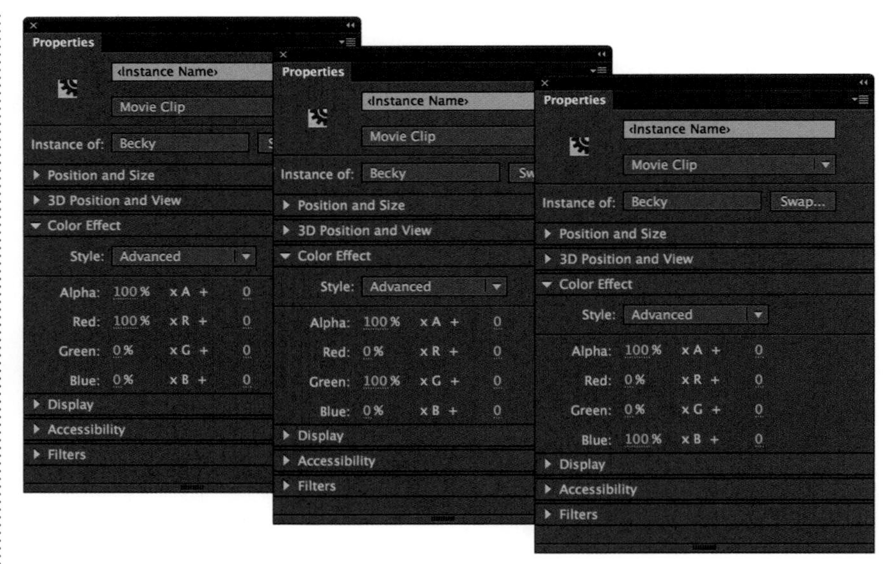

1 Select the symbol containing your artwork. Using the hot text sliders, change the value for red to 100% and both green and blue values to 0%. An overall hue of red will be applied to the symbol. Increasing the amount of green while decreasing red and blue will result in an overall greenish hue. Increasing the amount of blue while decreasing red and green will follow suit with an overall bluish hue.

VECTOR ILLUSTRATION: CHRIS GEORGENES

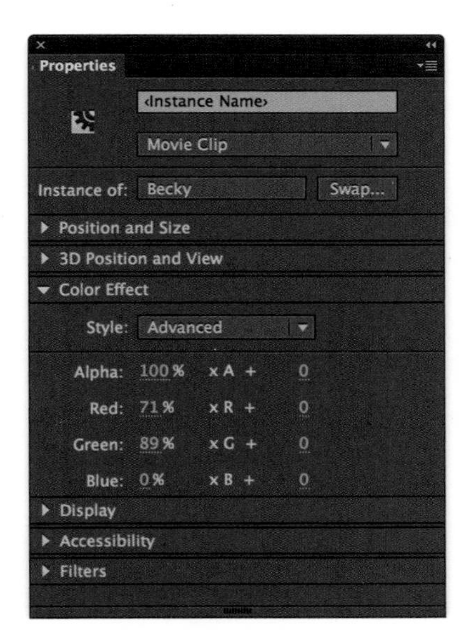

2 Red, green, or blue will not always satisfy your color needs. By varying the amount of red, green, and blue you can come up with almost unlimited variations of color tones. Here I have an almost equal mix of red and green but no blue at all.

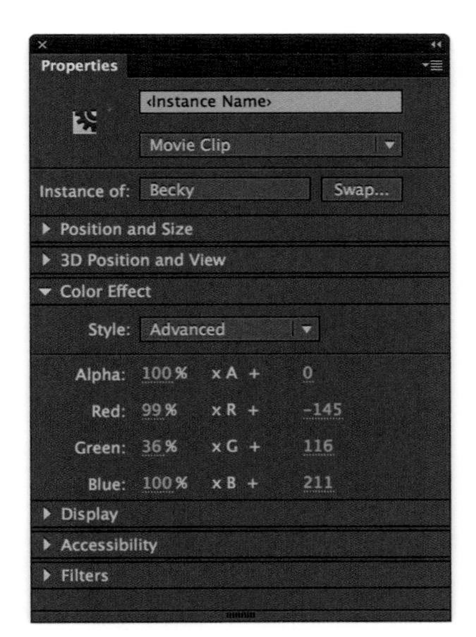

3 If the red, green, and blue percentages aren't enough, you can produce more values by adjusting the values in the right column. These values will get added to the percentage values in the left column. For example, if the current red value is 100, setting the left slider to 50% and the right slider to 100% produces a new red value of 150 ([100 × 0.5] + 100 = 150).

HOT TIP

The advanced color values can also be animated over time using Classic and Motion Tweens. Check out the animated example in Animated Color Effect.

Animated Color Effect

1 As animators, we occasionally need to find ways to visually suggest the passing of time. One of the easiest approaches is to change the overall hue of an entire scene or background. As we know, this process naturally takes several hours, but through animation we can speed up time to convey the effect. In its initial shot, this quaint suburban home is designed to represent daytime, probably early afternoon given the angle of the shadow across the front door. The entire background has been converted to a symbol, and a Motion Tween has been created by right-clicking over the symbol and selecting Create Motion Tween. Insert frames in the tween span by clicking on a frame further down the Timeline and clicking the F5 key. With the tween span extended, the hue of the entire scene can now be changed via the Color Effect section of the Properties panel.

VECTOR ILLUSTRATION: CHRIS GEORGENES FOR BIG PINK

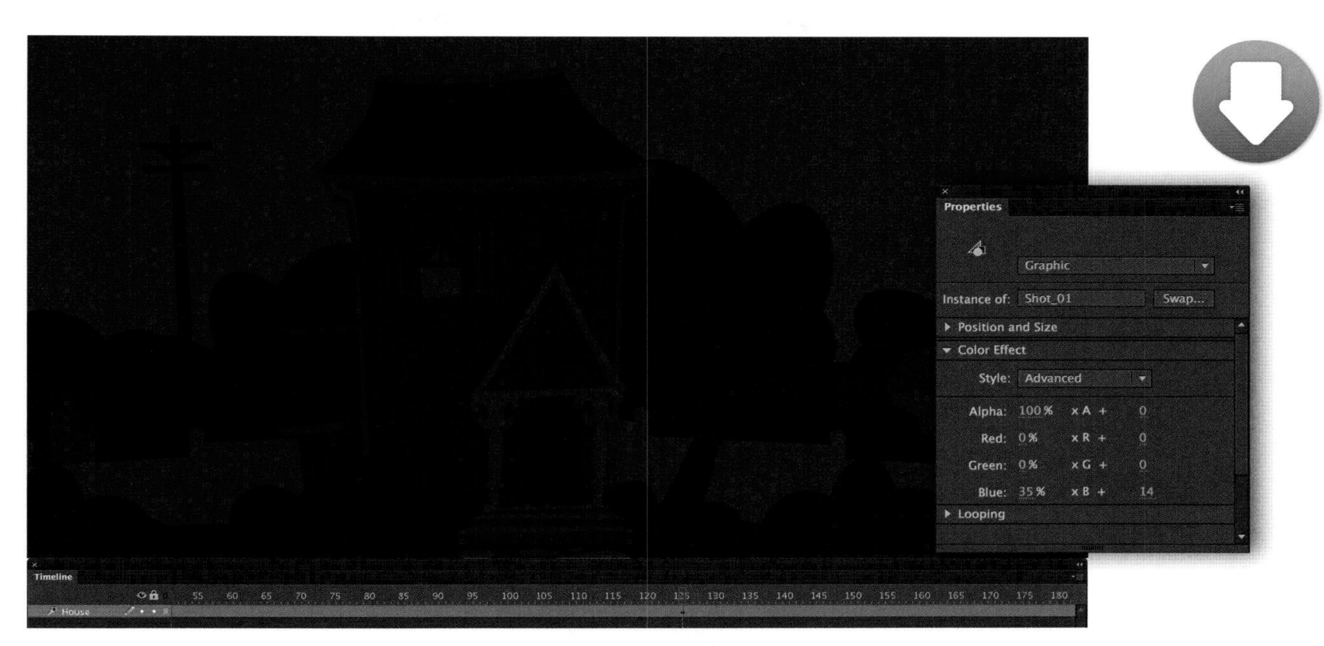

2 Make sure the frame indicator is at or near the end of the tween span. With the Properties panel open and Color Effect section expanded, select the symbol containing the background image. Using the hot text sliders, adjust the hue of the symbol instance. Here I have removed the red and green values by entering a numerical value of "0" for both and increased the amount of blue to suggest a cooler range of colors across the entire image. These settings imply a lack of sunlight and create a convincing nighttime mood. Position the frame indicator back at frame 1 and press the *Enter* key to play back the animation. The Motion Tween span will interpolate the difference in color values between the keyframes, resulting in a dramatic time lapse animation similar to the transition from day into night. You are not limited to just day and night as this technique can be used to imply a change of mood for dramatic effect.

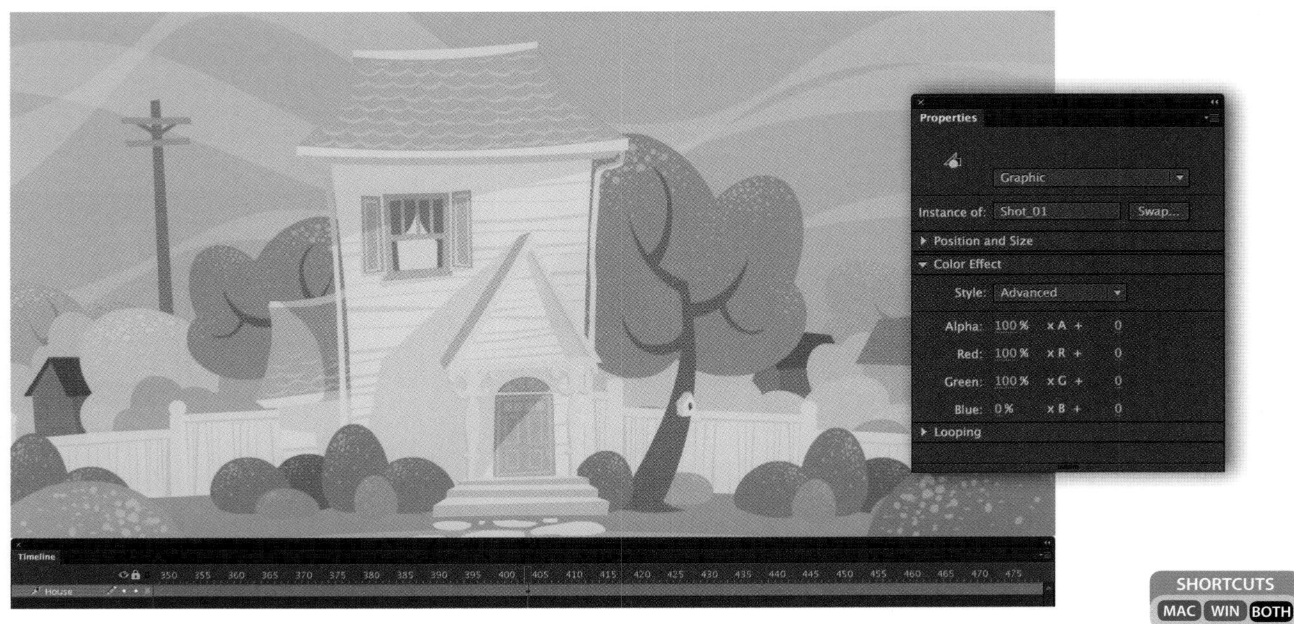

SHORTCUTS
MAC WIN BOTH

Using Gradients

GRADIENTS CAN BE VERY EFFECTIVE WHEN you want to break away from the flatness of solid color fills. They can be used to add a sense of depth and dimensionality to your characters, backgrounds, and graphics in general. Gradients can also work against you due to their ease of use, resulting in generic and often lackluster images. When in the right hands, however, both linear and radial gradients can contribute to a very effective and sometimes realistic design.

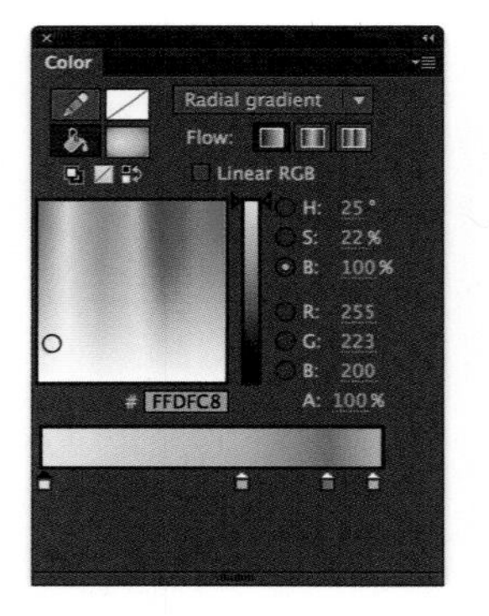

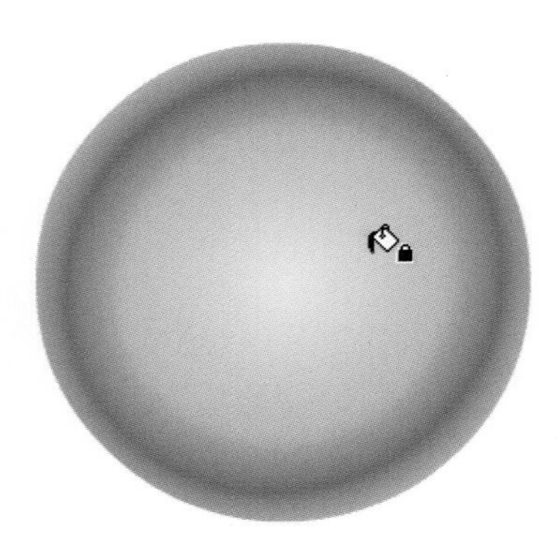

1 A simple radial gradient is used to fill most of the shapes that make up the monkey. The trick here is providing the illusion of a 3D object in a 2D environment. Four colors are used for this gradient. The critical color for this illusion is the fourth color (far right). It represents a light source coming from behind the sphere, suggesting the sphere is truly round.

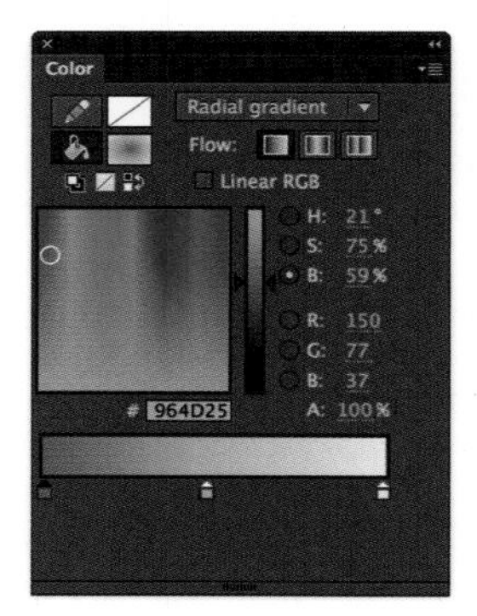

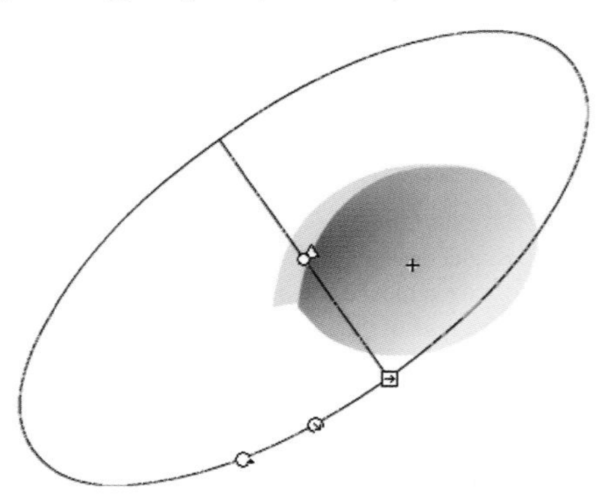

4 To make the ear look concave, mix another radial gradient going from darkest in the center to a lighter value on the outer edge. Fill the shape with this gradient and position it off-center so that only half of the gradient is shown. Since darker colors will recede and lighter colors will appear closer to us, this otherwise flat shape now gives us the impression it is concave.

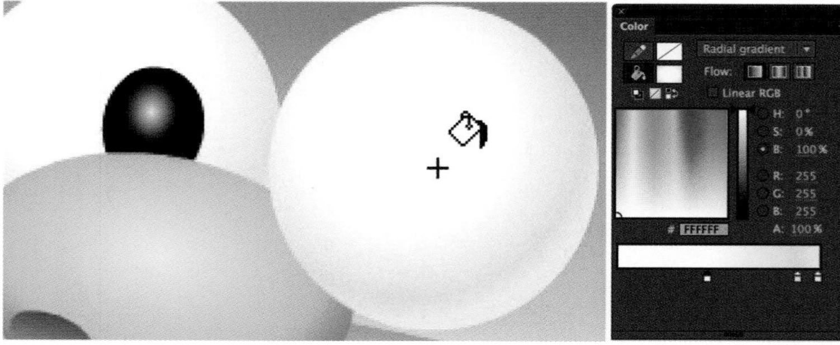

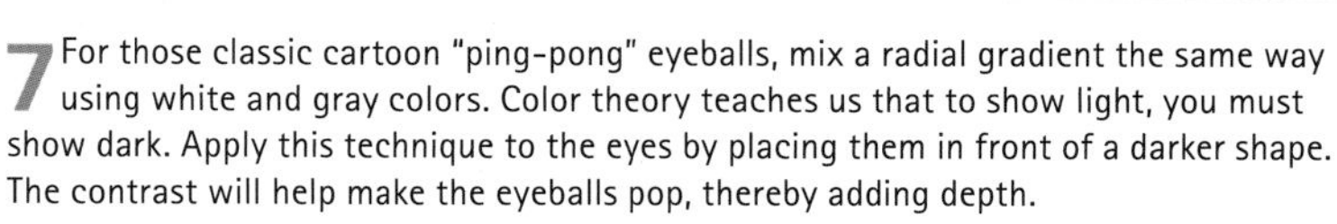

7 For those classic cartoon "ping-pong" eyeballs, mix a radial gradient the same way using white and gray colors. Color theory teaches us that to show light, you must show dark. Apply this technique to the eyes by placing them in front of a darker shape. The contrast will help make the eyeballs pop, thereby adding depth.

MONKEY CHARACTER: MUDBUBBLE LLC

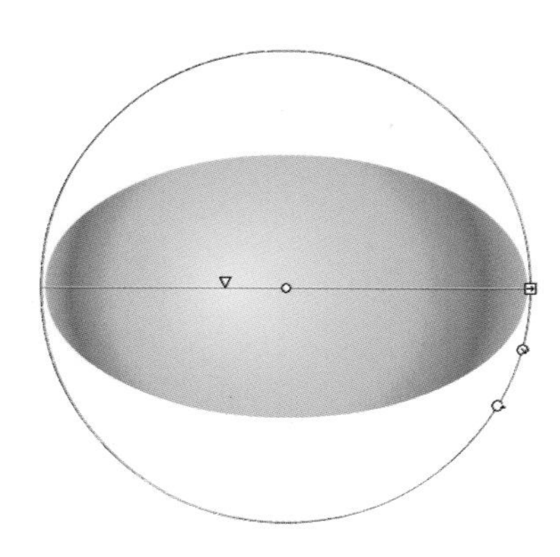

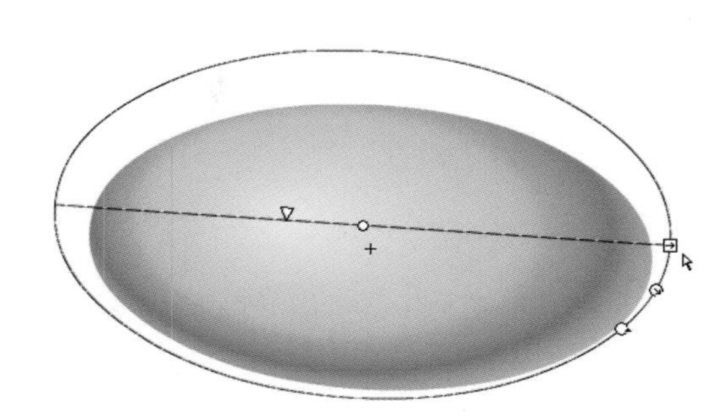

2 Edit the gradient to conform to the shape using the Gradient Transform Tool **F**. Use the handles to rotate, scale, and skew the gradient so that it is slightly larger than the shape. Select the center control point, drag the entire gradient, and position it slightly off-center from the shape.

3 Click and drag the focal point tool so that the highlight is positioned between the center of the shape and its edge. This position suggests that the light source is at more of an angle. Notice the fourth color of our gradient is showing along the bottom and right edge, which implies light wrapping around the sphere from behind.

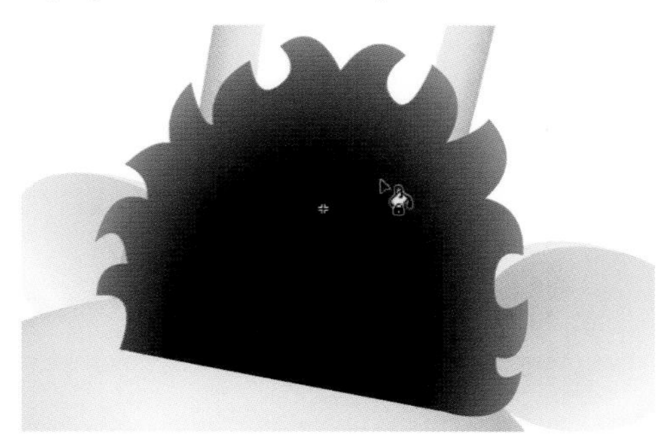

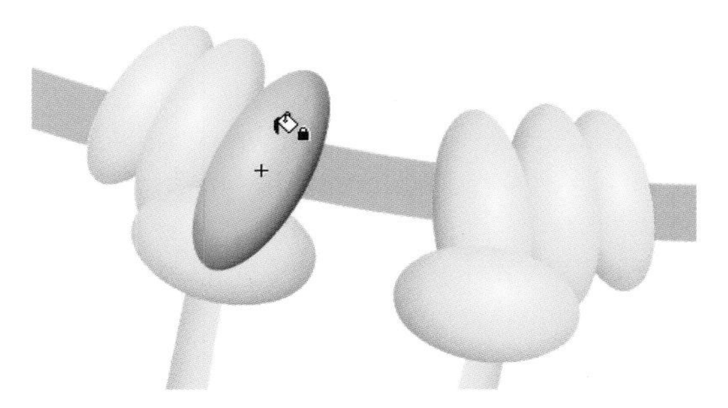

5 The hair is a shape filled with another radial gradient. Most of this shape will be hidden behind other graphics, so you only need to concern yourself with how the outer edge looks when the character is fully assembled.

6 The hands are really not hands at all. A few strategically positioned spheres with the same radial gradient as the face and body are used to suggest hands.

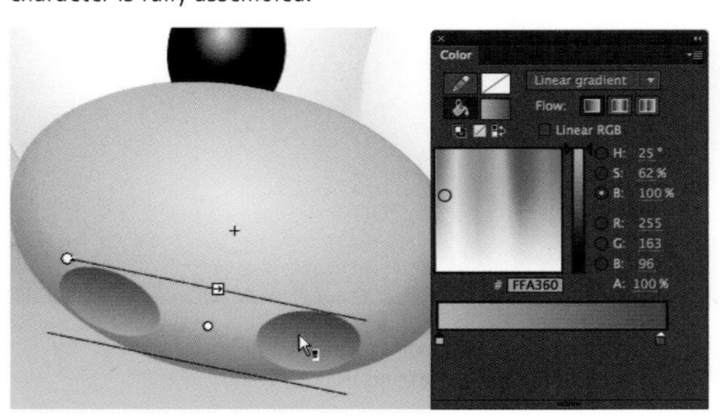

8 The nose is a combination of spheres filled with radial and linear gradients. To create the nostrils, use a linear gradient and edit it so that the darker color is above the lighter color. By themselves, the spheres are just shapes. But placed against the radial sphere, they become holes.

9 Good designs are consistent in technique. When each element is composed of the same graphical style, the overall result is typically consistent and fluid. Don't deviate from your plan; choose a technique and stick with it.

HOT TIP

Gradients, in my opinion, look more realistic when the change in color values is subtle. Gradients that have strong contrasting colors have a tendency to look unrealistic.

Gradients and Blur

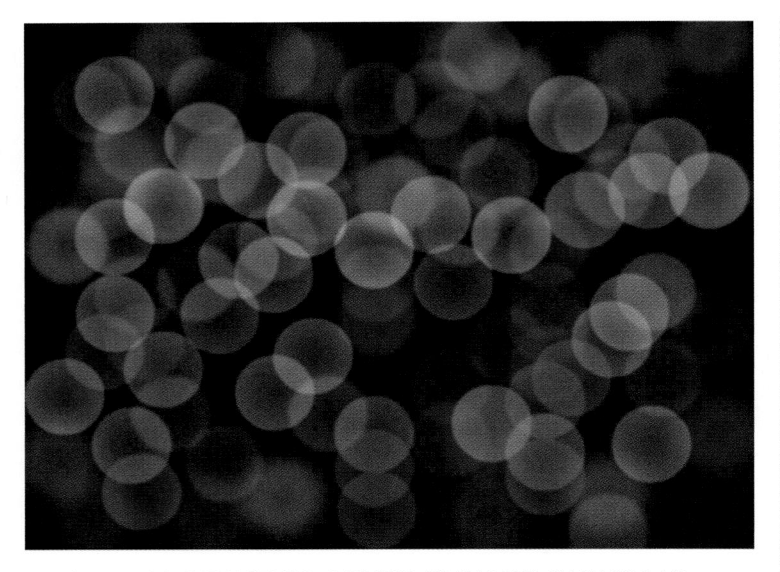

YOU MAY HAVE NOTICED A TREND IN IMAGES SHOWING UP with lots of circles. In photos, they're in the background and a little blurry. That blurry background circle effect is known as a *bokeh* and is produced in the out-of-focus areas in photos. The shape of the bokeh varies based on the type of lens used, but it's usually a circle or a hexagon. Because a real bokeh is an artifact of a shallow depth of field, the effect can be simulated in order to bring focus to a subject placed in the foreground. It can also be used to project a variety of styles like a romantic atmosphere, a softened image, an ethereal effect, a whimsical feel, or a futuristic look.

1 Let's start by using the Rectangle Tool (R) to make a rectangle the same size as the Stage on a layer named "bg." In the color panel (Window > Color or ⌘/ctrl Shift F9), set the drop-down menu to Linear gradient. Change the stroke to no stroke.

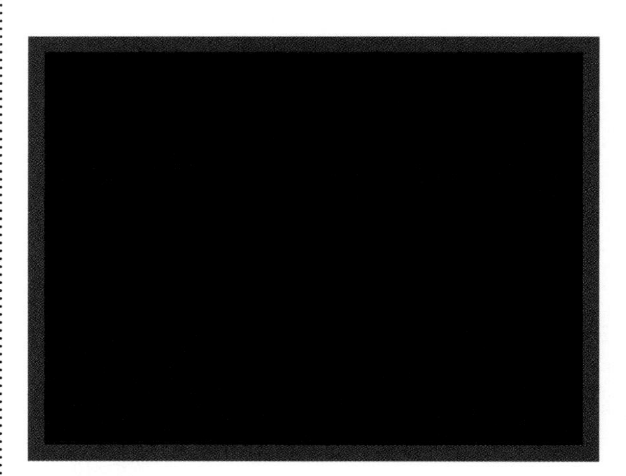

4 We're going for a look where the ground gets darker in the distance as the sun is setting in the evening sky.

VECTOR ILLUSTRATION: MYRA FERGUSON

2 By default, the gradient is drawn from left to right. Rotate it 90° counterclockwise with the Gradient Transform Tool F. Hover over the white circle on the end of the blue line until the cursor changes to the rotate icon. Drag to rotate. Hold down the Shift key to constrain the rotation to 90°. Make sure the gradient fill is the same size as the rectangle where the blue lines of the gradient are even with the top and bottom edges of the rectangle.

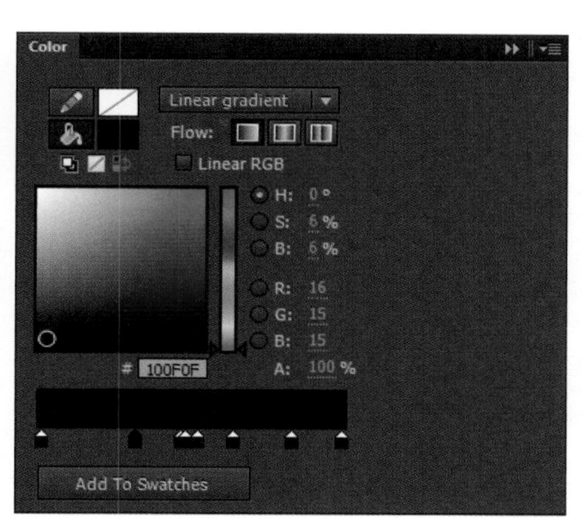

3 Set the color stops of the gradient in the Color panel to simulate the ground section going from lighter brown to black about two-thirds up the rectangle followed by an immediate transition from teal to dark bluish then a slightly lighter blue section. End with a dark section of navy blue.

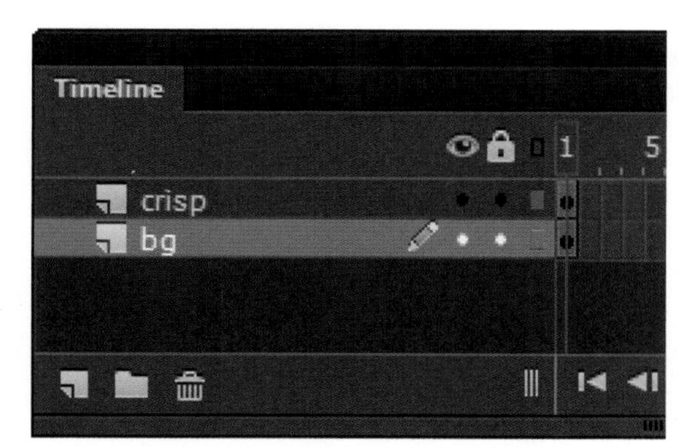

5 Make a new layer on top of the background called "crisp," which will contain the sharpest of the blurred circles.

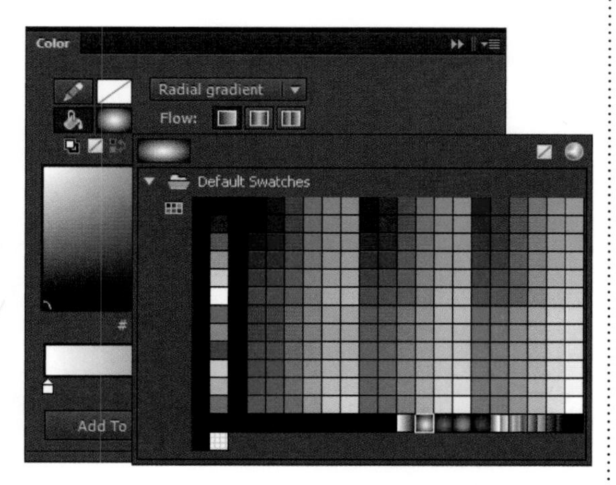

6 On this layer, draw a circle with no stroke. Click the Fill Color to access the Swatches and select the preset grayscale radial gradient.

HOT TIP

While the gradient fill is selected with Gradient Transform Tool, the blue lines indicate the edges of the gradient as applied to the shape. If the shape and the Gradient Transform Tool are both selected but you don't see the blue lines, then the gradient is larger than your viewable area. Zoom out to find the edges. Click on the square handle with an arrow inside it and drag inward toward the center point to make the gradient smaller or drag outward to make it larger within the shape.

Gradients and Blur (cont.)

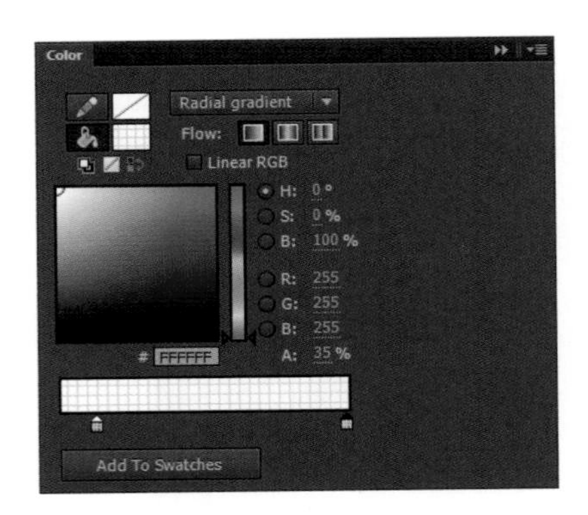

7 Now switch to the Color panel and change the black stop to white. Adjust the alphas to make the circle slightly transparent. With the color stop on the right still selected, change the alpha to 35%. Select the left color stop and move it a little to the right. Change its alpha to 20%.

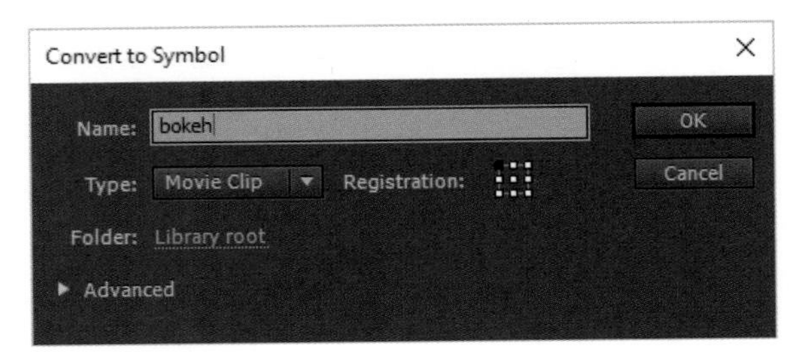

8 Turn the circle into a symbol by going to Modify > Convert to Symbol or F8. Name the symbol "bokeh" and make it a Movie Clip.

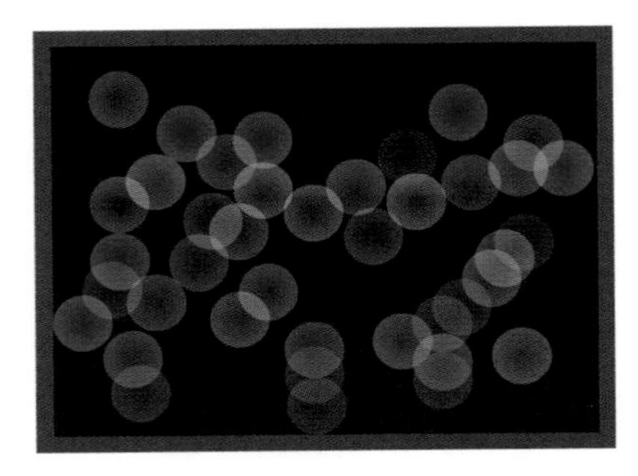

11 Since we're making what looks like an evening scene, you might want to pick colors you'd see as lights in the background, like signal lights which would be greenish-bluish, yellowish, and pinkish-reddish. Sprinkle variations of these tints on all the instances in this layer. Adjust the amount of tint applied through the percentage slider next to Tint.

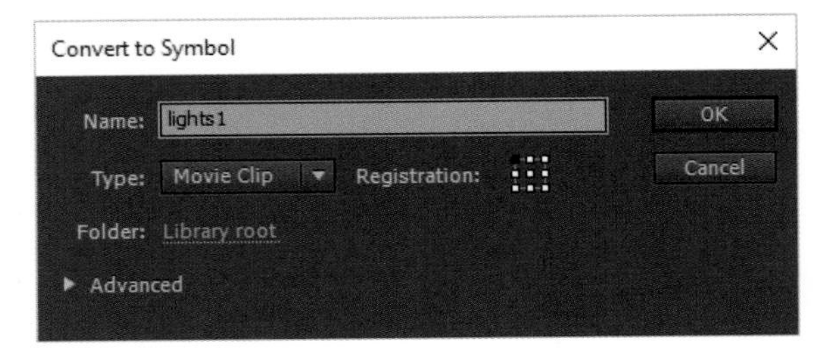

12 Select all the instances and make a new Movie Clip symbol and call it "lights1." As a Movie Clip, it can have a blur filter applied.

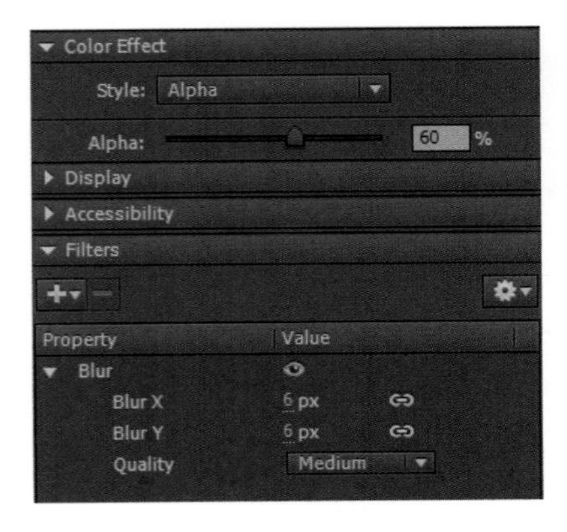

15 Select the keyframe on this layer to select all the instances on it and convert it to a Movie Clip symbol. Call it "lights2." Add a Blur filter to it with a setting of 6 pixel for both Blur X and Blur Y. Set the quality to Medium. In the Color Effect section of the Properties panel, set the Style to Alpha and the percentage to 60%.

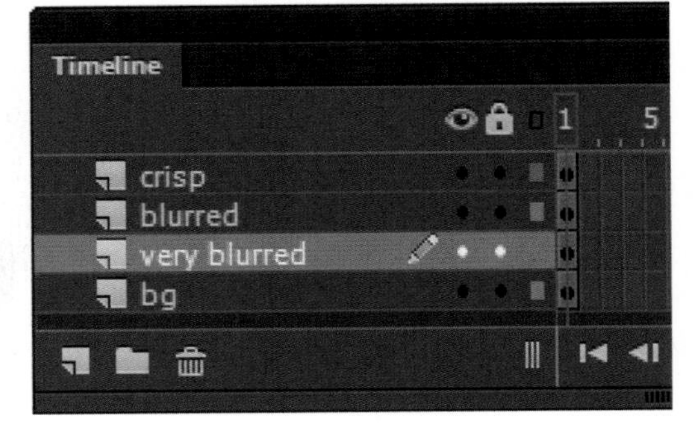

16 Make one more layer and name it "very blurred." Again add instances of overlapping circles, add tints, select the keyframe for the layer to select all the instances, and convert to a Movie Clip symbol. Call this symbol "lights3."

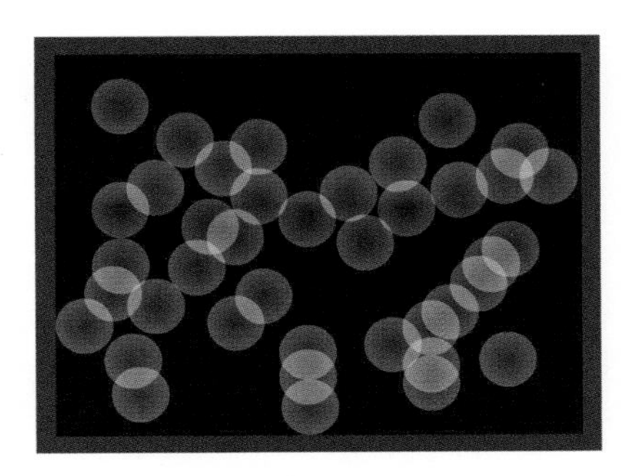

9 To simulate the lights in our scene, we'll need to add several instances of this circle. It's a best practice to name the instances of the Movie Clips, but it isn't necessary to make it work in this example. With the instance selected, Copy and Paste or alt + drag to make copies and spread them out around the Stage. Overlap some of the edges of the circles with other circles.

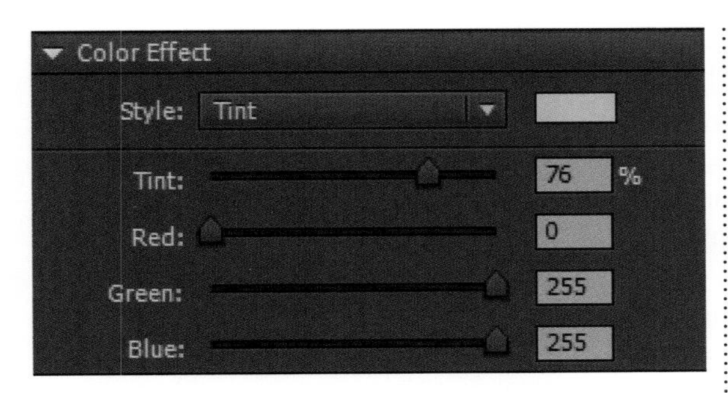

10 With one or more instances selected, go to the Properties panel in the Color Effect section. Change the Style type to Tint through the drop-down menu. Select color to apply as a tint to the instance(s) selected.

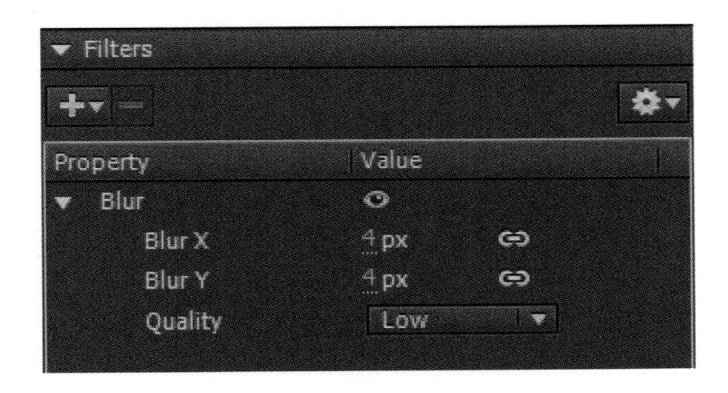

13 With the instance of the Movie Clip selected, go to the Filters section in the Properties panel. Click the + in the drop-down menu to add a filter. Select Blur and make both Blur X and Blur Y 4 pixel. The quality can be set to Low.

14 To make the effect more realistic, add another layer, name it "blurred," and add multiple instances of the circle. Overlap the instances on both the blurred layer and the crisp layer. Apply a variety of the tints to these instances as in step 11.

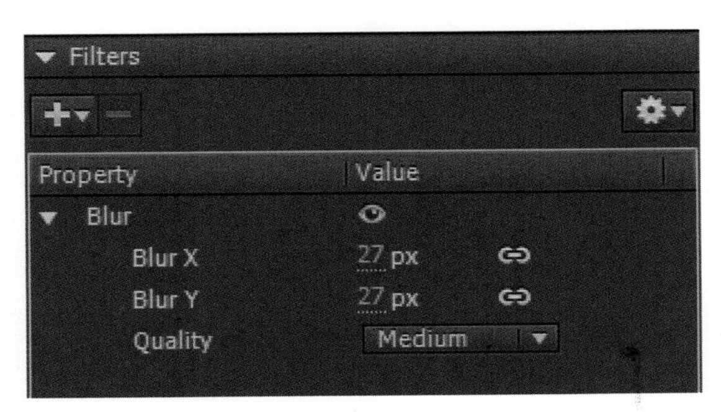

17 Add a Blur filter to the instance with a setting of 27 pixel for both Blur X and Blur Y on Medium quality.

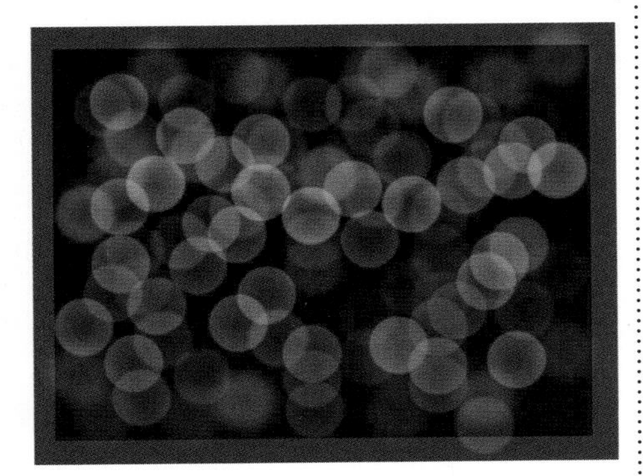

18 Adjust the spacing and tint of the various instances of the circle as needed. Use your bokeh image as a background for any text or images that you'd like to be the focus like in an ad, an announcement, or an eCard.

HOT TIP

To simultaneously deselect the current selection and what isn't selected on a layer, use Edit > Invert Selection, If you find you use it often, map it to a keyboard shortcut by going to Edit > Keyboard Shortcuts... and assign it a shortcut that's easy to remember. When the Keyboard Shortcuts dialog opens, look up the menu item Edit under Command and twirl down to expose the command Invert Selection. Click in the Shortcut area and press whatever key combination you want to assign. You'll be alerted if that shortcut is already in use and able to undo if what you entered isn't what you wanted.

Advanced Gradients

IF YOU'VE BEEN USING Animate for a while, you know there two kinds of gradients, linear and radial. Of course, you have some options like repeating the color stops, but even then you wind up with either stripes or a bullseye. What do you do if you want a gradient that follows the curve of a wavy stroke or irregular shape? You cheat.

The effect really is a cheat since it isn't technically a gradient. It's a filter that applies a gradient. That filter is called Gradient Glow. Let's make a glowing streak of light to illustrate how it works.

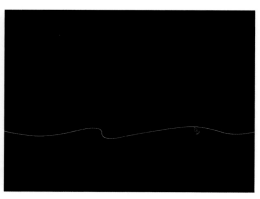

1 Start with 1 pt. white stroke with a width of 800 pixels on a black 800 × 600 pixels. Stage. I placed mine at 400 pixels on the *Y* axis.

2 Add some points along the stroke with the Add Anchor Point Tool = and use the Selection Tool V to drag out some wavy curves.

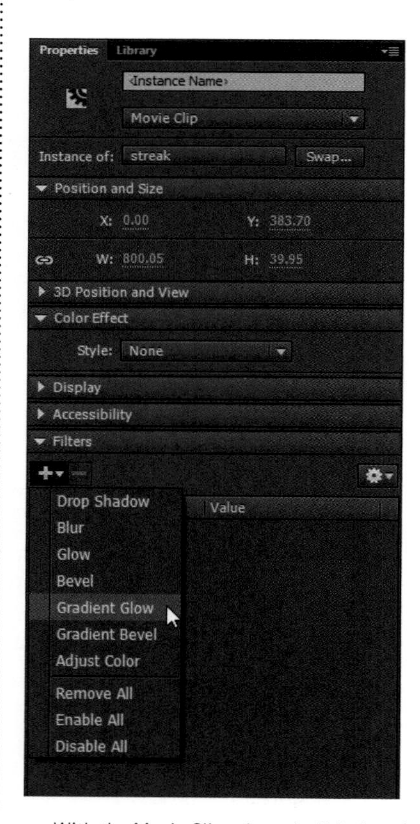

5 With the Movie Clip selected, click the + in the drop-down menu under Filters in the Properties panel and select Gradient Glow.

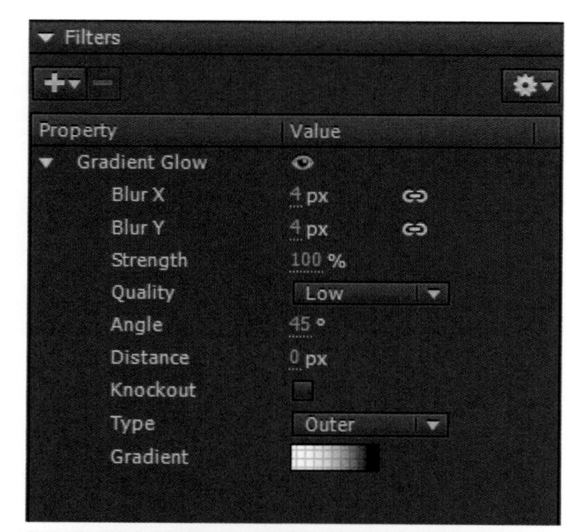

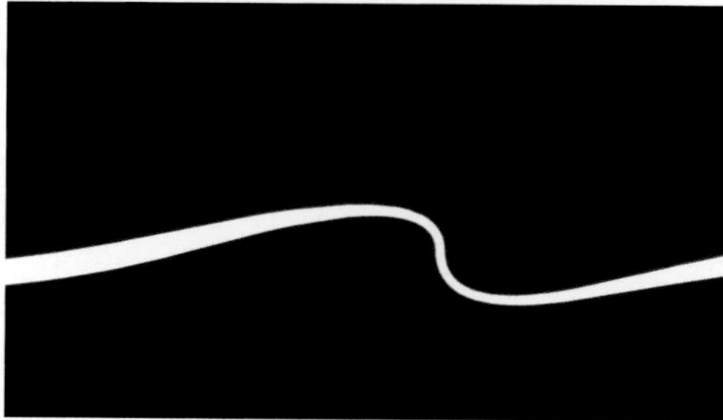

6 Let's set it so that you can see edge coloration before we blur it for the glow effect. We can leave most of the default settings for now, but change Distance to 0. You'll see a faint gray edge outlining our stroke.

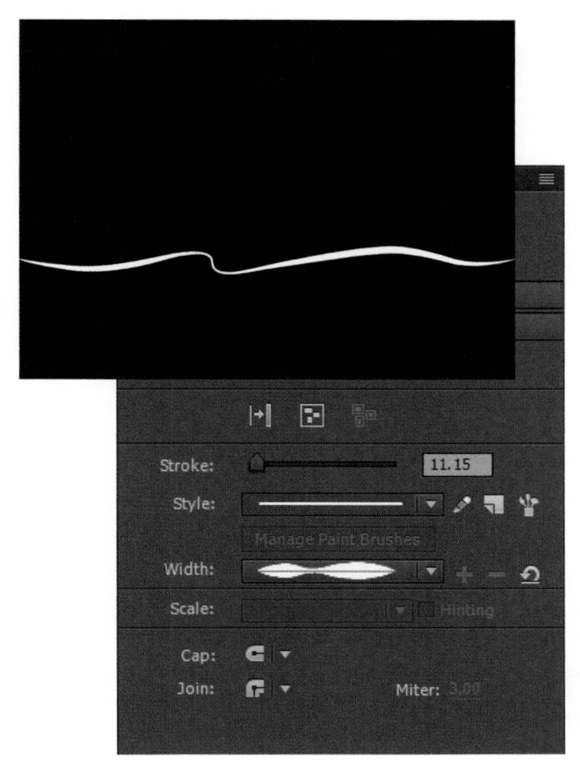

3 Select the stroke and change the Variable Width Profile under Fill and Stroke to Width Profile 2.

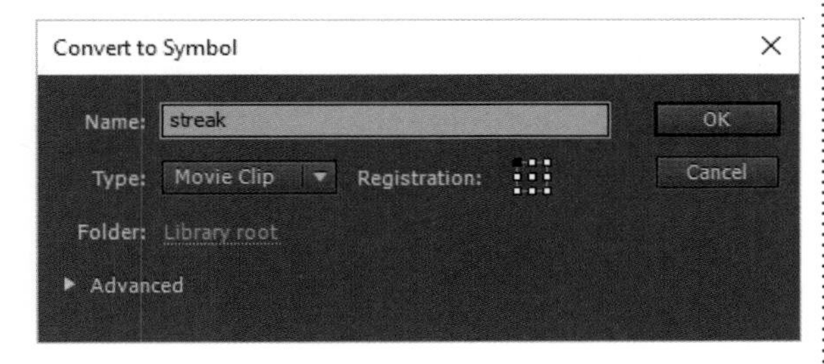

4 Convert the stroke to a Movie Clip, so we can add a filter to it.

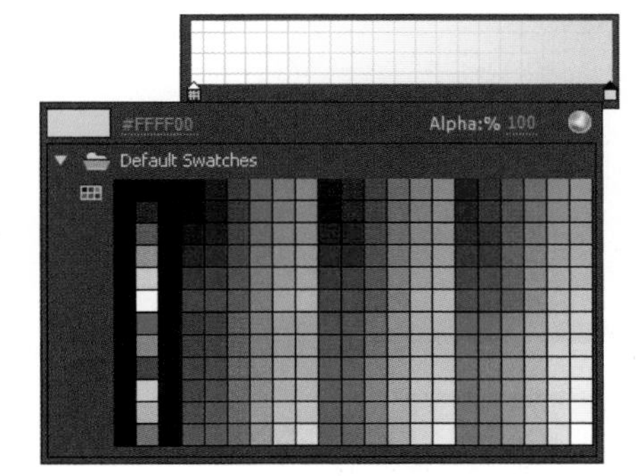

7 When the Gradient Glow is set to Type: Outer, the Gradient shown in the thumbnail is applied to the outer edges with the left color stop at the outermost edge. Click on the thumbnail, so we can change it to our colors. Make the right color stop yellow #FFFF00. Notice the Alpha is 100%.

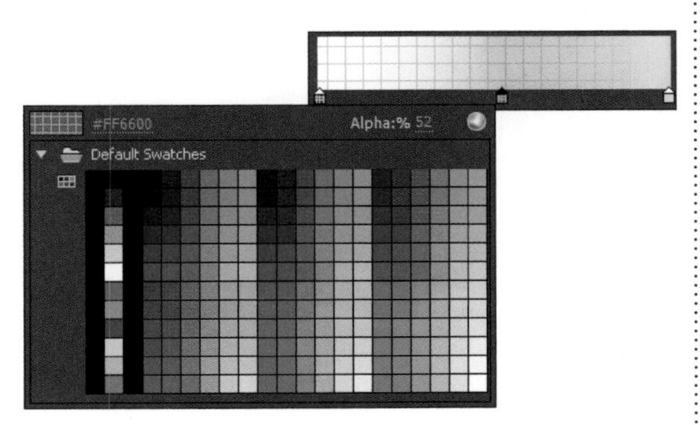

8 Now add a color stop to the middle in orange #FF6600. Its Alpha is somewhere between 100% and 0% depending on where in the middle you clicked. Change it to 100% at the top of the Color Picker.

Advanced Gradients (cont.)

9 The left stop is set to white #FFFFFF at 0%. You can change the color, which affects the blend between it and the next stop, but you can't remove it. It provides some smoothness to the edge of the gradient, so let's leave it as is. We can scoot the orange closer to it and the yellow to a little left of center.

13 Let's add one more filter, Blur. The default settings work to provide enough blending to make our streak look like it is glowing.

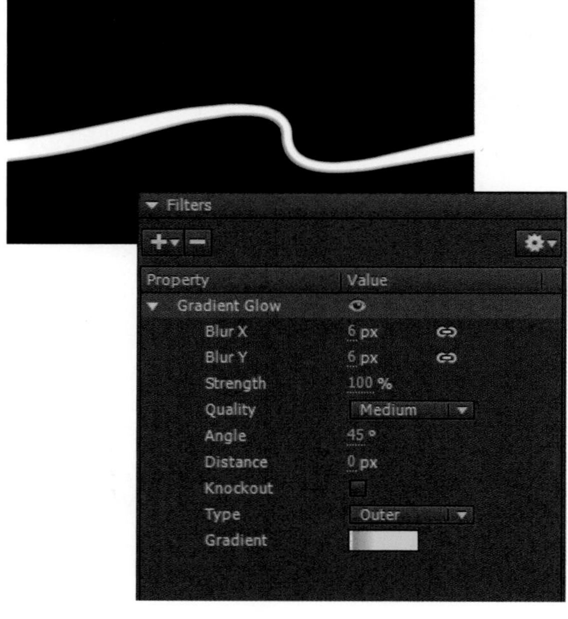

10 Let's make the outlines a little larger by changing the values for Blur X and Y to 6 and changing Quality to Medium, so it shows up better when we're not zoomed in.

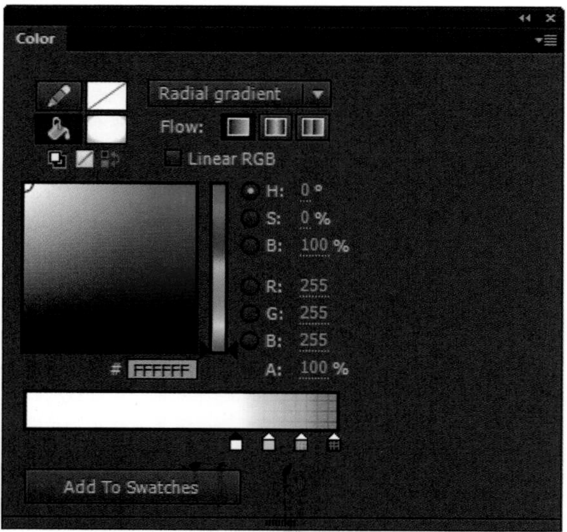

14 Make a circle with a radial gradient based on samples of the colors in the streak, and convert it to a Movie Clip.

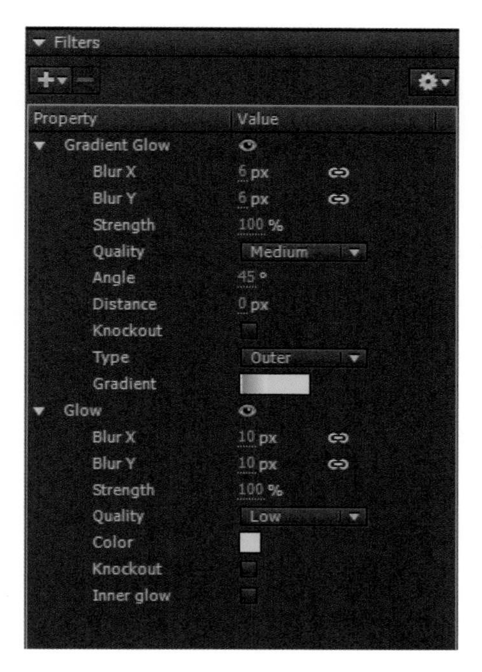

11 The edge color looks great, but let's take it to the next level by making it look more glowy. With the Movie Clip selected, add another filter. This time, let's add Glow. Make the Blur X and Y 10 pixel. and change the color to yellow #FFFF00.

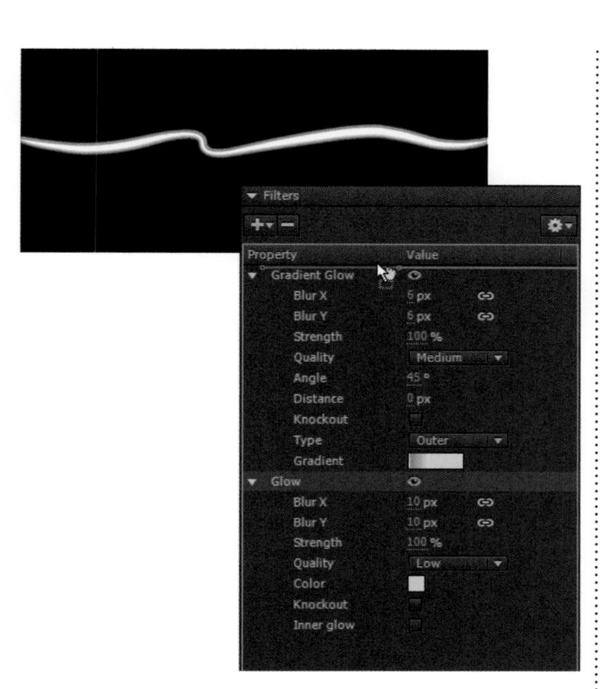

12 We're getting there, but the glow isn't blending in that well because Animate applies the filters from the top down. Grab the Glow filter and drag it up above Gradient Glow just like you would if you were moving a layer up to the top of the stack.

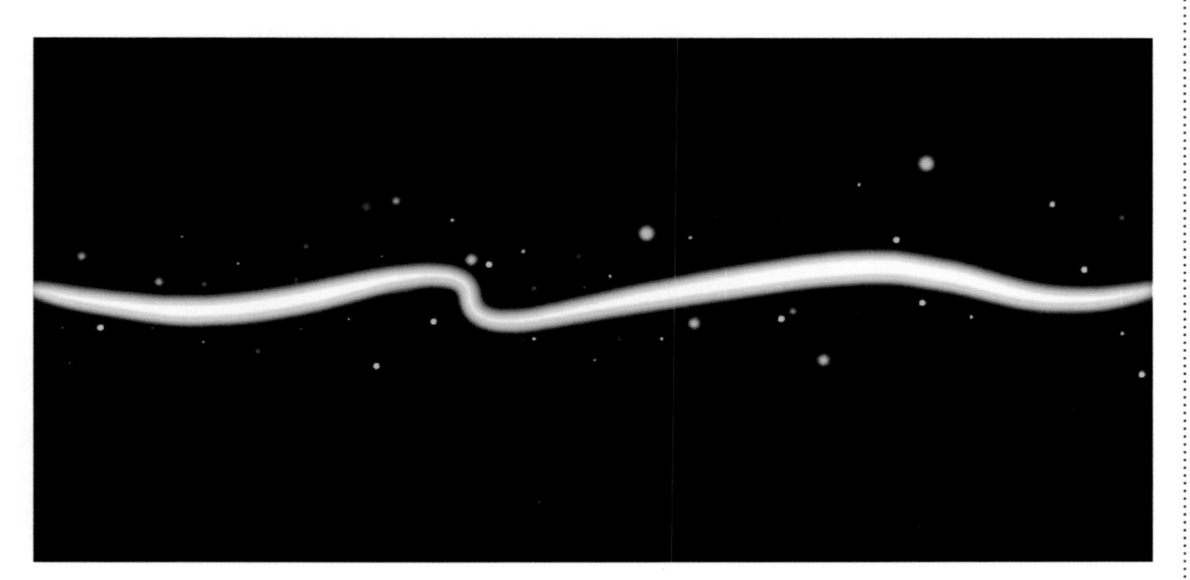

15 Add multiple instances of it at varying sizes, tints, and amounts of Blur filter. If you make the larger ones blurrier, it will look like they are being affected by depth of field.

HOT TIP

If you want to increase the size of the edging, change the values for Blur X and Blur Y. You can also get some cool effects by changing the other settings. Try switching the Type to Full, increasing the Blur X and Y values, and decreasing the Strength. Playing around with the various settings helps you to discover your own techniques for making additional color effects.

Realism with Gradients

ANIMATE IS MUCH MORE THAN A TOOL FOR designing cartoon characters. Its full array of vector drawing tools is suitable for many styles of illustration. Here we'll go step by step creating a realistic flower illustration. Flowers are always appealing to draw and at the same time challenging due to the subtle variations of color they often contain. The main tools used in this example are the Pen Tool and Gradients. Animate has adopted the core functionality of Illustrator's Pen Tool including identical shortcut keys and hot key modifiers—not to mention identical pen cursors as well. Integration is bliss.

ILLUSTRATION: CHRIS GEORGENES

1 The first step is to outline the basic shape of the flower's petal with a stroke color that is high in contrast to the original image. Be as precise as you want, but I recommend using the original image as a guide, simplifying where needed along the way.

2 The Pen Tool (P) is perfect for this task simply because it is quick and easy to manually trace the contour of the petal by clicking and dragging along the contour of the image.

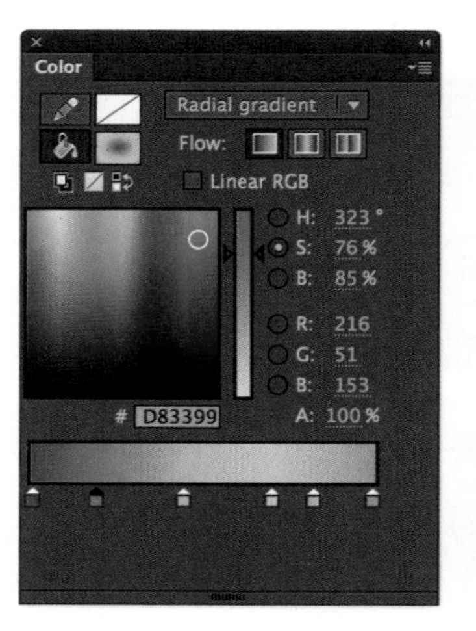

6 The initial gradient will provide the overall hue and tonal range of the flower petal. Animate lets you apply up to 15 color transitions to a gradient.

7 Fill your shape with your radial gradient and then use the Gradient Transform Tool (F) to edit its size, position, and rotation. You can delete the stroke at this stage as it is no longer needed.

3 To close the path, position the Pen Tool over the first anchor point. A small circle appears next to the Pen Tool pointer when positioned correctly. Click or drag to close the path.

4 Use the Subselection Tool A to refine your path if you desire. To adjust the shape of the curve on either side of an anchor point, drag the anchor point, or drag the tangent handle. You can also move an anchor point by dragging it with the Subselection Tool.

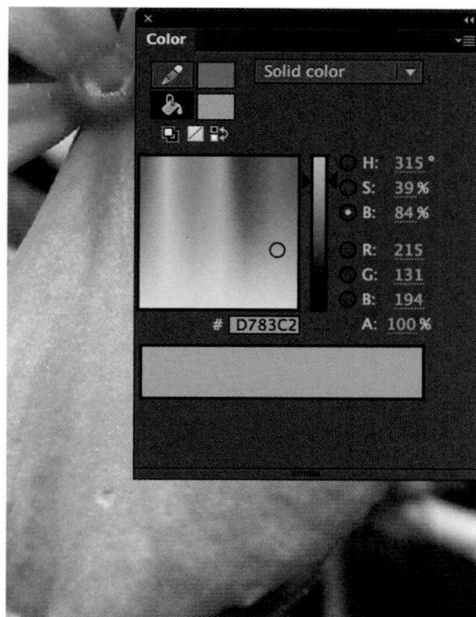

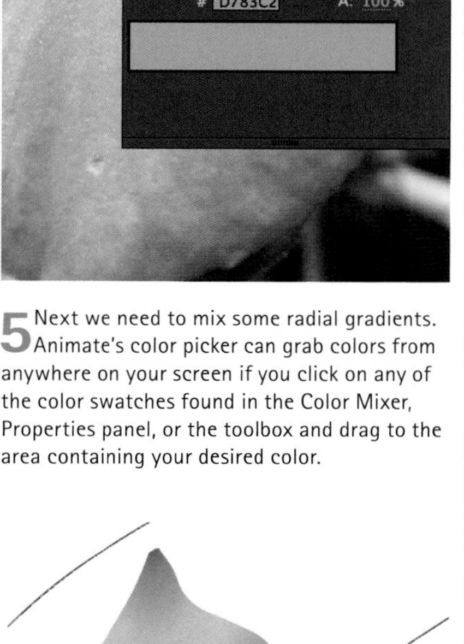

5 Next we need to mix some radial gradients. Animate's color picker can grab colors from anywhere on your screen if you click on any of the color swatches found in the Color Mixer, Properties panel, or the toolbox and drag to the area containing your desired color.

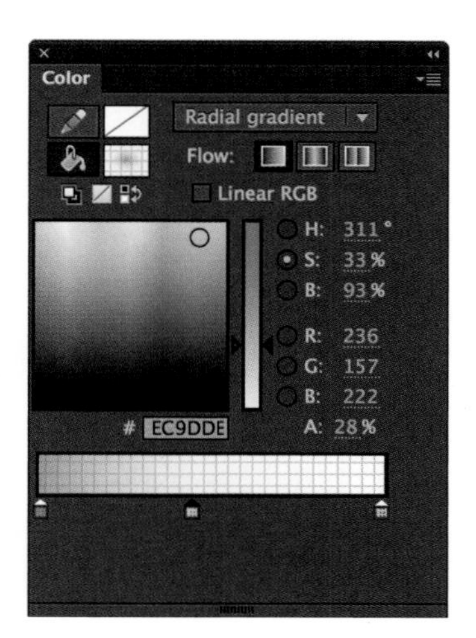

8 Copy ⌘ ctrl C and Paste in Place ⌘ ctrl Shift V this shape to a new layer as you will be layering several gradients on top of each other to create a realistic effect. The following gradients contain varied amounts of alpha to create subtle transitions in color.

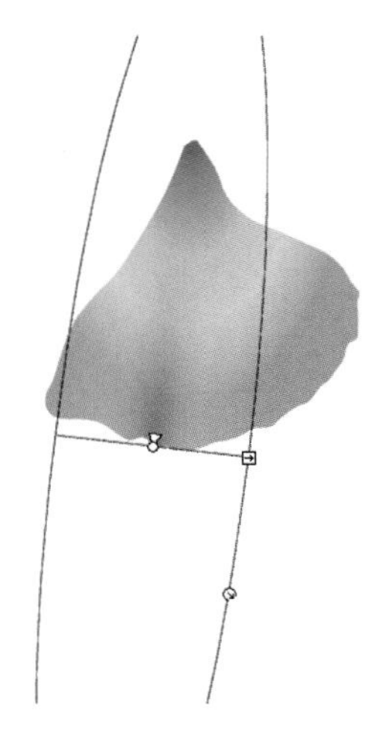

9 Fill the duplicated shape with your new gradient and use the Gradient Transform Tool F to create the suggestion of subtle undulations within the shape. Repeat the process of copying and pasting in place this shape to new layers for each new gradient.

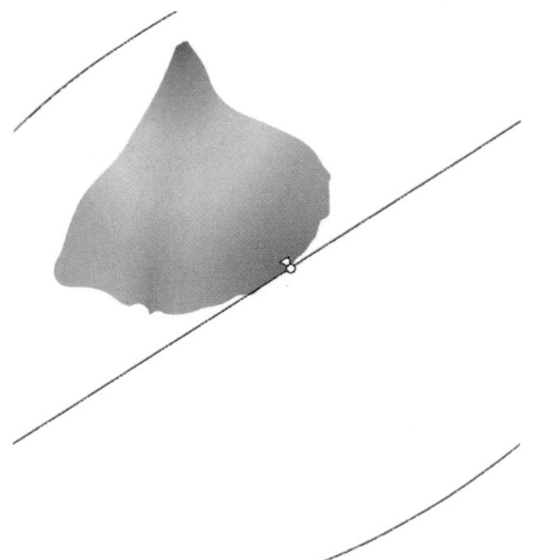

10 You can manipulate each new gradient using the Gradient Transform Tool F to create soft shadows and highlights. In almost all cases, you will use only partial gradients to create subtle transitions of light and shadow.

HOT TIP

To constrain the curve to multiples of 45°, hold down the Shift key while dragging. To drag tangent handles individually ⌥ alt +drag.

Realism with Gradients (cont.)

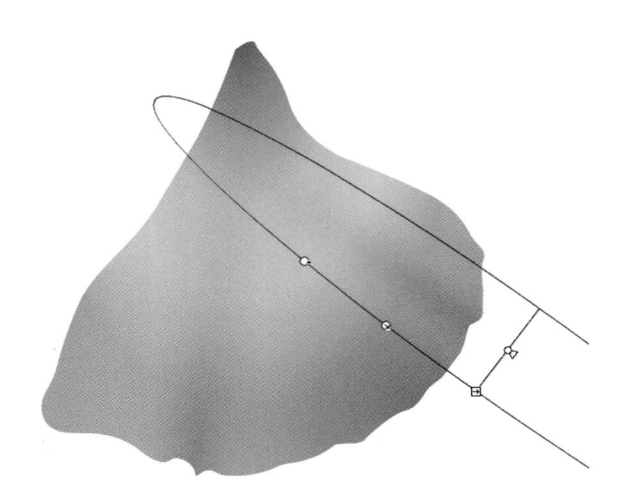

11 It's always convincing to position soft shadows where the edge of the shape contains an imperfection. The combination of gradient colors and irregular contours makes for a very convincing imperfection.

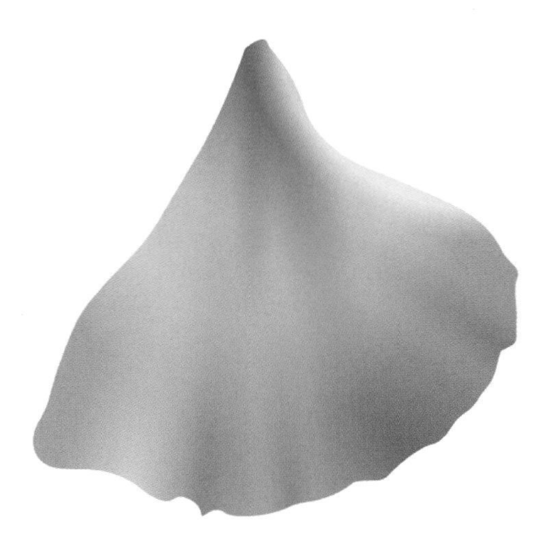

12 This end result is achieved by using several variations of layered radial gradients, producing beautiful and convincing variations of color.

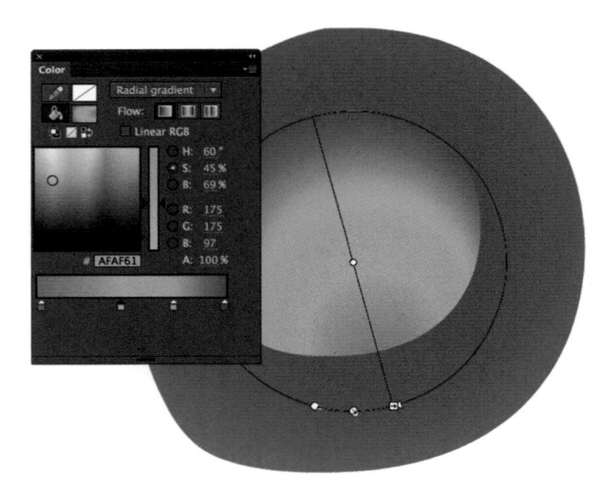

15 To achieve the effect of depth in the center of the stigma, drag the little white arrow in the radial gradient's center to move the focal point toward the edge.

16 Here's what the flower image looks like once all the petals and stigma have been illustrated. But you don't have to stop here. Let's have some fun with Animate's filters. Convert the entire flower to a Movie Clip symbol.

ILLUSTRATION: CHRIS GEORGENES

13 Repeat the same procedure for each petal of the flower image. To keep your main Timeline layers to a minimum, convert each layer to a group or an object drawing and convert each petal to a symbol.

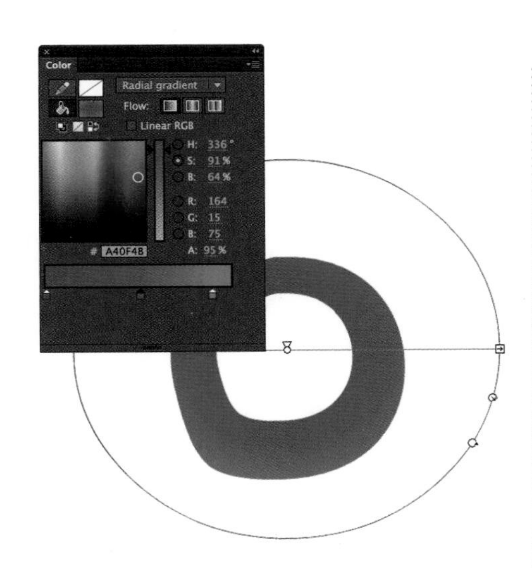

14 The center of the flower, technically named the stigma, was created with a doughnut-shaped fill containing a radial gradient.

17 From the Filters panel, add a Drop Shadow. Set the blur, alpha, and distance to your desired amount. You may want to also add a Blur filter to soften the overall image of the flower.

18 Duplicate the instance of the flower Movie Clip. Scale and rotate them to create an appealing floral arrangement. It's almost hard to imagine this style of illustration can be made entirely in Animate, right?

HOT TIP

The technique of mixing gradients with transparency and layering them so that they overlap each other can produce effects that otherwise wouldn't be possible with just radial and linear gradients. You can actually use this technique to create gradients with abstract shapes and curves that go beyond what the default gradients were designed to look like. It takes a measure of trial and error to achieve the look you want, but in the end the final results may be worth the extra effort.

SHORTCUTS
MAC WIN BOTH

Adding Texture

BITMAPS DON'T ALWAYS HAVE TO BE imported as static elements in your projects. Instead, they can be an effective source of adding texture to your designs. Since any image could be a potential texture, the possibilities are endless. For this frog character, I wanted a slightly more sophisticated look while still maintaining a cartoon feel. Instead of using solid color fills and some spot color shading, the use of imported bitmap textures added that extra sense of depth and richness.

ED THE FROG: COPYRIGHT LEAPFROG INNOVATIONS - VECTOR ILLUSTRATION: CHRIS GEORGENES

1 The first task is to design your textures. A digital camera is a very handy device for this purpose. Take a walk around your neighborhood, and you'll quickly find an unlimited supply of interesting textures that can be used for your designs. Use Photoshop to adjust the color, add filters, and crop your images. Remember to keep the image small enough for web output.

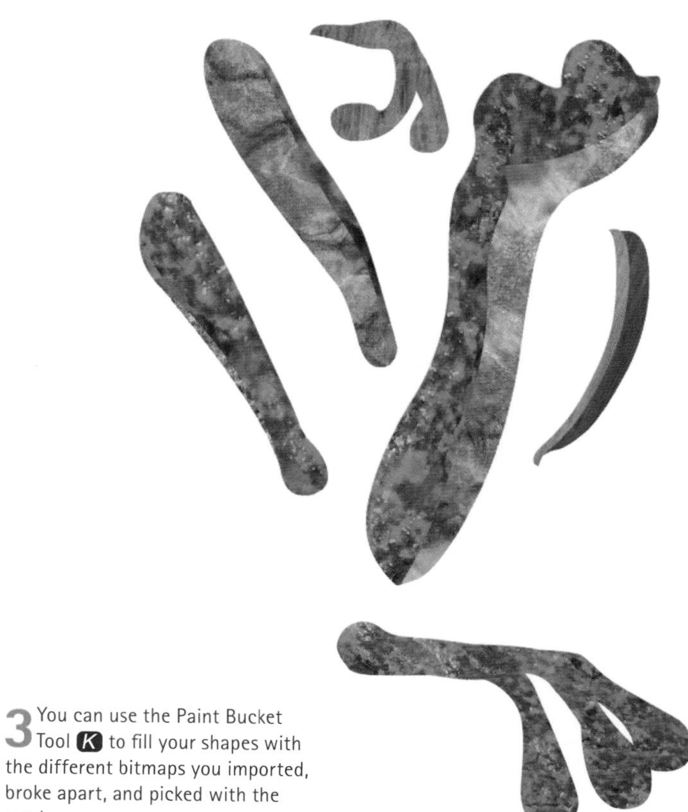

3 You can use the Paint Bucket Tool (K) to fill your shapes with the different bitmaps you imported, broke apart, and picked with the eyedropper.

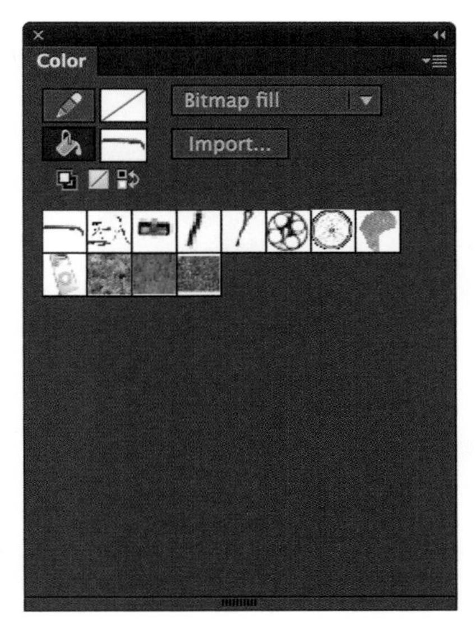

2 Using the Brush Tool **B**, draw your shapes using the bitmap as the fill color.

HOT TIP

As an option, set the quality of your movie to "BEST" by adding one line of code to frame 1 of the main Timeline. Your bitmaps will look their best but will demand more from your processor during playback.

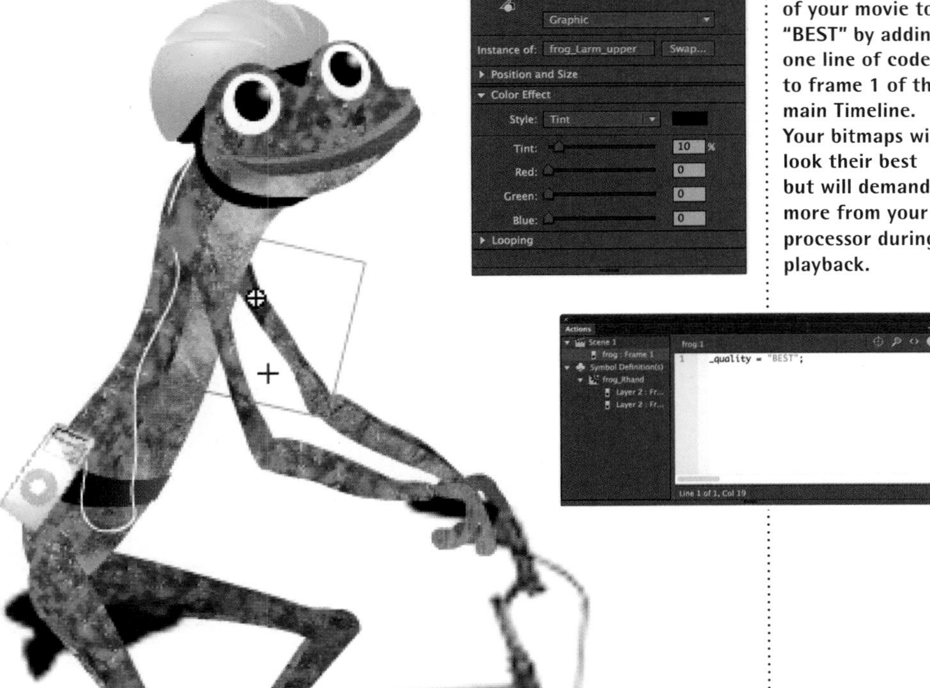

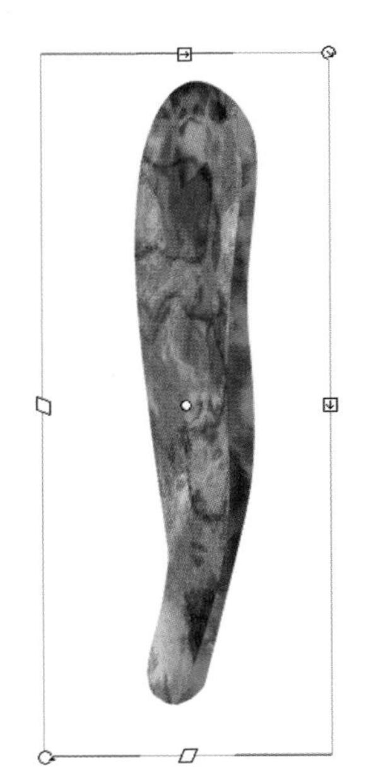

4 Most likely the bitmap fill will need to be scaled, rotated, or re-positioned. Select the Gradient Transform Tool **F**, and edit your fill using the various handles around the bounding box.

5 The final step is to convert all parts to symbols and add a slight amount of dark tint to the instances behind the character. The tint helps separate similar bitmap textures from each other and adds a touch of depth.

Adding Texture (cont.)

BITMAPS DON'T ALWAYS HAVE TO look flat. Introducing "Grotto," a character made almost entirely of bitmap fills and some carefully placed Animate gradients, which provide the illusion of form, volume, and most of all, texture. Here we'll look at how to give otherwise flat bitmap textures a bit more depth using some basic gradients and alpha.

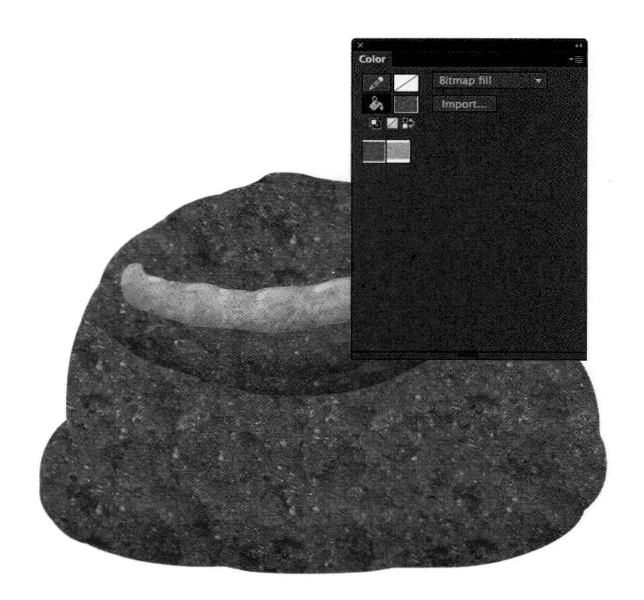

1 The first step is to create your texture in Adobe Photoshop, import it into Animate, break it apart, and then select it with the Eyedropper Tool I. I created the shape for Grotto's body with the Brush Tool and the bitmap swatch as my fill "color." Select the body shape and convert it to a Graphic symbol.

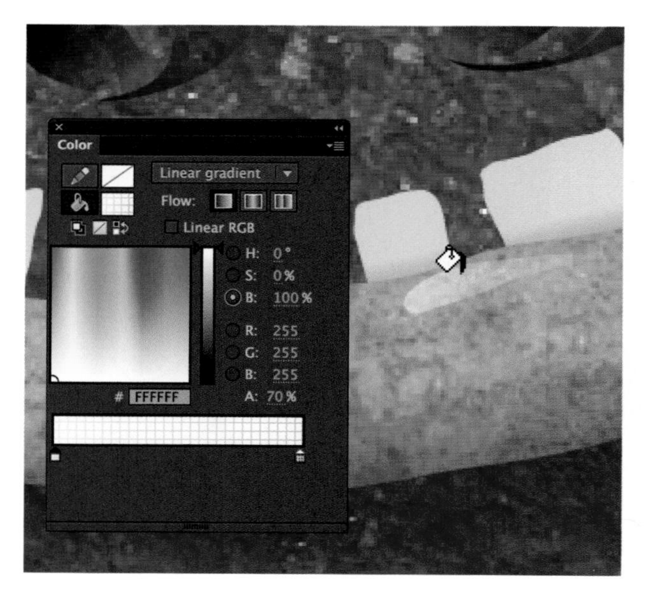

4 Sometimes the devil is in the detail, which is evident here with the addition of some subtle highlights to the lip. On a new layer use the Brush Tool B to paint some shapes and then fill them with a linear gradient containing 30% white to 0% white. Use the Gradient Transform Tool F to edit the gradient as necessary.

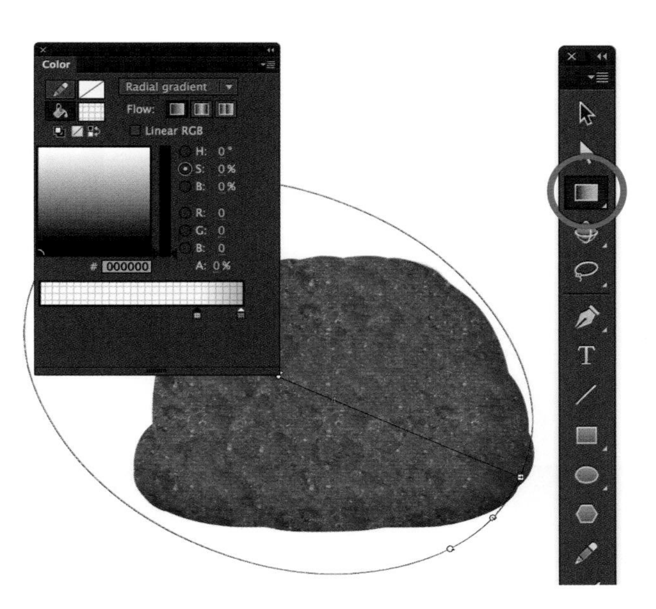

2 Edit the symbol by adding another layer above the shape layer. Copy ⌘ ctrl C and paste in place ⌘ ctrl Shift V the body shape into this new layer. Fill it with a radial gradient with two colors: black with about 30% alpha and black with 0% alpha.

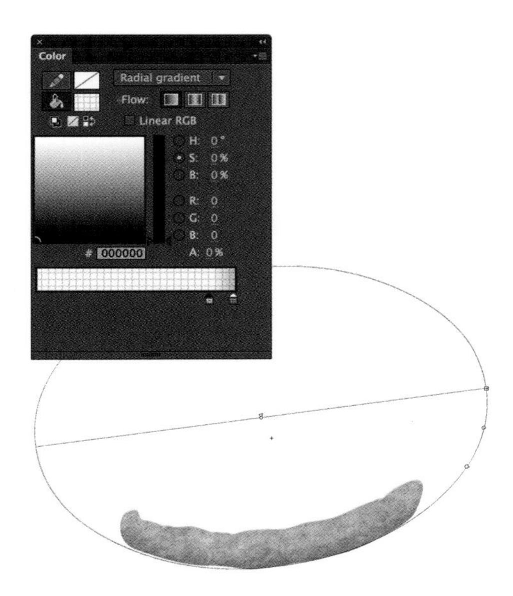

3 The mouth/lip symbol was made the same way by layering a radial gradient over the bitmap fill shape. Use the Gradient Transform Tool F to position the gradient so that it forms a shadow along the bottom half of the shape.

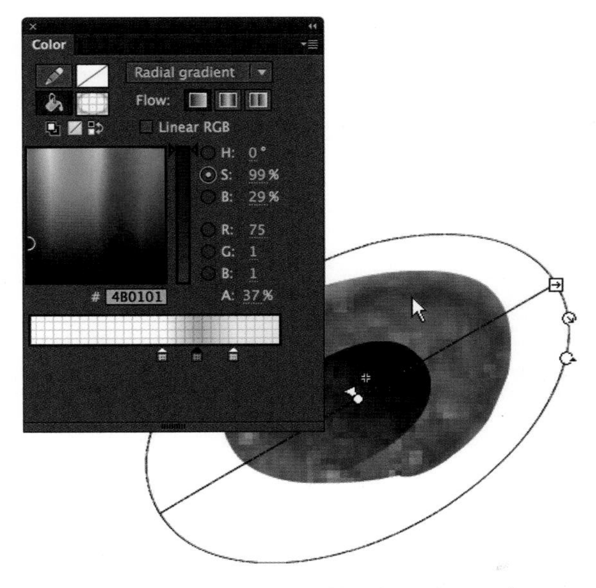

5 The nostril is another example of layering various gradients over the original shape containing the bitmap fill. Here I used a linear gradient for the inner nostril shape and a radial gradient to provide some shading for a more realistic effect.

6 When all these subtle details are combined, they can add up to a very sophisticated image. The shapes that make up Grotto are simple yet convincing and achieved simply by layering some basic gradients over our textures.

HOT TIP

You may also want to adjust the properties of the imported bitmap. (Double-click the bitmap icon in the document library and make sure "Apply Smoothing" is checked.) This property will apply anti-aliasing to your image and make it appear smoother.

The Pen Tool

SO FAR IN THIS CHAPTER WE HAVE LOOKED AT several ways of achieving different styles of drawing, from the basics of snapping simple shapes together forming bigger, more complex shapes to using bitmaps as textural fills. Most of the time the design process demands a combination of tools and techniques to get the job done. For this character design, I went from a rough pencil sketch to a fully rendered vector drawing using the Pen Tool and basic shapes. The Pen Tool, in combination with the Selection Tool, offers infinite flexibility when it comes to manipulating strokes and shapes.

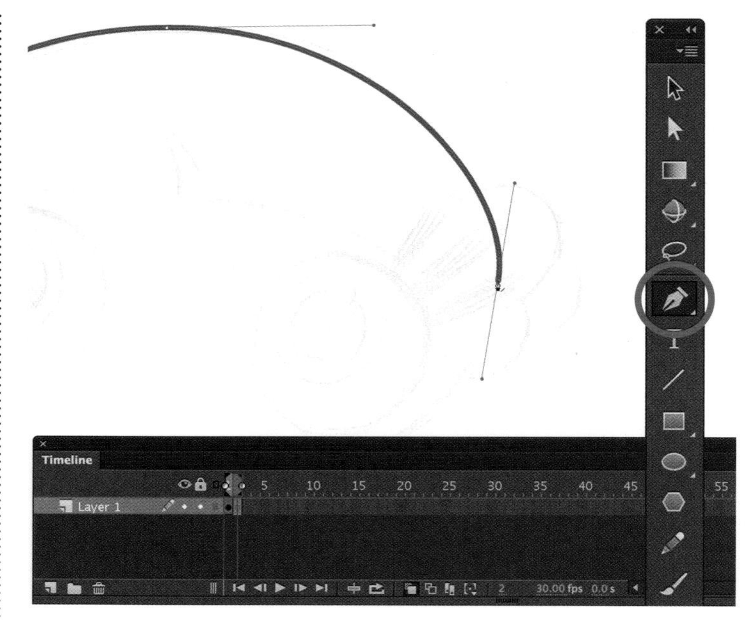

1 Start with a scanned sketch or draw directly into Animate. Create a blank keyframe on frame 2 and turn on Onion Skin ⌥ alt Shift O. Using the sketch as reference, trace the hair using the Pen Tool P by clicking and dragging each point as you go. This technique will automatically create curves with Bezier handles, allowing you to manipulate the stroke each time a point is made.

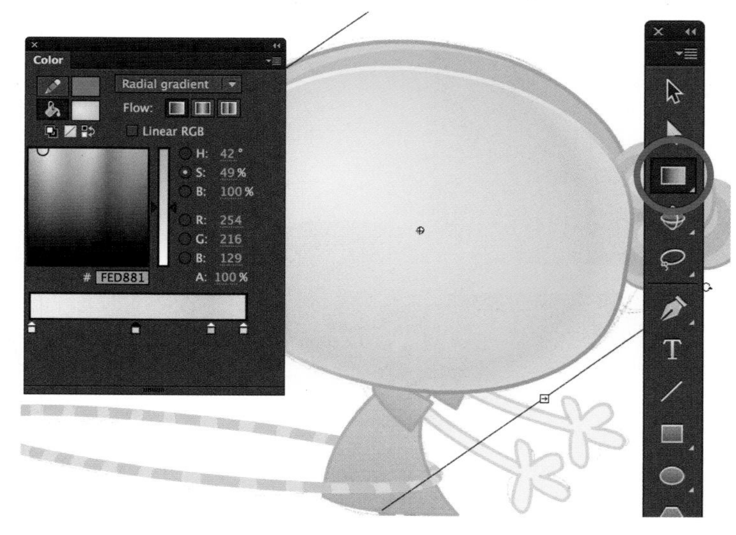

4 A linear gradient can be applied to a path without converting it to a shape like in older versions. For this gradient I chose to mix three colors: light, mid, and dark tones. With this gradient selected in the stroke color swatch in the Color panel, click on the path using the Ink Bottle Tool S to apply it. Edit the gradient using the Gradient Transform Tool F.

VECTOR ILLUSTRATION: CHRIS GEORGENES

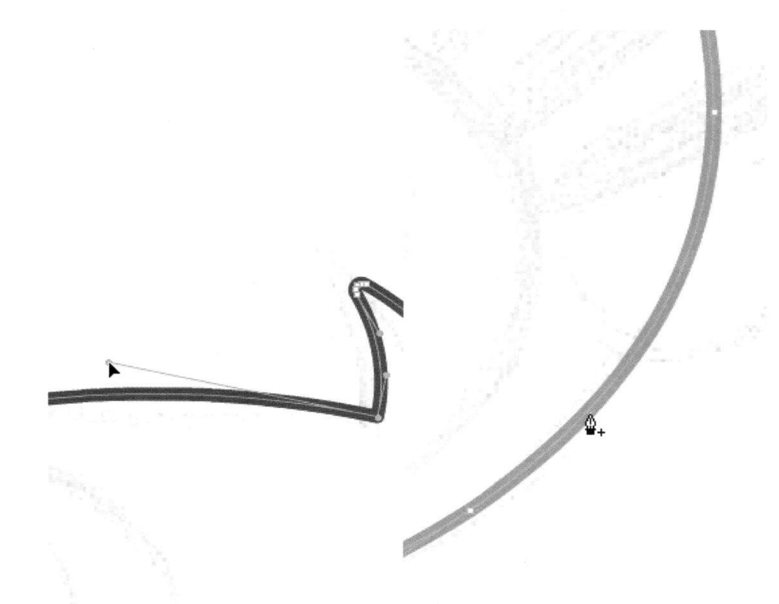

2 Using the Subselection Tool A, modify the contours of the hair by clicking an anchor point and adjusting its Bezier handles. Once this shape is complete, temporarily cut and paste it to a new layer and lock it to avoid editing it unintentionally.

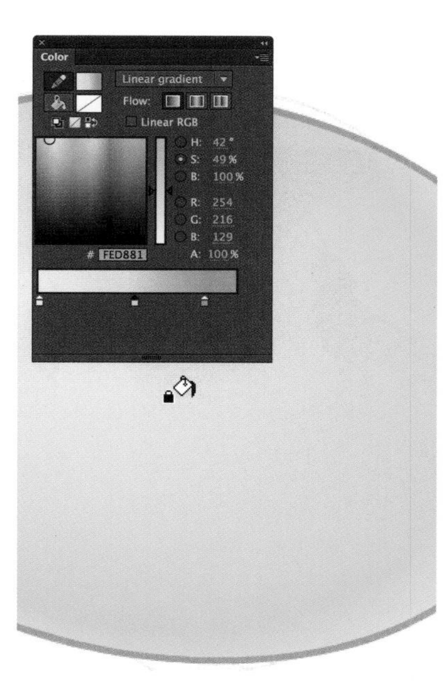

3 Once you have closed the path, fill it with a color. Here I have mixed a radial gradient to provide a sense of volume to the shape.

HOT TIP

Go to Edit > Preferences > Drawing and make sure the "Show Pen Preview" option is checked. This option allows you to see a preview of what your lines will look like as you are drawing with the Pen Tool. Hold down the Shift key to snap your lines to 90° and 45° angles as you draw. To designate a control point as the end of your line, hold down the ⌘/ctrl key while clicking.

5 The Pen Tool P is clearly a useful tool for drawing paths, but in some situations the Oval Tool O and Rectangle Tool R are better and faster alternatives. The Selection Tool V can be used for basic editing of paths made with the shape tools.

6 The final result is a combination of shapes and paths created with the Pen, Oval, and Rectangle Tools. Editing of these paths and shapes was the result of using the Selection, Subselection, and Pen Tools.

Importing and Manipulating Adobe Stock

I CAN'T THINK OF A BETTER WAY TO CHEAT at drawing than not actually doing the drawing—just start with the artwork already made for you. Adobe Stock includes vector images—along with photos, videos, templates, 3D, and premium and editorial images—that we can customize with some simple changes. You can search for assets on the Adobe Stock site or directly in Animate CC via CC Libraries. If you know you're going to be using Adobe Stock for your assets, you can buy one image or a multi-image subscription. If you wait to purchase images after your search, the License and Save button is replaced with a Buy and Save button.

I'd like an image of a howling coyote. I've done some searching and found a howling wolf which appears in the pose I envisioned as a silhouette in front of the moon, but there are some visual differences between wolves and coyotes. I can still use the image, but it will need a few tweaks to make the muzzle a little longer and more narrow, the ears a bit larger and more pointy, and the head larger in proportion to the body because coyotes are generally smaller than wolves.

Let's step through the process of searching for an Adobe Stock image, working with a comp, licensing it, and manipulating it.

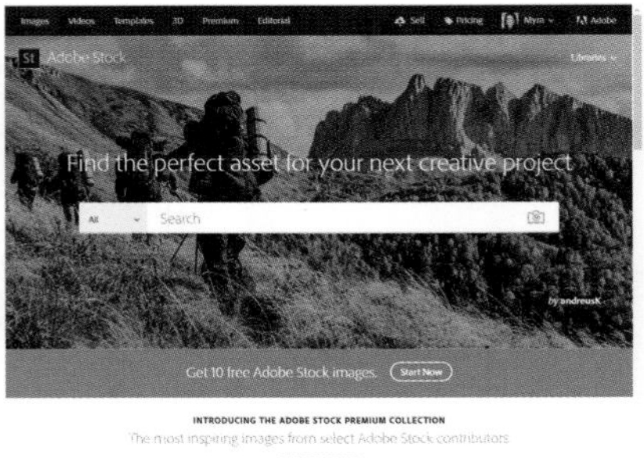

1 Go to the Adobe Stock website at stock.adobe.com. You don't have to be logged in to search, but you will if you want to save a preview or license an image. Enter the keywords "howling wolf" in the search field.

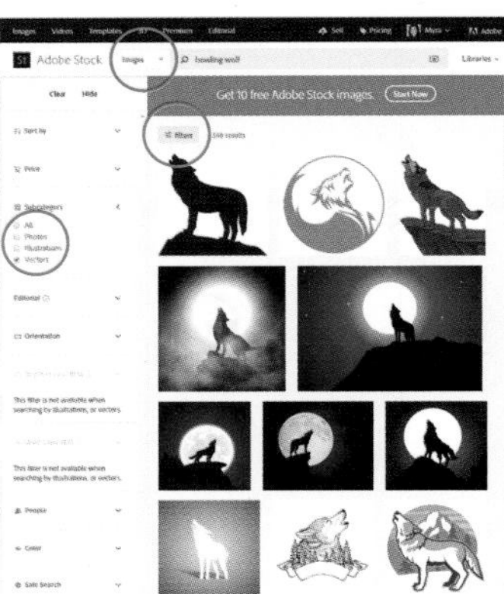

2 Refine the search by changing the asset type from "All" to "Images" from the drop-down menu. Click the filters button (it looks like three stacked sliders) to open the submenu. In the Subcategory section, select "Vectors."

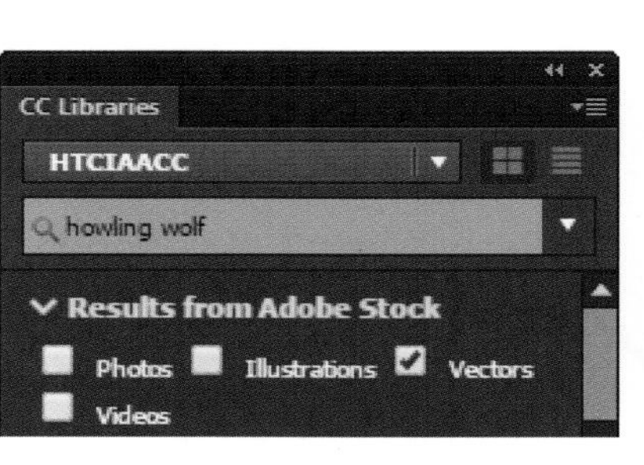

5 To search within Animate, repeat the above steps by entering the keywords in the search field in the CC Libraries panel. Set the search field to "Search Adobe Stock." After an initial search, filter your results by selecting Vectors.

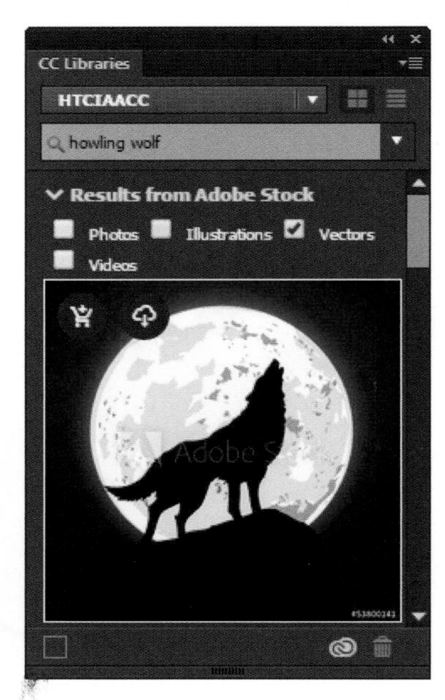

6 Hover over the image to see the buttons to license or save as preview. I already had images available in my account, so the License and Save button appeared instead of Buy and Save.

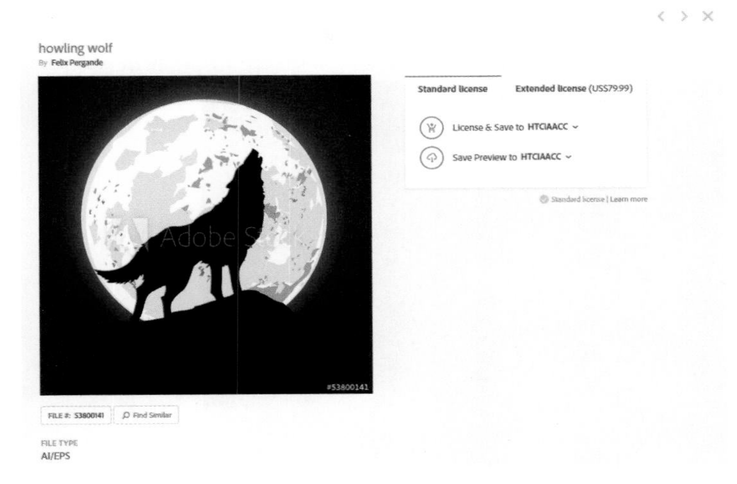

3 Select one of the silhouettes of a howling wolf in front of a moon with a dark blue sky. I've clicked on Wolf on Moon background. Now click the Find Similar button.

4 From this revised search, I found "howling wolf" by Felix Pergande. Save a preview of it to a Creative Cloud Library. If you don't have a designated CC Library for this project, create a new library by typing a name for the library in the drop-down menu.

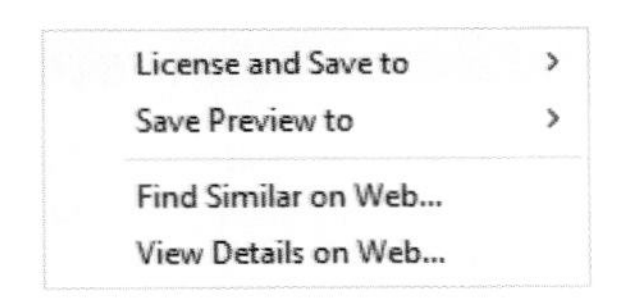

7 You can also right-click to get the License and Save to and Save Preview to options. You'll also find the Find Similar on Web... and View Details on Web... options by right-clicking.

8 Once you find the image you'd like, drag the preview image that you saved to your CC Library onto the Stage. Even though the stock art is a vector graphic, when you drag the image onto the Stage, you see the preview is a rasterized, low-resolution, flattened, watermarked version.

9 If you decide to license the image, you'll see a confirmation. After confirming that you want to license it, the vector graphic becomes available in your CC Library. The thumbnail isn't watermarked, and a checkmark indicates that it's licensed.

HOT TIP:

As the Adobe Stock collection grows, it may become more difficult to find this specific image. Try adding additional keywords like "blue moon Halloween." When looking for this or other images, try other search parameters like orientation, people as included or not, and color. The Sort by feature can help you find images that are most relevant to your keywords, that have been added to Adobe Stock most recently, that are most popular, that are downloaded the most frequently, and that have yet to be discovered.

Importing and Manipulating Adobe Stock (cont.)

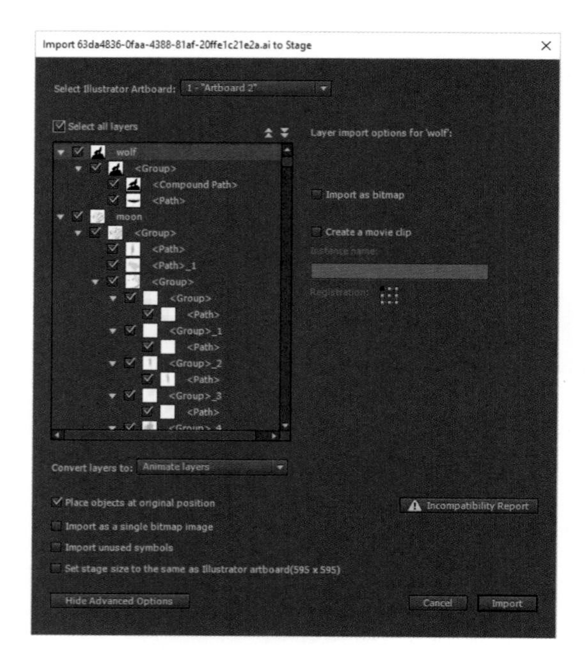

10 Some Creative Cloud applications automatically update the preview with the licensed image. However, in Animate CC you have to update it manually. So drag the licensed version onto the Stage. This image was created in Illustrator, so on import check preferences for layer selection, importing as a bitmap, creating a movie clip, converting layers, and other importing details.

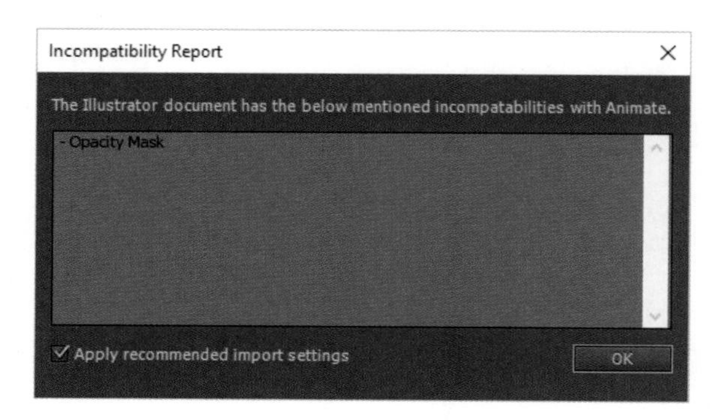

11 Animate alerts us this image has an incompatibility issue. This report warns that the image uses an opacity mask that is incompatible with Animate. Check Apply recommended import settings to instruct Animate to do its best to import the image despite the incompatibility. In this case, it removes the glow around the moon and turns it into a bitmap with transparency. The rest of the vector shapes are intact.

14 Select the points on the muzzle to taper the nose and jaw and to elongate it.

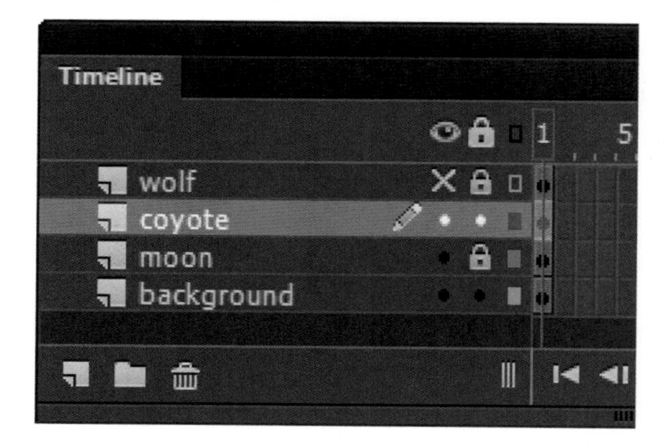

15 To compare your adjustments to the original, make a copy of the wolf and put it on a new layer. Click Show Outline and lock that layer.

12 Convert layers to Animate layers was selected, so each of the shapes becomes a layer. Select the wolf layer.

13 Notice it's grouped. You can double-click to access the anchor points or ungroup ⌘ ctrl Shift G.

16 Keep the shape of the ear in a similar downward position but make it larger. Make the head larger compared to the body. Delete the original when you no longer need it for comparison.

17 Extend the background so that the rest of the Stage is blue. If you try to scale the background rectangle, the circle gradient will scale too and transform into an oval. Instead, use the Subselection Tool A to select each point of the rectangle and move it to its corresponding edge of the Stage.

HOT TIP

To make your modifications available to your team, share the updated graphic as a symbol through CC Libraries. Select the symbol from the Stage, then click the + symbol on the lower left of the CC Libraries panel. A small dialog opens. Make sure the option for "Symbols" is selected and click Add. From the CC Libraries flyout menu, select "Collaborate" to open it in a browser where you can invite your team members, set permissions, and add a message. Make the CC Library public by selecting "Share Link" from the flyout. It opens in a browser where you can set the link to private or public, allow downloads, or send the link to an email address.

Shading 1: Line Trick

CELL SHADING IS COMMONLY REFERRED to as "toon shading." This style of shading is popular with comic book–style artwork and classic Disney films. I have discovered four different ways to achieve cell-style shading in Animate for you to consider. This particular example demonstrates a stroke drawn across an existing fill color. The stroke can be edited without disrupting the shape below it. Once the stroke has been defined and a shadow color added, the stroke can easily be removed, leaving behind the shadow and original fill color.

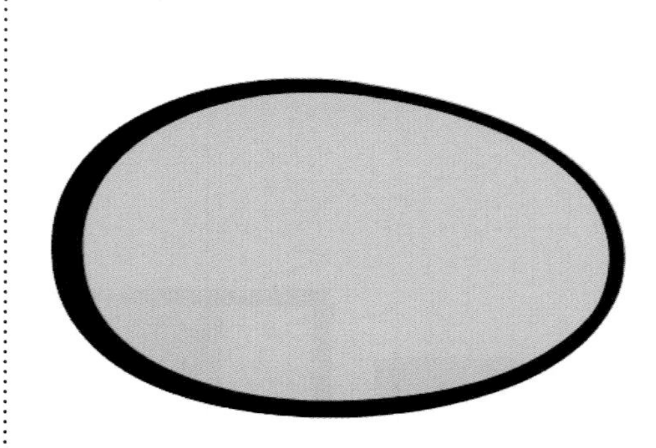

1 Start with a basic shape that contains a fill and outline. This technique will work just as well with shapes that have no outlines.

2 Select the Line Tool (N) and make sure Snap to Objects is also selected in the toolbox.

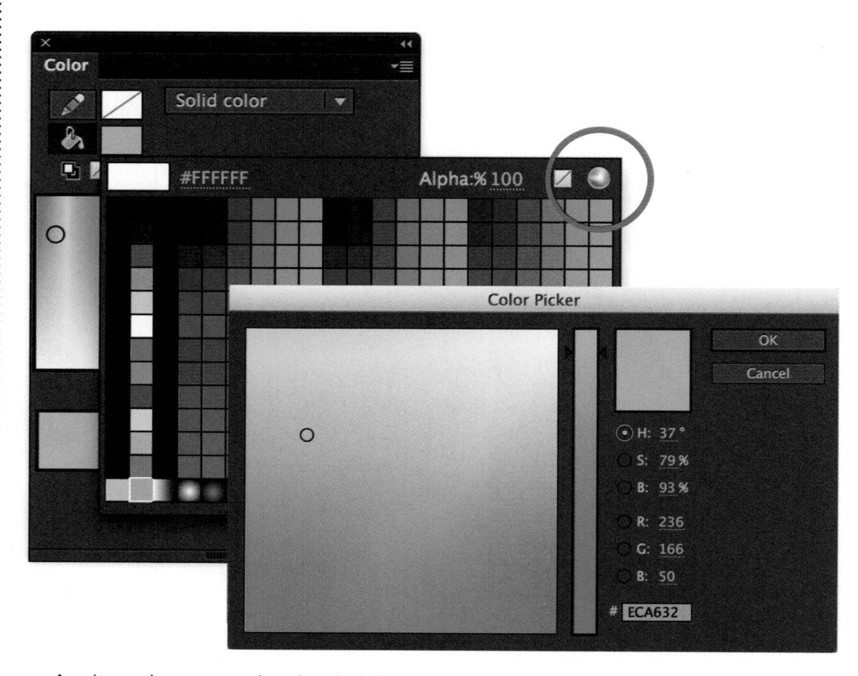

6 An alternative way to mix colors in Animate is to click the color wheel button in the upper right corner. This button will open the color palette mixer that is native to your operating system. Mix your new color and click OK.

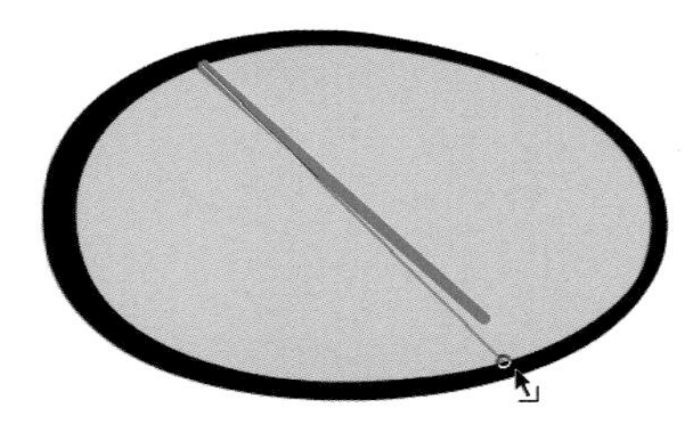

3 Draw a diagonal line inside the fill of your shape. Use the Selection Tool **V** to drag each endpoint of the line so that they snap to the edge of the fill.

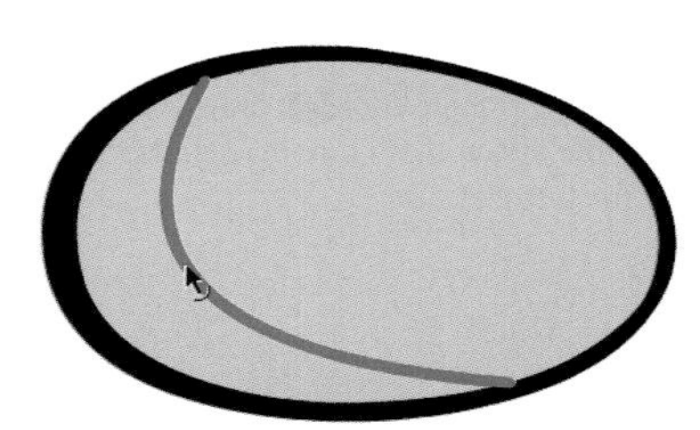

4 Use the Selection Tool **V** to bend the line so that its arc reflects the shape of the oval.

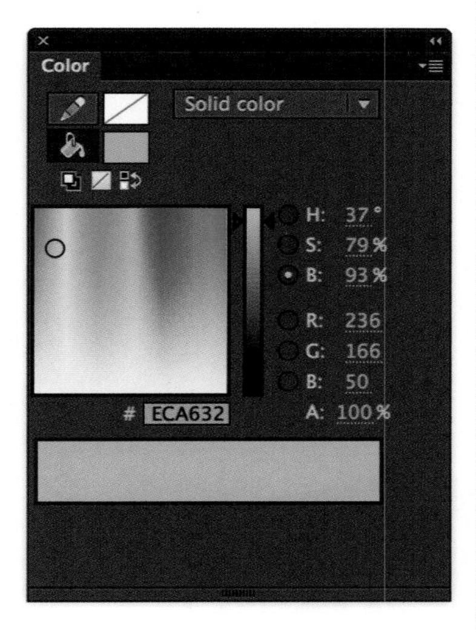

5 With the fill color selected, mix a slightly darker color using the Color panel mixer.

HOT TIP

Cell-style shading can be difficult to achieve. You have to imagine that your two-dimensional shapes have a third dimension and they are affected by light and shadow. Choose a light source and keep it consistent throughout your design when adding shading.

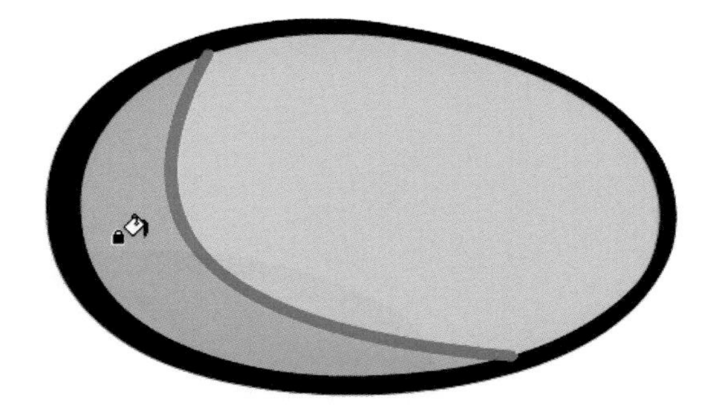

7 Use the Paint Bucket Tool **K** to fill the shape you created with the Line Tool.

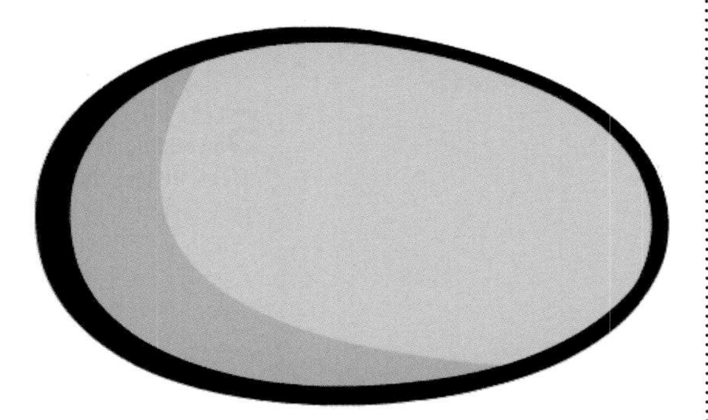

8 Select the line and delete it. Easy right? If it still isn't perfect, you can continue to use the Selection Tool to edit the edge of the new fill you created.

Shading 2: Shape It

HERE'S ANOTHER VARIATION ON CELL-STYLE shading in Animate. This technique involves the Rectangle Tool and allows for more complex shading. This approach may be preferable if your shapes require more complex shadows.

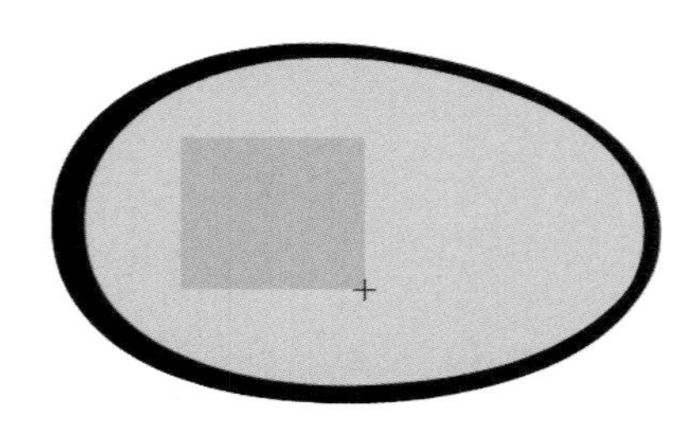

1 Using the Rectangle Tool (R), draw a box inside your shape that contains a darker fill color (no outline).

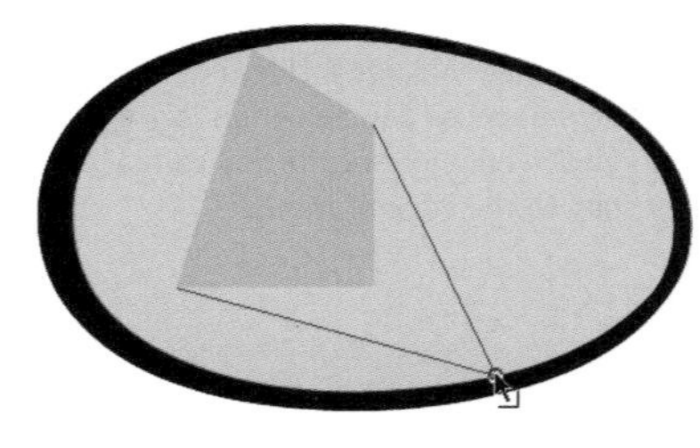

2 Use the Selection Tool (V) to pull the corners until they snap to the edges of the shape (make sure the Snap feature is turned on).

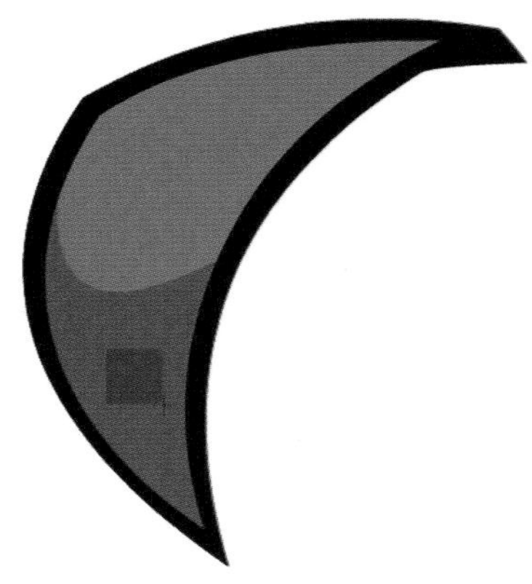

5 Let's take this technique one step further by adding more shading for a more realistic effect. Repeat the above procedure using an even darker color inside the shaded area.

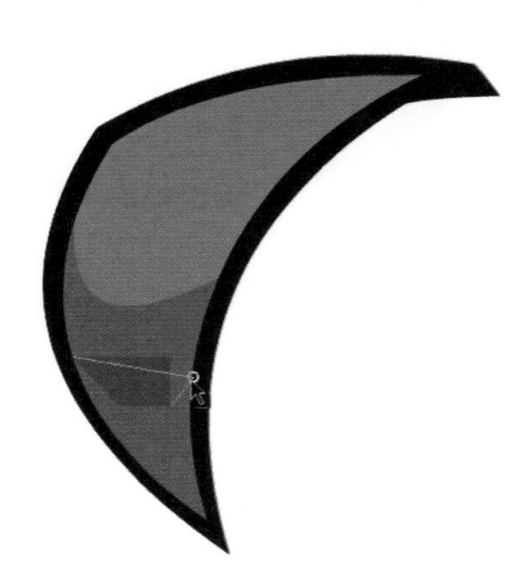

6 Use the Selection Tool (V) to pull the corners until they snap to the edges of the shaded shape.

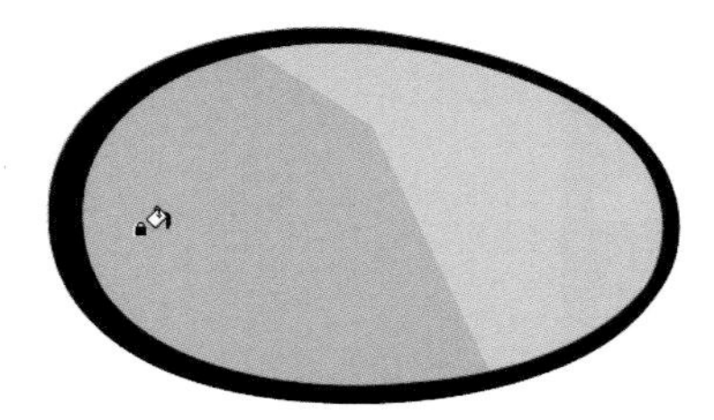

3 Fill the gap area created after snapping the corners to the edge of the shape.

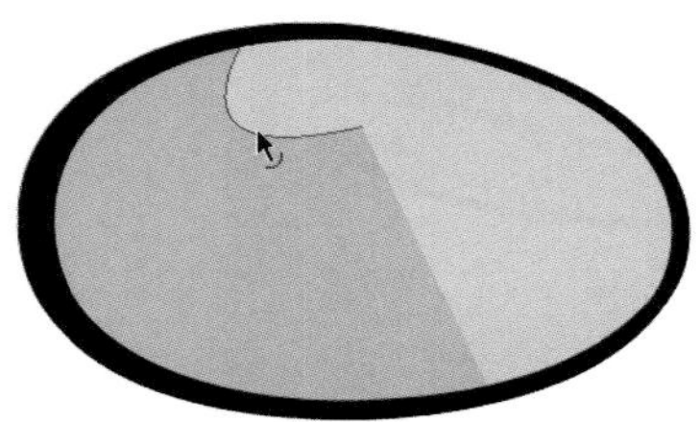

4 Use the Selection Tool to bend the edge of the darker fill color so that its arc reflects the shape of the oval. Having used the Rectangle Tool, you have an extra corner to play around with. The extra control can be useful for creating more complex shading such as with the ear shape.

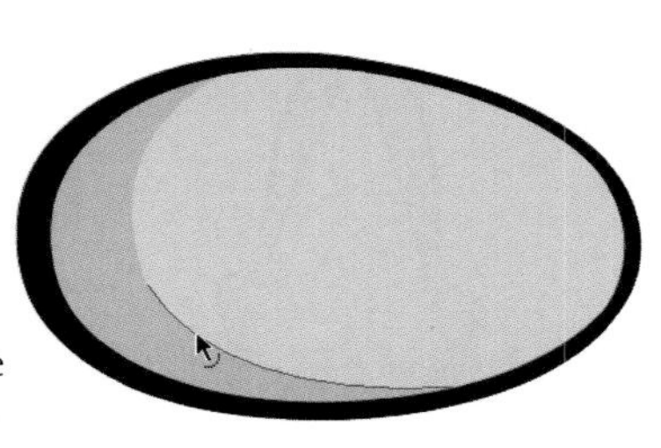

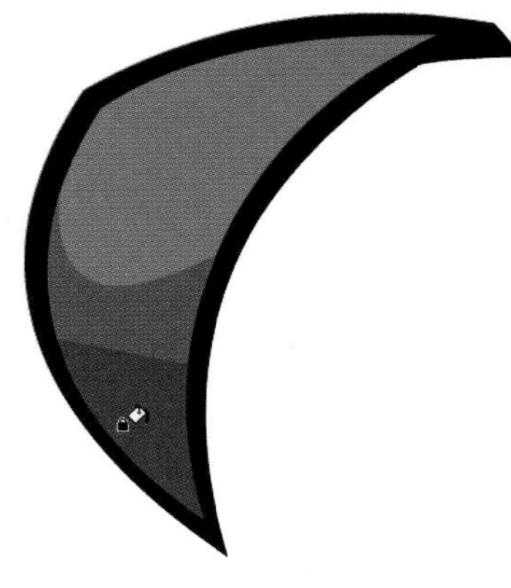

7 Fill the gap area created after snapping the corners to the edge of the shape.

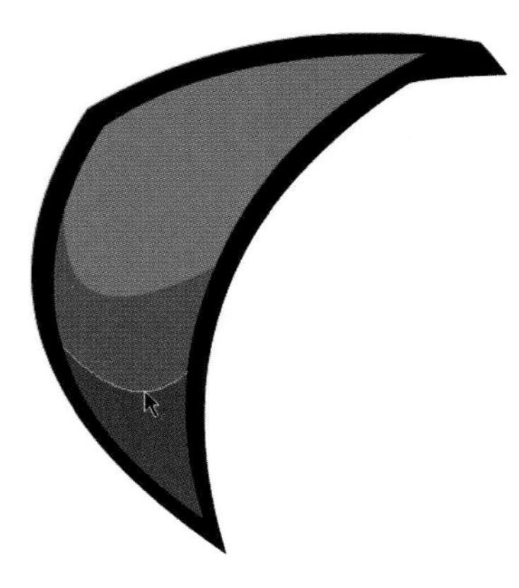

8 Use the Selection Tool to bend the edge of the darker fill color so that its arc reflects the contour of the shape.

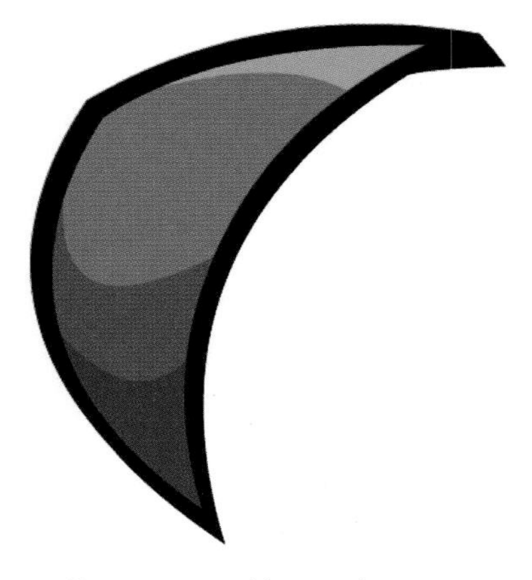

9 You can repeat this procedure as many times as you like. The more color values you add, the more realistic the image will be.

HOT TIP

If you would like a cool and easy way to create various hues based on your original color, give Adobe Color CC (as a web service at color.abobe.com) or Adobe Capture CC for mobile (available on the App Store for iPad, iPad Pro, and iPhone and on Google Play for Android) a try. You can mix shades of color very easily or capture them from your camera or existing images. Name your color theme and save it to a CC Library. Open the CC Libraries panel in Animate and navigate to the library where you saved your theme to access your colors.

Shading 3: Paint Selected

WE'RE ALL DIFFERENT, AND WE TEND TO find different ways of using the same tools. Certain techniques become familiar to our workflow, and we become comfortable in our individual habits. Here is yet another technique for creating cell-style shading that you may prefer over the previous versions. It lends itself well to designers who like a more hand-drawn feel to their work.

1 Start with a shape.

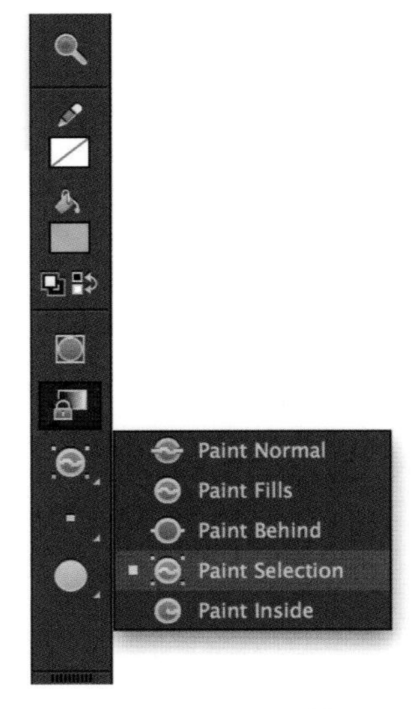

2 Select the Brush Tool B and then from the brush mode subselection menu, select Paint Selection. This subselection will restrict any paint to selected fills only.

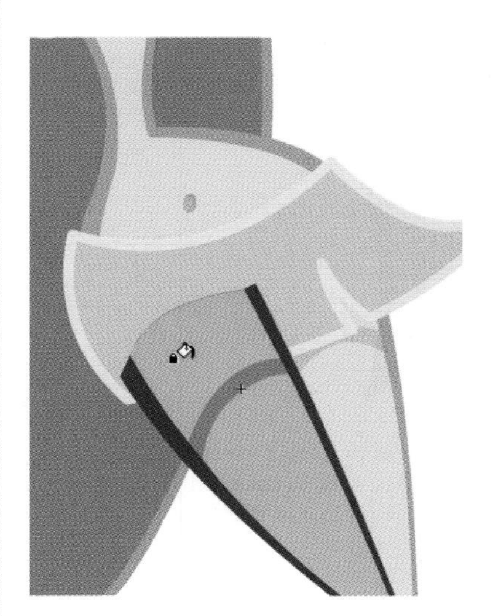

6 Next, simply fill the space created with the new fill you just painted.

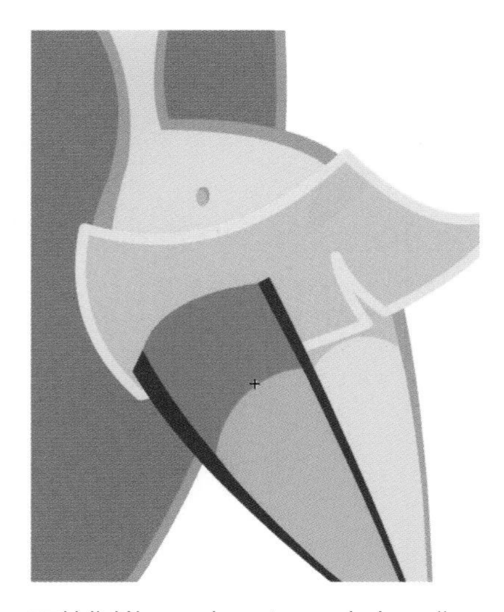

7 Voila! Now you've got a convincing cell-style shading for the leg.

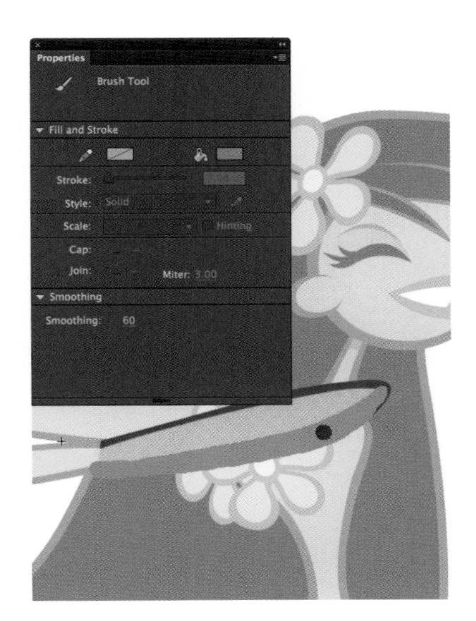

3 Use the Selection Tool V to select the fill color where you'll be adding the shade color. Now use the Brush Tool and adjust the amount of smoothing desired for the shape you'll paint. Next, paint inside the selected fill.

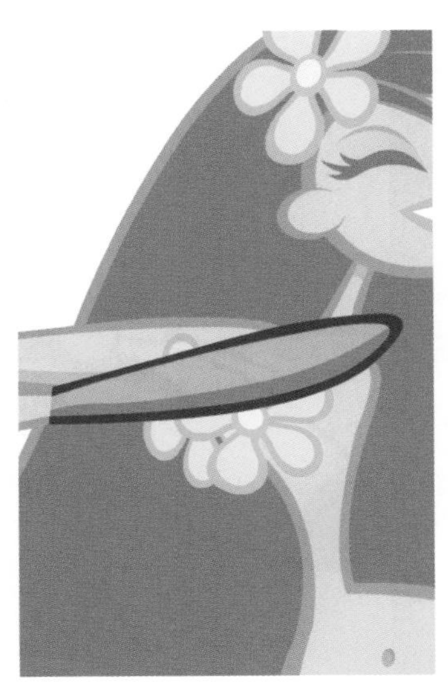

4 Don't worry about being sloppy. Once you release the brush, the painted fill will exist only inside the selected area you intended.

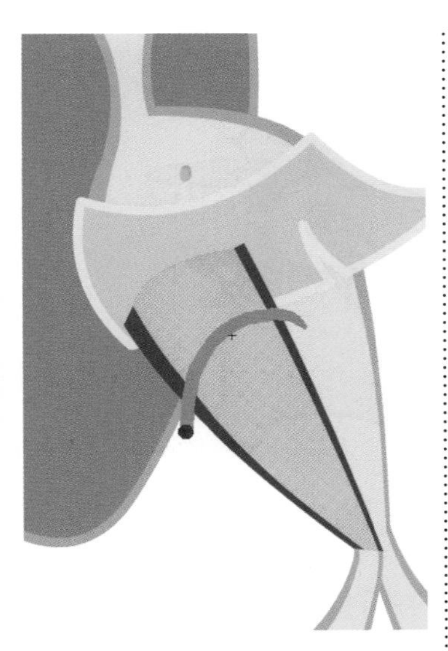

5 Sometimes the area may be too large to paint entirely by hand. In this situation, just draw the contour of the edge for the shaded area.

HOT TIP

Consistency is important when it comes to your light source. It helps to limit yourself to one light source if possible and create your shading based on the angle where the light is coming.

8 The face shading can be drawn the same way. Remember the direction of your light source and paint a crescent fill.

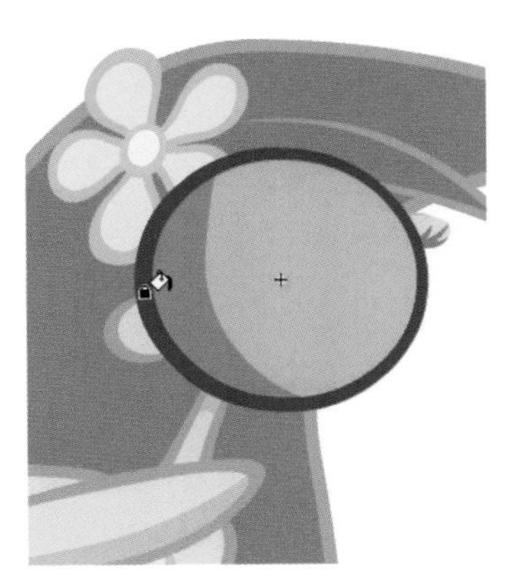

9 Fill the space created by the new fill, and you are done.

10 Cell shading can add that extra dimension to your designs, giving them depth and realism.

Shading 4: Outlines

THIS VARIATION ON CELL-STYLE SHADING works well for both simple and very complex shapes. If you have line work that is very loose in a hand-drawn style, this technique may be the one for you. You'll use the Ink Bottle to create a line around your fill. Then you can reposition this line off-center and fill the space created with a darker shade of color.

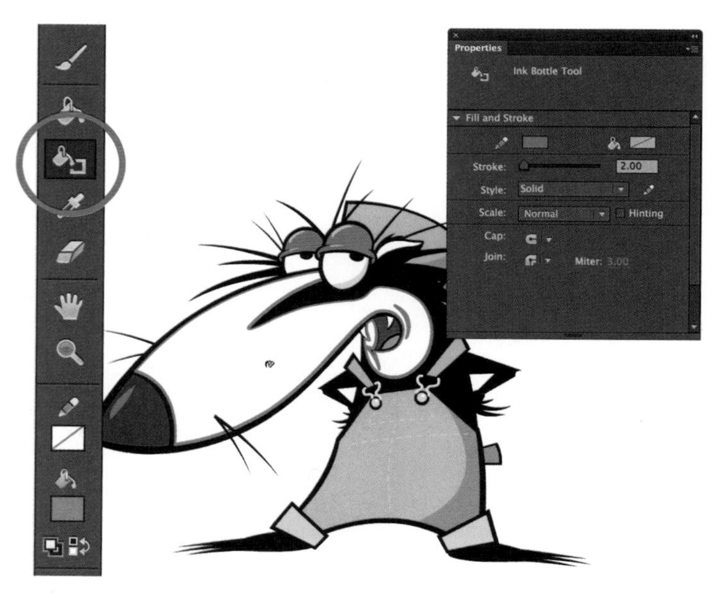

1 Start with the Ink Bottle Tool (S) and a stroke color that doesn't exist anywhere in your design. Set the stroke height to around 3 or 4 pt. Click anywhere within the fill to outline it with a stroke in the color you chose. Don't worry about how it looks because you will eventually delete this line entirely after you are done.

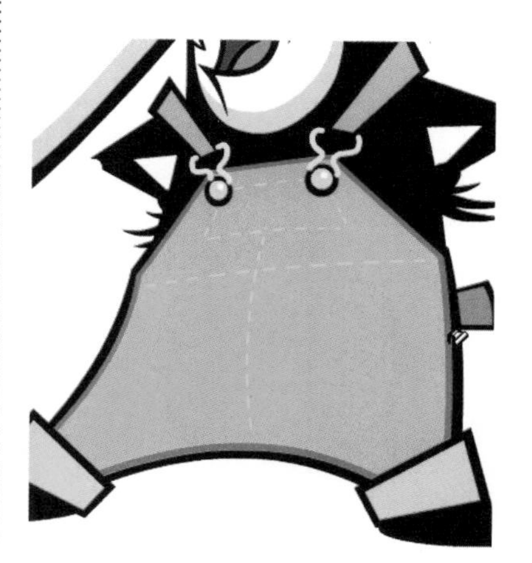

4 For this character's outfit, I applied a stroke outline to the overalls as well.

5 The stroke is selected and repositioned based on the same light source as in the previous example.

2 Select the line by double-clicking on it with the Selection Tool V. Next, use the arrow keys to nudge it away from the original shape in the direction of your light source. Fill this area created between the stroke and the original edge of your shape with your shade color.

3 Delete the entire stroke by pressing the Delete key. If your stroke has been deselected, select it by double-clicking on it with the Selection Tool. Double-clicking the stroke will select the entire stroke, while single-clicking on it will select a segment of it if it contains multiple points.

6 A darker shade of color is mixed and filled to create the illusion of form and realism.

7 With the stroke still selected, delete it. In some cases, the resulting shape created may need some tweaking.

8 Use the Selection Tool V to further refine the shading as needed.

HOT TIP

Set your stroke height large enough to make working with the stroke easier. A larger value will allow you to select it more easily. Choosing a bright color that is high in contrast from your original design will make it easier for you visually.

UI Design: Almost Flat

DESIGN TRENDS CHANGE. EARLY DIGITAL media was often created as skeuomorphic design which imitated real-life interfaces and materials. As mobile devices grew in popularity, flat design with its minimal look and smaller file sizes became the norm. Flat design, however, had its limitations in terms of providing visual cues to users for such tasks as differentiating labels from buttons or identifying what has focus. As we approach a post-flat era, the emerging trend is almost flat or nearly flat. Simple UI elements remain but may be embellished with a slight gradient or use a drop shadow. The result retains the simplicity of flat design while employing subtleties of depth for functional cues and being more visually pleasing.

You might recognize this first graphic from previous editions of this book. Let's look at how to make a comparable flat version and transform it to the almost flat look.

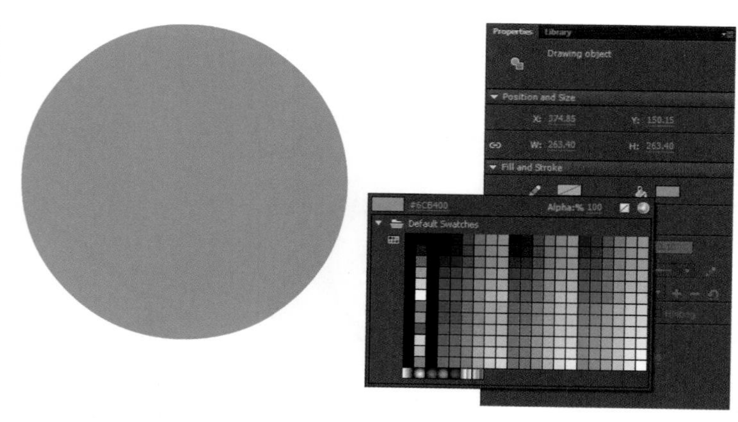

1 Start by drawing a circle with the Oval Tool O that has a diameter of 263.4 pixel and set the fill to green. I used #6CB400 which is a mid-tone of the original.

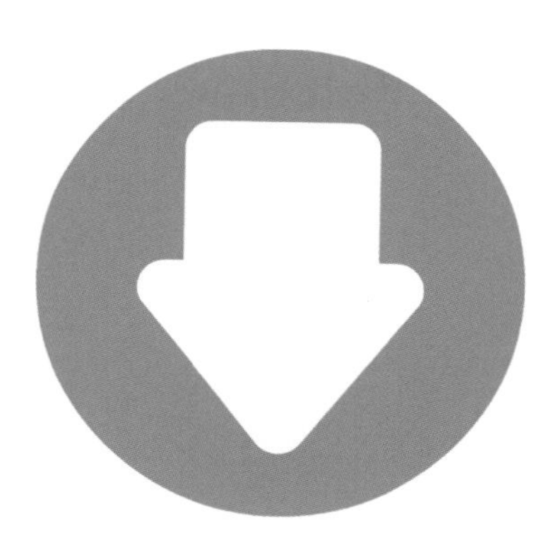

5 Deselect the arrow shape and select the Ink Bottle Tool S. In the Properties panel, select Solid as the Stroke Style. Bring the stroke height down to create a rounded edge around the arrow. I set mine to 30 pt. Apply the stroke to the arrow. Click Expand to fill again so that the arrow is all one shape.

8 Convert the green circle to a Movie Clip symbol F8. As a Movie Clip rather than a Graphic, the symbol can have Filters applied through the Properties panel. With the instance on Stage selected, click the + sign in the Filters section of the Properties panel. Add a Drop Shadow.

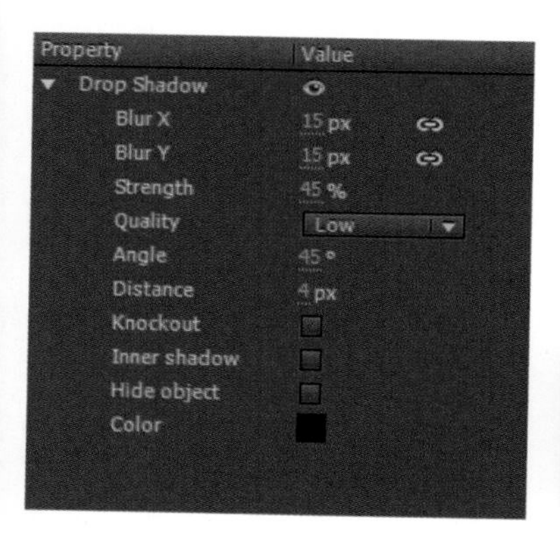

9 It's going to be a subtle shadow, so set the Blur X and Blur Y to 15 pixel and the Strength to 45%. The Quality can remain on low.

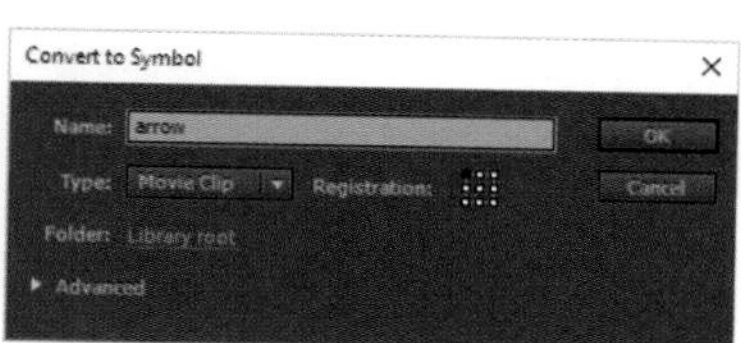

10 Select the arrow and convert to a Movie Clip symbol F8 so that a filter can be added to it for a little extra contrast with the background.

2 On a new layer, draw a white vertical stroke centered over the circle.

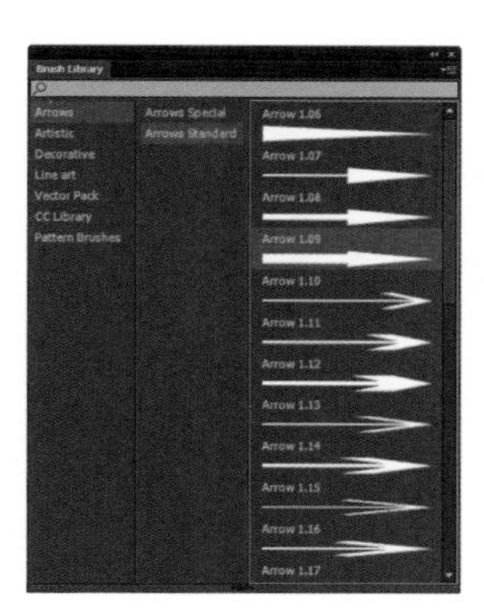

3 While the stroke is selected, open the Brush Library either by clicking the button in the Properties panel or by going to Window > Brush Library. Go to Arrows > Arrows Standard and double-click on Arrow 1.09.

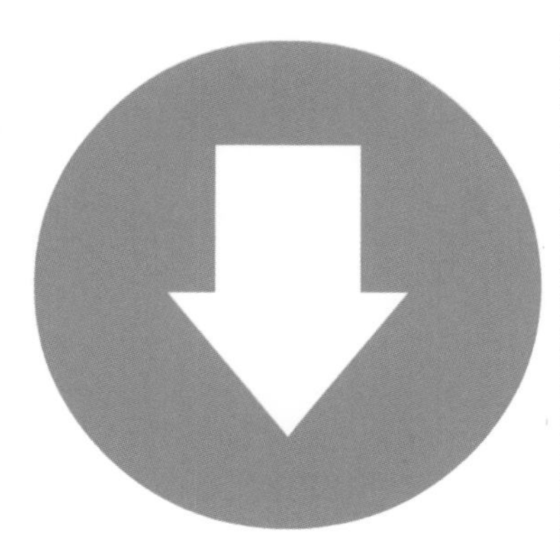

4 In the Properties panel, set the width of the stroke to where it creates the desired fullness. I used 125 pt. Click Expand to fill.

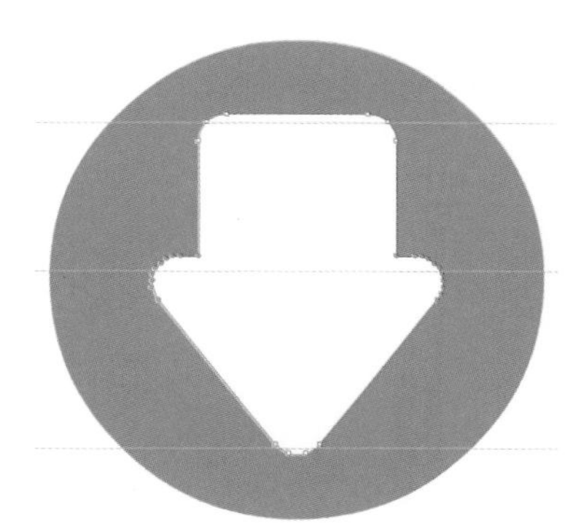

6 To change the length of the arrow tail and/or head, use the Subselection Tool A to grab the edges and nudge them.

7 The flat version is done. Now let's make one that's almost flat. Make a copy of the green circle and white arrow. Select the green circle and make the fill a linear gradient going from #3A7800 to #8FDF00. Use the Gradient Transform Tool F to rotate the gradient putting the lighter green on the top and the darker green on the bottom.

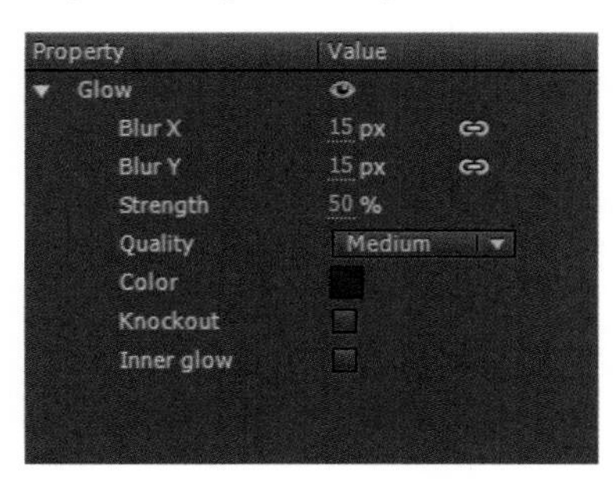

11 To make a soft shadow all the way around the arrow, apply a Glow filter—although it seems counterintuitive. Glow distributes a feathered application of whatever color you select, whether it's light or dark. Make the Blur X and Blur Y 15 px., the Strength 50%, and the Quality Medium. Pick a dark color. Black works, but a dark green at #213800 keeps the saturation.

12 We could have easily re-created the indented feeling of the original instead with a Bevel filter set to Inner and the angle of the light at 245°, but that isn't really necessary. The slight shadow we added all around the arrow is sufficient to make the arrow stand out yet does so in a subtle way.

HOT TIP

Efficiently make multiple buttons or one button for multiple projects by making the gradient for the background gray. Convert it to a symbol and add a tint to customize the color. Then add whatever icon—like play, pause, etc.—on top. If it's a Graphic symbol, it'll need to be converted to a Movie Clip. If your icon is white with a shadow or glow that has been turned into an all-around shadow like our arrow, set the color to a dark gray. Now change the Blending in the Display section of the Properties panel to Hard Light. This blend mode will screen the light part and multiply the dark part, so the white stays white and the shadow darkens whatever color you've made the tint.

On Being Creative—Where to Start

VECTOR ILLUSTRATION: MYRA FERGUSON

IT SURPRISES ME WHEN I HEAR PEOPLE SAY THAT THEY DON'T CONSIDER THEMSELVES creative. I think we all have our own expressions of creativity. We might just prefer to create in different ways and have various levels of comfort with trying something new. In digital media, the trick to getting better is making more projects. The same is true in a lot of disciplines—it takes practice to get better. It doesn't even really matter what you make. Just start making things. No one has to see what you've made unless you decide they should. It is the process of creating that produces confidence that in turn helps you believe that you can create whatever you envision. Then the more you create, the more ideas you have for creating, and the more confidence you gain to bring those ideas to fruition.

You can start by looking at other digital media projects for inspiration in places like Bēhance or *Adobe Create Magazine*. After a while, you'll find that you gather ideas not just from other digital media projects, but from design you encounter in everyday life. I've gotten inspiration from how a museum display was lit, conceptual interfaces from movies, and even a design on an area rug. When I see something that resonates with me, I take pictures and refer to them later. Eventually you'll not only start to notice these details around you but think of new ways you can use them in your own work.

But what should you create? Again, look around you for inspiration. Maybe there's a project you could make with photos you take from your phone. It could be a slideshow or the backdrop to a story you want to tell. Are you connected with an organization that could benefit from some volunteer design work? You could make an animation that explains the goal of their project or build an app that advances their mission. Maybe you could figure out a way to simplify a complex idea with visuals that explain how a process works.

What should you use to make your project? Of course, this book is about Animate CC, so you know I'm going to recommend using it. But really, what you use depends on what you want to create. You could incorporate Animate, but there are lots of other apps in the Creative Cloud that you could use by themselves or in conjunction with it. The obvious other app choices would be Photoshop and Illustrator to bring in images and Audition for audio. I've used After Effects to create looping effects for backgrounds in some of my projects. Now we have more tools available through the Creative Cloud like Adobe Stock and the mobile apps. You can create artwork to bring into your project with Adobe Touch Apps like Adobe Capture CC, Adobe Illustrator Draw, Adobe Photoshop Fix, Adobe Photoshop Lightroom, Adobe Photoshop Mix, and Adobe Photoshop Sketch. If you combine assets from these other apps into Animate, you can output your work to be included in a website that you can build with Muse or Dreamweaver. You can output a video that can be inserted into a larger video that you're editing using Premiere. Your video could be used in an interactive PDF or eBook made with InDesign. You can export an image from Animate to be used in a print layout in InDesign. Or you could come up with some completely different and amazing workflow. And you should.

Be creative and share your experience. Showcase your work—even your works in progress—on Bēhance. The exposure demonstrates your creative process and provides a forum for feedback that can help you improve. Getting your work noticed might just land you your next project that'll give you another chance to be creative.

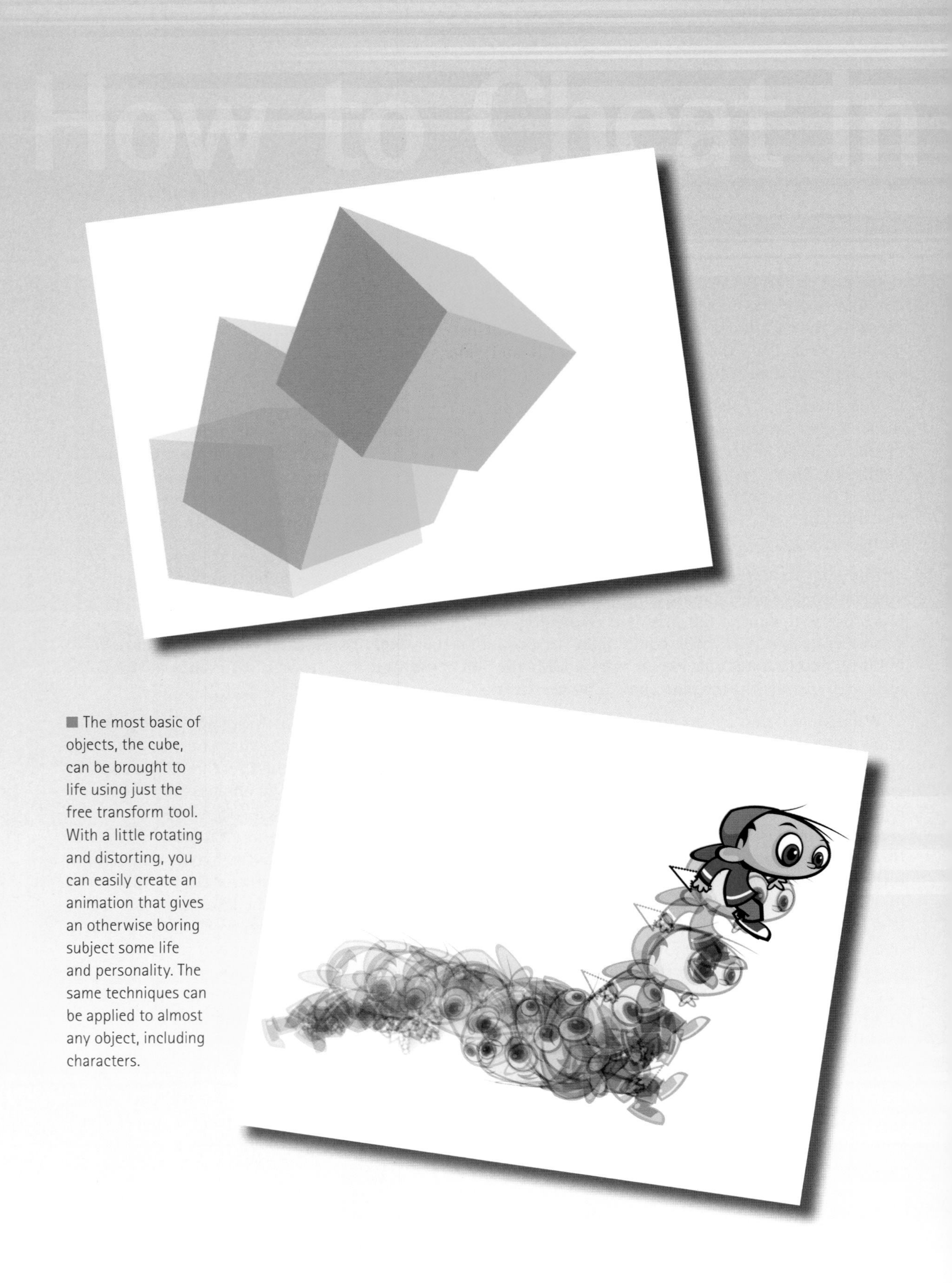

The most basic of objects, the cube, can be brought to life using just the free transform tool. With a little rotating and distorting, you can easily create an animation that gives an otherwise boring subject some life and personality. The same techniques can be applied to almost any object, including characters.

3 Transformation and Distortion

SQUASH, STRETCH, BULGE—WHAT DO ALL THESE transformations have in common? Hint: it's not how you felt after eating that second baked bean burrito. Answer: it's the Free Transform Tool, the single most efficient and versatile tool Animate offers, and it will prove to be one of the most used tools in your daily animation workflow. This chapter examines various ways of using the transform tools to edit drawings and animate them.

Distorting Bitmaps

AS A DESIGNER AND ANIMATOR, I frequently use the Free Transform Tool in Animate. It is the most multifaceted tool in the toolbox and is critical to the transformation and distortion of objects. Free Transform is perfect for scaling, rotating, shearing, and distorting your images. Free Transform is also used to edit the center point of instances of symbols. You can also use it to transform imported bitmaps or graphics created with the Animate drawing tools. There are a variety of modifier keys used with the Free Transform Tool that allow you to transform objects in different ways, as we discuss here.

1 Enter Free Transform mode by selecting the Free Transform Tool in the toolbox or by pressing the keyboard shortcut Q. Let's start by transforming an imported bitmap image.

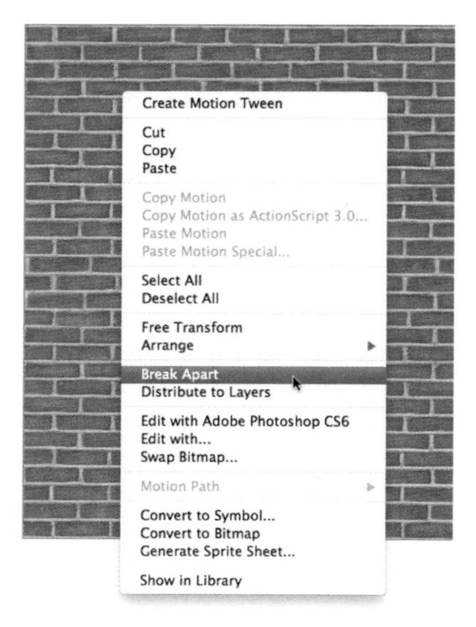

2 Break apart your imported image ⌘ ctrl B before transforming it. If you want, you can convert it to a Drawing Object (Modify > Combine Objects > Union).

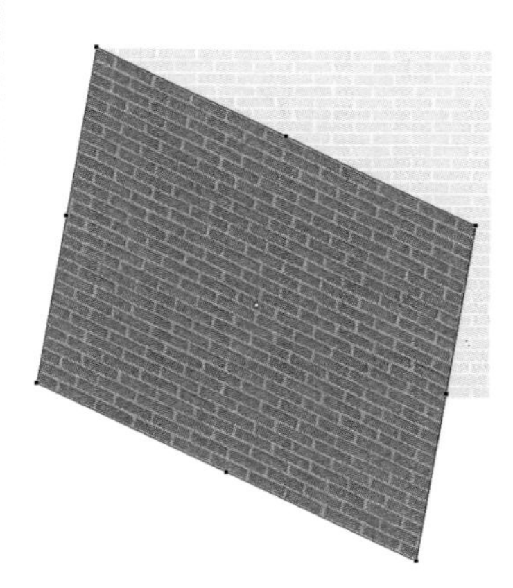

6 Position the cursor outside the bounding box between the handles and drag to shear the object. Hold down ⌥ alt to shear based on the center of the object.

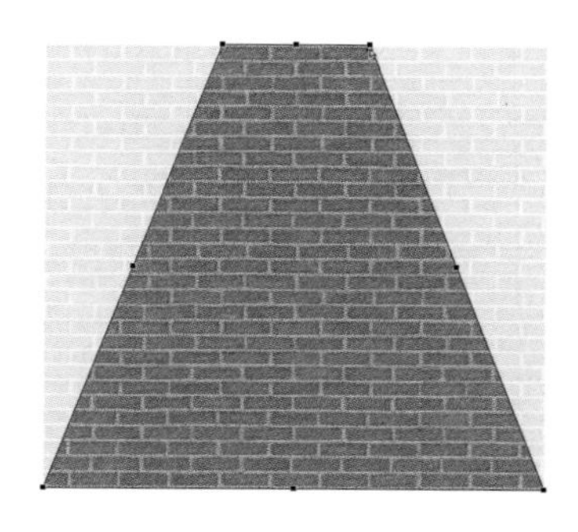

7 Hold down ⌘ ⌥ ctrl alt Shift and drag a corner handle to distort the object's perspective equally on both sides. However for bitmap images, Animate does not distort the image but crops it instead.

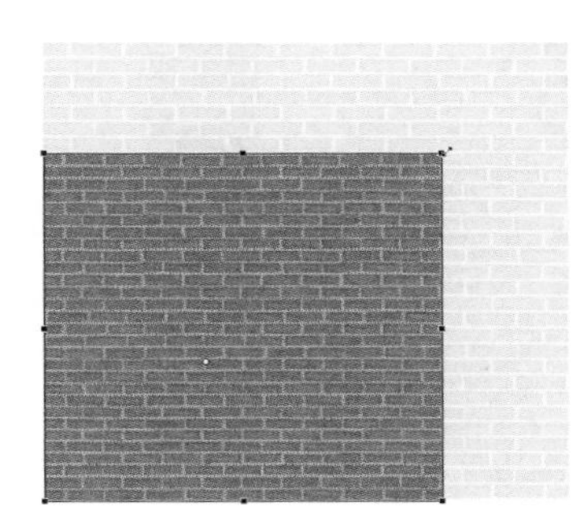

3 When you drag any of the four corner handles, you will scale the object. The corner you drag will move while the opposite corner remains stationary. Hold down the Shift key to scale based on the object's center.

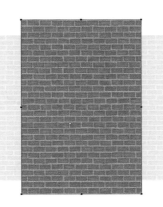

4 If you grab any of the four center side handles, you will scale the object horizontally or vertically which is great for squashing and stretching the object.

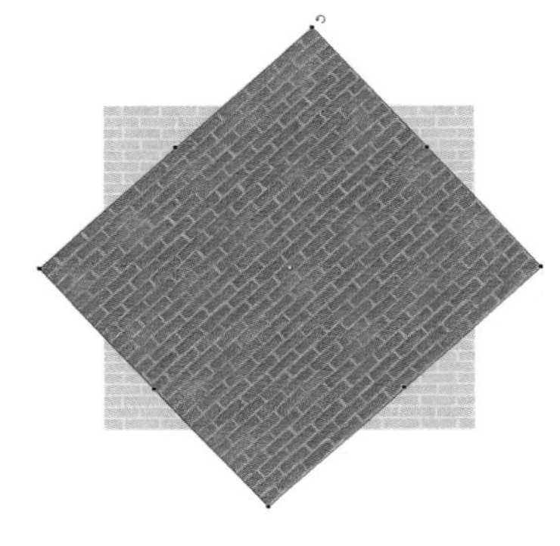

5 Grab one of the corner handles to rotate the object. Hold down Shift to constrain the rotation to 45° increments. Hold down ⌥ alt to hinge the object at the opposite corner.

8 Hold down ⌘ ctrl to distort the object in a freeform manner. But unfortunately again, Animate doesn't truly distort a bitmap image but rather, crops it.

9 Select the Envelope Tool (subselection of the Free Transform Tool). The Envelope modifier lets you warp and distort objects.

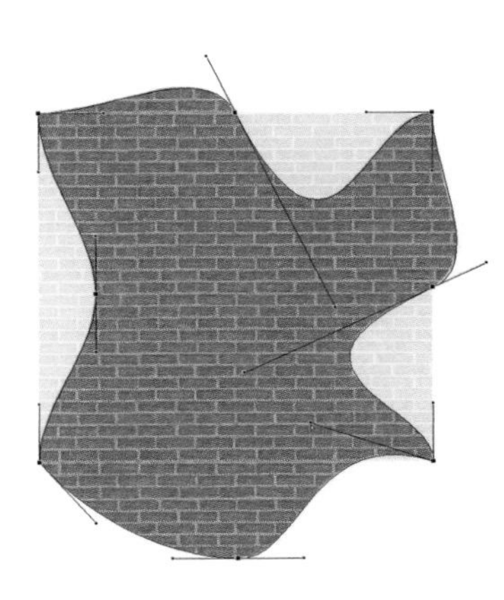

10 Drag the points and tangent handles to modify the envelope. Changes made to the envelope affect the shape but not the bitmap image itself.

HOT TIP

Some of the Free Transform Tool features cannot modify instances of symbols, sounds, video objects, or text. If you want to warp or distort text, make sure to break apart the text field into raw shapes first.

The Envelope Tool

WHEN YOU USE THE FREE TRANSFORM Tool with raw vector objects the Distort and Envelope subselection tools become available. Using these tools is where you can really have some fun warping and deforming shapes as if they were clay. Think of how your reflection looks in a funhouse mirror, and you'll start to get an idea of ways to use these tools. If you need to be precise with how your images are scaled, rotated, or skewed, use the Transform panel to type in your values for the respective transformation.

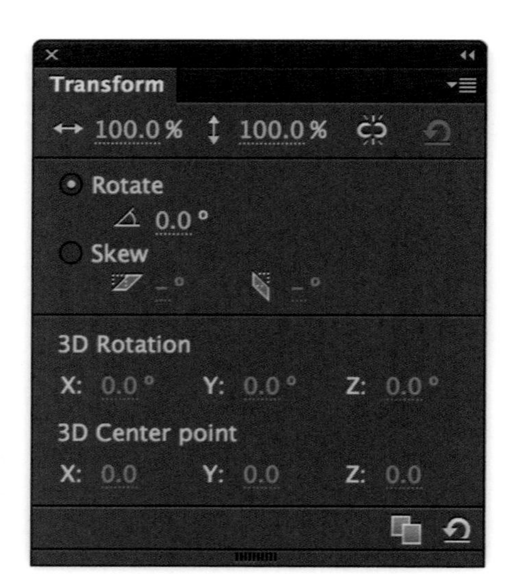

1 Enter Free Transform mode by selecting the Free Transform Tool in the toolbox or by pressing the keyboard shortcut Q. Select the Distort subselection tool at the bottom of the toolbox. Click and drag any of the corner handles to distort your shape.

4 The Envelope modifier is great for warping and distorting shapes. When you select the Envelope subselection tool, you will notice multiple handles attached to the bounding box. Manipulating these handles will affect the shape contained within. Click and drag a corner handle to start warping your shape.

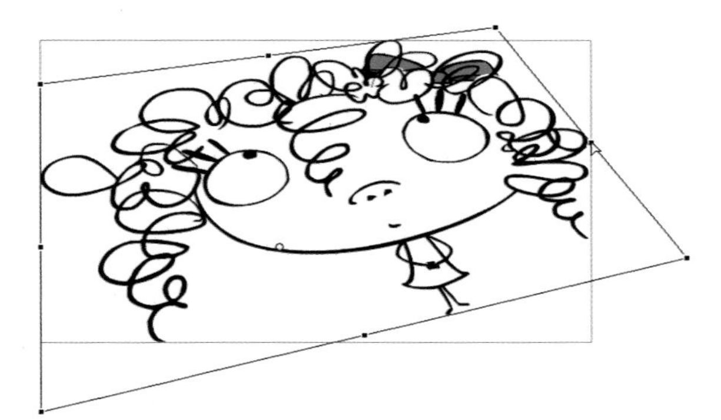

2 The Distort Tool is useful for manipulating the perspective of a shape by clicking and dragging the corner handles.

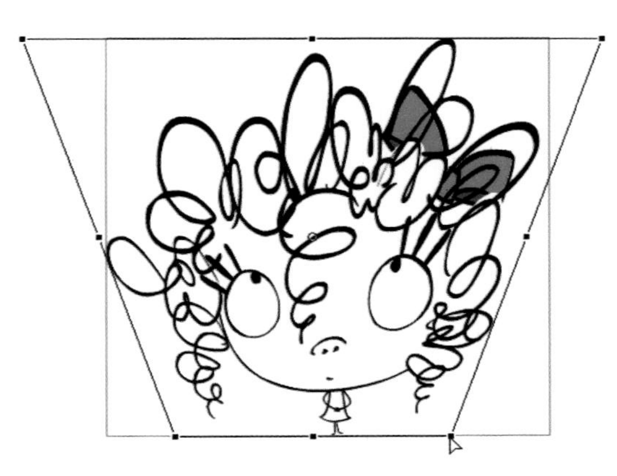

3 Hold down the Shift key while dragging a corner handle to constrain the adjoining corner an equal distance and in the opposite direction from each other. Think of it as tapering your shape.

5 Drag any of the eight tangent handles to warp your shape in almost any direction. These tangent handles are located at each corner and along both horizontal and vertical sides as well.

6 You can move any of the points to a new location to further warp your shape. But be careful, once you click outside of the selected shape, the transformation will end. You can select it again and continue to warp and distort it, but the previous point and tangent positions will be lost.

HOT TIP

Holding down ⌘ ⌥ ctrl alt when dragging a corner point will lock the tangent handles to its current position. Holding down the same keys while dragging one of the side handles will constrain that entire side and all its points.

Warping

THE ENVELOPE TOOL CAN HELP shave some time off your production schedule. In this case, the Envelope Tool was used to deform the head of the Evil Mime character to represent the effect of being hit by a self-imposed upper-cut. Sure, the entire head could have been drawn, but not often do we have the luxury of time when a deadline is looming. It was much easier to start with the head already drawn and warp it to suit our needs.

1 Duplicate the artwork of the head by creating a new keyframe in the head symbol. Select the entire head and the Free Transform Tool (Q), then select the Envelope subselection tool.

2 Using the Envelope Tool, you can move the handles to deform the relative area of the head.

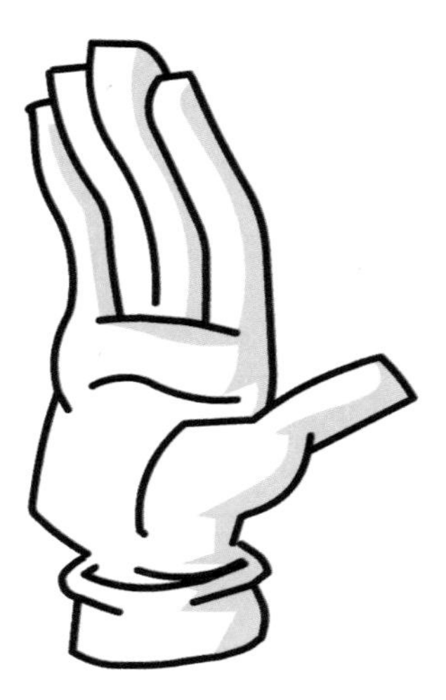

6 Here's the hand drawn in Animate using the Line Tool (N). You may find the need for a variation of this same illustration and need to make it quickly.

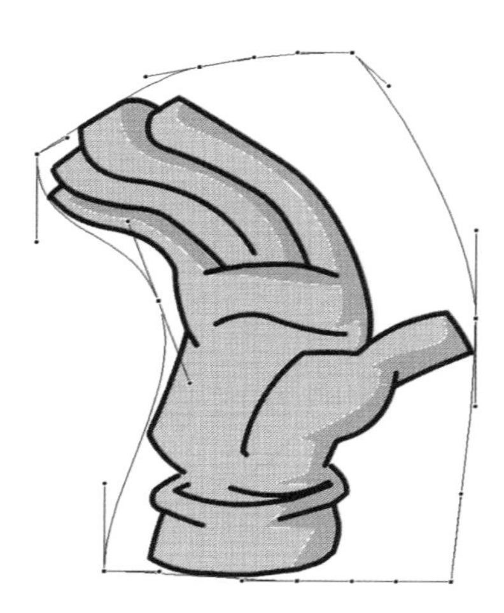

7 Using the Envelope Tool allows you to quickly distort the drawing into a different shape.

3 Continue to push and pull the Envelope's anchor points and control handles to deform the shape to your liking.

4 You can restart the envelope process by deselecting the artwork and selecting the Envelope Tool again. Reselecting the Envelope Tool resets anchors and handles, which allow you to distort your image further.

5 Don't be afraid to manually go back into the artwork and adjust your linework using the Selection Tool. Often it's your own eye that is the best tool for the job.

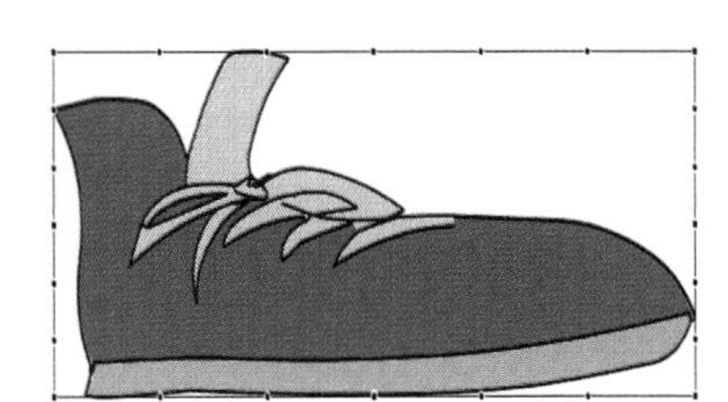

8 Here's the foot in its default state. Depending on your animation, you may need several feet in different shapes.

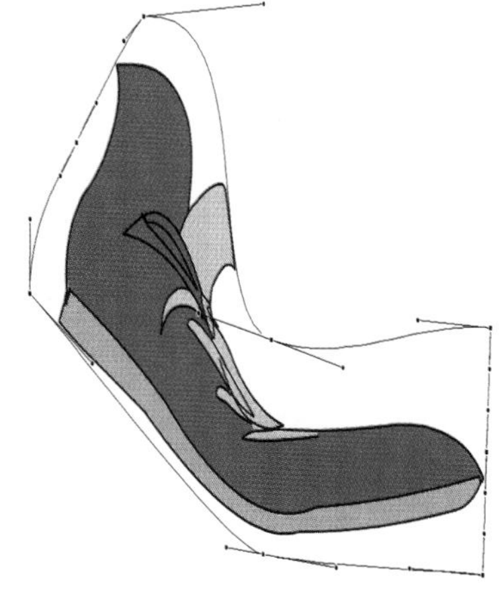

9 Once again, the Envelope Tool gets the job done quickly and efficiently.

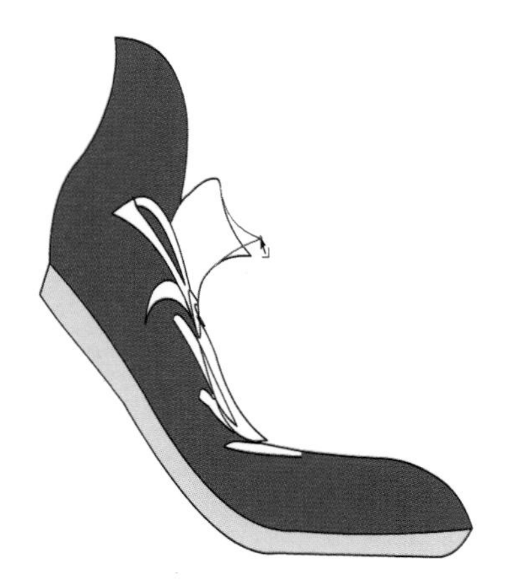

10 Don't rely completely on the transform tools. In most cases, they only go so far. You may want to further refine the details of your image manually by using the drawing tools.

HOT TIP

Don't rely on the Envelope Tool for everything. In a situation like this, where a complex shape is being warped, you will probably find that upon ending your transformation, you will need to refine your shapes manually by using the Selection Tool or any of the drawing tools.

Card Flip

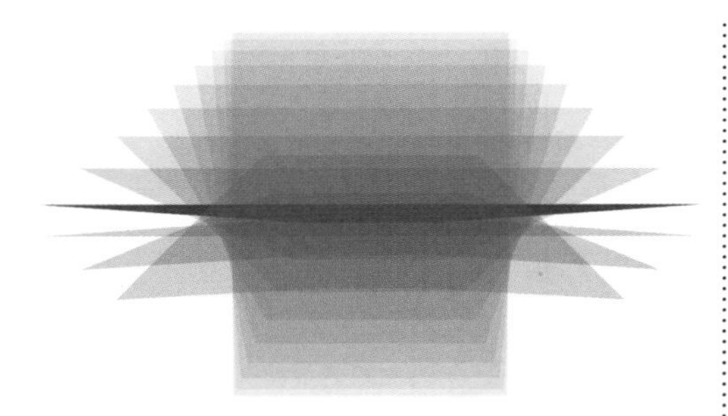

A POPULAR ANIMATION REQUEST IS HOW to animate a flat card rotating or flipping 360°. What makes this animation often difficult to understand is the initial approach to actually creating it. It is easy to assume, since Animate is a two-dimensional program, adding a third dimension simply is not possible unless the object is redrawn manually one frame at a time. But with Animate, it's all in the approach, and it doesn't have to be taken literally. Two dimensions are plenty to work within for this animated effect.

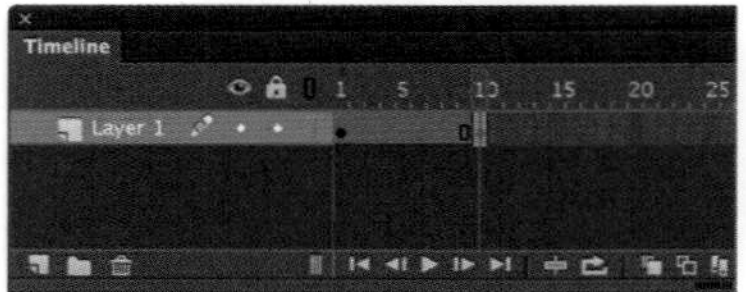

1 Start with a simple rectangle with no stroke around it. Add a second keyframe on frame 10. Select the Free Transform Tool Q and then the Distort subselection tool.

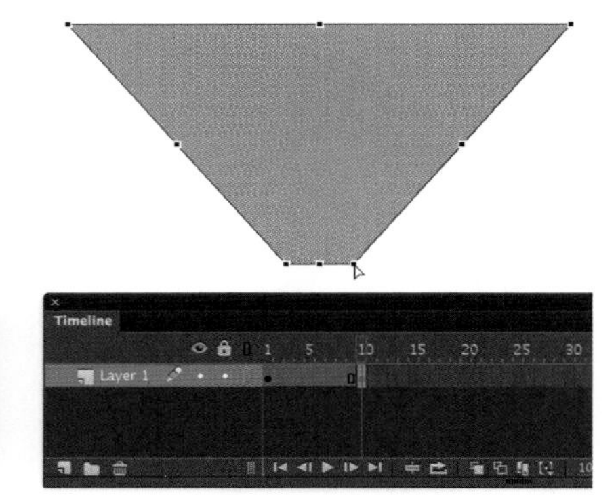

2 Hold down the Shift key and pull a top corner point away from the shape. With the Shift key still pressed, pull a bottom corner in the opposite direction.

5 In Animate CC you have the ability to apply a Shape Tween from the context menu in the Timeline. So go ahead and apply one.

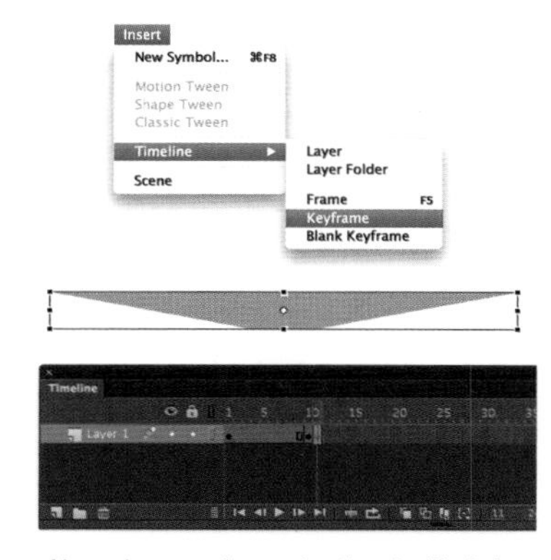

6 Now that you have the first half of the animation, you need to create the second half. Select frame 11 and insert a keyframe.

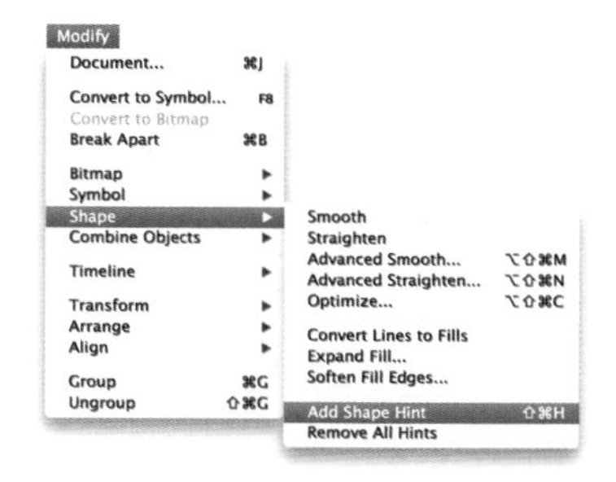

10 Let's add some shape hints to correct the problem. Select the first frame in the faulty tween and then go to Modify > Shape > Add Shape Hint .

11 Drag the red "a" hint to one of the corners of your shape until it snaps.

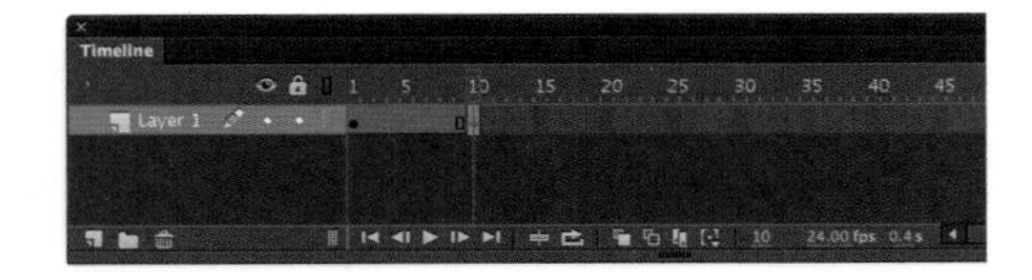

3 Click outside the shape to end the transformation. Select it again, hold down the Shift key and drag the bottom middle handle upward. The Shift key will constrain the shape vertically.

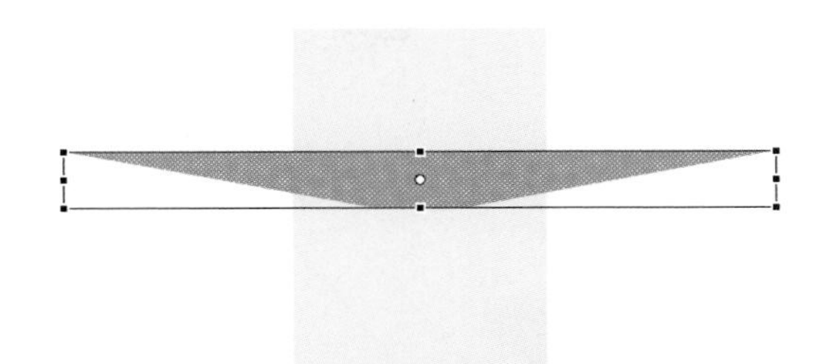

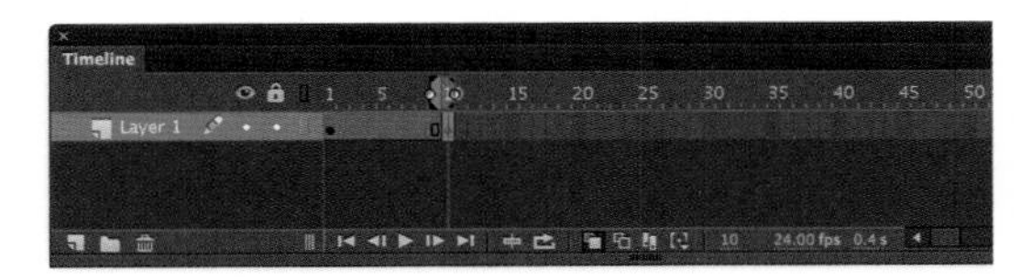

4 Turn on Onion Skin ⌥ alt Shift O, so you can see the previous frame. Position the newly transformed shape so that it is centered over the original shape seen through the Onion Skin.

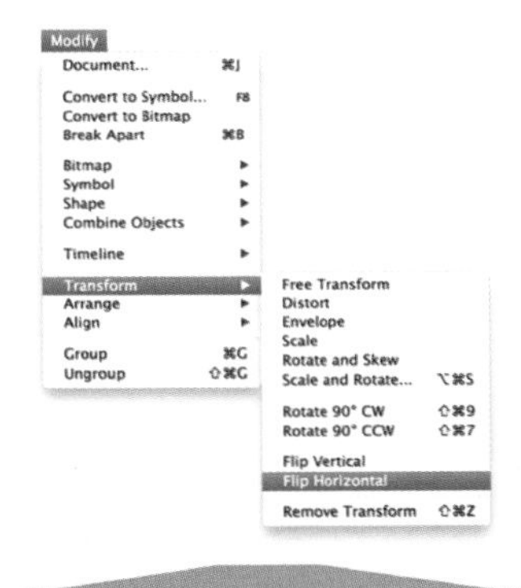

7 Modify the shape in frame 11 by flipping it vertically.

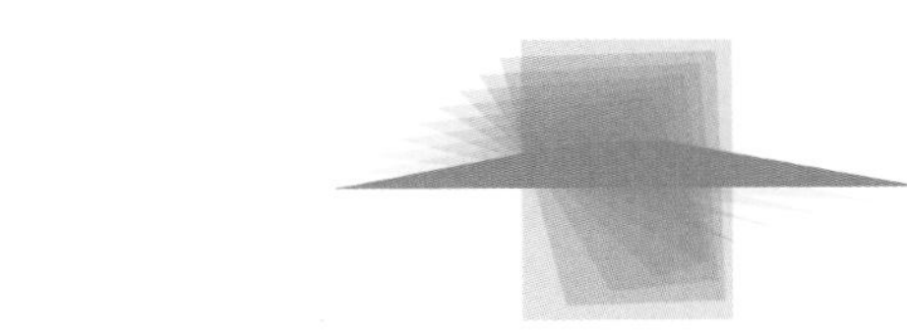

8 Select the keyframe in frame 1 and copy the frame ⌘ ⌥ ctrl alt C. Next, select frame 20 and paste the frame ⌘ ⌥ ctrl alt V.

9 Apply a Shape Tween to the latter half of your frames. You may experience a misbehaving tween like I did when writing this topic. Let's fix it.

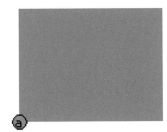

12 Go to the last keyframe in your tween and drag the green "a" hint to the same respective corner. Repeat this procedure again for the opposite corner.

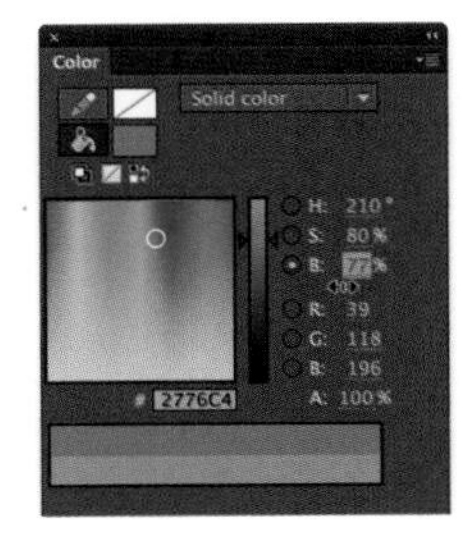

13 The final visual effect is to mix a slightly darker version of the color of the card, and then use it to fill the shapes in frames 10 and 11.

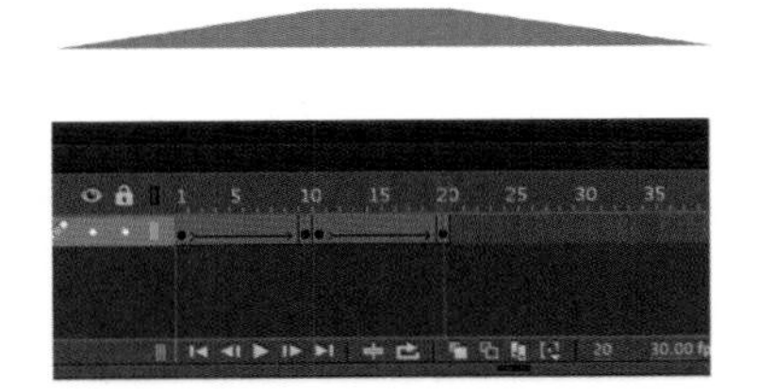

14 The card will not only tween its shape but also its color from light to dark. This color change makes for a convincing three-dimensional effect.

HOT TIP

Due to the nature of vectors and how Animate tries to calculate what it thinks you want to achieve, sometimes the tween implodes or twists in ways we never anticipated. Shape hints exist for this very reason, and they are easy to learn about in the Animate Help docs. An alternative solution for this example would be to convert frames 1–10 to keyframes, copy and paste them in frames 11–20, and then reverse them.

3D Rotation

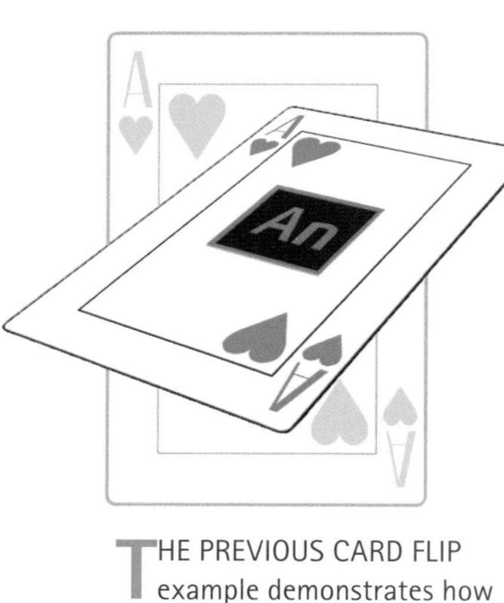

THE PREVIOUS CARD FLIP example demonstrates how to transform a vector shape with the Free Transform Tool and Classic Tweens. Adobe Animate CC provides tools to simplify the same process. The 3D Rotation tool lets you transform objects not only along the *X* and *Y* axes but the *Z* axis as well.

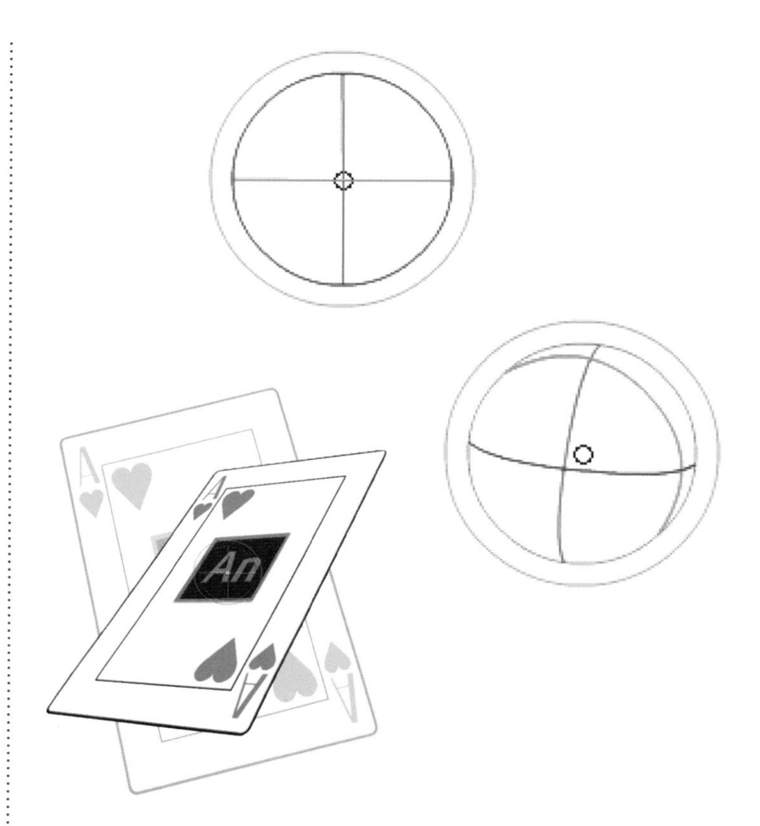

1 The 3D Rotation tool (W) rotates Movie Clip instances in 3D space. A 3D rotation control appears on top of selected objects on the Stage. The X control is red, the Y control is green, and the Z control is blue. Use the orange free rotate control to rotate around the *X* and *Y* axes at the same time.

The default mode of the 3D Rotation tool is global. Rotating an object in global 3D space is the same as moving it relative to the Stage. Rotating an object in local 3D space is the same as moving it relative to its parent Movie Clip if it has one. To toggle the 3D Rotation tool between global and local modes, click the Global toggle button in the Options section of the Tools panel while the 3D Rotation tool is selected. You can temporarily toggle the mode from global to local by pressing the (D) key while dragging with the 3D Rotation tool.

ILLUSTRATION: CHRIS GEORGENES AND MYRA FERGUSON

2 The first thing to do is to right-click over the Movie Clip and select Create Motion Tween. Animate CC will automatically insert frames based on the document frame rate to achieve a full second in the Timeline. This document is set to 24 fps; therefore, the duration of my Motion Tween is 24 frames.

3 Position the frame marker on frame 12. Select the 3D Rotation tool W. Click on the instance of the card and notice the 3D rotation controller that appears on top of the symbol. Click inside the 3D control and drag along the *Y* axis to rotate the card in 3D space. Notice that Animate has inserted a keyframe automatically for you.

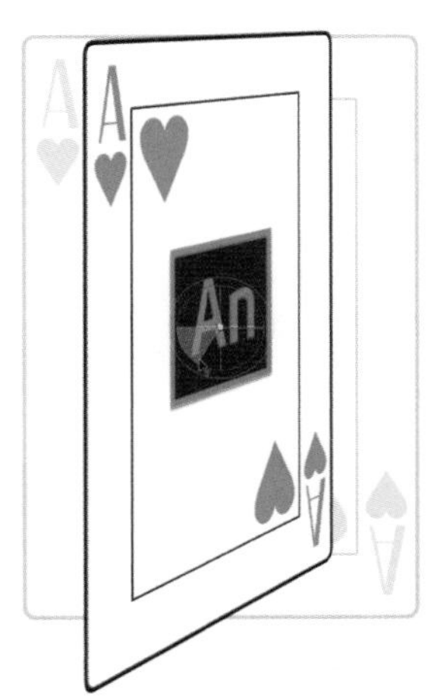

HOT TIP

Press the D key to toggle between global and local mode.

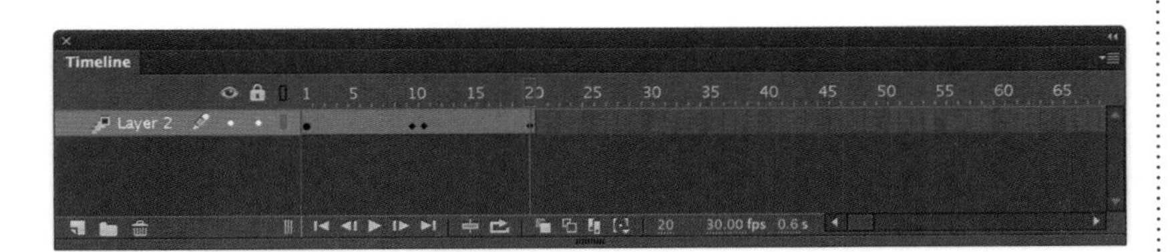

4 Position the frame marker on the last frame and continue to rotate the Movie Clip along its *Y* axis in 3D space until it is 180° from its original orientation. Repeat these steps as often as needed depending on the number of rotations you want to animate.

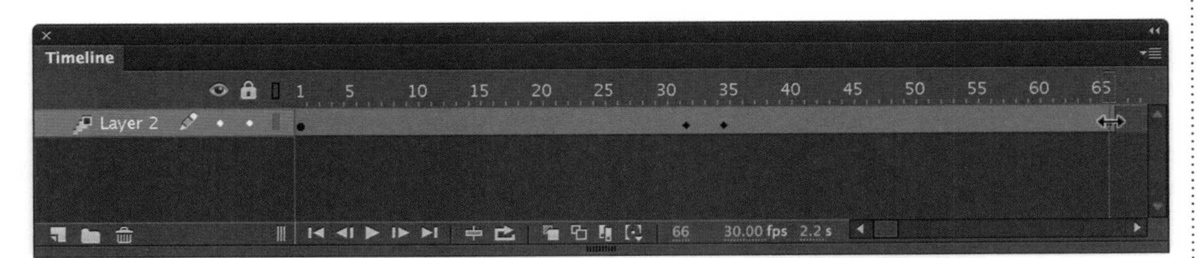

5 If you want to extend the Motion Tween in the layer without affecting the existing keyframes, simply drag the right edge of the tween. Another way to do the same thing is to click on a frame further down the Timeline and press the F5 key to insert frames up to the selected frame. Another way to add frames is to click the Timeline where you want to insert frames and press the F5 key.

Butterfly

IT'S POSSIBLE TO ANIMATE THE BUTTERFLY'S WINGS using the Distort Tool (subselection of the Free Transform Tool). With the 3D tools in Animate CC, however, it is much more efficient to use the 3D Rotation tool for the flapping wing animation. Here I have converted the original wing graphic to a Movie Clip symbol and applied a Motion Tween using the Motion Model. The advantages of using the 3D Rotation tool for this animation are faster results and a smaller file size. The smaller file size is on account of using Motion Tweens and several instances of the same symbol. Previous methods required each frame to be redrawn, resulting in a frame-by-frame animation using raw vector art for each keyframe, which created larger file sizes since each frame contained all new data that needed to be loaded sequentially when viewing online.

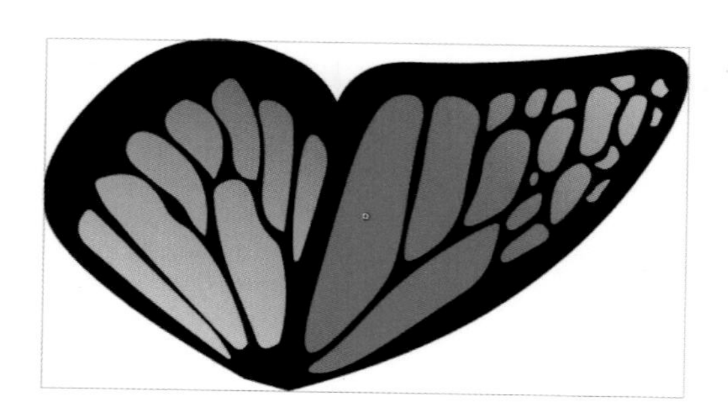

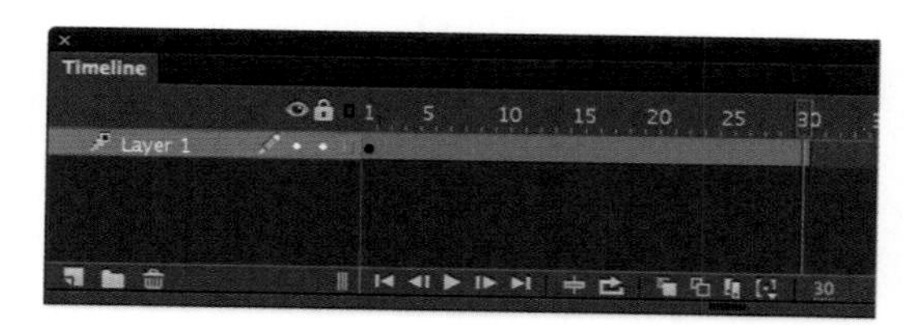

1 Convert the wing into a Movie Clip symbol twice so that you end up with a Movie Clip inside a Movie Clip. You will want to animate the wing inside a symbol, so a second instance can be used for the other wing later.
Select the 3D Rotation tool (W). Click on the instance of the wing and notice the 3D rotation controller that appears on top of the symbol. Reposition the controller by dragging it to a new location. The controller's position determines its center point. Right-click over the symbol and select Create Motion Tween. Animate will automatically insert frames based on the document frame rate to achieve a full second in the Timeline. This document is set to play back at 30 fps; therefore, the duration of my Motion Tween is 30 frames. The speed of the animation can be easily changed by dragging the right edge of the Motion Tween left or right.

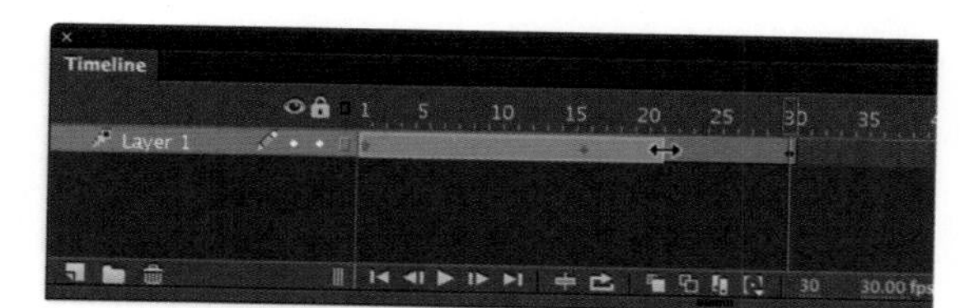

4 To adjust the speed of the wing animation, click and drag the leading edge of the motion span. Here I've decreased the length of the Motion span, which increases the speed of the animation.

BUTTERFLY ILLUSTRATION: CHRIS GEORGENES

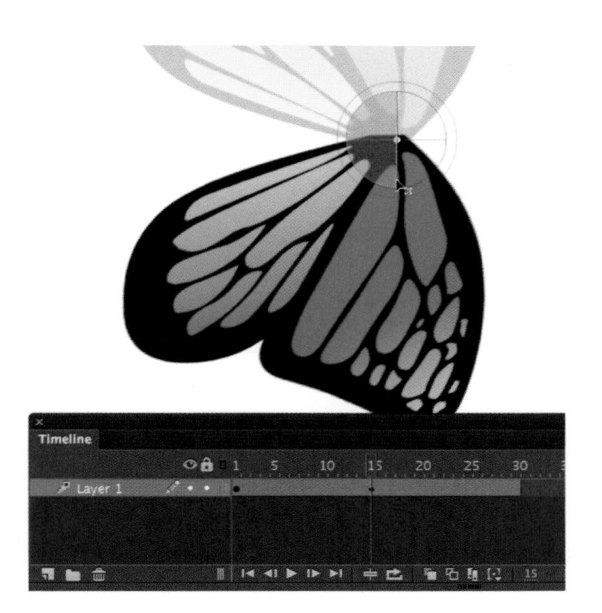

2 Position the frame marker about mid-way between frame 1 and 30 (frame 15 will work). Click inside the 3D control and drag along the *X* axis until the wing is 180° from its original position. Notice that Animate has inserted a keyframe automatically for you.

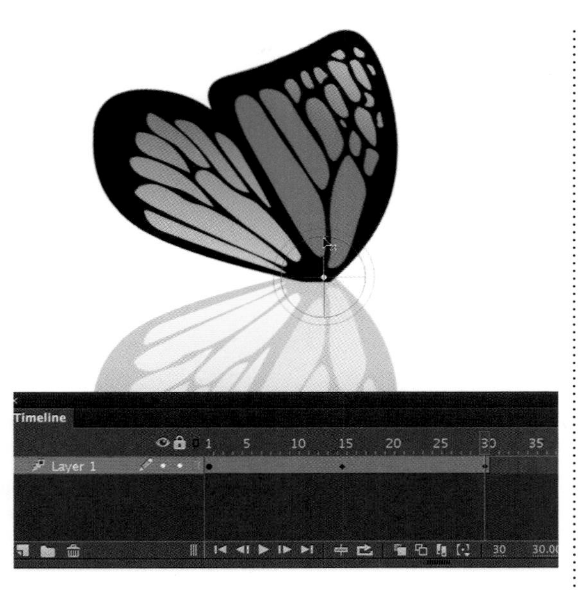

3 Position the frame marker on the last frame in the tween. Drag along the *X* axis inside the 3D control until the wing is back in its original position. Play back your Timeline by pressing the E key to see the wing flapping along the *X* axis.

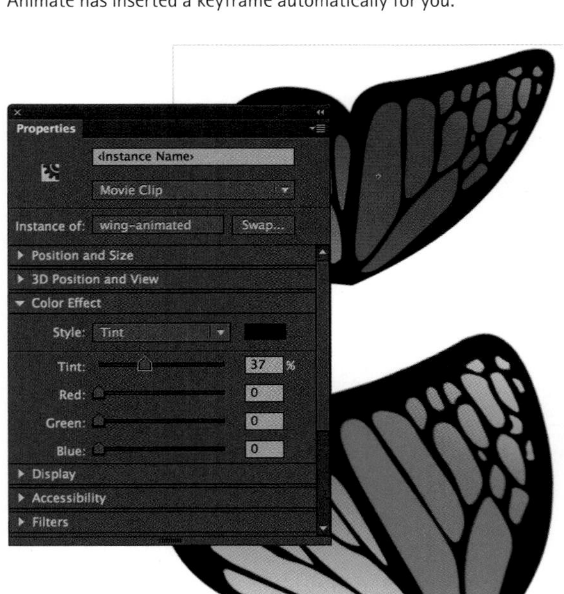

5 Copy and paste ⌘ ctrl C ⌘ ctrl V the Movie Clip containing the wing animation to use as the second wing on a new layer below all existing layers. Select it and using the Tint color effect in the Properties panel, darken it slightly to provide a sense of depth.

6 Create a body shape, align the wings, and publish your movie to see the butterfly take flight. To add some depth to the butterfly, move the back wing to the right a few pixels and skew it slightly. You can also move the front wing to the left and skew that a little also.

HOT TIP

Double-click the center point of the 3D control to move it back to the center of the selected Movie Clip.

Squash and Stretch

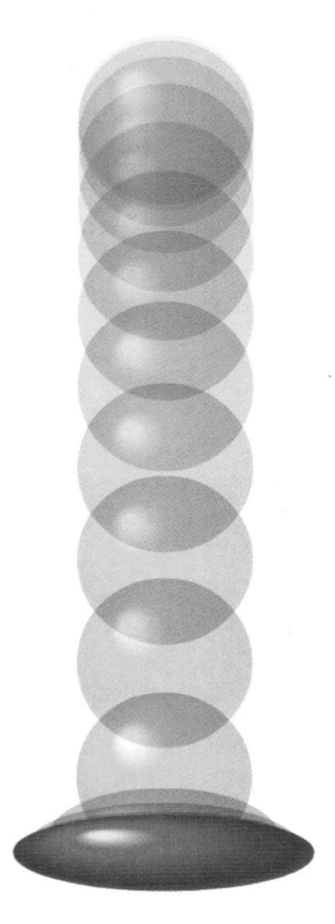

SQUASH AND STRETCH IS A TRADITIONAL technique that is widely used to give animations more realism and weight. When a moving object comes in contact with a stationary object, it will deform on impact, unless it is completely rigid. It's important to remember that no matter how much an object squashes or stretches, it always maintains the same amount of volume. The amount of squash and stretch depends on how much flexibility your object has. Traditional animation usually contains exaggerated amounts of squash and stretch. A good example of squashing and stretching is a bouncing ball. When it hits the ground, it actually deforms and gets squashed. It will then become stretched as it propels itself upward. With a little Motion Tweening and frame-by-frame animation in Animate, we can achieve convincing realism with relatively little effort.

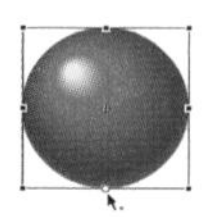

1 Start with the object in its highest position. Convert it to a symbol and then edit its center point using the Free Transform Tool (Q). Move the center point to the center of the bottom edge.

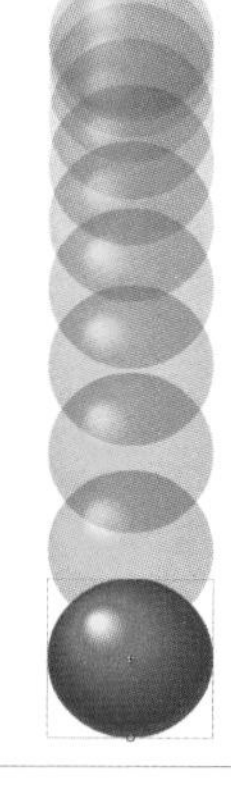

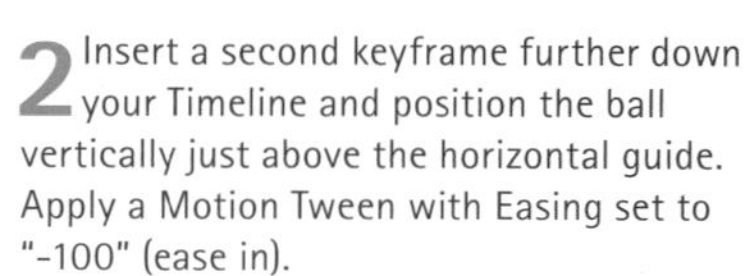

2 Insert a second keyframe further down your Timeline and position the ball vertically just above the horizontal guide. Apply a Motion Tween with Easing set to "-100" (ease in).

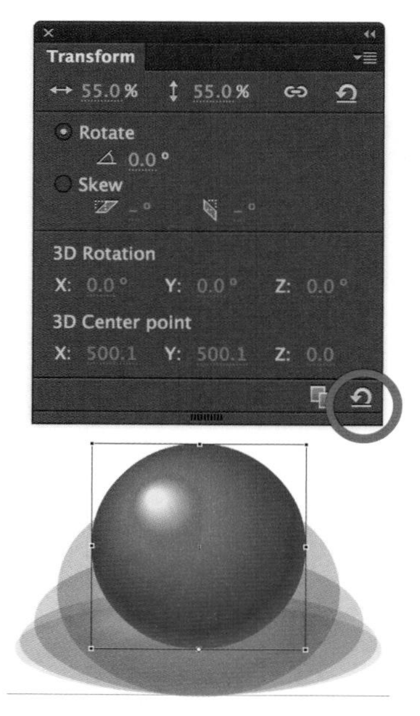

6 Start the ball's ascent by inserting yet another keyframe and removing all transformations. The Transform panel has a Remove Transform button to make this a one-click solution.

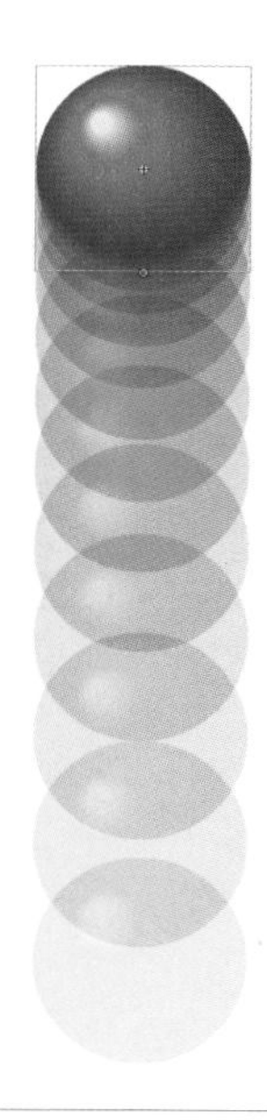

7 Copy the first frame and paste it as your last frame to position the ball at the end of your Timeline in the exact same position as it started. Apply a Motion Tween and set the Easing to "100" (ease out).

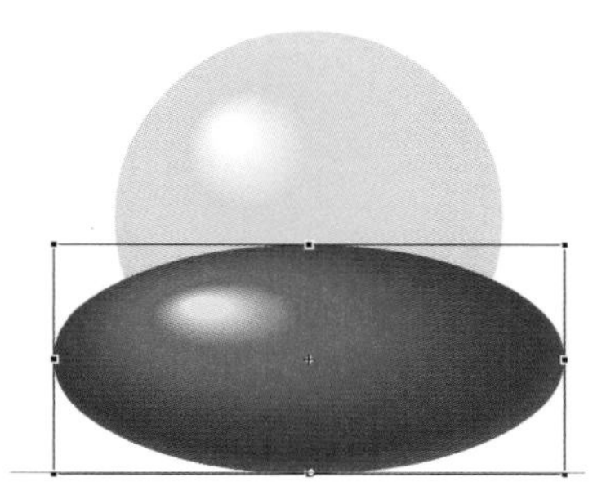

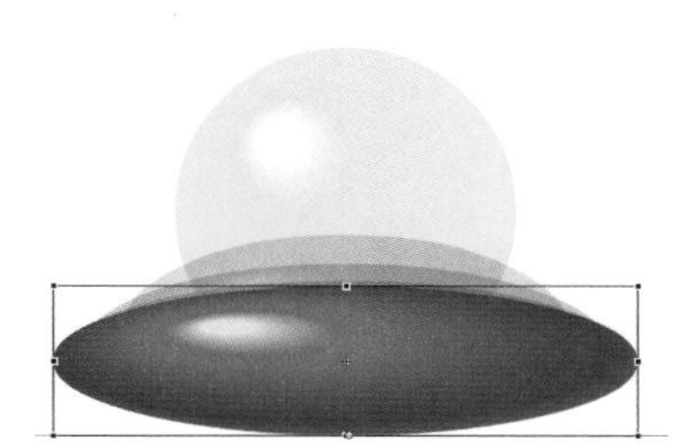

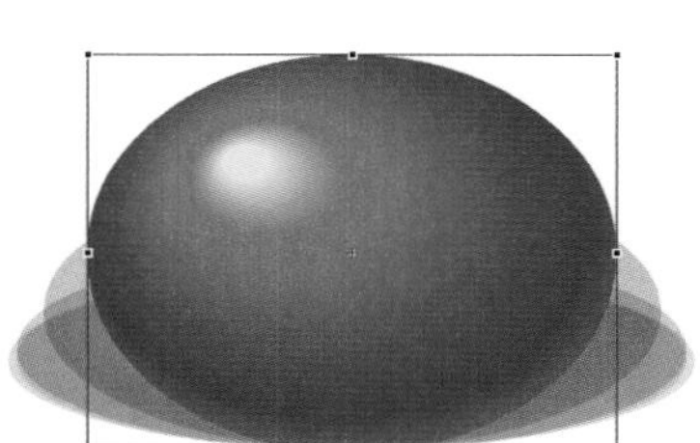

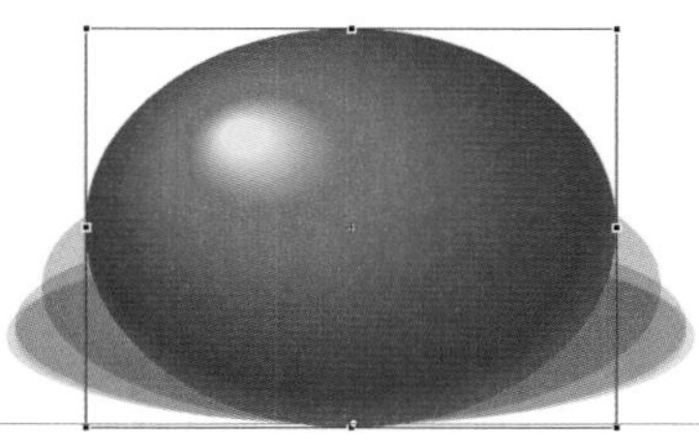

3 In the next frame, insert a keyframe and turn on Onion Skin ⌥ alt Shift O. Use the Free Transform Tool Q to scale the ball, so it becomes wider and shorter. It's important to keep the volume of the ball consistent.

4 Insert another keyframe about four or five frames further down the Timeline. Squash and stretch the ball even more. Apply a Motion Tween and set the Easing to "100" (ease out).

5 Insert another keyframe a few frames down your Timeline and transform your ball in the opposite direction. Make sure it still has some deformation applied to it.

Edit

Undo Select Frames	⌘Z
Repeat Create Classic Tween	⌘Y
Cut	⌘X
Copy	⌘C
Paste in Center	⌘V
Paste in Place	⇧⌘V
Clear	⌦
Duplicate	⌘D
Select All	⌘A
Deselect All	⇧⌘A
Find and Replace	⌘F
Find Next	F3
Timeline	▶
Edit Symbols	⌘E
Edit Selected	
Edit in Place	

Remove Frames	⇧F5
Cut Frames	⌥⌘X
Copy Frames	⌥⌘C
Paste Frames	⌥⌘V
Clear Frames	⌥⌦
Select All Frames	⌥⌘A
Cut Layers	
Copy Layers	
Paste Layers	
Duplicate Layers	
Copy Motion	
Paste Motion	
Paste Motion Special...	

8 Animate CC offers a way to reuse animations. Copy Motion allows a Classic Tween, its frames, and symbol information to be pasted to another object. Select all the frames in your squash and stretch animation. Select Edit > Timeline > Copy Motion.

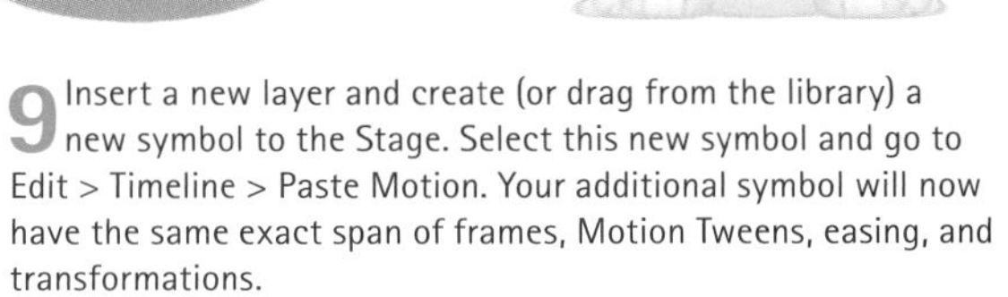

9 Insert a new layer and create (or drag from the library) a new symbol to the Stage. Select this new symbol and go to Edit > Timeline > Paste Motion. Your additional symbol will now have the same exact span of frames, Motion Tweens, easing, and transformations.

HOT TIP

Save and reuse animations using Motion Tweens by right-clicking over the tween span and selecting Save as Motion Preset in Animate CC. It's also a good idea to keep all your most used animations in a single FLA document, so they are easier to locate.

Why Join Your Local Adobe User Group

I'VE BEEN AN ADOBE USER GROUP MANAGER FOR 13 YEARS—3 YEARS IN COLORADO AND 10 years in Missouri. The group in Missouri started out as a Macromedia User Group prior to Adobe's acquisition of Macromedia. My friend, previous co-worker, and business partner, Matt Kerner started that group and persuaded me to join. I later became co-manager and assumed the role as manager when he moved. It's a purely volunteer role that entails scheduling venues, posting meetings, presenting, inviting other speakers, encouraging participation, etc. So why on earth would anyone spend all this time on a user group?

Well, it's fun. Fun for me means getting to spend time with other people who like being creative and using the software I use, learning new techniques, inspiring others, and becoming inspired. Being a part of an Adobe User Group is a chance to be social, to learn, and to be creative.

A lot of my career has been spent working either in a small department, as a remote member of a team, or as a freelancer. Networking and socializing can be extremely limited in these scenarios, so the Adobe User Group gives me the opportunity to interact with people I might not otherwise have a chance to meet. Once I started meeting more people in the Adobe Community, then I found out about regional events and met even more people. I also started going to MAX (originally Macromedia MAX and now Adobe MAX). The connections I made at MAX have been some of the most influential in my personal and professional life. Some of my dearest friends are those I've met in the Adobe Community even if we live in different states or different countries. Professionally, I've also gotten several contracts through the connections I've made in the Community. My work on this book is the result of meeting Chris Georgenes at Adobe MAX several years ago.

So what do you do at an Adobe User Group meeting? Well, that depends on the type of group it is and the manager. My groups have been general Adobe User Groups. In other words, we haven't focused on one particular technology. I try to change the topics that I present frequently so that people with different interests have the opportunity to join us. I often invite various speakers and welcome members to share a topic or project if they feel comfortable presenting. In the past, we've celebrated product launches and the birthdays of our favorite software with food, games, and giveaways. Even if there isn't a celebration of some sort, we still get to do giveaways. As a User Group Manager, meetings with giveaways are some of my favorites. T-shirts, hats, bottles, chargers—among other swag—are frequent prizes, but the big giveaways have always been the software. For most of my time as a manager, the User Groups have been able to do semiannual raffles. In my role as an Adobe User Group

Manager, I've had the distinct honor of being able to give away tens of thousands of dollars' worth of software on Adobe's behalf to our raffle winners.

That's what we do, but it's more than presentations and freebies. It's Community. It's finding your people. One year at Adobe MAX, I was describing a pair of pants to a friend. The pants were Lucky Brand Jeans in a paisley print. I explained that if I had used Adobe Kuler (now Adobe Color) to capture the colors of lasagna and applied those to the design, then those would have been the colors in the fabric. Instantly she understood what I meant. Communicating and connecting—that's what happens when you're a part of the Community.

■ The hula hoop appears to be around the hulagirl's waist, or is it? In the original image above, the hula hoop is clearly in a layer above the hulagirl. By creating a mask for the hula hoop, we can hide the portion of it that overlaps the girl's waist, making it appear to be around her.

4 Masking

MASKS ARE POWERFUL. THEY CAN BE USED IN MYRIAD WAYS to achieve limitless results. Masks can make your daily workflow easier, less time-consuming and, in most cases, become your most indispensable tool.

Having the ability to control the way two or more layers interact with each other through the use of masks is vital to your abilities as a designer and animator. The coolest thing about using masks in Animate is that not only do they help you to create stunning images, they can also be animated, a very powerful concept that can be mastered quite easily.

Cinemagraph

THERE NEVER SEEMS TO BE ENOUGH SYRUP ON PANCAKES, RIGHT? IT SOAKS IN, AND THEN YOU CAN'T SEE IT. WHAT IF YOU could have never-ending syrup? Let's make that happen in a cinemagraph. You've probably seen these popular GIFs online. They combine a portion of movement with a still image. You can use Photoshop or proprietary software like Flixel to make them, but at their most basic level they are an animated series of images and a masked still. It sounds like a job for Animate.

What I've found to be the biggest trick in making a good cinemagraph is getting the right shot. First, plan out what you want to be still and what you want to move. Eliminate other movement as much as possible. Use a tripod to take your shot. You can use either a burst of stills or video. Then use the minimum number of frames needed to complete a repeatable sequence. What we mask in Animate is what shows, so if we apply the mask to the image that remains motionless, we only need to make one mask. Put the mask and masked layer above the image sequence layer, and voilà, you have a cinemagraph. Export your animated GIF, and if you're impressionable like me, take a break and go eat some pancakes.

PHOTO SEQUENCE: MYRA FERGUSON

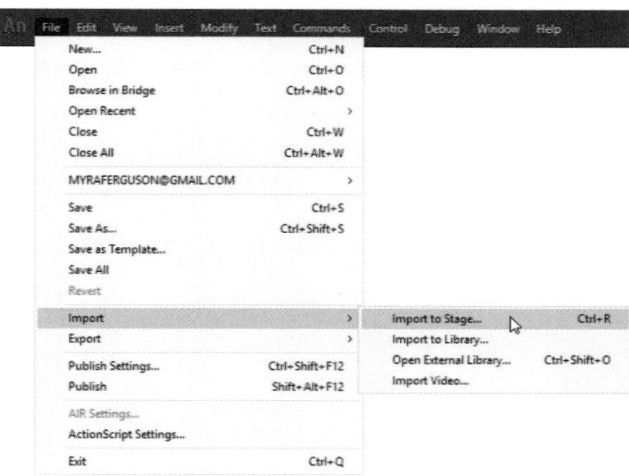

1 Make a new document with a Stage size of 550 × 367. Import the frames to the Stage.

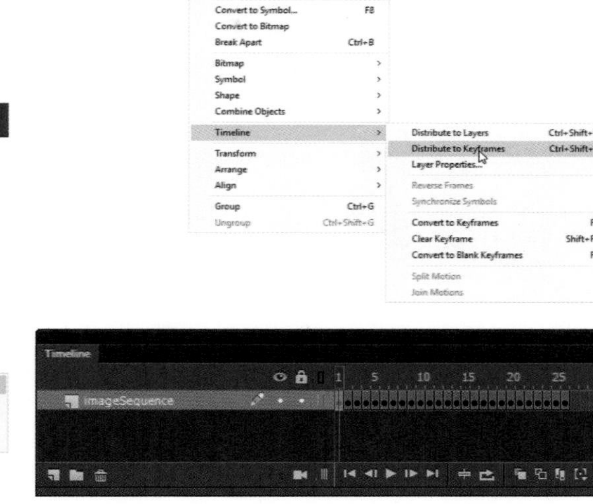

2 With all the frames selected, go to Modify > Timeline > Distribute to Keyframes ⌘ ctrl Shift K and remove the first frame Shift F5, which is empty after the distribution.

3 Pick one of the frames to be the still area. The last frame has a nice saucy pool of syrup. Let's use that one to reinforce the idea of overabundance. Make a new layer and copy the image in frame 26 into it.

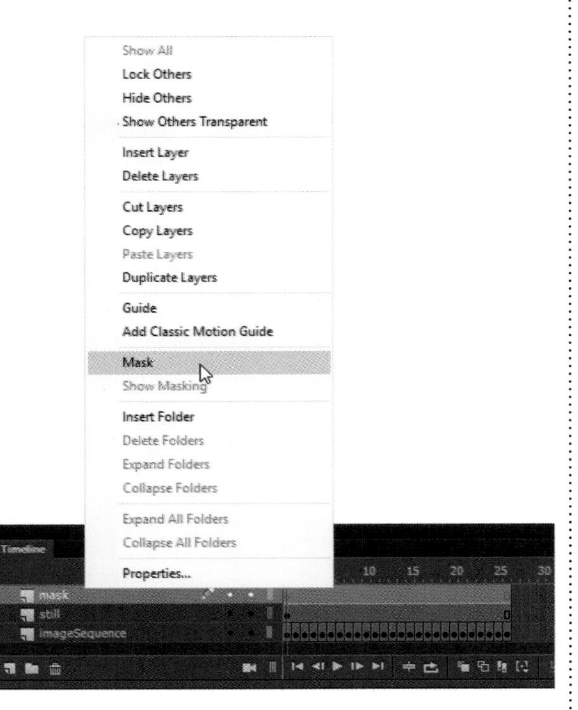

4 Make another layer for the mask. Right-click and select Mask. Unlock the mask layer.

Cinemagraph (cont.)

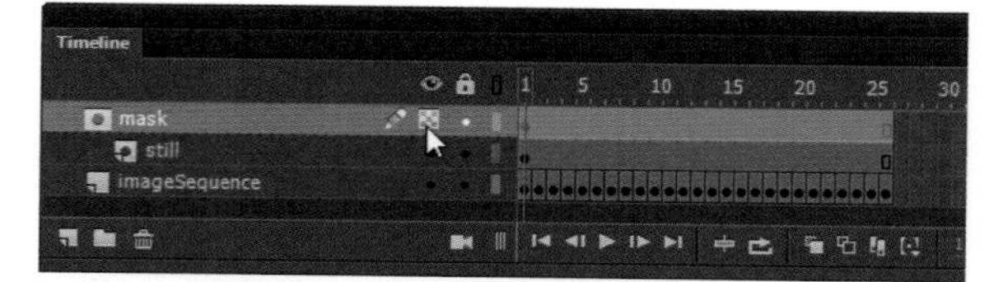

5 Because we want to show the still portion only and that takes up most of the image, start with a rectangle the size of the Stage (550 × 367 px.).

6 Animate now lets us make a layer transparent while we work, so set the mask layer to 50% opacity by *Shift*-clicking on the Show or Hide Layer dot. Now we can easily see what to erase. Erase the part that moves, which would include the stream of syrup to the edges of the butter.

9 When your mask is good, go to File > Export > Export Animated GIF... which opens the Export Image dialog.

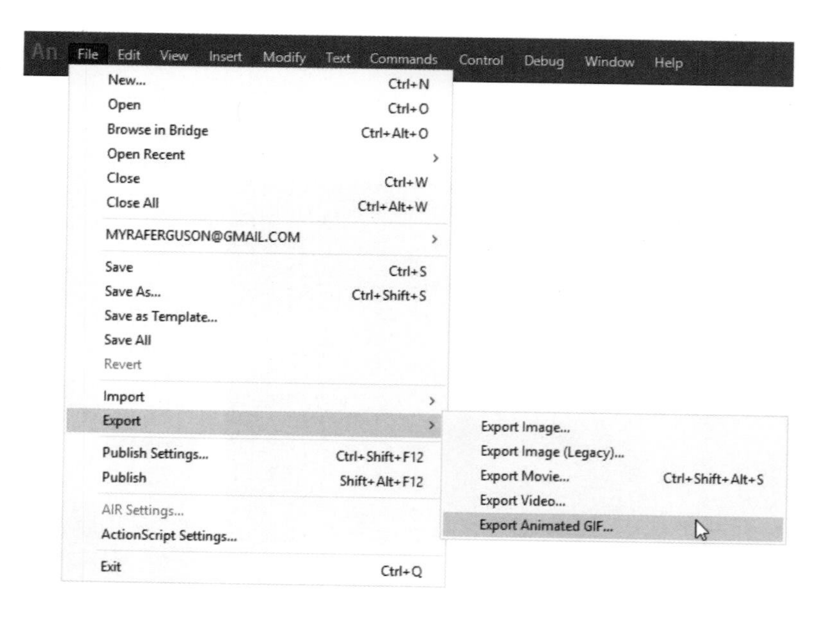

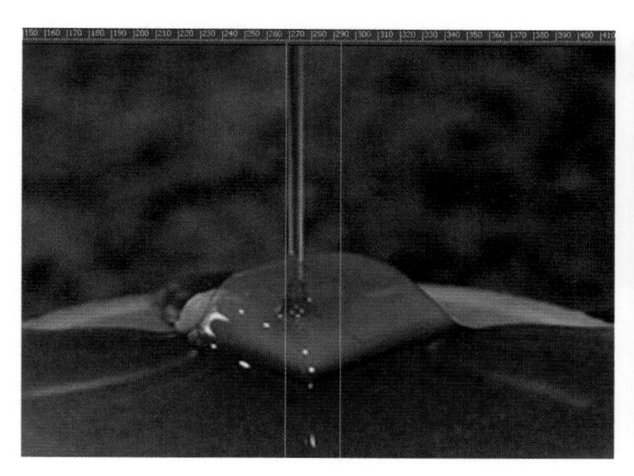

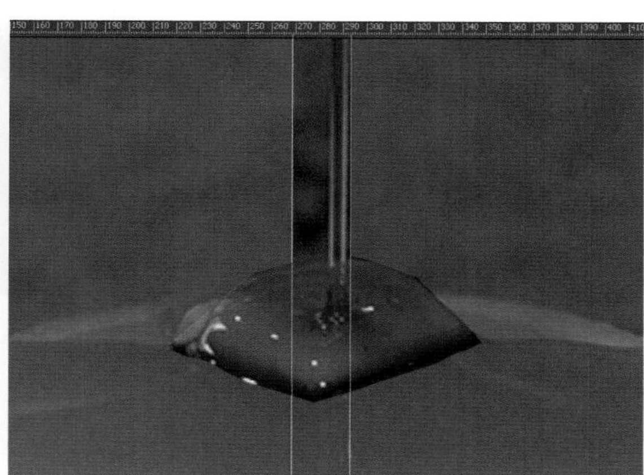

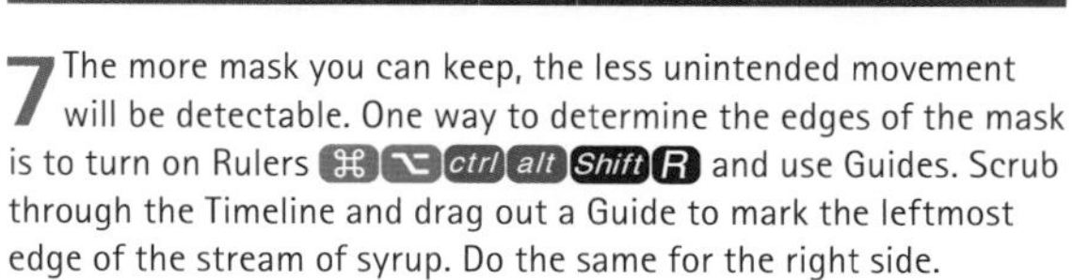

7 The more mask you can keep, the less unintended movement will be detectable. One way to determine the edges of the mask is to turn on Rulers ⌘⌥ ctrl alt Shift R and use Guides. Scrub through the Timeline and drag out a Guide to mark the leftmost edge of the stream of syrup. Do the same for the right side.

8 Erase what's in the middle down to the butter. Then erase where the syrup makes contact with the butter. Make sure your mask and still layers are locked, and test your movie Control > Test ⌘ ctrl Enter to see if your mask needs any refining.

10 In the Preset section select GIF. Either Perceptual or Selective at 256 Colors looks great with Diffusion on and 100% dithering, but the GIF file size may be larger than you'd like. Test to see what looks best at the smallest file size. The Export Image dialog indicates what the file size will be in the lower left corner. Increase the size of the preview in the dialog with the drop-down menu. Click the Preview... button to see what it looks like in the browser. Adaptive at 64 colors and 100% dithering reduces the size by about 30%. Remove frames or change the image size to reduce it even more. Click Save and become internet famous by posting your cinemagraph.

HOT TIP

Subtle movement seems to make the best subject matter especially if it doesn't interact or intersect anything else that might be moving.

Double Exposure

PHOTOGRAPHERS HAVE BEEN USING THE technique of superimposing one or more images over another since the days of film. This effect has re-emerged in large part thanks to the show *True Detective*. The title sequence for the show uses semitransparent overlays on silhouettes to create eerily haunting images while informing viewers of the backstory.

While some designers may use the effect to evoke a spooky sentiment, double exposure can also be used to tie ideas together like the shape of a bear filled with a forest scene or a person with a cityscape. In these examples, the juxtaposition of the two images gives the viewer more information such as where the subject lives or what the subject is thinking. You can create this effect either in film or with Photoshop, but masking in Animate makes this effect a pretty simple cheat.

Let's combine a vector graphic of a member of a marching band with a picture of the band practicing. The idea for this image is that the time invested rehearsing strengthens their skills, unites the band, and builds character—all of which the performer brings to the field.

1 First we'll need to select our two images. I'd recommend picking one that's a fairly close-up shot and the other that's more of a long shot.

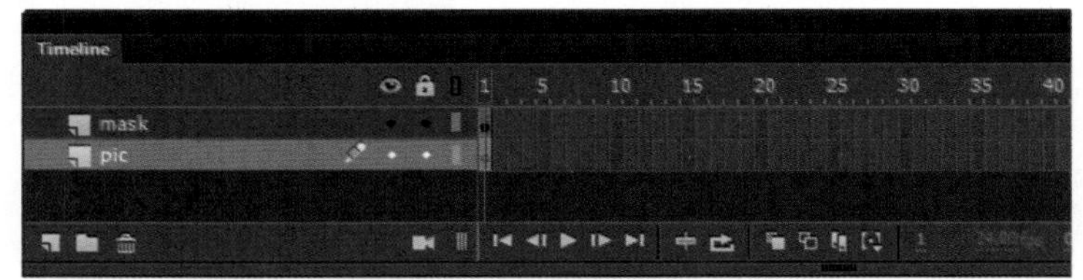

4 Make a new layer. Name it "pic" and drag it below mask. Import ⌘ ctrl R your secondary image, which can be either a raster image or vector graphic.

DOUBLE EXPOSURE EFFECT IMAGE: MYRA FERGUSON | MODEL: THOMAS FERGUSON

2 The close-up will need to be a vector, so you can either select a vector to start or use Illustrator to convert your image. When creating your vector graphic, looking for stock art as vectors, or tracing your image in Illustrator, keep some details beyond the general shape. The details might be facial features, or like our image they are the instrument and shako with the plume. The main shape of the vector is what masks the secondary image, but the extra details can improve the overall effect.

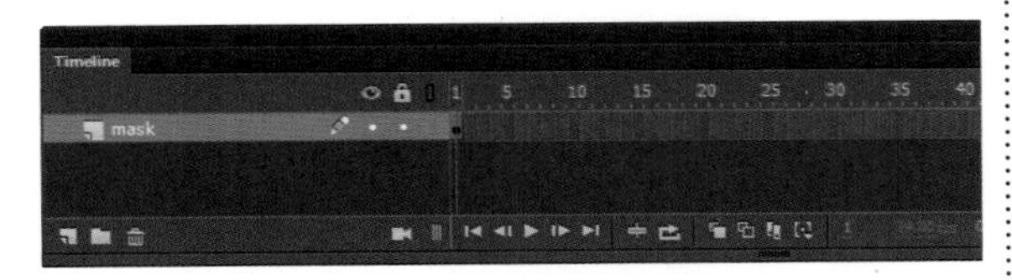

3 Import ⌘ ctrl R your main vector shape to the Stage, and position and scale it. Name the layer "mask."

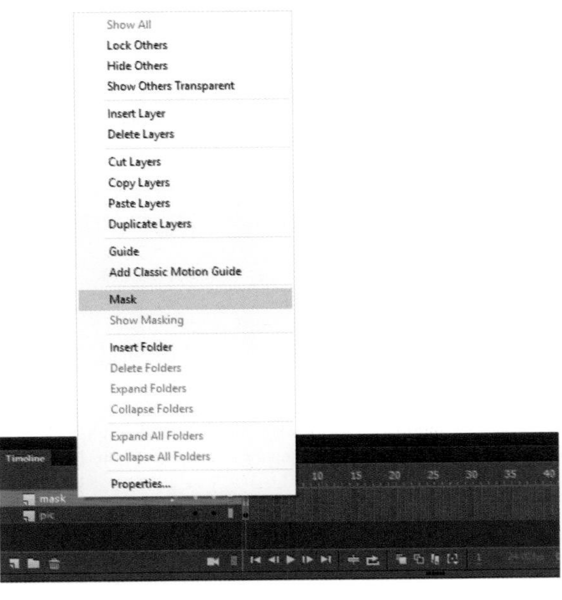

5 Select the mask layer, right-click, and select Mask from the contextual menu.

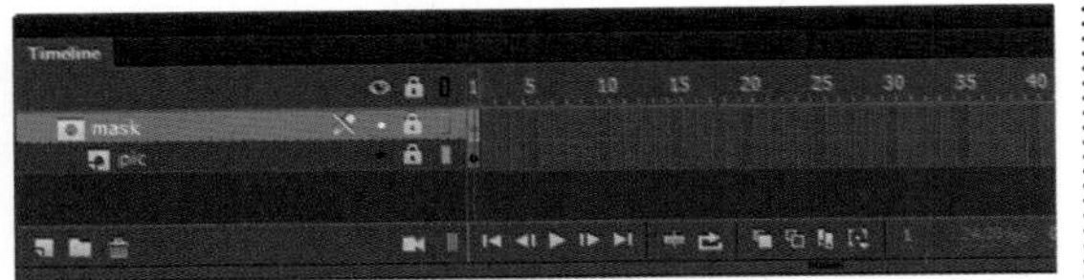

6 The icons for the layers change, the image below the mask layer becomes indented, and both layers become locked. The shape masks the image so that only where there is a shape, the image below shows through.

Double Exposure (cont.)

7 You might want to resize and/or reposition your secondary image for it to show through the masked area better. Unlock the pic layer by clicking on the lock, and change the mask layer to outlines by clicking on the solid rectangle. When your image is where you want it, toggle the lock back on the pic layer.

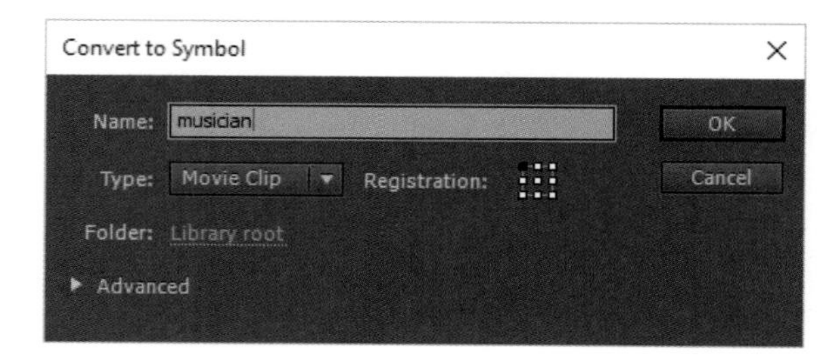

8 Really, you could stop here, but we could improve the image with a few tweaks. Let's bring back some of the detail from our main image. Unlock the mask layer. Convert the shape to a Movie Clip. Copy ⌘ ctrl C the Movie Clip and lock the mask layer.

10 Adding the tint made him opaque, so we aren't seeing the picture underneath anymore. We could change Tint to Advanced and adjust the amount of alpha, but let's play with the Blending. The Blending mode Add works well to show the underneath image and brighten it with the gold.

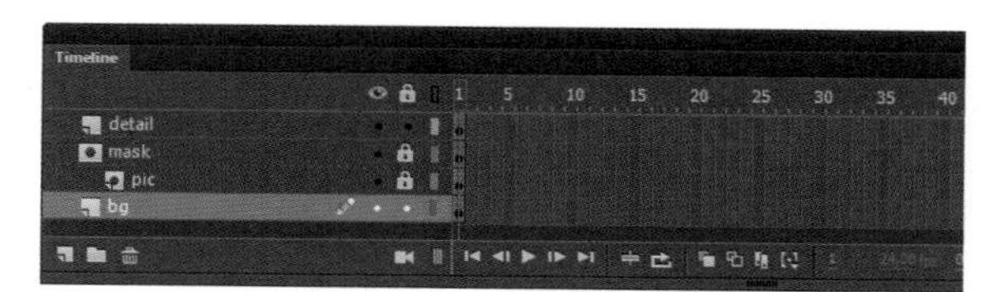

11 One more embellishment finishes the image. Add a new layer and drag it to the bottom. If it indents, drag it to the left until you see a black line showing it aligning to the far left.

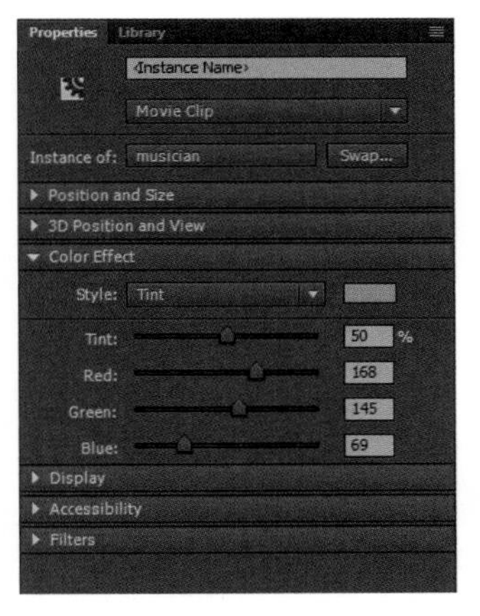

9 Make a new layer and Paste in Place ⌘ ctrl Shift V the musician. To incorporate the school's colors of black and gold, add a tint of #A89145 at 50% to the musician.

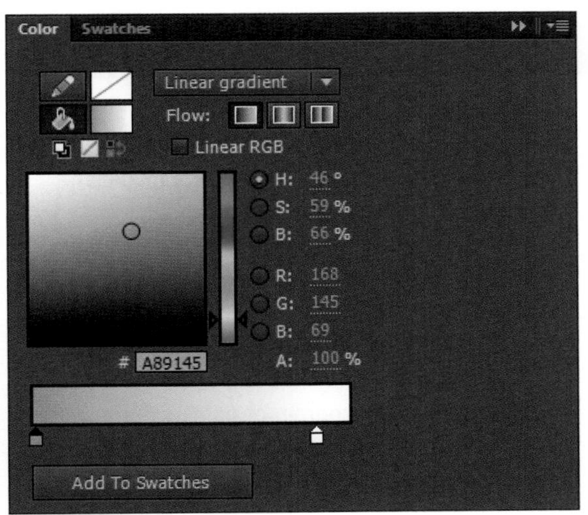

12 Add a rectangle the size of the Stage and fill it with a gradient that goes from white to our gold where the transition starts at about the height of the instrument.

HOT TIP

Quickly test out which blend mode works best for your image. With your Movie Clip selected, go to the Properties panel and under the Display section click Normal from the Blending drop-down menu and release. When it is highlighted, use your down and up arrows to step through all of the blend modes. I like to refer to this process as shopping for blend modes.

Rotating Globe

WHENEVER I WORK WITH MASKS, I FEEL like a magician. Masks provide the ability for you to create illusions, much like a magician's "sleight of hand" technique. It's all about what the viewer doesn't see, and you, as the designer, have the ability to control that. One of the more popular animation requests is how to make a rotating globe. The first thought is that a globe is a sphere and to animate anything rotating around a sphere requires either a 3D program or painstaking frame-by-frame animation—not so if you can use a mask. Remember, it's not what you see, but rather, what you don't see.

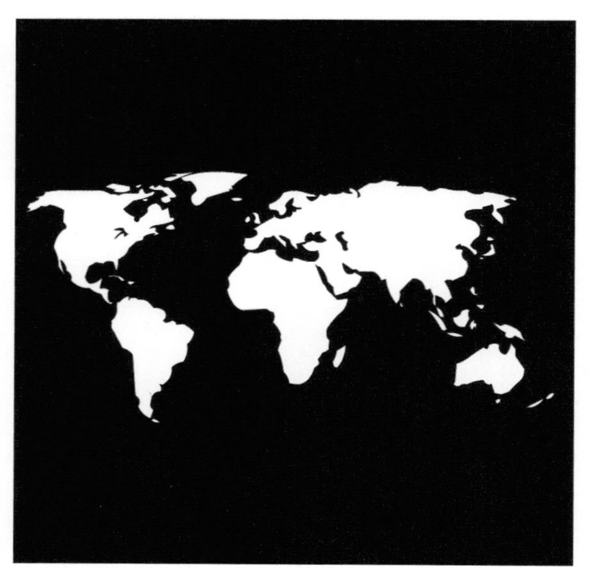

1 The first step is to create the continents. A quick online image search will yield plenty of examples. Import the image into Animate and leave it as a bitmap, use the Trace Bitmap feature, or manually trace it using Animate's drawing tools. Convert it to a symbol.

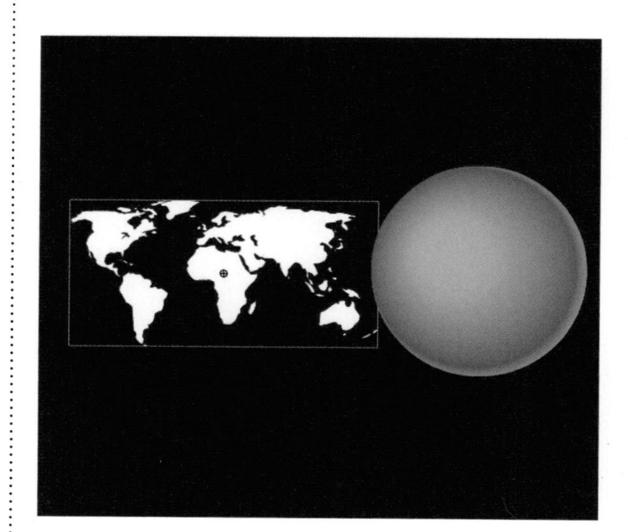

4 The next step is to create a mask layer using yet another copy of the circle in the bottom layer. Create a new layer above your continents, paste in place the circle, and then convert this layer to a mask layer. This layer mask prevents the continents from being visible outside this circle. All you need to do now is Motion Tween the continent symbol across this circle.

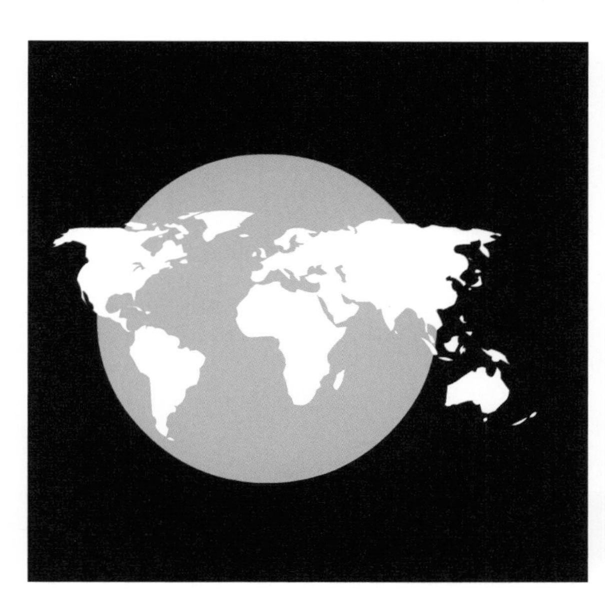

2 Create a new layer and move it below your continents. Draw a perfect circle using the Oval Tool O while holding down the Shift key. Select this circle and copy it, and paste it in place on a new layer above your continents.

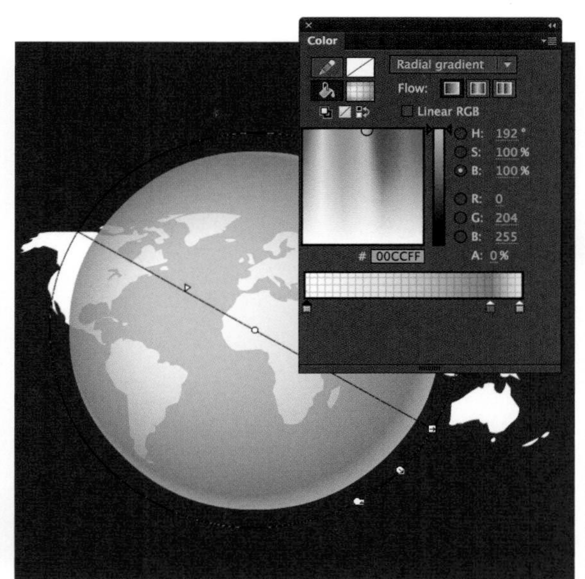

3 Mix a radial gradient similar to the one shown and fill the circle in the layer above your continents. Make sure to mix enough alpha into each color, so the continents will show through. Using the Gradient Transform Tool F, edit your gradient so that the highlight edge is off-center to one side.

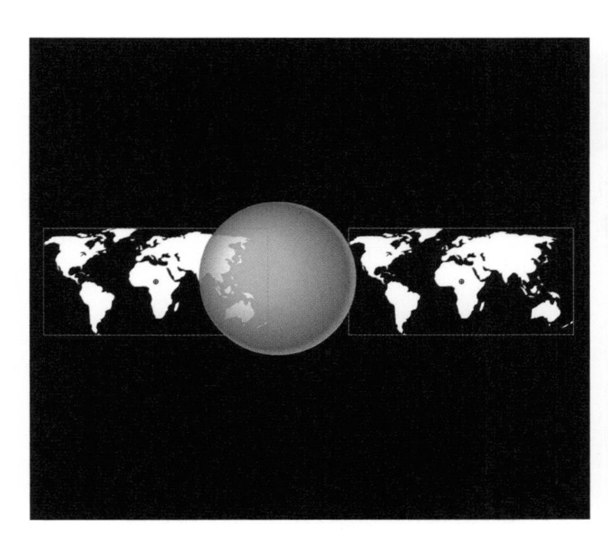

5 To avoid too much delay in the animation between the first and last frames, add a new masked layer with a new instance of your continent symbol. The best way to make this looping animation as seamless as possible is to copy the first frame of the continents and paste it in place into the last frame of your Timeline. Work backward in the Timeline and position the continents outside of the circle to the right.

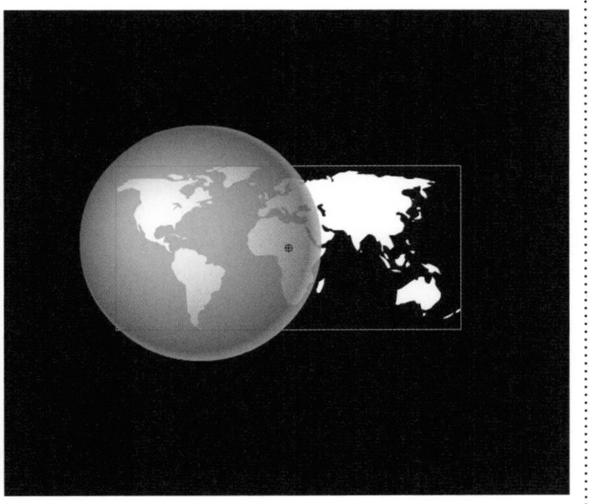

6 Since the first frame is exactly the same as the last frame and each frame in between represents a slightly different position for the continents, select the symbol in the last frame and use the arrow keys to nudge it to the right a few pixels. Moving it over takes into account a two-frame "hesitation" in the movement of the continents every time the playhead returns from the last frame to frame 1.

HOT TIP

You can always move your entire animation into a Movie Clip symbol so that it can be easier to position, add multiple globes, and/or target with ActionScript. To make it a Movie Clip, drag across all frames and layers to highlight them in black. Right-click or Command-click over them and select "Copy Frames" from the context menu. Open your Library and create a new Movie Clip symbol. Right-click or Command-click over frame 1 of this new symbol and select "Paste Frames."

Flag Waving

THE WAVING FLAG IS A POPULAR "how do I...?" request. To be honest, it plagued me for quite some time as to how best to achieve this animation. My initial reaction was to use Shape Tweens and frame-by-frame animation, but that proved time-consuming and had unconvincing results. Then one day, out of the blue, it hit me. If I slide the right shape across a masked area, I could create the illusion of a flag waving without having to kill myself animating it in a traditional way. It suddenly became so easy anyone can do it.

1 You will begin by making a nice long repeating ribbon shape. Start with a simple rectangle with any color fill and no outlines. Make it a little wider than it is taller.

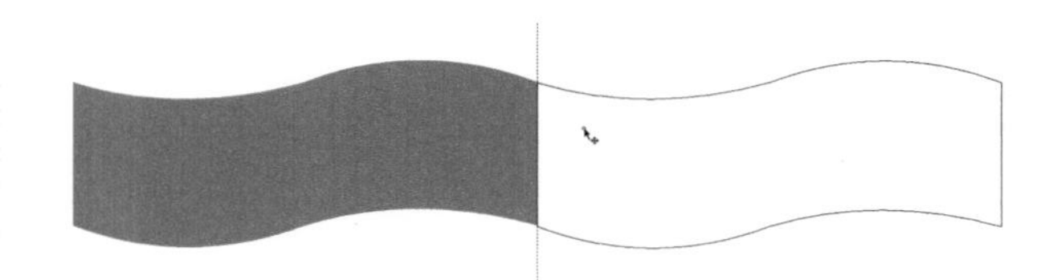

4 Repeat step 3 by pasting your new shape and flipping it vertically. Then attach it to the side of the shape again. See the ribbon pattern taking shape? But your ribbon is a solid color and lacking some depth, so let's continue by adding some shading.

7 Create a mask layer above the ribbon layer. Using the Rectangle Tool (R), make a shape big enough to cover a section of the ribbon as shown. It helps to use a high contrast color.

10 Test your movie using ⌥ ctrl Enter to see the effect of the flag waving as it passes through the mask. But let's not stop there. Let's animate the mask using Shape Tweens to further emphasize the left and right edges of the flag waving. Use the Selection Tool (V) to bend the left and right edges. Create a keyframe further down the mask layer.

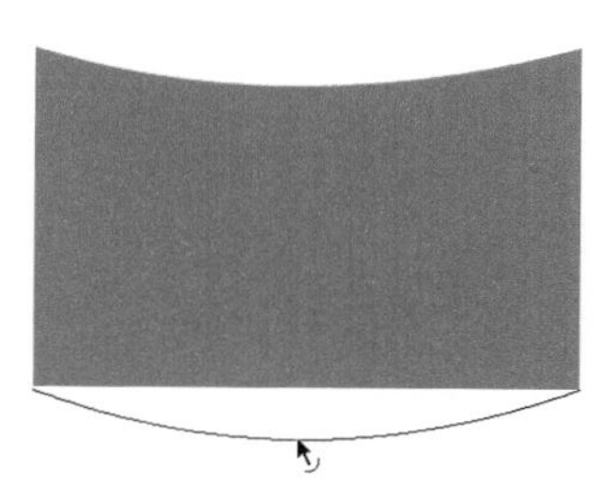

2 Use the Selection Tool V to bend the top and bottom edges slightly, so they have a nice arc to them. You will want to repeat this shape to create a pattern, so select it and copy it.

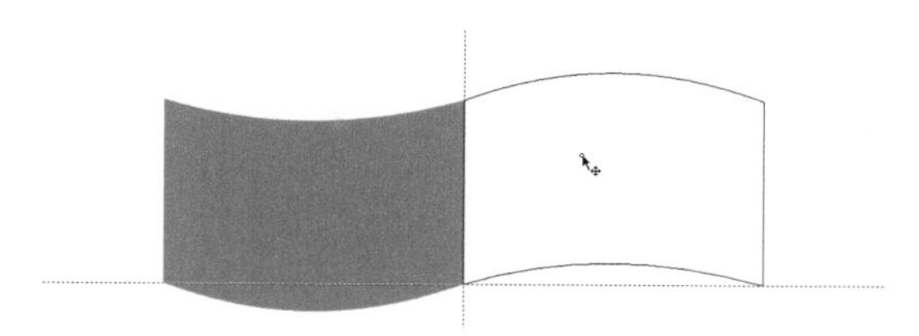

3 Paste your shape and then flip it vertically. Use the Selection Tool to drag it so that it connects to the original shape. Once these shapes are joined together, select it and copy it.

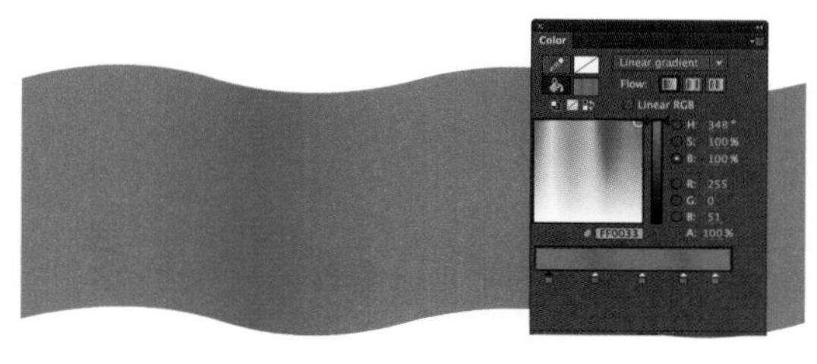

5 Mix two colors and add them to the Swatch panel. Mix a linear gradient with several color pointers alternating between these two color values. Fill your ribbon shape with this gradient and edit it so that the darker tones are in the concave sections of the ribbon shape.

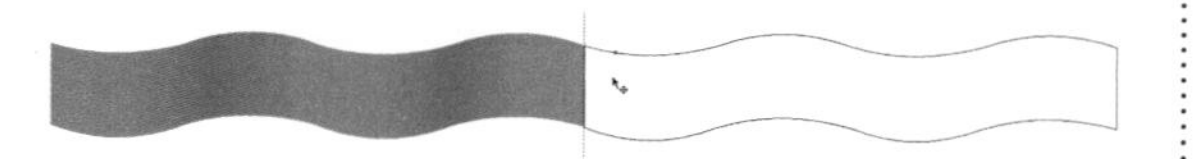

6 Once you have the ribbon the way you want it, select it using ⌥ ctrl A, copy it using ⌥ ctrl C, and then paste it using ⌥ ctrl V. Align it edge to edge with the original shape to essentially double its length. Convert it to a symbol.

8 Next, create a keyframe somewhere down the Timeline and reposition the ribbon to the left of the mask shape. Apply a Motion Tween.

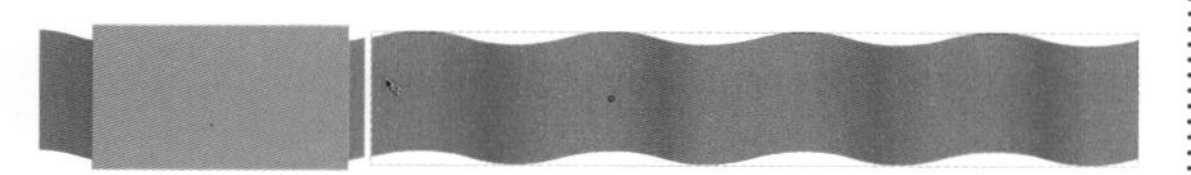

9 To create a seamless loop of the ribbon, copy and paste in place a new instance to a second masked layer (using the same mask). Motion Tween it so that it follows the original ribbon shape without creating any gaps.

11 In this new keyframe, bend the left and right sides of the mask shape in the opposite direction. Apply a Shape Tween. Repeat this procedure until the last frame is reached. The animated mask adds an extra animated touch to the overall flag waving effect. Presto! You are done.

12 Don't forget to add a flag pole and sky background for an even more convincing illusion. Try placing this animation in a Movie Clip symbol and drag a few instances of it to the Stage. Scale them and arrange them in perspective for the ultimate flag waving effect.

HOT TIP

This example is a looping animation. For best results make sure the first and last frames are identical by using copy frames and paste frames or by copying the object in the first frame and pasting it in place in the last frame.

Iris Transition

THERE ARE USUALLY SEVERAL WAYS TO go about creating the same animations and effects in Animate. Whether it be animated on the Timeline or dynamically generated using ActionScript, Animate allows us as users to work within our own comfort zones. A simple iris transition is an example of an effect that could be done several different ways. Using a mask for this example provides us with even more options. We can easily control the direction and focus of the iris itself, where it starts, and where it ends. Animating the iris can be a nice touch to your storytelling if you want to focus the viewer's attention to a very specific area of the screen.

1 The first step is to create a simple circle using the Oval Tool (O). The fill color is insignificant. Hold down (Shift) while dragging to constrain its proportions. Do not convert this shape to a symbol but, rather, convert the layer to a Mask layer.

4 Add a new layer and drag it over the mask layer, so it becomes linked to it as a "masked" layer. This layer is where your content will reside. If your content requires multiple layers, then make sure they are all masked or move all content into a new symbol and drag an instance of the symbol to the masked layer.

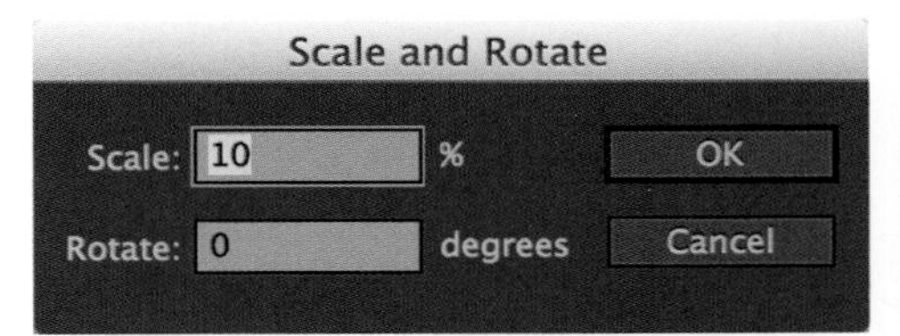

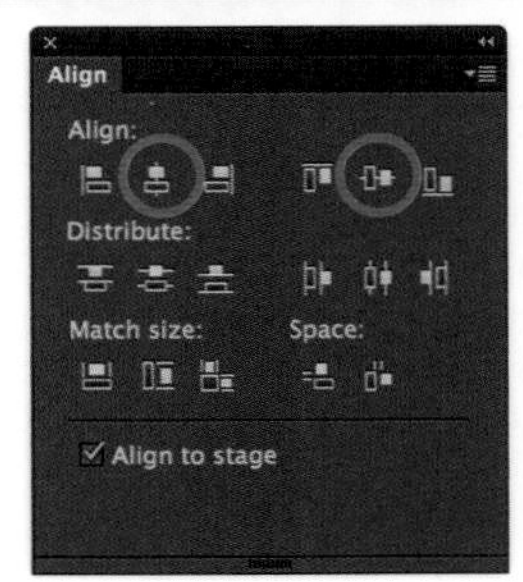

2 In frame 1, scale this circle as small as possible. Open the Scale and Rotate panel using ⌥ alt ctrl alt S, type in a percentage, and click OK. Use the Align panel using ⌥ ctrl K to center the circle to the Stage.

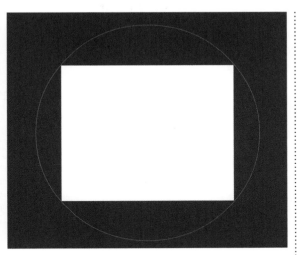

3 Create a keyframe a few frames down your Timeline in the same mask layer. Scale the circle so that it covers the Stage completely. Convert the shape to outlines, so you can see the Stage underneath it. Apply a Shape Tween so that the circle grows from small to large, filling the Stage completely.

HOT TIP

Feel free to experiment with colors other than black. Sometimes radial gradients can add some fun depth to this transition effect. It is easy to substitute different colors or textures by changing the background layer art to whatever you want.

5 Create a new layer that's not masked below all the other layers and create a black rectangle the size and shape of the Stage. The color can be anything you choose, but black typically works well for this type of effect. At this Stage you can reverse the animated mask by copying keyframes in reverse order and applying another Shape Tween.

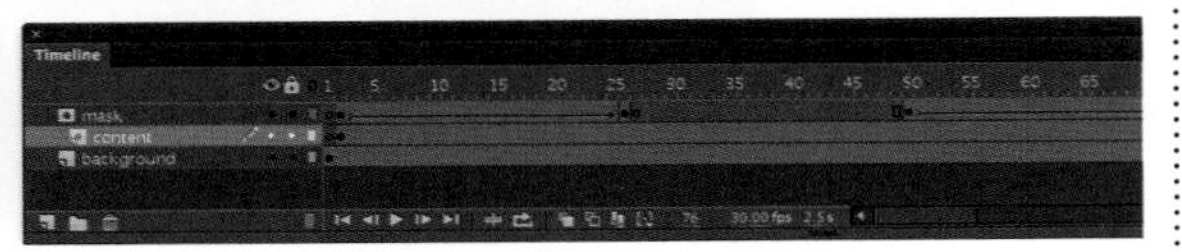

6 Since you are creating the iris effect with an animated mask, you can easily control the iris' focus on a particular area of the Stage. In the last keyframe, position the circle in the last frame over the character's eye. When the animation plays, the iris will animate and close in on the eye—a typical technique used in several cartoons.

Handwriting

THIS ANIMATED EFFECT IS one of my favorites because I am asked frequently how it can be achieved, yet it is quite simple in technique. Every time I demonstrate how to make text "write" itself, the reaction is almost always the same: "Oh wow! That's all there is to it?" The example here uses an animated mask, which yields a very small file size, ideal for large blocks of text.

How to cheat in Adobe Animate

1 The first step is to type some text on the Stage. It doesn't matter what it says. Just choose a font and start typing. If an effect doesn't render properly when you test it, check which kind of text block it is. If it's set to Static text in the Properties panel, it should be fine. Some effects like masking, alpha, rotation, and scaling text may not render correctly. One work-around would be to convert the text to shapes by breaking it apart. However, if you need to use Dynamic text, you can embed the font outlines.

How to cheat in Adobe Animate

3 Add a new layer above your text layer and convert it to a mask layer. The text layer will automatically be linked to it as a "masked" layer. In frame 1, draw a rectangle just to the left of your text, making sure it is as tall as the text itself.

How to cheat in Adobe An

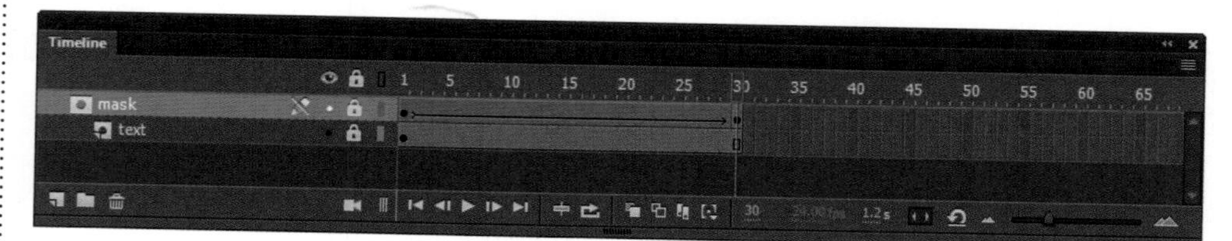

5 Now apply a Shape Tween in between the two keyframes. Lock both layers and play the Timeline to see the effect of the text appearing to write itself. If you want the animation to play faster or slower, insert more frames or remove frames, respectively.

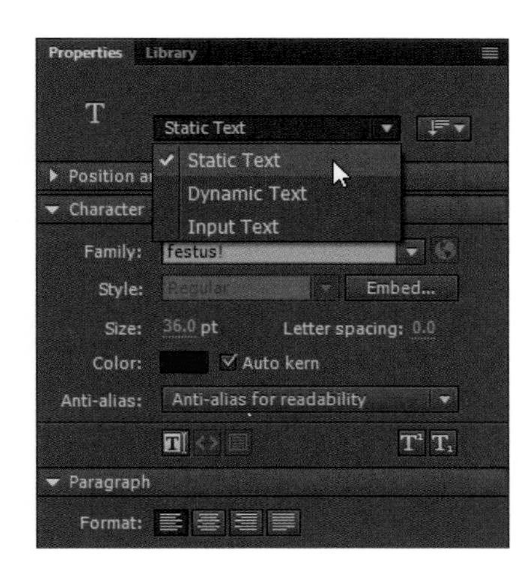

2 If you choose to change the behavior of your text field to Static, the font will be embedded in the compiled SWF, and the Flash Player will render it correctly even with an effect added to it. Another option is to break apart the text until it becomes raw shapes. Breaking it apart will ensure the text renders correctly but also creates a larger file size, and it will be harder to edit the text if need be in the future.

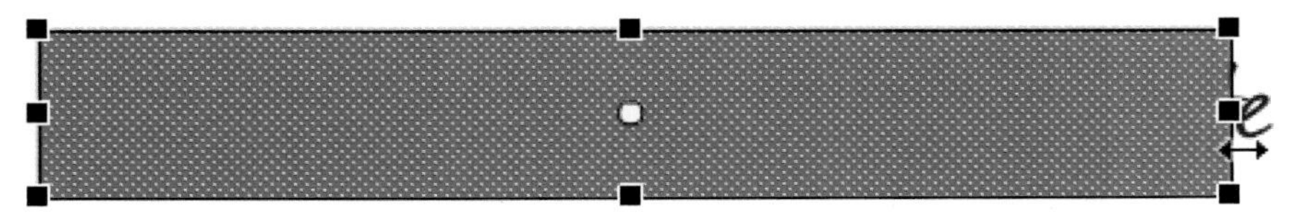

4 In this same layer, create a keyframe further down the Timeline and select the Free Transform Tool Q. Hold down the ⌥/alt key while using the Free Transform Tool to anchor the left edge of the shape in place. Grab the middle transform handle on the right side of the selected shape and drag it to the right until it spans the width of the text.

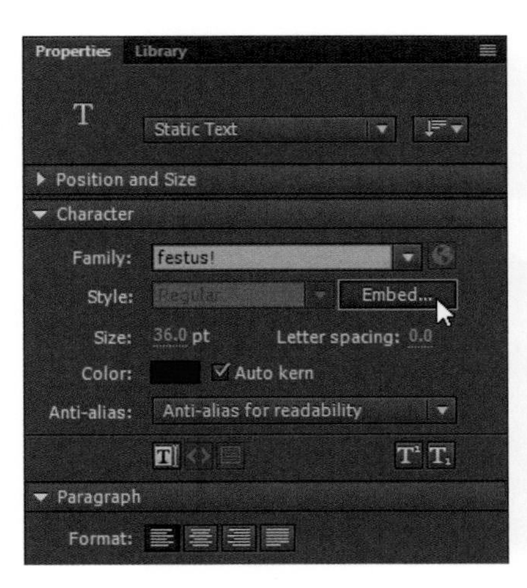

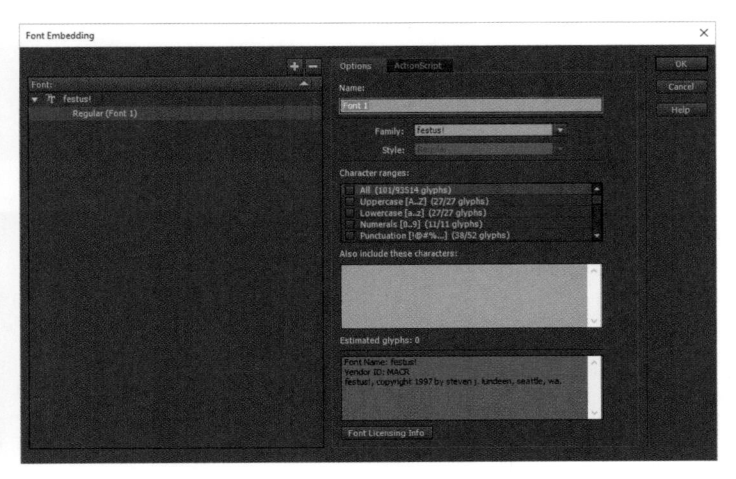

6 If you need to use Dynamic text, you must include the font outlines so that the text renders correctly in the Flash Player. To embed the font, select the Dynamic text field and then click the "Embed..." button in the Properties panel. The Font Embedding panel will appear, allowing you to choose the range of characters used in your animation. Try to select the minimum number of characters because embedding all characters can increase file size significantly. There's a section in the Options panel that allows you to type in just the characters that you are using on the Stage. These are the only characters that will be embedded and keep the file size as small as possible as a result.

HOT TIP

You can create a more realistic writing effect with a frame-by-frame technique where you start with the whole word, add a new keyframe, and erase a bit of it in the reverse order in which it should appear. Keep adding keyframes and erasing from the end of the word until it's completely gone. Then select all the keyframes, right-click, and select Reverse Frames from the context menu.

Spotlight

ANIMATED MASKS, AS WE'VE seen, can provide an interesting dimension to your animation. It really doesn't take much effort to create various visual effects using an animated mask, such as this spotlight effect for a client's logo.

1 The first thing you need is some text or other image where you can shine a spotlight. Convert it to a symbol. The background should be dark if not completely black. In order to show light, we first need to create darkness. This technique wouldn't have the same effect if the background was very light.

2 Create a new layer above your image layer and convert it to a mask layer. The image layer will automatically be linked to it as a "masked" layer. Draw a shape using the Oval Tool O while holding down the Shift key to constrain its proportions. Convert it to a symbol.

3 Add a keyframe further down the Timeline and position the mask shape to the opposite side of the image. Apply a Motion Tween so that the mask shape passes across the image.

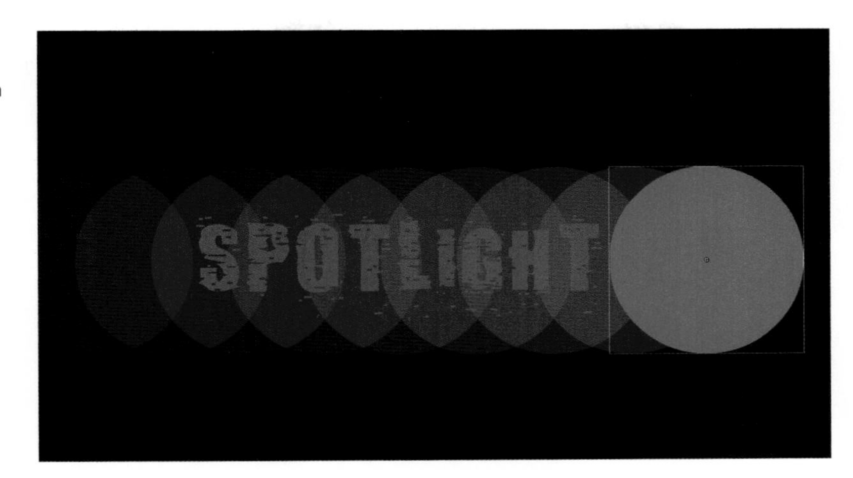

4 The key to making this technique convincing is to copy and paste in place the image to a new layer below the original layer. Make sure it is a normal layer (not masked). Select the symbol and tint it to a dark color. This layer will not be affected by the mask.

5 Test your movie to see your animated mask pass over the original image layer while the darker instance remains unmasked and visible throughout the animation.

HOT TIP

Don't be afraid to add more keyframes in your mask layer and position the mask symbol in various positions relative to the image it is revealing. You can also animate the mask getting larger and smaller by scaling it. Be creative and change the shape of the mask to, say, two circles side-by-side to suggest we are looking through binoculars.

Focus

ONE OF THE MOST EXCITING features in Animate is the PSD and AI importer. For this example we will edit an image in Photoshop, save it as a PSD file, and import it into Animate via the PSD Importer wizard.

We will also add a slight touch of ActionScript for some added interactivity. If you suffer from ActionScript phobia, don't panic. Adding only a couple of lines of code will be painless. The code hides the cursor in the Flash Player and allows us to drag a Movie Clip around the Stage. The trick here is the mask itself, allowing us to see the sharper image through the mask shape only. Open wide and say "Ahhhh." This won't hurt a bit.

1 First you need to start with an image, of course. This might be a good time to browse your hard drive or grab your digital camera. It doesn't have to be a raster-based image or even a photograph. It can be vector art drawn in Animate or imported from a different program. Whatever image you choose, you will need two versions, the original and a blurred version of the original.

4 Once the import process is complete, your Animate document should contain both images on different layers. Make sure the blurred image is below the sharper image.

5 Create a new layer above the sharper image, draw a shape on that layer, and convert it to a Movie Clip symbol F8. Convert that layer to a mask to automatically link it to the layer below. Both layers will be locked to show the effect of the mask.

PHOTO: CHRIS GEORGENES

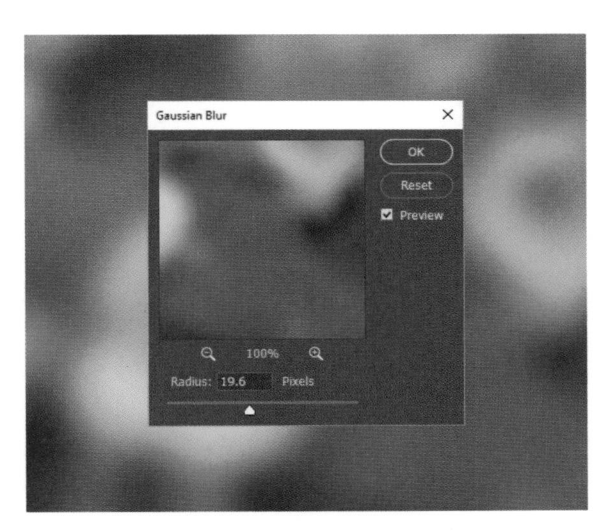

2 Open your image in Photoshop and duplicate its layer, so you have two copies of the same image. Apply a Gaussian Blur to one of your images. Save the file as a PSD file.

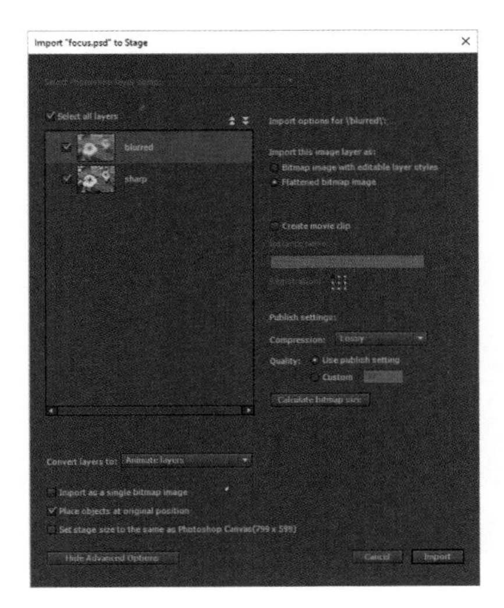

3 In Animate, import the PSD file you just created. The PSD import wizard will appear and prompt you with a variety of options. The left panel will display all the layers of the PSD file. Click on them to display options for each. You will also want to convert layers to Animate layers, place layers at original position, and set your Animate Stage to the same size as your Photoshop image.

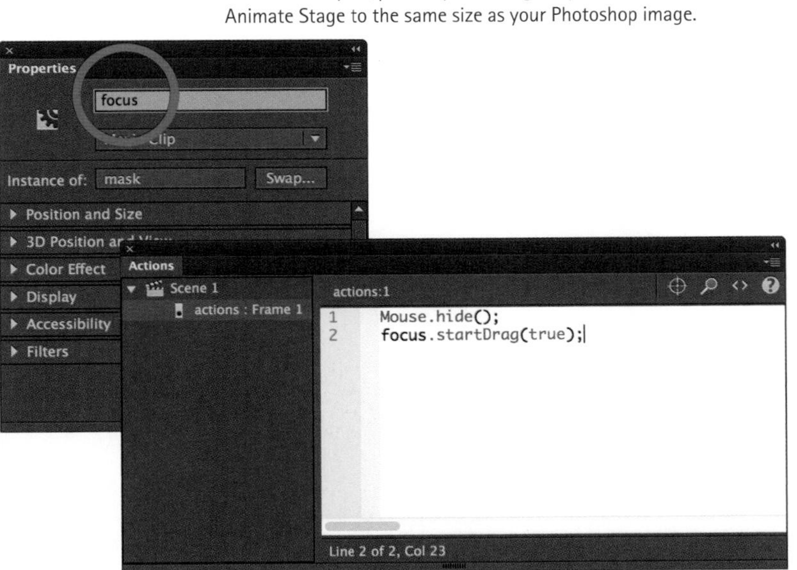

6 You are almost done! Lock all layers to see the effect. It works, but it is pretty boring as the mask just sits there. Time to add some functionality.

7 Use the Selection Tool V to select the Movie Clip symbol containing the mask shape. In the Properties panel, type in an instance name. I chose "focus" for this example. With the Movie Clip still selected, open the Actions panel and type the following ActionScript exactly:

ActionScript 3.0:

```
Mouse.hide();
focus.startDrag(true);
```

HOT TIP

The shape of your mask doesn't have to be a circle. It can be as simple or as complex as you wish to make it. Experiment in Photoshop with image effects beyond blurring. There's enough to choose from to keep you busy for a while. I particularly like the Glass filter (Filter > Distort > Glass...).

Feathered Mask (ActionScript)

A FEATURE CALLED "RUNTIME BITMAP CACHING" gives us the ability to create masks with that desired feathered edge. I know that oftentimes when the designer world overlaps the developer world, things can get a little blurry. To be honest, even the most code-phobic designer can use ActionScript to integrate dynamic masks into their designs. All that is required is a few lines of very simple code.

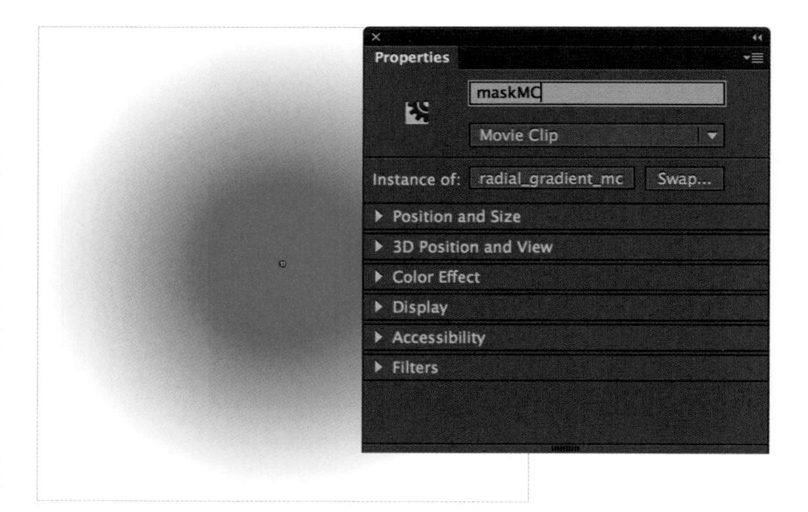

1 The first step is to create a radial gradient with two colors. The middle color should be solid, and the outer color should be mixed with 0% alpha. The alpha transition from 100% to 0% creates the feathered edge that gets used later for the mask. Using this gradient as your fill color, select the Oval Tool (O) and draw a circle on the Stage. To constrain the circle so that it is perfectly round, hold down the Shift key while dragging. Convert this shape containing your radial gradient to a Movie Clip symbol. With this Movie Clip symbol selected, give it the instance name "maskMC" in the Properties panel.

3 You will need two different images to make the transition. Place both images on different layers, one directly over the other. For clarity, I will refer to these as "Image A" and "Image B." Image A resides on the bottom-most layer. Image B gets revealed with the feathered mask using ActionScript.

4 Since the mask itself is controlled with ActionScript, we need to use ActionScript to composite it to the image that gets revealed during the transition. Convert Image B to a Movie Clip symbol and use "mask_image" as the instance name. The only thing left to do is apply the code that tells the radial gradient to act as a mask and apply itself to Image B.

PHOTO: CHRIS GEORGENES

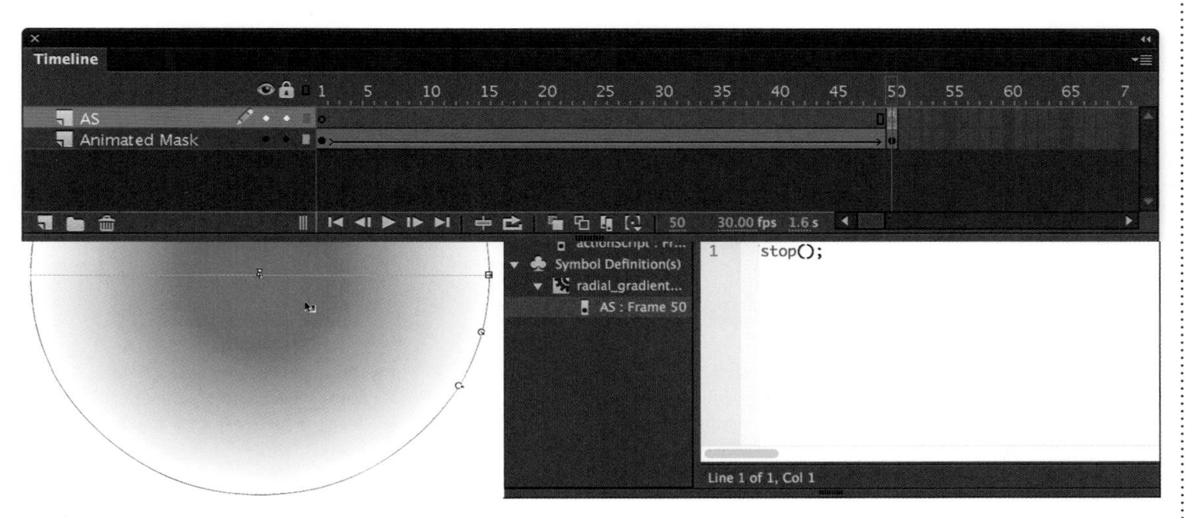

2 Double-click the Movie Clip to enter Edit mode. Select the radial gradient again and convert it to another symbol. Now we can create a nice transition effect by animating it. Using a tween, scale the symbol from very small to very large, large enough so that it covers the Stage completely. Place a stop(); action at the end of this Timeline.

5 In the Actions panel F9 type in the following code:
mask_image.cacheAsBitmap = true;
This code caches the image so that it can be masked at runtime in the Flash Player.
maskMC.cacheAsBitmap = true;
The code on Line 2 will assign the Movie Clip "maskMC" to act as a mask at runtime.

mask_image.mask = maskMC;
This last line of code assigns the mask and the image to be composited together. That's all there is to it. Make sure you open the source file "feathered_mask_actionScript.fla" from the downloadable files to see this effect in action.

HOT TIP

Caching Movie Clip symbols has huge advantages in Animate. You will gain significant performance increases because there is less demand on the processor to calculate the math necessary to render certain property effects. Caching also allows for more advanced levels of compositing that cannot otherwise be done.

Medical Pack

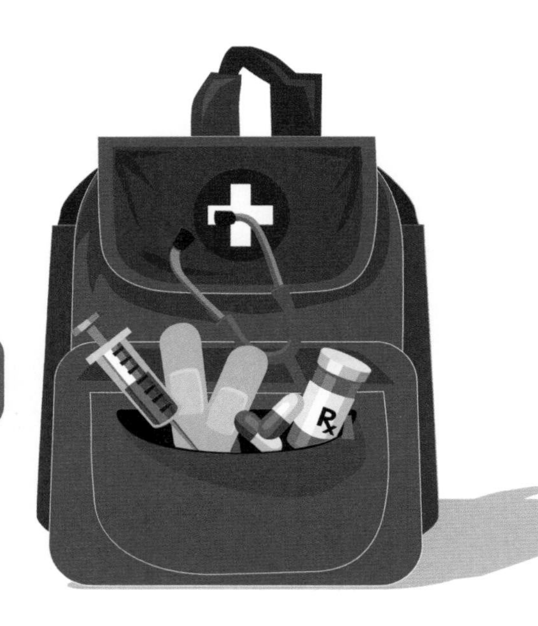

AS WE'VE SEEN THROUGHOUT THIS chapter, masks can be used to help create compelling animations. Often the best animated effects are a combination of different techniques that come together to perform a single effect. In this medical pack animation, I needed to animate the front pocket unzipping and then opening to reveal the items inside. I used a combination of Shape Tweens, Motion Tweens, and animated masks. Each of these techniques alone isn't as compelling as when used together harmoniously.

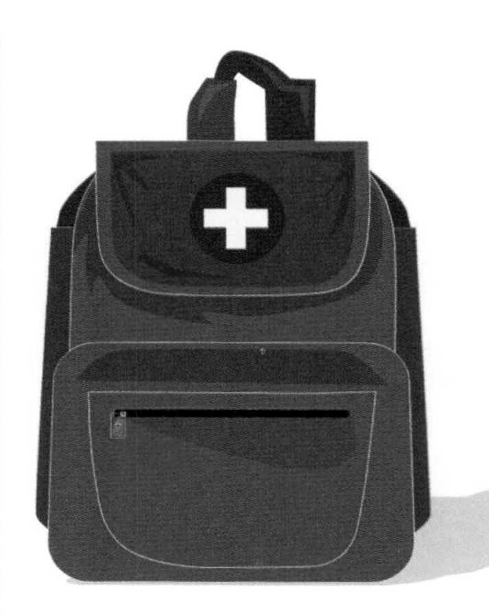

1 The medical pack is drawn as vectors inside Animate. The front pocket and zipper are the only objects to be animated, specifically the zipper, the shadow, and the white stitching. Each of these objects is placed on a different layer.

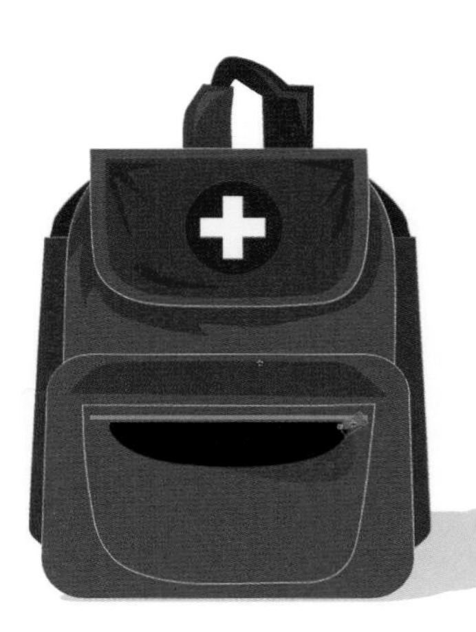

2 The zipper requires just a horizontal Motion Tween across the pouch opening. The black shape represents the opening of the pocket. I created a Mask layer above the pouch opening and drew a thin green rectangle shape inside it.

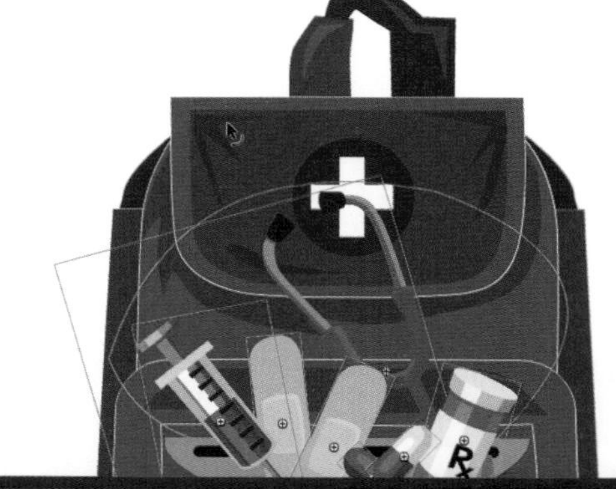

6 Using Motion Tweens, animate each object vertically over the "opening" of the pocket area. As long as each object is inside the mask shape, they will be visible. If by chance one or more objects needs to animate beyond the shape of the mask, you can edit the mask shape to accommodate the space needed. Make sure each object layer is assigned to the Mask layer.

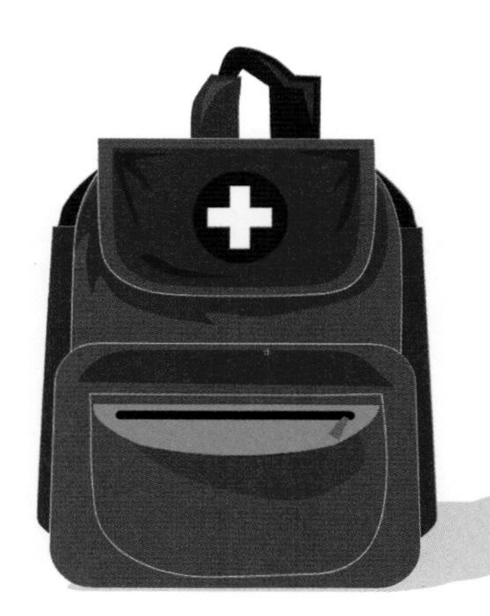

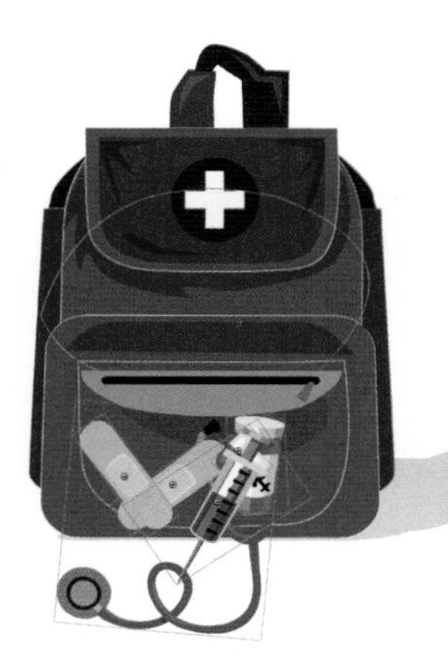

3 Using a Shape Tween, animate the green shape in the Mask layer to span the black pocket opening below it. Make sure the pocket layer is assigned to the Mask layer. Lock both layers and play back the Timeline to see the mask reveal the black pocket, providing the illusion of it opening.

4 Create a second mask shape that generously occupies the area above the pocket. The mask is drawn in the same shape of the opening from step 3 as well as a larger area to accommodate the space the objects will eventually occupy.

5 With the mask layer converted to outlines, we can position the objects "inside" the pocket just below the shape of the mask. The objects aren't seen because they are outside the area of the mask. Each object is a symbol on its own layer.

HOT TIP

The shadow of the pocket along with the white line that represents the stitching is animated using Shape Tweens independent of the masks and masked layers. It's just an extra step I like to take to provide a sense of added realism to the animation.

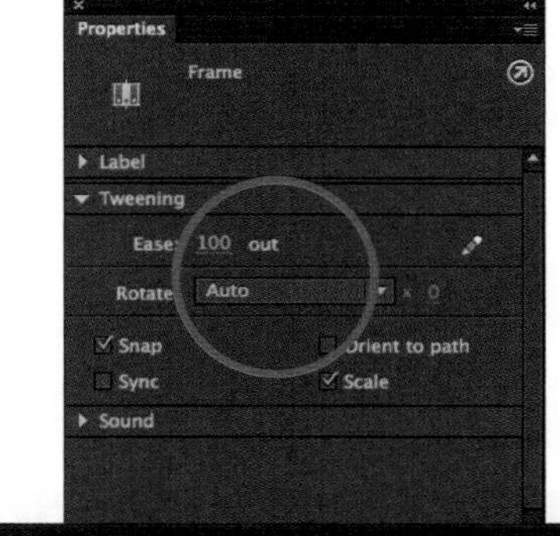

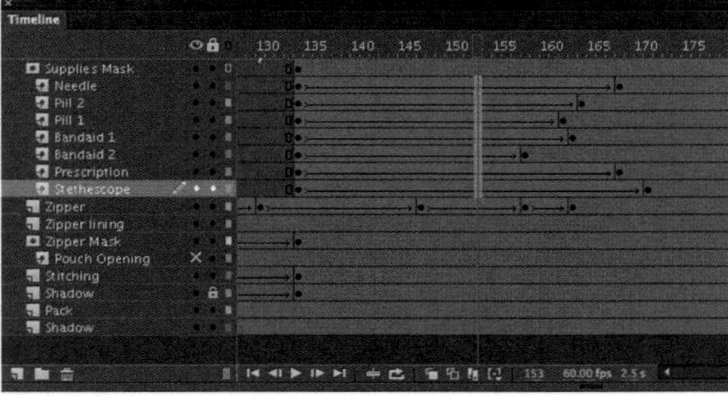

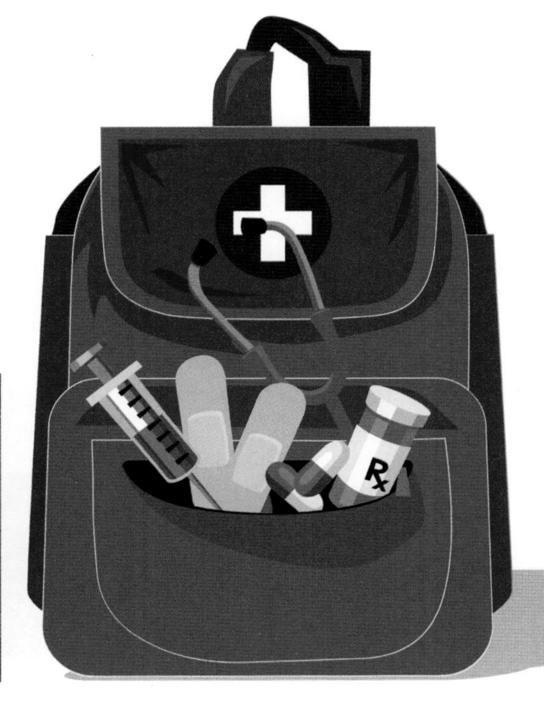

7 Add some Easing out to the Motion Tweens and some rotation to each symbol. Lock both the mask and all masked layers to watch the objects appear to rise up from inside the pocket of the medical pack.

8 Here's the final frame of the animated effect. The use of masks helped solve the issue of literally creating a pocket for the medical pack.

Animated Background Masking with Text

NO ONE KNOWS MASKS BETTER THAN SUPERHEROES! SO we're going to approximate the style of the Marvel logo animation. I say "approximate," because we would need to add a lot more detail to really replicate the effect, but this combination of a few simple techniques is a cheat that gives our animation a similar appearance fairly easily.

The Marvel logo animation uses a flipbook metaphor to make the transition from the world of print comic books to cinema. Pages of comic book panels flicker, and the motion creates a sort of frenetic energy that both forms and symbolizes the Marvel Universe. This rapid sequence of images is woven into the text and background of the logo screen and settles into the traditional logo and coloring.

We're going to focus on a few key visuals in this Marvelish effect. First is the content, which includes the collection of comic book panels and the logo and the text. Second is the movement of these elements. Third are the details like coloring and motion blur that complete the effect.

COMIC BOOKS BACKGROUND TEXTURE BY DEBERARR – STOCK.ADOBE.COM

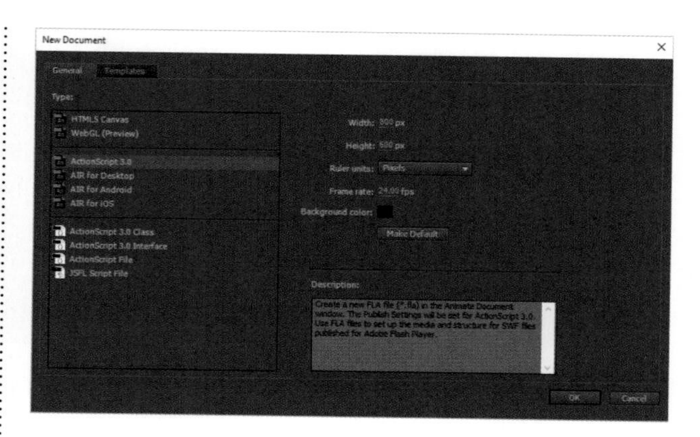

1 Create a new ActionScript 3.0 document with an 800 × 600 pixels Stage and set the Stage color to black, which makes it easier to see the text we add later.

4 Convert the image to a Movie Clip symbol F8 and name it "comicStrip." Name this layer "bg." Proportionally scale the instance of the comicStrip by linking the height and width in the Properties panel and setting the width to 2000 pixels Align the top and left edges with the Stage.

2 Turn on Rulers ⌘ ⌥ ctrl alt Shift R and drag guides out to line up with all the edges of the Stage to help when we add larger assets. Make sure Snap to Guides ⌘ ctrl Shift ; is enabled.

3 For the content, we can either use some stock art like Adobe Stock's Comic Book Background Texture (File #108823700) by deberarr or make our own. The striped format of the background image works well because it resembles layered pages of panels without having to feature characters. If you're using the Adobe Stock image, save a preview to your Creative Cloud Library. In Animate, drag the image from your CC Libraries to the Stage.

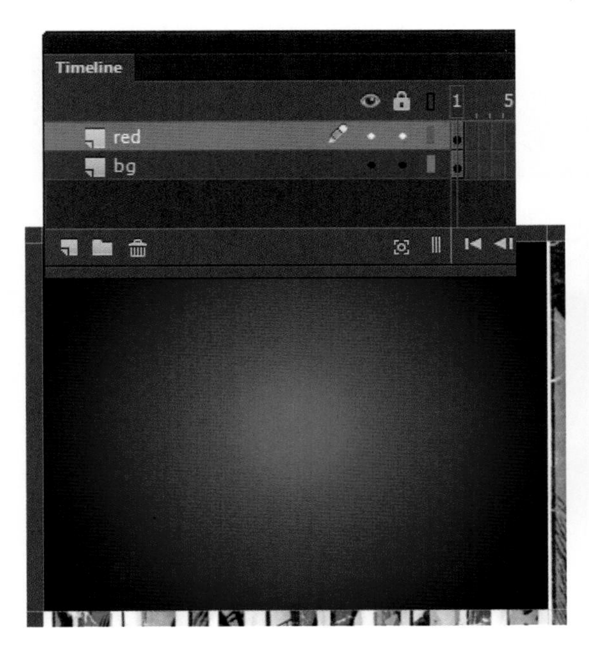

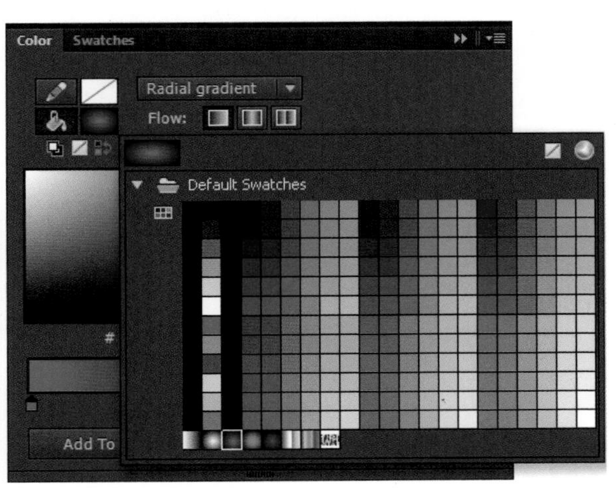

5 Make a new layer called "red" and draw a rectangle the size of the Stage. Select the red and black gradient swatch for the fill and no stroke. Convert it to a Movie Clip and name it "background."

Animated Background Masking with Text (cont.)

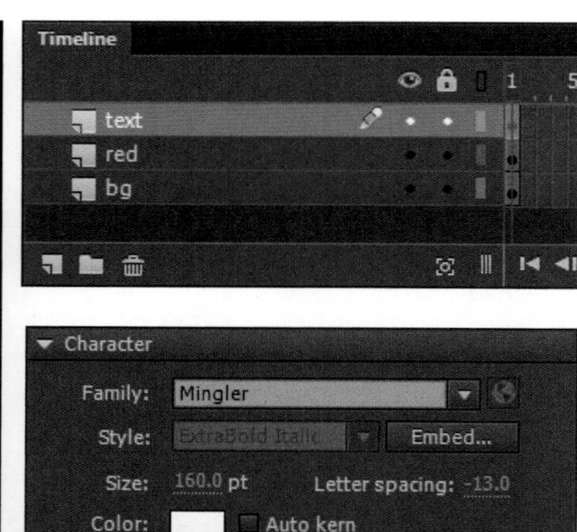

6 Make a new layer called "text." Let's use our own text instead of a logo. I'm using Mingler ExtraBold Italic which is available through Typekit and looks comic-like. Type "REVEAL" since this example is about using masks. I've set the text at 160 pt. in white and adjusted the Letter spacing to -13 to more tightly kern the type.

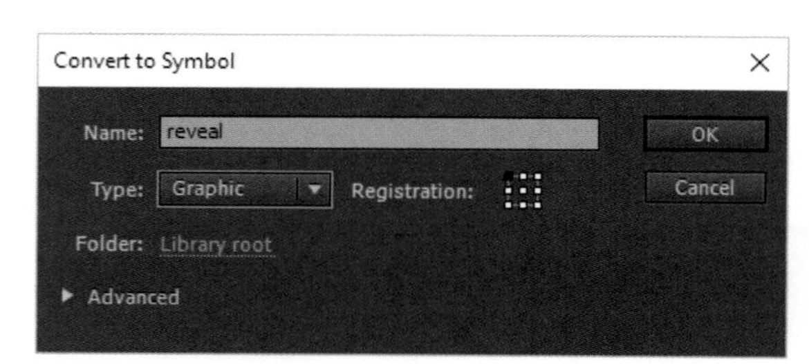

8 Align the text with the Stage so that it's horizontally and vertically centered. Convert it to a Graphic symbol named "reveal." Making it a Graphic symbol allows us to scrub the main Timeline and see it animate.

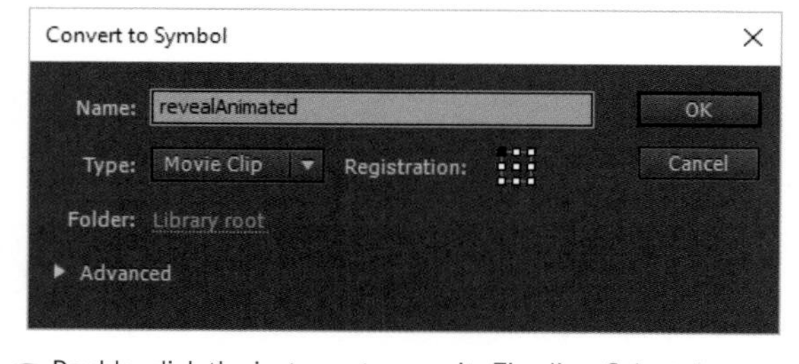

9 Double-click the instance to open its Timeline. Select the text. Convert it to a Movie Clip symbol again. Call this one "revealAnimated."

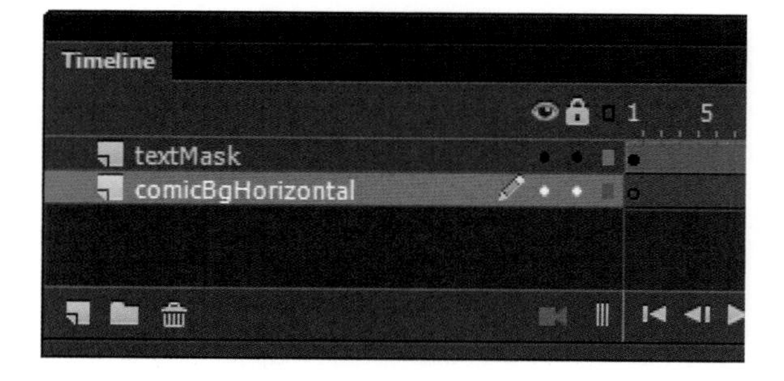

10 Insert a frame (F5) on frame 60. Name the layer "textMask." Add another layer below textMask. Name it "comicBgHorizontal."

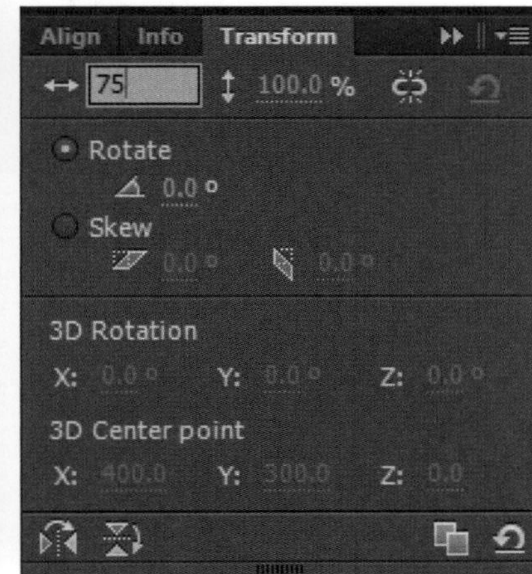

7 In the Transform panel ⌘ ctrl T unconstrain the height and width by clicking the chain icon to unlink them. Scale the width to 75%.

11 Drag out another instance of comicStrip. This time place it on the comicBgHorizontal layer. Relink the width and height in the Properties panel, so you can scale the background proportionally with a width of 2000 pixels Drag the background so that it aligns with the guides on the right and top of the Stage.

HOT TIP

Another way to adjust kerning is to Break Apart ⌘ ctrl B the text once. Animate will separate the characters into individual text boxes that you can nudge independently. If you break the text apart again, Animate will transform the type into editable vectors. However, once you break the text apart into vectors, you can no longer edit it as text.

Animated Background Masking with Text (cont.)

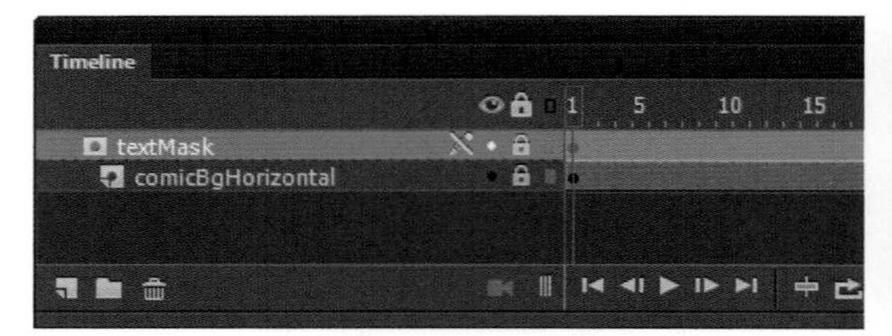

12 Right-click on the textMask layer and select Mask to make it mask the instance of the comicStrip background. Animate will automatically indent our background layer and lock both of the layers. We're going to make some changes to the text layer, so unlock the textMask layer.

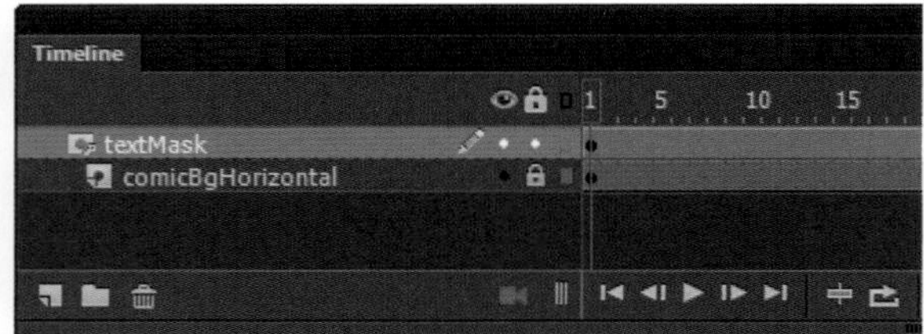

13 Select anywhere on that layer, right-click, and Create Motion Tween. Select the last frame, right-click, and Insert Keyframe > All.

16 Select anywhere on the layer, right-click, and Create Motion Tween. Select the last frame, right-click, and Insert Keyframe > All. Select the first frame and Shift + drag the comicStrip instance to constrain the movement and align the left edge to the guide at the 0 mark on the ruler.

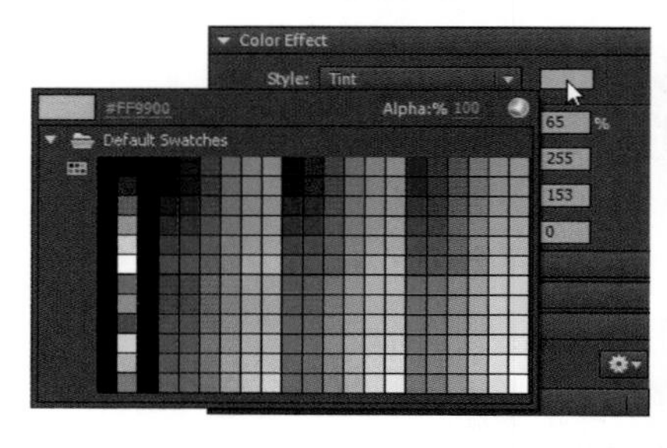

17 While still on the first frame, select the comicStrip instance and change the Tint in the Color Effects section of the Properties panel to #FF9900 at 65%. Select frame 30, then select the comicStrip instance on the Stage, and change the Tint to #FFFF99 at 80%. Do the same for the last frame to change the Tint to white at 100%.

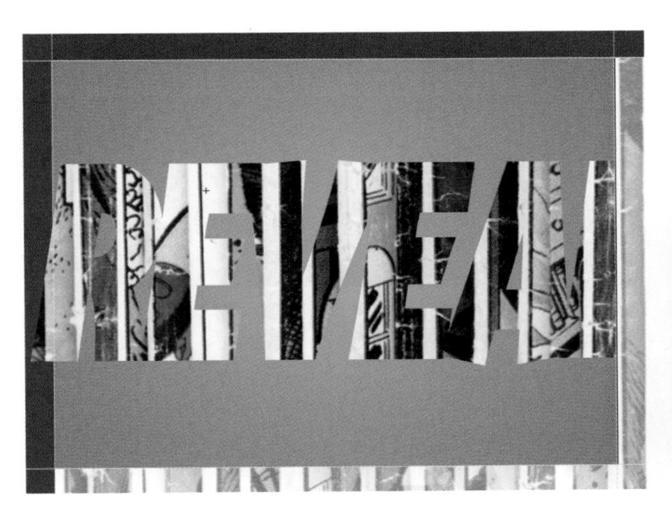

14 Select the first frame, open the Transform window ⌘ ctrl T, and scale the text shape proportionally to 250% to make the text animate zooming into place. The change automatically inserts a keyframe. Lock the layer.

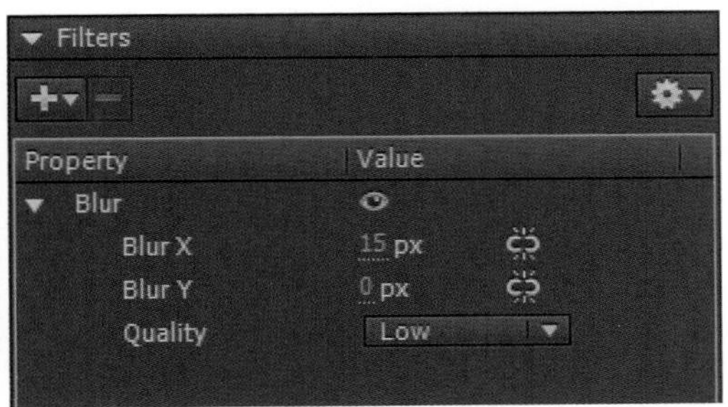

15 Unlock the comicBgHorizontal layer and select the instance on the Stage. Add a Blur filter in the Property panel by clicking on the + and selecting Blur from the drop-down menu. Unlink Blur X and Blur Y. Set Blur X to 15 pixels and Blur Y to 0 pixel.

HOT TIP

Use guides instead of Align to Stage when you're inside the Timeline for a symbol. Align works differently here. It uses the crosshairs of the registration point as opposed to the Stage's edges to determine where to align.

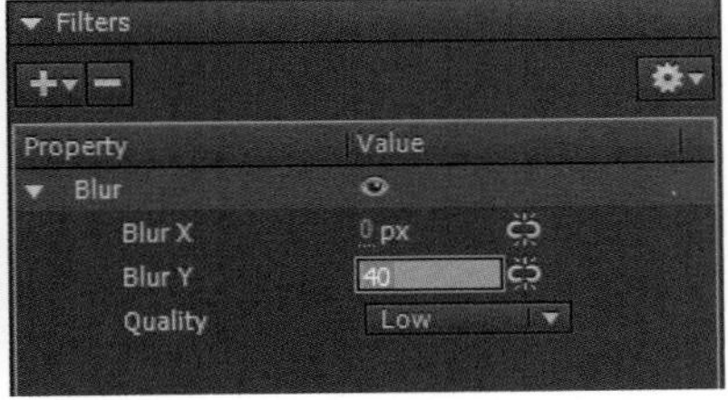

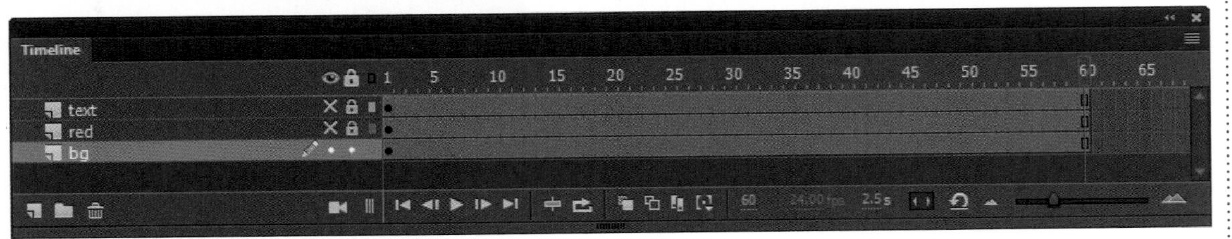

18 Lock both layers and go back to the main Timeline by clicking Scene 1 above the Stage. Select frame 60 for all three layers and Insert Frames F5. Hide and lock all the layers except for bg. Select the instance of the comicStrip on the Stage and add a Blur filter. Set Blur X to 0 and Blur Y to 40.

Animated Background Masking with Text (cont.)

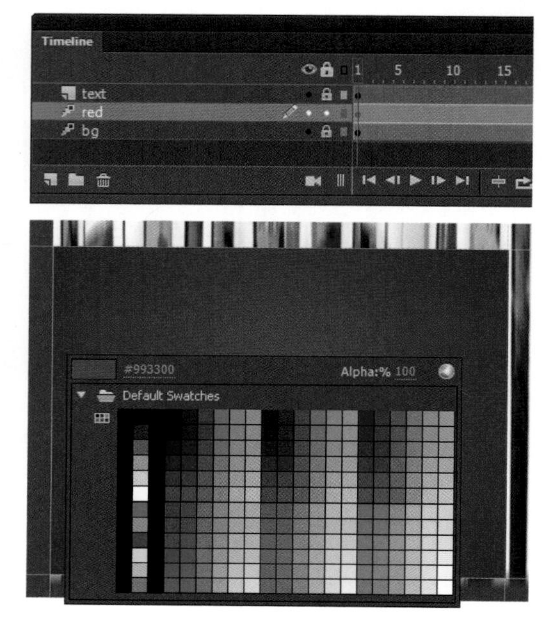

19 Select any frame on the BG layer, right-click, and Create Motion Tween. Select the last frame, right-click, and Insert Keyframe > All. Go to the first frame, select the comicStrip instance on the Stage, and Align it to the bottom of the Stage.

20 Now we're going to make the red gradient start as a semitransparent, desaturated orange and transition to the red and black gradient. Lock the bg layer, and unlock the red layer. Create a Motion Tween. Select the first frame and click on the instance of the background on the Stage to change the contextual menu in the Properties panel. In the Color Effect section select Tint from the drop-down menu. Click on the Tint color and select #993300.

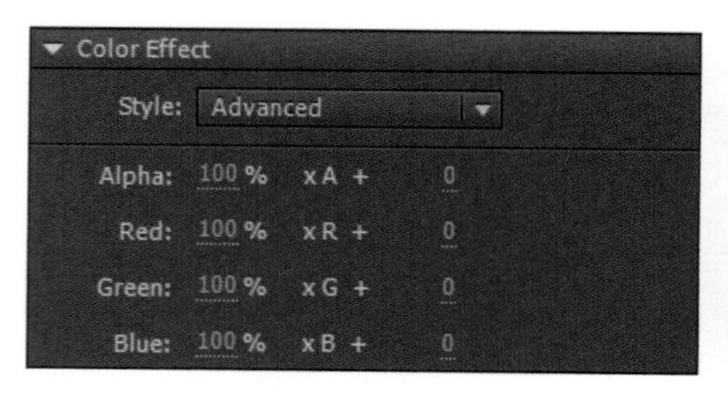

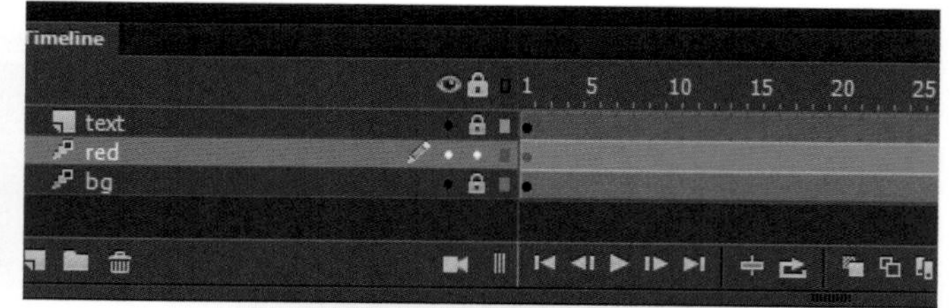

22 Select the last frame of the layer and click the instance of the background again. We want to remove the tint and make the rectangle fully opaque. You might think we'd need to set the Color Effect back to None; however, if the change isn't made to the same parameter, in this case the Advanced Color Effect, Animate will remove the keyframe we previously set. So let's use the Advanced setting to restore it. Set the Alpha to 100% which makes it opaque again. Then set all the values on the left to 100% and make all the values on the right 0. Our image only contains red, so we could just change the red value. For other images that contain some green and blue, it's good to know that these settings restore them to their original colors.

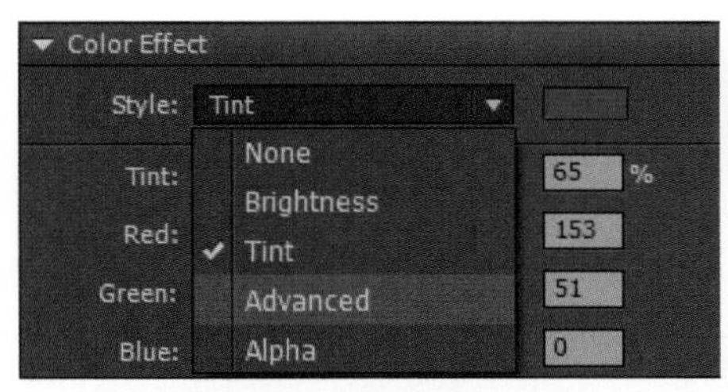

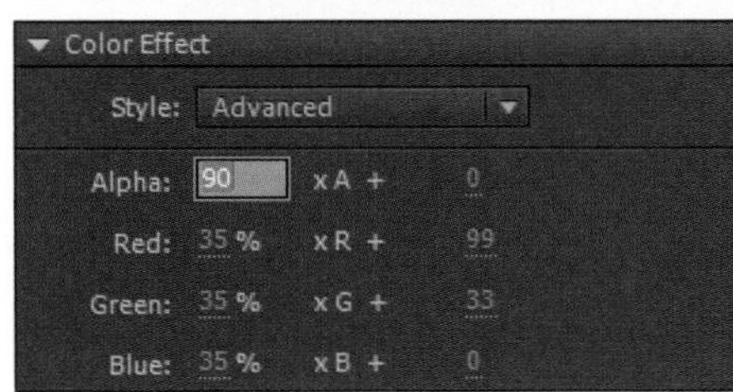

21 We want some of the comic background to show through from underneath, but the only way to make our rectangle semitransparent is to change Tint to Advanced in the Color Effects section in the Properties panel and adjust the Alpha there. Set the Alpha to 90%.

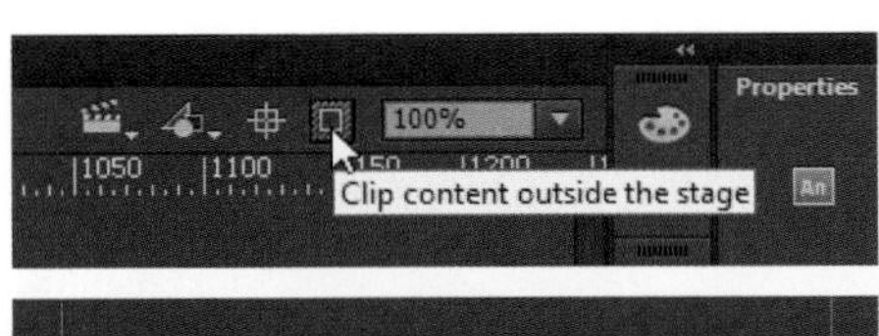

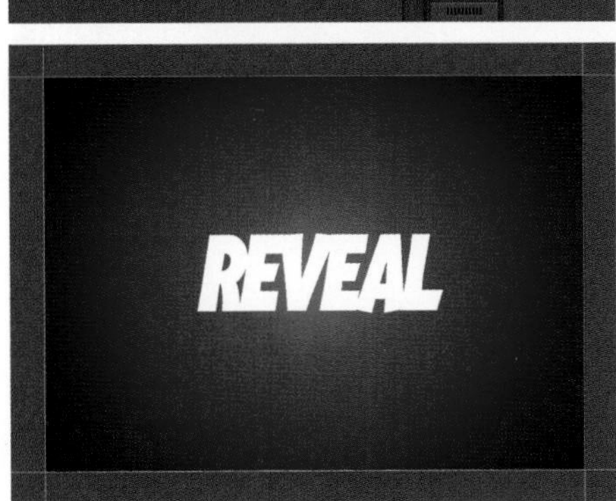

23 Let's hide anything that goes off the Stage by selecting the Clip content button.

24 Lock all the layers and Test ⌘ ctrl Enter it out.

HOT TIP

You may have noticed the names I'm using are lowercase or in the case of phrases start with a lowercase letter, have no space between words, and subsequent words have their first letter capitalized. I'm using what's known as camelCase. It's a naming convention that isn't required, but it can be a good habit if you start to write ActionScript.

A Remote Possibility

VECTOR TORNADO: VECTOR ILLUSTRATION: MYRA FERGUSON

JUST A FEW YEARS OUT OF COLLEGE AND NOT LONG AFTER GETTING MARRIED, I STARTED thinking about what it might be like to work from home. I wasn't sure I was ready to freelance at that point, but hardware and software prices were becoming more reasonable. It wouldn't be long until I would have my own tools.

Fast-forward a few years to the mid-1990s, and I was working on more complex projects beyond graphic design and desktop publishing. I was entering the world of interactive digital media, 2D and 3D animation, and video. It seemed like even high-end hardware and software were starting to become more affordable. Connecting to the internet was getting better, too, with faster speeds at better prices. I thought for sure these trends would make it possible to work in digital media from just about anywhere.

What I really wanted to do was visual effects for movies. The problem was I lived in Columbia, Missouri. Don't get me wrong. COMO, as it's known to the locals, is a great town. It's the home of the University of Missouri as well as headquarters for several established insurance companies. But a large market for digital media it was not.

I was working on my master's degree which included courses on 3D. I had gotten a Windows NT machine and thought I might be able to find companies at SIGGRAPH that were looking for talent who could work remotely. The trade publications were full of articles about a talent shortage. What surprised me was that companies were really only willing to look for and work with people who were local. Of course, if the talent pool is limited geographically, then yes, I could see how they could consider that a shortage.

A few years after that, I did get full-time remote work in St. Louis and later Kansas City. Columbia is located about halfway between them, so I could drive the 2–3 hours either way for the occasional in-person meeting. Although telecommuting was doable, it was not the preference of either company to make remote work a permanent arrangement. Interestingly, in both cases the offices were satellite locations under remote corporate management.

In the last few years, I've seen more companies warm up to the idea of remote workers. For those who manage it well, there are significant benefits. It generally makes for a happier work group as the team is entrusted to do the work assigned without being micromanaged. Happy workers are loyal workers, and loyalty translates into less turnover. The company doesn't have to worry about the overhead of office space and in most cases, equipment. Team members don't have to struggle with traffic issues or weather. There's greater flexibility and the end result is a productive working relationship.

I've heard some concerns that remote groups sacrifice a sort of creative synergy. That hasn't been my experience. Video conferencing, screen sharing, and messaging have allowed for that same flow of ideas at times when collaboration is needed. In fact, meetings with web technology might be even better in that you can chat an idea that can be read after someone speaks so that it neither gets forgotten nor interrupts the speaker. Meetings and chats also can be saved, which makes referring to the ideas discussed and confirming that you're on the right track possible. When your meeting is done, you can set your online presence to "do not disturb" so that you can work without interruptions.

I know there are some clients who just feel more comfortable with face-to-face time. That's fine. If they find meeting in person to be a necessity, they usually take care of the expense of bringing the remote teams onsite for a project kickoff.

One consideration with working from home is making time for being social. Being a part of an Adobe User Group and getting to spend time with friends in the Adobe Community helps as well as volunteering for other organizations. Some people work from coffee shops just to be around other people. If working from home becomes part of your lifestyle, find ways that work for you to cultivate your creative and social side.

■ Animating movement often requires tricking the viewer's eye into thinking the motion is there when it is merely implied. The rocket isn't actually moving forward, but your eye thinks it is because the background is animated in the opposite direction the rocket is pointing.

5 Motion Techniques

LET'S FACE IT, ANIMATE IS ABOUT MOTION. IN SOME CASES, the more motion, the better. Motion can emphasize the intensity of an action sequence and can add a measure of realism to your animations. Whether it's making text fly around a website or animating a character in an action sequence, providing convincing motion effects can be critical to their visual success.

In this chapter, we examine the differences between the Motion Tween and the Classic Tween methods as well as look at a few of what I consider the most valuable motion effects that you can use in your everyday life as an Animate designer and animator.

Frame-by-Frame Animation

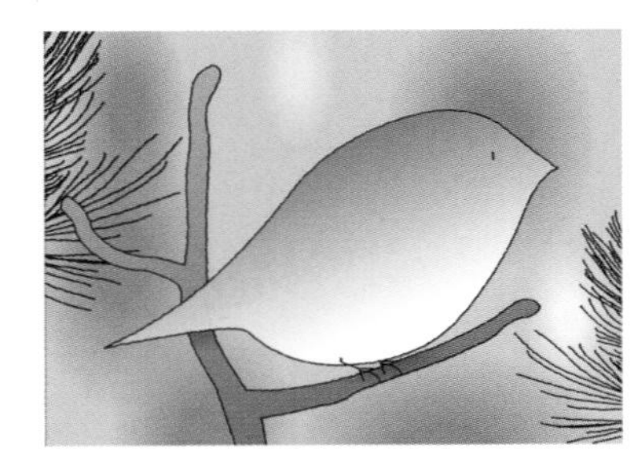

TRADITIONAL CEL ANIMATION was created by drawing on transparent plastic sheets known as cels and then by making slight changes on each new sheet to introduce movement. Characters were placed over a background sheet, and the composite image was captured by a movie camera. When a character held its position, multiple pictures could have been taken, but the result would have been an unnatural stillness. Instead the artists traced a copy of the character onto other cels in what was known as a traceback to give the lines a continuous liveliness, also known as line boil, while the character remained still.

More recently, line boil has become a popular technique for digital 2D animation to introduce movement into otherwise still shots. Let's draw a cute little bird and use frame-by-frame animation for quick stroke changes as a cheat for creating line boil.

VECTOR ILLUSTRATION: MYRA FERGUSON

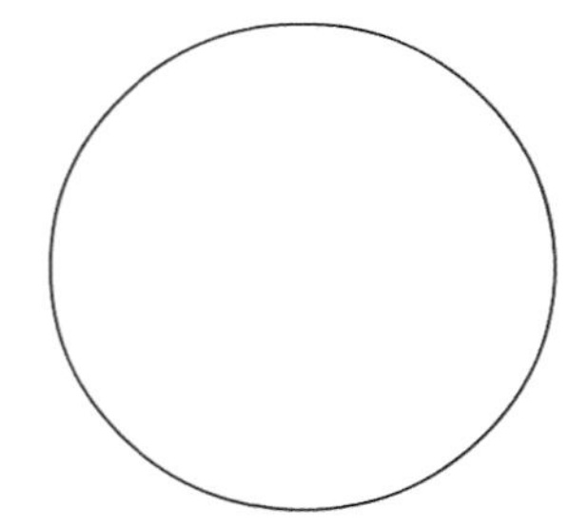

1 With the Oval Tool O, place a circle with a 2 pt. solid black stroke and no fill in the center of the Stage.

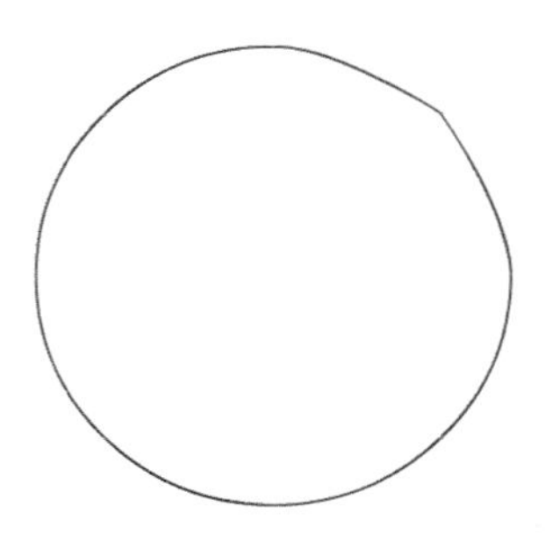

2 Select the circle with the Subselection Tool A. Select the Convert Anchor Point Tool C and click the anchor point on the upper right of the circle.

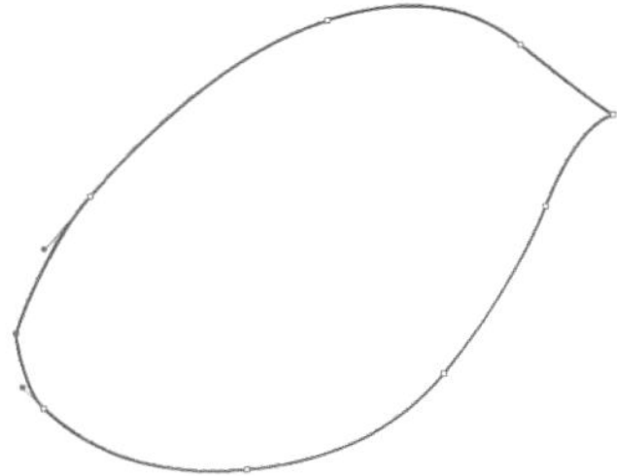

5 Select the Convert Anchor Point Tool C and click on the point opposite the beak to make a tail by pulling it out with the Subselection Tool A. Reshape as needed.

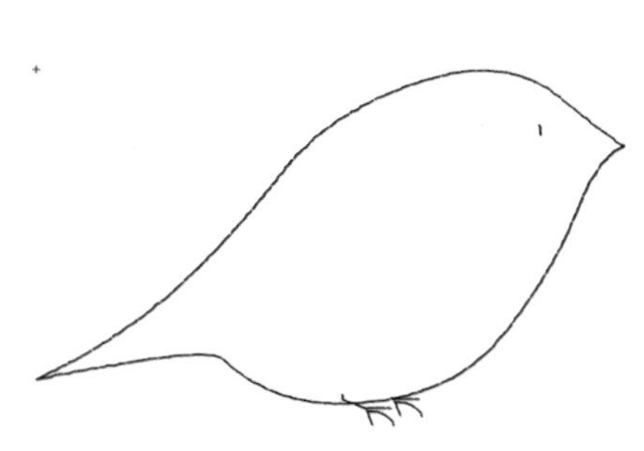

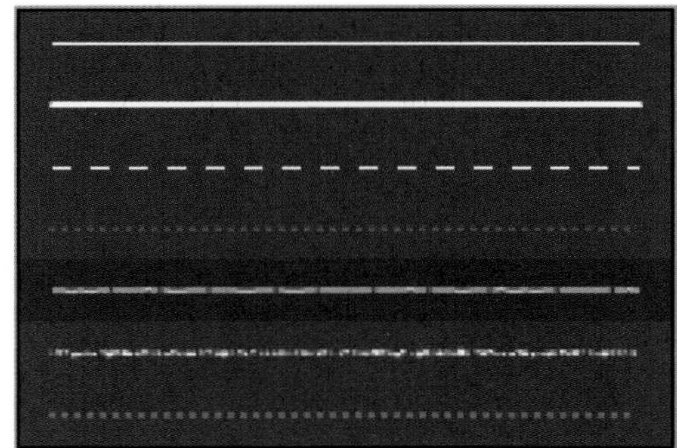

8 Double-click the bird instance on the Stage to enter Isolation Mode. In the Property panel, use the Stroke style drop-down menu to change the stroke to Ragged.

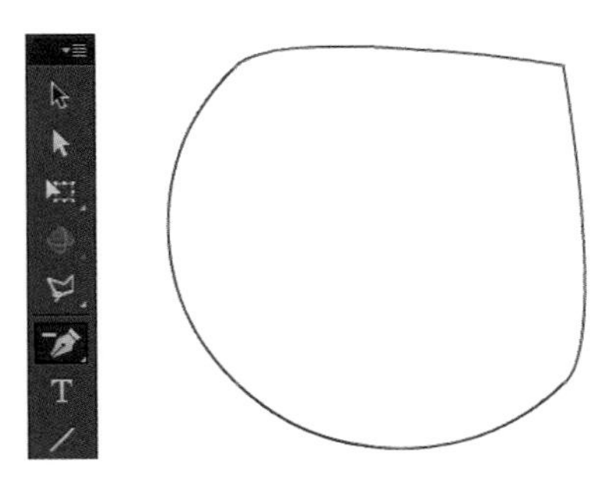

3 Use the Delete E L E T E Anchor Point Tool—to remove the anchor points at the top and on the right.

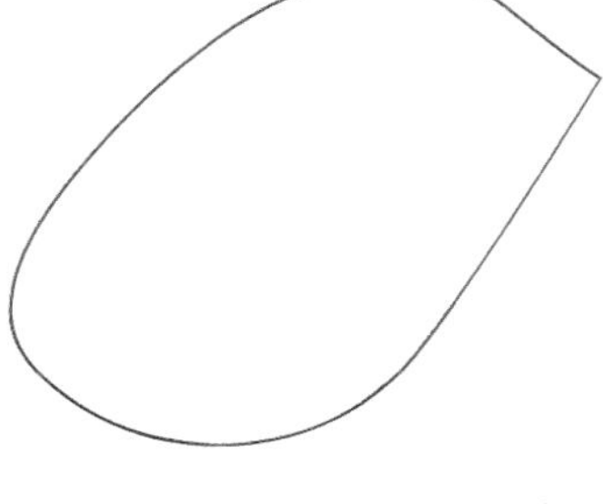

4 Adjust the shape so that the point becomes a beak and the rest of the shape becomes a head and body for the bird.

6 Use the Pencil Tool Shift Y or Paint Brush Tool Y to add bird feet and a line for an eye with the stroke still set at solid, black, and 2 pt.

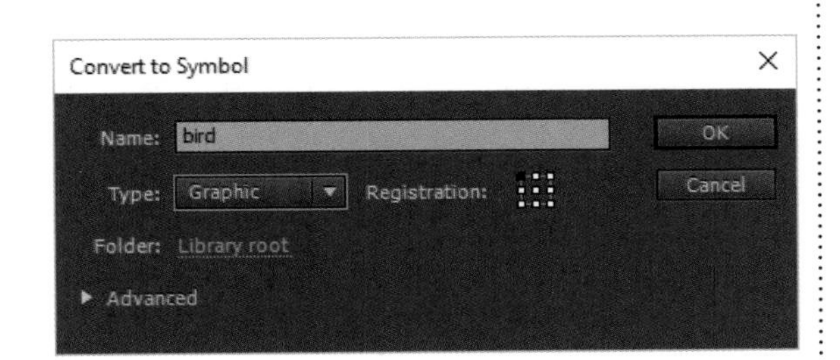

7 Use ⌘ ctrl A to select all of the bird and convert it to a Graphic symbol F8.

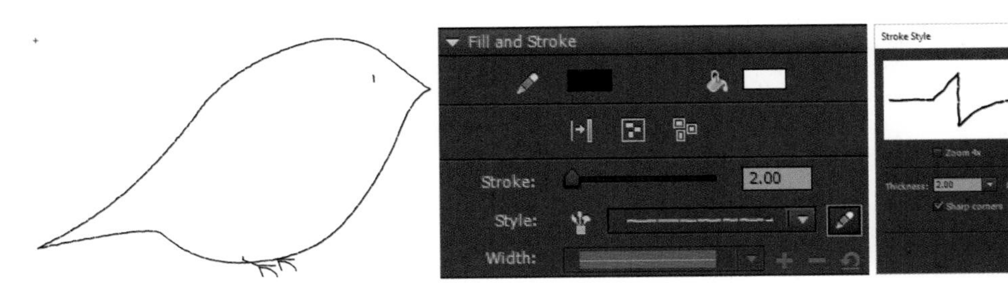

9 In the Timeline, insert a new keyframe F6 at frame 2. Select all ⌘ ctrl A and click the Edit Stroke Style button in the Property panel. Keep all the settings but change Pattern to Random.

Frame-by-Frame Animation (cont.)

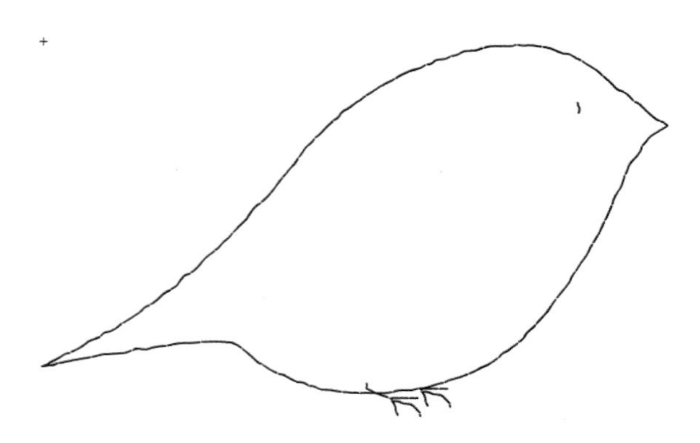

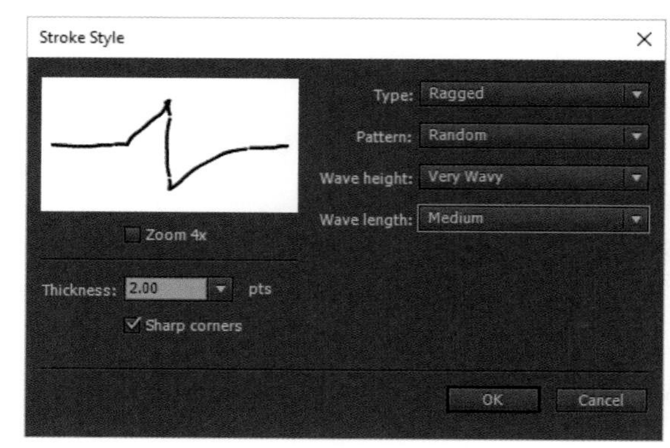

10 Insert another new keyframe F6 at frame 3. Select all ⌘ ctrl A and edit the stroke again. This time change Pattern back to Simple, Wave height to Very Wavy, and Wave length to Medium.

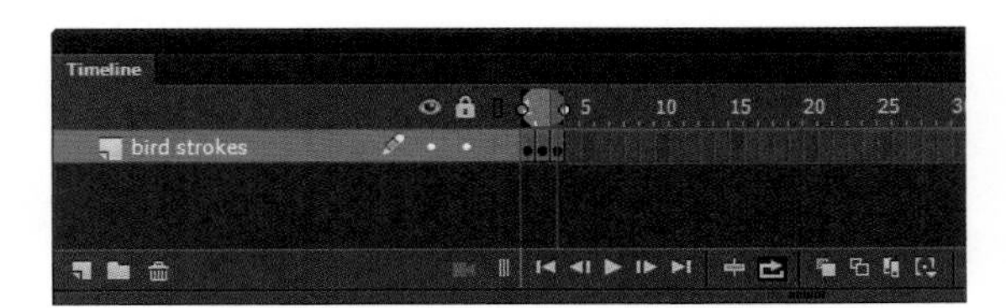

11 At the bottom of the Timeline, press the Loop button ⌥ alt Shift L and Play Enter. If the fps (frames per second) are set to 24 in the Properties panel, Pause Enter and set it to 12 FPS.

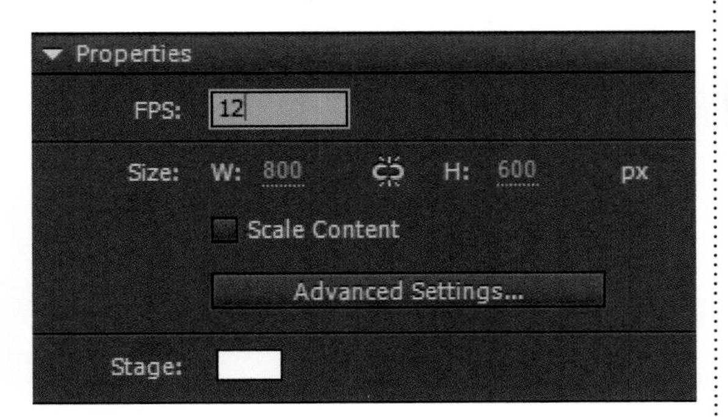

12 Return to the main Timeline. The graphic instance should be set to Loop from the first frame. Add as many frames in the Timeline as needed to make the segment the duration you need.

HOT TIP

Apply the same ragged stroke to any other lines you add to your image for consistency; however, keep the background elements motionless in order to draw attention to your character. To further distinguish the background from the foreground, you can desaturate the background colors.

Distribute Symbols and Bitmaps to Keyframes

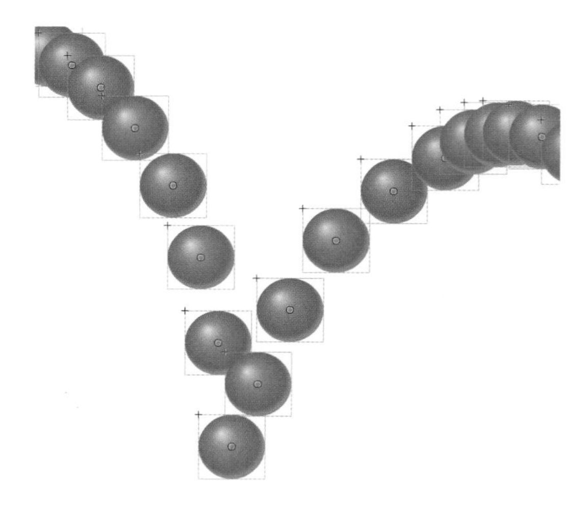

SOMETIMES CERTAIN FEATURES COME ALONG that allow you to take advantage of them in ways they may not have been originally designed. It took some thinking on my part to come up with an example to showcase the new Distribute to Keyframes feature. Once the idea came to me, I quickly realized how much of a game changer this feature could be for anyone using Animate for frame-by-frame animation. Typically, frame-by-frame animation requires an image or a series of images to be drawn or positioned across individual subsequent keyframes, a technique that requires frequent testing to make sure the timing is right. With Distribute to Keyframes, you can create all your "animation" on a single keyframe with the convenience of seeing the spatial relationship of the object throughout each pose or in this example, each position.

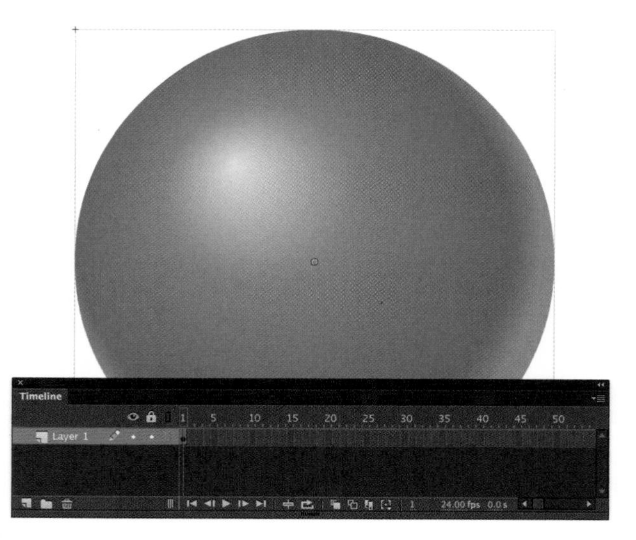

1 In frame 1 of a new document, I created a simple ball graphic using the Oval Tool O and a radial gradient for depth. The plan is to animate this ball bouncing from left to right across the Stage.

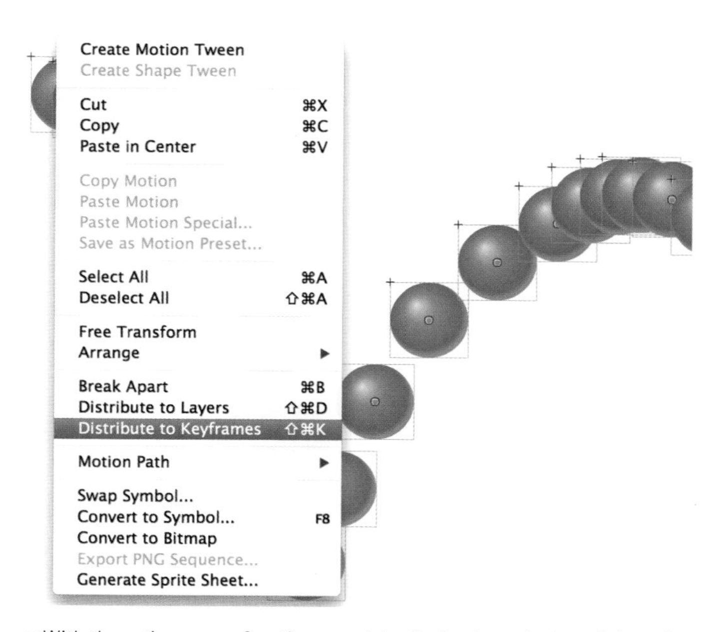

4 With the entire range of motion complete, the hard part is done. Select all ⌘ ctrl A, then right-click over any of the selected objects on the Stage and select Distribute to Keyframes from the context menu.

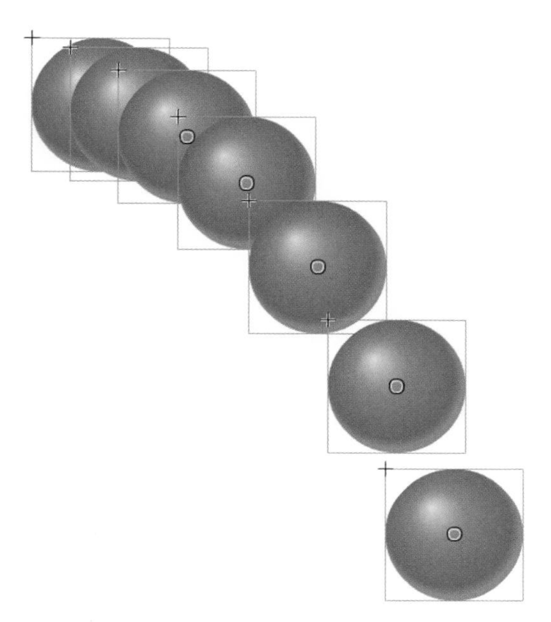

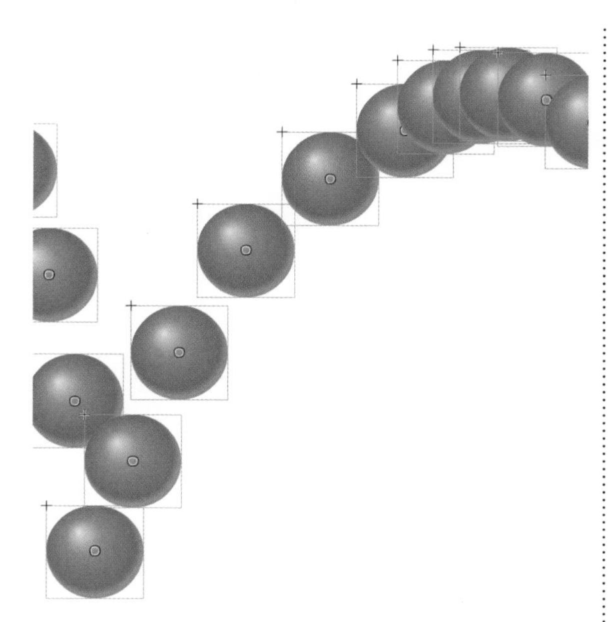

2 Hold down the Option/Alt key ⌥ alt and then click and drag the symbol to duplicate it. Position it using the Selection Tool V. To simulate gravity the ball must increase speed as it descends, otherwise known as an easing in effect. The distance between each ball gradually increases as the ball arcs downward.

3 Here the duplicate ball symbols are positioned in an ascending arc with the space between each of them decreasing to simulate an easing-out movement. The advantage to animating this way is seeing the entire range of motion of the object, which provides an overall sense of timing based on the intended action.

HOT TIP

Distribute to Keyframes works with objects other than symbol instances. You can distribute grouped objects, Object Drawings, and imported bitmaps. Distribute to Keyframes even works with multiple objects of various formats. Select any combination of bitmaps, symbols, grouped objects, and Object Drawings, and you can still distribute them all to keyframes with a single command.

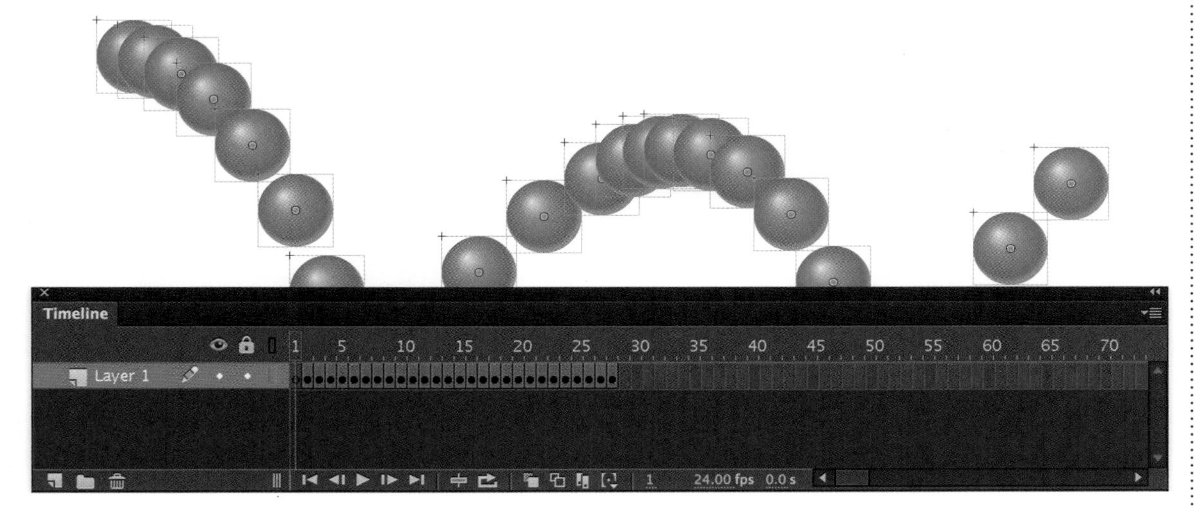

5 Animate CC will distribute each selected object to its own keyframe. Play the Timeline to see the animation of the ball bouncing. The timing will be dictated by a combination of the document frame rate as well as the relative placement of each object. Creating animation using the Distribute to Keyframes method has become a part of my workflow whenever possible. In situations such as the ball bouncing example, it can be a real time saver to create your animation as a single image first, and then let Animate do the hard part by distributing everything to keyframes.

Variable Stroke Width Animation Guide

SNAPPING A MOVIE CLIP to a guide to animate movement is a technique that's been around for a while, but now you can apply the Width Tool to the path to get a new effect—animated scaling based on the variable stroke width Animation Guide.

To illustrate how the variable width affects scaling, let's animate something that appears to move away from and then toward you. We'll use a firefly (also known as a lightning bug if you're from anywhere near Missouri). I didn't realize until I moved to Colorado that there aren't many fireflies here (at least not the ones that produce much light), but in Missouri when the sun goes down in the summer they come out. They light up and fly around and kids try to catch them. It's fun!

VECTOR ILLUSTRATION: MYRA FERGUSON

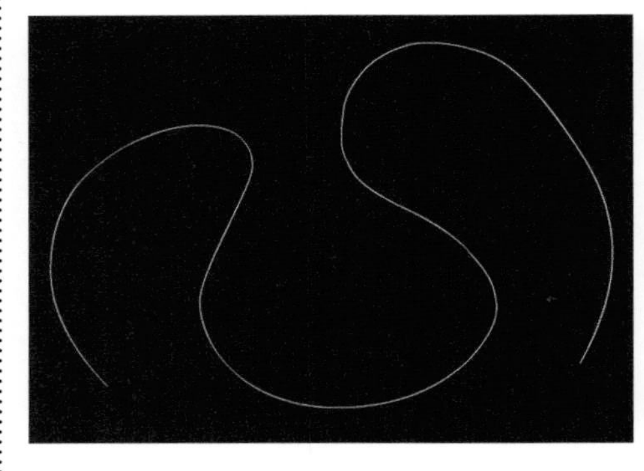

1 Let's draw a swirly stroke. You can use the Pencil Tool Shift Y set to smooth or the Paint Brush Tool Y to draw some big curves. This stroke will be the path where the firefly travels.

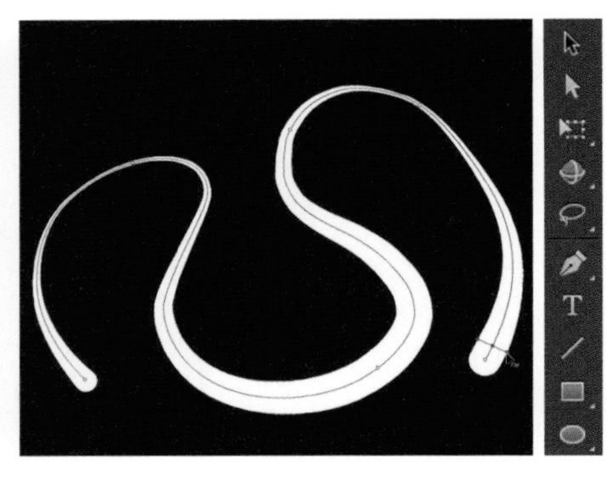

2 Select the Width Tool U (or choose a Variable Width Profile from the Width drop-down menu in the Fill and Stroke section of the Properties panel), click on various lengths of the curve to change parts of it to be very wide and others to be very narrow.

6 The firefly could have been a Graphic instance, but let's add an extra yellow glow filter. To add a filter, the instance needs to be a Movie Clip.

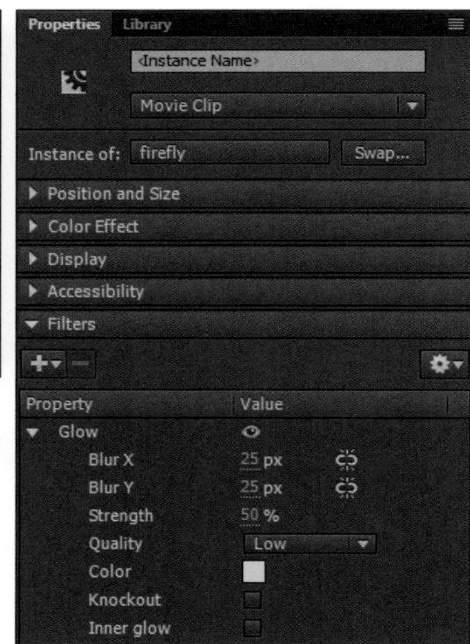

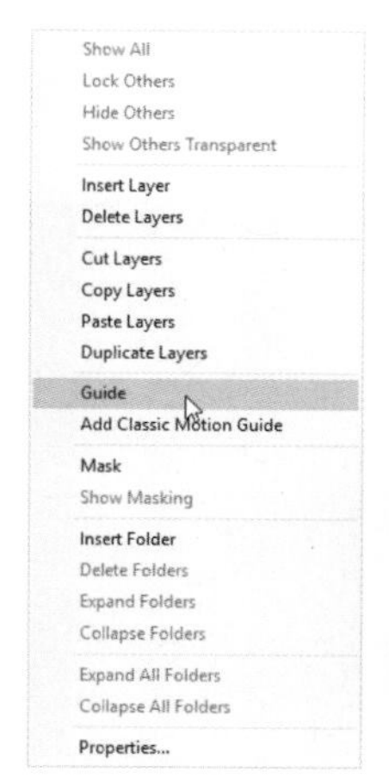

3 Right-click on the layer and change it to a guide layer.

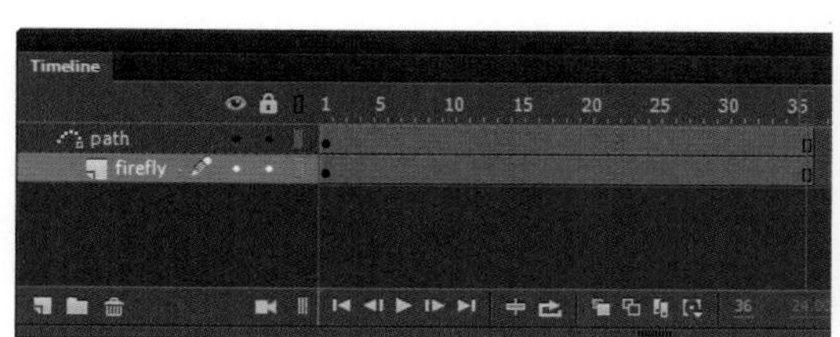

4 Now let's add a layer for the firefly. Move this layer beneath the guide layer so that it indents. Insert frames up to frame 36. Click the Show Layer as Outlines box on the path guide layer, so you can more easily see the firefly and the path.

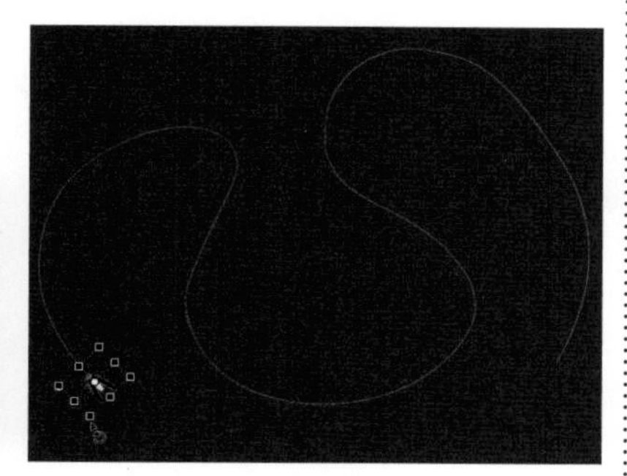

5 Drag the instance of the firefly Movie Clip out to the Stage where it snaps to one end of the path. Rotate it so that it orients to the direction of the path.

7 On frame 36 on the firefly layer, add a keyframe and move the firefly to the end of the path where it snaps. Rotate it again, so it maintains its orientation.

8 Along the firefly span, right-click and Create Classic Tween. Notice the options in the Properties panel after the tween is created. We'll want Snap, Orient to Path, Scale along Path, and Scale selected.

9 Turn on Colored Onion Skin ⌥ alt Shift O to see how the width affects the scale of the firefly. I changed the past color to gold by going to Edit > Preferences... ⌘ ctrl U under Onion Skin Color.

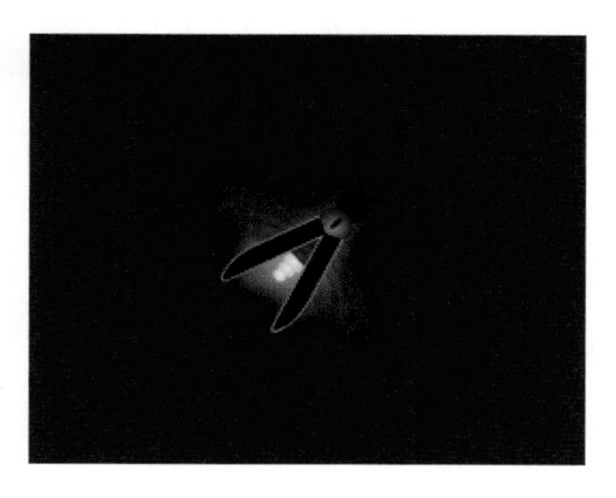

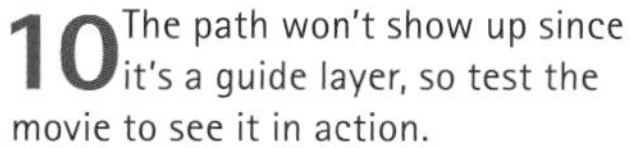

10 The path won't show up since it's a guide layer, so test the movie to see it in action.

HOT TIP

Scale isn't the only attribute of the guide path that can affect the animation. Color can affect it too. Set the stroke color to the rainbow linear gradient and with the tween span selected, check Color Along Path in the Properties panel. It may be an exaggerated example, but it helps you to more clearly see the effect.

Motion and Classic Tweens

SO MUCH HAS CHANGED with Animate, yet so much has remained the same. One of the fundamental features of Animate animation is tweening, and we have two different tween models. What are the differences between these? What tween model should you use and when? If you remember one thing about these two tween methods in Animate CC, the Classic Tween is frame based while the Motion Tween is object based. There are advantages and disadvantages to using either, and the difference depends on what kind of object you are animating and what that object needs to do. This example compares both tweening methods to show how they can both be used depending on your animation needs.

Motion Tweens have more than one type of keyframe. The black circular dot in the first frame of the span indicates the assigned target object. If this dot is hollow (white), it means the object has been removed and a new object can be assigned.

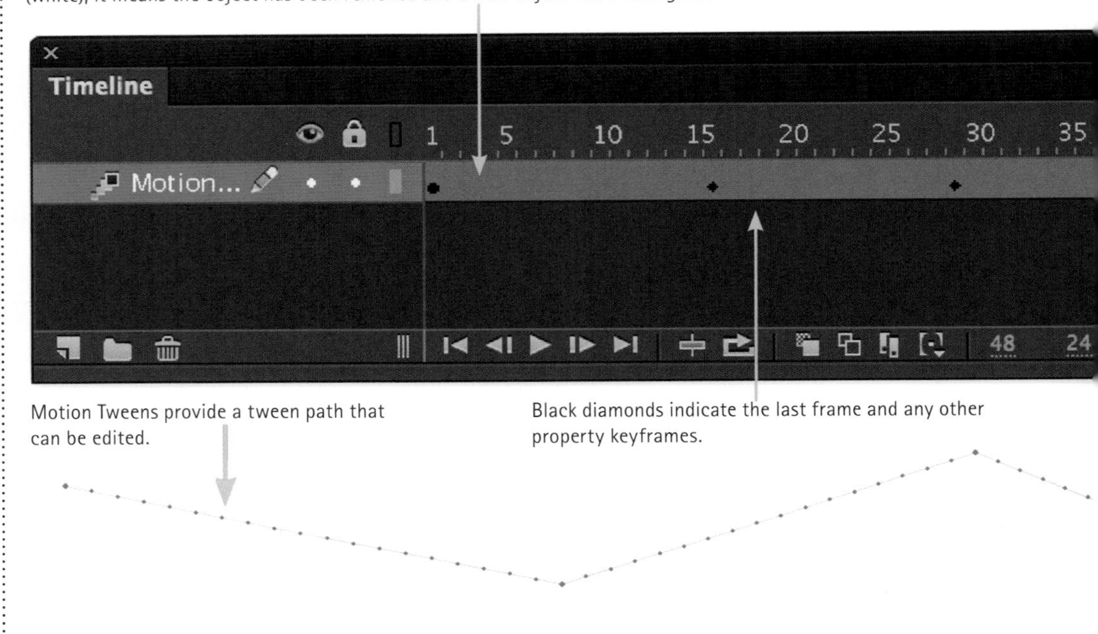

Motion Tweens provide a tween path that can be edited.

Black diamonds indicate the last frame and any other property keyframes.

A black dot at the beginning keyframe with a black arrow and blue background indicates a Classic Tween.

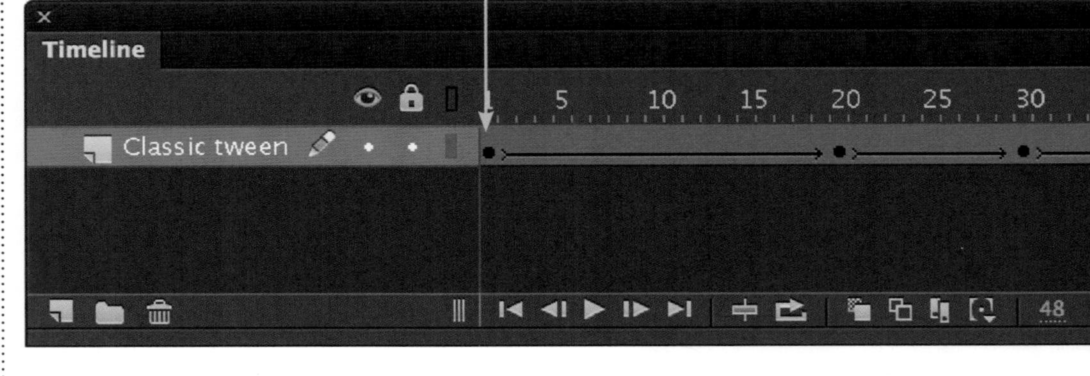

Use Classic Tweens to animate between two different color properties, such as tint and alpha transparency. Motion Tweens are limited to one color effect per tween.

Motion Tweens are indicated by a solid light blue colored layer span. Unlike the Classic Tween span, there are no horizontal dashed or solid lines or arrows indicating a broken or completed tween.

Classic Tweens cannot be saved as Motion Presets.

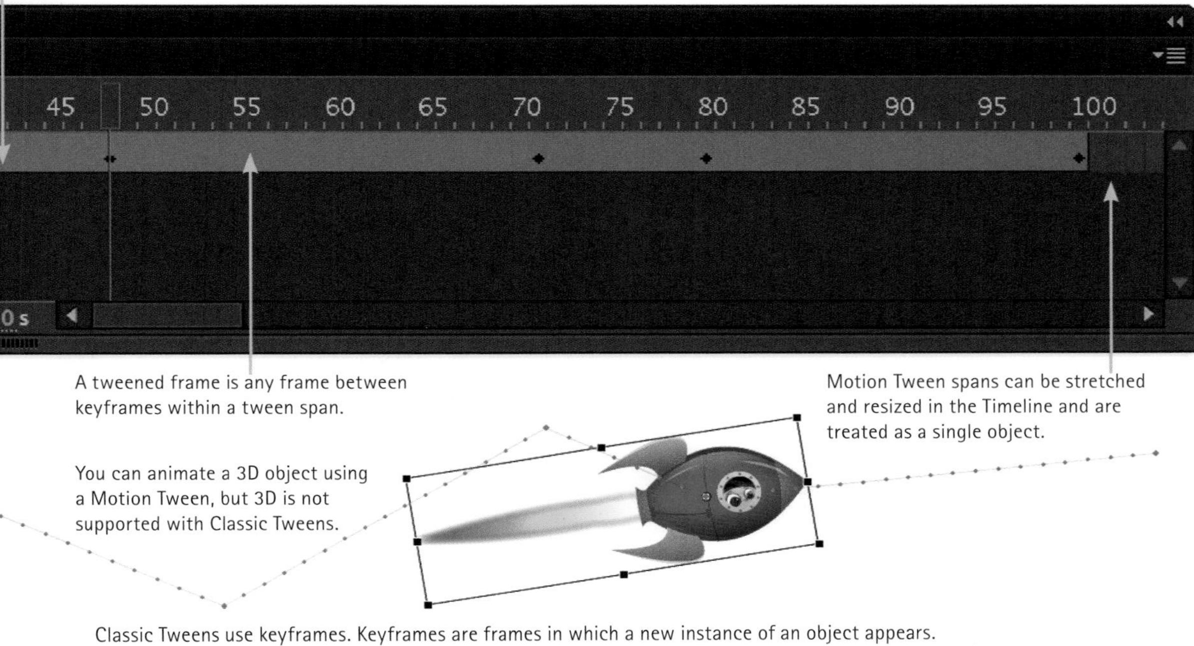

A tweened frame is any frame between keyframes within a tween span.

Motion Tween spans can be stretched and resized in the Timeline and are treated as a single object.

You can animate a 3D object using a Motion Tween, but 3D is not supported with Classic Tweens.

Classic Tweens use keyframes. Keyframes are frames in which a new instance of an object appears.

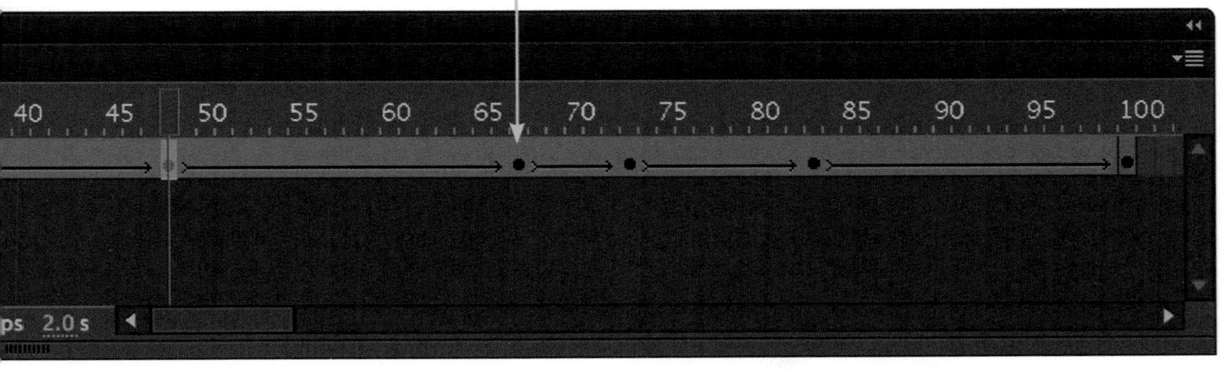

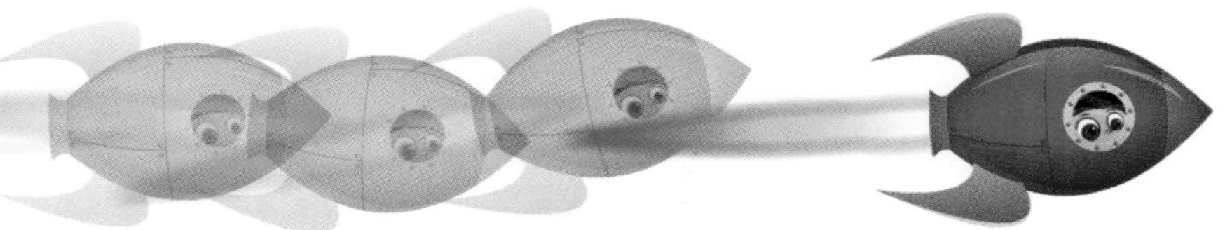

Classic Tweens cannot be stretched and resized in the Timeline like Motion Tween spans can. Classic Tweens are composed of frames that have to be selected individually and inserted or removed in order to stretch or shorten the animation.

HOT TIP

It's a little tricky but possible to hack the one color effect per Motion Tween limitation. Use the Advanced style, which combines all the settings for Brightness, Tint, and Alpha numerically by channel. If you're not sure what values to use, that's okay. Animate can tell you. Say you want to set both Tint and Alpha. Set the style to Tint and select your color. Then go to Advanced and adjust the Alpha value. Before going on to another frame, jot the values down for what you intend to make each keyframe. Then you can set your keyframes by selecting Advanced and enter those values. If you try to get the values while on different keyframes, Animate thinks you meant to switch the color effect property and removes the previously set Advanced property keyframe.

Creating Motion Tweens

THINK OF THE MOTION Tween as a Classic Tween on steroids, allowing you to animate each property individually across an entire motion span, which was difficult if not impossible with Classic Tweens. One of the most popular Timeline-related enhancement requests is now a reality—the ability to lengthen and shorten the Motion Tween and have all keyframes interpolated automatically. With Classic Tweens lengthening and shortening can only be done manually—and the more layers, frames, and keyframes, the more of a nightmare this process can be. Let's take a look at more differences between these two tweening methods.

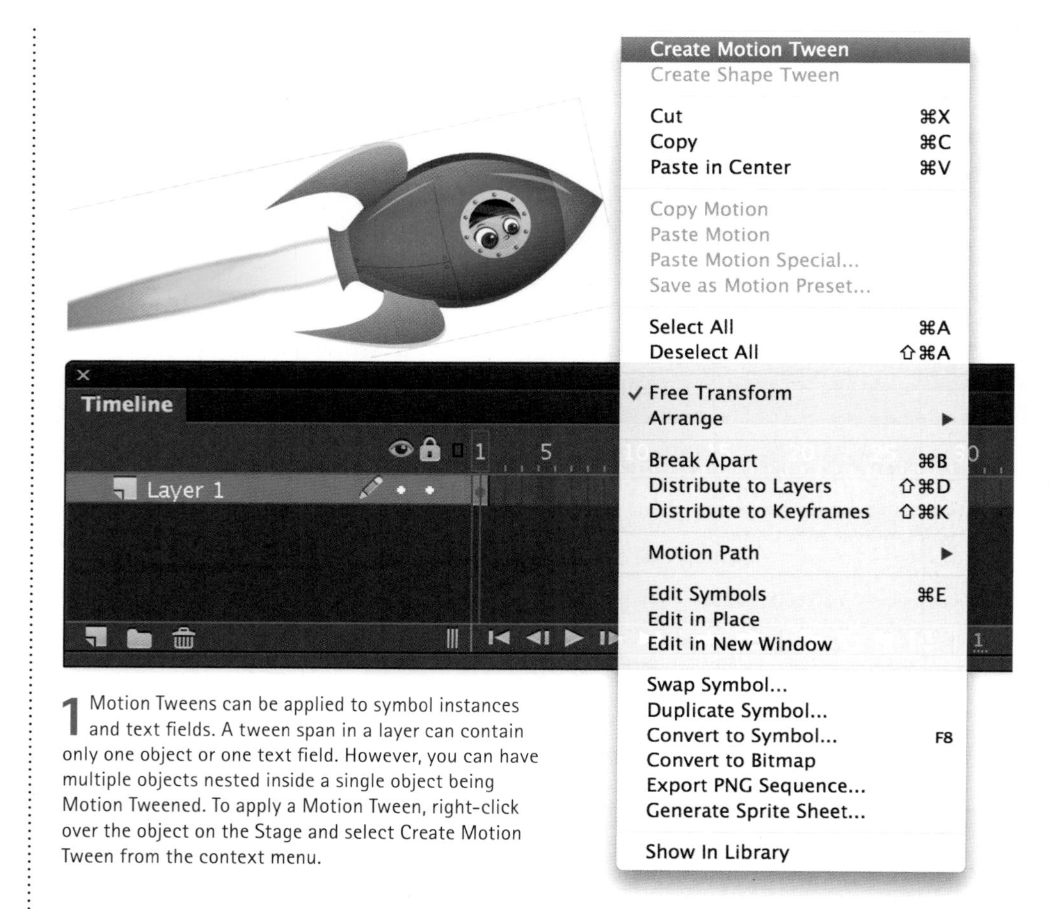

1 Motion Tweens can be applied to symbol instances and text fields. A tween span in a layer can contain only one object or one text field. However, you can have multiple objects nested inside a single object being Motion Tweened. To apply a Motion Tween, right-click over the object on the Stage and select Create Motion Tween from the context menu.

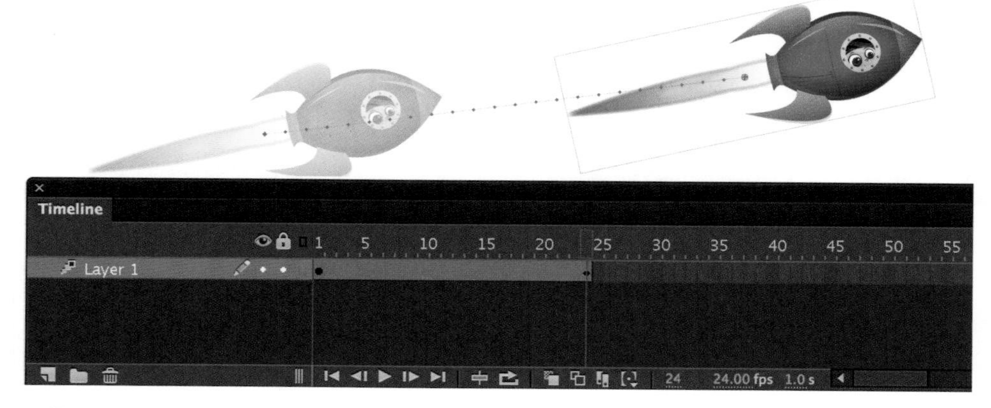

3 The quickest way to create an animation is to simply move the object to a new position on the Stage. Animate will automatically create a motion path that can be edited using the Selection Tool V and the Subselection Tool A.

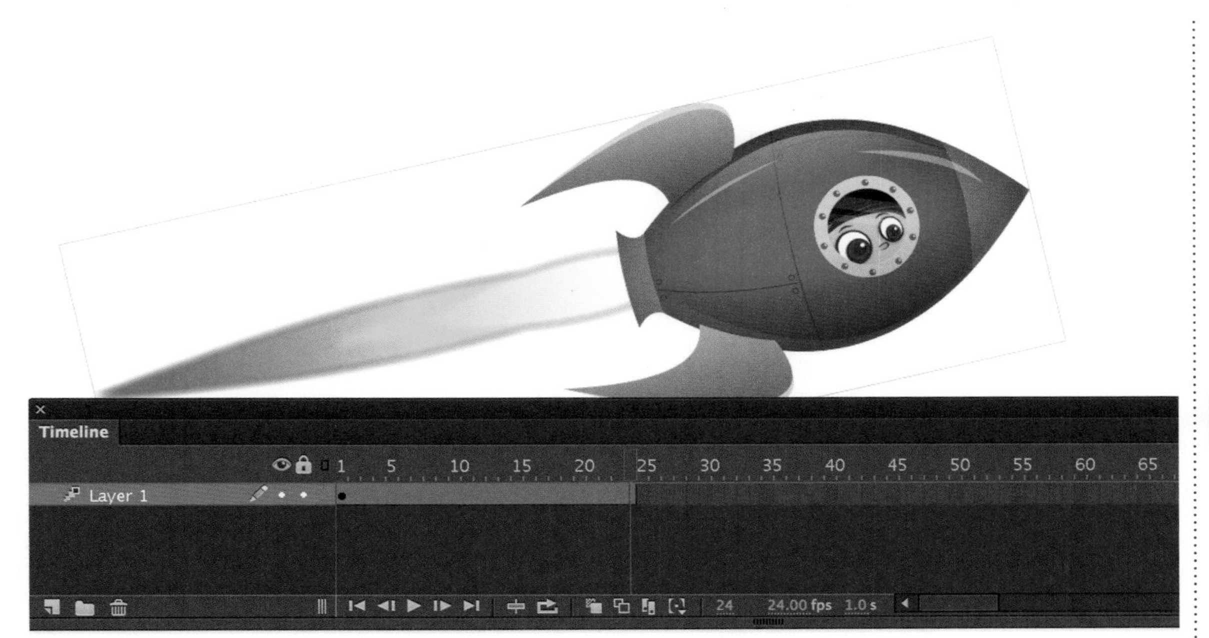

2 Animate automatically lengthens the tween span to accommodate a full second's worth of frames based on the document's frame rate. If your frame rate is set to 24 fps then your span becomes 24 frames long. The playhead is automatically positioned at the end of the tween span.

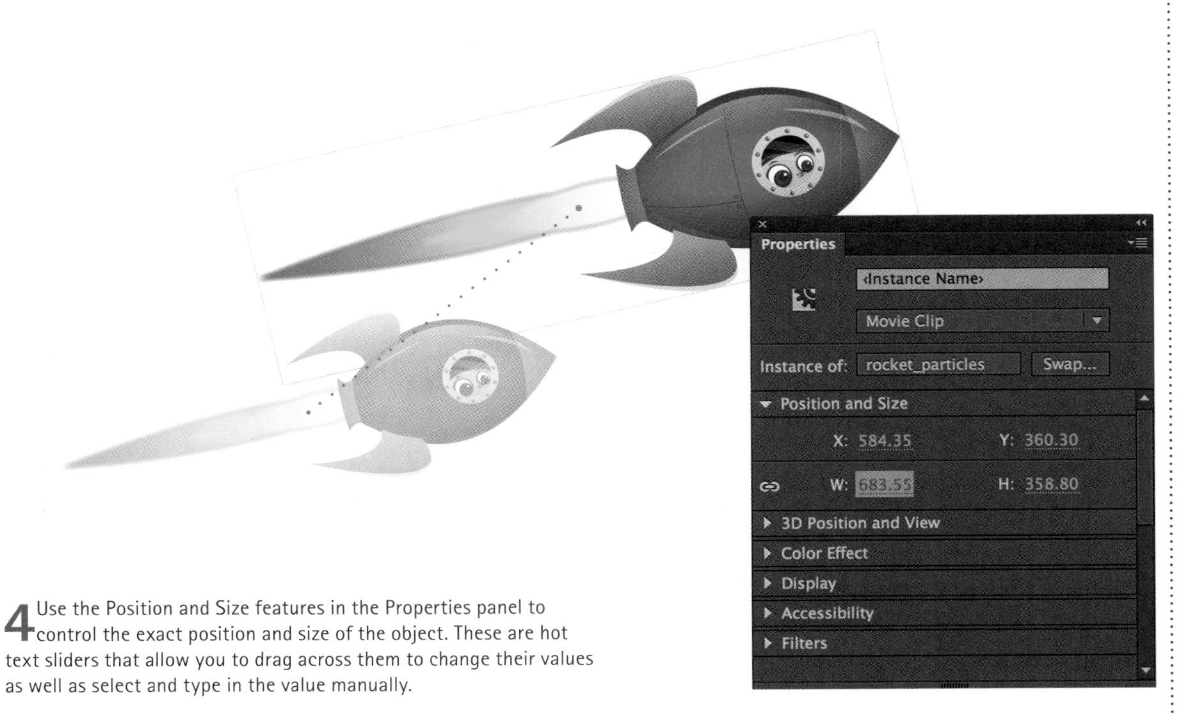

4 Use the Position and Size features in the Properties panel to control the exact position and size of the object. These are hot text sliders that allow you to drag across them to change their values as well as select and type in the value manually.

HOT TIP

The terms "keyframe" and "property keyframe" have two different meanings in Animate CC. The term "keyframe" refers to a frame in the Timeline in which a symbol instance appears on the Stage for the first time. The separate term "property keyframe" refers to a value defined for a property at a specific time or frame in a Motion Tween.

Working with Motion Spans

SO HOW DOES THIS MOTION Tween model work anyway? Not only has Adobe changed how tweens are created and applied but also how we work with frames, keyframes, and the tween span itself. The Motion Tween is very different from its predecessor visually, sans any dashed or solid horizontal arrows or vertical lines indicating the "sync" feature being turned off. The Motion Tween span is simple and straightforward, uncluttered, and unadulterated, yet provides the ability to create sophisticated animations that go beyond the capabilities of the Classic Tween method.

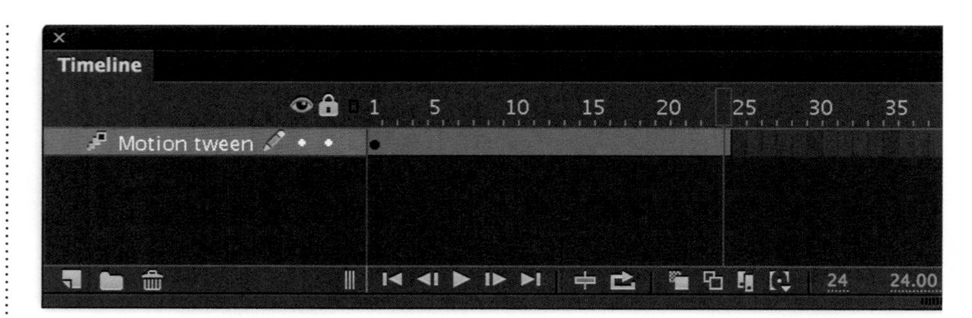

1 It's ironic that the Motion Tween span looks so plain and simple yet offers so much power and flexibility. You will not find horizontal lines with arrowheads between keyframes. You will not see dashed lines signifying broken tweens or vertical lines representing non-synced keyframes. Motion Tweens offer a brave new world for Animate tweeners, and to steal a line from animation legend Laith Bahrani, "All of your tweens have finally come true."

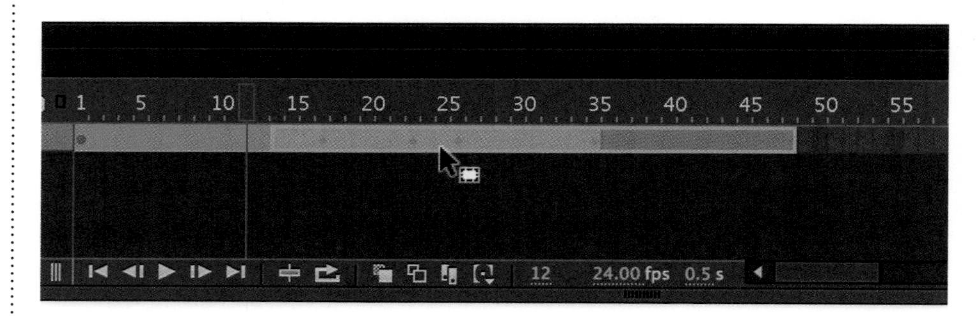

4 To move a span in the Timeline, ⌥ alt + click to select it and then click and drag it to a new location in the layer.

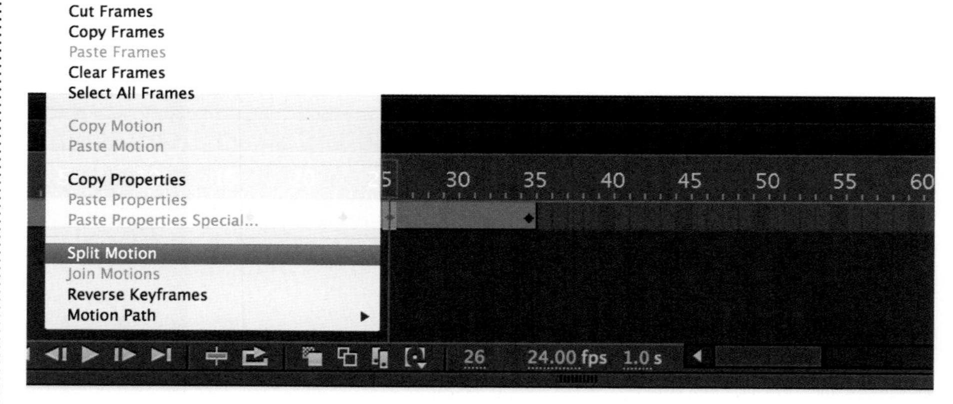

7 To split a tween span into two separate spans, ⌘ ctrl + click a single frame in the span where you want to split it, and then choose Split Motion from the span context menu.

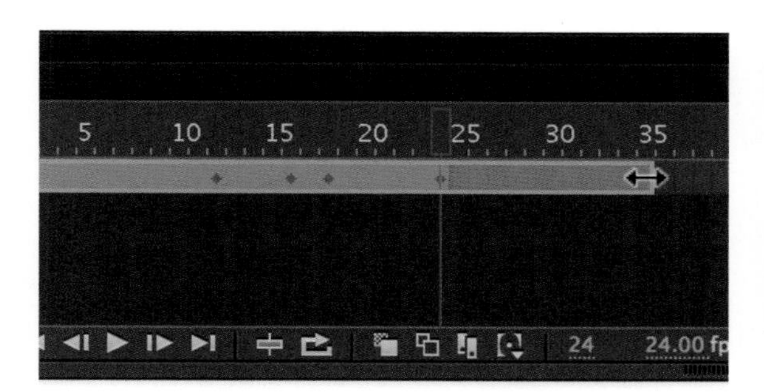

2 To lengthen the duration of your animation, drag either the left or right edge of the span to the desired frame. Animate will automatically interpolate all the keyframes in the span according to its new length. To add frames to a span without interpolating the existing keyframes, hold down Shift while dragging the edge of the span.

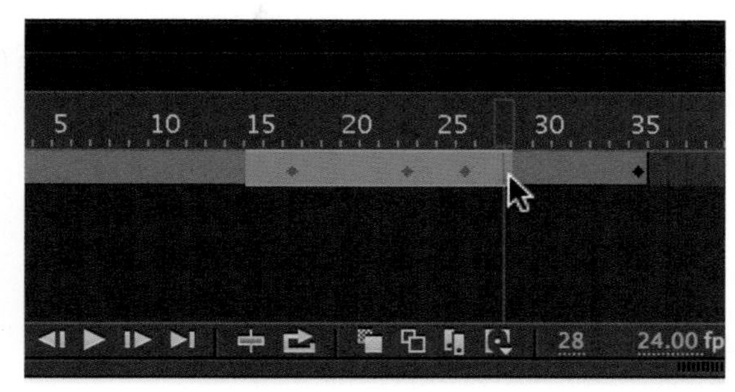

3 You can select a range of frames in a Motion span by dragging across the desired frames.

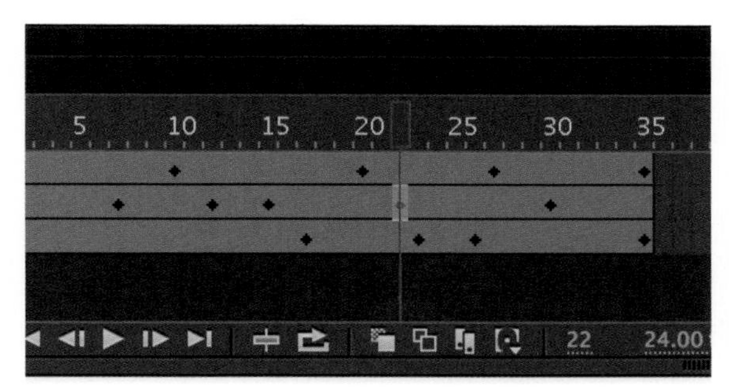

5 To select a single frame or keyframe in a Motion span, ⌘ ctrl + click the frame or keyframe. Once it's selected you can drag the keyframe to a new frame or ⌥ alt + click to duplicate it while dragging it to a new frame.

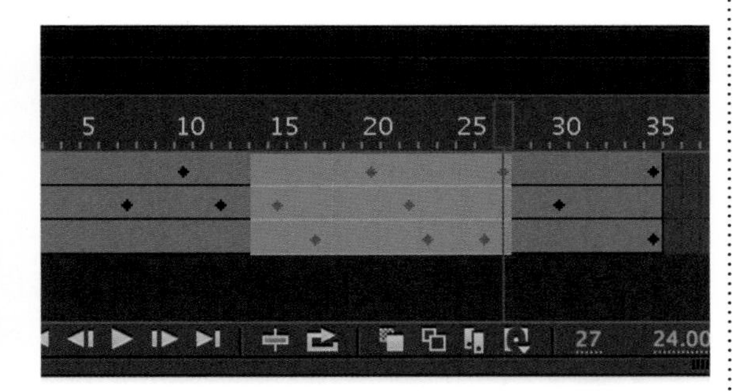

6 To select a range of frames in a Motion span, ⌘ ctrl + drag across the range of frames and layers you want to select.

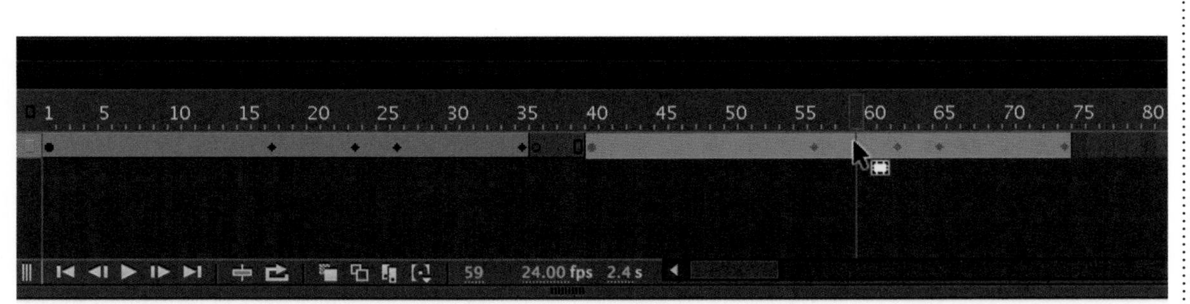

8 You can duplicate a Motion span by selecting it and then holding down the ⌥ alt key while dragging it to a new location. Using ⌥ alt + drag is a super easy way to duplicate an animation across layers and other Motion spans. If you drag a Motion span and overlap it with an existing span, the frames shared by both spans will be "consumed" by the span being moved into this position.

HOT TIP

When working with Motion spans, keep in mind that controlling nested animations inside a Graphic symbol (see "Lip Syncing, nesting method"), is very limited. Any settings for Graphic symbols (Loop, Play Once, and Single Frame) are applied once to the entire span. They cannot be applied to individual property keyframes in the span. Therefore, your ability to control nested animations is lost, which is the main reason why Adobe retained the Classic Tween method.

Editing Motion Paths

IF YOU'RE ALREADY FAMILIAR with Animate and the Classic Tween method, then you may have at one time or another experienced some frustrations trying to work with a frame-based tween model. Throw in the need to animate your object along a path, and your workload just increased even more. Previously, if we needed to animate an object along a path, a guide layer was first created, then the guide was linked to the object layer, and then the object was manually snapped to both ends of the path with the aid of the Snap tool. The Motion Tween method eliminates the need for all of these extra steps.

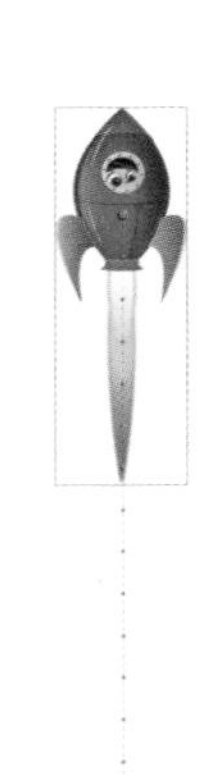

1 Right-click over the object and select Create Motion Tween. Animate automatically creates a Motion span in the Timeline. With the playhead over the last frame of the span, drag the object to a new location to expose the Motion path on the Stage.

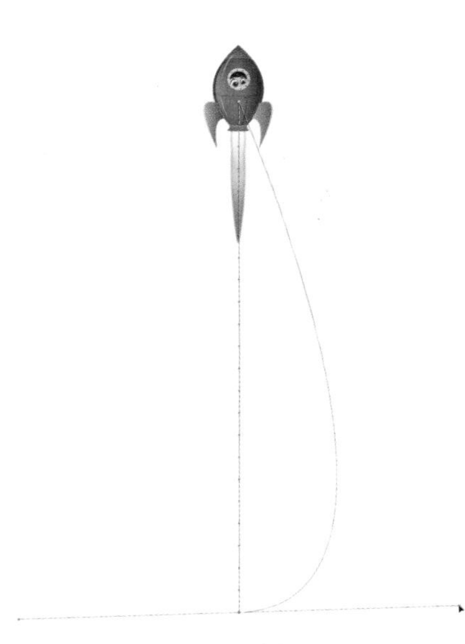

2 Use the Selection Tool V and click anywhere on the Stage away from the Motion path to ensure it is deselected. Reshape the path by simply dragging it anywhere along the segment.

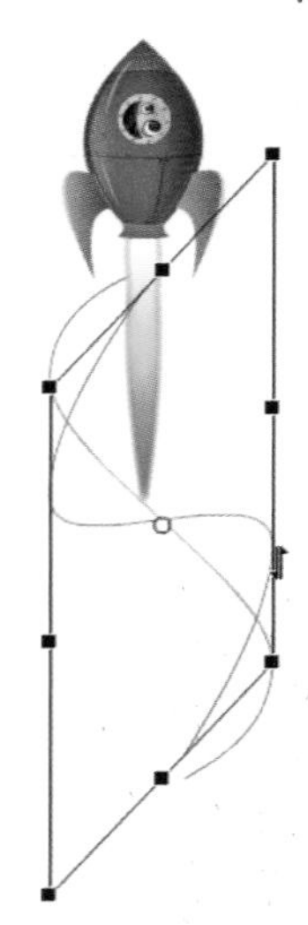

6 Use the Free Transform Tool Q to scale, rotate, and skew the Motion path as you would an object.

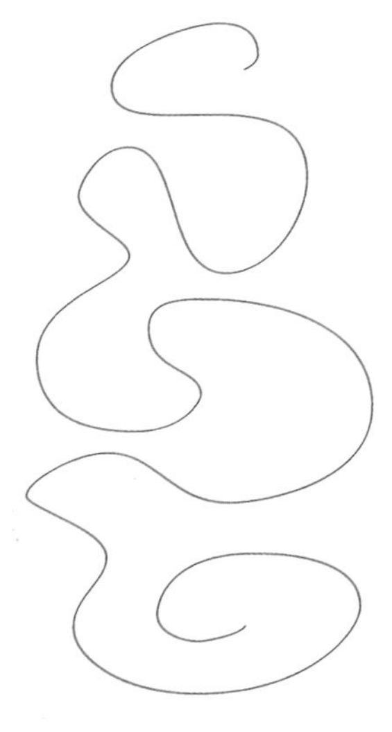

7 In some cases it may be easier to create a complex path by drawing it on a new layer with the Pencil Tool Shift Y or Pen Tool P.

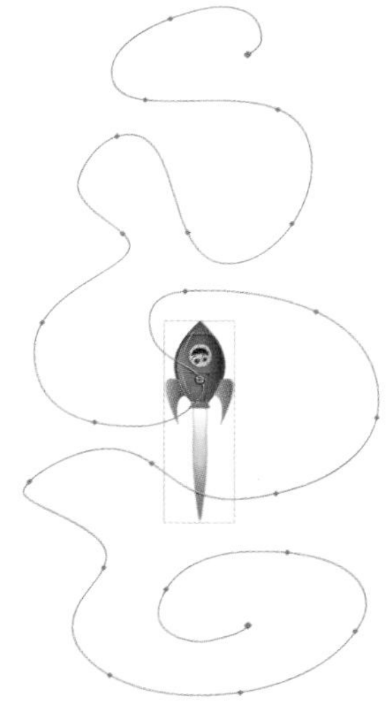

8 Select the stroke and then copy it ⌘ ctrl C. Select the Motion span in the Timeline or the object on the Stage and paste your stroke ⌘ ctrl V.

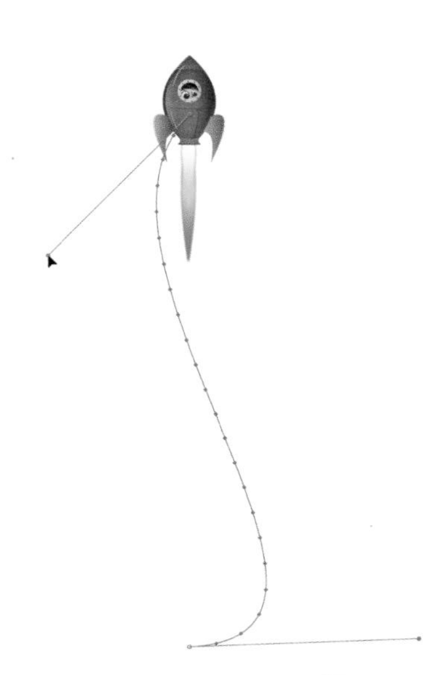

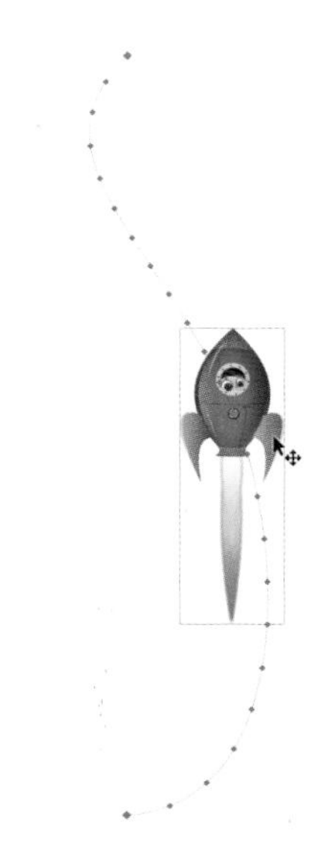

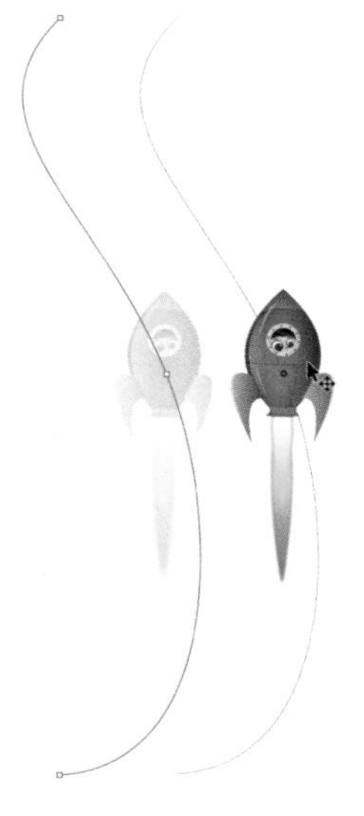

3 With the Subselection Tool (A), you can expose the control points and Bezier handles on the path that correspond to each position property keyframe. You can use these handles to reshape the path around the property keyframe points.

4 Position the playhead on a frame where the object resides midpoint along the path. Drag the object to reshape the path automatically.

5 You can reposition the entire Motion path and the animation by selecting it with the Selection Tool (V) and then dragging it to a new location.

HOT TIP

With the Subselection Tool (A) selected, hold down the ⌘/ctrl key to temporarily perform free transform to the Motion path.

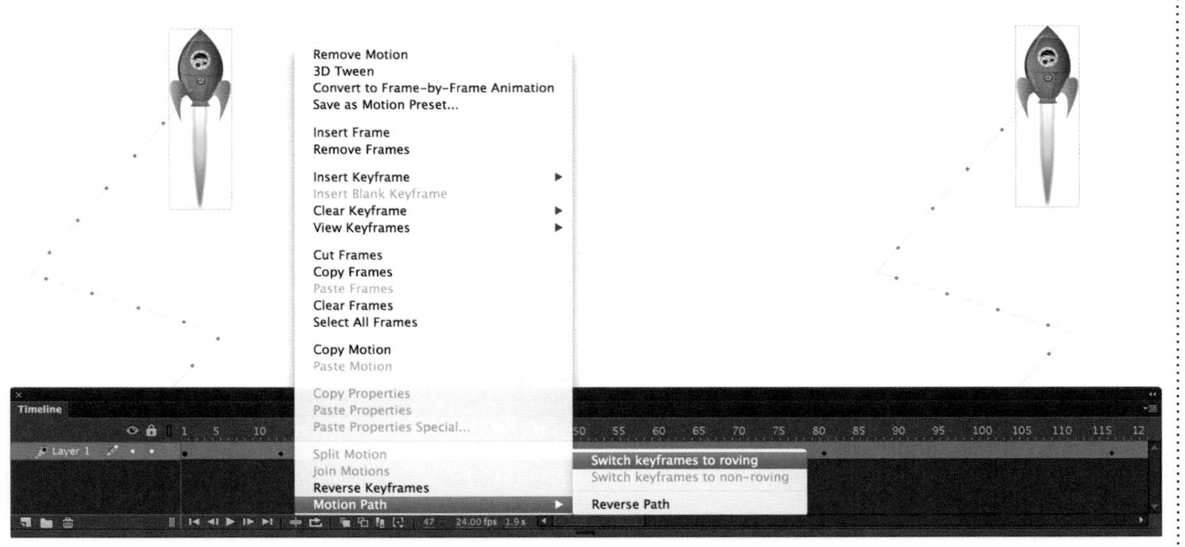

9 If you dig a little deeper into Animate CC's context menu, you may discover yet another feature called "switch keyframes to roving." The dictionary defines *roving* as "not assigned or restricted to any particular location, area, topic, etc." In keeping with that definition, Animate describes a *roving keyframe* as a "keyframe that is not linked to a specific frame in the Timeline." What a *roving keyframe* means in Animate terms is as follows: say you create an animation like the one pictured above where an object is following a path with several unequal segments. Each segment spans a different number of frames causing the object to travel at different speeds along each segment. If you want the object's movement to be constant, then right-click over the span and go to Motion Path and select *Switch keyframes to roving.*

Motion Presets

MOTION PRESETS ARE pre-built Motion Tweens that can be applied to an object on the Stage. With the object already selected, choose the desired preset from the default list in the Motion Presets panel and click the Apply button. The preset animation has been applied to your new object. The default presets provide a great starting point, but you'll likely want to make your own. Animate CC provides the ability to save your custom animations as presets that can be reused over and over. You can build up libraries of animations that are not only easily applied to any object on the Stage but can also be shared across the entire Animate design community.

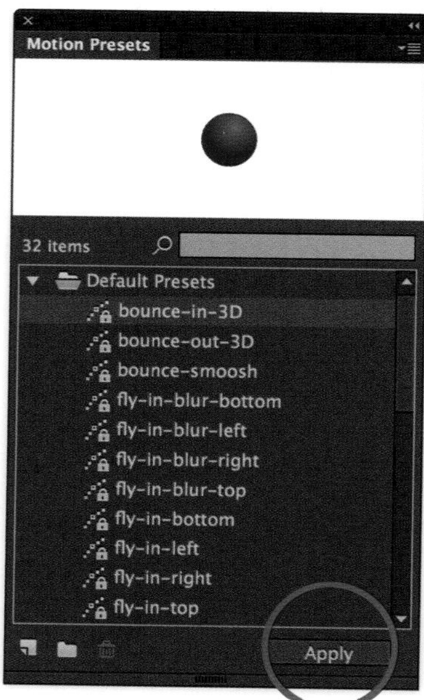

1 Go to Window > Motion Presets to open the Motion Presets panel. This panel looks a lot like the Library panel with its preview window on top and list of folders and preset objects below. Select a preset to preview it, and then select a Movie Clip symbol on the Stage. Click the Apply button to assign the motion to the object.

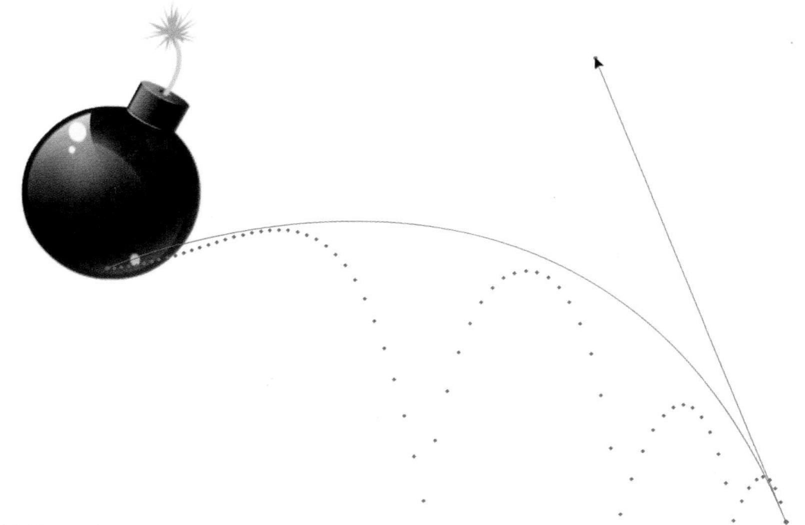

3 The Motion path can be edited using the Selection Tool V and Subselection Tool A. Here the Selection Tool is used to edit the curve of the path by dragging between its endpoints. Make sure you click on the Stage away from the path to make sure the path is deselected first. Use the Subselection Tool A to edit the control points using the Bezier handles that appear when selecting an endpoint or a property keyframe along the path. You can use these handles to reshape the path around the property keyframe points.

2 Once the preset is added, Animate applies a Motion Tween to the selected object. You can leave the animation as is or use it as a starting point by editing the Motion span in the Timeline as well as the spline path that the object now follows.

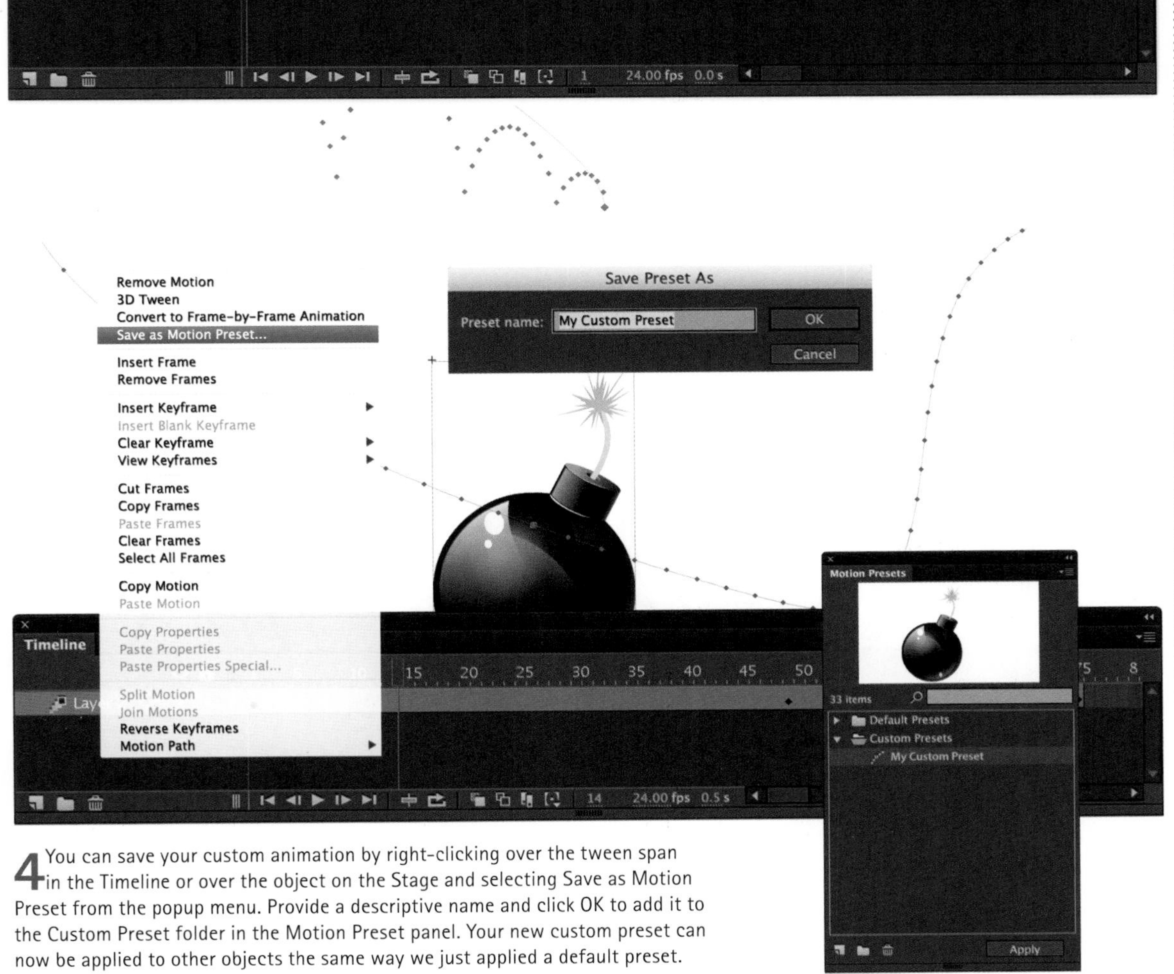

4 You can save your custom animation by right-clicking over the tween span in the Timeline or over the object on the Stage and selecting Save as Motion Preset from the popup menu. Provide a descriptive name and click OK to add it to the Custom Preset folder in the Motion Preset panel. Your new custom preset can now be applied to other objects the same way we just applied a default preset.

HOT TIP

To apply the preset so that its motion ends at the current position of the object on the Stage, select "End at current location" from the Motion Preset's drop-down menu located in its upper right corner.

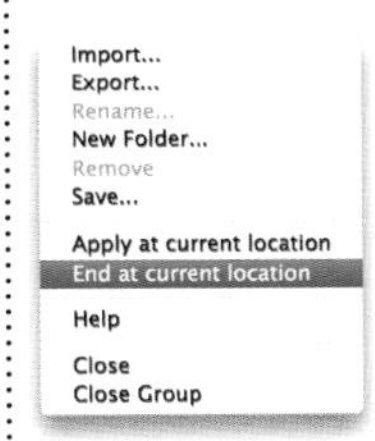

Motion Tweens and 3D

ANIMATE IS A 2D DESIGN and animation program. Making a 2D object appear to spin in a 3D space is a popular effect but very difficult due to the lack of that third dimension. Animate offers 3D capabilities in the form of 3D Rotation and Transformation tools.

1 Let's start with the image we want to spin. It can be anything you want, but I have chosen a coin because it is often the exact object many people want to animate spinning anyway. I'm using a bitmap of a 1 cent US penny, but you can use a coin of any currency either as an imported bitmap or drawn with Animate's drawing tools. Either way, make sure to convert the artwork to a Movie Clip symbol. Then right-click over it and select Create Motion Tween.

4 Next, position the playhead on the last frame and rotate the object the rest of the way so that it is facing us as it was in frame 1. Play back your animation to see the coin spin in 3D space.

5 But wait! Something's not right. Animate spins the coin to the right during the first half of the animation but then reverses direction during the second half. This reversal is easily corrected by placing the playhead on the frame just after the second keyframe and rotating the object slightly more.

2 Select the 3D Rotation tool **W** and with the playhead on a frame other than frame 1 drag the object along its *Y* axis (horizontally).

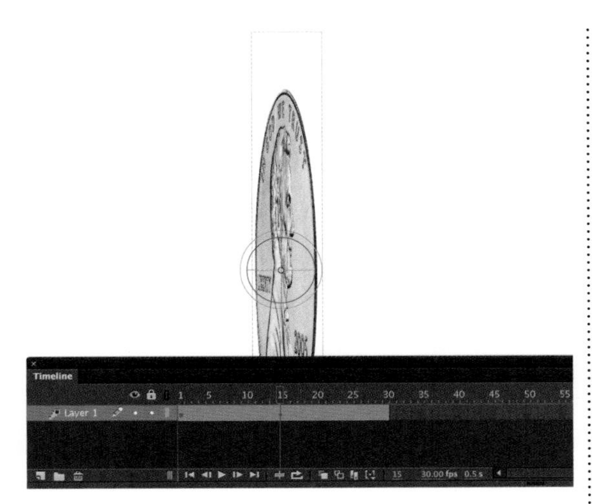

3 Do not try to rotate the coin 360° and expect Animate to know what you want it to do. You will need to divide the animation in half by stopping the coin rotation just short of the halfway point.

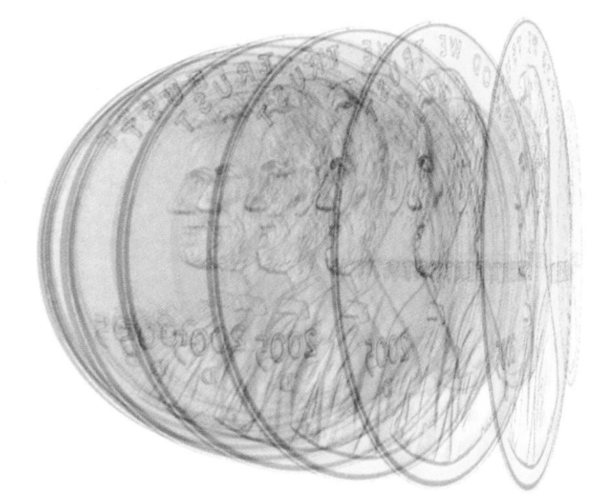

6 With the 3D rotation complete, try experimenting by editing the object's position relative to its center point. Edit the instance of the object by double-clicking on it. Move the object away from the center point (represented by the "+" crosshairs).

The farther you move the object from its center point, the more dramatic the effect of the 3D rotation. Here I turned on Onion Skin, so you can see each frame of the effect when the symbol has been moved horizontally from its own center point.

HOT TIP

Experiment further by adjusting the Perspective angle and Vanishing point in the "3D Position and View" section of the Properties panel. You can get some very interesting 3D perspectives by applying more depth to your object.

3D Position and View

ALTHOUGH THERE'S A GREAT NEW CAMERA in Animate that zooms and pans easily through a scene and that requires the movement of only one single object (the camera), it doesn't allow you to dolly into and out of or truck left and right through a scene. To simulate dolly or truck camera movements requires moving all the contents around the Stage. Having the ability to build scenes involving a background, middle ground, and foreground has always been a part of the production process.

Cameras only work in 3D environments, and up until now Animate has never supported 3D except for ActionScript-generated 3D engines. But if you are like me, that level of ActionScript prowess is beyond reach.

You can simulate a camera dolly in Animate CC with 3D Position and View, specifically a *Z* axis that we can utilize to create a virtual 3D Stage.

1 Setting up your Stage is the most time-consuming part of the process. The more elements in your scene, the more convincing the 3D effect will be. Here I have built a landscape consisting of background and middle ground elements, all converted to Movie Clip symbols and each residing on its own layer.

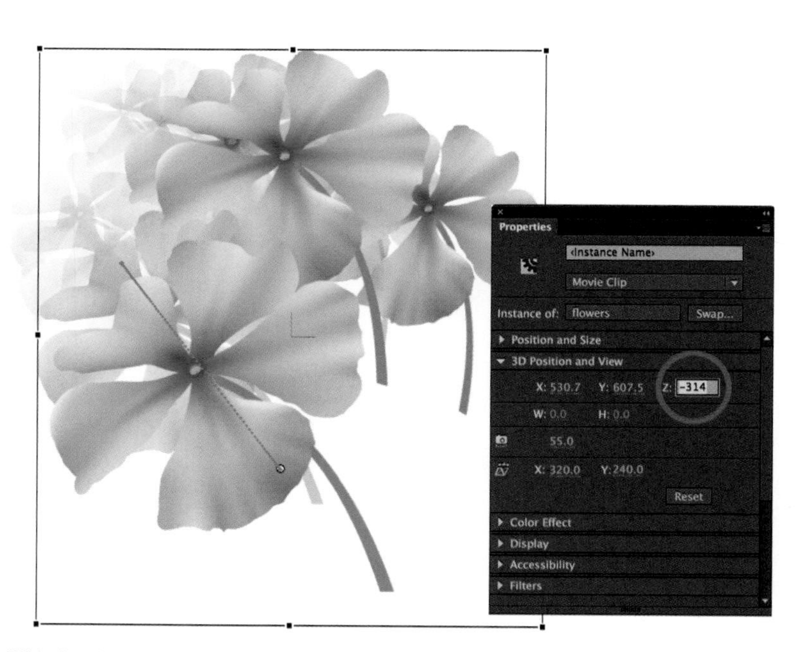

4 With the playhead in the last frame of the Motion span and the Properties panel open, select each Movie Clip individually and use the *Z* axis hot text slider to scale and position each object outside the Stage. You will likely need to edit the *X* and *Y* axes to position the object precisely where you want it.

2 To suggest an even more convincing sense of depth, I have included several foreground objects by adding several instances of a Movie Clip containing the flower graphic from Chapter 2.

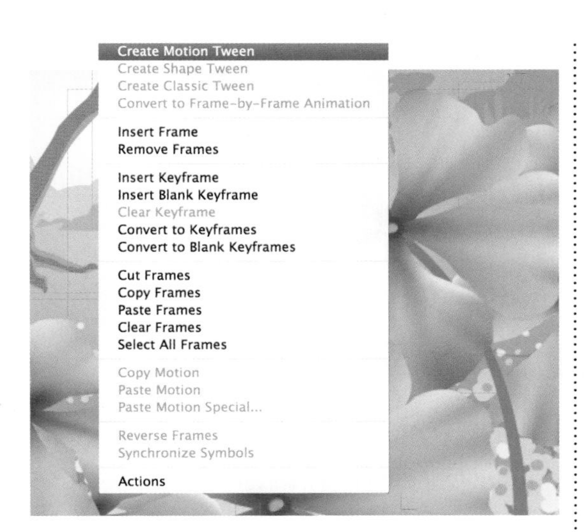

3 Determine what frame you want the "camera" dolly to begin and insert keyframes for all of the layers containing the objects that will eventually be moved along the *Z* axis. Apply Motion Tweens to each of the Movie Clips.

5 For this shot we are simulating a camera dolly, meaning the shot will move us into the scene. We simulate a dolly by scaling each object from its original size to a larger size. The direction of the dolly is dictated by the final position of each Movie Clip. The key to the success of this effect is how much the objects move in relation to each other. Foreground objects move faster and scale larger than the objects farthest away from us in the background. The sky and largest mountain range do not move at all, while the flowers closest to us move and scale the most. These differences in movement give the viewer a sense of true depth in the scene.

HOT TIP

Locate this source file from the downloadable assets. Scrub the Timeline with various layers turned on and off to see just how each object is animated relative to other objects on other layers. The parallax motion is a sophisticated effect viewable when all objects are seen together in motion.

The Bone Tool

EVERYDAY THINGS ARE JUST FUNNIER when you put a face and arms on them. Maybe you've seen these cute little GIFs of ordinary live-action objects with hand-drawn arms, legs, and faces expressing their reactions while engaged in otherwise run-of-the-mill activities. They are known as Real Life Doodles and have their own community on Reddit (www.reddit.com/r/reallifedoodles). These amusing animations started out as a pastime for David Little, aka SooperDavid, and have grown into an internet obsession. Of course you can make your own with nothing more than a little frame-by-frame animation, but if you want to speed up the process try adding bones.

You'll want video footage of a subject in some sort of motion and that you can envision being personified based on that motion. For this example, I'm using footage of an earthquake machine test used in a classroom science, technology, engineering, and mathematics (STEM) project. At the highest frequency of cycles, the structure stays intact, but the washers come loose and make the tower shake and scoot all over the floor. Now imagine if the tower were alive. It would probably be experiencing a high level of anxiety while trying to collect its body parts that have just been shaken loose and flung across the floor.

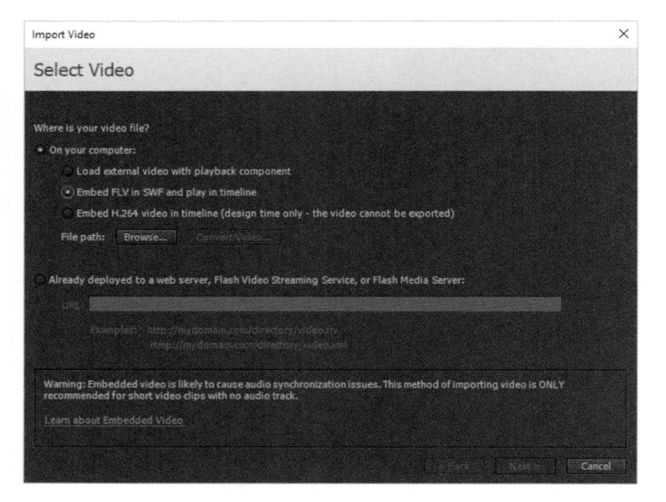

1 I already did some initial setup before getting to the Bone Tool. The first step included preparing my video as an FLV and using File > Import Video... and selecting Embed FLV and play in Timeline. This option lets me scrub the Timeline to sync reactions to what happens in the video.

4 I cut these layers and pasted them into their own Graphic symbol named "doodle." Then back on the Main Timeline, I created a Motion Tween for that layer. Using the Motion model, I scrubbed the video and nudged the character's features as a means of tracking it with the moving structure.

VIDEO: MYRA FERGUSON

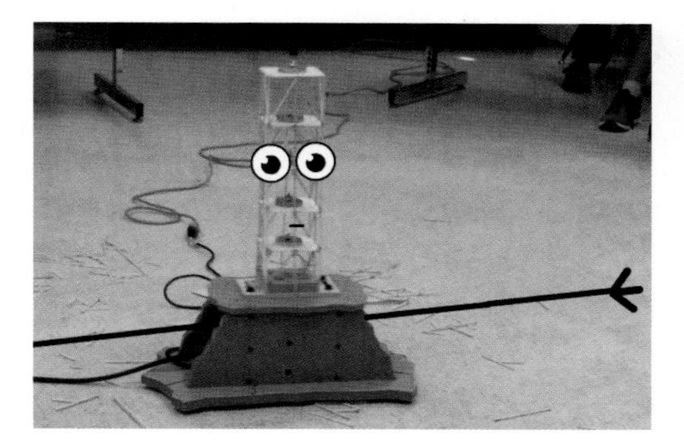

2 I made the basic face and upper body for the character which included the eyes, a mouth, and the arms with simple hands. The eyes and arms each have a layer for the right side and left side.

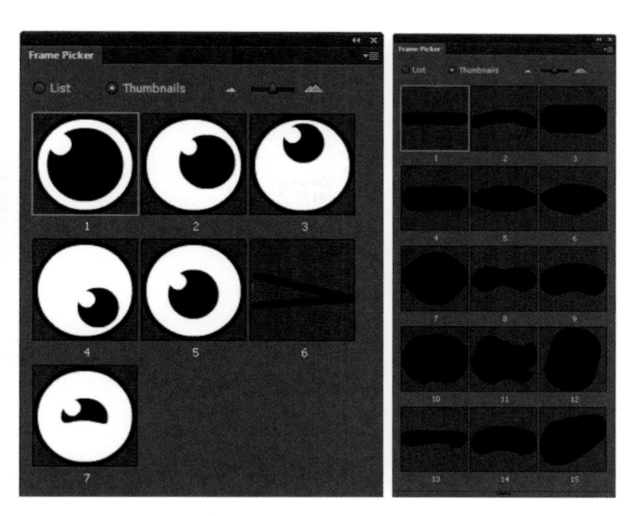

3 I set eyes for the tower character within the doodle instance. Each eye image is a keyframe in a Graphic symbol. In their own layer throughout the Timeline for the duration of the video clip, I placed keyframes of the eye instance for the left eye and right eye and set the options in the Properties panel. Under Looping, I set the Options to Single Frame. I clicked Use the Frame Picker... to open the Frame Picker panel. With Frame Picker, I don't need to keep track of which shape corresponds to which frame number. I can immediately see which eye shape I want to use from the Thumbnails and select it. I repeated the previous step to select the mouth shapes.

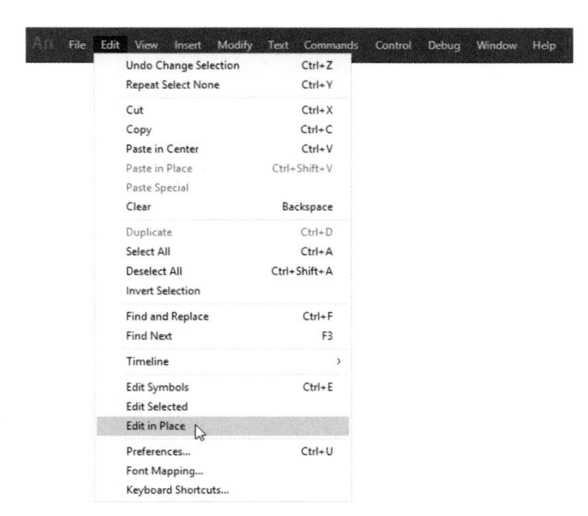

5 Now, let's talk about bones! I'm using the bones to set the poses for the various segments of the arm. Edit in Place the doodle instance by going to Edit > Edit in Place or by double-clicking on it.

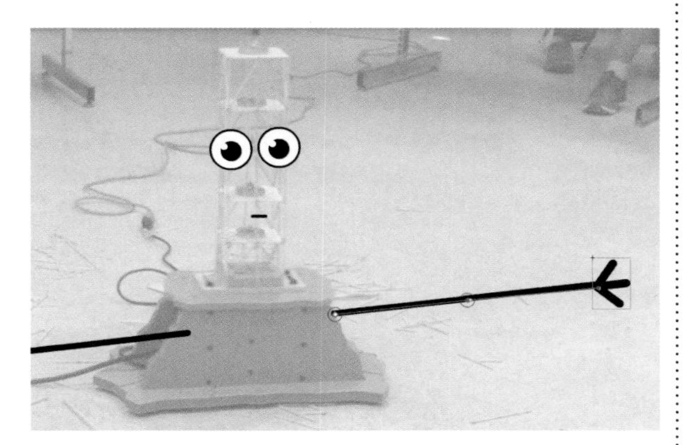

6 Use the Bone Tool to connect the parts of each arm segment. Start from where the shoulder (in this case the base of the tower in the video) would connect to the arm.

The Bone Tool (cont.)

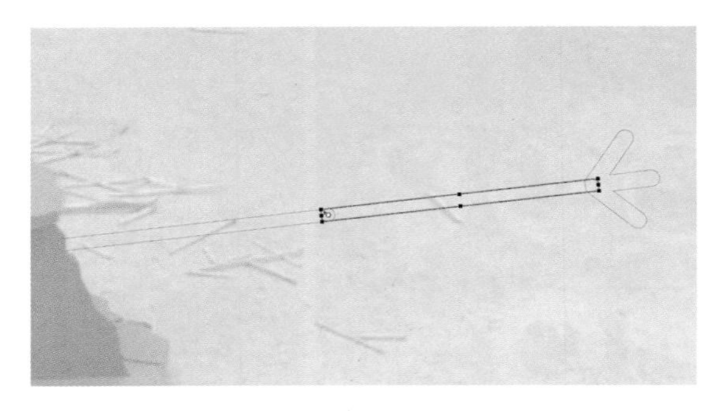

7 If you're having issues getting the bones to connect where you want, check the pivot point of the instance. Select the instance with the Free Transform Tool Q, and if the white circle isn't where you want the bones to connect, you can move it. Zooming in close and switching to Show Layer as Outlines help, too.

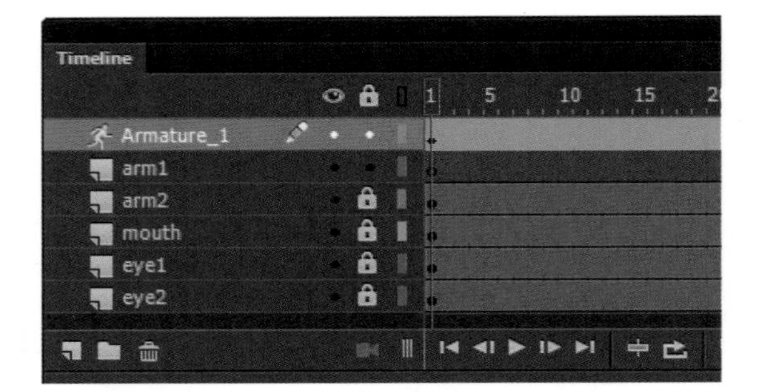

8 Once we've connected all the Movie Clips on our layer, notice it no longer has any content and a new layer has appeared starting with "Armature_" and a person icon. The layer itself when unselected is green (otherwise it's yellow when selected), and Animate automatically sets our first keyframe for us. We can delete the other layer.

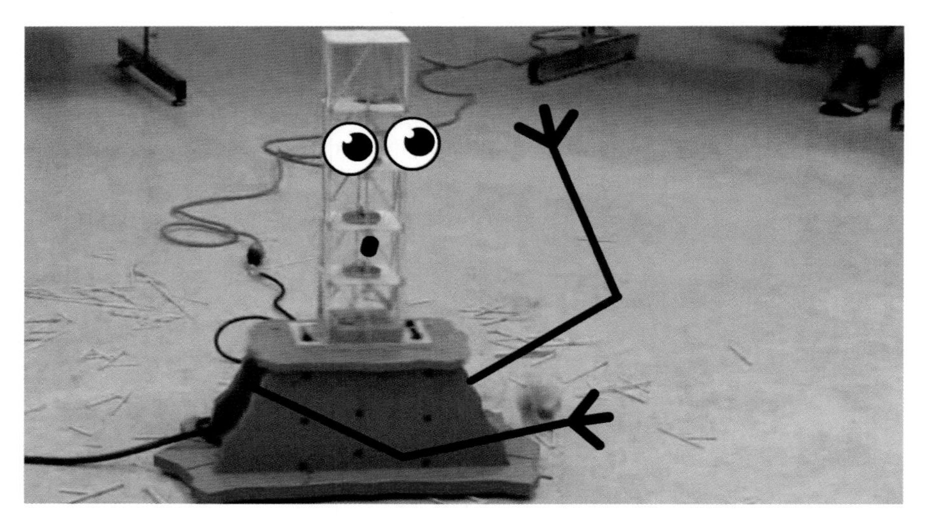

11 Continue Editing in Place to add keyframes for the arms throughout the Timeline.

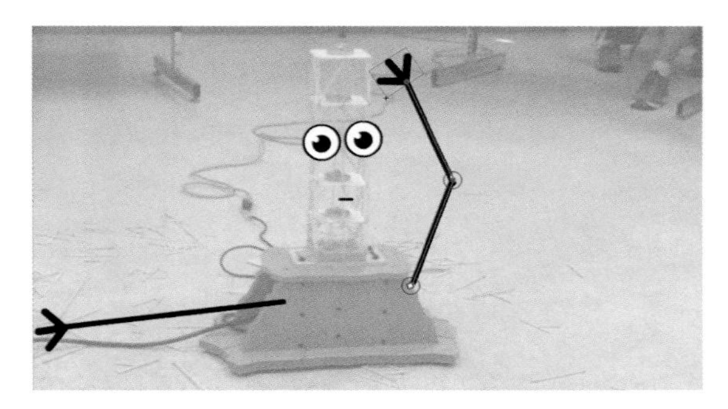

9 Let's help our guy strike a pose. Posing multiple segments is what makes Bones so helpful. Take his hand and drag it up toward his head. His forearm and upper arm stay attached and lift with the hand. When you move the armature, Animate automatically adds another keyframe for you on the layer.

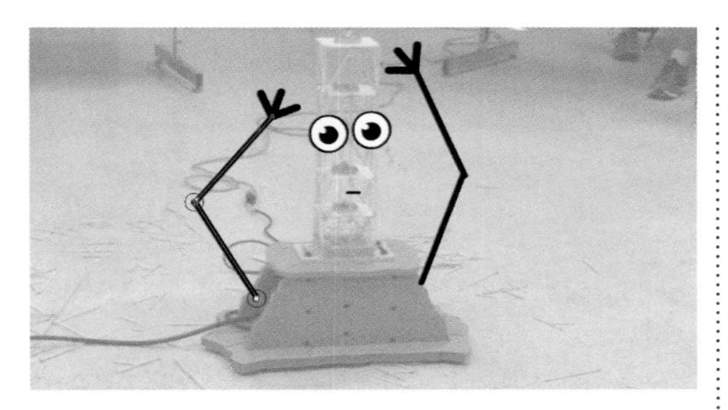

10 Do the same for the other arm. We can keep each arm segment separate since the base turns somewhat. Just nudge each arm segment as needed to keep it in place.

HOT TIP

If you want to avoid compensating for the wobble when animating over video, open it in After Effects and apply the Warp Stabilizer effect.

Basic Shadow

SHADOWS CAN ADD DEPTH TO YOUR PROJECT. This example is the most basic technique for adding a simple shadow to an animated character. Its simplicity does have its limitations, however. In this chapter you learn more advanced shadow techniques that give you greater flexibility, but some approaches may not be supported in older versions of the Flash Player. Depending on your target audience and your client's technical requirements, you may need a technique that allows you to publish to older player versions. This effect demonstrates one such technique.

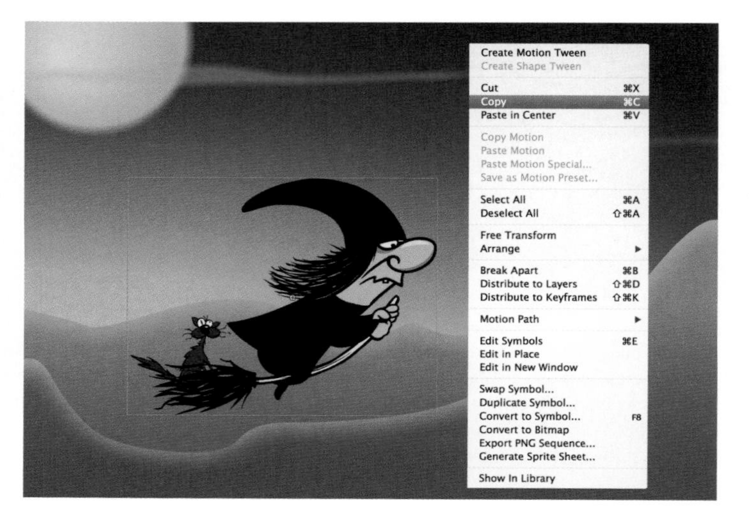

1 For the best result, place your character animation inside a symbol, which is commonly referred to as *nesting*. The next step is to simply copy the symbol of your character using ⌘ ctrl C. Create a new layer and move it below the character layer. Paste the copy of the symbol using ⌘ ctrl V into this new layer.

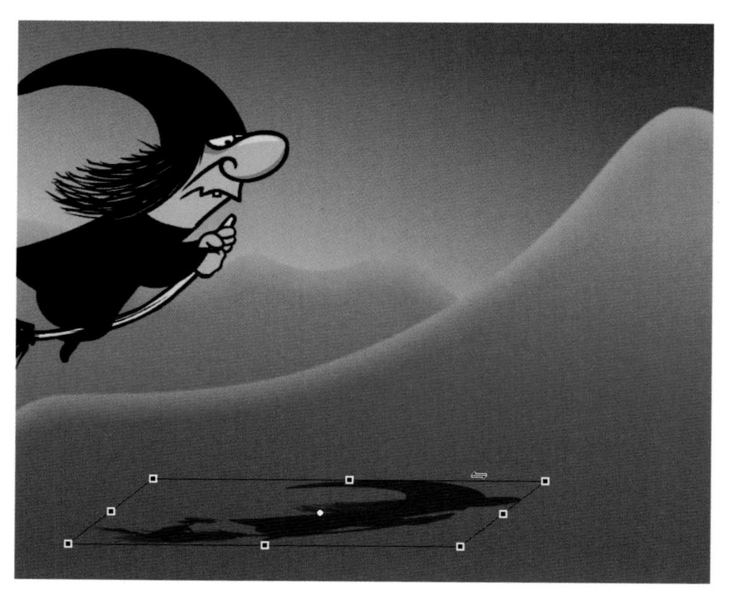

4 With the Free Transform Tool Q still selected, click and drag horizontally outside the bounding box in between the handles to skew the shadow.

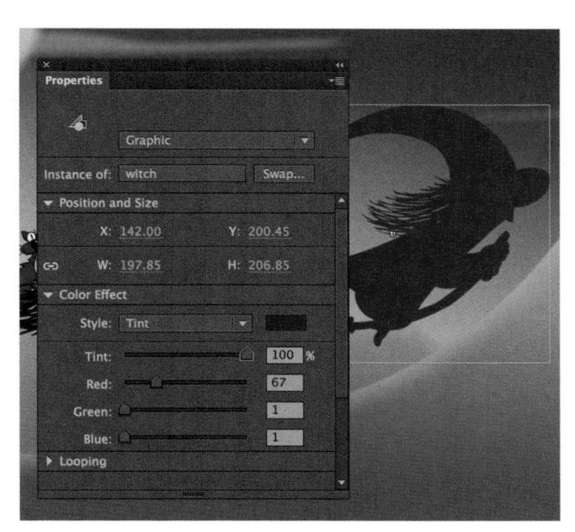

2 Next, apply a tint to the symbol instance you just pasted. The tint needs to have a strength of 100% to completely hide the character's details. The color of the tint should also be a darker color value than the background.

3 Position the shadow instance, and with the Free Transform Tool Q, scale it vertically to suggest some perspective of it being cast against the ground.

5 You may want to scale your shadow slightly smaller to suggest more depth. Play around with its position relative to the original character for the best results. Because the shadow symbol is a duplicate of the original animated character symbol, it will also animate in sync with the character. This synchronization will result in a convincing shadow effect. Since you have not used any special filters, this shadow effect is supported by all versions of the Flash Player.

HOT TIP

This technique works great when your entire character animation resides in a symbol. Using a duplicate of this instance for the shadow serves a dual purpose. Since you are reusing a symbol, your movie will be efficient in terms of file size. Another advantage to using a duplicate symbol is evident when you revise or add more animation to the original symbol. Since both instances reference the same symbol in the Library, the shadow instance will be updated as well.

Drop Shadow

SEPARATION BETWEEN CHARACTER and background can be critical to the overall impact of your animations. There are several ways to approach adding shadows for characters, but with animation, the approach can seem a bit daunting at first. Animate CC makes adding shadows as easy as possible with the use of filters. For this example we take a look at the Drop Shadow filter in its purest form. The perspective shadow technique that follows this one provides a cool way to use the same filter that adds more depth and perspective.

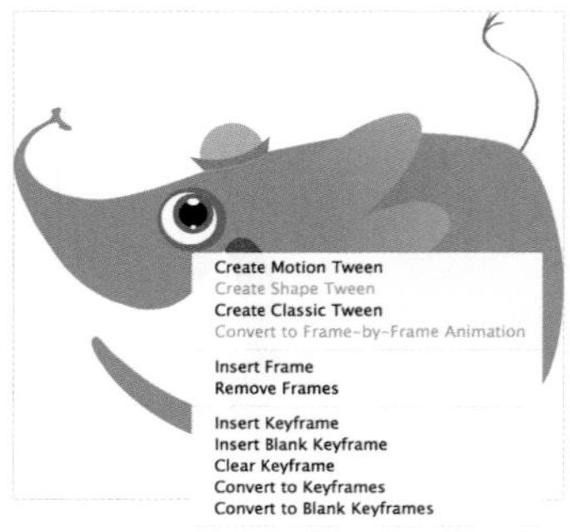

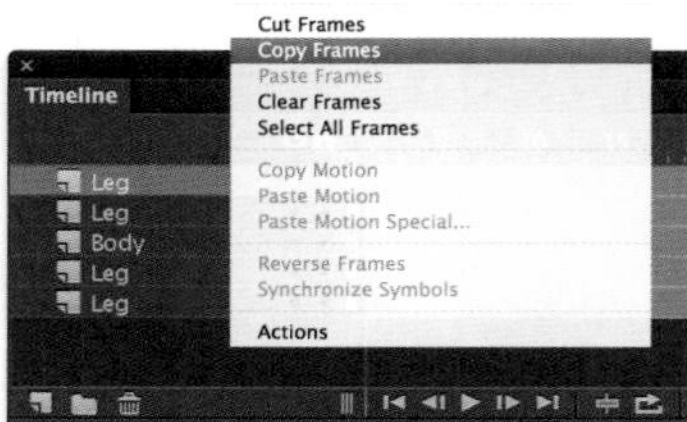

1 Filters can only be applied to Movie Clips. If your animation is not in a Movie Clip, you'll need to make it one by selecting the entire range of frames and layers and then Copy Frames from the right-click context menu. (If it is a Graphic symbol, you can change its behavior by going to the Properties panel and changing the drop-down menu to Movie Clip.)

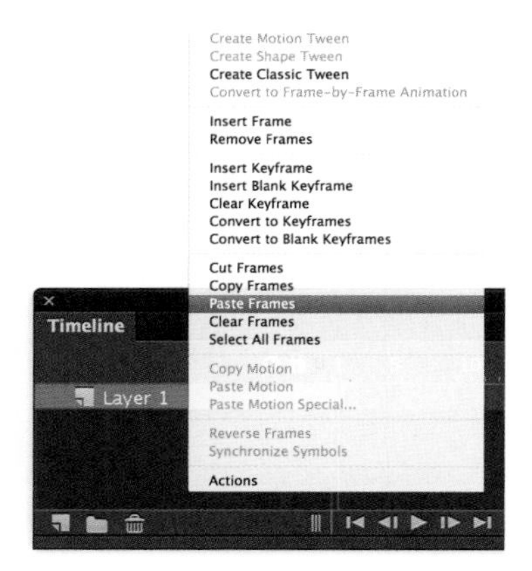

2 Create a new Movie Clip symbol from the Library panel. Select the first frame of this symbol, and from the right-click context menu, select Paste Frames.

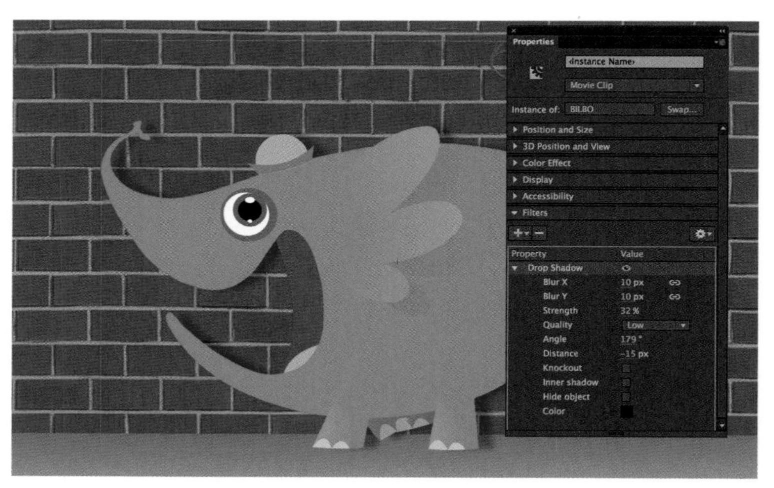

5 If you have a complex background, set the opacity to around 30% to 40%. This amount of transparency allows the background values to show through the shadow itself for a realistic effect. I usually spend most of my time adjusting the angle and distance of the shadow relative to my light source. Test your movie to see the Movie Clip and shadow animation.

3 Drag an instance of this Movie Clip to a new layer on the main Timeline. Delete all the original frames and layers as they are no longer needed. Select your new Movie Clip instance and from the Properties panel select the Drop Shadow filter from the Filters section.

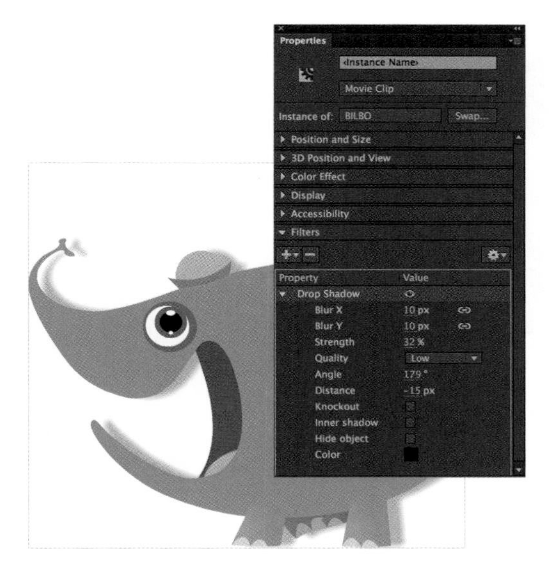

4 Adjust the amount of blur, opacity, angle, and distance to achieve your desired results. You can also select the color of the shadow by clicking on the swatch color.

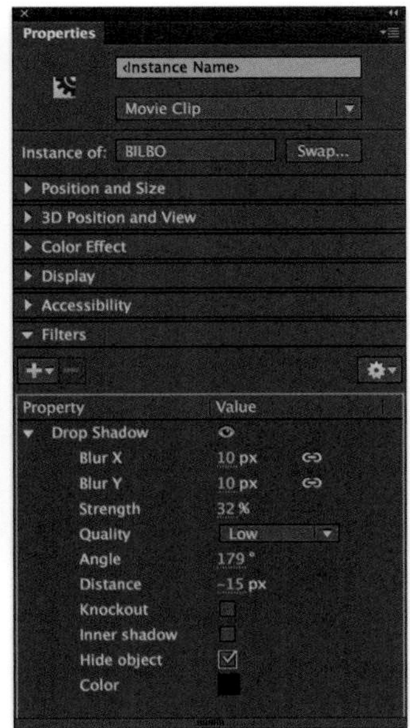

6 Select the Hide object feature to hide the Movie Clip. The drop shadow will remain on Stage. Test your movie to see just the shadow animation. Experiment with some of the other options, such as Knockout and Inner shadow. You can also click the little lock icon next to blur to remove the X and Y constraint. Apply more blur to X or Y for even more interesting results.

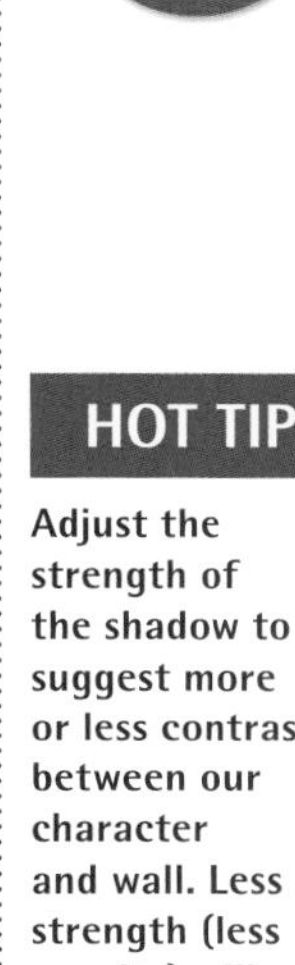

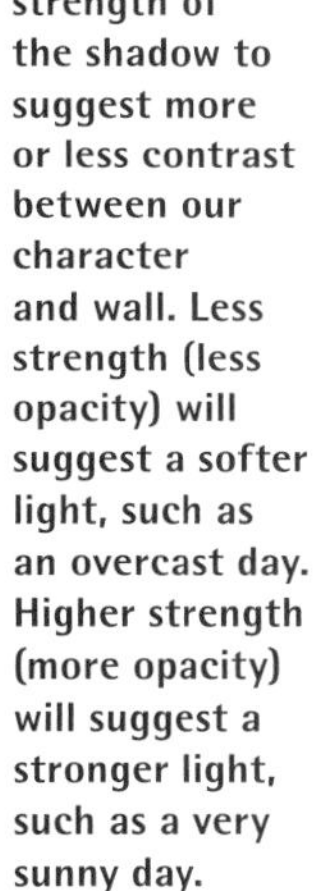

HOT TIP

Adjust the strength of the shadow to suggest more or less contrast between our character and wall. Less strength (less opacity) will suggest a softer light, such as an overcast day. Higher strength (more opacity) will suggest a stronger light, such as a very sunny day.

Perspective Shadow

SO FAR WE'VE LOOKED at how to add a Drop Shadow filter to an animated character using a Movie Clip and the Filters feature. But the Drop Shadow can be a little limiting in some situations. To place a character in an environment that has more depth and perspective, the Drop Shadow will not work very well since it tends to flatten the perspective. You may need a shadow that provides the illusion of perspective and depth.

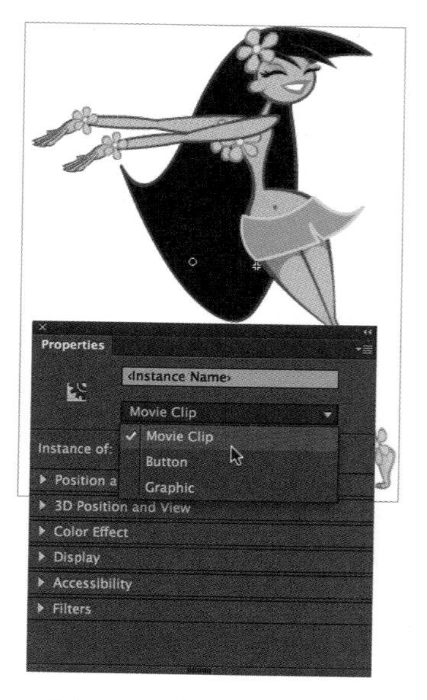

1 Select your Movie Clip instance and copy it using ⌘/ctrl C. Create a new layer below it and paste it in place using ⌘/ctrl Shift V.

2 Lock the top layer to avoid editing it. Select the instance in the layer below it, and using the Free Transform Tool Q, edit its center point so that it is positioned on the bottom edge.

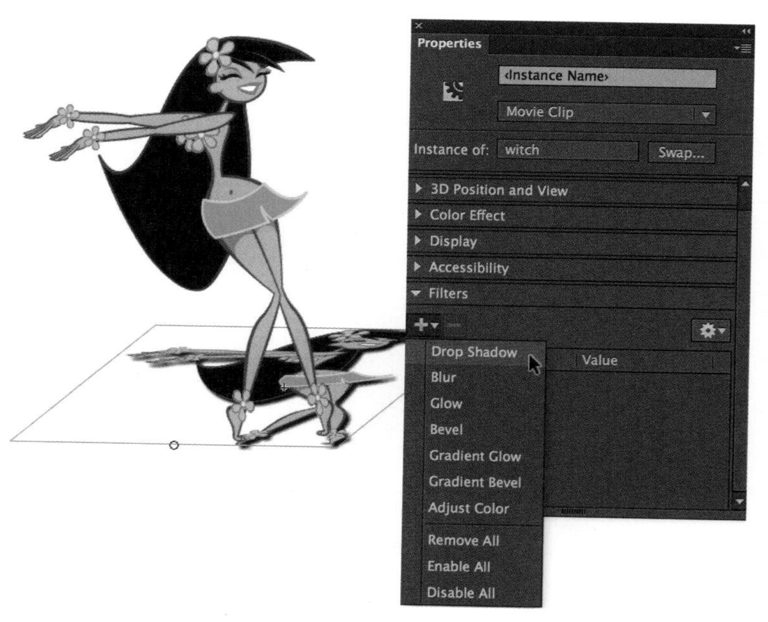

5 With the symbol still selected, apply a Drop Shadow filter to it.

MUDBUBBLE HULA GIRL CHARACTER

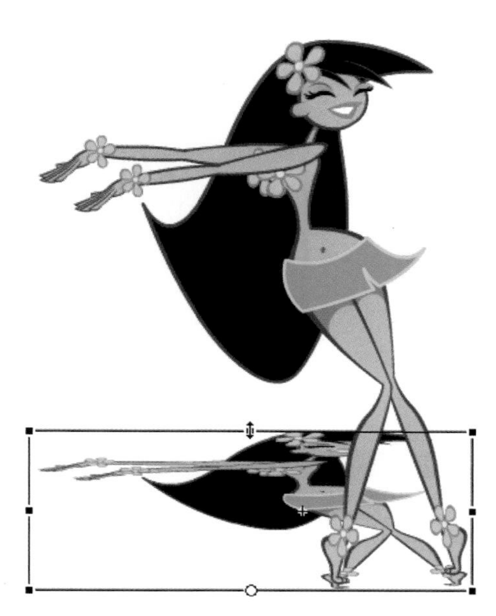

3 Scale the symbol downward by dragging the handle in the top center. Notice that the center point positioned on the bottom edge limits that edge from scaling.

4 Next, skew the symbol by dragging in between the handles outside the top edge.

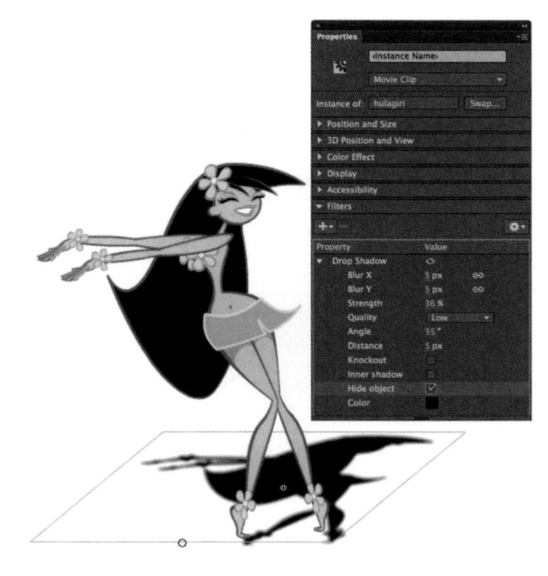

6 The "cheat" to this technique is to select the Hide object feature. Now all you'll see is the Shadow filter itself.

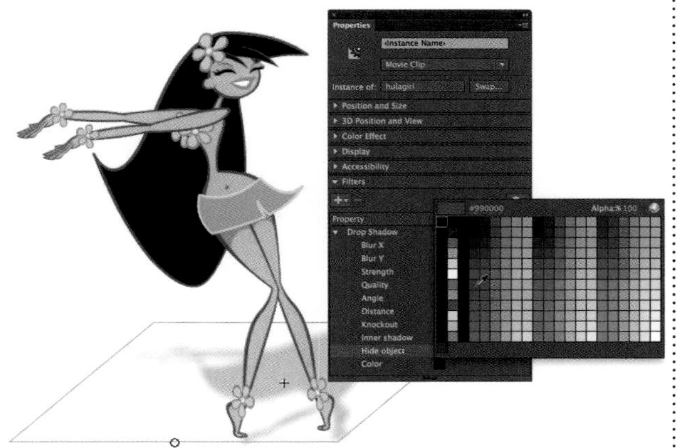

7 Play around with the options provided. You can adjust the amount of blur, opacity, quality, angle, and distance. You can even change the overall color of the filter itself.

HOT TIP

Not all Animate CC Filters are supported in HTML5 Canvas. Bevel, Gradient Glow, and Gradient Bevel are not supported. But if you can't remember, one way to know is to wait to apply the filter after you've converted it to a Canvas document. The unsupported filter will be disabled in the drop-down menu. If you've already applied a filter before converting it, Animate will remove the filter and tell you that it has been removed because it's not supported. While the Drop Shadow filter is supported, you'll get a warning that it's an expensive effect, which means performance will take a hit in order to render it.

Flying Text

REMEMBER THE FIRST TIME you learned to use a mouse? Or tie your shoes? These tasks seem so simple now, but some skills are just plain easier after someone shows you how. It's the "not knowing where to start" that can be frustrating. Well, consider this your start. I'm going to show you how simple it is to achieve some basic, cool motion effects in Animate CC—effects that look really difficult to build but are not so hard to create once you know how. Specifically, you'll make objects appear to move very fast using an animation effect known as motion blur. This blur is not the same filter effect as shown in the previous example, but rather a simple use of a linear gradient.

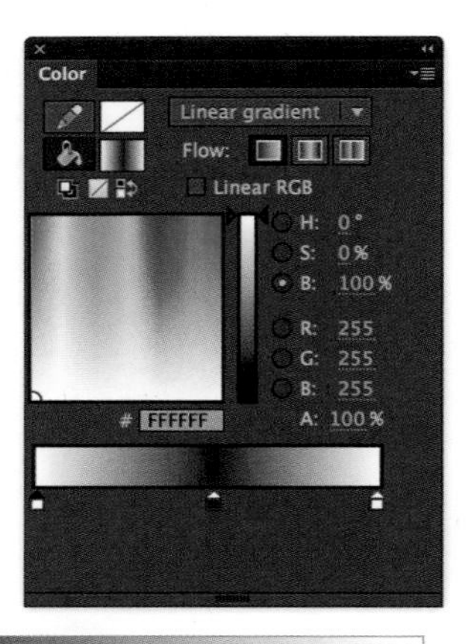

1 First, you need to create the two objects used for this effect: text and a linear gradient. The linear gradient should have at least three colors. The middle color should be a value similar to the main color of the object, and the left and right colors should be the same color as your background. If you have a complex background, mix these two colors with 0% Alpha so that the blur blends into the background.

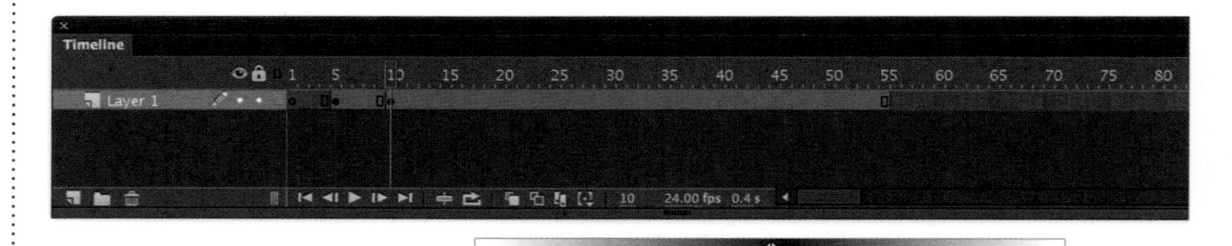

3 About three to five frames down your Timeline, add a new keyframe F6. Holding down the Shift key, use the right arrow key to move the gradient across the Stage. Position it wherever you like. Just make sure it remains on the Stage entirely (do not position it off the Stage).

5 This effect is not limited to a horizontal format. Rotate the gradient 90°.

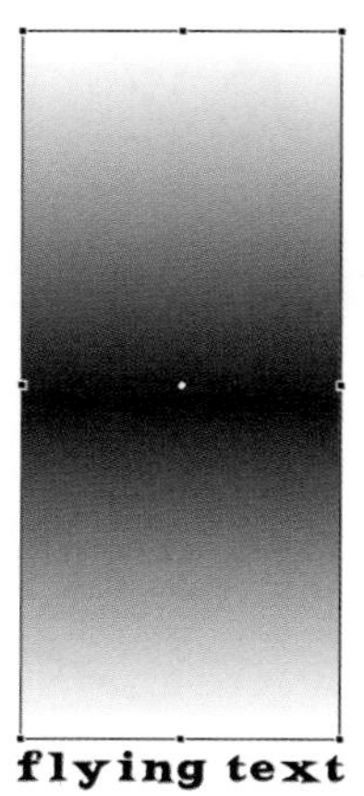

6 Align the text below (or above) the gradient using Onion Skin to help guide you.

HOT TIP

This technique works quite well with objects other than text. Balls, bullets, superheroes, cars, just about any object in action that requires a high rate of speed will work with this effect. You will likely want to play around with a combination of frame rate and the length of your Classic Tweens depending on your project. The advantage with this effect is you do not need a very fast frame rate (although it does help). You can achieve the same results with a lower frame rate as long as the number of frames in the Classic Tweens are fewer than compared to a higher frame rate.

2 To create the animation for this effect, convert the linear gradient to a symbol and place it about halfway off of one side of your Stage. You might want to start the animation on a frame other than frame 1 to provide a moment for the viewer to anticipate the action.

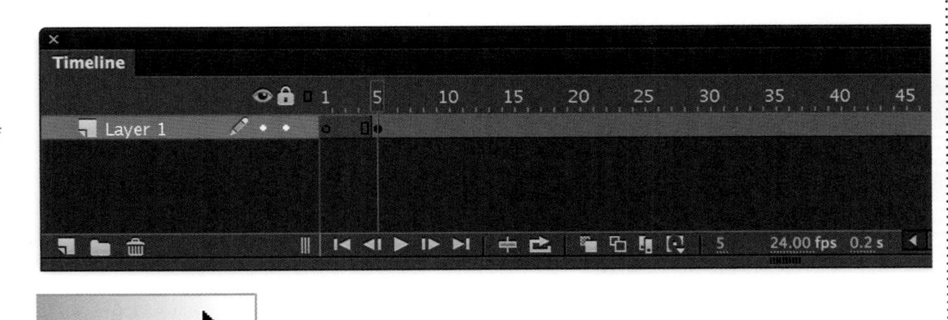

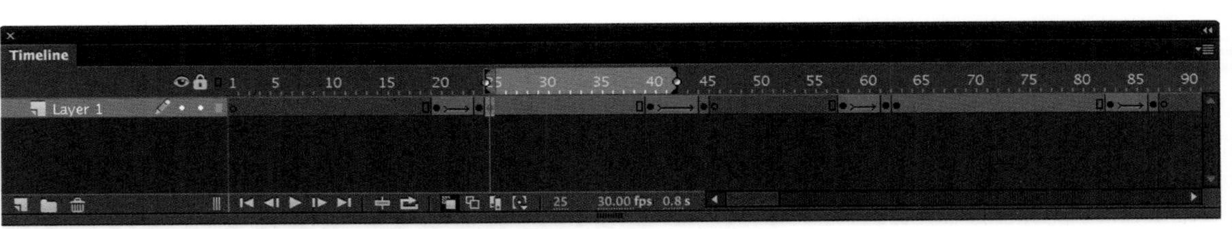

4 Apply a Classic Tween to make the gradient symbol move across the Stage. Next, create a blank keyframe in the frame after your second keyframe and drag your text symbol to the Stage from the Library panel ⌘ ctrl L. Turn on Onion Skin ⌥ alt Shift O, so you can see the previous frame and where the linear gradient is positioned. Align your text to the right of the gradient. Play back your animation.

7 Repeat the same procedure as you did for the horizontal effect. Classic Tween the gradient vertically from outside the viewable Stage area. Then in the frame after the tween, add a blank keyframe and position and align the text below the gradient. Reverse the procedure to make the text fly out and off the Stage. I'm sure you will have a lot of fun with this effect as it is one of the easiest to master, yet it looks so good!

Combining Effects

THERE ARE SOME ANIMATED EFFECTS that look so advanced, it's difficult to determine how they were actually made. It is often assumed the skill level necessary to create such advanced motion graphics is well out of reach for the average Animate user—not true in most cases. When we watch animated motion graphics, if the frame rate is fast enough, the human eye may not be able to see everything that is happening. As a result, our mind fills in what may not even be there. The good news is, we can use this natural shortcoming of the human eye to our own advantage when creating "advanced" motion effects. In my experience I have discovered that the most visually appealing animations are a combination of multiple techniques happening at the same time.

1 Type out your text using the Text Tool (T). This particular font is pretty complex and already suggests movement. Your text, however, can be hand-drawn graphics depending on the style of project you might have.

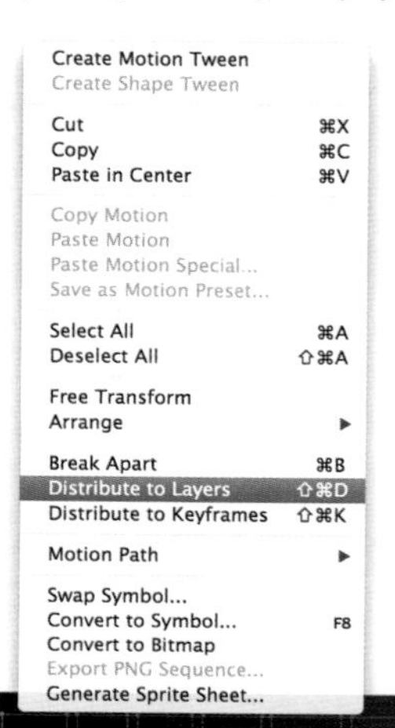

3 With every letter still selected, right-click over one of them and select Distribute to Layers, which will create a new layer for every letter, and each letter will be placed into its own layer for you. Distribute to Layers is a true time saver if ever there was one. Now is a good time to convert each letter to a Graphic symbol.

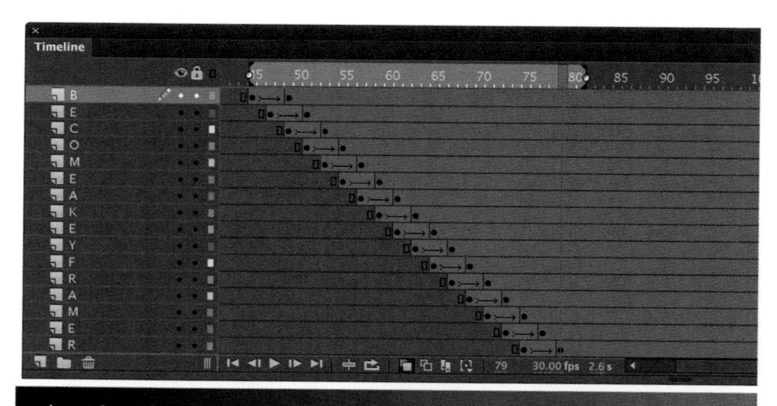

5 Next, to create the effect of each letter fading in one after the other, you will stagger each Classic Tween to overlap the one below it. Starting with your second letter, select the range of frames in the Classic Tween, then drag them down the Timeline a few frames. You can also select a frame before the tween and press (F5) (Insert Frames) to push each Classic Tween down the Timeline.

BECOME A KEYFRAMER

2 With the text field still selected, break it apart using ⌘ ctrl B once. Applying one break will split the text field into individual text fields per letter. One break retains the properties of the font, and you have the ability to edit each letter as such. If you wish, you can break it apart one more time to convert the font into raw vector shapes.

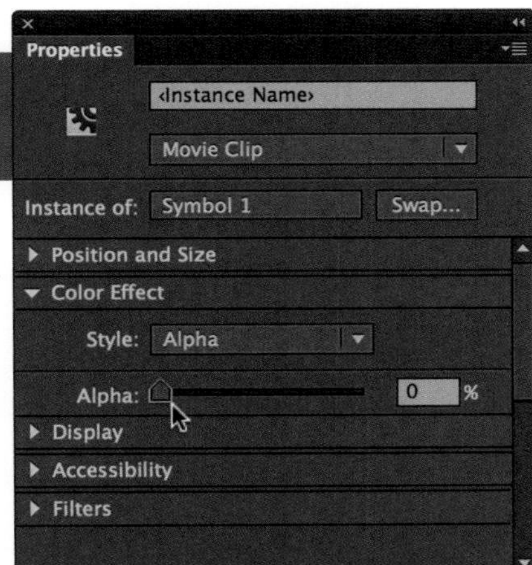

4 On each layer, add a keyframe about three to four frames down the Timeline. Now go back to the first keyframe containing your letter, select the letter symbol on the Stage, and apply some alpha via the Properties panel. Drag the Alpha slider all the way down to 0%. Repeat this procedure for every letter. Apply a Classic Tween for every letter so that they all fade in when you play back your Timeline. You can choose to use Motion Tweens for this effect if you prefer.

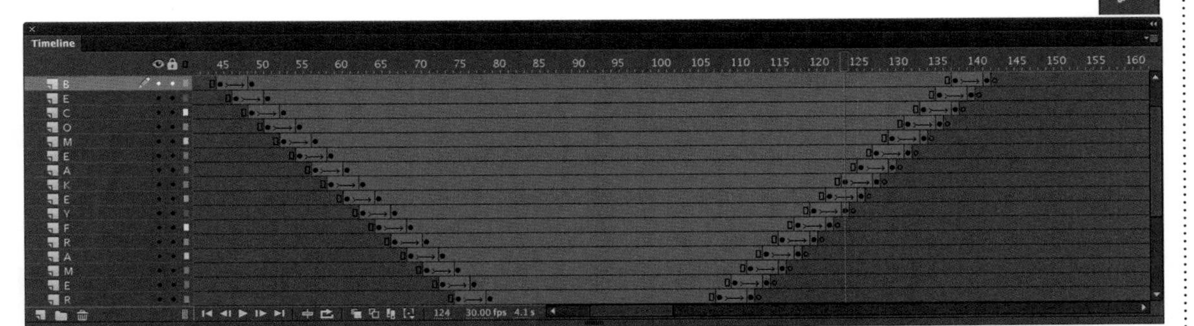

BECOME A K E

6 The final step is to select the first frame of each animation and use Shift while pressing the left arrow key ← to position each letter with 0% alpha to the left and on playback will create the motion of each letter flying into position while fading in at the same time. Once again, there is nothing particularly difficult about this effect. All you have done is use Classic Tweens with some alpha fades. This animation technique is still very basic. The only difference is the timing of each letter relative to each other. Throw in a slight amount of movement, and suddenly you have what looks like an advanced animated text effect.

HOT TIP

Create your own commands for repetitive tasks such as converting to a symbol and clicking OK. Open the History panel to see a list of recent steps. Select your steps and another object and click Replay to have those steps applied to it. However, steps listed with a red X can't be replayed, copied, or saved. With the steps you want to repeat selected, click on the button on the lower right of the panel to Save selected steps as a Command. Once your steps are an actual command, you can create a custom key shortcut for it. Even shortcuts that save you two clicks each time can add up quickly over a period of days, weeks, and months. Every minute saved is a minute earned in this industry.

Blur Filter (Text)

SOMETIMES YOU MAY NEED a blur effect that is more realistic than the linear gradient method. The Blur filter is perfect for creating realistic blurs, even animated ones. Before filters, we had to export an object as a PNG file, open it in Photoshop (or any graphics editor of choice), and apply a motion blur. Then we would have to export from Photoshop as a PNG file and re-import it. Thankfully, those days are long gone with the ability to not only apply filters but to animate them as well.

1 It is usually a good idea when creating animated effects to work backward. Start with the final frame, insert frames to extend your entire Timeline, and then add keyframes to the last frame.

3 In frame 1, select a Movie Clip symbol on the Stage and apply a Blur filter from the Filters panel. Click on the small black chain icon to unlock the blur constraint. Use the slider to adjust the amount of blur for the *X* axis only.

5 For objects that fly in vertically, limit the amount of blur to the *Y* axis. Remember to use your Shift and arrow keys to maintain alignment between keyframes, unless of course you want to have your object travel at an angle.

PHOTO: MYRA FERGUSON

2 Go back to frame 1 and begin the animation process by positioning the objects that will animate into view off the Stage. (Hide the shoes for now. We'll do something different with them later.) Hold down the Shift key while pressing the arrow keys to maintain alignment and move the object incrementally 10 frames.

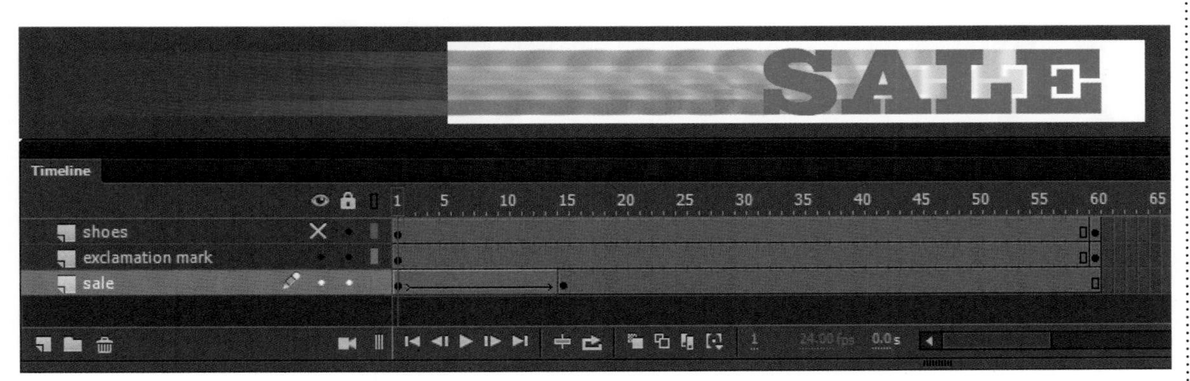

4 Drag the keyframe in your last frame closer to the first keyframe and apply a Classic Tween. The symbol will animate from outside the Stage into its original position. The Blur filter will also be tweened from the amount of blur in the first frame to no blur in the last frame.

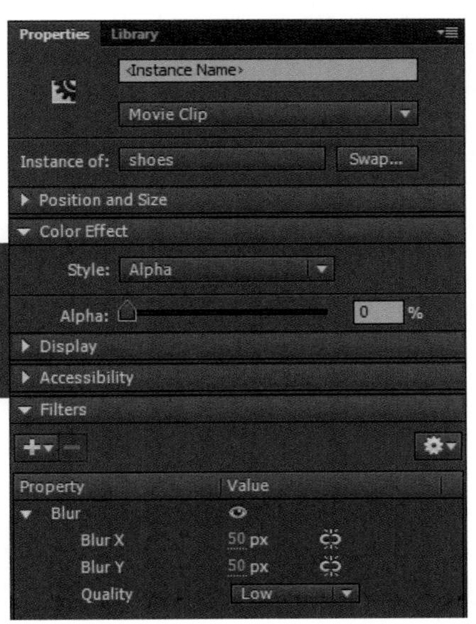

6 Objects that appear as if being focused from thin air use an equal amount of blurring for both the *X* and *Y* axes. Show the shoe layer again. Apply the Blur filter to the shoes in the first frame (the slider taps out at a value of 100, but you can type in your own value up to 255), change the Color Effect to Alpha at 0%, and Create a Classic Tween for the shoes.

HOT TIP

Be careful about the number of filters you apply to objects. The playback performance of the Adobe Flash Player may be affected if too many calculations are needed to render each of the filtered effects. Each filter has a quality setting: Low, Medium, and High. If you are unsure about the processor speed of your target audience, use the Low setting to ensure maximum playback performance.

Selective Blurring

HERE'S ANOTHER COOL TRICK TO SUGGEST movement between two keyframes. Open the "SelectiveBlurring-FINISH.fla" from the exercise files and play back the animation. The technique being used is basically a mixture of frame-by-frame animation with a variation of blurring and stretching. Look closely at the movement of his arm when he reaches for the gun. There are only two frames where this effect is used, and at 24 fps it's almost impossible to see. Yet the effect is still visually effective as it really smooths out the motion of his arm through the gesture of reaching and drawing his weapon.

1 The first step is to add a little anticipation. Rotate the arm into a position that suggests he is about to grab something. I also added some "itchy-finger" animation to build up the anticipation and focus the attention on his hand.

4 The next frame is similar to the previous frame. I used the Brush again to draw new shapes using the same colors. Turn on Onion Skin to see the previous frame as a reference.

2 Replace the arm with some very simple shapes drawn freehand style with the Brush Tool B. The fill for the arm is a mixture of black and about 30% transparency. The fill that represents the hand is the flesh tone mixed with some transparency as well.

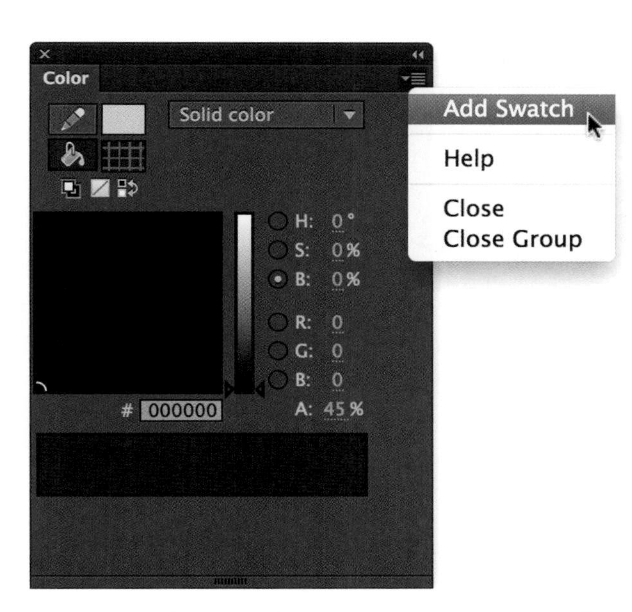

3 You can mix in a little alpha by typing in a percentage manually or using the handy slider bar. Add this new color to your Swatch panel using the upper right corner drop-down menu.

5 After two frames of blurring, it is time to bring the original arm back to the animation and in a new position. Notice that I also added some brush strokes behind the arm to suggest the arm is still moving but decelerating.

6 When a gun is fired, the resulting action is referred to as "recoil." We have Sir Isaac Newton to thank for showing us that every action has an equal and opposite reaction. This law of physics is critical for us to understand and, when necessary, incorporate into our work.

HOT TIP

The selective blurring technique works best when it is barely seen. If it stays on Stage long enough for the viewer to notice it as an object, it has performed a disservice to your animation effect. In essence, this technique should enhance the motion as a whole, not introduce an additional component. It should be subtle and used sparingly for a greater overall effect.

Background Blurring

IF YOU WATCH ANIMATED SHOWS ON TELEVISION, then I'm sure you've seen the manga speed lines where the characters remain relatively still while the background is being blurred. These streaks provide the illusion that the characters are flying through the air at an incredible speed. Visually it's a very dramatic effect and can be used in a myriad of ways during an action sequence. The illusion here is that the background is actually moving through the shot, but in fact it doesn't have to be. In this example the shapes that represent the motion simply wiggle slightly in a very short loop. What makes this effect convincing is a combination of color, linework, and of course the character itself.

1 Start with a radial gradient as the undertone of your shot. Use the Gradient Transform Tool (F) to position the gradient in the lower left corner. The character will fly in from that corner, and the radial gradient helps provide some needed depth to the scene.

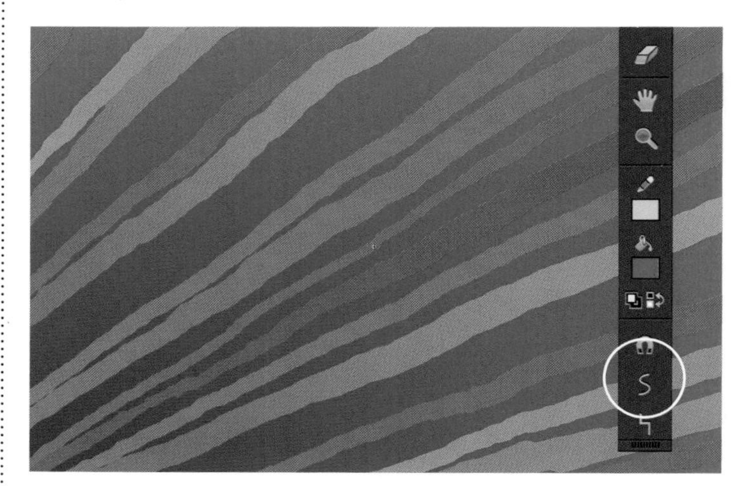

4 Select all lines and convert them to a Graphic symbol. Edit this symbol by adding several keyframes on the same layer. Each new keyframe will duplicate the lines for each added keyframe. Select all lines in each keyframe and click the "Smooth" tool (Brush subselection tool) a few times. Make sure the amount of smoothing is different for each keyframe. The idea is to create an oscillation between frames.

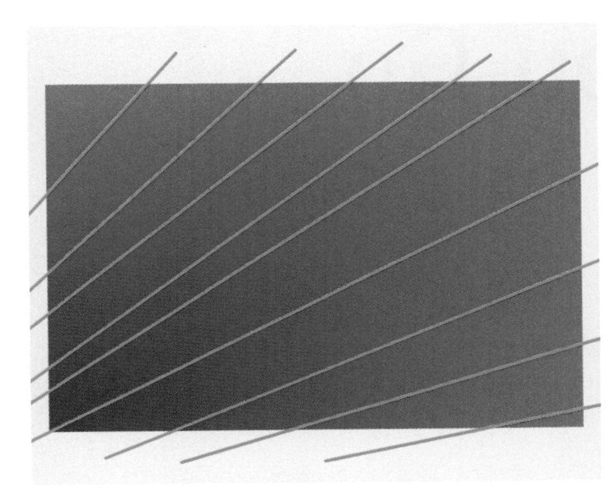

2 Create a new layer and use the Line Tool **N** with a stroke color high in contrast to your gradient colors. Draw some lines to use as directional guides.

3 Create a new layer above your guidelines and using the Brush Tool **B** and a large brush size, hand draw some thick lines that taper slightly toward the lower left corner.

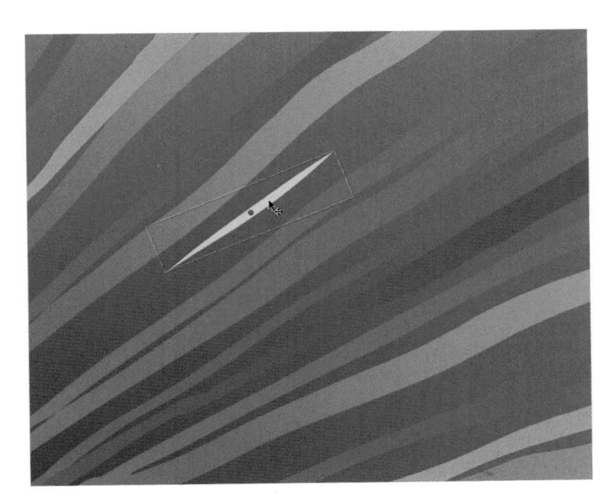

5 On the main Timeline, I added some random shapes flying through the shot in the same direction as the background lines. These shapes help emphasize the speed and direction that the character is moving.

6 The final touch is to add your character. This effect works best when your character is drawn in a way that reflects the speed and wind resistance the character would encounter.

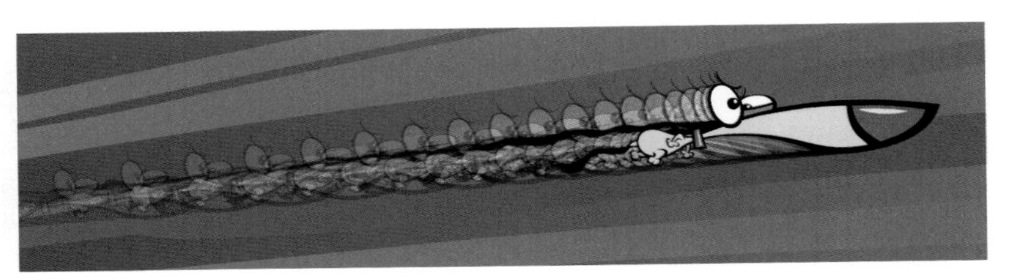

7 You can emphasize the dramatic effect by Motion Tweening the character from off the Stage into its final position. Combine this effect with some of the motion blur effects previously learned in this chapter, and you'll have a killer action sequence.

HOT TIP

With the background as a nested looping animation, you can easily reuse it for other similar shots that need to imply very fast motion. As a symbol, it can be transformed by scaling, skewing, and even tinting based on the design of your shot.

Where Do You Go from Here?

YOU MAY HAVE HEARD THE SAYING, "IT'S NOT WHAT YOU KNOW BUT WHO YOU KNOW." I'd like to add, "...and *where* you are." In his book "Outliers," Malcolm Gladwell (2008) suggests your success may also depend on when you are and to whom you were born, but let's focus on variables within our control.

Let me explain. I'm originally from Missouri. If you're not from the Midwest, what sort of image of Missouri just came to mind? Cornfields? Maybe cows? Missouri gets lumped into a category referred to as "fly-over states," meaning these are places you'd fly over if you're traveling from coast to coast. The phrase is somewhat disparaging. It assumes there's nothing much below the aircraft worthy of being an actual destination where you'd want to stop, visit, live, work—whatever.

Despite the misconception, Missouri has a lot to offer. Surprisingly, some people don't realize St. Louis is actually in Missouri (although there is an East St. Louis in Illinois, it's not the same, really). Likewise, Kansas City is also in Missouri. Both cities have rich histories and significant industry. Located approximately halfway between St. Louis and Kansas City is Columbia, the home of the University of Missouri and the distinguished School of Journalism.

Even though I grew up in St. Louis, Columbia was my home for the majority of my career. So I can say in my own personal experience that despite the benefits of its low cost of living, its high quality of life, and all the other amenities, Missouri being considered a fly-over state—at least when it comes to digital media opportunities—may not be entirely wrong.

So why did I stay there so long? Family and finances were among the main reasons, and those are pretty good reasons. Identifying priorities is important. Early in my career, I had gotten a job offer to work on feature films at Disney in Florida that I had to turn down because I just wasn't in a position to move. I sometimes wonder what might have been, but going would have meant missing out on some of the most significant experiences in my life. Instead, I found or made opportunities where I could in Mid-Missouri. I earned my master's degree. I sought remote opportunities whenever possible. I became an Adobe User Group Manager in order to connect with the worldwide Adobe Community. Making a career in digital media in a location that's not really a digital media hub is doable. It's just not that easy.

What then would I advise if your location is similar? Think about your priorities and your career goals. What's important to you, and what would you like to do? Now do some searches for where there are larger studios and more job postings. You'll see some cities come up more frequently than others. For the last several years, the main locations for animation jobs have been Los Angeles, California; San Francisco, California; New York, New York; and Vancouver, British Columbia. I've also seen large concentrations of animation jobs for Austin, Texas; Chicago, Illinois; Boston,

VECTOR ILLUSTRATION: MYRA FERGUSON

Massachusetts; and Orlando, Florida. Do you live near one of these cities? If not, decide if you'd consider moving to any of them. Would moving affect some of your other priorities? If those places don't work, then expand your search to other related jobs like interactive media, motion graphics, or UI design. See where those jobs are concentrated.

I'd also encourage you to think about moving sooner rather than later in your career. Whether you notice it or not, you're building your network in every position you have and every organization you join. That network can be instrumental in helping you get that next job or finding new clients. The longer you wait to move, the more difficult it can be as you may be abandoning those connections you've cultivated. Waiting can also be harder if you factor in how it affects a spouse, children, or extended family.

I can speak to the effects of moving later because I recently moved to Colorado. While it still isn't a major center for animation, much of the Front Range has a flourishing tech industry with a variety of digital media opportunities. While it's fair to say I'm still working on rebuilding my local network, remote work prospects have improved. One major benefit of the move is having nearby access to a major airport. And as an added bonus, Colorado's low humidity is amazing for my hair. It's all about priorities, right?

Reference

Gladwell, Malcolm. Outliers: the story of success. New York, NY: Back Bay Books, Little, Brown and Company, 2008.

■ From concept sketch to finalized animated body parts, just how does an Animate animator get from point A to point B? What is the workflow when it comes to animating characters in Animate? How do you make the character's movement or placement in a setting believable? This chapter looks at several real-world examples of actual characters, how they were built, and why.

6 Character Animation

IT'S TIME TO GET DOWN AND DIRTY. IN PREVIOUS CHAPTERS we looked at how to achieve a wide variety of design styles, transformations, and motion effects. But the concept of how to bring all these techniques together to create a successfully animated character can remain a mystery. When is it advantageous to nest certain animations and why? How can swapping symbols be effective? What exactly does the Sync option do? What is the most effective way to synchronize a character's mouth and lips to a voice-over soundtrack?

These questions and more are explained in the following pages. So roll up your sleeves and get ready for a fun ride into the world of Animate character animation.

2.5D Basics

TWEENING IS A GREAT WAY TO ADD QUICK AND SIMPLE ANIMATION to your Animate movie. But what if you could push the tweening method to its limits and give more realism to your character? What if you could harness its simplicity and make it work in ways not too many other Animate users have considered? What if you have learned everything there is to know about tweening, go back to the first 10% of that knowledge, and take a left turn? Where would that take you? In this example, I'm going to reveal a truly killer Animate animation technique that will actually create a 3D optical illusion known to fool even the most discerning eye. The cool part is you never leave the Animate environment and remain in the 2D realm. You are now in a dimensional limbo. If it's still 2D but looks like 3D, then what exactly is it? Welcome to what is commonly referred to as *2.5D animation.*

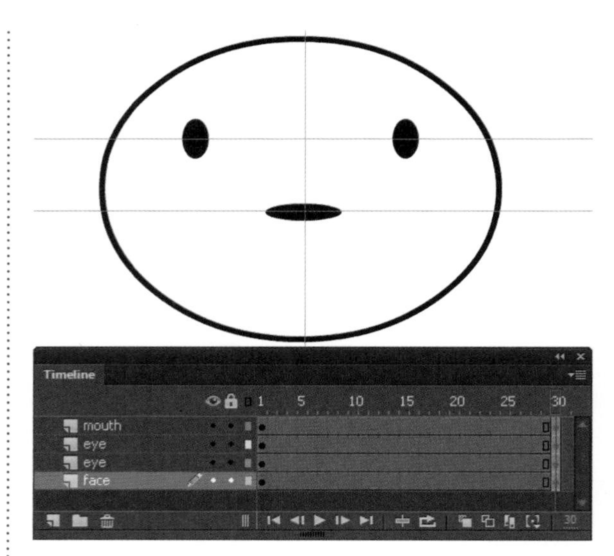

1 Let's start with a few basic shapes that resemble eyes and a mouth on a face. You can add some horizontal and vertical guides to help keep these objects aligned with each other. Before you start editing these shapes, insert keyframes a few frames down the Timeline across all layers. You will see why this extra time is useful later.

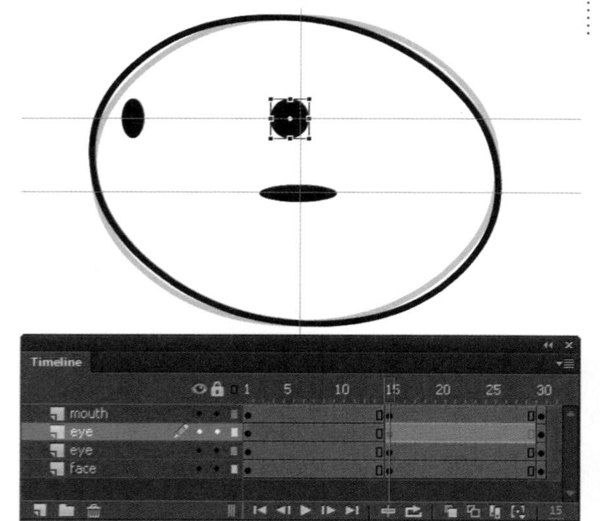

4 Move the other eye over as well but scale it slightly wider as it gets closer to the middle of the head. At this rotation, if it were truly mapped to the surface of a 3D sphere, it would be at its widest at the point where it is closest to us.

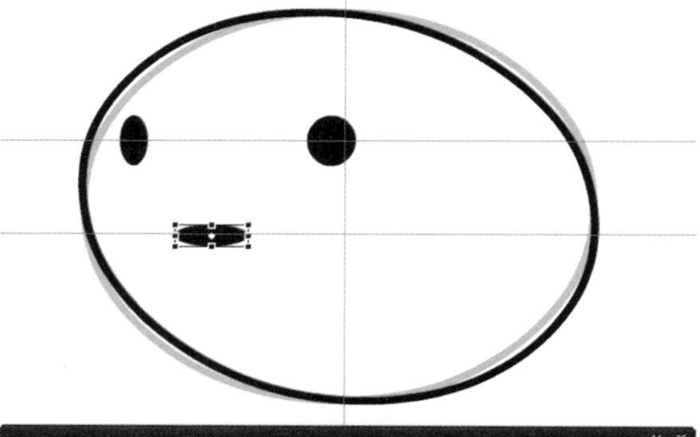

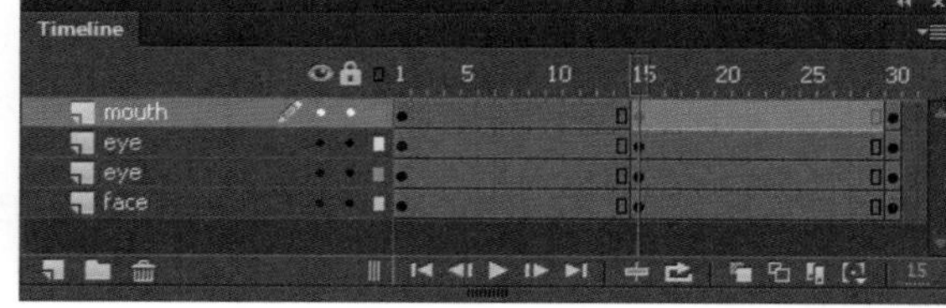

5 Next, move the mouth over in the same direction and scale its width slightly smaller like you did for the first eye. You might want to push the mouth closer to the left edge to provide more space between the mouth and the right eye. This trick will help make it feel as if the mouth is truly wrapping around the head like the left eye is starting to do.

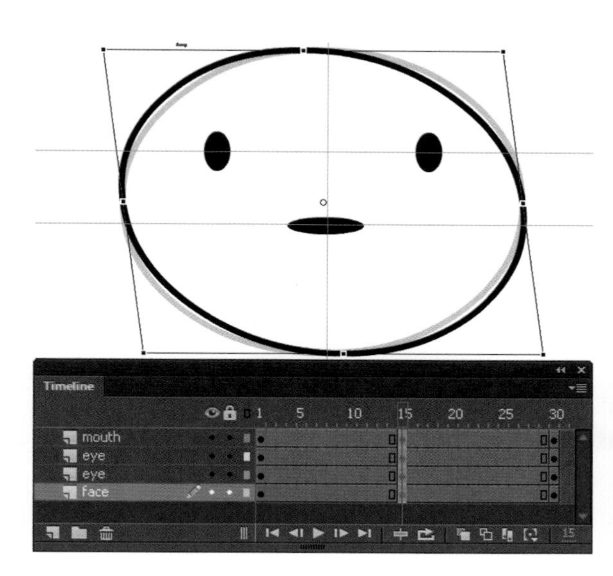

2 Insert keyframes across all layers between the first and last frames of your Timeline. Start with the head symbol by skewing it with the Free Transform Tool Q. Since you will be creating the illusion of the head turning to the left, skew this shape by clicking and dragging just outside the bounding box in this direction.

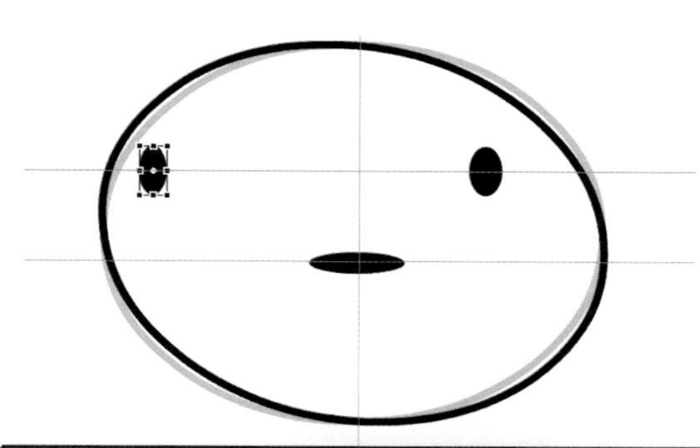

3 Next, select the left eye symbol and position it close to the left edge of the head shape. Use the Free Transform Tool to reduce its width slightly, creating the illusion of the eye moving away from us around the surface of the head.

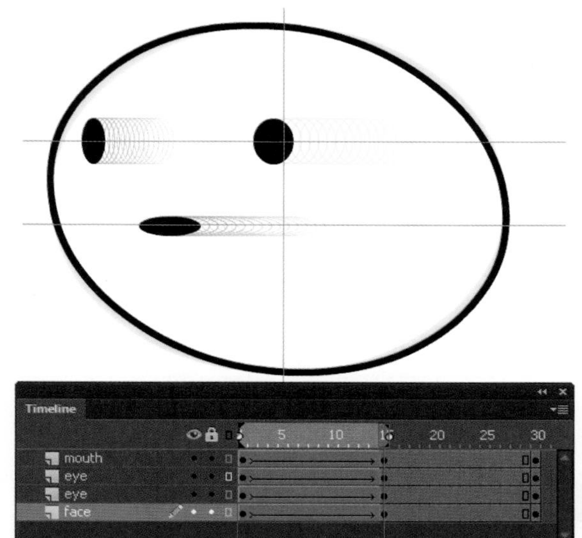

6 Now all you have to do is apply Classic Tweens to all the layers. Drag across all layers to select them and apply a Classic Tween from the context menu or Insert > Classic Tween. Remember when you added keyframes to the final frame in step 1? Now all you need to do is apply Classic Tweens to the latter half of your Timeline to return the head to its original position.

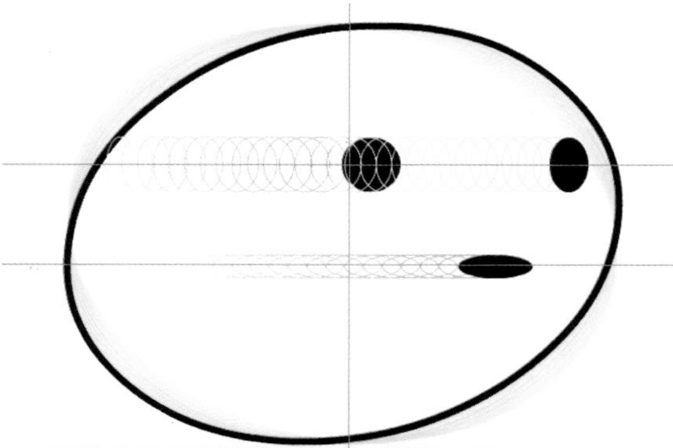

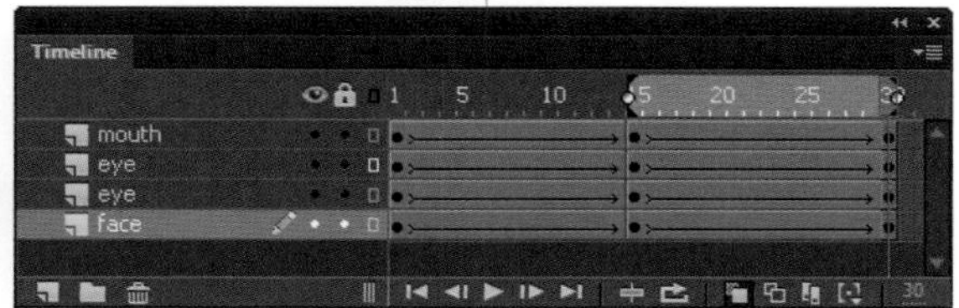

7 Repeat the same procedure but in the opposite direction to make the head appear to turn to the right. Experiment by making the head move from left to right by removing the keyframes in the middle of the Timeline.

HOT TIP

Don't be afraid to push the limits of this technique. I see my students attempt this style of animation, and all too often they hardly move the features across the face enough to make the illusion convincing. Play back your animation frequently to test the overall effect. You can always add or remove frames if the animation is too slow or too fast. Add a little easing to make it look even more realistic.

2.5D Advanced

LET'S APPLY THE SAME TECHNIQUE AS EXPLAINED in the previous example to a more sophisticated character. This character is composed of several individual objects, all of which were designed and composed with this animation technique in mind. The spacial relationship of each object to each other is important as they will all need to move, skew, and scale together but at varied amounts. The effect is based on the whole being greater than the sum of its parts. There's nothing overly sophisticated about creating this technique, but the result can look very complex on the surface.

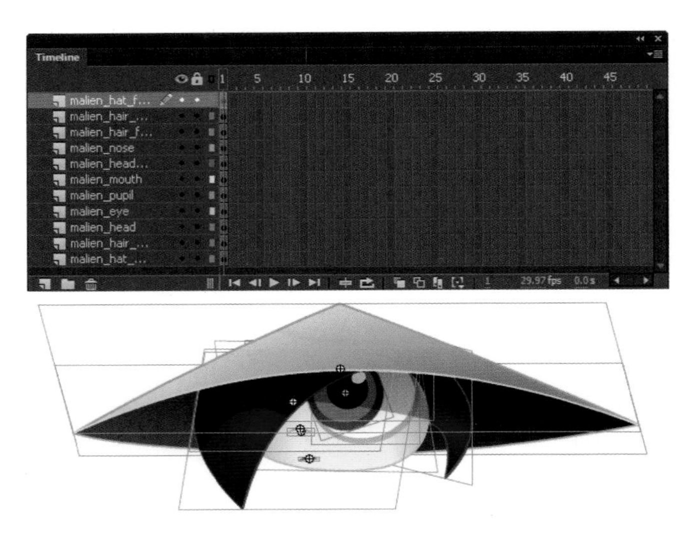

1 The first step is to make sure all objects have been converted to symbols and you have edited their center point to your desired location. For this technique to be successful, it's often useful to design your characters in three-quarter view as opposed to a profile view or facing us directly.

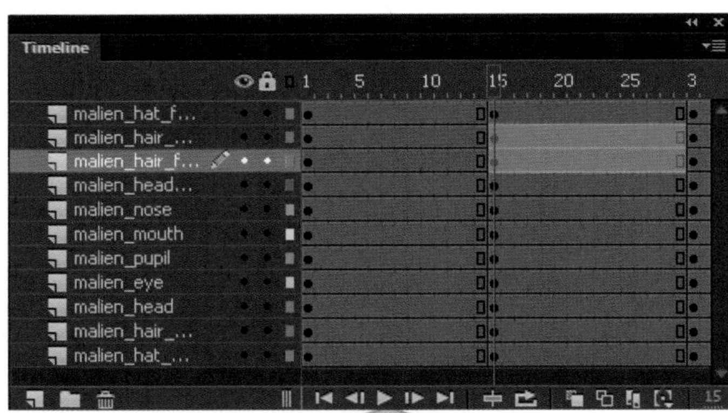

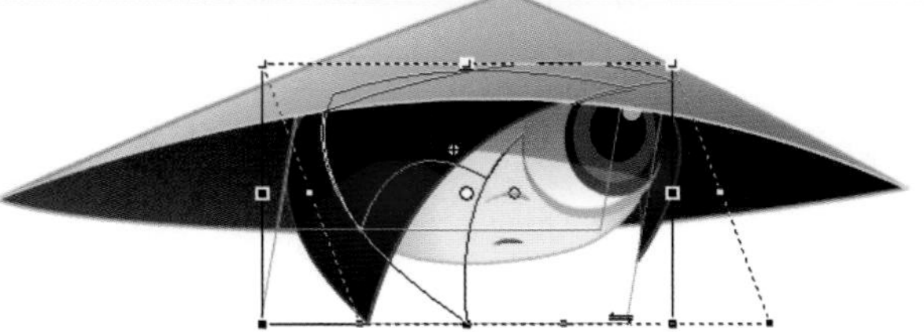

4 Next, skew the hair to the right from its bottom edge. Since you want to convey this object coming around the front of the character's face, move it over to the right and scale it horizontally to make it slightly wider than it is in the first frame. Moving and scaling horizontally creates the illusion that it is moving not only across the face but also slightly toward us as well.

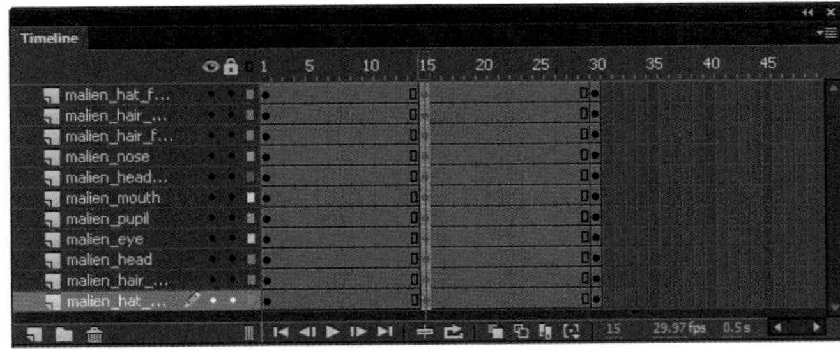

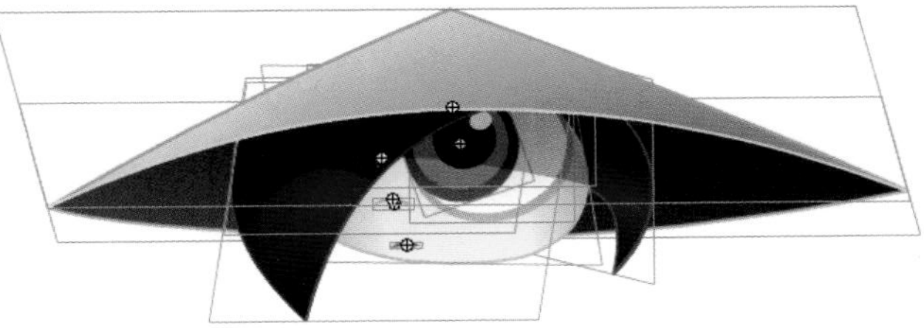

2 If you want to create a seamless loop by making the head eventually return to this exact position, select a frame (across all layers) somewhere down the Timeline and add a keyframe F6. It pays to think ahead because you avoid having to copy and paste the keyframes from frame 1 later. Select another frame (across all layers) an equal distance between your first and last keyframes.

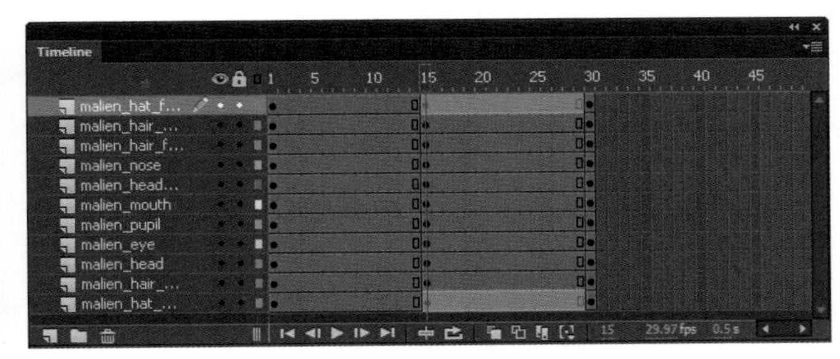

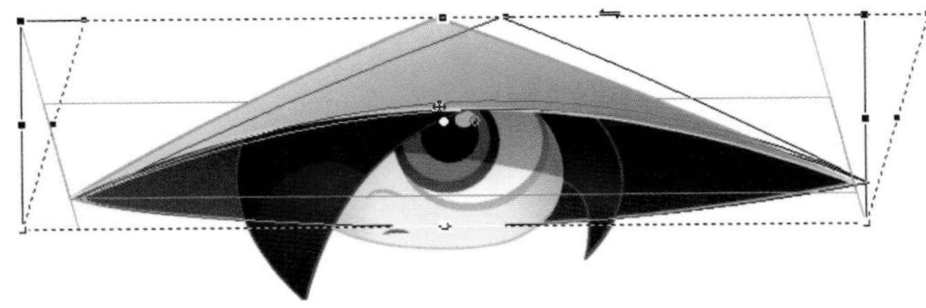

3 This middle frame is where you will edit your character. Start by using the Free Transform Tool Q to skew the symbol instances. Here I have skewed the hat, which is composed of two separate symbols, a front and a back. Selecting and skewing them together ensures that they remain aligned with each other. It's helpful to lock all other layers temporarily while you apply the transformations.

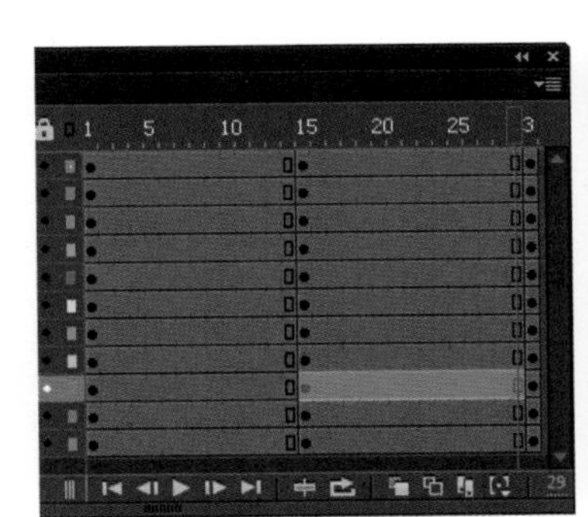

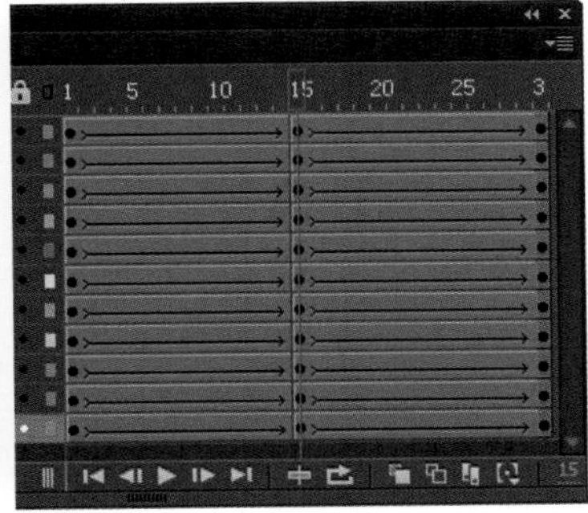

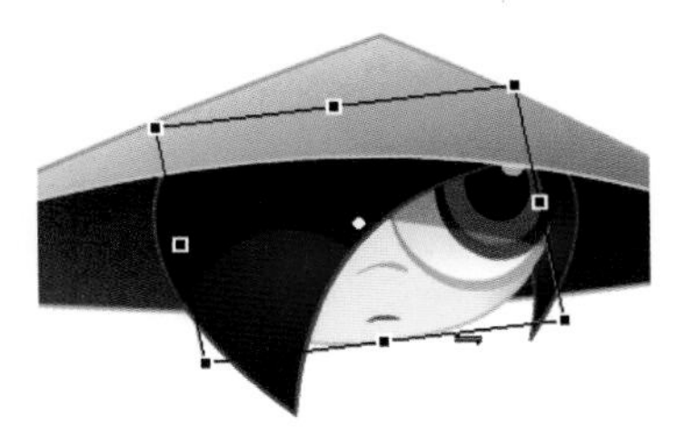

5 Repeat this process for each object, combining various amounts of skewing, scaling, and positioning. The smaller symbol representing the hair on the right side is the only symbol in this example that gets positioned to the left. Moving it behind the head emphasizes the illusion that the head is a sphere that objects can seemingly "wrap" around.

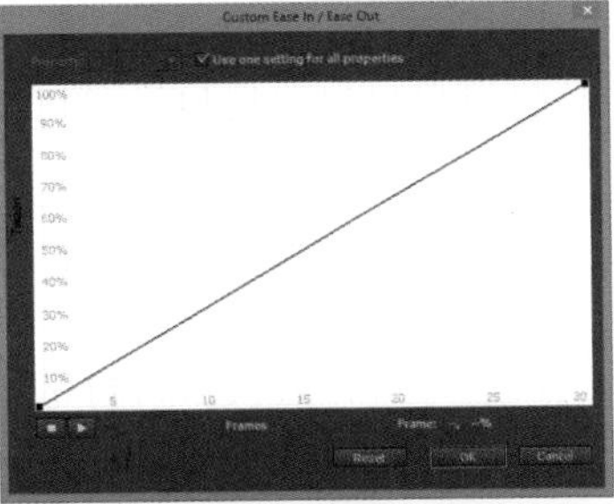

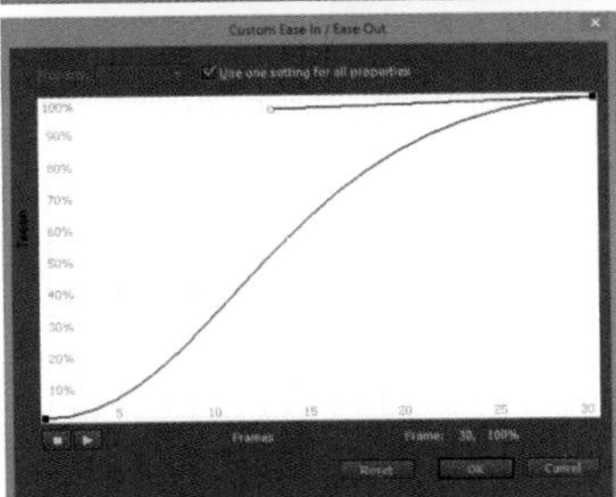

6 The final touch is to add easing using the Custom Ease panel. The straight path represents no easing. The S-shaped path represents easing in and out within a single tween.

HOT TIP

Character design is critical for this effect to be successful. Keep it simple and stylized because the more anatomically correct your character is, the harder it will be to animate in this style.

2.5D Monkey

THE KEY TO REALISM LIES WITHIN THE SHADING. The same 2.5D animation technique is being used here, but this time the graphics are drawn using gradients to promote an even more convincing faux 3D effect.

1 Start with the character at a three-quarter angle in frame 1. Let's call this "point A."

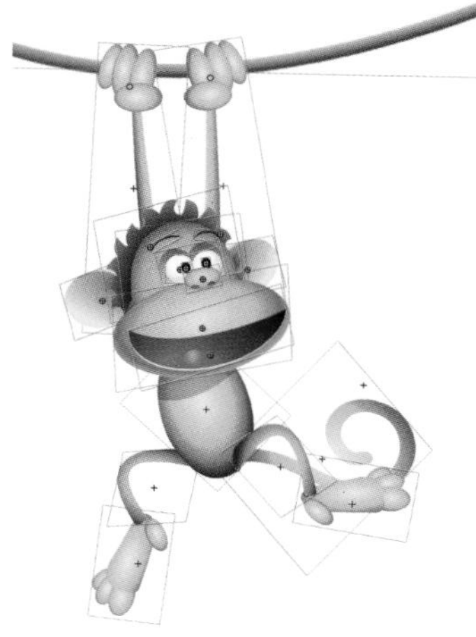

2 In your last frame, create what we'll call "point B." The challenge is getting from point A to point B through the use of tweens.

6 The ears play a pivotal role in this effect. At this new angle, we can see more of the left ear and less of the right ear.

7 Once the head symbols are transformed and positioned where you want them, lock their layers, select all the body parts, and rotate them.

8 Next, adjust the legs and tail individually by selecting and rotating them.

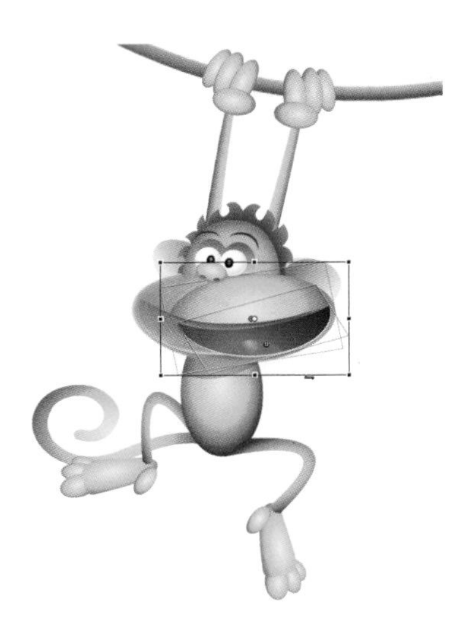

3 Using the Free Transform Tool Q, rotate, skew, and move each symbol into its "point B" position. Here the mouth symbols are transformed first.

4 Next, transform the nose, eyes, pupils, and eyebrows. Pay close attention to the spatial relationship between each of these objects and our perspective at this new angle.

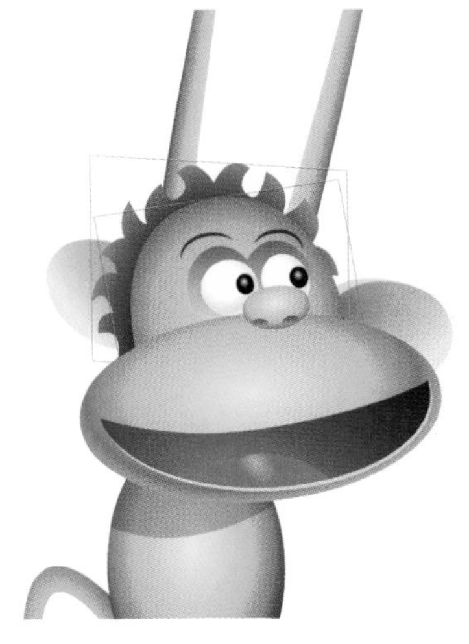

5 The head and hair symbols are rotated and positioned accordingly. At this angle, we see more of the hair from the left side and less on the right.

HOT TIP

Check out the "Using Gradients" topic in Chapter 2 to learn how to create and edit the radial gradients used in this example.

9 Select everything except the arms and hands and move the monkey over using the right arrow key →. Hold down Shift to move in 10-pixel increments.

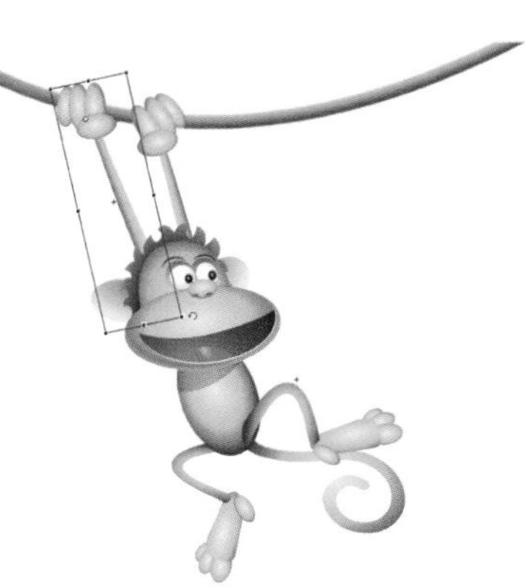

10 Rotate the arms so that they align with the monkey's new position. Their center point is positioned where the hands grab the vine to make the rotation even easier.

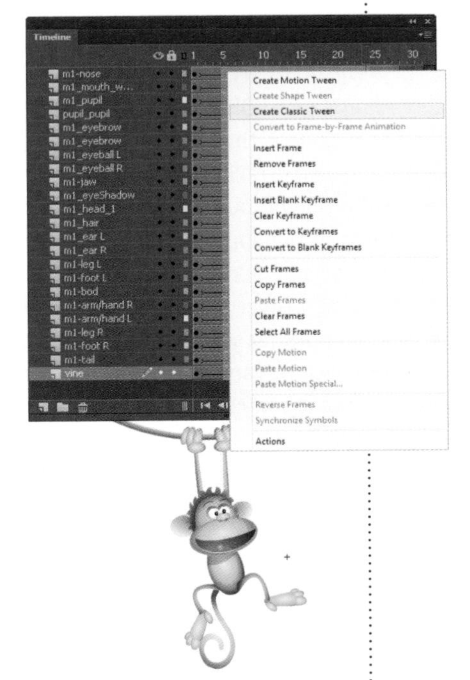

11 Apply Classic Tweens to each layer and play back your animation. Final adjustments are usually necessary at this stage.

Lip Syncing (Swap Method)

LIP SYNCING IS AN ART FORM IN ITS OWN RIGHT. It is the art of making a character speak to a pre-recorded vocal soundtrack. This technique involves the creation of various mouth shapes and matching them to the appropriate dialog. This technique can also be very time-consuming, especially if your dialog is very long. You can make it as simple or as complex as you want. There's a big difference between South Park–style and Disney-style animation when it comes to matching mouths to sounds. There are two basic methods of lip syncing in Animate, which we will look at here.

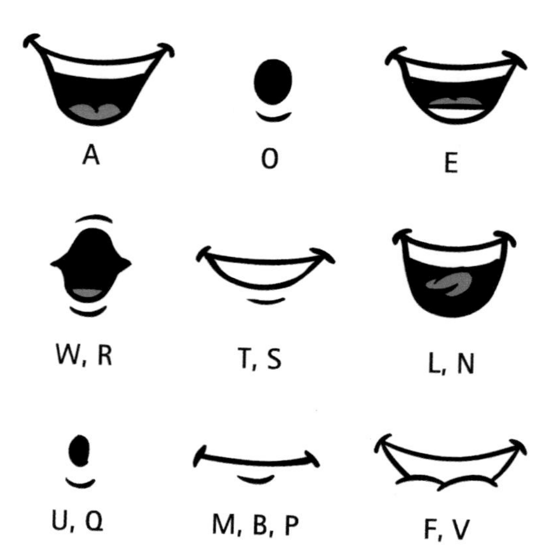

1 Here are the standard mouth shapes to use as a guide. Each shape corresponds to a specific sound or range of sounds. Each sound is noted below each shape. For most animation styles, you do not need to create a different mouth for each letter of the alphabet. In most situations, certain mouths can be reused for a variety of sounds.

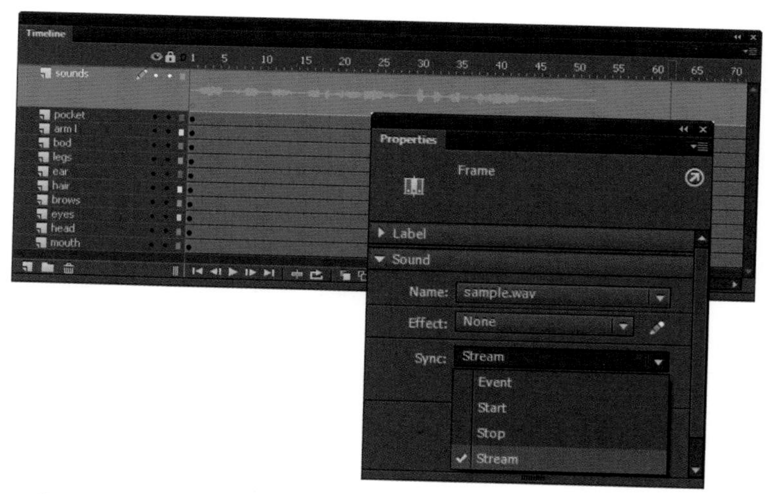

4 The next step is to import your sound into Animate. Sound formats supported are WAV, MP3, AIFF, and AU. Go to File > Import to Stage and locate the sound file on your hard drive. Once the sound is imported, create a new layer in your Timeline, and select a frame. Using the Sound drop-down menu in the Properties panel, select the sound you just imported. Next, set the sound from the default "Event" to "Stream."

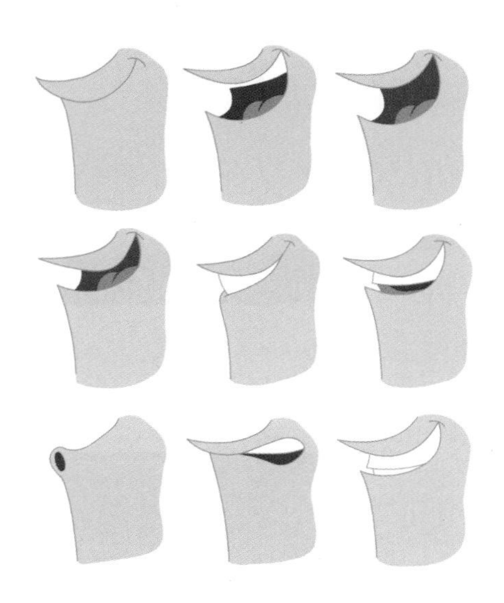

2 Using the standard mouth shapes as your guide, draw your character's mouth shapes, taking into consideration the design and angle of your character. After drawing each mouth, convert each one into a Graphic symbol.

3 Based on the design of your character, your next step will likely be to put the mouth instance on its own layer making it easier to edit for animation.

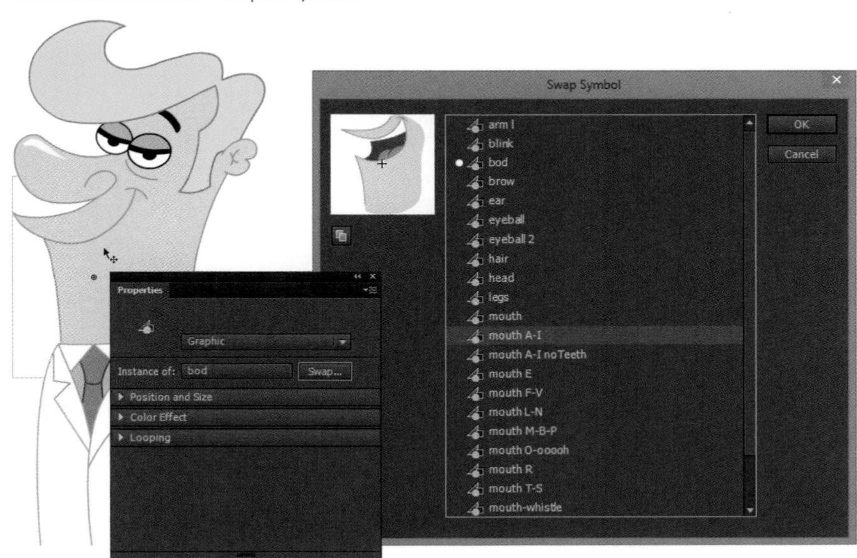

5 On the main Timeline where your character resides you can animate the mouth talking by creating keyframes and using the Swap Symbols method via the Properties panel. The Swap Symbol dialog will open and allow you to scroll through your Library.

6 Click once to preview each Library item and click OK to replace the instance on the Stage with this symbol. It helps to name your mouth symbols starting with the same three letters as they will be sorted by name in the Swap Symbol panel, making it easier to find the mouth you want.

7 Click OK to swap the symbol instance on the Stage with this new symbol from the Library.

HOT TIP

When you name each mouth symbol, include a description of what dialog sounds it should represent. This naming simplifies the process of choosing the appropriate symbol by allowing your eyes to scan down the list of names in the Library without needing to select each symbol to see the thumbnail.

Lip Syncing (Nesting Method)

THROUGH YEARS OF ANIMATING IN Animate, I have developed what I think is an even better and faster way to lip sync a character. A few years ago I was working in a full production environment with teams of animators producing several series for television and the web. Most of these episodes were 22 minutes in length with several characters and plenty of dialog. Lip syncing quickly became the most dreaded of tasks. Using the Swap Symbols method is certainly a useful approach, but when you have 22 minutes of lip syncing to do and only 2 days to finish it, finding a faster method becomes a production necessity. The Swap Symbols method requires a minimum of four mouse clicks for each swap.

1 Select the symbol instance.
2 Click the Swap button.
3 Select the new symbol.
4 Click OK.

Over the course of thousands of frames and symbol swaps, those clicks can add up to an enormous amount. Shaving off just one click per mouth shape can, over time, save valuable production costs (not to mention an animator's sanity). These situations are when "nesting" really shows its strength and versatility. By nesting all your individual mouths into a single symbol, you can control the instance of this symbol with the Properties panel. This method eliminates the need to swap symbols and also saves time.

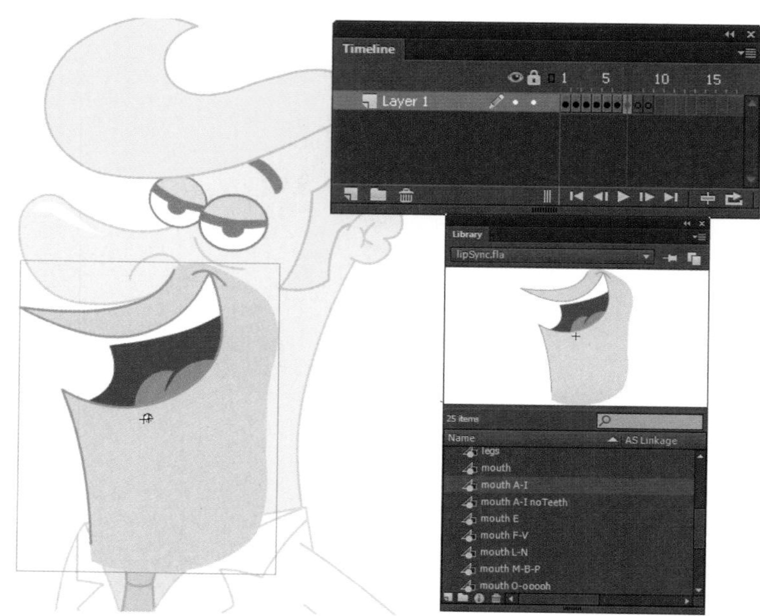

1 The first step is to place all your mouth shapes into a Graphic symbol. I recommend editing an existing symbol on the Stage to help you align your additional mouths to the character on the main Timeline. Double-click the mouth symbol on the Stage to enter Edit Mode. Create a blank keyframe for each additional mouth. If your mouths already exist as symbols, open your Library ⌘ ctrl L and drag each mouth to its own keyframe. Use Onion Skin ⌥ alt Shift O to help align each one.

5 The convenience of nesting is obvious when you transform (rotate, scale, flip horizontally or vertically, etc.) your character. All nested assets are transformed as well.

6 Often you may need a custom mouth animation, for example, a mouth that whistles. Right-click over your mouth and select Duplicate Symbol. Give it a descriptive name.

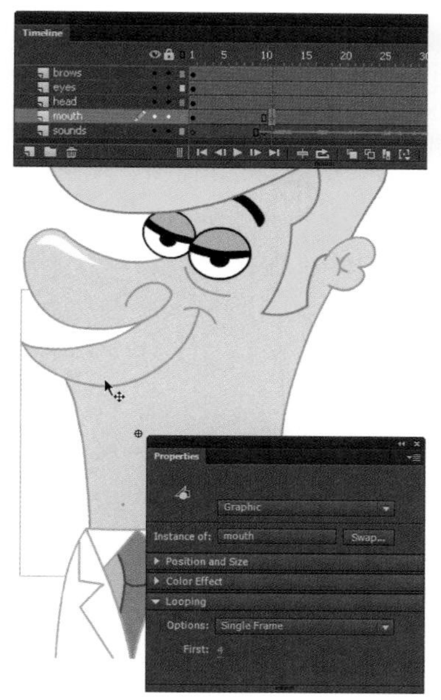

2 Back on the main Timeline, open the Properties panel and select your "mouth" instance containing all of your mouth shapes. The Properties panel will give you options specific to controlling the Graphic symbol instance.

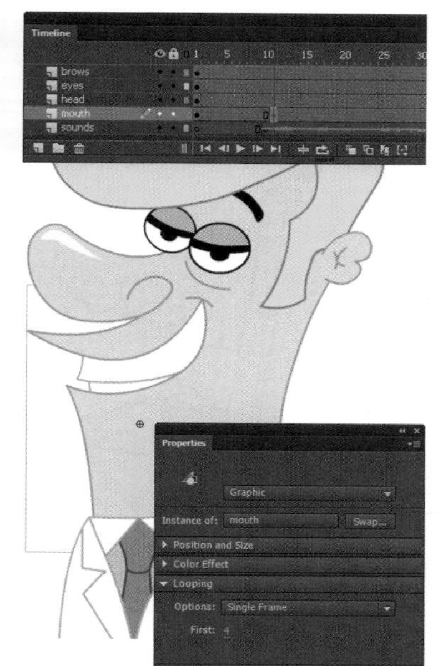

3 Add a keyframe to the mouth layer, select the mouth instance, and in the Properties panel select Single Frame. In the First frame input box, type the frame number corresponding to the mouth shape needed based on the sound at that keyframe. As of the June 2016 release, you can select which frame to use from the Frame Picker. Click the Frame Picker button from the Properties panel. The Frame Picker displays all the keyframes in your Graphic symbol. Click the thumbnail for the mouth you want to use and the frame number will automatically populate the First frame field.

4 Scrub the Timeline (drag the playhead back and forth) to hear the next sound. Repeat the same process by adding keyframes and picking the corresponding frame number for the mouth shape needed.

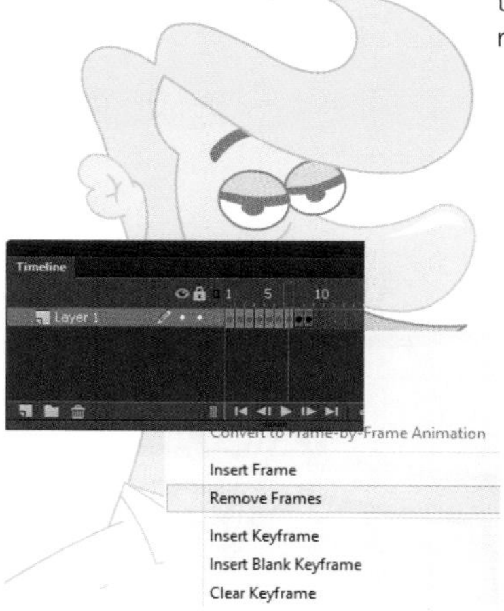

7 Remove the unneeded symbols by selecting them and choosing "Remove Frames" from the right-click context menu. Keep the symbol that closely represents a whistle shape.

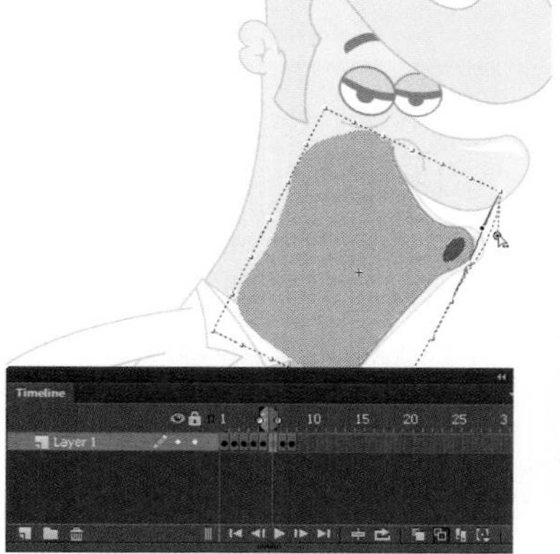

8 Animate the whistling mouth as a short loop. Here I used the Envelope modifier to distort my original mouth shape after breaking it apart.

9 On the main Timeline, add a keyframe, and select the "whistle" symbol containing your new animation. In the Properties panel select "Loop" from the drop-down menu.

HOT TIP

When designing your character, it's important to conceptualize how the character's features may work. Some mouths are designed so that they are independent of the jaw and nose, while other mouths are an integral part of these features. So ultimately your mouth may be drastically different in terms of design, yet follow these basic standards.

To Sync or Not to Sync

TO SYNCHRONIZE A NESTED ANIMATION INSIDE a Graphic symbol with the main Timeline, select the Sync option in the Property Inspector. Sync is a feature that is available when a Classic Tween is applied. Select a keyframe with a Classic Tween to find the Sync option in the Tweening section of the Properties panel. What Sync means for nested animations is that the nested frames will be synchronized with the main Timeline.

Animate CC consistently turns on the Sync option by default. However, if you're modifying an older animation, Sync may not have been turned on automatically depending on how the Classic Tween was applied.

So when would you use Sync? When would you want to avoid it? Let's first take a look at a situation where Sync would not be useful.

1 In order for you to see the effectiveness of the Sync option, you need to work with a nested animation. A mouth symbol with several mouths on different keyframes will do just fine. Thumbnail views of each frame were displayed using the Frame View drop-down menu in the upper right corner of the Timeline panel (to the right of the frame numbers) to select Preview. This view is a handy way to see the contents of each frame.

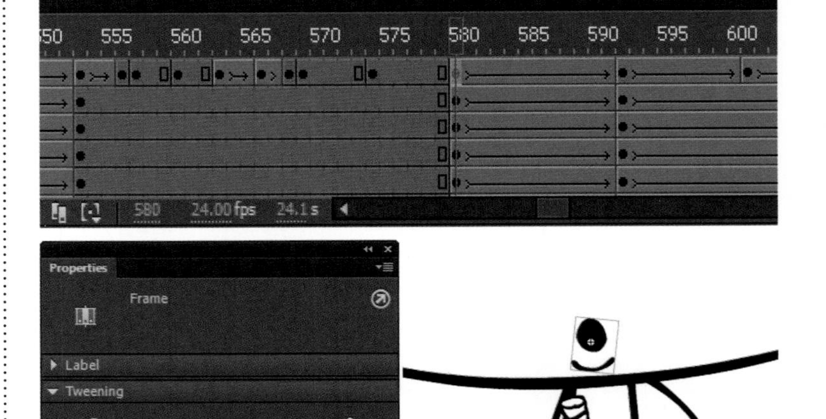

5 When you apply a Classic Tween and want the ability to control the frames nested inside Graphic symbols, select a keyframe in the tween and turn off the Sync option via the Properties panel. Note that this only applies to Classic Tweens and not the Motion Model.

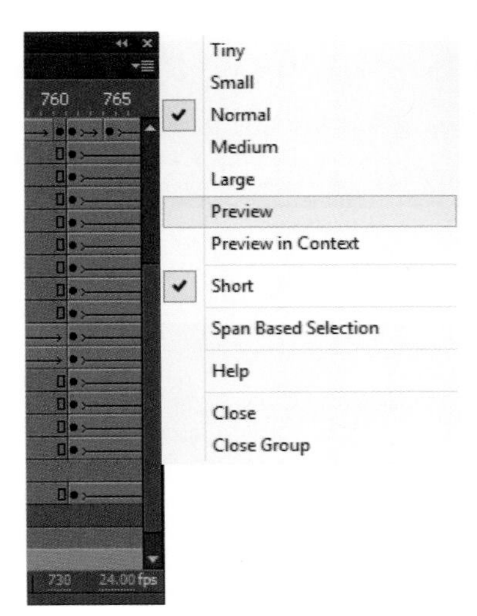

2 The Frame View drop-down menu offers several choices for you to customize the way your Timeline looks. My personal favorite is the "Short" setting, which lowers the overall height of each layer.

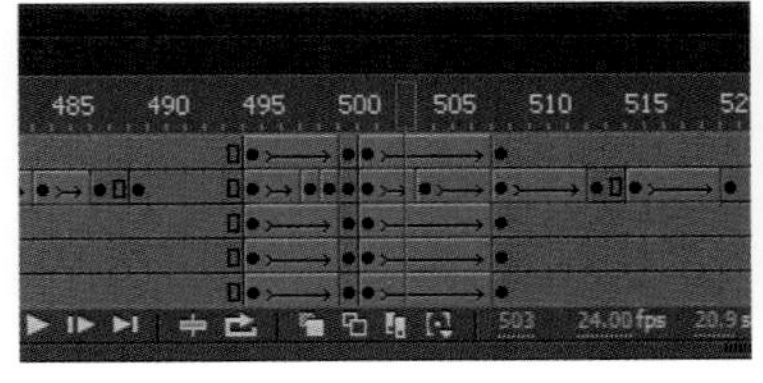

3 You can take lip syncing a bit further by tweening the mouth on the main Timeline. Tweening on the parent level adds a second layer of animation since this mouth symbol contains nested mouths as well.

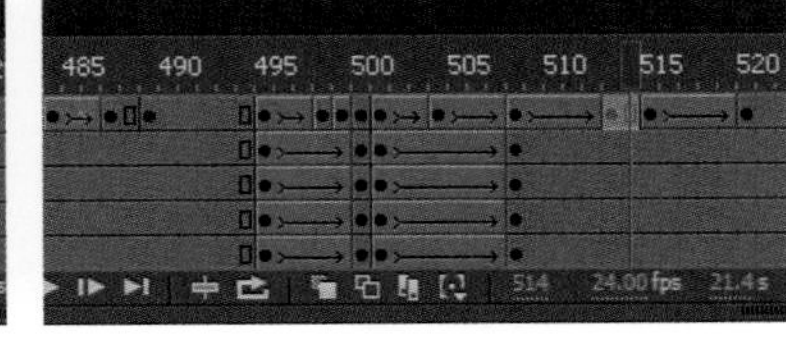

4 Using the Free Transform Tool **Q**, scale and/or skew the mouth depending on the vocal sound and apply a Classic Tween. Sync is an option when Classic Tweens are applied as shown in the next step.

HOT TIP

Check out these extensions updated for Animate CC—Anim Slider Pro ZXP by Warren Fuller (animonger.com/flashtools) and FrameSync by Justin Putney (ajarproductions.com/blog/2016/05/10/framesync-animate-cc). They are very useful extensions for controlling nested Graphic symbol animations and, personally, my favorite tools for Animate.

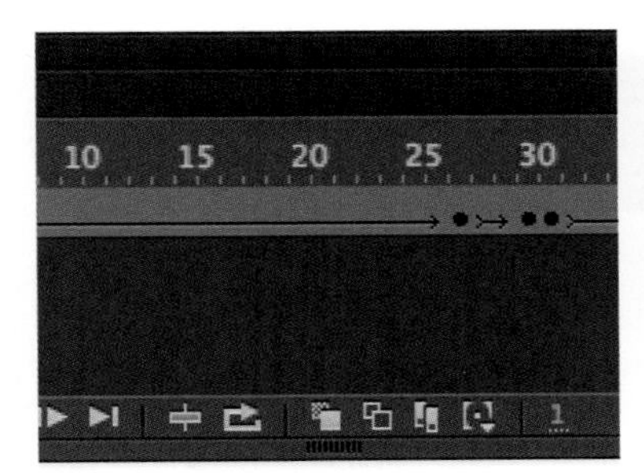

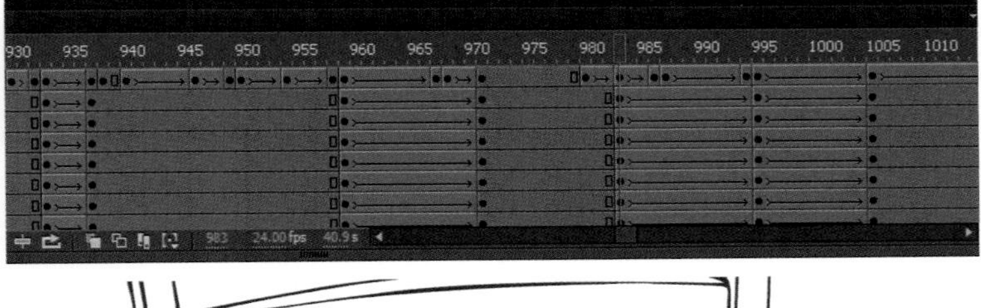

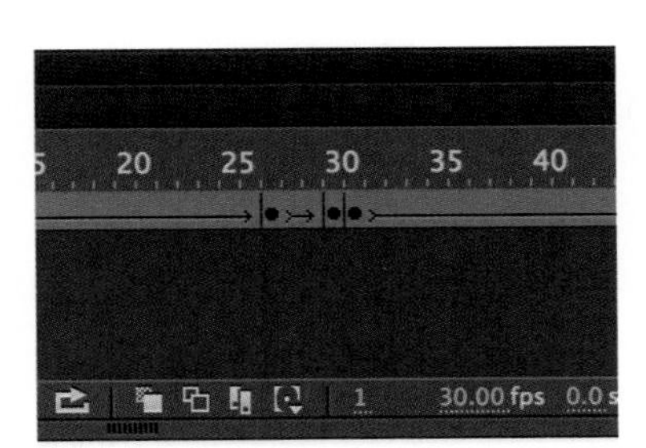

6 In the Timeline, the top image indicates a keyframe with Sync turned on. The bottom image indicates a keyframe with Sync turned off.

7 Having the ability to assign a specific frame number is critical for lip syncing. If Sync is selected, you will not be able to edit the current frame number. Once Sync is turned off, then you are free to change the frame number pertaining to the nested animation.

Sync (Classic Tweens)

ONE DAY THE CLIENT ASKS FOR YOU TO animate their company's character logo across their website. You use several keyframes and Classic Tweens to animate their character (nested inside a symbol) along a motion guide and deliver the final version to your client and await their feedback. Unfortunately the client changes their mind and asks if you could change the bee character to a dog with a jet pack instead. Do you have to do the entire animation over again? No, because you can always swap out the bee symbol for another symbol. But you have to swap out each instance of the bee for every keyframe you made in the animation. What a drag! The more keyframes on the Timeline, the more monotonous and frustrating this task can be. Sync to the rescue!

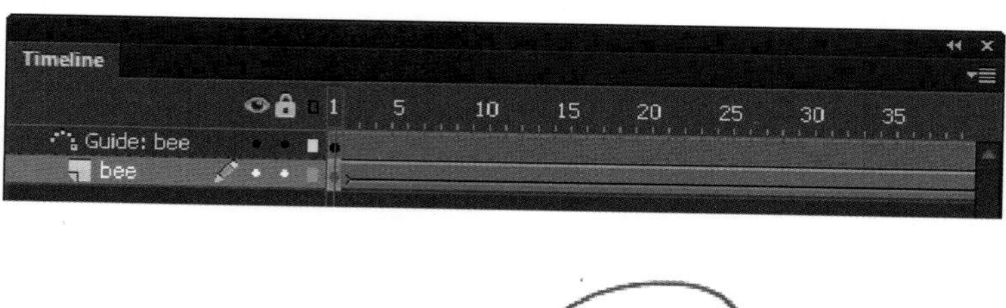

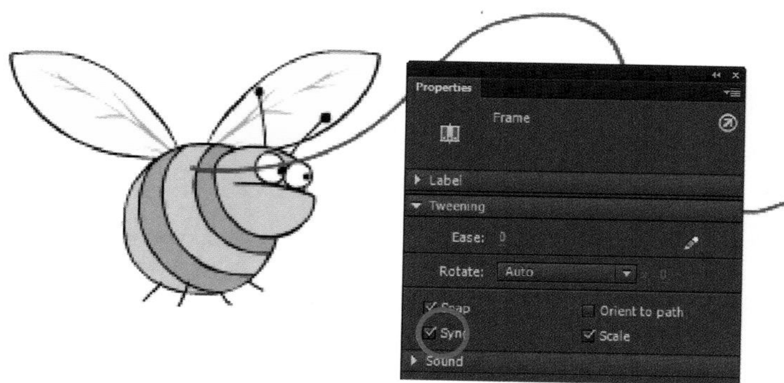

1 Let's start with a simple animation involving a nested character animation in a Graphic symbol Classic Tweened along a guided path. Apply a Classic Tween by right-clicking over the keyframe in frame 1 and selecting Create Classic Tween. Select frame 1 and turn on the Sync option in the Properties panel.

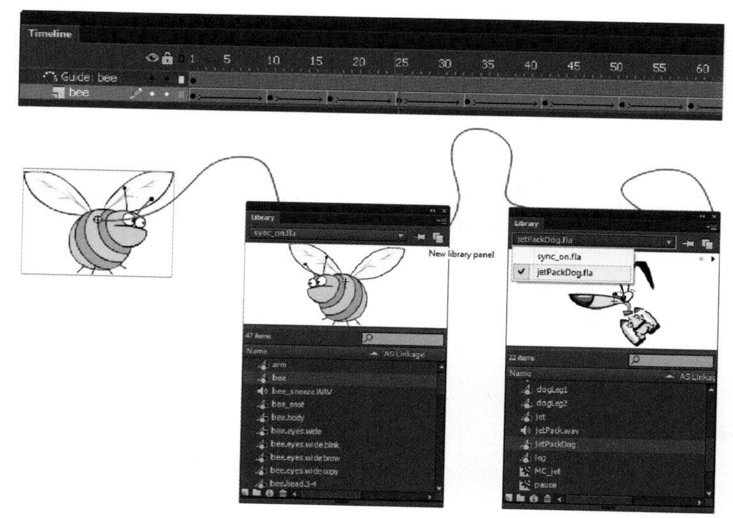

4 You just about finish the animation when the phone rings and your client informs you that they want to change the bee to a totally different character. Thanks to Sync, your time and hard work will not be wasted. Go to File > Import > Open External Library and navigate to your FLA containing the replacement symbol and click Open. You can also click the New Library panel button to open the Library of the FLA already open in Animate. A new Library panel will open displaying the symbols and assets contained in the selected FLA. Click and drag the preferred symbol from the external Library to the Library of your current document.

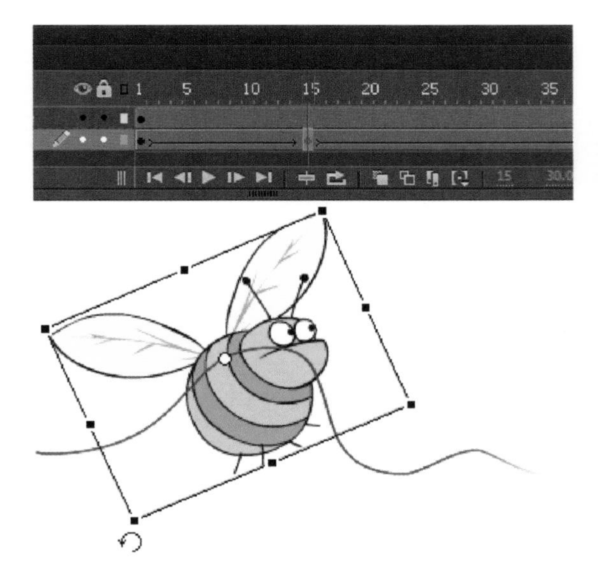

2 Insert a keyframe somewhere in the Classic Tween. Use the Free Transform Tool Q to rotate the symbol. Feel free to scale or skew the symbol as well. Because the first keyframe is "Synced," all subsequent keyframes will have Sync turned on by default as well.

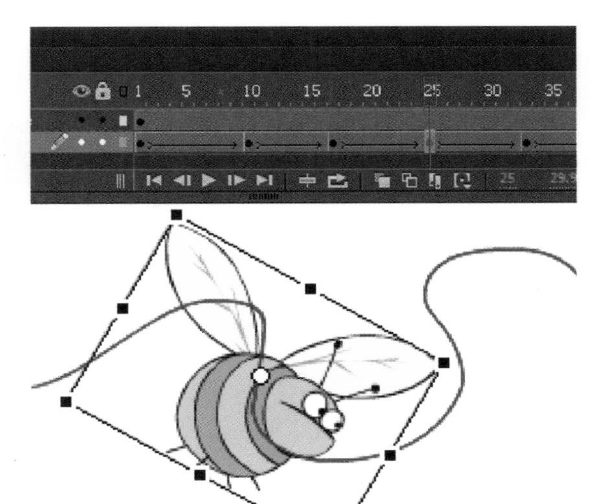

3 Continue to insert keyframes every few frames and transform your symbol by rotating and scaling. The idea here is to make this simple Classic Tween relatively complex for the example purposes.

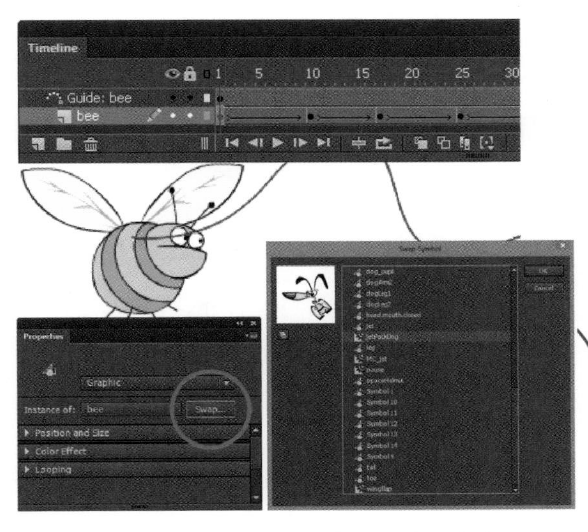

5 On the first frame of your Classic Tween, select the bee character on the Stage. In the Properties panel click the Swap button and locate the new symbol you just added to your Library and click OK.

6 Since every keyframe in the Classic Tween has the Sync option selected, your entire animation will be updated across all keyframes. Crisis averted, go and make yourself another cup of coffee, catch up on your email overflow, and get back to your client in a little while. Make sure to sound out of breath when you call them to tell them the changes have been made (just kidding).

HOT TIP

Use the Sync option to control different symbols within the same Classic Tween. Turn off Sync for certain keyframes if you want to swap to another symbol for that keyframe. Turn on Sync to keep the same symbol in sync with the main Timeline. This method will not work with Movie Clip symbols. Use only Graphic symbols because only Graphic symbols can be synced to other Timelines using the Sync option. Movie Clips have Timelines that are independent of all other Timelines and need ActionScript to be synced to other Timelines.

Sync (Motion Tweens)

THE MOTION TWEEN CHANGES EVERYTHING when it comes to tweens and what we can do with them. If you remember one thing about them, remember this: the Motion Tween is object based while the Classic Tween is frame based. Being frame based refers to the classic approach to animation in the Timeline through creating and removing keyframes, applying tweens, creating and applying motion guides, and copying and pasting frames. With Motion Tweens, most tasks are applied to the object on the Stage while Animate does most of the work for us. For this particular animation, the joke is always on the dog. Each of his meals are dropped into his dish and each time the meal is different (as well as revolting and inedible). I knew this scene would be reused, so it was critical to build it in a way that made it easy to swap out the object that falls into the bowl. If you thought using the Sync option to swap symbols across animations couldn't be easier, think again.

1 The first step is to draw the object that is to land in the bowl and convert it to a symbol. Position the symbol above the bowl and almost off the top edge of the Stage. Since the Motion Tween is *object* based, right-click over the symbol and select "Create Motion Tween." Animate will automatically create a motion span in this layer and insert a duration of frames equal to a full second based on the document's frame rate, which will likely be plenty of time as this animation won't last beyond 1 second.

4 Once you have the animation complete, swapping out the current symbol for an alternative symbol is surprisingly easier than using the Sync method from previous examples. Thanks to the Motion Tween, all you need to do is open the Library panel, find the symbol you wish to use in place of the current symbol, and drag it to the Stage (make sure the layer with the motion span is selected). Animate will prompt you to confirm that you want to replace the existing tween target object. Click OK.

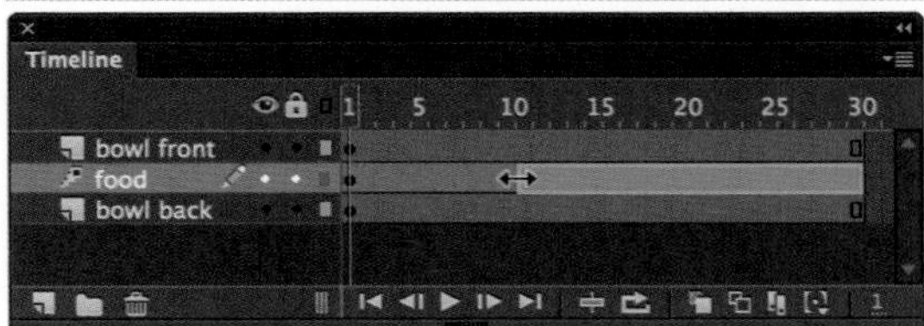

2 Insert some time before the animation actually starts, which can be a bit cumbersome when using Classic Tweens. With the Motion Tween all you need to do is click and drag the left edge of the motion span and drag it to a new frame. Position the frame indicator somewhere around frame 15, hold down the *Shift* key, and drag the symbol vertically so that it ends up inside the dog bowl.

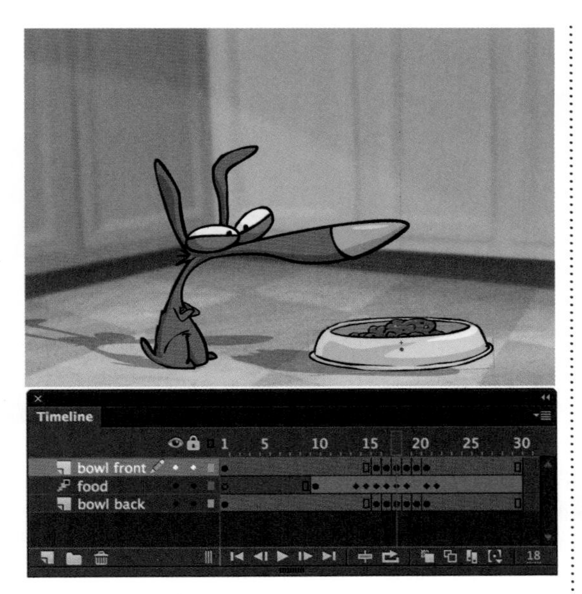

3 To provide the illusion of weight to the dog food, additional keyframes and positions were added as well as some squashing and stretching. To make the effect even more convincing, the dog bowl itself can be animated as if it is reacting to the impact of the food.

5 Your new object has now been applied to the entire motion span, replacing the original object across all keyframes and properties. Using this technique has obvious advantages over the Sync method. Instead of selecting the first keyframe in a Classic Tween and swapping out the symbol from the Library, the Motion Tween method is a simple case of dragging a new object to the Stage with the layer selected containing the animation.

6 You can even select the span and press the *Delete* key to remove the object entirely from the animation. All of the Motion Tween information is retained, allowing you to drag a new object to the Stage or copy and paste a new object into the existing span.

HOT TIP

To remove frames or cut frames from within a span, drag to select the frames and choose Remove Frames or Cut Frames from the span context menu. To extend the presence of a tweened object on Stage beyond either end of its tween, Shift-drag either end frame of its tween span. Animate adds frames to the end of the span without tweening those frames.

Hinging Body Parts

WITH FREE TRANSFORM, WE CAN edit the center point of a symbol instance, thus editing the point on which the symbol rotates or "hinges" itself. Any simulation to inverse kinematics is purely coincidental. This technique does not allow you to link objects together in a chain like the Bone Tool does but can be useful for manipulating objects individually.

1 Select the Free Transform Tool Q and then click on one of your symbols on your Stage. The center point of the symbol is now represented by a solid white circle. Simply click and drag this circle to a new location. In my example, I moved the center point of the arm to approximately where the shoulder is.

4 You can select multiple symbols across multiple layers and hinge them as if they were one single object. With the Free Transform Tool still selected, hold down the Shift key and click on multiple symbols on the stage. The center point will now be relative to the center point of all the symbols selected.

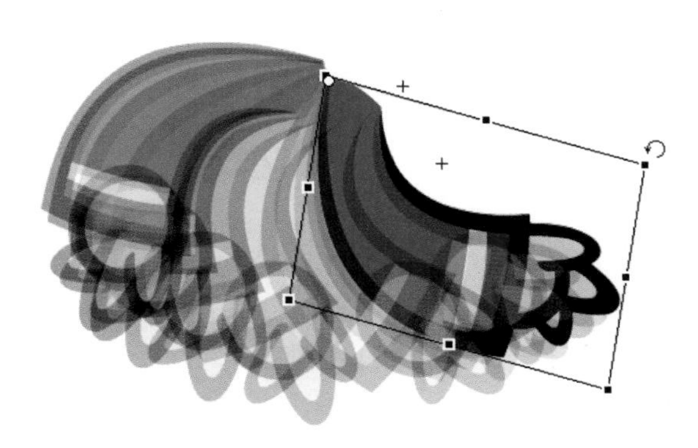

2 With the same tool, rotate the arm symbol. It will hinge based on its new center point, making it easier to position each arm movement in relation to the body symbol.

3 Repeat this process for each body part you want hinged. As you can see, I even hinged the ear symbol as well. Now you can start animating by creating additional keyframes and apply Classic Tweens throughout your Timeline.

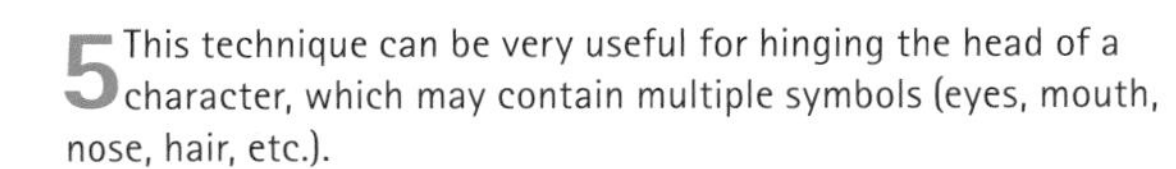

5 This technique can be very useful for hinging the head of a character, which may contain multiple symbols (eyes, mouth, nose, hair, etc.).

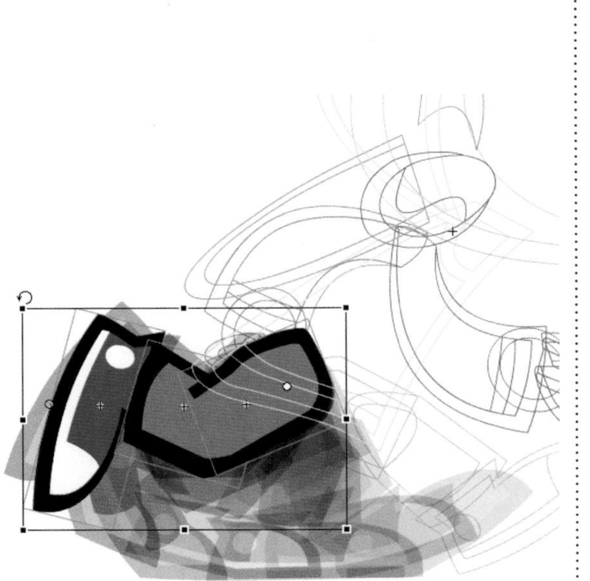

6 The center point for each individual symbol will be retained, but the center point representing multiple selected symbols will not be remembered once they are deselected.

HOT TIP

To select multiple objects, it is often easier to click and drag with the Selection Tool across the objects on Stage. Make sure you set the center point for each symbol on frame 1 of your Timeline. If the center point is different between keyframes where a Classic Tween is applied, your symbol will drift unexpectedly.

Closing the Gaps

FORM FOLLOWS FUNCTION IN Animate. The more stylized the design, the more flexibility you will have when it comes to adding motion. On the other hand, the more anatomically correct your character is designed, the less you can get away with when the time comes to animate it. Sometimes a project comes along where the design style demands realism. As a result, the animation technique demands attention to detail, which can be limiting to a certain degree. One particular issue is the unsightly gap that is often created when bending arms and legs at their respective joints. The solution, "caps." At least that's what I like to call them. An elbow cap for the arms and a knee cap for the legs can solve the dreaded gap problem.

EVIL MIME CHARACTER: YAHOO! SUPER MESSENGERS/MUDBUBBLE

1 The Evil Mime character for the Yahoo! Super Messengers project was designed in a very anatomically correct style. This style caused some problems during the animation process, specifically the joints between limbs. When the arms or legs are in their original positions (as they were drawn originally), there's no gap.

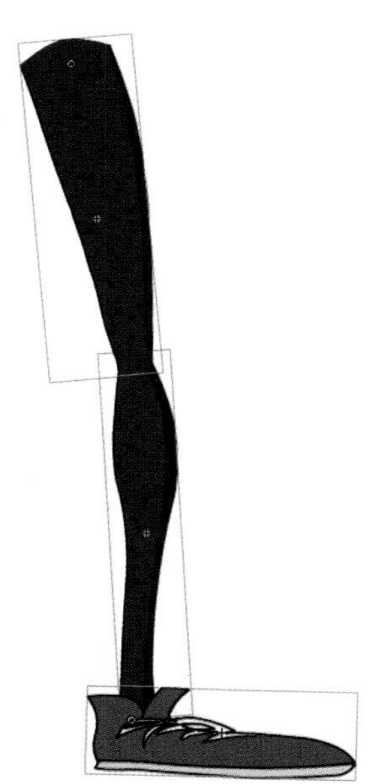

5 The leg, like the arm, works quite well when in a straight position. The upper thigh blends perfectly into the calf and shin.

6 The problem arises when these body parts are pushed to their anatomical limit when rotated and bent at the knee (or lack thereof).

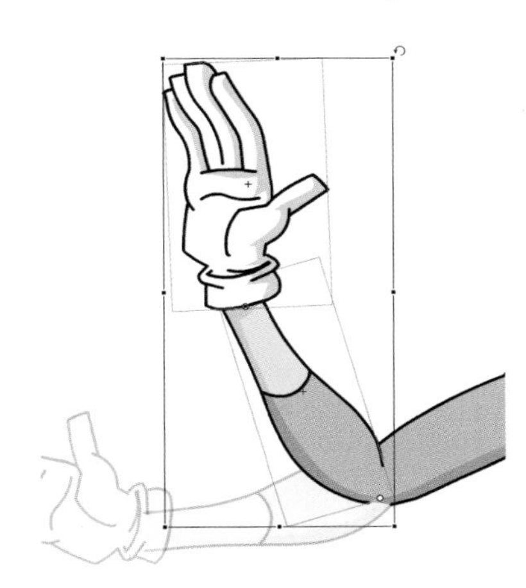

2 Once the arm is bent, the gap appears between the forearm and upper arm symbols. The gap is a problem inherent with this style of line work.

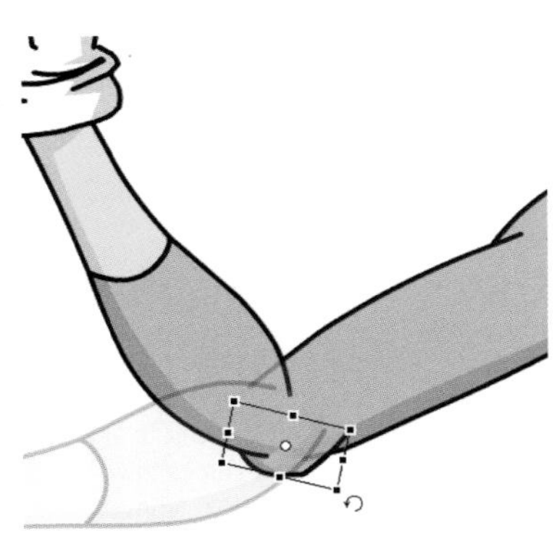

3 The solution is to add a new symbol in the form of an elbow. This new cap can be used as filler to hide that ugly gap between limbs when rotating.

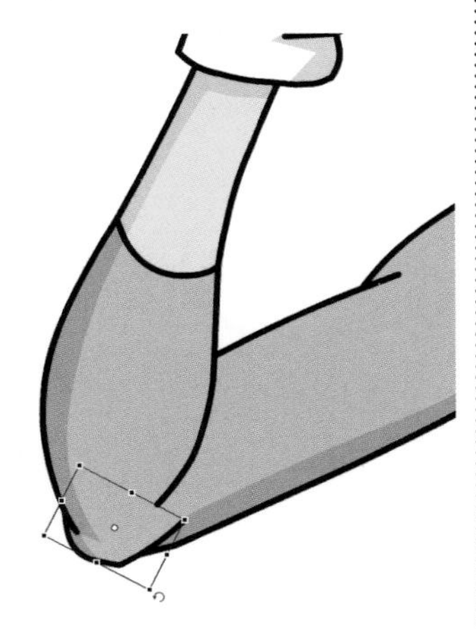

4 Use the Free Transform Tool Q to skew the cap symbol, so it aligns with both arm symbols bridging the gap between them, so to speak.

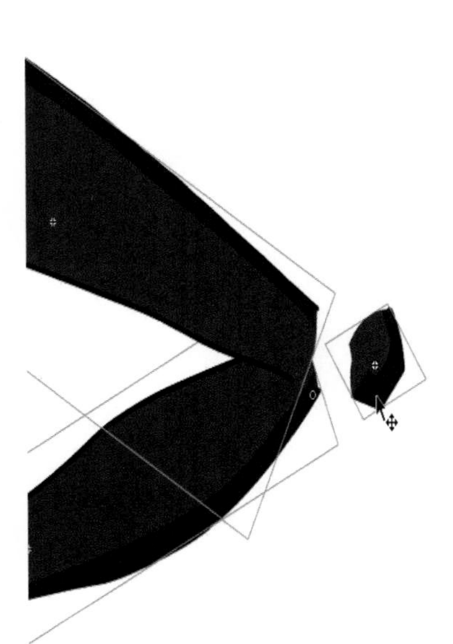

7 Once again, adding a knee cap symbol solves this problem quite nicely.

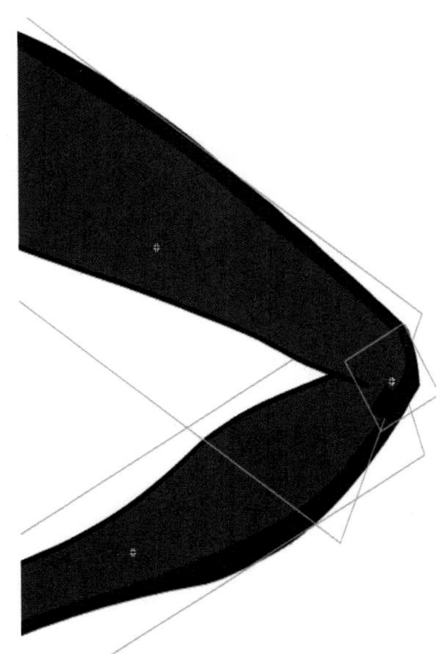

8 Position the knee cap in between the upper and lower leg symbols and align as necessary. Use the Free Transform Tool Q to skew and scale the knee so that it fits properly.

9 It may seem like a lot of work to add elbow and knee caps and subsequently more layers to your Animate document, but in the end, the results of your hard work and attention to detail will not go unnoticed.

HOT TIP

Cut-out style characters like this one are perfect for animating when linked together in a chain-like fashion.

Walk Cycle

LET'S FACE IT. AS AN ANIMATOR, YOU ARE eventually going to be faced with the task of making somebody or something walk. For whatever reason, newcomers to animation regard walk cycles as extremely difficult. Why? I won't lie to you, they are. Well, in an anatomically accurate way, they can be very challenging. As an animator, you will find it nearly impossible to avoid the walk cycle, so it may be best to face your fear head-on right now. You just might learn that walk cycles aren't all that difficult to accomplish. There are several ways to make the task of animating a walk cycle very difficult or relatively easy. Let's examine the easy way. The best way to create a walk cycle in Animate is to animate the character walking in place, as if on a conveyor belt. The main idea here is to drag an instance of this looping walk cycle animation to the Stage and use a Classic Tween to animate the character walking across the scene. We'll get more into that after we tackle the actual walk cycle.

1 Design your character in three-quarter view. At this angle the character is simply easier to animate, especially when it comes to walk cycle animations. Next, convert your entire character and all its parts into a Graphic symbol. You will be working entirely inside this symbol to create your walk cycle.

2 Let's concentrate on just one leg for now. In fact, turn all other layers off so that only one leg of your character is visible. This character's leg is made up of three different symbols: an upper thigh, a lower leg, and a sneaker. This straightforward setup is flexibility enough for a simple walk cycle.

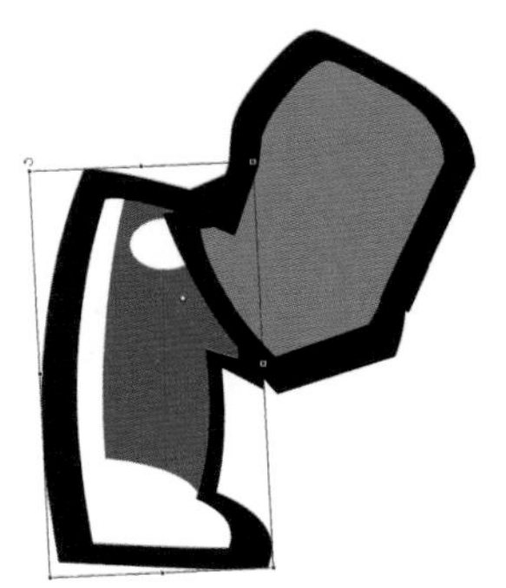

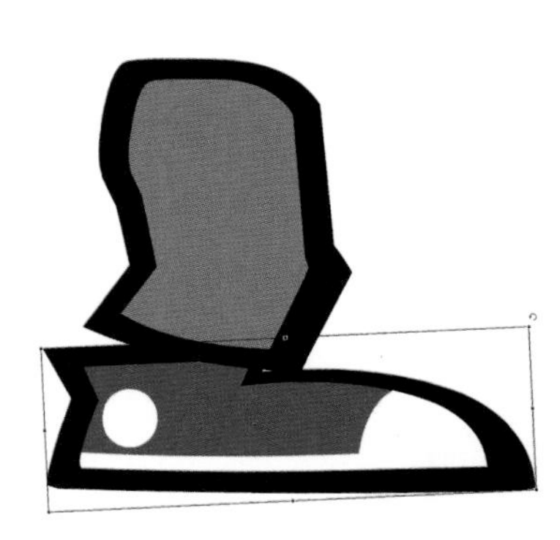

4 Notice that I didn't use the same sneaker for every frame. Depending on the position of the leg, I duplicated the original symbol, gave it a new name, and edited its shape to reflect its new position. This type of detail is what I love to add to my animations, and I really feel, as subtle as it may be, it adds a lot to the overall look and feel of the character's movements.

8 Feel free to experiment with the amount of frames between each of your leg positions. You can have more frames for when the foot is sliding back along the ground (so it travels more slowly) and fewer frames while the leg is off the ground (so it travels more quickly), returning it quickly to its initial position. This change in speed can create the illusion that the character is heavy, or perhaps carrying something heavy. If you do the opposite and have the foot slide quickly across the ground and slowly when off the ground, it may suggest your character is on a slippery surface, such as ice.

MUDBUBBLE BOY

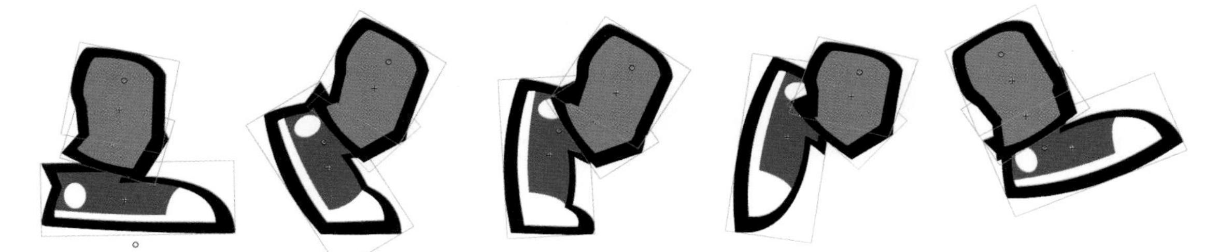

3 Position the leg into several major walk positions using keyframes. Start with the leg planted firmly on the ground. The next position is the foot still on the ground but bent so that the heel is up off the ground. Then create another keyframe and position the leg just before it is lifted off the ground. Next, position the leg completely off the ground and in its most rearward position. The final keyframe shows the leg is in its most forward position off the ground. Use the Free Transform Tool Q to rotate each leg instance until it is in the desired position. Notice there are several slightly different shapes to his sneaker based on the amount of weight (or lack of weight) being placed upon it. When it is fully compressed on the ground, its bottom edge is flat. Just before it's lifted off the ground, it is bent just after the toe. When it is entirely off the ground, its bottom edge is slightly rounded. These details may seem very insignificant, but in the grand scheme of things, they can make all the difference.

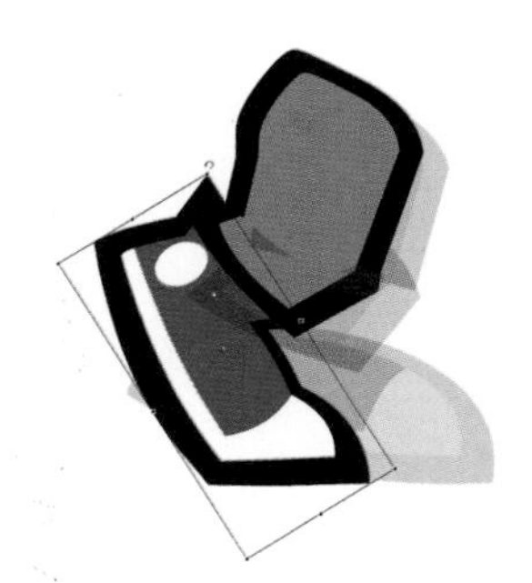

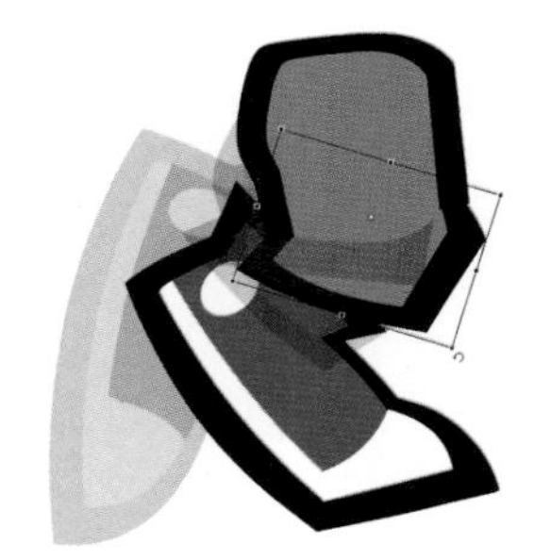

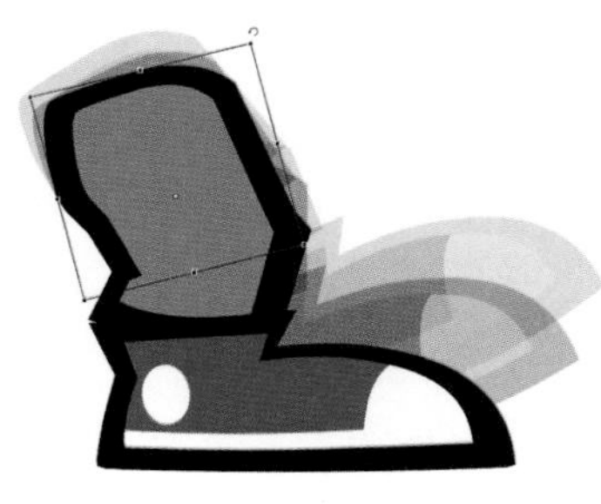

5 Turn on Onion Skin ⌥ alt Shift O and adjust the playhead brackets, so you can use your established leg positions as references. Create keyframes across all layers that contain your leg symbols.

6 Use the Free Transform Tool Q to rotate and move each leg symbol into an intermediate position relative to the keyframes you already created. The number of frames between the major leg positions will determine the characteristics of the walk cycle.

7 Experiment with the frames between each leg position. Adding more frames when the foot is sliding back along the ground will create the effect of the character gripping the surface. Add fewer frames while the leg is returning to its initial position.

9 Play back your animation constantly, so you can get real-time visual feedback as to your process. This type of animation work is trial and error and depends on your personal animation style to get the walk cycle to look and feel good to you. Don't get frustrated. It simply takes practice. Sometimes it helps to not think of it as an actual leg. Try to imagine it's not a leg at all but some kind of mechanical assembly like a basic pulley or lever system. This thought process can make animating less daunting and a lot more fun. Open the "leg_simulation.fla" from the downloadable assets. This FLA contains an example of a walk cycle experiment. I made it to show how a walk cycle can be thought of in mechanical terms. It was a fun experiment because it removes the intimidation factor that is associated with animating a walk cycle.

HOT TIP

Before you start, it may be a good idea to put down your stylus and go for a walk. I'm sure the fresh air won't hurt, but the intention is for you to study how your body moves during the act of walking. As an animator, you will find that studying from real life will be your greatest resource. Notice your right leg and left arm move in the same direction with each other. Same thing happens with your left leg and right arm. Noticing details like these will help your animation.

SHORTCUTS
MAC WIN BOTH

Walk Cycle (cont.)

ONCE YOU ARE FINISHED creating enough keyframes and leg positions and you are satisfied with the movement of your leg, we can now move on to the other leg. Since you already animated one leg, there is no reason to start from scratch with the second leg (unless the other leg is designed differently). Therefore, delete the other leg entirely from the Stage. Seriously, go ahead and delete it. We don't need it any more. Trust me.

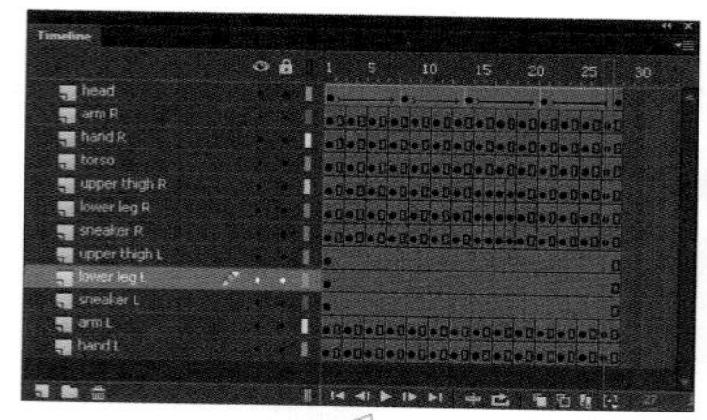

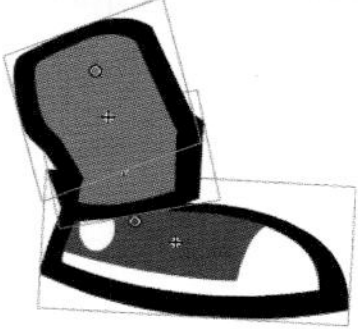

10 Hold down the Shift key to select multiple layers and drag them to the trashcan icon or click on the trashcan icon to delete them from the Timeline.

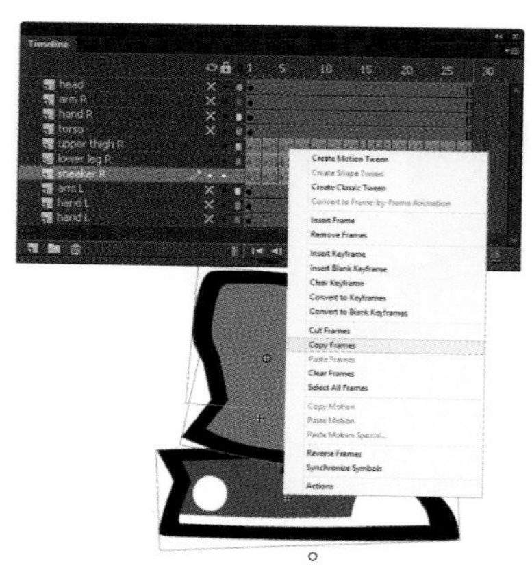

11 Select the entire range of frames and layers of the leg you previously animated. Right-click (^ + click) over the highlighted area and select "Copy Frames" from the context menu.

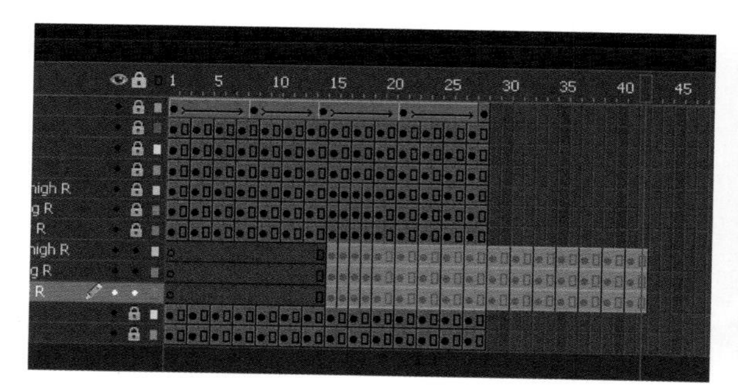

15 Select this entire range of frames and layers by clicking and dragging across all of them.

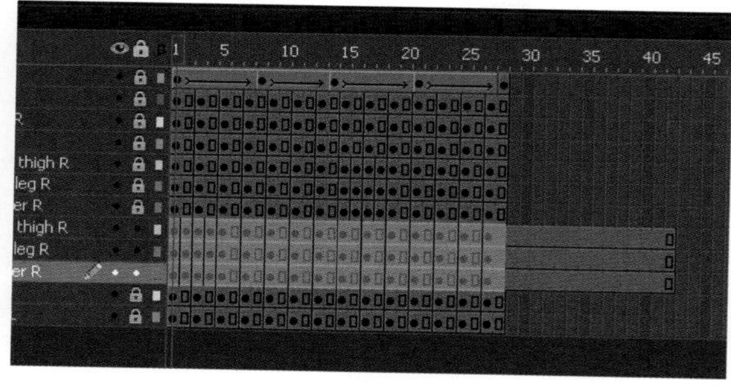

16 Click and drag this entire range of frames and layers to the left until they start on frame 1. Remove the residual frames by selecting them and "Removing" them from the right-click context menu.

20 As we did with the leg animations, animate just one of your character's arms and then copy and paste its keyframes into a new layer(s) to achieve the second arm. Select the first half of your arm/hand animation and place it after the latter half of the animation.

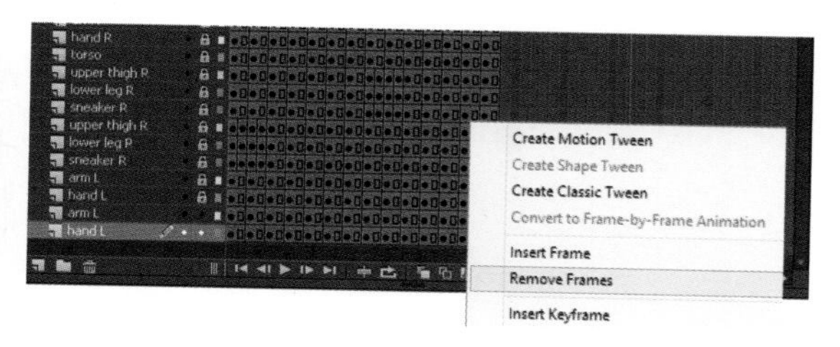

21 Select and drag the entire arm/hand animation, so it starts again on frame 1 and remove the residual frames that are left behind.

12 Add a new layer below your existing leg, select the entire range of frames, right-click over them, and select "Paste Frames" from the context menu.

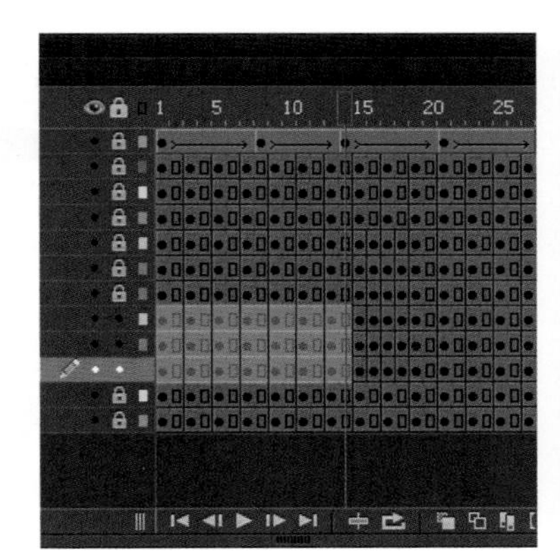

13 Lock all layers except these three you just copied and pasted. Select the first half of this duplicated leg animation by clicking and dragging across layers and frames.

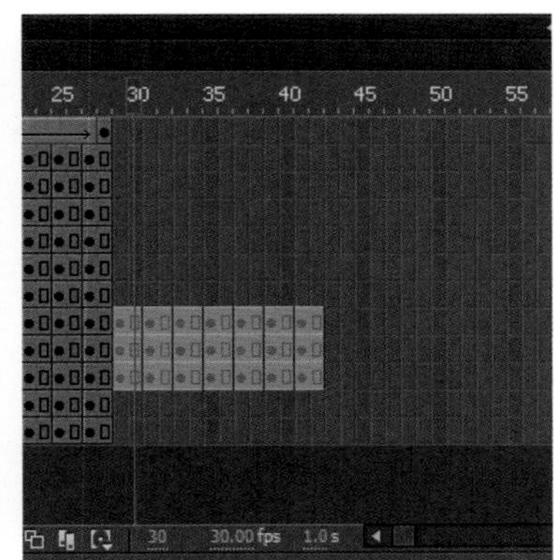

14 Click and drag the entire section of highlighted frames down the Timeline and place it after the latter half of the animation.

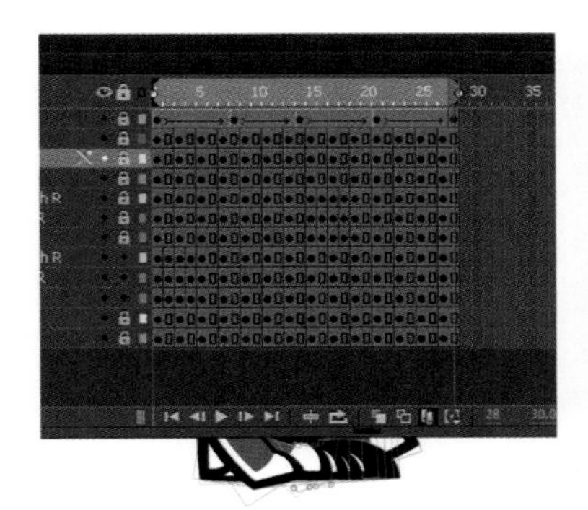

17 Using Edit Multiple Frames, select the new leg symbols and use the arrow keys to nudge them to the right and up slightly. Nudging will help separate the two leg assemblies.

18 Apply a color tint to the leg symbols using black with about 30% strength. The tint gives the illusion the back leg is in a shadow and helps create a sense of depth.

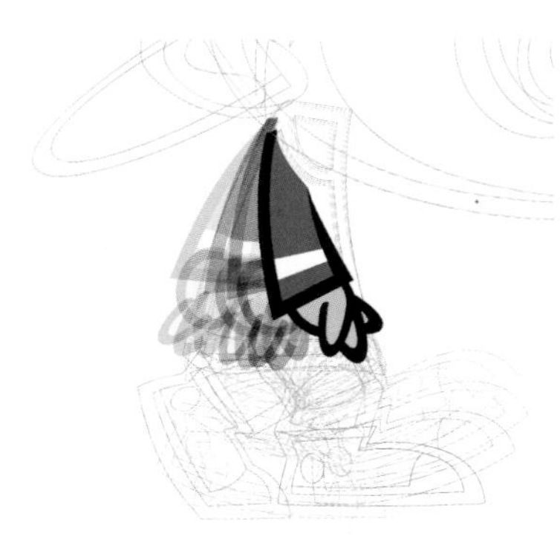

19 Animate the arm and hand symbols by rocking them back and forth. You can use frame-by-frame or Classic Tweens depending on your needs.

22 Turn on Edit Multiple Frames again and select this entire range of arm/hand symbols. Click on them once with the Selection Tool V and apply the same color tint as the legs.

23 With Edit Multiple Frames still turned on, use the arrow keys to nudge them up and to the right slightly.

24 You can add to your walk cycle animation by adding some motion to the character's head and body. It comes down to personal preference and your individual animation style.

HOT TIP

Be careful when using the Edit Multiple Frames feature. Make sure only the layers you want to edit are unlocked and all other layers are locked to avoid accidents.

Anticipation

BY DEFINITION, ANTICIPATION IS THE preparation for a particular action or movement. It can also be used in animation to attract the viewer's attention to a specific event that is about to occur. An example of anticipation would be an archer pulling an arrow back along its bow or a baseball player raising his arm to throw a ball.

Anticipation can also be used to build suspense in a scene. It tells the viewer something is about to happen, and the longer the anticipation is, the more suspenseful it can be.

Anticipation is critical to making believable animation. Without anticipation, your animation may appear too abrupt and unnatural. It is important as an animator to study from life and notice how we move and react anatomically.

1 Here the character is in its initial position. There's not much going on in terms of action, but we can assume he might do something due to the slight tension in his stance and his hands being in close proximity to both holstered guns.

4 The first step shows the character still on one foot but also leaning back a little further and crouching lower with all his weight on this one leg. This stance is obviously not a comfortable gesture that could be held for very long; hence, there is anticipation that something is about to happen.

COWBOY: MUDBUBBLE

2 To anticipate the action, animate the cowboy in the opposite direction he will be moving. Make a new keyframe across all layers where the next position change will occur and use the Free Transform Tool **Q** to rotate and position your character. Apply a Classic Tween and some easing out to imply physical tension within our character.

3 Sometimes an animation requires more than one keyframe position to achieve the right movement and gesture. For this particular animation, I used four different gestures for the anticipation animation, each with a Classic Tween and some easing applied.

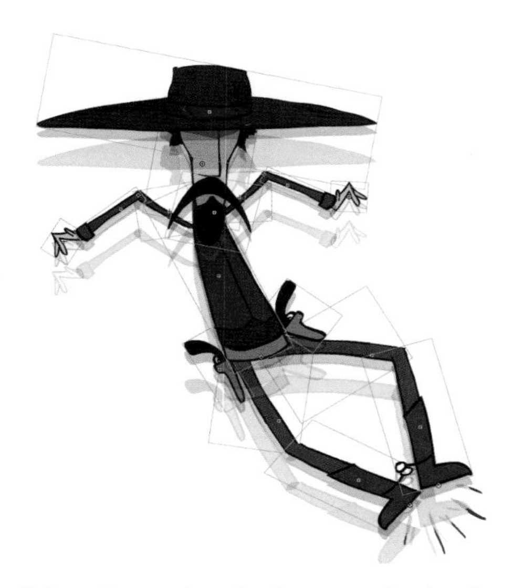

5 Here I am pushing the envelope by adding even more tension in the character's overall gesture. There's no doubt he is about to react in a very physical way.

6 Sir Isaac Newton showed us for every action there is an opposite but equal reaction. In keeping with this law of motion, animate the character moving in the opposite direction and ultimately performing the anticipatory action.

HOT TIP

Use Colored Onion Skinning to differentiate between previous frames, the current frame, and upcoming frames. Default colors are set to blue for past, red for current, and green for future. You can customize these colors, too. If you want to make it easier to see your character, set the previous and next frames to gray.

Tradigital Animation

THE FUSION OF TRADITIONAL AND digital animation has given us "tradigital" animation. I don't know who invented the term, but the effect was first shown to me by Ibis Fernandez, a well-known and talented animator who blew me away when he sent me a sample of this technique a few years ago. Up until that point in my career, I thought I knew every trick in the book. It was clear to me I had more to learn.

Tradigital animation is the result of traditional animation techniques translated by the use of digital tools. The end result may look traditional, but the process is very different and less time-consuming. When a client deadline is looming, traditional animation goes out the window. A common argument among traditionalists is that tweens are too easy to use and often become relied upon for every aspect of an animation. Dependence on tweens alone may result in your animation looking very mechanical and stiff. So where do you draw the line (sorry, bad pun)? What technique should you use? Classic Tweens? Motion Tweens? Shape Tweens? Frame-by-frame?

Answer: All of the above. Don't limit yourself to just one technique if you don't have to. Use the technique that the action calls for, even if it means combining two or more techniques. What is so impressive about this particular technique is the fluidity of the movement you can achieve. Draw image "A" and then image "B" with the Line (or Pencil) tool. Then with each line segment on its own layer, Shape Tween from "A" to "B." Merge all your layers, clean up your lines, and add some fills and shading—voilà! You're a "tradigitalist."

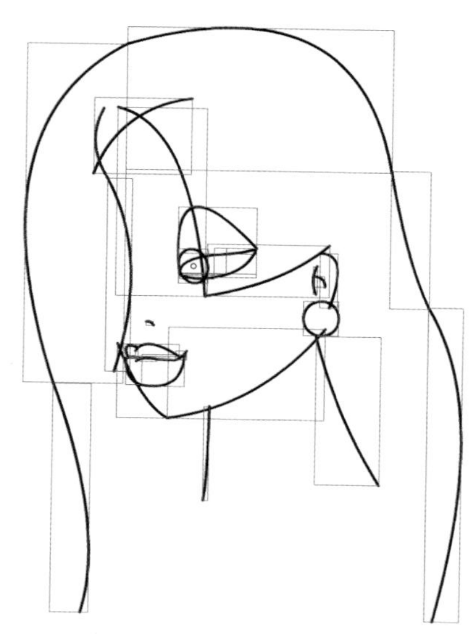

1 For this technique to be a success, you need two different drawings of your character or object. Object Drawing mode is highly recommended here as each stroke will remain as a separate object that can still be edited. It is also critical because you will later distribute each stroke to its own layer.

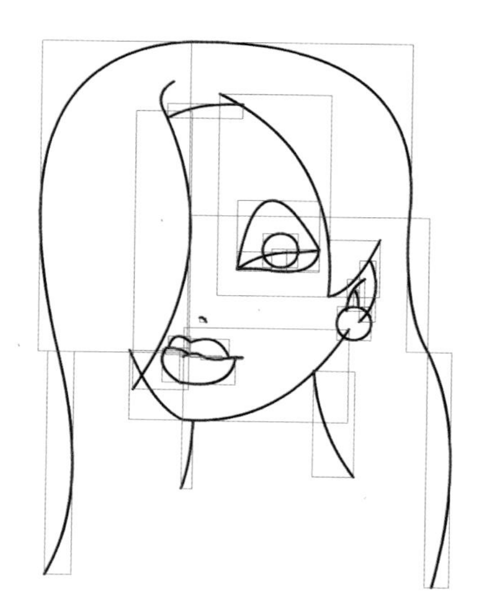

2 Insert a blank keyframe F7 in a new frame (frame 30 will do), and draw the new angle of your character or object. The trick here is to use the same number of strokes as you did in the first drawing. You could also choose to insert a keyframe F6 and edit the same strokes to reflect your new angle.

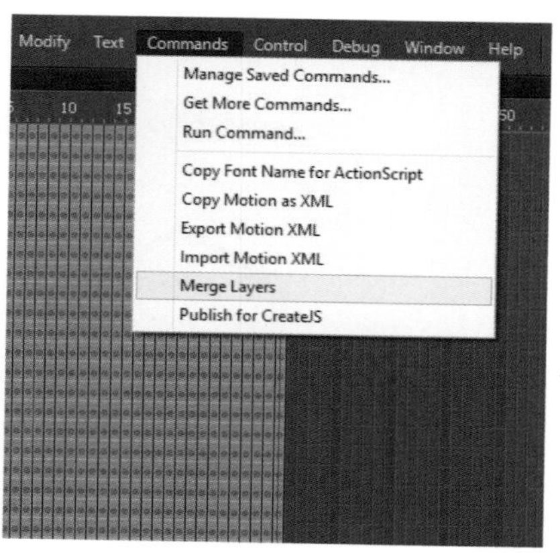

6 Make sure you have installed the Merge Layers extension that was mentioned in the HOT TIP. Select all layers and keyframes and go to Commands > Merge Layers. This extension will run the JSFL command that will compress all keyframes and layers to one single layer for you.

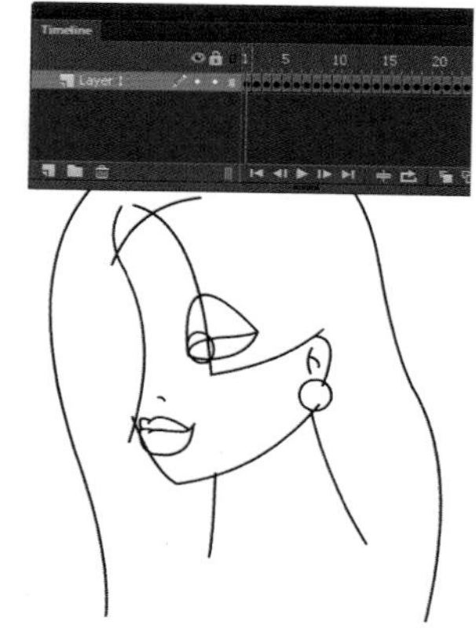

7 You can delete all the old layers as they will all be empty after the merge. Go to File > Save As and save this file with a new name, which is important because you may decide to make some changes to your image at some point in the future. After all layers are merged, making changes becomes very difficult.

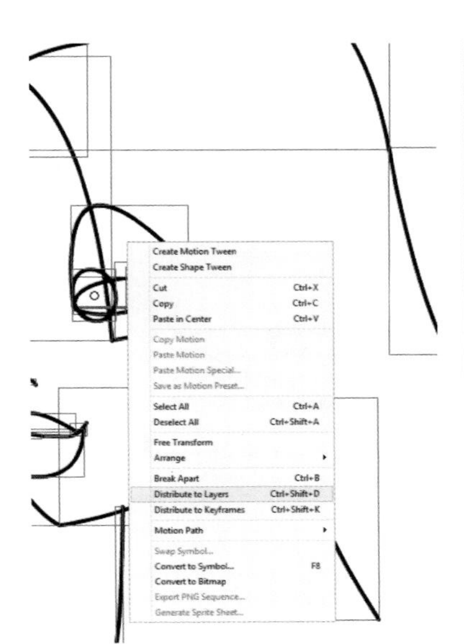

3 For both drawings, select all of your strokes, right-click over them, and select Distribute to Layers from the context menu. Since this process will create a whole new set of layers for each drawing, you will need to select all the keyframes for one drawing and drag them to the other drawing's layers.

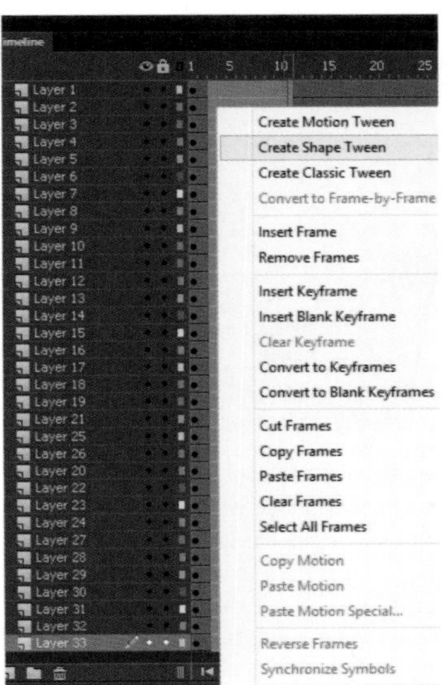

4 Drag across all layers, right-click, and select Create Shape Tween from the context menu or Insert > Shape Tween. Now is the time to add easing if preferred.

5 Next you need to prepare your layers for merging. Drag across all layers and frames, selecting them all in gold. Right-click over the highlighted area, select Convert to Frame-by-Frame Animation from the context menu to convert the entire animation to keyframes, and remove the tween spans in a single command.

8 Next, you need to break apart strokes from the Object Drawing mode. Why? Because if you have overlapping strokes and want to add color fills to your image, it needs to be flattened one step further for editing. Turn on the Edit Multiple Frames feature and adjust the frame indicator brackets to span all keyframes. Break apart ⌘ ctrl B to merge all strokes.

9 Use the Selection Tool V while holding down the Shift key to select all unwanted strokes and delete them. In this situation, it is simply a fact of life that as an animator, you eventually will have to perform the tedious chore of cleaning up after yourself or—even worse—someone else's work.

10 As tedious as the last step was, here's your reward, a very slick looking animation that looks like it was made using three dimensions. But it gets even better when you add color and shading.

HOT TIP

David Wolfe has created a "Merge Layers" extension for Animate that is available at www.toonmonkey.com/extensions.html. Download the Flash CC version, which has already been converted to the ZXP format, and install it with Adobe Extension Manager CC. Techniques like the "tradigital" topic would take at least five times longer to create without the use of a Merge Layers extension.

Tradigital Animation (cont.)

11 Once all your strokes are connected and cleaned up, mix your colors and start filling. You will need to apply all color fills across all keyframes by hand. Animate has no automatic way of applying these color fills for you.

12 Occasionally you may find an area of your image will not accept the fill color. Usually the cause is a gap between strokes that is hard to see. Make sure Snap is turned on and use the Selection Tool to drag their endpoints until they "snap" together.

13 Let's take this effect to the next level by adding shading. Add two new layers above your animation and draw two shapes in each new layer. Use the color black mixed with about 30% alpha. Make sure the brush has Smoothing set to 100. The fewer vector points, the better.

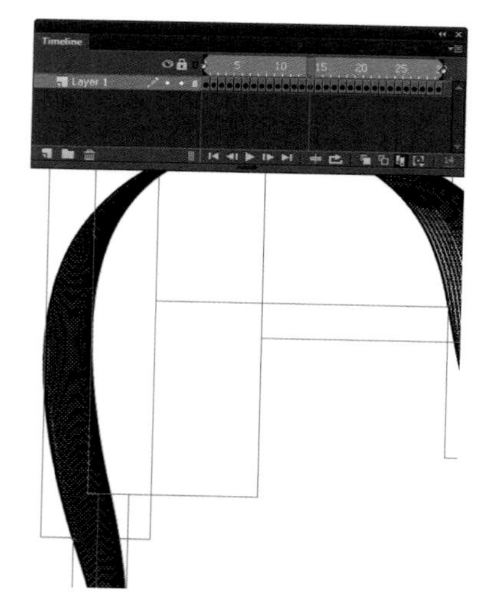

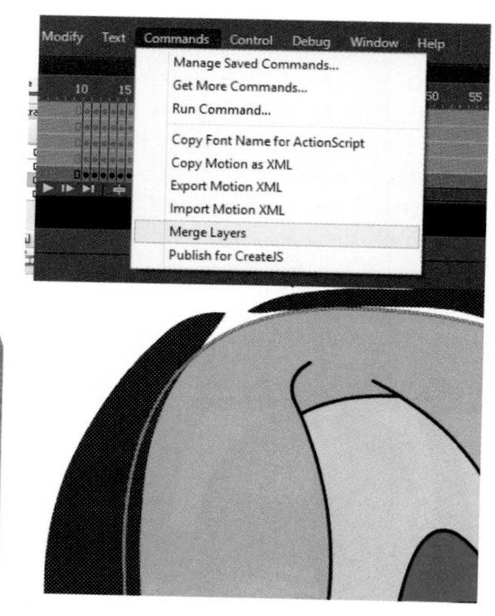

17 Turn on the Edit Multiple Frames feature and make sure the Frame Indicator brackets span all keyframes. Select all ⌘ ctrl A and break apart ⌘ ctrl B all Drawing Model objects to merge all the strokes together.

18 Copy all frames of your outline from the previous step and paste them into a new layer above your shading layers. Make sure all other layers are locked, turn on Edit Multiple Frames, select all strokes, and change their color to bright red or something in contrast to the character itself.

19 Turn off Edit Multiple Frames and unlock the two layers containing the shading animations. Select all frames across all three of these layers and go to Commands > Merge Layers to compress them down to one layer. Delete the remaining empty layers.

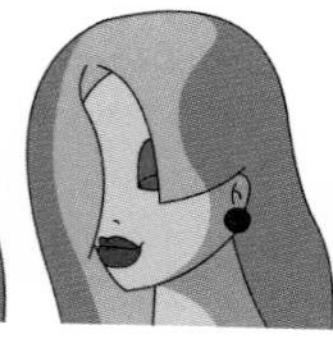

14 Insert a keyframe in both layers in your last frame of your animation. Move the left shape about 20 pixels to the left and the right shape the same distance to the right. Use the Selection Tool to bend their outlines to reflect the new contour of your character and apply Shape Tweens.

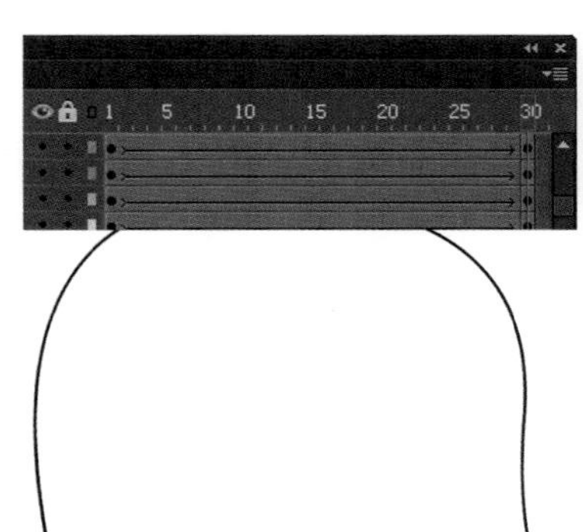

15 Remember the previously saved version of this animation? Open it and find the layers containing the outline strokes of your character. Select them and Copy/Paste Frames into a new document. You will use these strokes to "cut" away the shading you will not need.

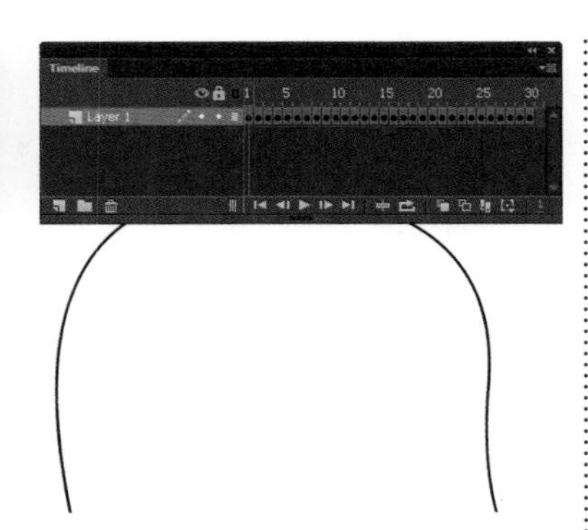

16 Select all frames and layers, right-click over the highlighted area, and select Convert to Frame-by-Frame Animation. Merge all layers using the Merge Layers JSFL extension Commands > Merge Layers.

20 Use the Selection Tool to click anywhere outside the shapes to deselect them. Select the shaded area outside of your character's outline and delete it. Repeat this procedure for every keyframe.

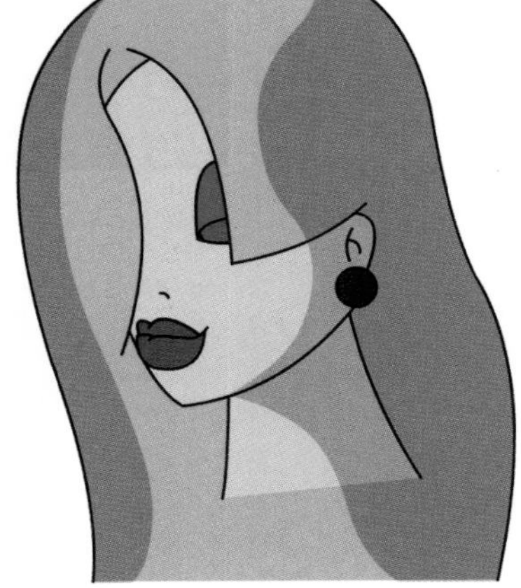

21 The final step is to double-click the red stroke (double-clicking selects all segments in the stroke), and delete it. Repeat this step for every keyframe until you are left with just the shading shapes inside the contours of the original character.

22 Next, test your movie and sit back to enjoy the fruits of your labor. This technique is great when you want to add some realism and drama to your shot. But remember to plan ahead carefully to avoid having to spend more time making revisions.

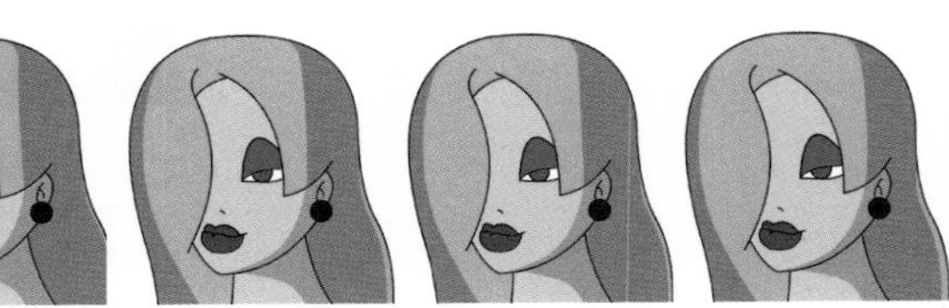

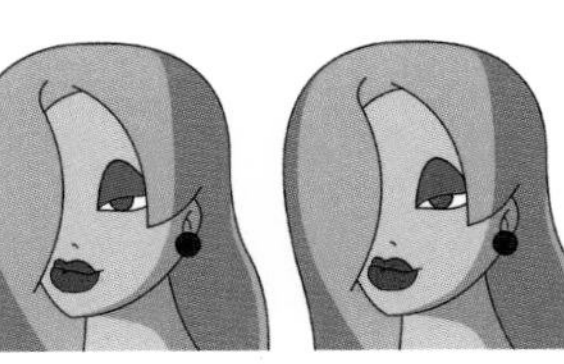

HOT TIP

Shape Tweening in Animate is a voodoo science. Results can often be unexpected depending on the amount of vector points that comprise the object(s). The biggest tip is to keep your shapes as simple as possible if you need to Shape Tween them. Simplicity is why in step 14 I chose to insert a keyframe and work with the exact same shapes from frame 1. I know they will have precisely the same number of points and increase the chances of my Shape Tween being successful. If any of the shapes "implode" during the Shape Tween, you may have edited them a bit too much.

Mixed Media

THE IDEA OF COMBINING HAND-DRAWN ANIMATION WITH live action has been around since the first motion pictures in the early 1900s. Even though the concept isn't new, the trends in implementation can vary. Borrowing from the recent trend of painting kitschy subjects over thrift store art landscapes, I've placed a hand-drawn Sasquatch in a reclining pose in a photo of a large rocky outcrop in the midst of a woodsy landscape. For this cheat, I show you how to position a character on a high-resolution photo and animate the zoom together to sell the idea of the character being in the setting.

PHOTO: MYRA FERGUSON | SUNBATHING SASQUATCH: VECTOR ILLUSTRATION: MYRA FERGUSON

1 Start by importing a photo that will work for your setting. Convert it to a Movie Clip. Make sure the resolution is high enough to still look good at your greatest amount of zoom. The zoom doesn't need to be very extreme.

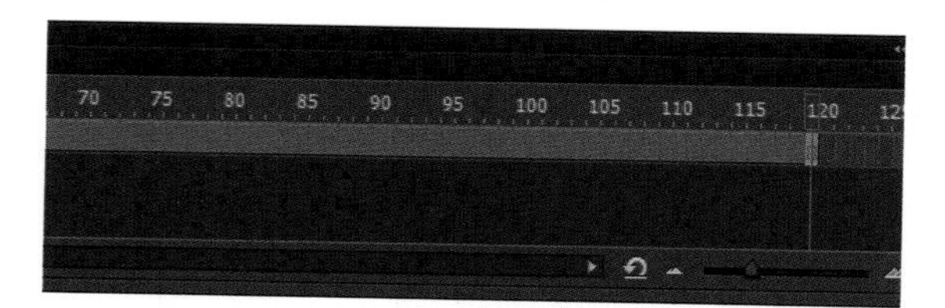

4 Go back to the Main Timeline. Extend the Timeline to frame 120. Click the "Clip the content to the Stage" button to only see what's on the Stage.

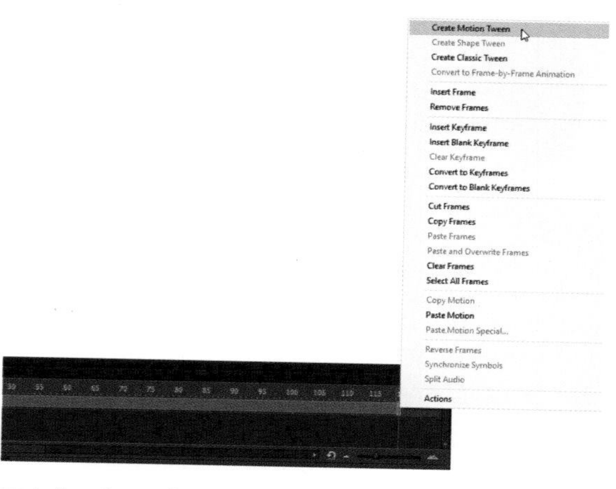

5 Let's animate the scaling of the Movie Clip, which affects everything inside it—both the landscape and the character. Right-click on the image to Create a Motion Tween.

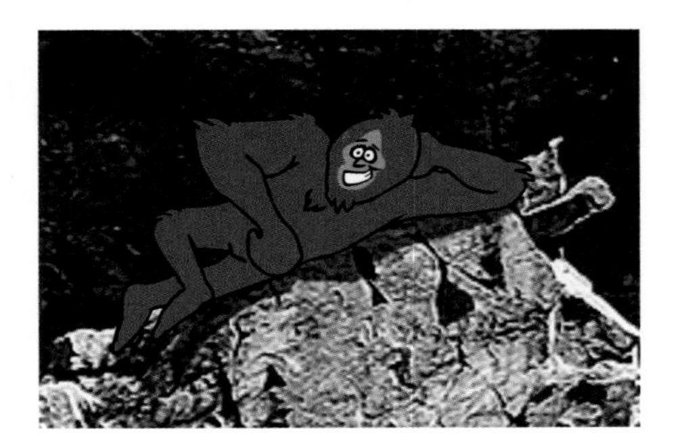

2 On a new layer inside the Movie Clip with the landscape, draw your character, import stock art, or modify imported stock art to fit into your scene.

3 Add a convincing shadow that takes into account the angle and the color of the other shadows in the image. For Sasquatch's shadow, I duplicated his shape, which consists of all fills (all strokes were converted to fills), and changed the fill to the single sampled color with the Alpha set to 70%. I flipped and rotated the shape to get close to the angle of the other shadows. With Transform > Envelope, I adjusted the shadow to make it align with where it was being cast. If you want it to blend into the landscape a little more, convert the shadow to a Movie Clip and add a little Blur filter.

6 While still on frame 120, position and scale the image where you want the animation to end. The end is where I want the payoff of catching a surprising glimpse of Sasquatch in all his reclining glory.

7 Select the first keyframe on the same layer. Adjust the position and scale of the image where you want the animation to start. I want the animation to start out looking like an ordinary landscape. Following along the incline of the outcrop heightens the interest of what could be waiting for the viewer at the top.

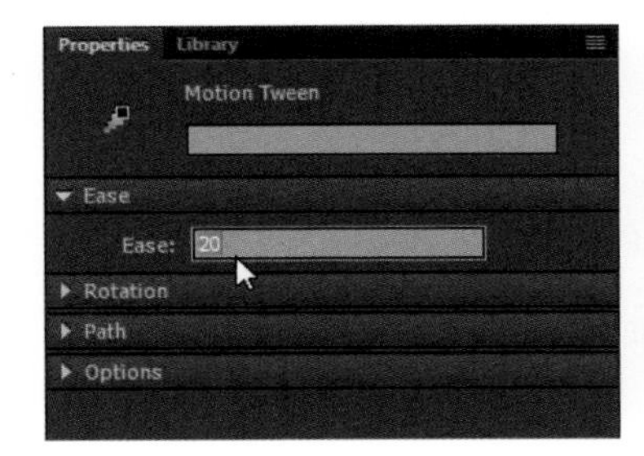

8 You can adjust the rate of the motion with easing in the Properties panel. I've set it to 20.

9 You can also adjust the motion path. Use the Selection Tool (V) to adjust the curve.

10 Hit (Enter) to test it out.

HOT TIP

It used to be that if you wanted to see only what was on the Stage, you would need to uncheck View > Pasteboard, which awkwardly scooted your workspace to the upper left corner. You could also create a mask to hide the excess, which could also be used as a sort of guide if you set the layer to show outlines. Now all you have to do is click the Clip content outside the Stage button in the upper right corner next to magnification.

INTERLUDE

Indelible Impressions

SOME MOMENTS MAKE SUCH A LASTING IMPRESSION THAT THEY INFLUENCE US THROUGHOUT our lives. One such impression made its mark on me when I was only about 4 years old. My dad bought the original Magnavox Odyssey gaming console. Let's just say that was a long time ago when playing console games on the TV was like living in the future. It didn't really matter that every game appeared to be some variation of PONG. I was mesmerized.

What stuck with me were the graphics. They were printed on transparent film and held in place on the TV screen by static electricity. Later when I got my own Atari 2600—which I still have—video games continued to make an impression. At this point, the graphics were at least displayed through the CRT, but they weren't very compelling images. However, the designs printed on the boxes were a different story. They captivated me. I remember longing for a day when the actual game graphics would rival the quality of their covers.

VECTOR ILLUSTRATION: MYRA FERGUSON

Fast forward to today. Video game graphics vary stylistically from hyper-realistic 3D to cutesy and everything in between—and possibly beyond. The genres and the possibilities are extensive. Some of the sports games are hard to distinguish from real broadcast sporting events.

One of the reasons I love Animate is that it gives me the freedom to create my own game graphics and build games in whatever style I like. I can gamify education or advertising. I have the flexibility to make about anything I can imagine and distribute it on the web, on mobile, on kiosks— just about wherever. And thanks to Animate I can also enjoy highly creative games others have made on a variety of platforms.

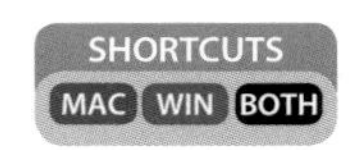

■ Surprisingly, the most impressive of Animate effects are often the simplest to create. The above characters are animated running in place as a looped sequence. It looks cool as it is, but if you copy and paste an instance of it, flip it vertically, and lower its opacity, you can achieve the sense that the surface they are running on is reflective and maybe even a bit slippery.

Adobe Animate CC

7 Animation Examples

I HAVE SPENT MY FAIR SHARE OF TIME ON VARIOUS animation forums, reading, learning, and providing my own perspective when needed. As a result, I've seen what animation techniques and examples Animate users frequently request. I will often create a sample FLA and make it available for everyone to download and dissect for themselves. It's very difficult to teach design and animation in text format and, often, a simple FLA can make all the difference.

This chapter contains some of the most popular "How do I..." animation requests from Animate users. If this chapter teaches you one thing, I hope that it teaches you think differently about how you approach Animate as a tool.

Super Text Effect

SO OFTEN THE SIMPLEST ANIMATION TECHNIQUE is the most effective visually. Take this website introduction for Superbusy Records as an example of simplicity at its finest and how to get the most bang for your buck with the basics of Animate animation. The text animation is composed of basic Classic Tweens and scaling, and the bee animation takes advantage of some old school blurring with a linear gradient. Timing is everything and the fast-paced editing of this animation makes it look more complicated than it truly is.

1 Start off with a text field set to Static and type in your text. There's nothing fancy here, just some basic text to get you started.

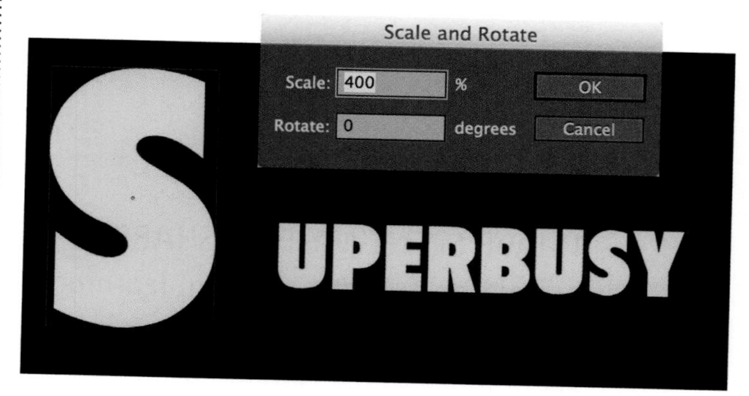

4 Select all layers on a frame somewhere down the Timeline (frame 30 will do) and insert a keyframe for every layer by hitting the F6 key. Go back to frame 1 and select your first letter. Use the Scale and Rotate ctrl alt Shift to scale it to 400% or greater.

7 The bee graphic is introduced using a simple linear gradient first. Then the bee "pops" into position. This technique is identical to the "Flying Text" topic in Chapter 5.

2 Break apart the text field once using ⌘ ctrl B and each letter will be broken apart but still editable. Break apart twice to convert your text to raw vector shapes. Your text will no longer be editable once broken down this far. You can choose to break apart only once if you think you might want to edit the text at a later time.

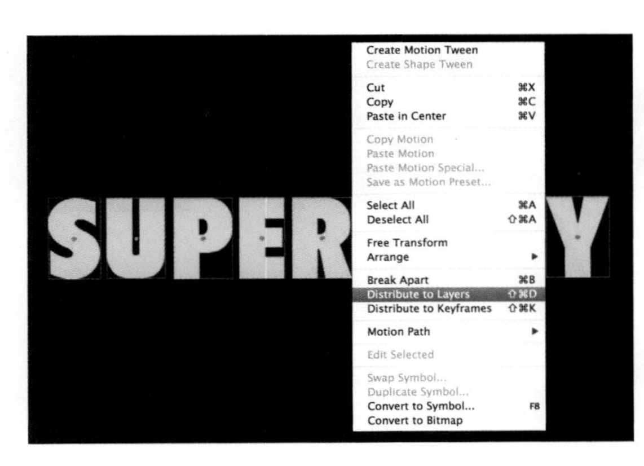

3 Select each letter individually and convert each to a Graphic symbol. Once all letters are converted, select them all, right-click over them, and select Distribute to Layers from the context menu.

5 Apply a Classic Tween to animate this letter scale from 400% to 100%. Select the keyframe in frame 30 and move it to around frame 5. Play back to test the speed based on your frame rate. Adjust the tempo as necessary by adding or removing frames in the Classic Tween.

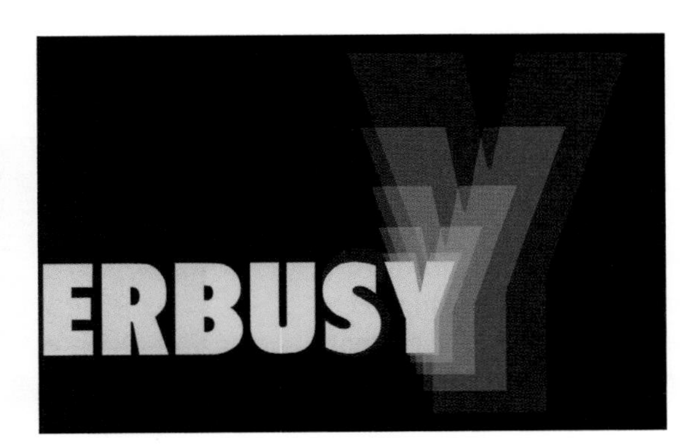

6 Repeat this procedure for each letter. Then stagger each letter's animation by sliding the Classic Tween down the Timeline so that each letter animates into place one after the other. Your Timeline tweens should resemble a staircase.

8 The bee is a Movie Clip containing a very simple, two-framed animation of the wings. The original wing is replaced with a radial gradient to provide the illusion that it is blurred because it is moving faster than our eye can see.

9 The blur animation is composed of only two frames with the radial gradient slightly rotated between them. The looping of these two frames at 30 fps is enough to convince us that they are oscillating at a very high speed. Adding the appropriate sound effect makes it even more convincing.

HOT TIP

You may want to break apart your text into raw vector shapes if you plan on sharing this FLA with someone else on a different computer. If the font you use is not installed on the other machine, then Animate will substitute that font for the default font or a font of your choice. If this project is for a client and they request the FLA, you should make sure they have the same font you are using or break apart the text into shapes.

Page Turn

PAGES THAT CURL UP AND AWAY TO REVEAL more pages are always an appealing effect (see what I did there?) for introducing content on your website or as buttons to other web pages. There are variations created entirely with ActionScript, but if you're not comfortable with scripting you can make a page turn without it. That doesn't mean you can't add some interactivity by placing this animation in a Movie Clip and controlling its playback when the mouse rolls over it.

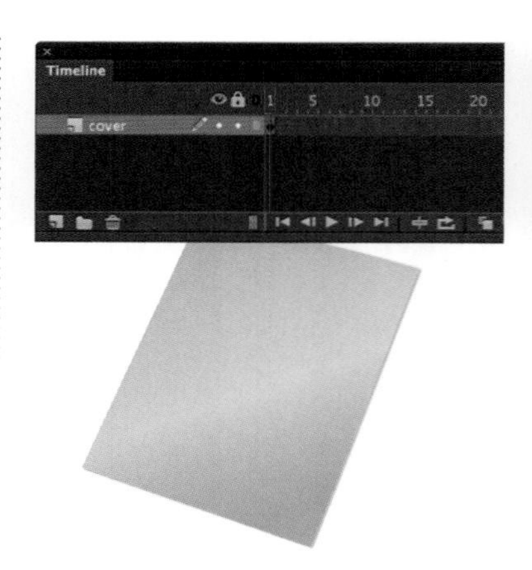

1 Start with a simple rectangle with a linear gradient fill or your own color fill preference. Convert it to a Movie Clip symbol F8 and apply a Drop Shadow filter to add a little depth.

2 Duplicate the cover symbol, and place it on a new layer above the original. Edit the graphic inside by filling it with a different color. Add some text or an image of your choice.

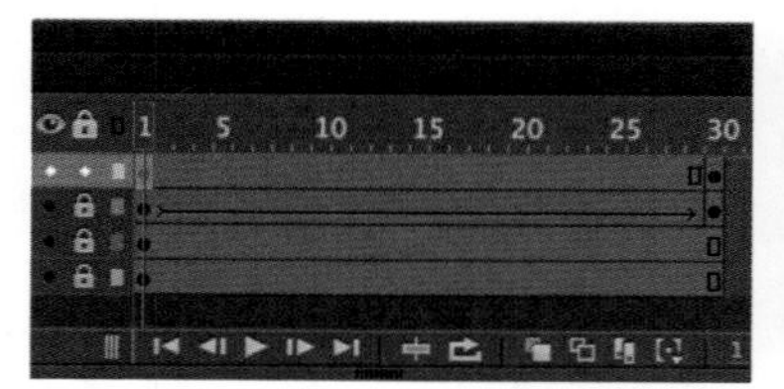

6 Insert a new layer and create a triangular shape that resembles a page curl similar to the example above. The easiest way to make this shape is to start with a rectangle. Turn on Snap to Objects and drag one corner until it snaps to another corner. Now that you have made a triangle, move the remaining three corners into the positions as seen in the above example.

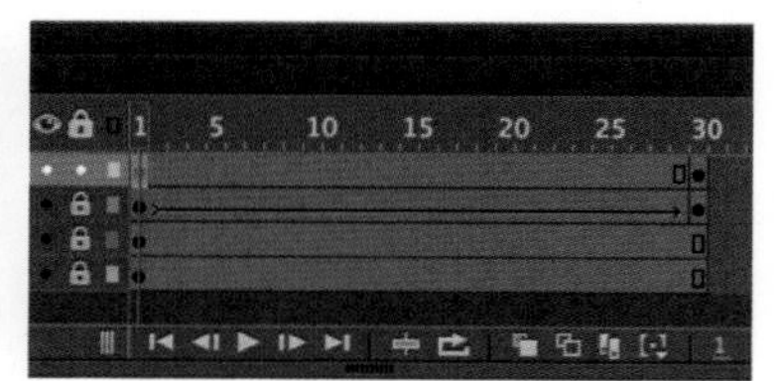

7 Mix a linear gradient using three colors. The first and last color swatches should be the brightest and similar in value. The middle swatch should be the same color but darker in value. Fill the curl shape and use the Gradient Transform Tool F to rotate and position the gradient so that its bottom edge shows a slight amount of the lightest value.

3 Insert a new layer again above your existing layers. Convert it to a mask layer and draw a shape that spans the lower right corner. Insert a keyframe in frame 30 so that a duplicate of this shape is created.

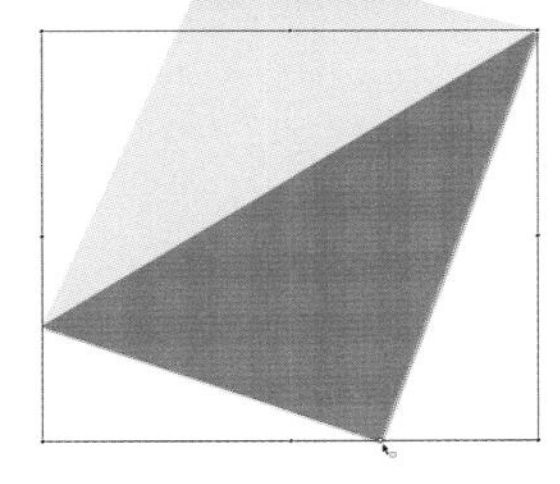

4 Select the shape in frame 1. With the Free Transform Tool Q, position the center point at the bottom corner. Hold down ⌥ alt and scale the shape until it is very small.

5 Holding down ⌥ alt will constrain the shape based on its center point. Apply a Shape tween, so the shape grows from small to large. This animation will reveal the content page.

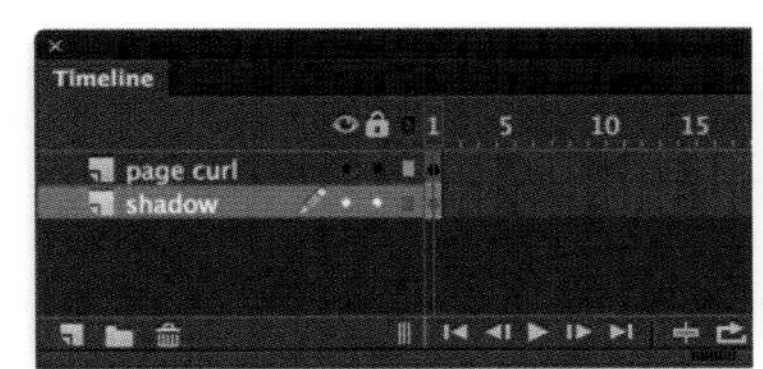

8 Convert the shape from step 7 to a Graphic symbol, double-click it, and add a new layer inside this new symbol. Create another shape in this new layer using the Rectangle Tool R for the shadow created by the page curl. This shadow will be cast onto the page below, so draw the shape to span only the area necessary inside the content page.

9 Fill this shape with a linear gradient consisting of two colors. Mix about 50% alpha into the first color and 0% alpha into the second color. Use the Gradient Transform Tool F to rotate the shadow so that it fades away from the curl. Convert both shapes to a Graphic symbol.

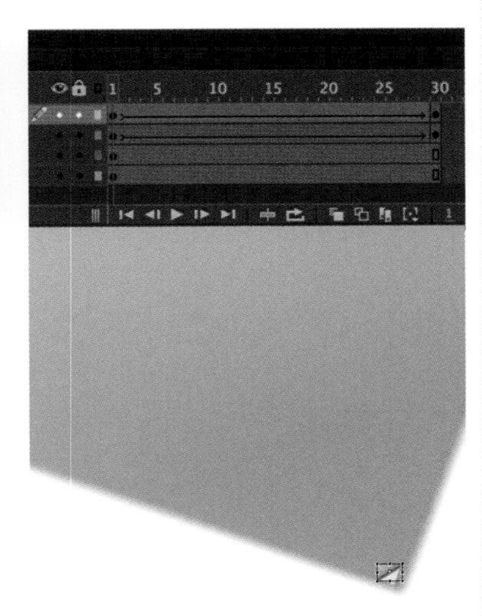

10 Animate the curl just as you animated the mask in steps 4 and 5. Insert a second keyframe in frame 30, and select the curl graphic in frame 1. With the Free Transform Tool Q, move the center point to the lower corner, hold down ⌥ alt, and scale it until it is the same size as the mask shape in this frame. Apply a Classic Tween.

HOT TIP

You can duplicate this effect to create additional page curls, allowing the user to turn more pages to reveal more content. Nest the page curl animation into a Movie Clip symbol and drag multiple instances of it to individual layers. With some basic ActionScript, you can control the page turns during runtime in the Flash Player.

Smoke with Gradients

THERE ARE SEVERAL WAYS TO ANIMATE SMOKE, and each technique is based on the style of the smoke. Do you need your smoke to be a cartoon-style smoke cloud? Maybe you want a more realistic billowing of soft puffy clouds? How about a very stylized smoke effect with curling hard-edged shapes simulating the basic movement of smoke? There are many different ways to achieve the same results in Animate, whether it's with ActionScript or animation. Animate has always been a blank canvas for us to express ourselves. Let's take a look at a few ways to approach the dynamics of the smoke cloud.

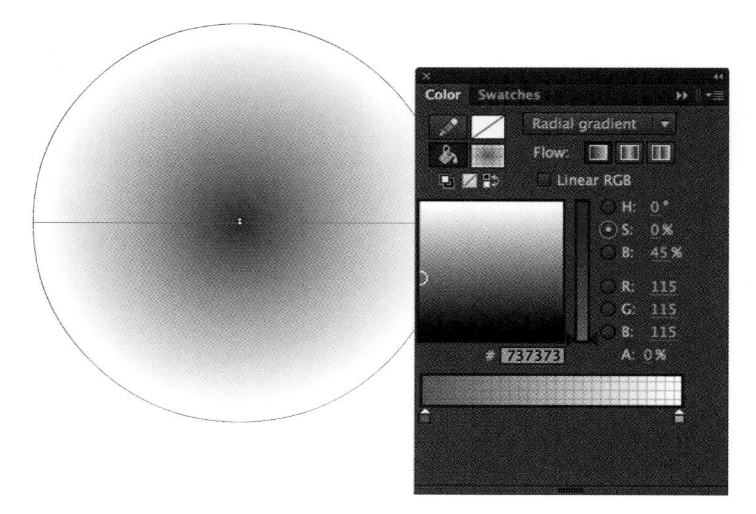

1 Create a radial gradient with a dark gray center and the outer color mixed with 0% alpha. Create a circle with the Oval Tool O with this gradient as your fill color and no stroke. Convert this shape to a Graphic symbol.

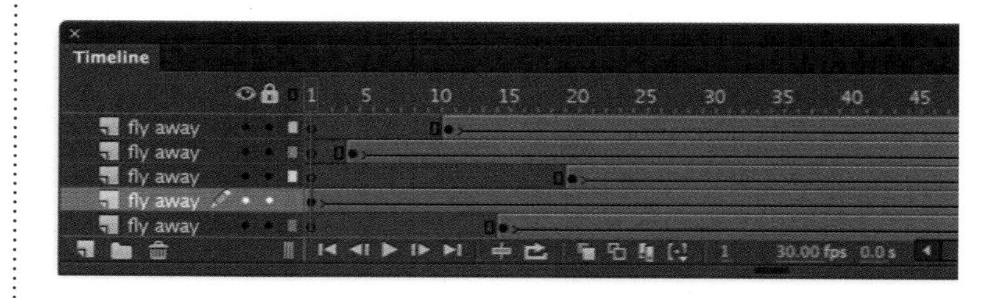

4 Select the entire Classic Tween, copy all frames and keyframes, insert a new layer, and paste all frames into it. Select the graphic in the first frame and move it a few pixels in any direction. Do the same for the Graphic symbol in the last keyframe. Select the entire Classic Tween and drag it down the Timeline a few frames. Repeat this procedure until you have several layers of slightly different animations of your gradient starting small and rising while fading out completely.

PHOTO: ADOBE STOCK PHOTOS

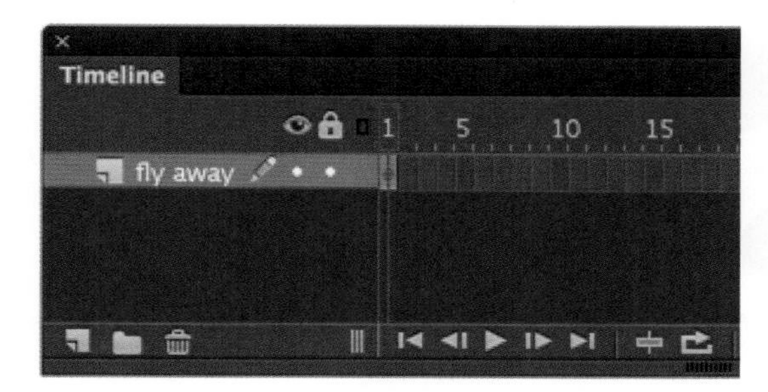

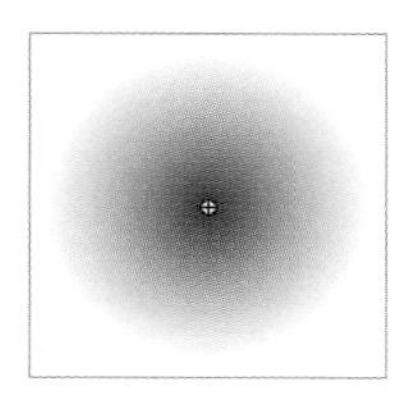

2 Select the Graphic symbol and convert it to a Movie Clip symbol. Double-click this Movie Clip to enter edit mode. This Timeline is where the animation will take place.

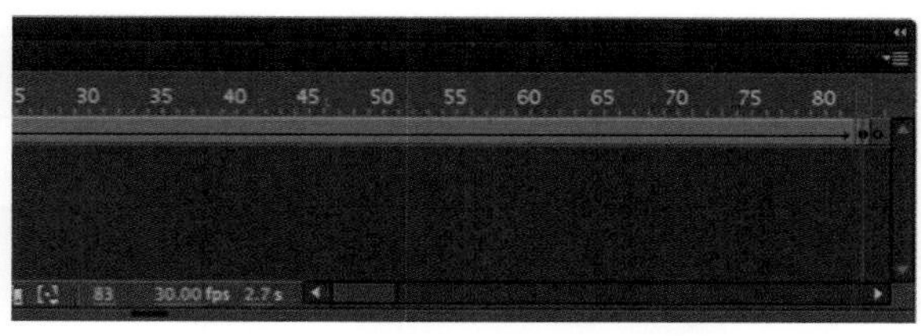

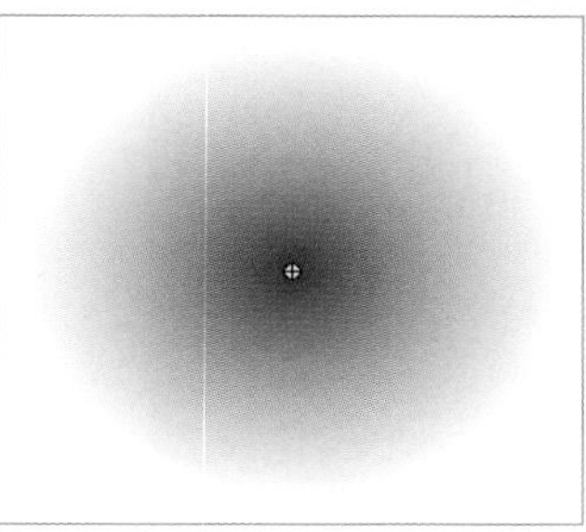

3 Insert a second keyframe several frames down the Timeline. Scale the Graphic symbol to about 200% and move it up about 75 pixels. Apply a Classic Tween.

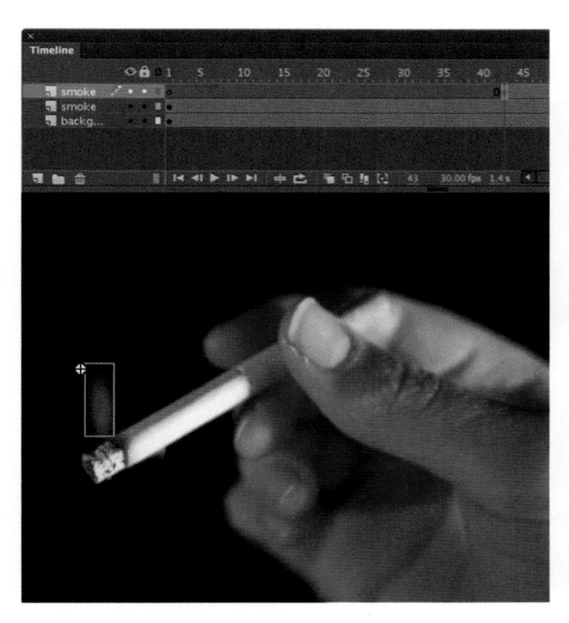

5 On the main Timeline, copy and paste the Movie Clip containing your "smoke" animations to a new layer. Drag the keyframe to a frame later in the Timeline. Frame 25 will work fine. Select the instance and flip it horizontally to help change its appearance from the original.

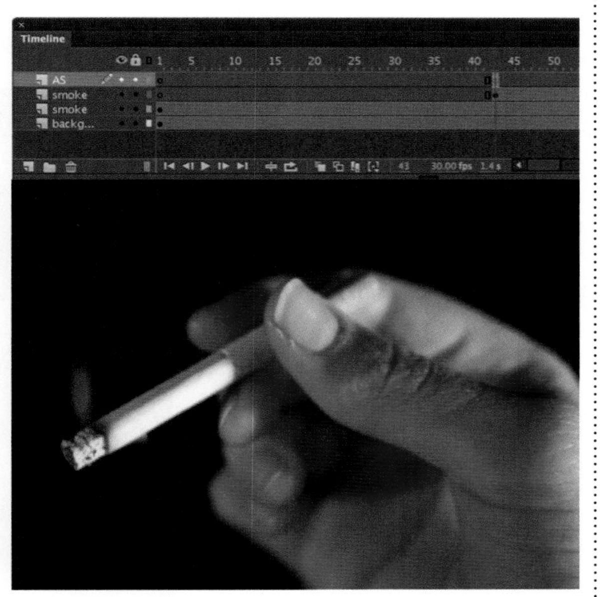

6 Since the animation is inside a Movie Clip, it is best to stop the Timeline once the second instance is introduced on the Timeline by adding a stop action. The Movie Clip instances will continue to play and loop. Since they start on different frames, they will overlap to produce a constant flow of smoke.

HOT TIP

The Blur filter, when used excessively, can cause potential performance issues during playback. Test your animation frequently to avoid causing a processor-intensive animation. Remember, the Flash Player is not like pre-rendered video format. Animate renders on the fly in the Flash Player, so too high a frame rate combined with complex animations can demand too much from the player. Optimize your shapes whenever possible, and use a realistic frame rate.

Smoke Stylized

STYLE WILL ALMOST ALWAYS DICTATE the animation technique. Often the client will request a specific artistic style based on a pre-existing logo or company identity. The challenge here is to be consistent, not only with the artwork but also with the animation style. A realistic smoke animation would look nice but not match the client's style preference. It's time to be inventive and to create a smoke animation that is stylized, yet simple and effective. Oh, and the client needs it yesterday.

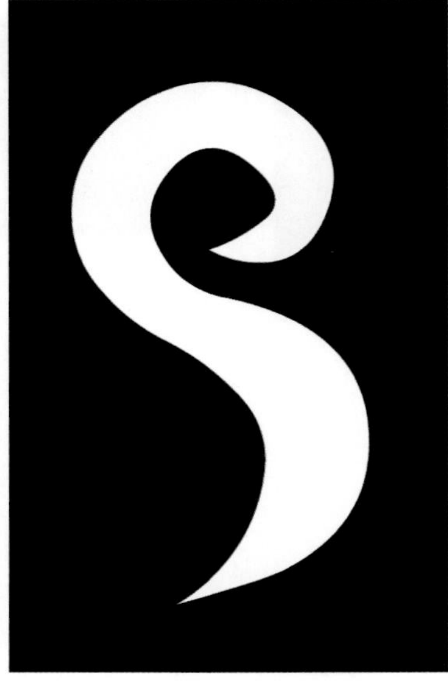

1 The easiest way to start is with the final shape you want as your stylized smoke. The shape can be drawn with any of Animate's drawing tools. Whatever you use, I recommend making a fill with no stroke.

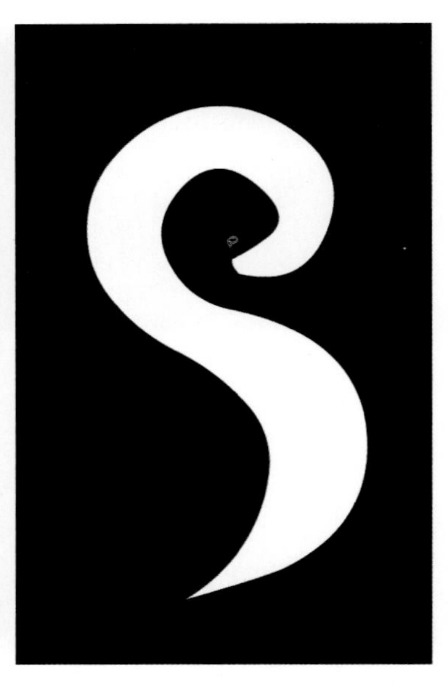

2 Insert a keyframe (F6) in frame 2, and with the Lasso Tool (L) select a small section at the top end of the smoke shape and delete it.

6 Copy and paste all frames into a Graphic symbol to reuse later. Create a second keyframe down the Timeline, and with the Free Transform Tool (Q) skew it and move it up about 30 pixels.

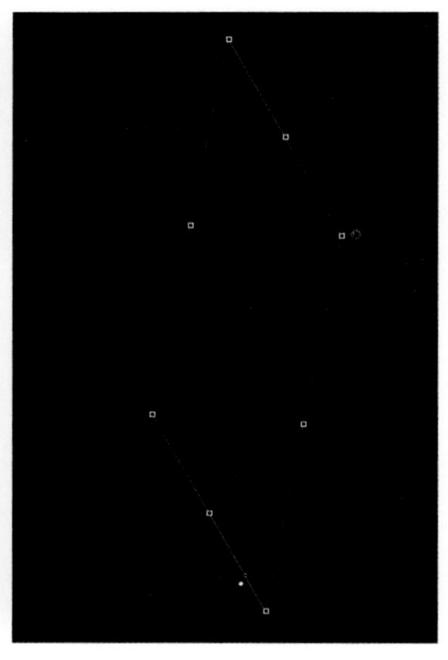

7 Create a third keyframe further down the Timeline and adjust the Alpha to 0% so that it fades out. Apply another Classic Tween and maybe a little more skewing.

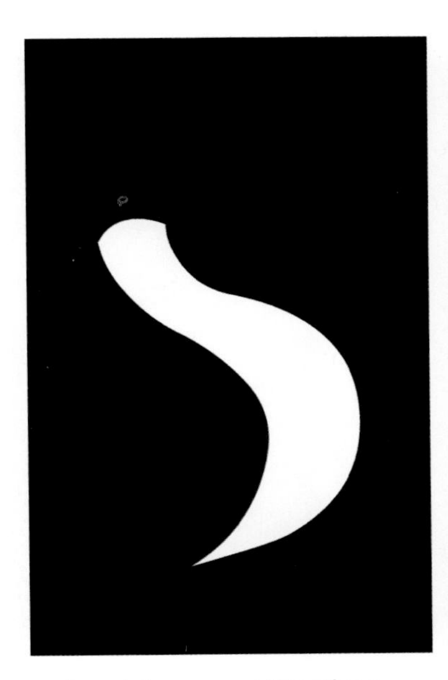

3 Repeat the process of inserting a keyframe and selecting a small section of your shape and deleting it. Use your keyboard shortcuts to make this task faster and easier.

4 Toggle between F6 and the Delete key while selecting sections of your shape until it has been completely removed from your Stage.

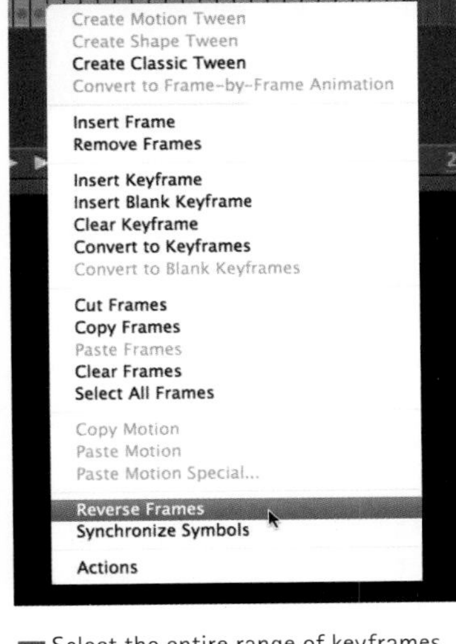

5 Select the entire range of keyframes and then right-click over them to bring up the context menu. Select Reverse Frames. Reversing the order will reveal your shape when you play back your animation.

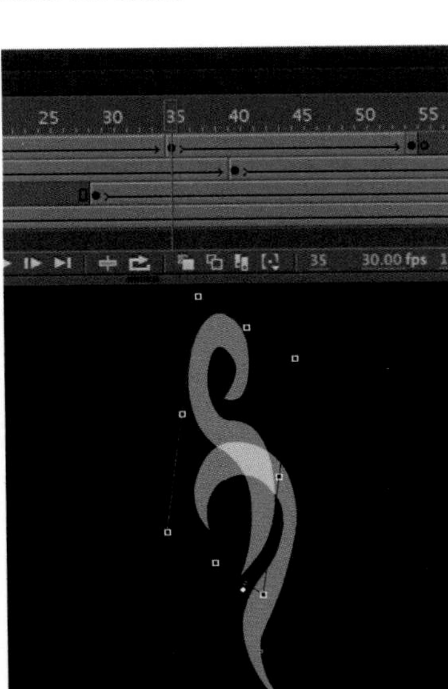

8 Add another layer and drag an instance of the same symbol containing your animated shape to the Stage. Flip it horizontally and repeat steps 6 and 7.

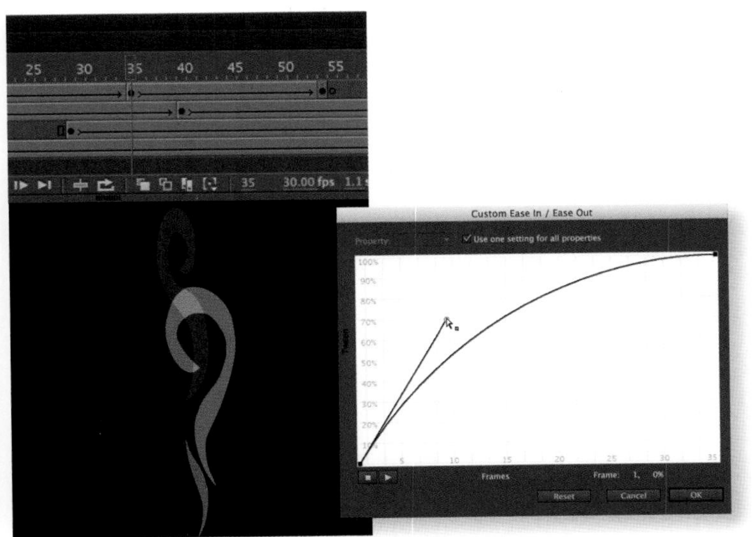

9 Add a third layer and repeat steps 6 and 7 again. Play back your animation frequently, and adjust the amount of skewing, tweening, and the overall timing as necessary.

10 You may want to apply a bit of easing out to the symbols as they fade away. Although it may not be necessary, it might just add that final touch to your overall effect.

HOT TIP

As you work through this example, you may realize at some point that you are creating a pretty sophisticated frame-by-frame animation sequence that looks like it was made by the hand of a very experienced animator. That's our little secret. You may choose to use the Eraser tool instead of the Lasso Tool and avoid having to use the Delete key entirely. If you have a pressure-sensitive tablet and a stylus with an eraser on one end, you may have the fastest way to pull off this technique.

Full Steam Ahead

FILTERS ARE ANOTHER GREAT WAY to create realistic smoke or, in this example, steam. Since the image we are working with is an actual photograph, the animation needs to be just as convincing. Without the presence of steam, this cup of tea looks cold and somewhat unappealing. Not only can you use filters to blur objects in Animate, but you can also animate these filters.

1 Start off by drawing some simple shapes with the Brush Tool B. They should be random and abstract.

2 Select this shape (or shapes) and convert it to a Movie Clip symbol. With this symbol still selected, convert it to a Movie Clip once again, so you end up with two Movie Clips, one nested inside the other.

6 Select the Movie Clip instance in the second keyframe and apply another Blur filter. Increase the amount of blurring, so it is slightly more than the blurring in the first keyframe.

7 Select the Movie Clip instance in the third keyframe and apply another Blur filter. Increase the amount of blurring even more than you applied in the second keyframe.

3 Double-click the Movie Clip symbol on the main Timeline to edit it. Insert a second keyframe a few frames down the Timeline and scale the original Movie Clip symbol as shown above.

4 Insert a third keyframe down the Timeline, scale the Movie Clip even wider, and position it a little higher.

5 Go back to the first keyframe and apply a Blur filter using the Filters panel (Window > Properties > Filters).

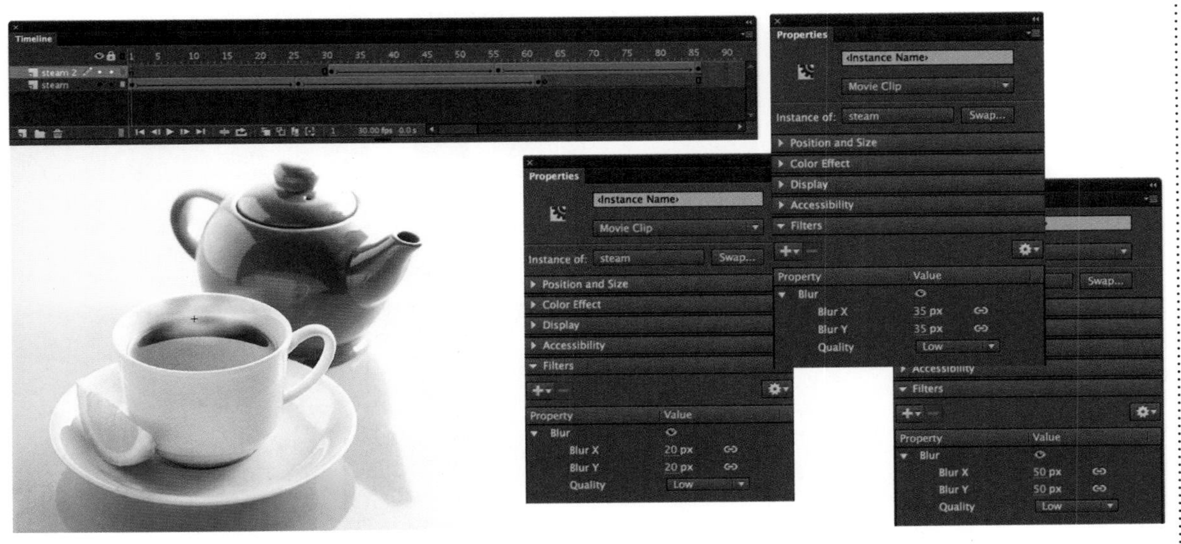

8 Apply Classic Tweens to all keyframes. Play back your animation and make adjustments as necessary. You may want to adjust the amount of blurring, alpha, or transforming to your animation. You can also create a second steam animation by creating a new layer and drawing more shapes. Convert them to a Movie Clip symbol F8 and repeat steps 1 through 7. Then select and drag the entire range of keyframes and frames down the Timeline so that they start after the original animation. Staggering the sequence will help eliminate the repetition of one single looping steam effect.

HOT TIP

Filters can only be applied to Movie Clip symbols, and you must publish targeting Flash Player version 8 or higher. Animated effects involving filters can be very processor intensive. Use them sparingly and test often to make sure playback performance remains acceptable.

Fireworks

EVERYBODY LOVES FIREWORKS. There's nothing like a warm summer night under the stars watching the skies light up with the brilliance of pyrotechnics. You can make every day the Fourth of July by animating your own fireworks display, and they'll be legal in every state. With some simple gradients, a little masking, and some tweens, you'll be hearing "Oohs!" and "Ahhhs!" in no time.

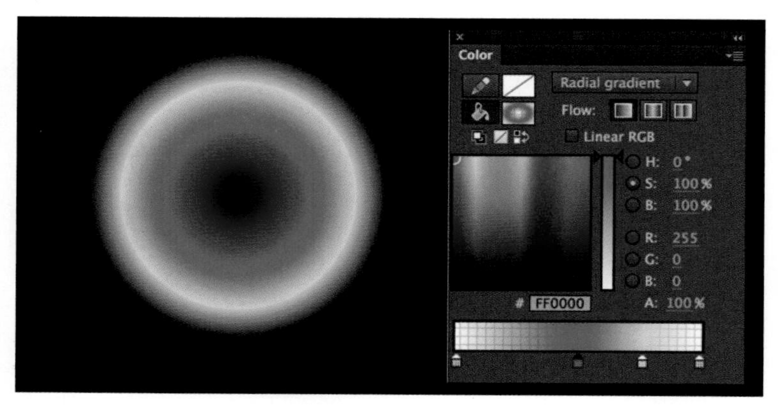

1 Start with a radial gradient with at least four colors. The middle and outer colors should be mixed with 0% Alpha. The second and third colors are based on your own fireworks color scheme. Convert the gradient to a Graphic symbol.

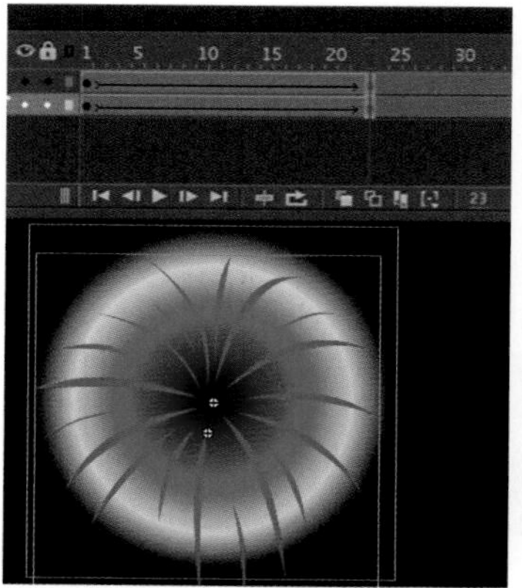

5 Insert keyframes for both layers somewhere down your Timeline and scale them both up about 300%. The gradient should be at least as big as the mask.

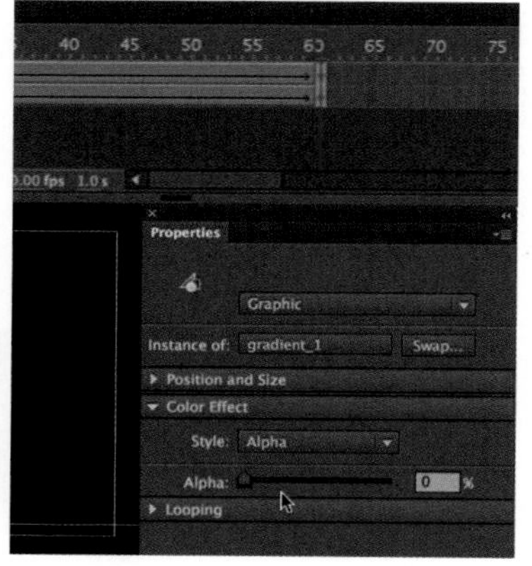

6 Insert two more keyframes much farther down the Timeline and scale both the mask and gradient about 125% more. Fade out the gradient to 0% Alpha.

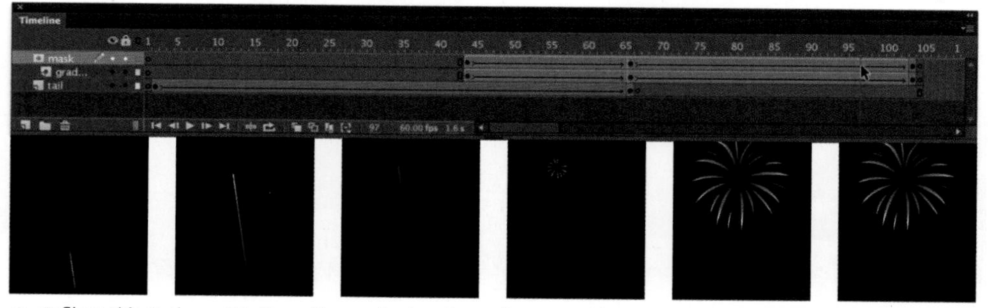

10 Since this stroke and its Shape Tweened animation simulate the ascending explosive, you will need to slide the actual fireworks animation down the Timeline to make room for it. At this point, it comes down to artistic license and how you want the entire animation to play out. Here I have the ascent disappear just before the burst effect appears. The speed of the ascent can be adjusted by adding or removing frames during the Shape Tween.

2 You need to create a mask that resembles the shape of exploding fireworks such as in this example. Convert it to a Graphic symbol.

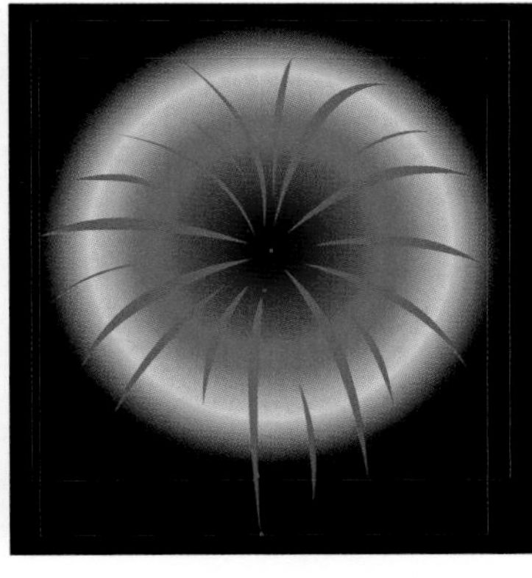

3 Place the radial gradient in the masked layer so when the layers are locked, the gradient shows through the mask only.

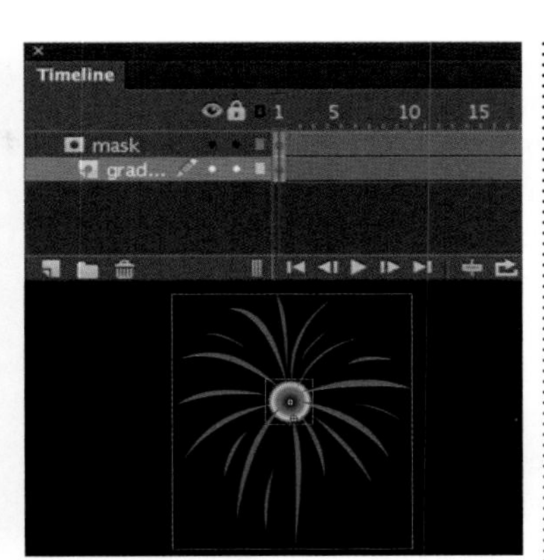

4 Scale both the mask and gradient in frame 1, so they are very small. Scale the gradient even smaller than the mask.

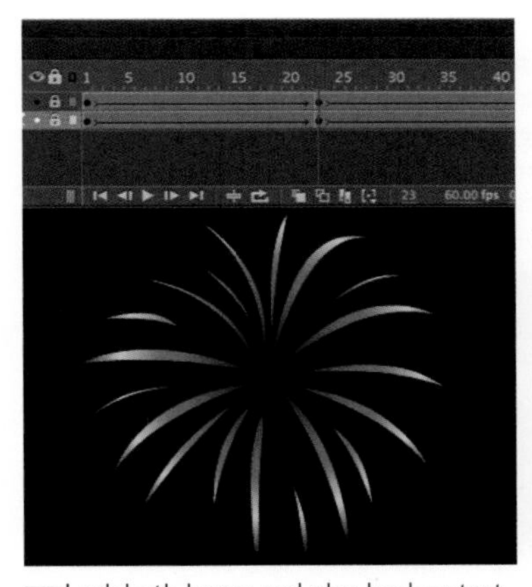

7 Lock both layers and play back or test your movie. You should have a pretty convincing fireworks explosion.

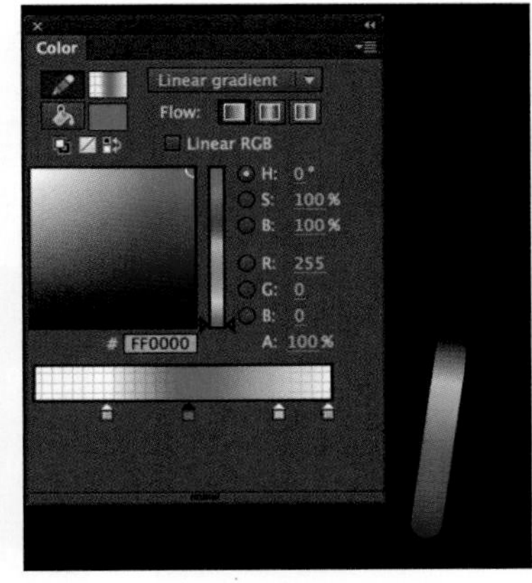

8 Draw a stroke and fill it with a linear gradient that contains two swatches mixed with 0% Alpha at both ends.

9 Shape Tween the gradient so that it starts at the bottom of the stroke and ascends until it reaches the top and beyond which is where it disappears.

11 If you nest this animation in a symbol, you can duplicate it in the Library to create additional fireworks with different colors.

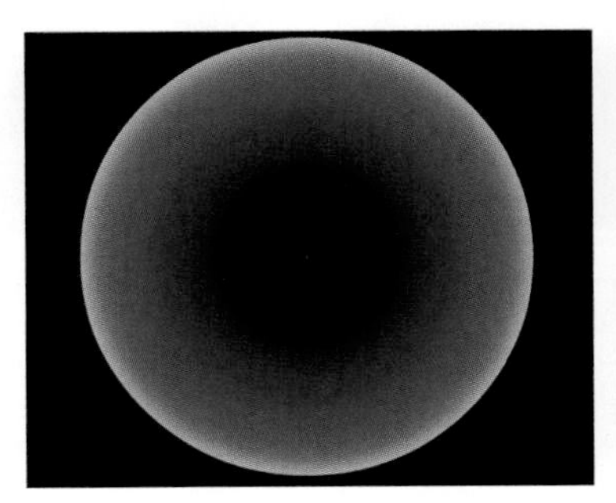

12 Edit the duplicate symbol(s) with a new radial gradient. The darker the background, the more vivid the fireworks will be.

13 Drag multiple instances of your fireworks to the Stage and start them on different frames to vary their timing.

HOT TIP

If you have a solid color background such as black, it is best to avoid Classic Tweens with alpha because they can be very processor intensive—especially if multiple animations are overlapping. Instead of alpha, tint to the same background color instead. Tint is much more processor friendly and playback will always be better as a result.

Star Wars Text

TEXT EFFECTS ARE ALWAYS a popular request among Animate users—specifically the "Star Wars" effect made famous during the opening scene in the original 1977 film. The effect is relatively simple to create but comes with a price: playback performance can suffer. Proceed with caution and test your animation often. Remember, the text must be legible without giving the reader a headache.

This is how to make a "Star Wars" style opening text effect. It ain't too hard once you know how. This is how to make a "Star Wars" style opening text effect. It ain't too hard once you know how. This is how to make a "Star Wars" style opening text effect. It ain't too hard once you know how. This is how to make a "Star Wars" style opening text effect. It ain't too hard once you know how. This is how to make a "Star Wars" style opening text effect. It ain't too hard once you know how. This is how to make a "Star Wars" style opening text effect. It ain't too hard once you know how. This is how to make a "Star Wars" style opening text effect. It ain't too hard once you know how. This is how to make a "Star Wars" style opening text effect. It ain't too hard once you know how. This is how to make a "Star Wars" style opening text effect. It ain't too hard once you know how. This is how to make a "Star Wars" style opening text effect. It ain't too hard once you know how. This is how to make a "Star Wars" style opening text effect. It ain't too hard once you know how. This is how to make a "Star Wars" style opening text effect. It ain't too hard once you know how. This is how to make a "Star Wars" style opening text effect. It ain't too hard once you know how.

1 Start by typing your block of text. Try to use a simple and bold font that is easy to read. You will be transforming this text and animating it. Since it will be constantly moving, the priority should be making sure it is legible and easy to read for the viewer. Select your text field and break it apart until the text becomes raw vector shapes. The amount of vector information will be substantial and will most likely cause some performance issues during playback. The effect on performance is another reason to choose a font that is as simple and clean as possible as it will produce fewer vector points.

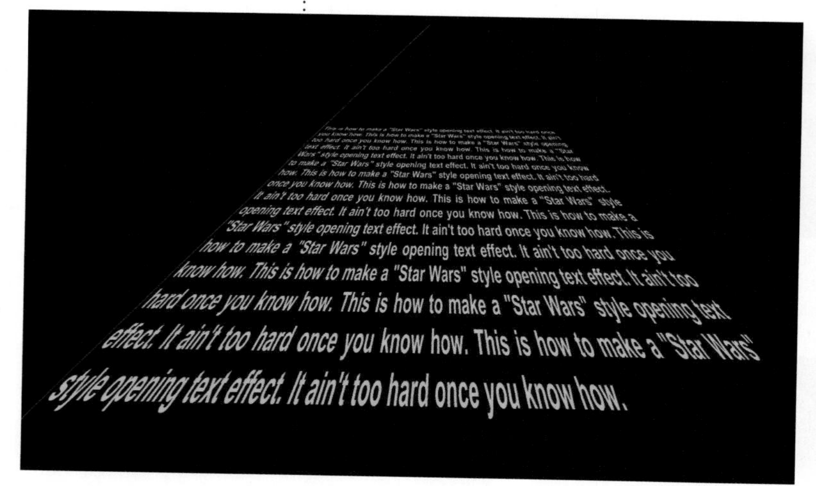

3 Insert a new layer and convert it to a guide layer. Make sure the layer containing your text is not "guided" or linked to it. You can drag the guide layer below your text layer to prevent them from being linked together. Anything on a guide layer will not be included when you export your movie. Animate offers a nice feature that provides the option to export or not export hidden layers. This option is accessible by going to File > Publish Settings and selecting Flash (.swf) and twirling open the Advanced options. On this layer use the Line Tool (N) to draw a stroke at the same angle as your text field. Copy and paste it in place, flip it horizontally, and position it on the opposite side of your block of text.

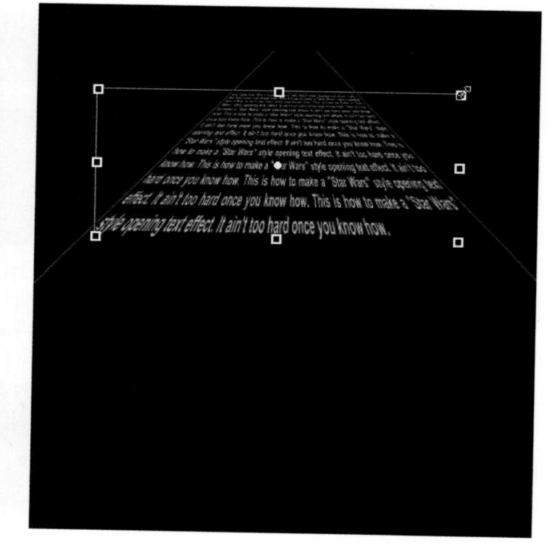

4 Add a second keyframe and scale your text until it fits inside your guides at their smallest point. You will need to insert several frames between these two keyframes and apply a Classic Tween.

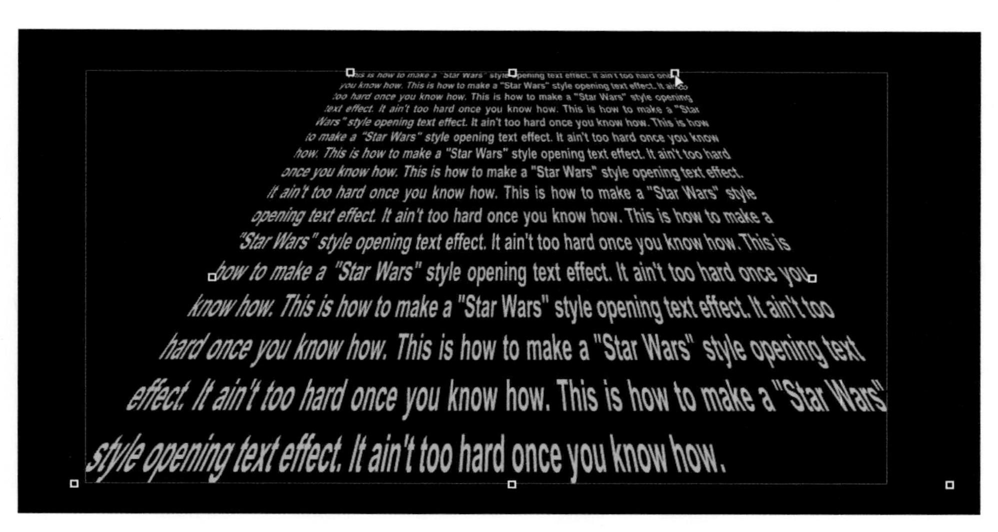

2 The next step is to simulate the perspective needed to provide the illusion that the text is receding. Select the Free Transform Tool Q and then the Distort (subselection) tool. While holding down the Shift key, drag one of the upper corners horizontally toward the middle of the text. Holding down the Shift key constrains the proportions of the transformation by distorting the adjacent corner in the opposite direction. Convert this block of text to a Graphic symbol. If you have several blocks of text, it might be best to keep them as smaller individual symbols.

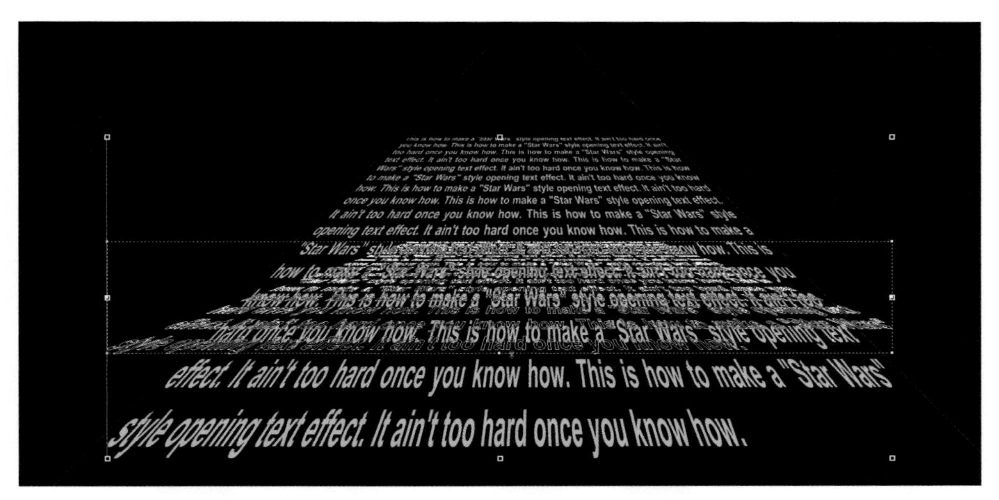

5 The final step actually breaks the one and only perspective rule crucial to this animation. I also think it is the most important step since it really helps provide the illusion of the text disappearing into infinity, yet it is so simple. In the very last frame of the tween, select the symbol containing the text field, and using the Free Transform Tool Q scale it vertically using one of the two middle handles along the top or bottom edge. In essence you will be squashing the symbol to make it flatter (do not widen it). For smooth playback, you will need a combination of hundreds of frames and a high frame rate. The exact amount depends on the amount of text, the font style, and how large (width and height) your movie is. The larger the movie, the more processor intensive it will be. Any animated effect that uses a combination of these factors can cause poor playback performance. Test often and know your target audience.

HOT TIP

You could try this effect with a block of text made in Photoshop that is distorted in the same perspective. Import the text as a bitmap with the same solid color background as your Animate movie. It may result in a more processor-friendly animation sequence but will suffer from loss of quality when scaled. Animate doesn't scale imported bitmaps very well and the results may not be visually appealing. The trade-off is using crisp vector text with some possible performance issues during playback. Testing often is your best defense.

Vertigo

CAUTION: THIS EFFECT may cause temporary headaches and possibly some minor nausea if you stare at it too long. Well, perhaps it won't cause sickness, but it's a great effect for representing vertigo, a balance disorder that causes a spinning sensation. If you're familiar with Alfred Hitchcock's film "Vertigo," you will already be familiar with how this visual effect can be used to show something or someone spinning out of control. With animation, it can also represent time travel, a wormhole, or even the beginning of a dream sequence or hallucination.

1 The success of this effect is in the one single graphic, the spiral. It was created in Adobe Illustrator using, you guessed it, the Spiral Tool. Animate does not have a tool like this one, so Illustrator proved to be a huge time saver. Of course, you can always draw this spiral graphic by hand using the support of a pressure-sensitive stylus, but that would certainly require a very skilled hand.

3 This effect makes a great place to superimpose a character or an object. Place the object in a Movie Clip symbol and rotate it in the opposite direction as your swirl. Switching the rotation will enhance the effect by providing the illusion of the object traveling through time or space.

2 Convert your spiral graphic to a symbol. Insert a second keyframe about 100 frames from the first keyframe. Apply a Classic Tween. Nothing will happen on playback because no change has been made to either instance of the spiral. Select a frame anywhere along the Classic Tween and in the Rotate drop-down menu, select CW (clockwise) or CCW (counterclockwise). Type in the number of rotations desired.

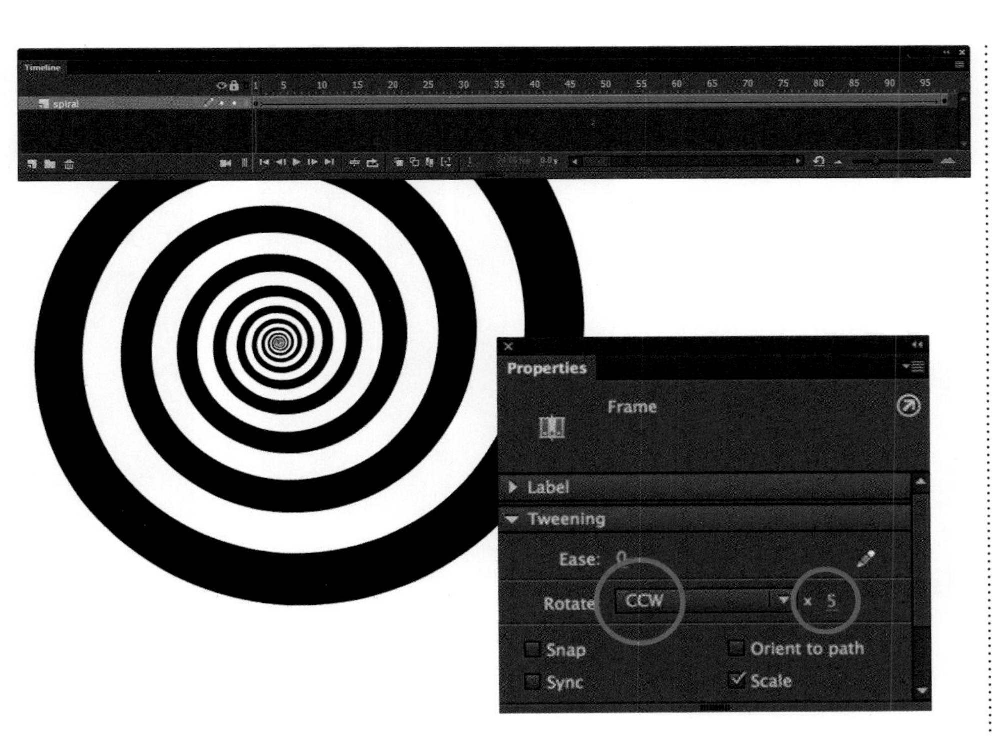

4 It's time to have some fun! Change the colors of your spiral and then select the character or object (make sure it is in a Movie Clip) and experiment with some of the Blend Modes available from the Properties panel. There are some interesting effects to play around with here that may provide some cool results.

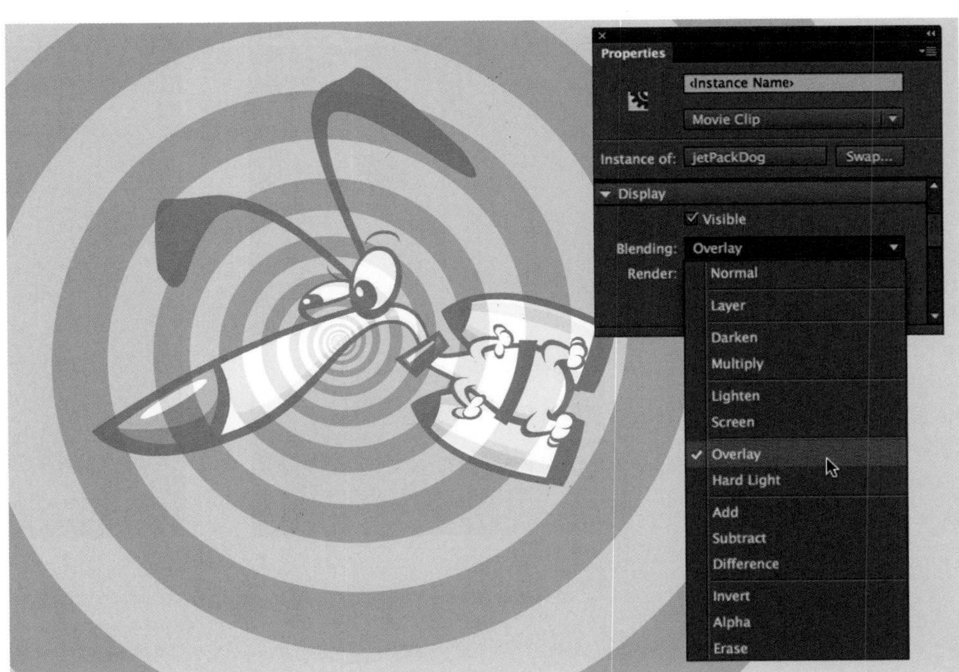

HOT TIP

You can get a lot of mileage from this spiral effect by adding objects that do more than just spin in the center of the spiral. You could add a rocket that is Classic Tweened from outside the Stage into the center of the spiral. You'd want to scale it very small as it reaches the center point of the spiral.

Let It Rain

THERE ARE SEVERAL WAYS TO APPROACH animating rain, probably because rain falls in several ways depending on wind conditions. I chose an average style of falling rain that can easily be expanded upon based on your own needs. Rain, to our advantage as animators, is repetitive. Reusing assets is one of the strengths of Animate. You only need to animate one raindrop and then populate your scene with multiple instances of it. You can then control how your rain acts by adjusting the angle at which it falls, its speed, and how many instances of it appear at any given time.

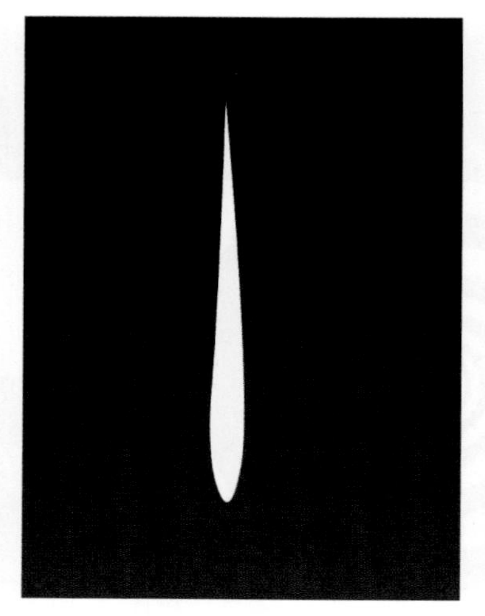

1 Use the Brush Tool (B) to draw your raindrop. Gravity suggests that the shape of the drop is thicker and rounder at its bottom. Fill your raindrop with a solid color or a radial gradient for some extra realism. This style choice is for you to decide.

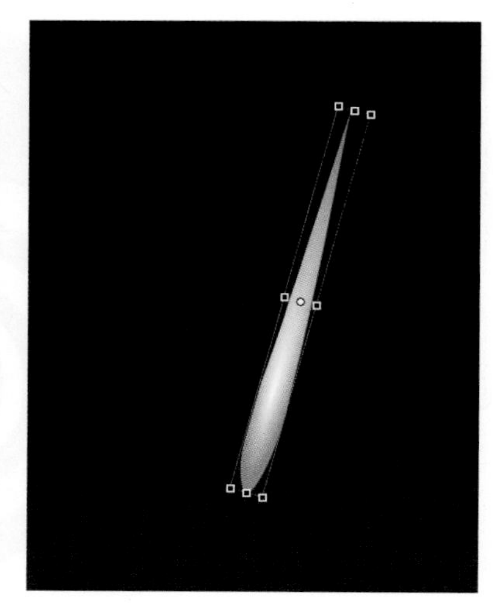

2 Convert your drop to a Graphic symbol and rotate it slightly. Base the amount of rotation on how strong of a rainstorm you want to have. The more angle your rain has, the more wind is suggested.

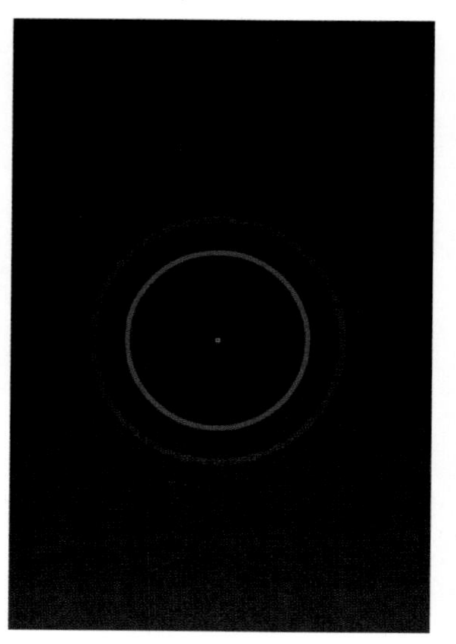

6 Copy all frames of your circle animation. Insert a new layer and paste the frames into it. Select all the frames in this new layer and drag them about five frames further down the Timeline.

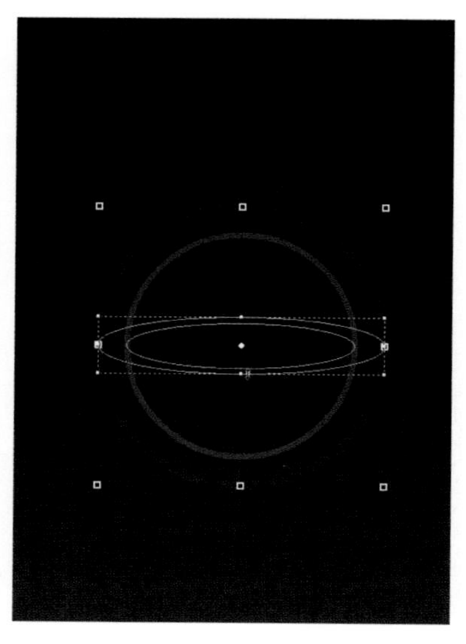

7 Navigate back to the main Timeline and transform your water drop symbol (containing its animation) by dragging the middle handle along the top or bottom edge with Free Transform Tool (Q).

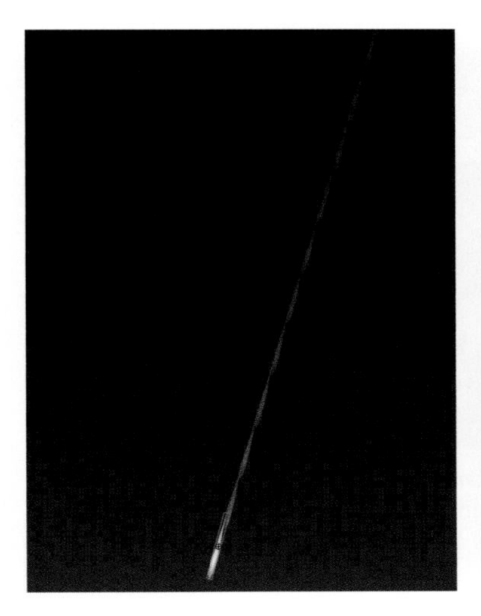

3 Insert a keyframe further down the Timeline. In frame 1, position the drop outside of the Stage. On your second keyframe, position it near the bottom of your Stage area. Apply a Classic Tween.

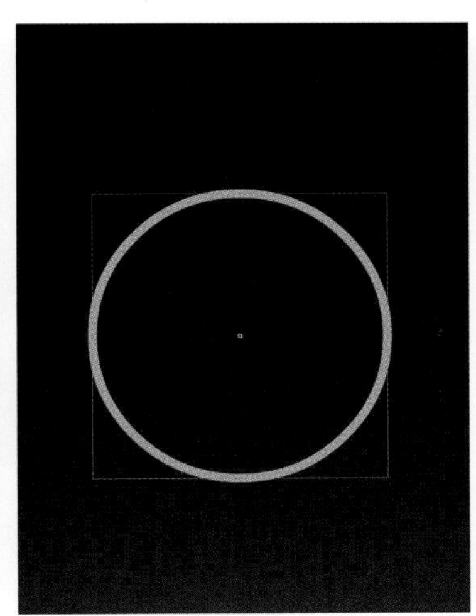

4 Let's create a ripple effect for the raindrop after it reaches its destination. Using the Oval Tool (O), draw a circle with a stroke color only. Hold down (Shift) to constrain its proportions. Convert it to a Graphic symbol (F8).

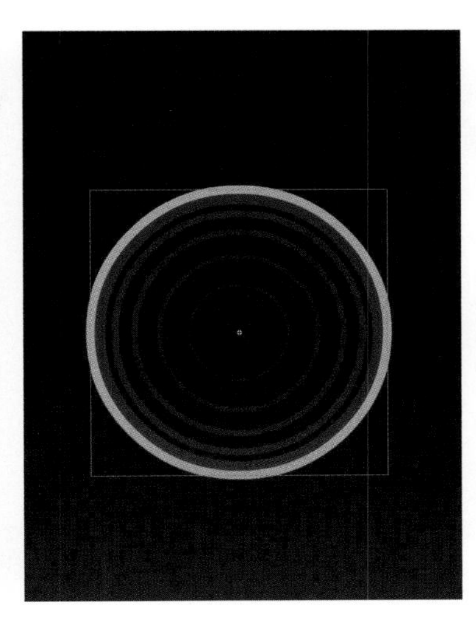

5 Convert it to a Graphic symbol again and double-click it to edit it. Insert a second keyframe and Classic Tween it from small to large over approximately 10 frames. Select the instance in the last frame and apply 0% alpha so it fades out completely.

8 Place the symbol containing your ripple animation in a blank keyframe (F7) in the frame after your raindrop animation. Position the ripple just below the raindrop in its last frame. Copy all frames in this layer.

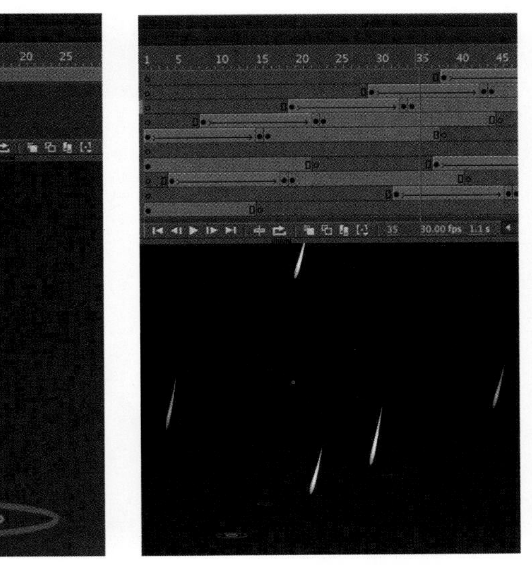

9 Paste these frames into a new symbol. Add several layers and continue to paste your animation into each one. Select and drag each layer's animation so that they each start on their own unique frame number.

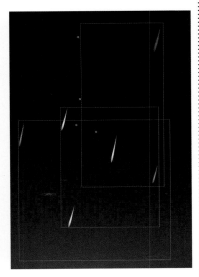

10 Now that you have a rain sequence nested in a symbol, drag as many instances of this symbol as you need to the Stage. Scale them and even tint some darker to suggest more depth to your scene.

HOT TIP

Nature isn't perfect. You simply can't find lines in nature that are exactly horizontal or vertical. Rain is the same way in the sense that it rarely falls perfectly straight down. Even a slight breeze will cause raindrops to fall at an angle. You can suggest stronger wind conditions by increasing the angle and speed of your raindrops. Decreasing the angle and speed of your rain animation will suggest a light shower.

SHORTCUTS
MAC WIN BOTH

Playing with Fire

NO ANIMATE ANIMATION BOOK IS COMPLETE without a topic involving fire. How many times have you ever wanted to animate fire and had no idea how to even approach it? The first technique that comes to mind for animating flames is Shape Tweening. It just seems like the appropriate choice because of the nature of fire and how flames dance and flicker. But in my experience, Shape Tweening doesn't seem to ever produce realistic results. Often, the shapes "implode" or simply morph in all the wrong ways. The effect of fire is simply not achievable using tweens.

Tweens are not an option for the obvious reason that they can only be applied to instances of symbols.

ActionScript might be a solution, but, if you are like me, your scripting skills are not up to the challenge of producing fire from within the Actions panel.

Don't be frightened by what I am about to say, but frame-by-frame is the best option for animating fire. Don't be fooled. It's not that hard or time-consuming.

1 Start by making several overlapping rectangles with no stroke. Don't concern yourself with color at this stage of the process. Any color will do.

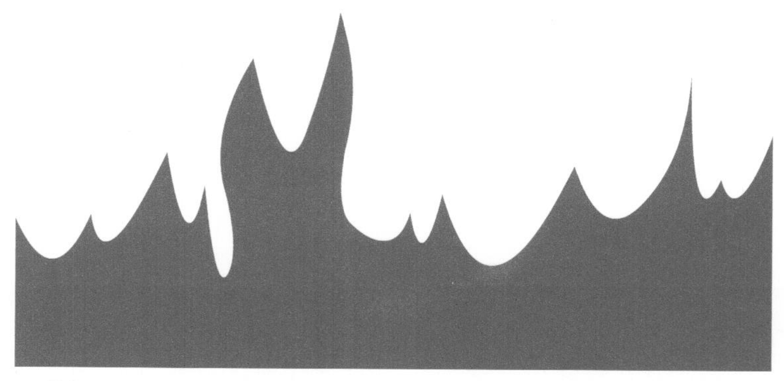

5 Ultimately your flames in frame 1 should look something like this. Try to alternate the direction of each flame. Fire is random and travels in unpredictable ways.

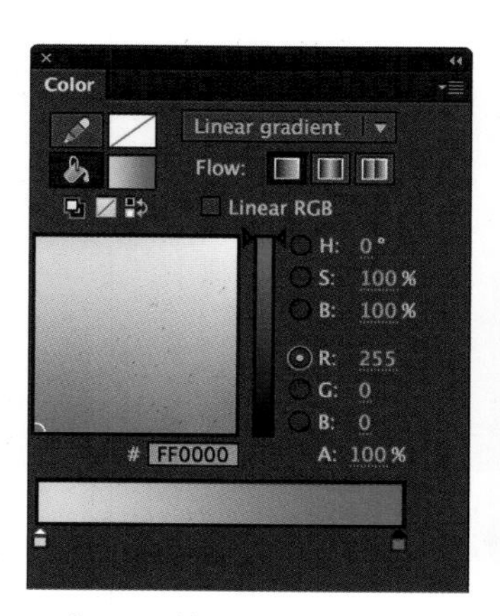

9 Create a Linear gradient using bright red and bright yellow as the two colors.

10 In each keyframe, select all and drag the Paint Bucket Tool (K) vertically inside your flames to fill them. The gradient will be applied in whichever direction you drag.

2 Use the Selection Tool V to pull edges to create peaks.

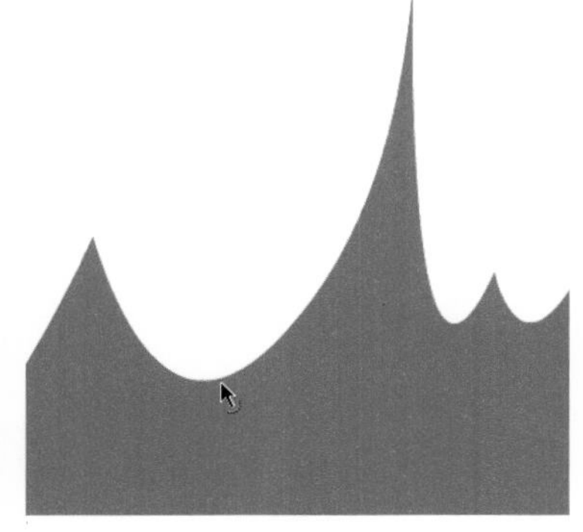

3 Fire is naturally unpredictable. Avoid repetition with your shapes.

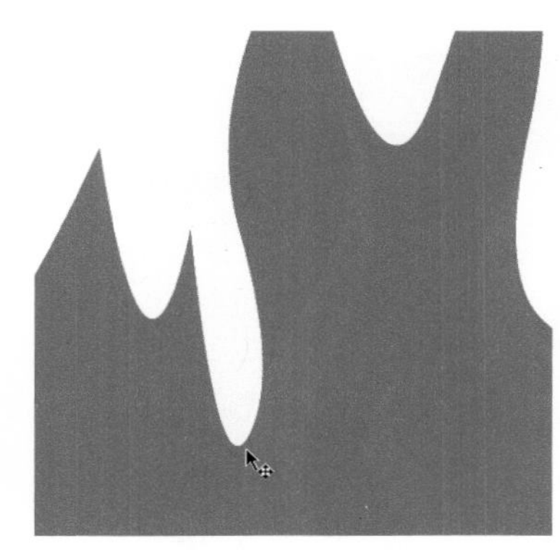

4 Try to incorporate some shapes with S-shaped curves for some added realism.

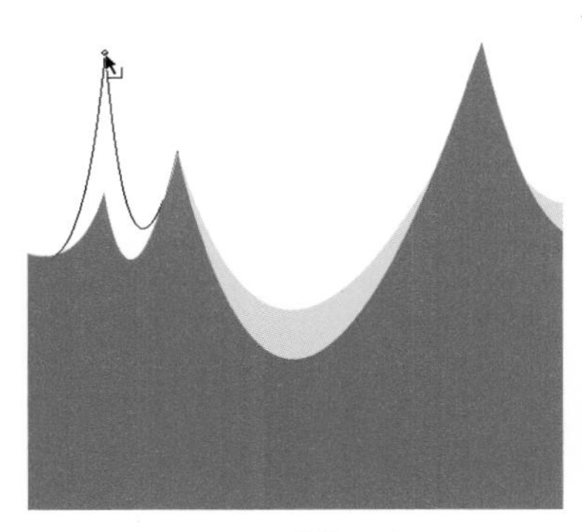

6 Insert a keyframe F6 on frame 2, turn on Onion Skin ⌥ alt Shift O, and begin editing the next frame by pulling each point higher and lower.

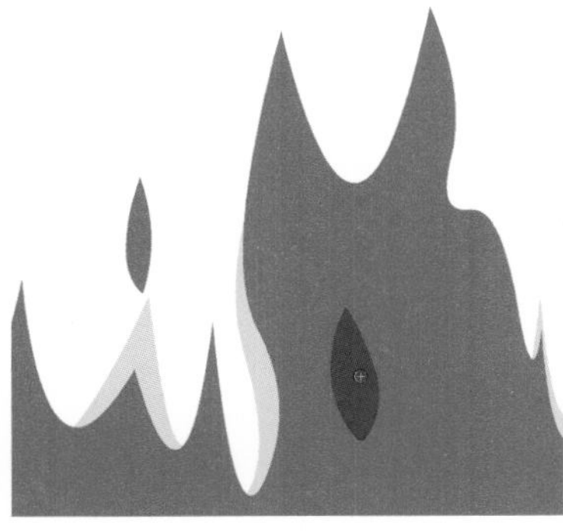

7 Punch holes in the flames by drawing different colored shapes and deleting them. Fire is not solid. It will break up as it rises into the air.

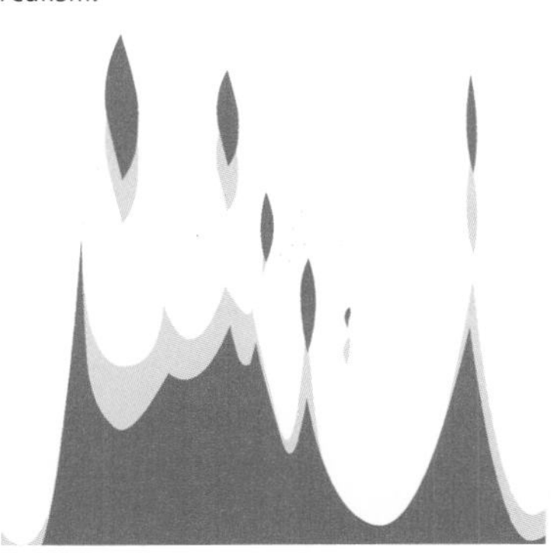

8 Continue to create keyframes and edit the shape of your flames in each one by pulling and pushing with the Selection Tool V.

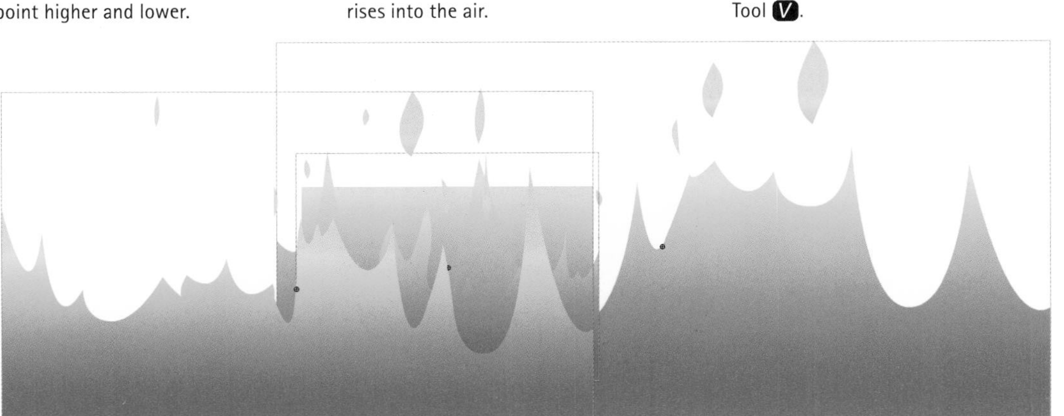

11 Copy all frames of your animation and paste them into a new Graphic symbol. Add three new layers to the main Timeline and drag instances of this symbol to each of them. Delete your original layer. Select one of the instances and flip it horizontally. Scale two of the instances so that they are much wider than the Stage. Position them off-center from the Stage while leaving one of the instances at its original size and position. Create a background shape with the same linear gradient to make it look like the entire scene is ablaze.

HOT TIP

Art imitates life, and there's no substitute for studying the flames of a real fire. Just as Disney's animators went to Africa to study real animals in preparation for production of "The Lion King", you should also study from life as much as possible. Although your budget may not allow for world travel, something like fire is a bit more accessible.

Torch

CREATING ANIMATIONS FOR GAMES often requires creating short looping animations that do not generate large file sizes. These short looping animations work well when they can be reused over and over again throughout the game. This flame example was created for a game where the character carried a torch. The tricky thing about fire as we know from the previous example is that it is unpredictable. Animating elemental effects usually requires a hand-drawn technique because automated tools such as tweening are too consistent in their interpolation to be used for the creation of anything random such as fire. But don't be intimidated by the thought of hand-drawing each frame because you can use the random nature of fire to your advantage.

1 The first frame is drawn using the Brush Tool (B) and a graphics tablet with pressure sensitivity. The idea here is to draw a single shape that has long whispy flame-like shapes coming off of it vertically. I try to make each flame different from the next with the tallest flames toward the center and the shorter flames to the sides.

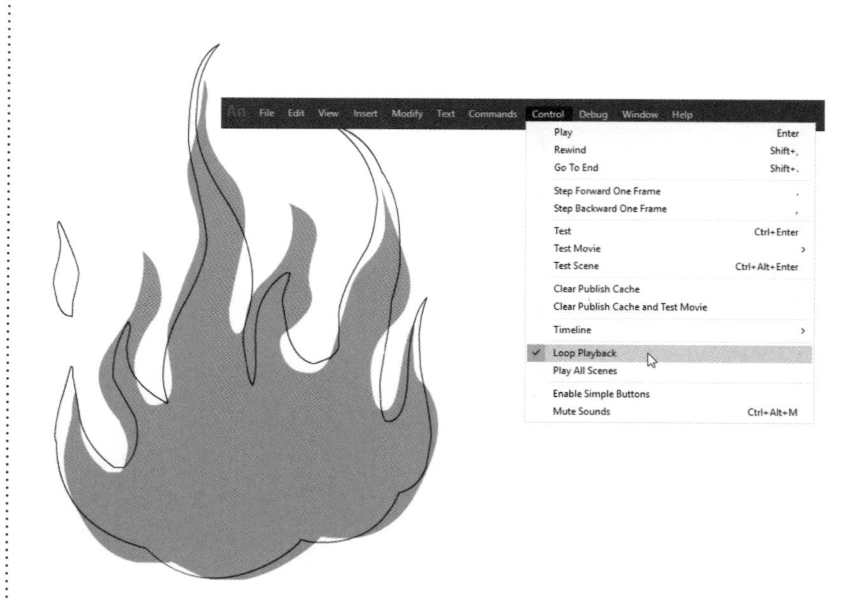

4 Once you have a few frames drawn it is always a good idea to play the animation in a loop to see how it is shaping up. You can loop the Timeline within Animate by choosing Control > Loop Playback.

2 Here I have the original fire drawing on a layer that is being shown as outlines. In a new layer below it is where I make the next fire drawing. Having the original drawing outline on the layer above helps me use it as a guide. Onion Skin would normally be used in this situation, but the current drawing will often hide the edges of the drawing in the previous frame. With an image such as fire, you can draw it much more easily when you can see the entire outline of the previous drawing.

3 Fire is unpredictable. Keeping this in mind, draw the individual flames so that they are animating in different directions. If the flames move in an unpredictable way, then it will look more realistic.

5 This flame animation required seven individual drawings to complete the loop. The flame color was changed to white to appear on a black background.

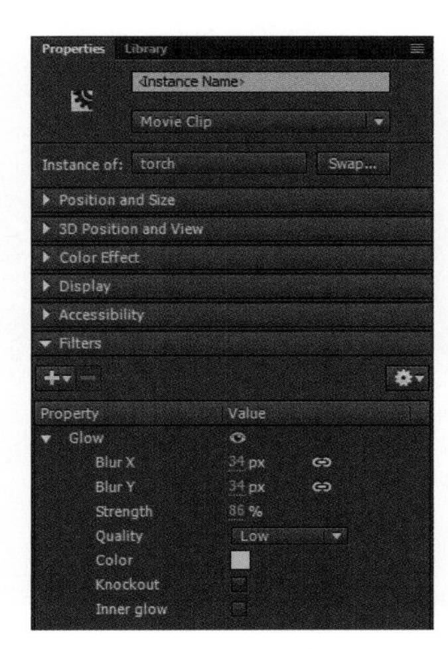

6 All frames were copied into a Movie Clip symbol in order to apply a Glow filter. Using yellow as the glow color, adjust the amount of Blur and Strength to create a soft glow effect.

7 Test the movie to see the torch flame come to life complete with the Glow filter for added effect.

HOT TIP

Animating natural elements often requires practice, patience, and ultimately skill. If you are going for a realistic effect, then be prepared to take the time to study actual flames and how they move in the natural world. Most often elements such as fire, smoke, and clouds react to environmental conditions as opposed to influencing them.

Lightning

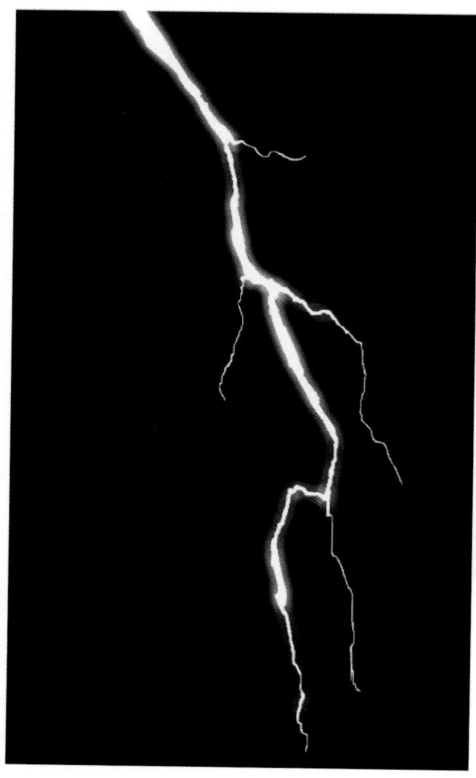

LIGHTNING IS ONE OF THE EASIEST and most fun elemental effects to animate. Lightning can be used in scenes for atmospheric effect, and it can be very effective to say the least. Once you master the techniques for making lightning, you can borrow the style for more than merely storms. Use it for scenes to demonstrate electricity, create science fiction effects, or illustrate superhuman powers.

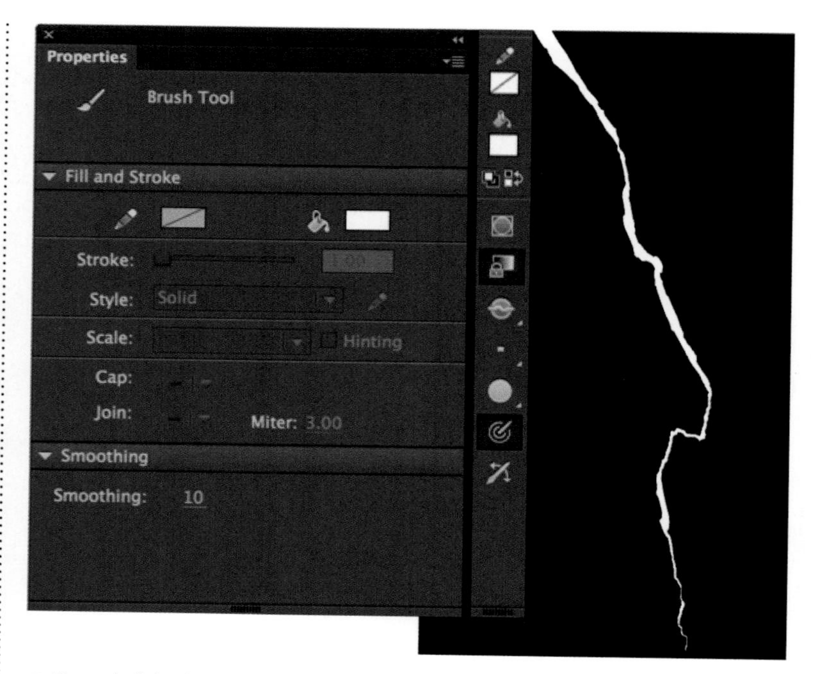

1 The main lightning bolt is drawn using the Brush Tool (B) and a graphics tablet with pressure sensitivity. Lowering the amount of smoothing helps achieve a realistic looking bolt due to the imperfections caused by the human hand. Nature is not perfect, and therefore your lightning bolt should have imperfections also. Try to vary the weight of the bolt as well as the direction it goes by drawing with a loose, carefree hand.

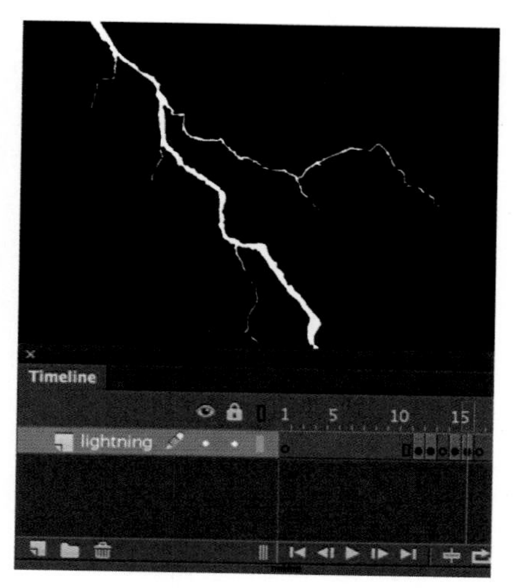

5 Insert a keyframe (F6) and select the Eraser Tool (E). Carefully remove areas of the lightning bolt from the outside edges to create the illusion that it is breaking apart.

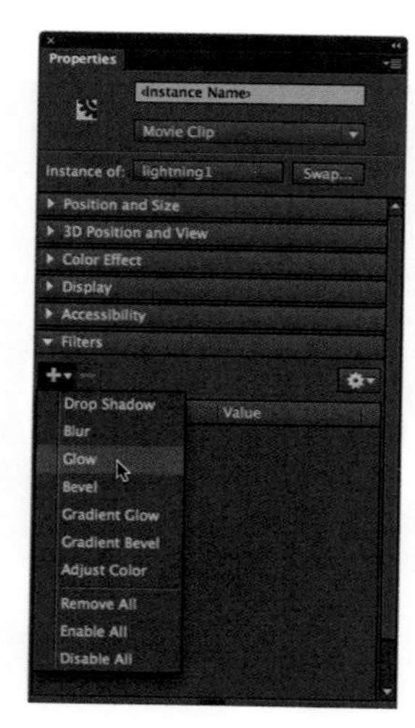

6 As an added effect, convert the first bolt of lightning to a Movie Clip symbol and then apply a Glow filter to it from the Properties panel.

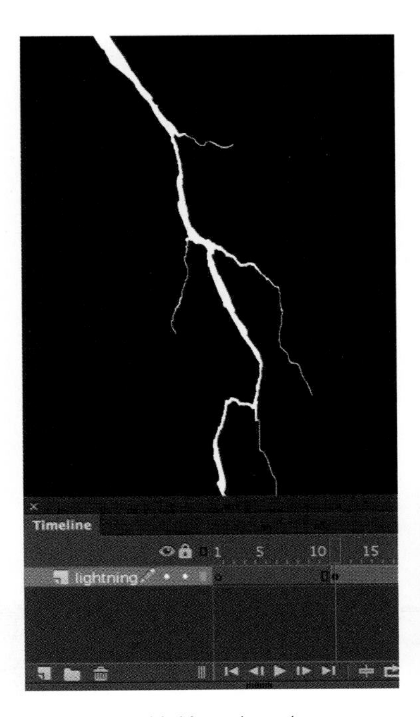

2 You can add thinner branches breaking off from the main lightning bolt itself. These branches are usually very thin, so reduce the size of the Brush before drawing them.

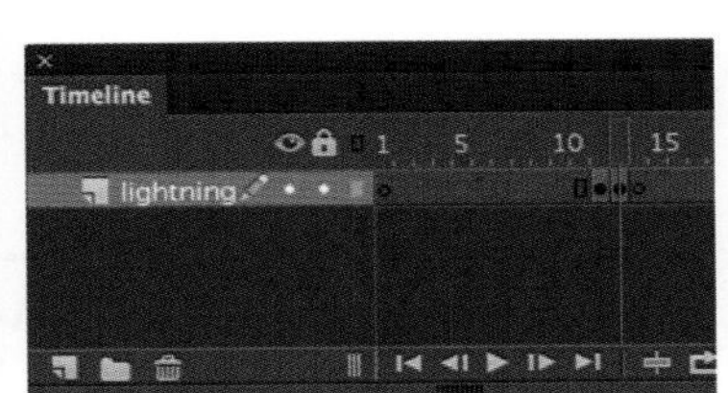

3 The frame following the lightning should be completely white. This white frame creates a high contrast effect that leaves a residual image in the viewer's eye. It is a very powerful and easy effect to create.

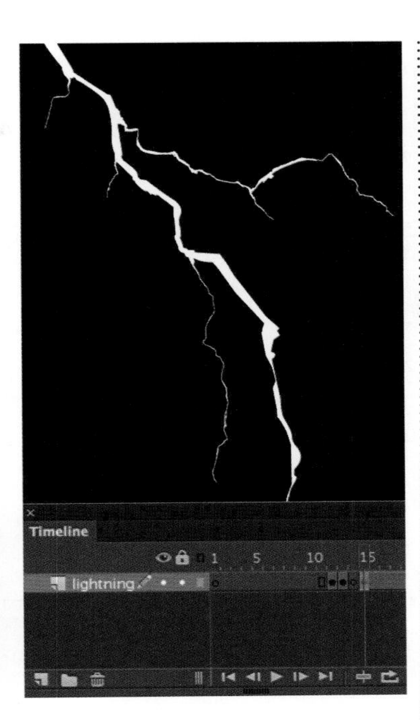

4 The next frame is left blank, exposing just the black background. The frame after that contains a new lightning bolt drawing.

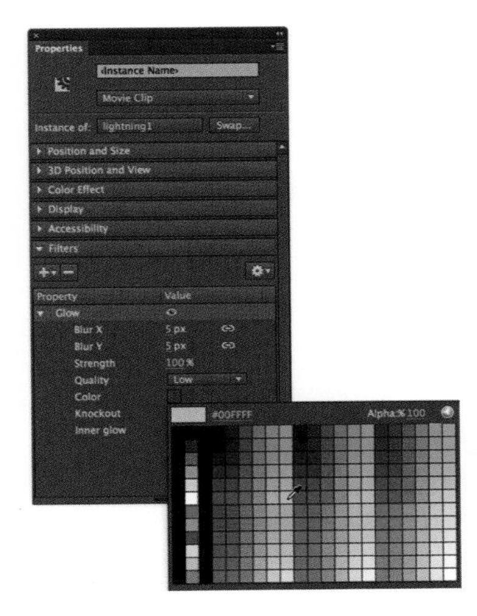

7 The color of the glow is entirely up to you. It can be almost any color depending on the subject matter. Green or blue can suggest a fantasy theme while red may look more real-world.

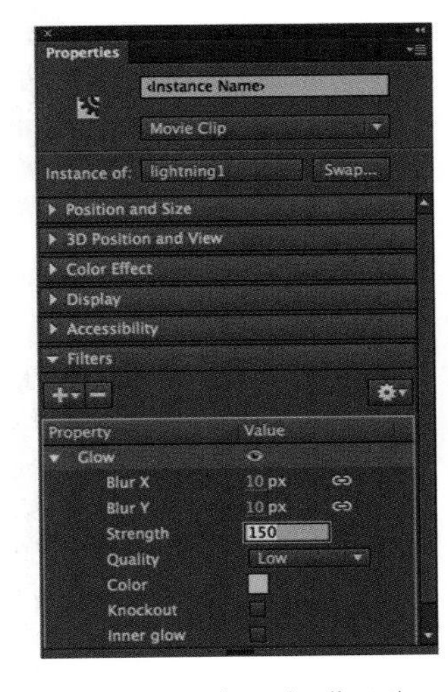

8 With the color selected, adjust the amount of blur and strength using the hot text sliders. It is easy to abuse the blur effect, so remember that being subtle usually works better here.

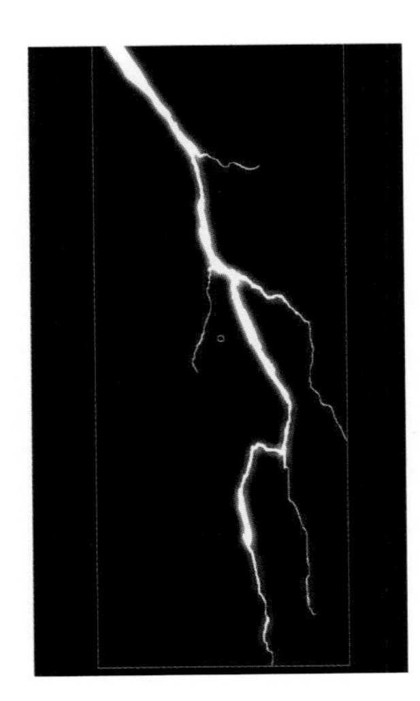

9 Test the movie to see the lightning bolt in action.

HOT TIP

Lightning is a very quick and simple animation technique that can easily be overanimated. Don't try and animate the lightning bolt into the frame by building it up over a sequence of keyframes. The entire bolt should enter the scene in a single frame fully drawn. If you've ever had the opportunity to stand and watch a lightning storm on the horizon, then you've noticed that lightning bolts strike within the blink of an eye. Keeping it simple will yield the best results.

Sausage Grinder

APOLOGIES IN ADVANCE TO ALL vegetarians. Sausage Kong is an Animate game developed by Thibault Imbert and myself. This type of game is what gets created when two guys go completely rogue and put their creative minds together sans a babysitter (and when I say "creative" I really mean "twisted"). The reason I chose the grinder animation for this example is because it takes advantage of several design and animation tools in Adobe Animate CC. From the Pencil Tool to Motion and Classic Tweens, you don't have to limit yourself to a single tool. It is often the combination of several techniques that make for a better product.

SAUSAGE GRINDER FROM THE GAME SAUSAGE KONG - THIBAULT IMBERT & CHRIS GEORGENES

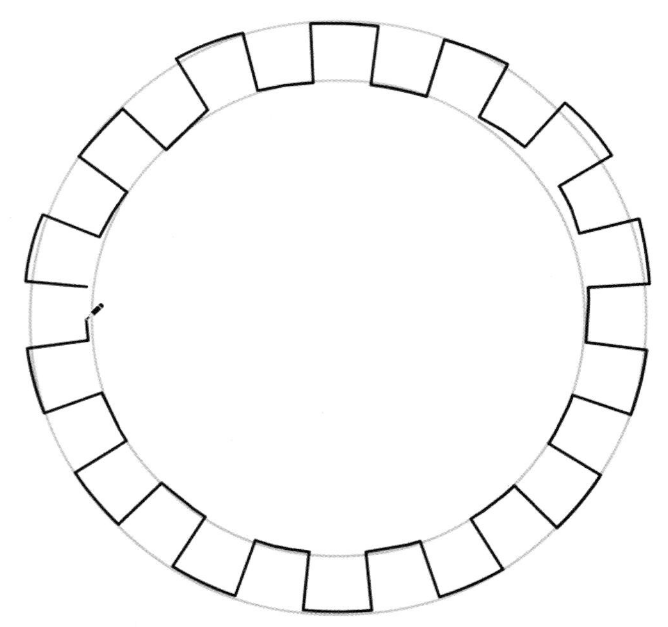

1 The gear was drawn using the Pencil Tool Shift Y. The light blue circles were used as my guide and drawn using the Oval Tool O with an outline color only on a different layer below the actual gear layer.

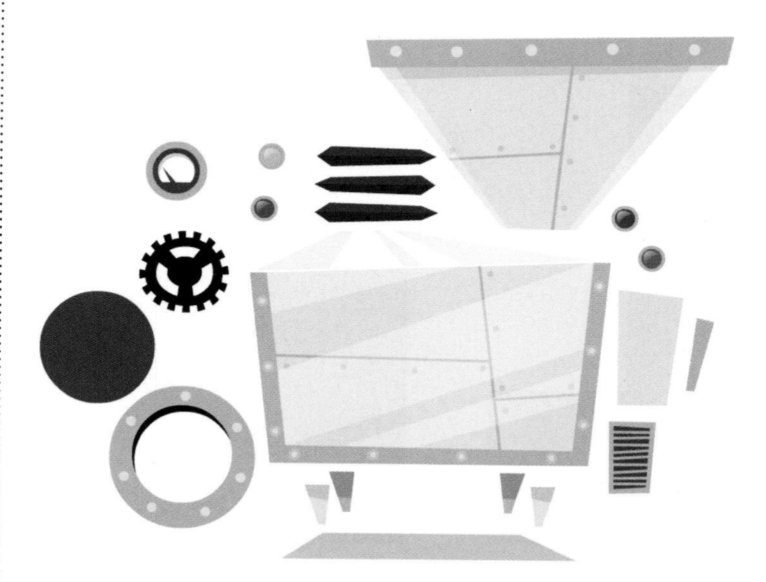

4 The important aspect to this animation is identifying the parts that need to move. Once identified, draw each part separately and convert them to symbols. Here is an exploded view of all the individual parts of the grinder.

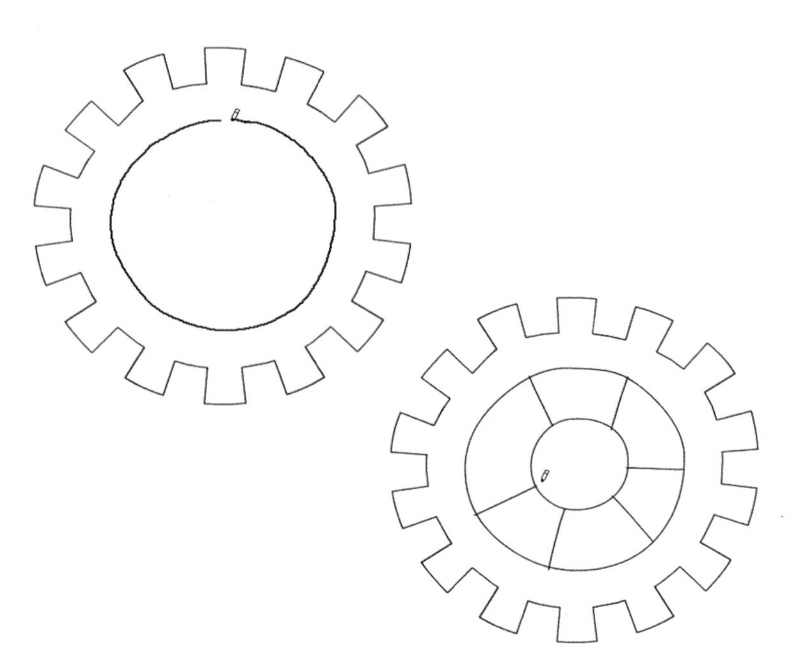

HOT TIP

I chose to hand draw the gears as a design choice. Drawing freehand has inherent imperfections and thereby lends itself to a looser style.

2 Using the Pencil Tool Shift Y and the same stroke size, draw two inner circles and then attach them by drawing some support sections.

3 Select any overlapping stroke segments and delete them. You can then fill the gear with your color(s) of choice.

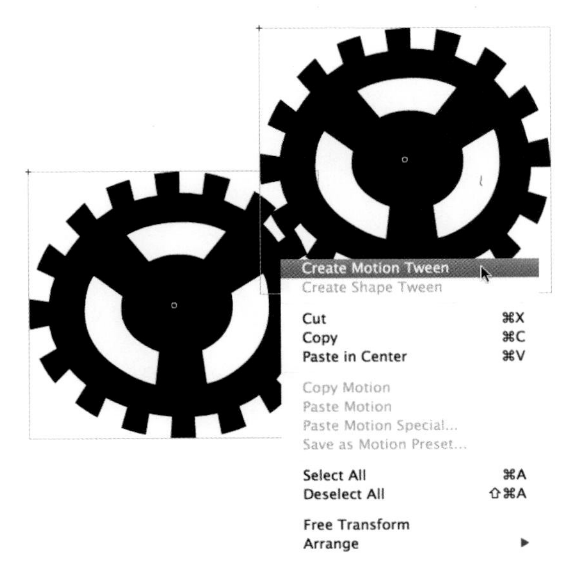

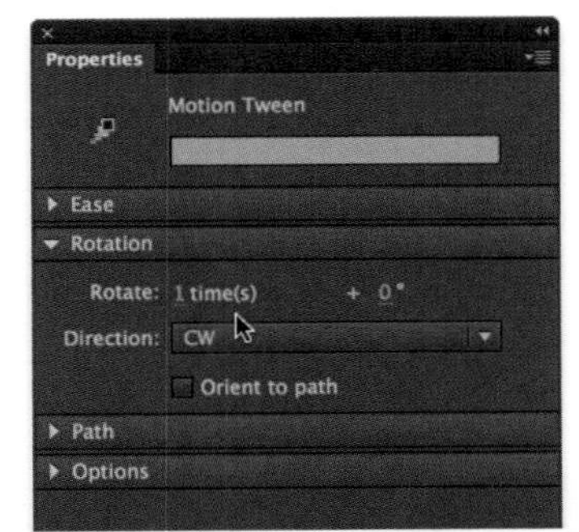

5 Convert the gear to a symbol and then copy and paste it to create a second gear. Distribute each gear to its own layer. Right-click over each one and select Create Motion Tween.

6 Select each motion span for each gear and in the Rotation section of the Properties panel enter each gear's rotation settings. Type in the number of rotations as well as the direction (clockwise or counterclockwise).

Sausage Grinder (cont.)

7 Both gear animations were converted to a single symbol. I wanted them to be viewed "inside" the grinder so I designed a porthole-style window as separate assets. The red shape is the mask that limits the visibility of the gears to the window area only. The gray circle is the background color, the irregular shape seen on top of the gray shape is the window highlight, and the bezel is shown at the very top.

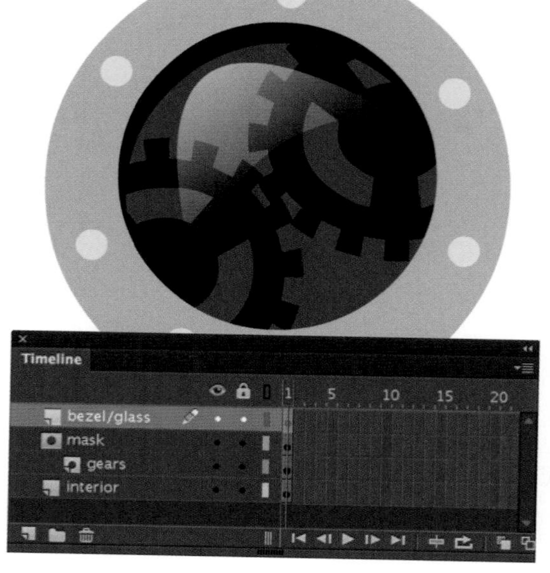

8 Here is the assembled window porthole with the masked gears. You can see the layer ordering of each object in the Timeline. The irregular shape with the alpha gradient is the only artwork inside the bezel. There was no need to provide anything else as this small piece of art was enough to provide the illusion of glass.

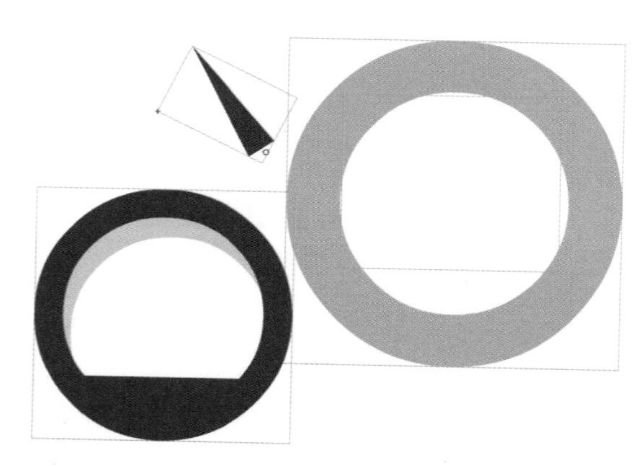

11 Here's the exploded view of the pressure gauge. Once again I have used very simple shapes to build this gauge while keeping in mind that it will be scaled down quite small, so keeping it simple was crucial. The needle was kept as a separate object because I intended to animate it.

12 With each object distributed to layers, I was able to animate the needle moving back and forth. Notice the center point was positioned at the bottom of the needle to allow it to rotate based on where it would be normally hinged.

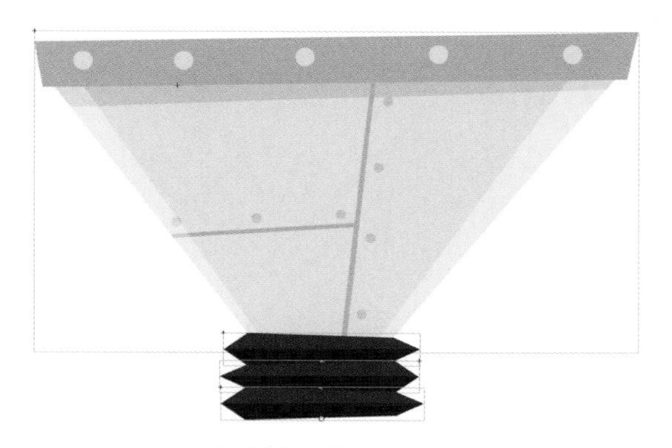

9 The meat catcher is made up of four different graphics each converted to a symbol and is distributed to layers. An eight-frame animation was created of the catcher moving up and down in a slightly erratic nature. Those eight frames were copied and pasted to lengthen the animation Timeline.

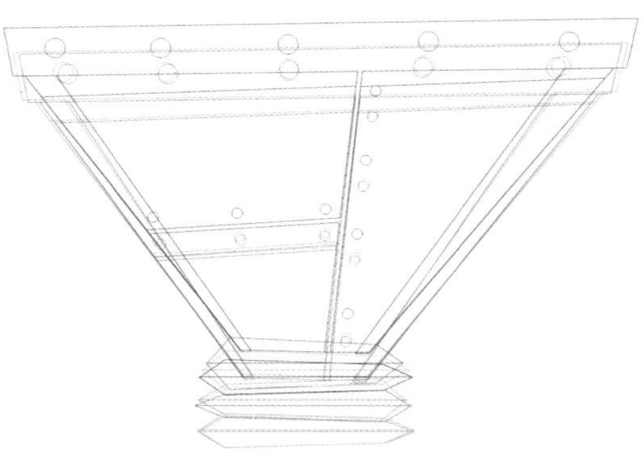

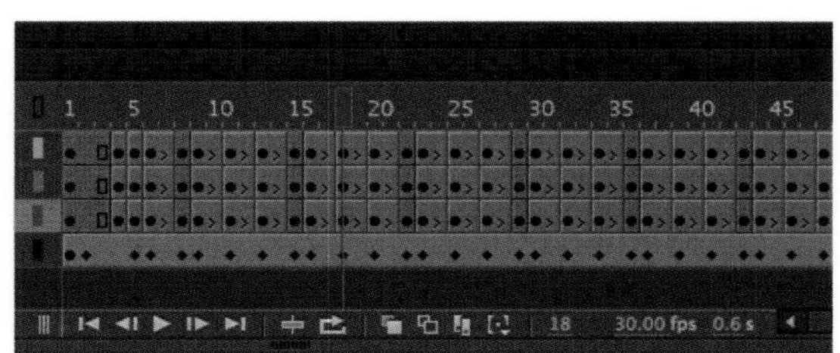

10 With the layers converted to outlines, you can see more clearly the subtle motions of the catcher between the frames. A combination of Motion and Classic Tweens was used to create this effect.

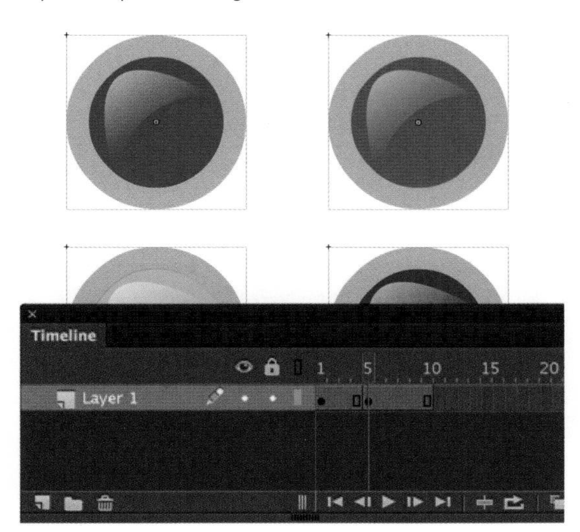

13 The flashing lights couldn't be simpler to create. The glass highlight was reused from the porthole (gears) example, and the light flashing effect was simply a second keyframe with a brighter color for the simulated lens.

14 Here's the entire grinder assembled and in fine working order. Check out the source file from the downloadable exercises to see the entire animation.

HOT TIP

Usually several different short looping animations can create a more compelling experience than a single larger motion. I prefer to make everything move small amounts simultaneously, as opposed to animating the entire object as a single asset. It's a lot more work but usually provides a better result.

Brush Animation

CREATING ANIMATE ANIMATIONS for Animate game titles sometimes involves creating ambient effects such as explosions, flying birds, floating clouds, and rolling fog, to name a few. This example deconstructs the creation of a specific effect animation where a brush is needed to provide a transition effect. As the game is launched and cards are dealt across the screen, the brush moves across the screen to "dust off" the back of the cards to reveal their face value. The original brush reference was drawn at a single angle by an illustrator in the form of a layered Adobe Photoshop file. The brush needed to be re-created at a different angle and animated as if it were directly in front of the user. This animation is fairly complicated, requiring extensive hand-drawn animation combined with some Animate ingenuity.

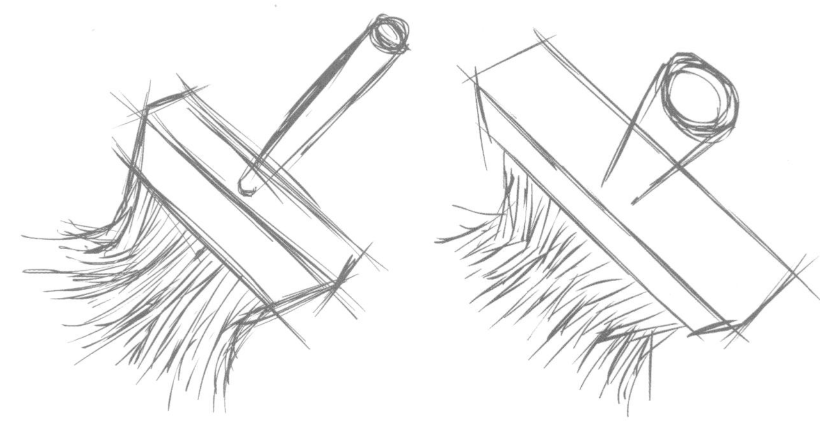

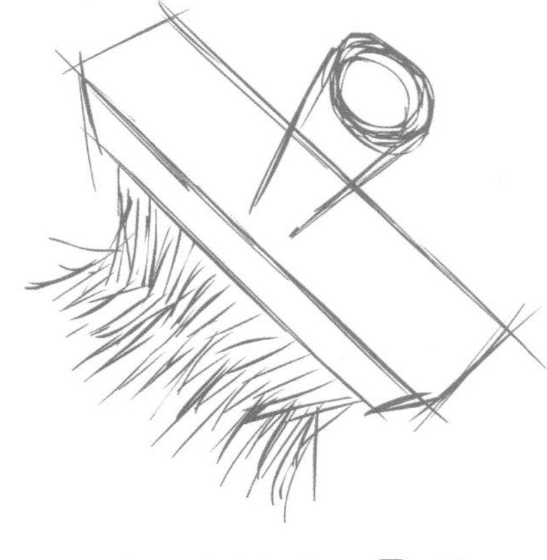

1 Ironically the Brush Tool (B) was used to sketch the brush image at the angle shown above. Keeping the drawings loose helped to achieve the basic motion of the brush.

2 Inserting a blank keyframe (F7) while Onion Skin was enabled helped during the process of sketching the brush at a slightly different angle. Starting with the circular butt end of the handle that appeared closest to the viewer gave a point of reference for continuing drawing the rest of the brush.

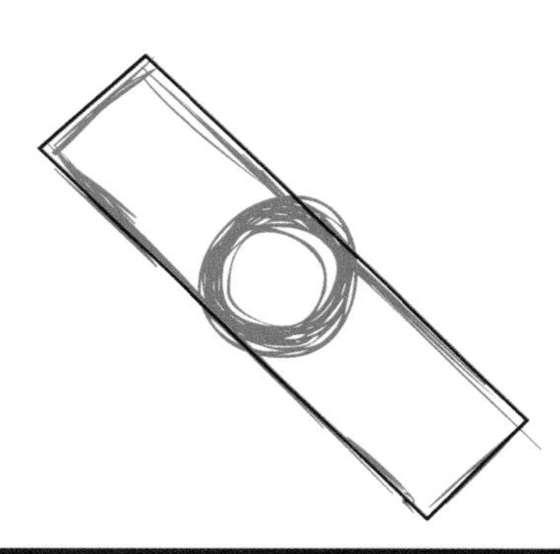

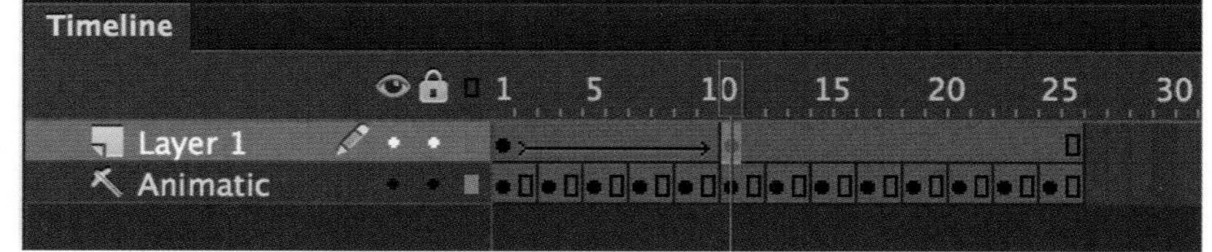

6 After the animatic stage was completed, the creation of the tradigital brush for the animation could begin. This next step borrows from the previous tradigital technique from the example on the previous pages. This step focuses on defining just one plane of the handle using the Rectangle Tool (R) with black as the stroke color and no color for the fill in frame 1. Each corner of the rectangle was clicked and dragged using the Selection Tool (V) to create the perspective with the sketch as a guide. In frame 10 a blank keyframe was inserted (F5), and another rectangle was drawn using just strokes in the shape of the plane also with the sketch as a guide.

3 In the next frame the brush was drawn at an angle where the butt end of the handle is almost completely facing the viewer. The top plane representing the body of the brush is almost at a 90° angle to the viewer.

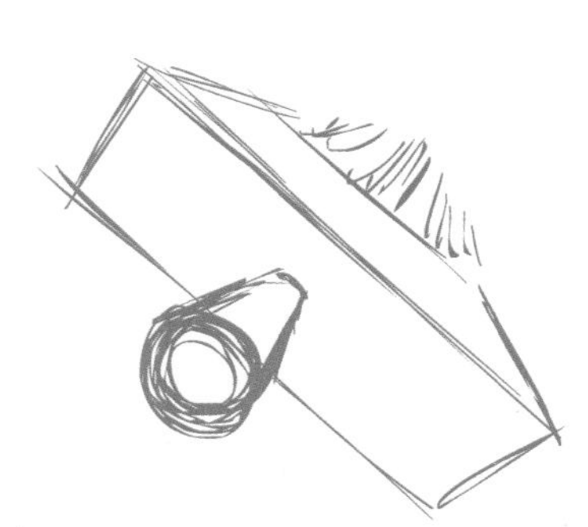

4 Here the brush has rotated at an angle sufficient to show its opposite side.

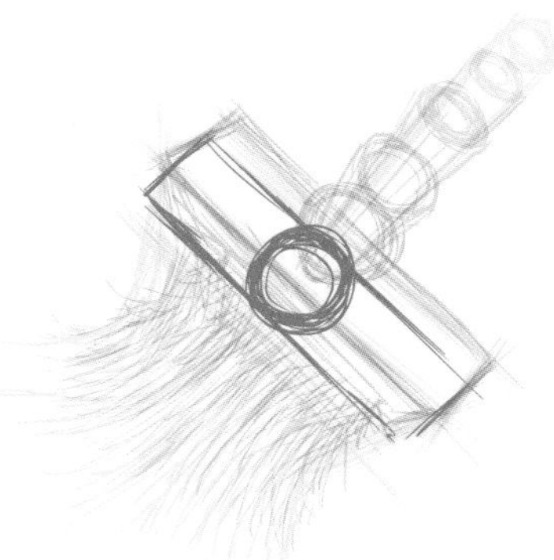

5 Onion Skin is useful for making sure the alignment of the handle is in check during this phase. A point of reference like the circular end of the handle can serve as a visual aid to keep the brush aligned throughout the rotation in each frame.

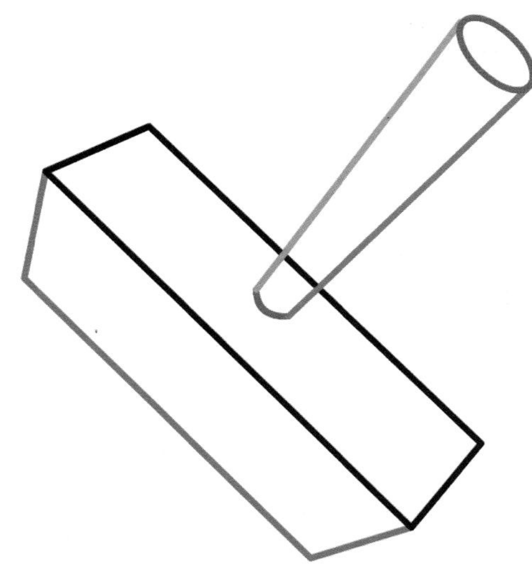

7 Repeat step 6 by inserting new layers for every new stroke or plane. The body of the brush required a total of six new layers. The different strokes for each layer are shown above in different colors for illustration purposes.

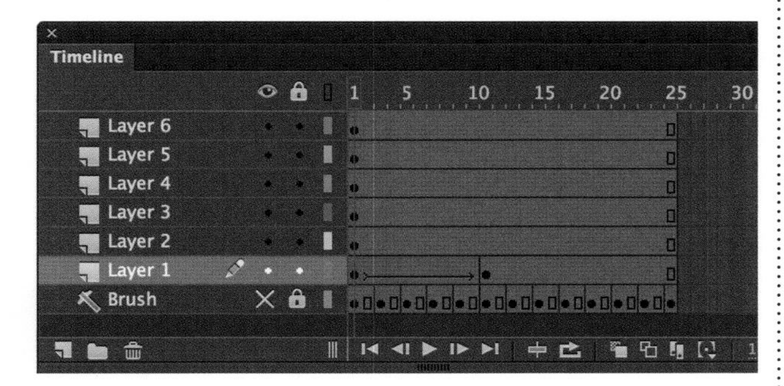

8 Here is how the Timeline layers look at this stage of the process. Each layer contains a different segment of the brush. The reason for keeping the strokes on separate layers is to make it easy to animate each stroke using Shape Tweens in the following steps. In most cases, a layer will contain more than one stroke segment which is OK. The idea is to limit the number of vector points to as few as possible to ensure the Shape Tweens have a better chance of working in the next steps.

HOT TIP

When you're trying to figure out what works in your animation, it helps to make rough sketches. Test your ideas by combining these sketches in what is known as an "animatic". It's basically an animated storyboard. By reviewing and revising the sketches in your animatic, you'll have a better idea of how your animation will look and how to approach creating it.

Brush Animation (cont.)

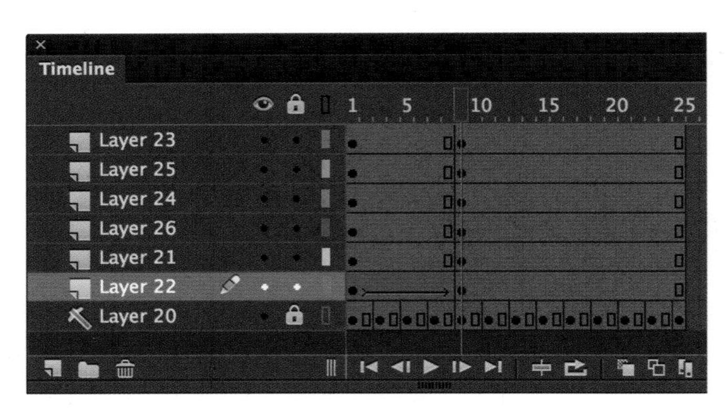

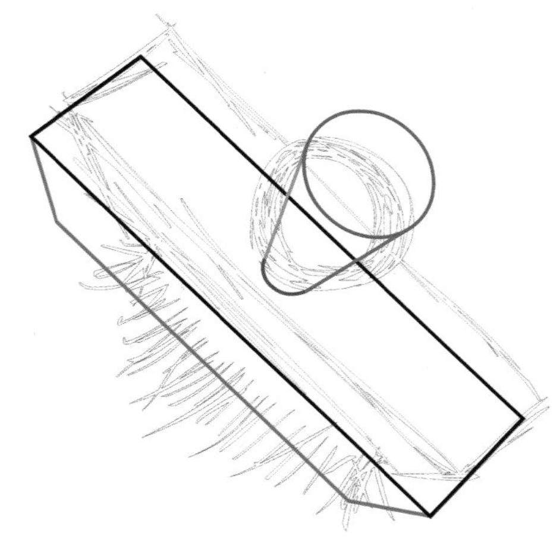

9 Keyframes are inserted across each layer on frame 9. This frame is where the tween span should ultimately end. The decision to animate to this point is based on the angle of the brush in this frame. As seen above, the brush angle in the original sketch is at an angle right before it travels past its own axis. In the following frame, the opposite side of the brush becomes visible as the handle moves past the viewer down to the left. Shape Tweening vector points beyond this angle have a history of being problematic, so it was better to animate the first half of the brush movement and worry about how to animate the second half later.

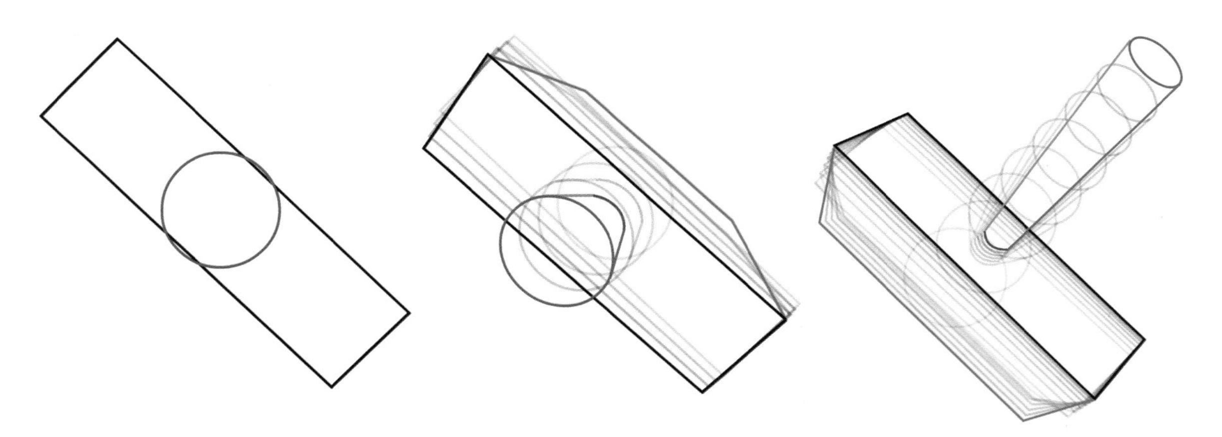

11 I continued the rest of the brush animation using the same process as described in the previous steps. Keyframes were inserted, lines were drawn, and Shape Tweens were added using the original animatic as my guide. With the brush animation complete, my Timeline consisted of mostly Shape Tweens and a few keyframes. Blank keyframes were the result of when the brush was at an angle where neither of its sides could be seen.

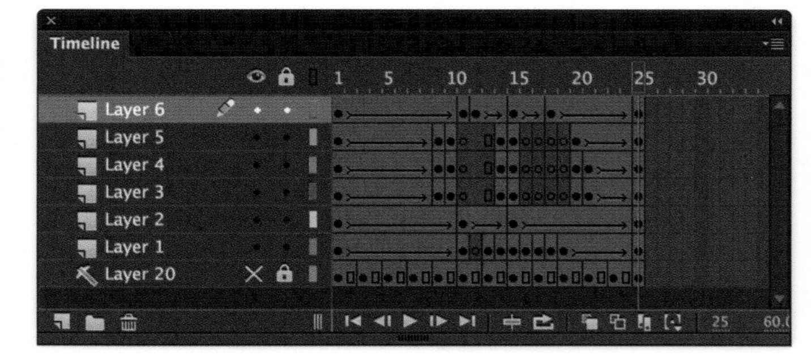

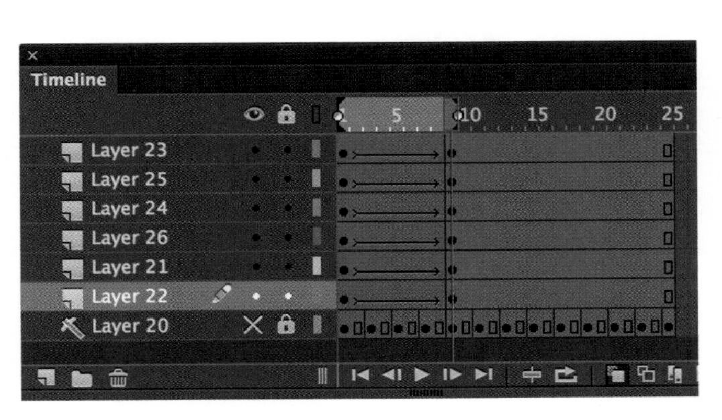

HOT TIP

You may not be sure when you start an effect like this if it will work out or even look good. The important thing is to start somewhere and keep it simple. Challenge yourself because with failure or success comes learning either way.

10 With each stroke in place on frame 10, apply Shape Tweens across each of the layers between the keyframes. Play back the animation to see the brush appear to change angle across a faux 3D space. Applying an easing in value of -100 at this point will create a more realistic motion.

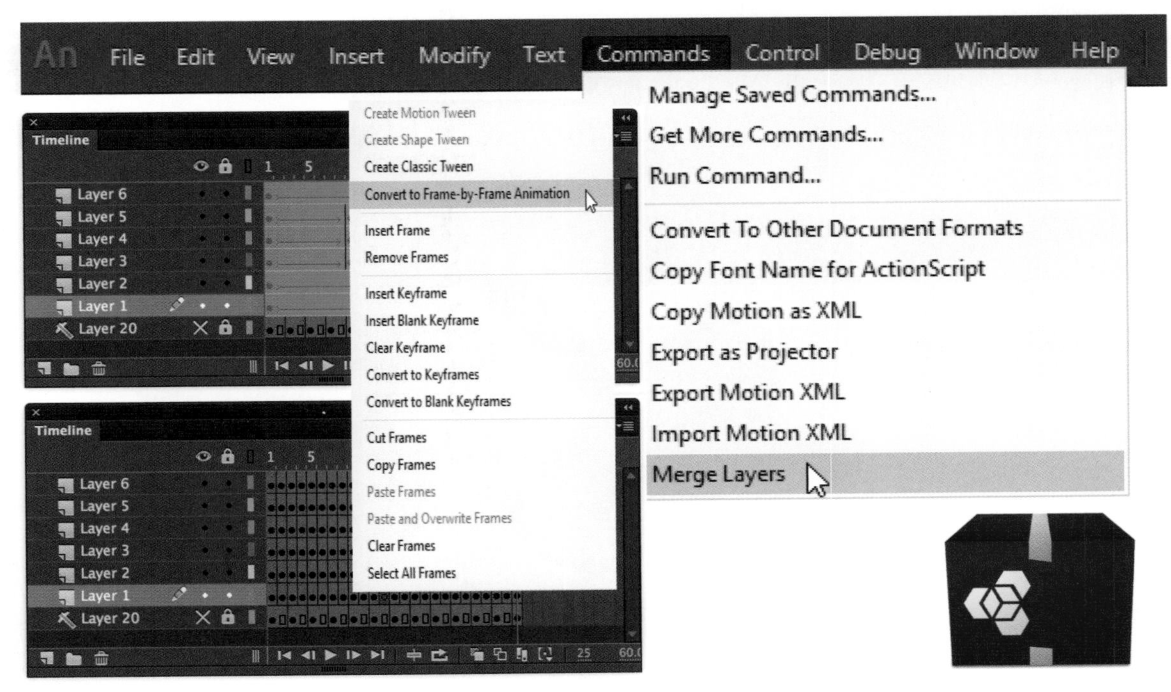

12 The next step was to merge all the layers down to a single layer. The reason for merging is to have each stroke on the same layer so that the Paint Bucket Tool K can be used to fill the closed shapes. To merge all keyframes across all layers manually would be painfully redundant work. Since Animate doesn't have a native feature for this specific task, we luckily have David Wolfe to thank for his handy Merge Layers extension that is available on his website (toonmonkey.com/extensions.html). With the extension installed it can be accessed from the Commands menu. Select the entire range of frames and layers and then choose Commands > Merge Layers.

Brush Animation (cont.)

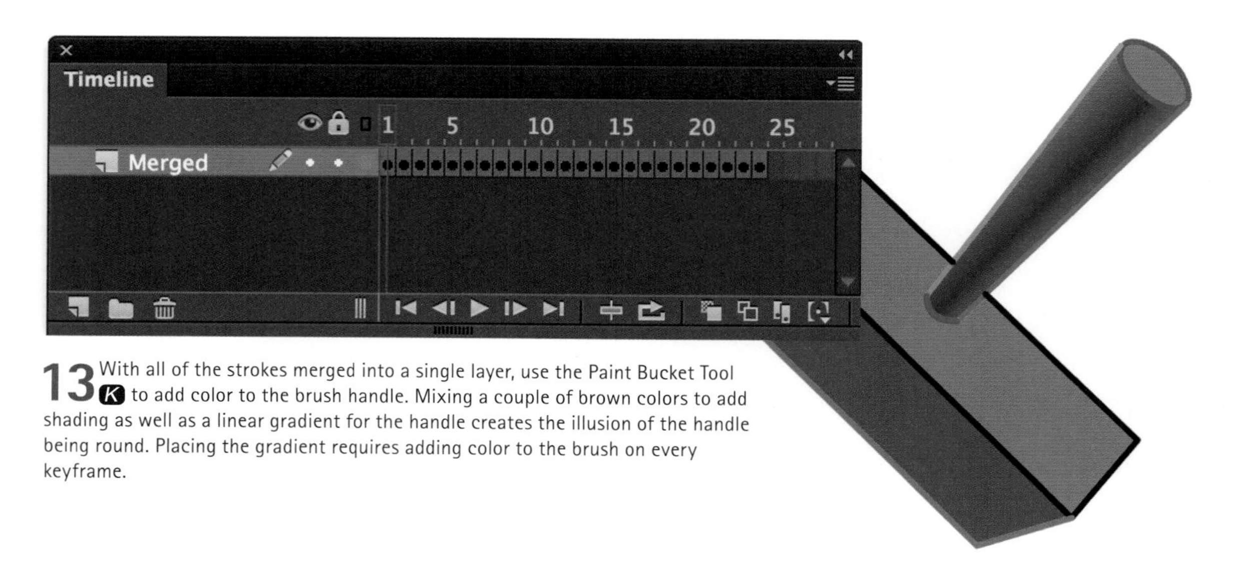

13 With all of the strokes merged into a single layer, use the Paint Bucket Tool K to add color to the brush handle. Mixing a couple of brown colors to add shading as well as a linear gradient for the handle creates the illusion of the handle being round. Placing the gradient requires adding color to the brush on every keyframe.

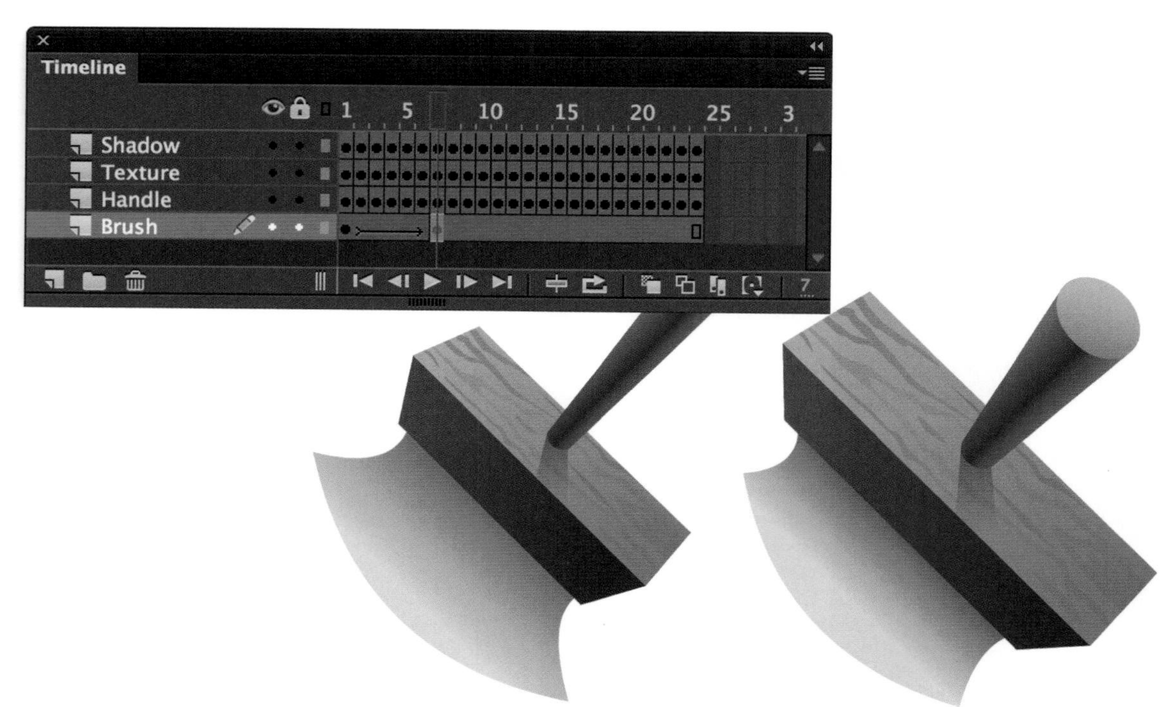

16 The next challenge was to create and animate the bristles of the brush. Use the Rectangle Tool R to draw a simple square fill. Then use the Selection Tool V to manipulate the corners and sides to look like the shape in the image above. Insert a keyframe F6 in frame 7 and use the Selection Tool V again to manipulate the shape as seen in the second image. Then apply a Shape Tween to these frames to animate the shape. Limiting the animation to seven frames helps to prevent the Shape Tween from breaking apart, which can happen when the shape is transformed too much from one frame to the next. The remaining bristles animation was created the same way using Shape Tweens across short sequences of frames.

14 Using the Selection Tool V, manually select the strokes from each frame and delete them, leaving behind just the fill colors.

15 Adding some texture to simulate wood and casting a small shadow from the handle creates a stronger illusion of this being a 3D object. This step was not necessary, but going the extra mile takes an animation to the next level.

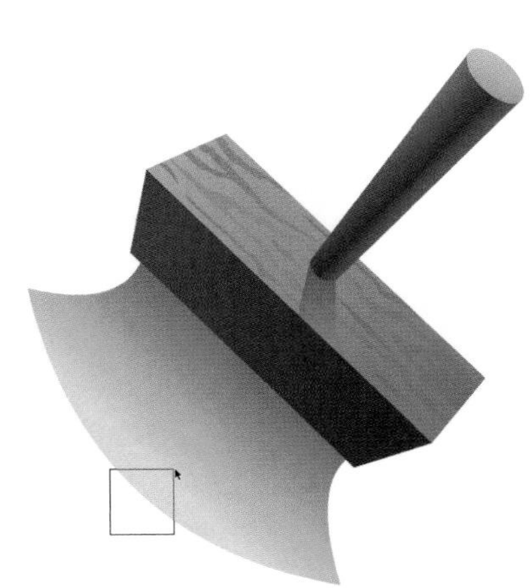

17 Once the overall bristle animation is complete, select all the frames in the layer across all the Shape Tweens and convert them to keyframes. Next use the Selection Tool V and select a small portion of the shape.

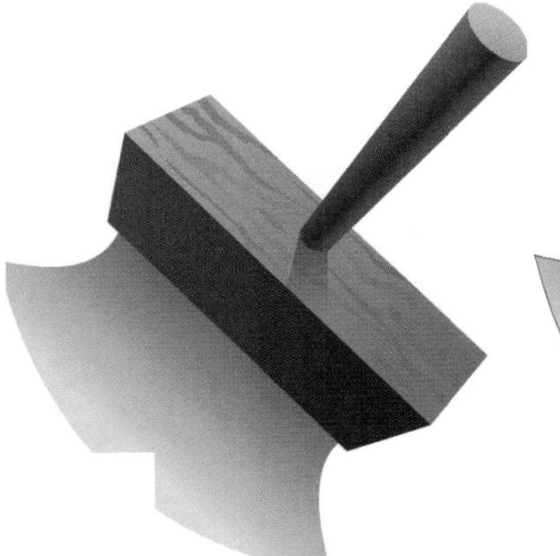

18 With the shape selected, press the Delete key to create a notch in the shape to allow for further manipulation on the bristles.

19 Using the Selection Tool V, drag the corners to create a thin notch.

HOT TIP

It's difficult to see, but the solid colors in the brush handle are really linear gradients. Creating gradients with subtle variances in color values helps create the illusion of various amounts of light reflecting off each surface. It's a tiny detail that adds a lot to the overall effect.

Brush Animation (cont.)

20 Repeat steps 18 and 19 to add additional notches in the shape to create the illusion of the bristles spread out.

21 Go to the next keyframe in the Timeline and repeat steps 18 through 20, but in this keyframe the notches should be slightly thinner.

22 In the next keyframe the same steps are applied, but the notches should be smaller and fewer in number. The idea is that the bristles are coming together and the spaces between them are going away over time.

26 The final step is to add the dust animation. Using the Brush Tool **B**, draw the dust as solid shapes using the brown color as shown.

27 With each keyframe draw the dust over again using Onion Skin as a guide. In this keyframe the dust is slightly smaller in volume.

28 Over time the dust begins to disappear. The trick to making dust look real is to slowly animate the edge of the dust closest to the brush faster than the leading edge of the dust.

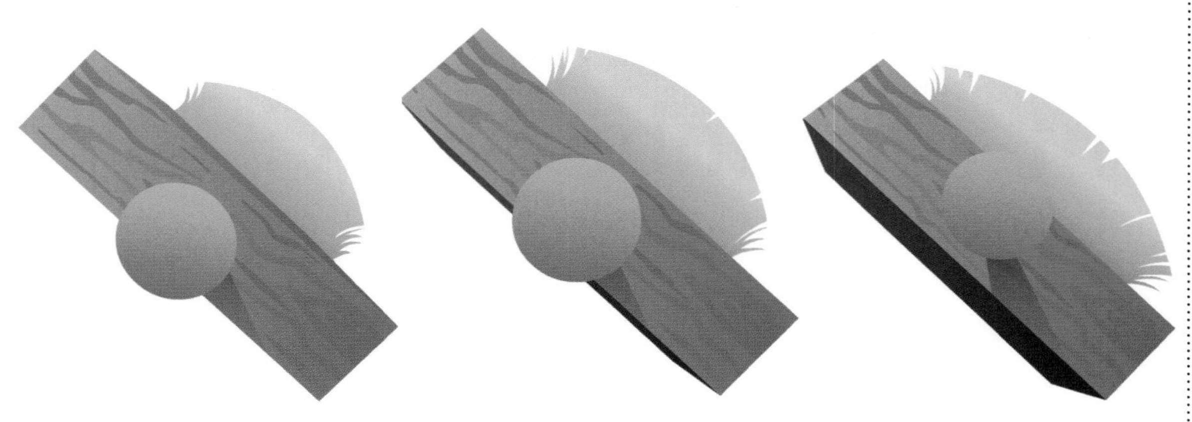

23 As the brush changes direction, so do the bristles. As the bristles extend away from the brush handle, the notches begin to appear. Repeat steps 18 through 20 to create the illusion of bristles once again.

24 In this keyframe only add a small number of notches. The animation is very quick during playback, and not much detail can be discerned by the human eye.

25 Here is the keyframe where the bristles are spread out the most. This frame contains the biggest notches and the largest number of them as well.

29 With the trailing edge of the dust moving faster, more of the dust particles break apart and start to disappear from the direction where they originate.

30 Here the dust is mostly small blobs, which continually get smaller and break apart.

31 In the final keyframe the dust is almost completely gone. Open the example file if you haven't done so already, and in the last scene you will find the dust animation.

HOT TIP

Keep it simple! If you're unsure how to animate something like bristles, start with a basic rectangle shape to make the animation process much simpler. Having drawn and animated each individual bristle would look realistic but is not necessary. It's also possible to make something like the dust animation not so difficult by keeping it as simple solid shapes drawn with the Brush Tool. The trick here is to not overthink the design.

How to Get the Most out of Adobe MAX

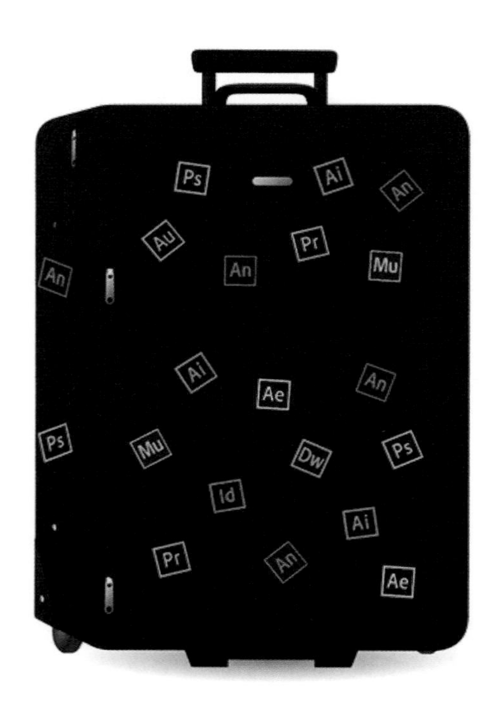

ADOBE MAX IS THE ANNUAL CREATIVE CONFERENCE for Adobe users. It originated as a developer conference, gained traction as a designer/developer conference, and has since morphed into a visual feast and concentration of creative stimuli. The gathering has grown to about 11,000 attendees. With so many participants, sessions, session types, tracks, technical levels, activities, events, etc., it can be overwhelming for some—especially first-timers. So, here are some strategies for navigating the MAX landscape and maximizing your experience.

1. If it's your first time at MAX, start with an objective or two like these:
    - Get familiar with a specific application.
    - Learn a new technique.
    - Meet others who are doing similar work who can share experiences.
    - Meet others who could be a resource.
    - Find out how to improve your portfolio.
    - Meet vendors who can provide services your company needs.

    Register as early as you can, so you can sign up for the sessions you want and tailor your schedule to accomplish your goals. Look for specific sessions or labs that feature that application or technique. However, once you get to MAX if you see a demo at the Community Pavilion or as part of another session that might help you with a particular project, change your schedule. Even if you've signed up in advance for a different session, it's flexible. Follow that lead if you find out there's something better suited to equipping you with the information you need.

2. Know what to bring with you.
    - Always have your registration badge with you.
    - Bring your laptop with the Creative Cloud apps installed if you're signed up for a BYOL (Bring Your Own Laptop) hands-on lab. If you need assistance with installation, go early to see the tech helpers.

- Make sure you bring business cards with you and keep them somewhere that's easily accessible so that you can quickly trade them with people you meet.
- Wear comfortable shoes in anticipation of a lot of walking.
- Take a jacket. Convention center rooms are notoriously chilly.
- Lug the lip balm. With lots of talking, especially in some of the dryer climates where MAX has been hosted, chapped lips are a frequent occurrence.
- Bring your phone charger. A full day of activity and an intermittent Wi-Fi connection can run down your battery. There are outlets and comfortable seating in the Community Lounge which make for a great place to recharge.

  Unless you've signed up for a BYOL lab, you likely won't need a laptop. If it's heavy, you might not want to tote it around all day. If you're a note-taker, use a lighter-weight tablet with a Bluetooth keyboard instead or go old school and use pen and paper. Why not take a picture on your phone? Just be sure not to use the flash. Best of all, barring unforeseen technical difficulties, the sessions are recorded and made available online. Be aware, however, that the hands-on labs aren't included in the recordings and the uploaded content isn't permanently available.

3. If a hands-on lab you wanted was full, you might still have a chance to get a seat.
   - Check the MAX scheduler to see if there's a waitlist. Get signed up if there is.
   - Stand outside the door. If people who were registered don't show up just before the lab, you'll get their seat at 5 minutes before the start of the lab.

   Sometimes, if there's enough interest in a lab, additional times will be added. So check the Scheduler and Adobe MAX via social media on Twitter, Facebook, and Instagram.

4. Make MAX your evening plans.
   - Attend the Welcome Reception where you can grab a bite to eat and mosey around to see the vendors at a time that won't interfere with your sessions.
   - Talk to the people who make the applications you love at Meet the Teams. Ask questions, make feature requests, and generally bask in the presence of greatness.
   - Whatever you do, do not miss Sneaks! Sneaks are a MAX favorite for many attendees including myself. It's a showcase of features or apps that may or may not become part of an actual product. In what is often a light-hearted series of presentations emceed by a celebrity, you get to witness the potential of new ideas and influence these emerging technologies through the collective response of the audience.
   - Attend the MAX Bash. The MAX Bash planners seem to outdo themselves every year. The event starts immediately after Sneaks. You're surrounded by a variety of food choices, imaginative spaces, and talented performers all concentrated in one place where you get to experience the synergy of all the activity with your friends and colleagues. If that weren't enough, you can expect top name bands to appear for a show as well.
   - Hang out or grab a bite to eat with your new MAX friends.

One of the most enjoyable aspects of Adobe MAX—and one that distinguishes it from other conferences I've attended—is how friendly it is. At other conferences, I've noticed most people wander in small groups consisting mainly of their co-workers. If you're attending those types of conferences by yourself, they can be lonely and isolating. But Adobe embraces community. In fact, you'll find an abundance of Adobe Community Leaders at MAX. There are Adobe Community Professionals (ACPs), Adobe User Group Managers (UGMs), and Adobe Education Leaders (AELs). We Adobe Community Leaders like to help, get involved, and meet new people. We are often speakers or teaching assistants at MAX, so we're not hard to find. We'll likely be the ones to strike up a conversation with you. I believe our passion for learning and engagement encourages other attendees to interact with each other, too.

5. Look for alternatives if there's a conflict in your schedule with sessions you want to attend.
   - Many sessions are available more than once. Check the schedule for alternate times or days.
   - All the sessions with the exception of the hands-on labs are recorded and made available online shortly after MAX, so you can attend the ones you missed or refer back to ones that made an impression.
   - Check out one of the bazillion other happenings instead. Check out the Community Pavilion where you can hang out in the play area, try out new devices, catch demos of software, or make something cool. Peruse the displays of the work being created at MAX, get a professional social media picture taken, or buy a souvenir at the MAX store.
6. Find ways to save money at MAX.
   - Sign up early to take advantage of the Early Bird Pricing.
   - See what deals are available for registration. Usually there are discounts for education, government, and nonprofits. Full-time college students get an amazing deal. There is also special pricing for teams of 3–10 people. There may also be a discount for local Adobe User Group members.
   - Find a roommate by bringing a co-worker or making friends in the Adobe Community who will help split the cost of a hotel room.
   - Take advantage of discounts on software and learning materials. Many vendors offer show specials.
   - Check your email after MAX for a previous attender discount for the next year.
   - Listen for details on attendee benefits. Big giveaways have been a part of MAX in the past. Some freebies have had specific details on eligibility and procurement that you'll need to know. Of course, there's no guarantee that every year MAX attendees will get a new device or software, but it doesn't hurt to offset the cost of attending.

7. Follow some general suggestions to make a better MAX experience.
   - Do not be late to or miss the General Sessions. The most important information and announcements come from these Keynotes.
   - Check out the various exhibits and stations at the Community Pavilion. You'll discover useful products and services and get to bring home some fun giveaways.
   - Plan ahead to drop your stuff off between the last session of the day and the Sneaks, which is immediately followed by the MAX Bash. The shuttles can take a while, and you won't want to miss anything or have to carry around all your belongings plus your swag at the festivities.
   - Be heard! Fill out your MAX Survey. Your feedback helps shape the future of MAX.

Once you've gone to MAX, you'll figure out what works best for you. Start a tradition like a pre-conference dinner with friends, a last-night-of-MAX outing, or a morning-before-you-fly-home breakfast. Maybe do all three. Have fun, learn lots, and get inspired.

Having the ability to record your own high-quality sound effects, vocals, and musical soundtracks opens up a world of artistic possibilities. Recording your own child can inspire original animations.

8 Working with Sound

FOR ME, ANIMATION IS ABOUT TIMING AND RHYTHM. I've always been visually sensitive to the moving image. As a drummer for over 35 years, I'm very fixed on musical patterns. The combination of animation and the right soundtrack can be a wonderful experience for both senses. When the right sound complements the perfect animation, it can produce a most memorable experience for the viewer.

In this chapter, we look at how you can incorporate sounds into your animations, where to find them, and how to record, edit, and load them dynamically.

Recording Sounds

SOUNDS CAN ENHANCE YOUR ANIMATION in wonderful ways. Recording and designing sounds is an art form all its own and a job typically left to dedicated sound editors who have an innate ability to edit, mix, and craft sounds into works of audible art. But chances are you don't have a dedicated sound designer at your disposal 24 hours a day. Since Animate does not record or create sound files, you need to find or record your own and import them into Animate. So the best way to find, edit, and incorporate sounds into your Animate projects is to purchase sound effects from your local music store or online. A quick search on Amazon for "sound effects" will return a few dozen audio CDs available for purchase. These are handy to have around but may include some legal restrictions as to how you can use the sounds. Some publishers may retain the royalty rights to the contents of CDs, limiting you to noncommercial usage. These limits

Get yourself a good microphone. I'll be honest—you get what you pay for when it comes to the quality of recording. There are several different microphones designed to record sounds for almost every situation imaginable. The cheapest solution would be something like the Logitech USB microphone that can be found at your local computer supply store for around $20. A microphone like that is great for transferring your voice during an internet phone conversation, but I wouldn't rely on it for high-quality recordings.

On the other hand, you don't need to spend your next five paychecks on the most professional studio microphone either. The microphone pictured on the right is an AKG Perception and retails for around $249. It produces great sound whether you are recording voice, sound effects, or musical instruments. It is a condenser microphone, which tends to be more sensitive and responsive making it well-suited to capturing subtle nuances in sounds. The best feature of all is being able to switch between the three different recording settings depending on the recording situation. You can set it to record only what is directly in front of the microphone, which is great for voice, sound effects, and instruments. If you have two voices or instruments next to each other, there's a setting to record bidirectionally. The third is an omni-directional setting that will record sounds in a 360° pattern around the mic. This setting is great for picking up general room or ambient sounds.

PHOTO: AKG PERCEPTION 400 | PHOTO: M-AUDIO FIREWIRE SOLO

may pose some legal issues for you and most importantly your client, who would rather avoid paying legal fees for a few *thumps*, *swooshes*, and *pops* sound effects. Another potential issue with published sound effect CDs is their sound quality. Depending on the equipment used to record and edit the sounds, there is no guarantee they are of high enough quality to justify using them. It's always a good idea to try to find out the technical information regarding the actual sound files before you purchase the CD. You will want sounds that are high quality, usually 44 kHz, 16-bit stereo. You may also want to edit your sounds by applying effects or editing loops, or you may even want to compose original soundtracks. For editing you'll need to choose decent audio editing software. Some of you may already be using an audio editing application, but for those of you who are unfamiliar in the area, we take a look at what's available a bit later in this chapter.

Next, you need a way to get your shiny new microphone to connect with your computer. Once again you have a variety of audio interfaces to choose from. Assuming you don't need every bell and whistle available, a good choice is something like M-Audio's FireWire Solo mobile audio interface. It has a standard XLR microphone input and a 1/2″ guitar input, allowing you to record guitar and vocals simultaneously. There are also dual line inputs for effects, drum machines, and other outboard gear. The biggest decision to make when purchasing an interface like this is whether you want to use USB or FireWire connectivity. FireWire may provide faster data transfer over USB, but double-check that your computer's hardware supports FireWire. If not, you can purchase a FireWire card separately.

So now how much can you expect to spend? An audio interface is between $200 and $400 depending on how many features it offers.

The M-Audio FireWire Solo mentioned here will set you back about $250, but I found one on sale for $200 at my local music vendor. Throw in a microphone stand and cable, and you could be looking at spending around $600. Keep in mind this information is based on equipment I feel provides the best bang for your buck. There are many less expensive microphones to choose from, some with USB connectivity that avoid the need to purchase a FireWire interface. It's a balance between the level of quality you prefer and the size of your budget.

SHORTCUTS
MAC WIN BOTH

Samson USB Microphones

CONDENSER MICROPHONE technology is becoming increasingly sophisticated. There are a number of quality microphones that connect to your computer using USB only. There's no need to purchase additional hardware and cables, and in most cases the microphones are extremely portable due to their small size.

Any one of the following microphones is an affordable way for the casual or professional animator to capture high-quality sounds for their animations. Learn more at www.samsontech.com.

The best bang for your buck may be the Samson Go Mic. The Go Mic is a portable USB condenser microphone that literally fits in the palm of your hand. The microphone chassis alone is only two and a half inches in height and just over an inch wide. The microphone is attached to a weighted base using a ball joint, allowing it to be angled in almost any direction. The base can sit on any flat surface or be mounted to the top of your laptop screen using the integrated clip. The base has four integrated rubber feet to help limit external vibrations and a hole that lets you mount it to a microphone stand.

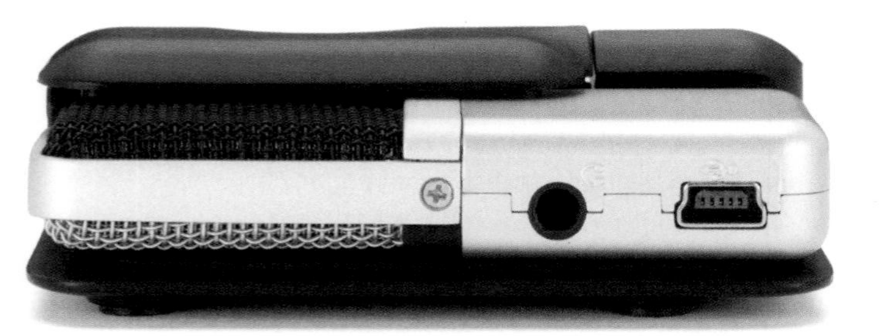

The Go Mic provides a 1/8″ output, so you can connect your headphones. The Mini-B size USB connector is also located on the same side of the microphone.

The Go Mic comes bundled with Cakewalk Music Creator software, but I opted to stick with Adobe Audition because of my familiarity with it. The Go Mic is designed to work with a variety of editing software such as Apple Logic, Garage Band, Sony Sound Forge, Cubase, and more. Out of the box, the Go Mic connected to my MacBook Pro was instantly recognized by OS X and Adobe Audition. No need to download drivers. The Go Mic just works. I was recording within seconds, and my initial spoken-word tests were surprisingly crisp and balanced.

What good is portability if it doesn't come with some form of protection when bouncing around the bottom of your laptop bag? Samson includes a zipper case with the Go Mic to eliminate the fear of the microphone getting dirty or damaged in transit.

You can also tailor the Go Mic to your recording environment by switching between cardoid and omni-directional polar patterns. The cardoid setting records sound in one direction while omni-directional captures sound in all directions. Use the cardoid setting for recording vocals in front of the microphone. Sounds from the sides and behind the Go Mic will be rejected. Omni-directional is great for situations where you are recording the environment—perfect for ambient sounds or live music situations. For those of you on a limited budget, I have good news. The Go Mic can be found on Amazon for under $40. The Samson Go Mic is an outstanding product for recording high-quality sounds with portability. With a Go Mic and a laptop, the world is your stage.

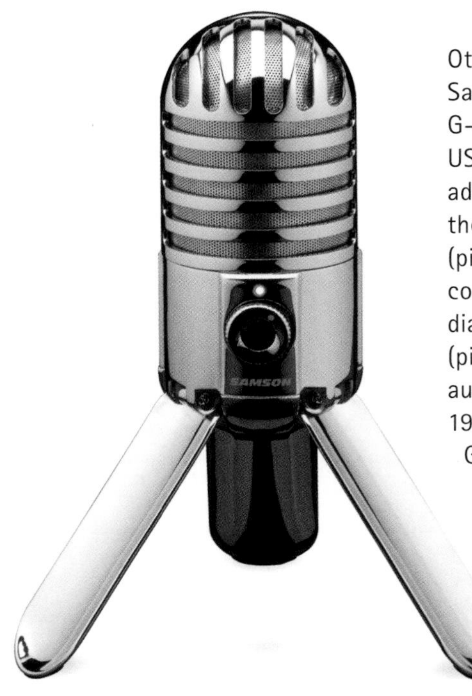

Other quality products from Samson are the Meteor Mic and G-Track microphones. Both are USB condenser microphones with additional features that go beyond the Go Mic. The Meteor Mic (pictured left) has a large 25 mm condenser diaphram (the Go Mic diaphram is 10 mm). The G-Track (pictured right) boasts a built-in audio interface and mixer and a 19 mm diaphram. The power of the G-Track is its ability to record vocals and an instrument at the same time, making it ideal for studio musicians.

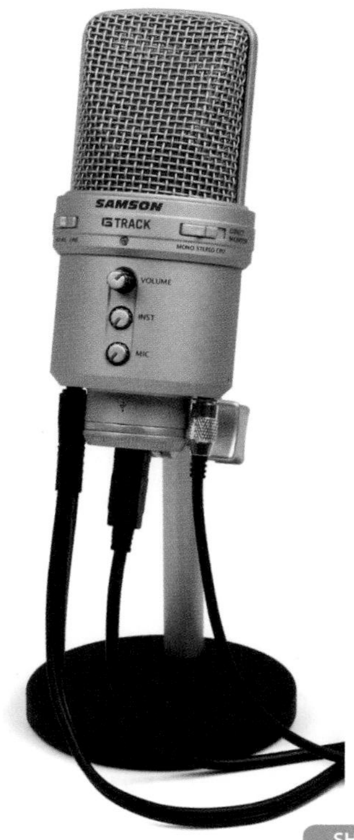

Audacity®

AUDACITY IS A FREE DOWNLOADABLE AUDIO editing application that boasts a surprisingly robust feature set. Audacity can record live audio through a microphone or mixer or digitize recordings from cassette tapes, vinyl records, or minidiscs. With some sound cards, it can also capture streaming audio. Audacity supports several popular audio file formats, allowing you to cut, copy, splice, and mix various files together as well as change their pitch and speed. If you have a limited budget, look no further—and even if you can afford software that offers more, Audacity still might be enough to satisfy your needs. Go to audacity.sourceforge.net/ to learn more and download the installer.

Audacity can record live audio through a microphone or mixer, or digitize recordings from cassette tapes, vinyl records or minidiscs. With some sound cards, it can also capture streaming audio.

Audacity offers a variety of editing tools consisting of a Selection, Envelope, Time Shift, Zoom, and Draw.

These sliders control the mixer settings of the soundcard in your system. The Output slider (left) actually controls the output setting of the soundcard driver, while the Input slider (right) controls the recording level setting of the soundcard driver.

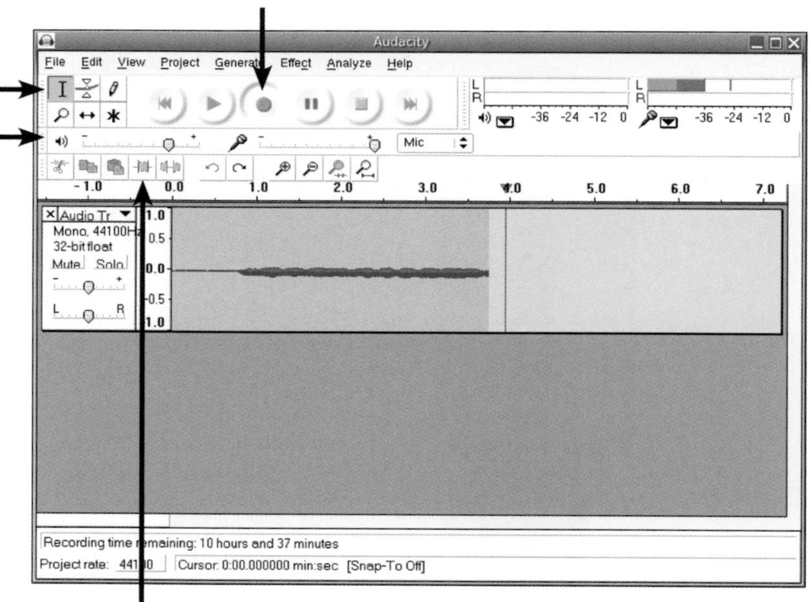

Audacity's handy Edit Toolbar allows you to cut, copy, paste, trim, and silence your audio and more.

Audacity certainly doesn't make its most basic of controls hard to find. Cursor to Start, Play, Record, Pause, Stop, and Cursor to End are all oversized and easy to find.

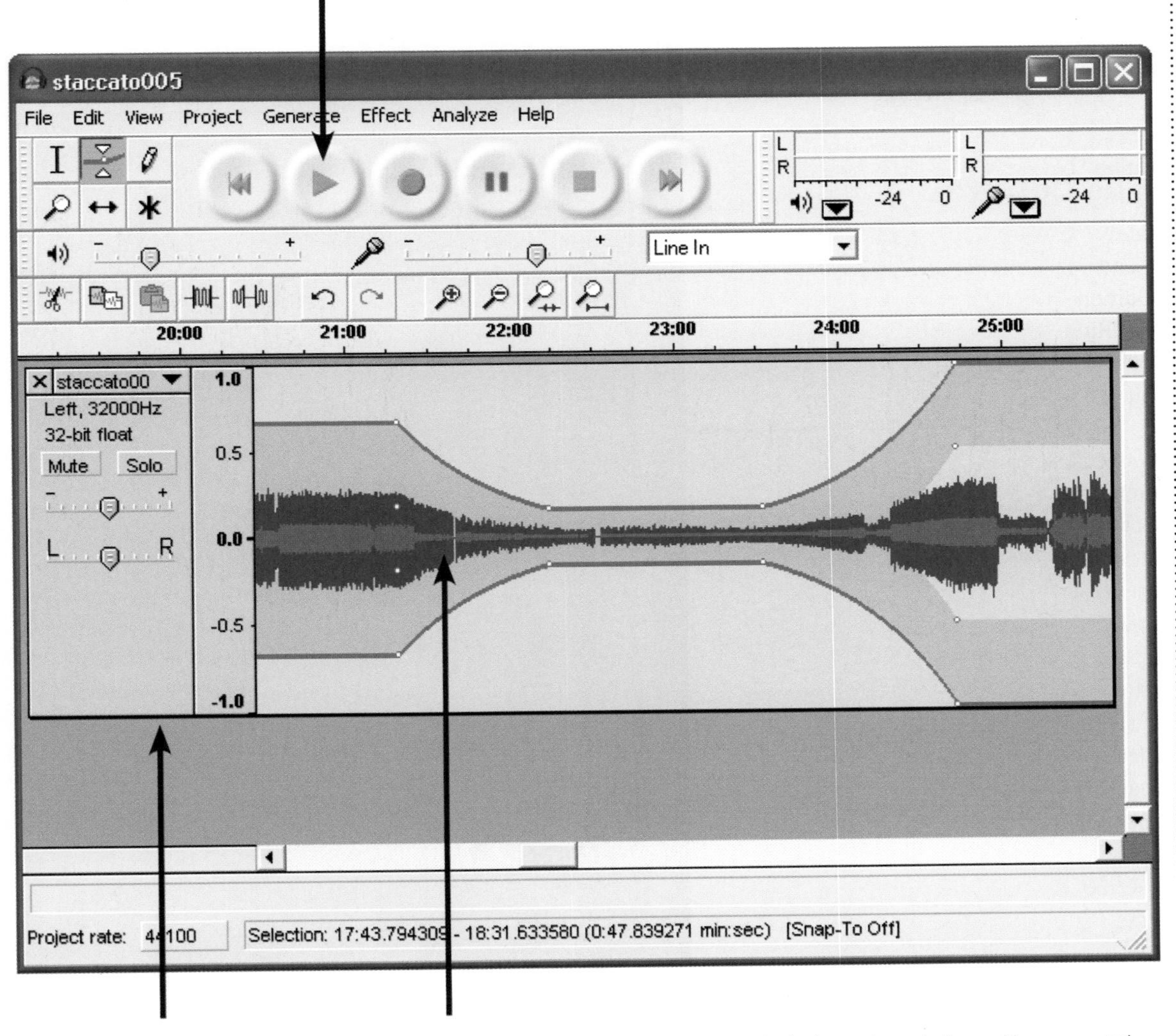

You can mute and solo (isolate) when working with multiple tracks.

Audio tracks contain digitally sampled sounds. In Audacity, a channel of sound is represented by one mono audio track and a two-channel sound by one stereo audio track. You can specify a different sample rate for each track. You can import audio of any sample rate or bit depth, and Audacity will resample and convert it to the project rate and bit depth on the fly.

HOT TIP

It's free! I can't think of a hotter tip than that. Audacity does a great job of handling a majority of your audio editing needs.

Adobe® Audition® CC

AUDITION IS A VERY robust audio editing program from Adobe that offers a fully integrated set of audio-editing and restoration tools. Audition is a complete audio-editing program, from recording and editing to mixing and exporting.

If you're an experienced sound editor and composer, Audition delivers a full suite of features that rivals the competition. I use it for recording voice-overs, sound effects, and also sounds from my digital keyboard. I can then switch over to Multitrack View and mix all my sounds together using an unlimited amount of stereo mixing tracks.

Audition offers over 50 real-time audio effects including echo, flange, reverb, and more. You can even record and edit MIDI.

Simply put, if you need a complete audio studio out of the box, Audition delivers.

The workspace in Audition is completely customizable. You can scale and drag panels to new locations and in configurations that suit your working needs. As you rearrange panels, other panels will resize themselves automatically to fit the workspace.

Switch between Edit, Multitrack, and CD views easily.

Work with more than 50 real-time audio effects including echo, flange, reverb, and more. Manipulate recordings with digital signal processing (DSP) tools, mastering, and analysis tools and audio restoration features.

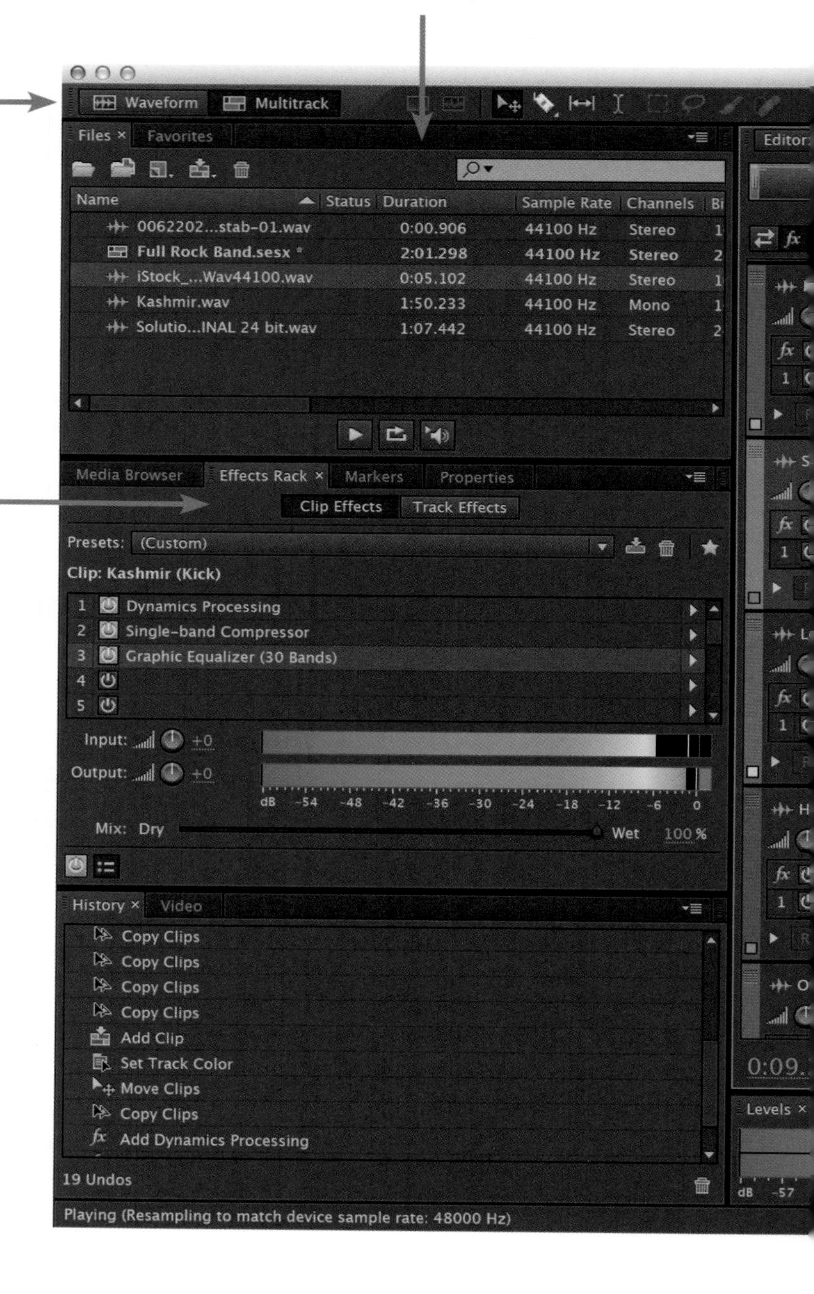

Apply various colors to your layouts similar to how you can in Animate.

Manage your customizable workspace with the Workspace drop-down menu. You can add or remove workspace layouts similar to how you can in Animate.

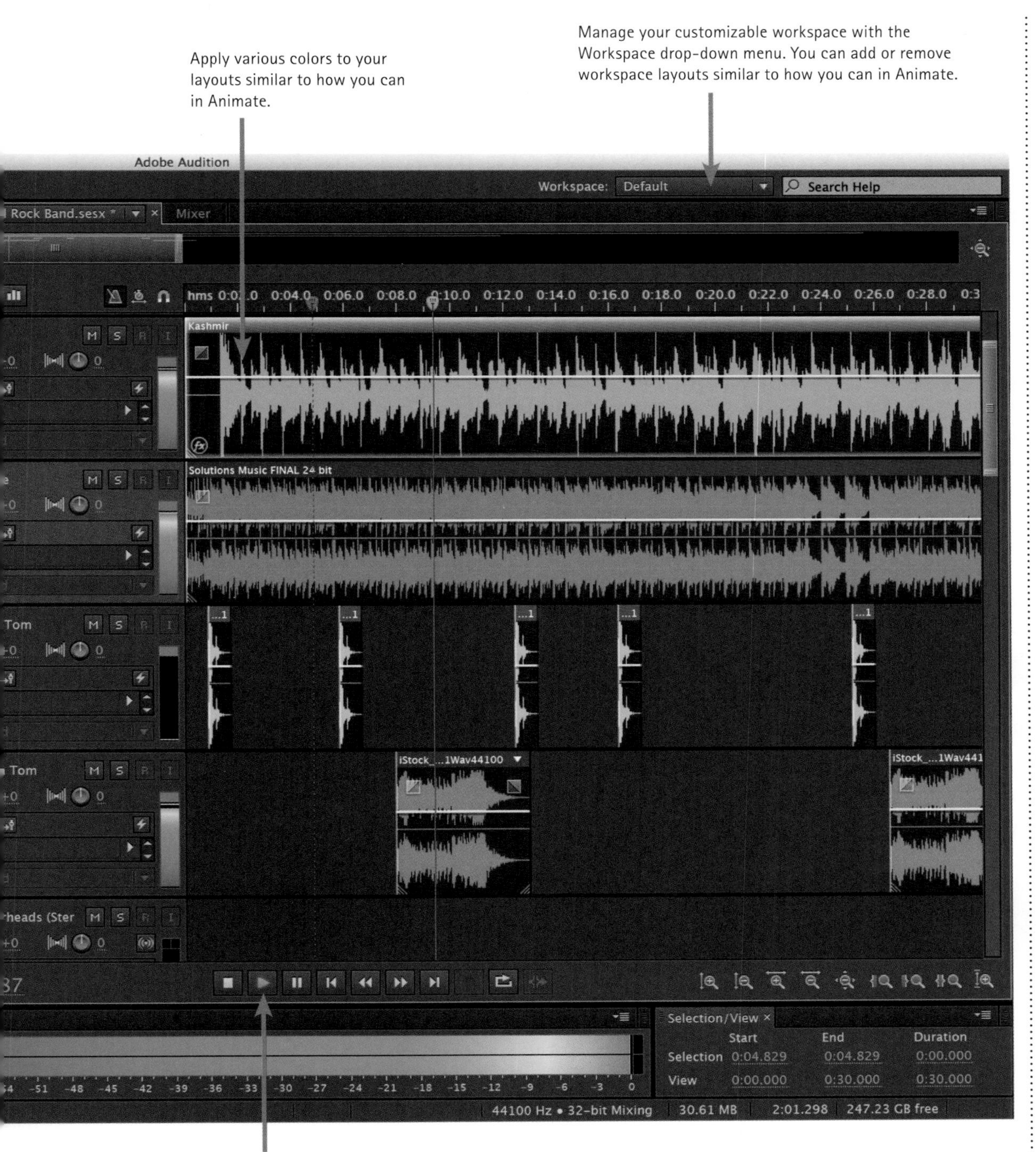

View and zoom controls provide a helpful way to isolate and focus on specific portions of your audio track(s).

HOT TIP

When I'm creating Animate animations for video export, I'll often export a mixdown of the soundtrack from Adobe Audition in MP3 format to animate to in Animate. An MP3 version helps keep the source file smaller. I'll then export a mixdown of the soundtrack in high-quality WAV or AIF format for when it comes time to edit the animation to the audio in Premiere Pro.

Sound in Animate

THE EDIT ENVELOPE WINDOW offers some limited sound editing features without having to leave the Animate environment. There are enough features here to control the starting and ending points of your sound file, as well as some basic fading effects. But don't expect much more beyond that.

As much as Animate could use a few more bells and whistles in this area, it was never meant to be a sound editing program in the first place. Let's leave that for the dedicated sound editing applications and use Animate for what it is. We can't expect Animate to do everything can we?

1 Select frame 1 in your Animate document, and then go to File > Import > Import to Stage and select your WAV or AIF file. Your sound will be in frame 1, but you will need to insert enough frames to accommodate its length. By default, the sound will be set to Event. Use the drop-down to change the sound's behavior.
Event: This setting is used to play a sound at a particular point in time but independently of other sounds. An Event sound will play in its entirety even if the movie stops. An Event sound must be fully downloaded before it will play.
Start: This setting is the same as Event except that if the sound is already playing, no new instance of the sound plays.
Stop: This setting stops the selected sound.
Stream: This setting is used to synchronize a sound with the Timeline and subsequently the animation. Streaming sounds will start and stop with the playhead.

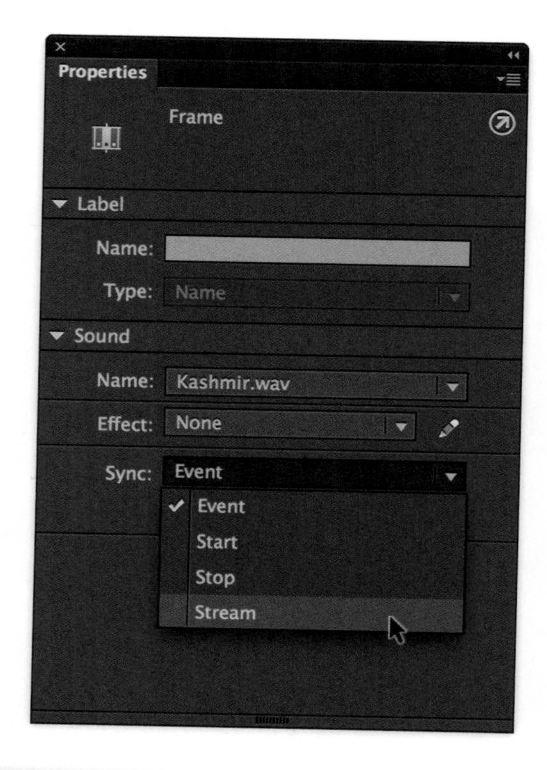

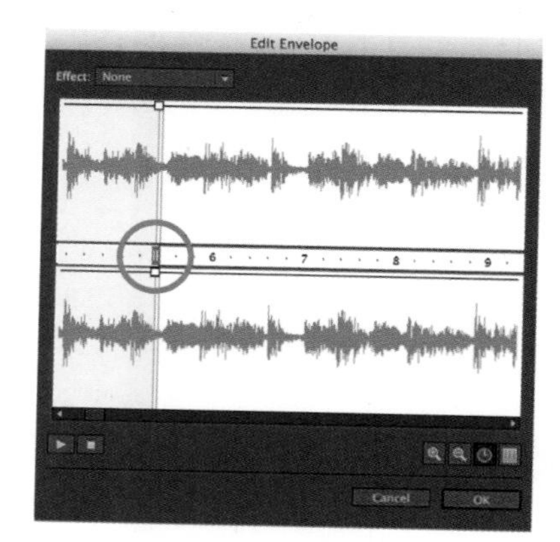

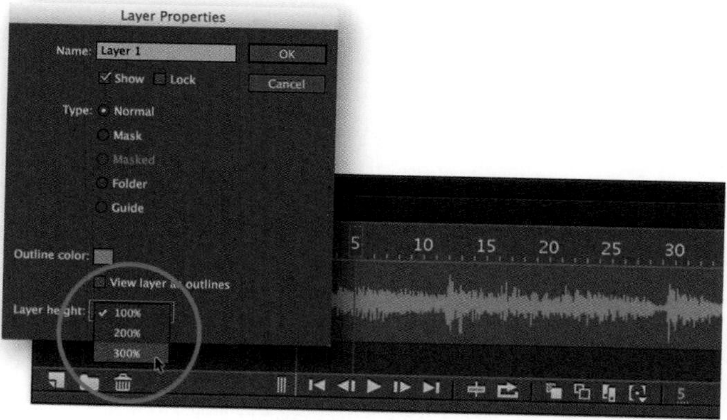

4 To change the start and end points of a sound, drag the Time In and Time Out controls in the Edit Envelope. The tricky part about moving these points is that it's a game of hit or miss (mostly miss) without the ability to scrub the waveform in the Edit Envelope window. If you need to continue a long sound file across multiple Scenes, you will have to add a new instance of the sound to each Scene. Next, determine where the sound ended in the previous Scene and manually adjust the Time In controller for the current Scene so that the sound starts where the previous Scene ended. It's not an exact science and not an ideal solution if your audio file is one continuous sound such as a musical score.

5 In some situations, having the ability to view the waveform is helpful. For example, having a clear visual indicator of when sounds start and stop can help speed up this tedious process. Right-click over the layer name containing your sound and select Properties from the context menu. In the Layer Properties panel, locate the Layer Height drop-down menu and select 300% to increase the height of the layer to its maximum.

2 Click the Edit button in the Properties panel to open the Edit Envelope window. Here you will see the waveform of your sound file and a few basic control features. The Effect drop-down menu offers some convenient effects to add to your sound; however, Effects won't work in WebGL and HTML5 Canvas documents.

None: Removes any previously applied sound.

Left Channel/Right Channel: Plays sound in the left or right channel only.

Fade Left to Right/Fade Right to Left: Shifts the sound from one channel to the other.

Fade In/Fade Out: Gradually increases/decreases the volume of a sound over its duration.

Custom: Lets you create custom in and out points of sound using the Edit Envelope.

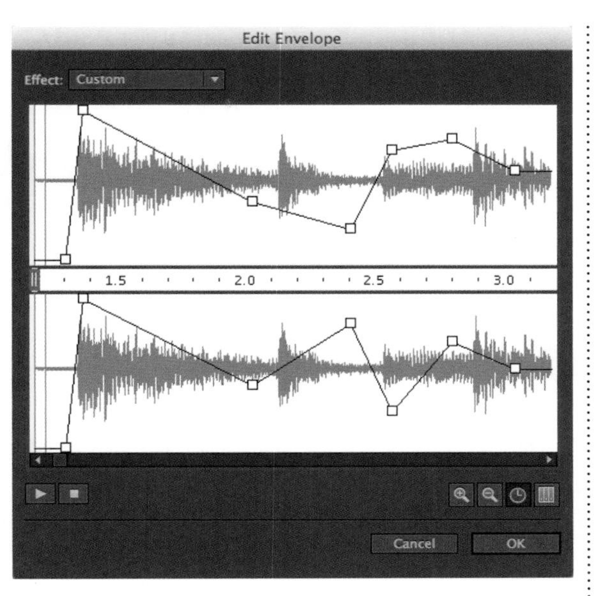

3 You can add up to eight envelope handles by clicking anywhere within the sound window. Each handle can be dragged around to control the volume of the sound at that point in the sound file. The higher the handle is positioned, the louder the sound. To remove a handle, drag it out of the window. To change the sound envelope, drag the envelope handles to change levels at different points in the sound. Envelope lines show the volume of the sound as it plays.

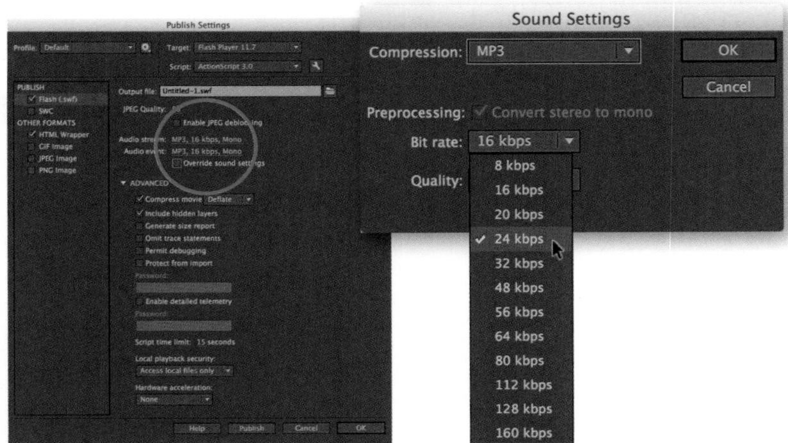

6 Many have experienced an issue with sounds when set to Stream that manage to fall out of sync with the animation in the Flash Player. The only solution I have found to keep the sound in sync is to change the default MP3 compression in the document's Publish Settings panel. Go to File > Publish Settings and check Flash under Publish. The default MP3 compression is 16 kbps, Mono. Click the "Audio stream:" link and change the bit rate to 20 kbps or higher. I personally recommend 24 kbps as the minimum compression setting. Click OK and test your movie.

HOT TIP

Once the sound has been set to Stream behavior, you can then drag the playhead across the Timeline, which is an action also known as "scrubbing" to hear your soundtrack. The default Event setting sends the sound to your system's soundcard and forgets about it. It is no longer part of the Timeline and will not maintain sync with any animation. The only way to stop an Event sound from playing while in the Animate authoring environment is to hit the esc key. Event sounds are typically used with shorter sounds and attached to buttons.

Dynamic Sounds (AS3)

IT'S ALWAYS FUN WHEN sound and graphics come together to create an engaging and dynamic experience. This example uses ActionScript 3.0 to assign sounds to invisible buttons. The sounds are triggered when you roll over individual drums and cymbals. Each sound file in the Library is exported for ActionScript, allowing you to assign each sound to a different keyboard command as well. As a result, the Animate movie converts your keyboard to a musical instrument.

This example is just one of an infinite number of ways sound and ActionScript can be combined to create a fun, interactive experience.

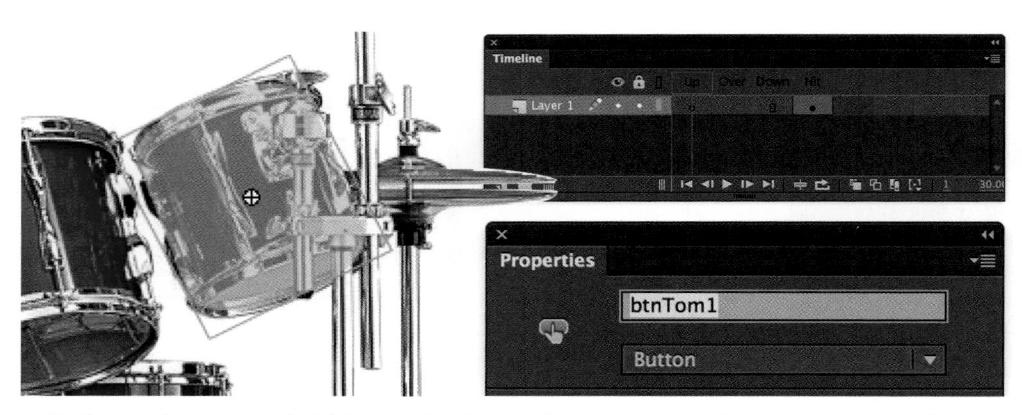

1 The first step is to create an invisible button for the area where you want to assign a mouse command. On a new layer above your image, draw a solid color in the same shape as your image. Convert the shape to a Button symbol and then double-click it to enter Edit Mode. Drag the Up keyframe to the Hit frame. The Hit state dictates the active area of the Button symbol and will not be visible in the compiled movie. Back on the main Timeline the button is semi-transparent for editing purposes. With the instance of the Button selected, type in a descriptive instance name in the Properties panel, so you can assign some commands to it.

4 The first line creates a suitably named variable and sets it to an instance of Tom1. You'll do this step for each sound clip Class, which preps each sound for play. The other lines here show how to trigger the sound with a keystroke. Set the focus to the stage and then add a "key down" event that checks for the event's charCode. In case it's 68 or 100, play the sndTom1 sound. What are 68 and 100? These happen to be ASCII codes for the letter D. See www.asciitable.com for a chart. (You'll want the Dec column for decimal.)

6 After creating a hit area and assigning a mouse and key command to trigger a sound dynamic_sounds_AS3.fla provided in the downloadable source file, I created an additional 12 invisible buttons "mapped" to specific areas of the image of the drum set. Each Button was given a unique instance name.

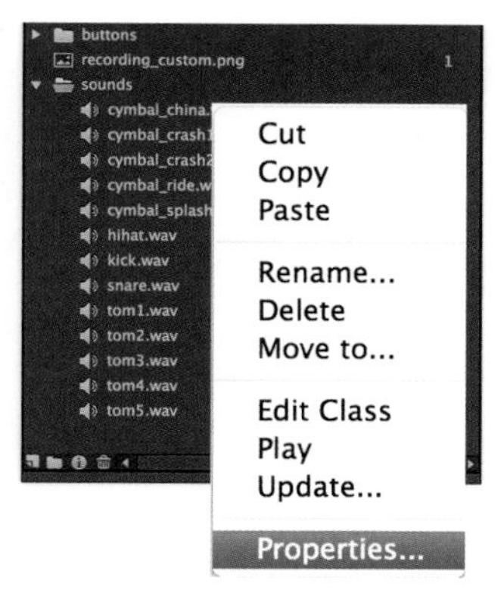

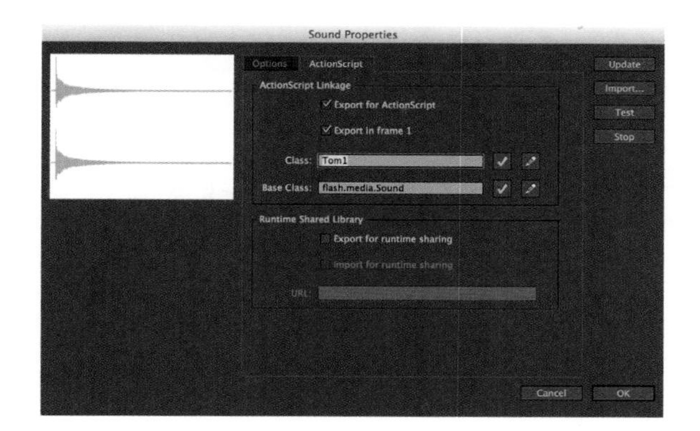

2 Import your sound file into your Animate document. In the Library panel, right-click over the sound and select Properties from the context menu.

3 In the Sound Properties dialog on the ActionScript tab, click the Export for ActionScript checkbox. That checkbox will automatically check the Export in the first frame for you. Provide a unique Class name. Here, I've named it "Tom1." The Base Class must be "flash.media.Sound," but Animate is smart enough to fill that in for you. When you click OK, Animate may give you a warning about a missing Class in the classpath. That's the Tom1 Class you just named, so let Animate generate its automatic fix. If you like, check "Don't warn me again" to avoid a repeat warning. Click OK.

HOT TIP

Choose instance names carefully to help organize your code. At a glance, it's easy to see that the Tom1 Class relates to the sndTom1 instance which is a sound and to the btnTom1 instance which is a button.

5 If you want to trigger the sound with a mouse movement, add the desired mouse event handler to your btnTom1 button and have the function play the corresponding Sound instance. Check out the sample file to see how easy it is to repeat this small block of code as often as necessary.

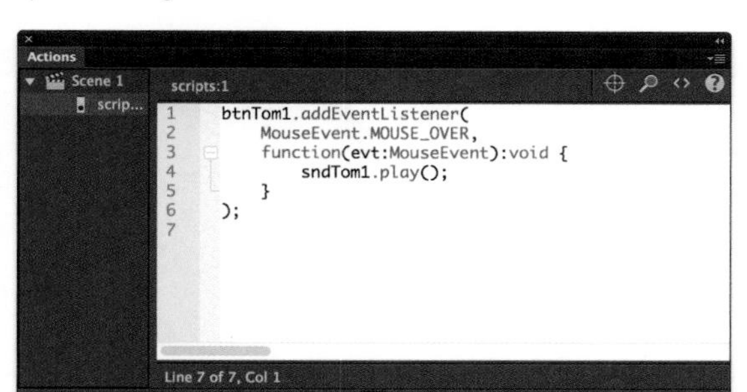

7 Open the Library, and you'll find a total of 13 sounds each exported to ActionScript and given a unique Class name. Open the Actions panel, and you'll see all the ActionScript has been provided as well.

This example was written by David Stiller (quip.net) in AS3. We hope that these samples will provide a springboard for your own dynamic sound projects and experiments. Have fun!

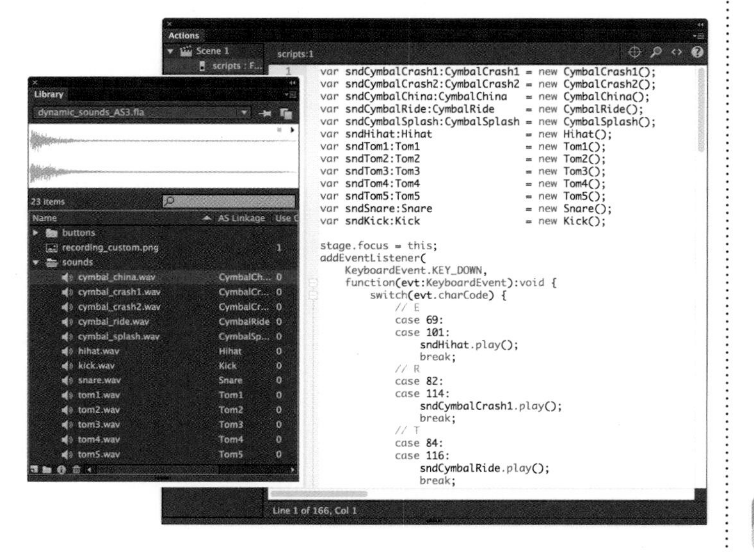

Is a College Degree Necessary to Work in Digital Media?

I'VE HEARD THIS QUESTION A NUMBER OF TIMES. I THINK IT SPEAKS TO SEVERAL ISSUES in our society—the cost of higher education, the quality of higher education, the lack of jobs (or lack of well-paying jobs) for many college graduates, the proliferation of free training online, and the availability of numerous other means of becoming self-taught. These are all valid considerations, but before you rule out college based on negative perceptions, I think you first have to evaluate your situation and your goals. Ask yourself these questions:

- What do you really want to do for your career?
- Is digital media something you only want to dabble in while you work toward something else?
- Do you aspire to eventually hold a leadership role in digital media?
- What is your stage of life or career?
- Is money for college an issue?

VECTOR ILLUSTRATION: MYRA FERGUSON

With the first couple of questions, I want you to think about where you want your career path to go. If digital media isn't it, then I wouldn't necessarily recommend you go to college to study it. That's not to say college is a bad idea. It just means it might not be the best path to get you where you want to go.

What about earning a little pocket money working up some logos or a website? There's nothing wrong with that, but does it require a college degree? Not really, but at the same time, I wouldn't expect to get paid very much—not unless you've been doing it for a long time and have built up a stellar portfolio or clientele. In that case, you're probably no longer really dabbling. Digital media has become your career.

Leadership roles are where college is going to make the most difference. While your skills and experience might get you into technical positions, hiring managers are going to look at what differentiates you from others when they're filling upper-level roles. If you think you'd like to to teach, in most cases, you'll need a minimum of a bachelor's degree. Many higher education institutions require a master's degree. To some extent, it doesn't really matter what your area of emphasis was. Having fulfilled the requirements to earn a degree demonstrates a greater maturity and a higher level of perseverance. However, your major could make a difference if you're competing for a spot with other college graduates.

The reason your stage of life or stage of career matters is because your experiences, if relevant, could be equated with formal training. Not having a degree can still hold you back from leadership roles, despite your age and experience. Another reason stage of life matters relates to your other responsibilities. If you know what you want to study and can go to college while you're young, do it. Studying gets harder if you get married and exponentially harder if you have kids. It's doable, but it's difficult. I started my master's degree after I was married, took a break when my son was born, and graduated when he was 3.

Money for college is always a concern. Regardless of your age, I would recommend looking for scholarships that might help. You might see if there's a work-study program at whatever school you're hoping to attend. Look at your local Community College. Some offer free or very affordable tuition. Having lived and worked in a college town, I know that full-time university employees often get discounted tuition as part of their employment benefits. Working full time while going to school may take longer, but it may just be the path that gets you to goals.

One day your client may request that their online content be converted to HTML5 or re-purposed for video. They may look to you for answers as to how possible either process is. Rest assured, Animate offers a wide assortment of output and conversion options. Update your older content and make it available on newer devices and modern browsers. And Animate-to-video is widely produced for a variety of broadcast content. These output options make the most of your Animate projects by giving you the greatest flexibility for delivery of your content.

9 Output Options

ANIMATE'S VERSATILITY IS INDISPUTABLE. YOU CAN USE Animate for animation, advertising, games for the web, eLearning, mobile, or desktop. For animators, exporting video for DVD and broadcast television is a high priority. For communications professionals, distribution to devices and modern browsers is a must. Now that Animate is here, the types of output have not only increased but have also gotten better. So you may want to grab your old files, update them with Animate, and output them to one of these new formats. Or if you're new to Animate, start creating projects with the knowledge that you have a myriad of output options.

Converting Your Document to HTML5 Canvas

DID YOU KNOW THAT ANIMATE CAN output to HTML5 Canvas? When you open Animate, the Welcome Screen displays a variety of types of documents you can create: HTML5 Canvas, WebGL (Preview), ActionScript 3.0, AIR for Desktop, AIR for Android, AIR for iOS, ActionScript 3.0 Class, ActionScript 3.0 Interface, ActionScript File, and JSFL Script File. But what do you do if you already created a file and want to change it to a different type? Just convert it. I'll show you how. The trick here is knowing which features can't be converted, so you can re-create effects in another way.

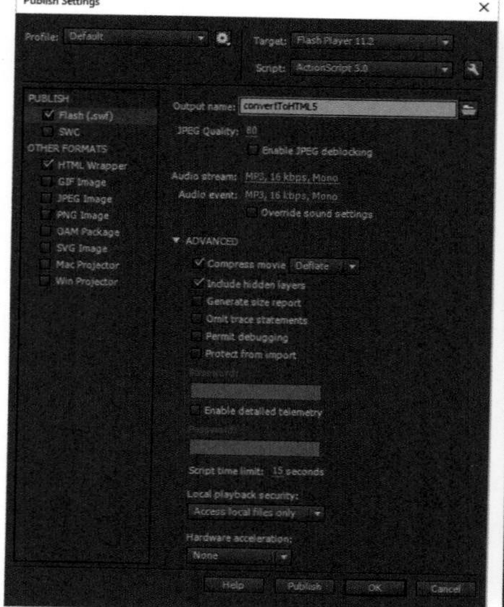

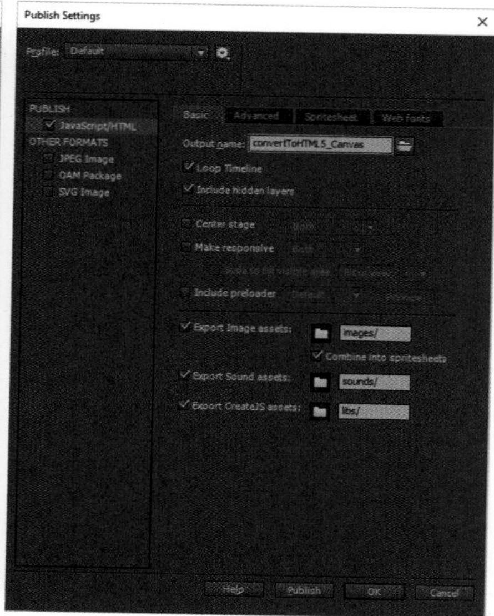

1 We'll start with an ActionScript 3.0 document that contains an ad for a coffee tasting event and convert it to an HTML5 Canvas document. If you're not sure whether you've already converted a file to HTML5 Canvas, first, you can look at the name of the file. Animate will create a new document using the same filename plus "_Canvas" at the end in addition to displaying "(Canvas)" after the filename. Another way to check is to open the Publish Settings. Instead of seeing "Flash (.swf)" under "PUBLISH," you'll see "JavaScript/HTML."

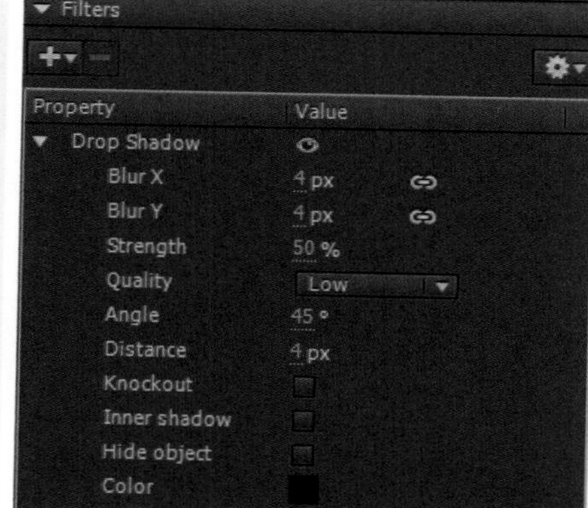

4 Notice that the logo is a Movie Clip with a Drop Shadow filter applied. While Canvas will support Drop Shadow, it defaults to Low Quality. It also will only recognize the Strength at 100% instead of the 50% set here.

VECTOR ILLUSTRATION: MYRA FERGUSON

2 Let's take a look at what we have in the ad before we convert it to see if we have any effects that could be problematic. Our document includes a layer of text, a logo layer, a layer with coffee rings with a drip, and a background layer.

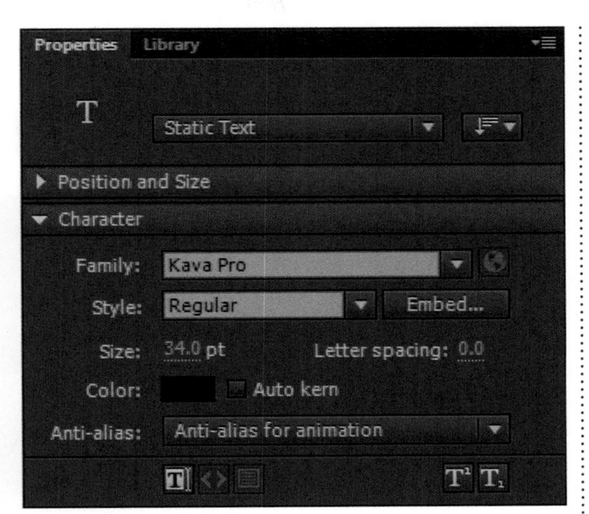

3 The text uses the TypeKit font, Kava Pro, for the copy. All the type is centered, and all the text boxes are set to Static Text. The type for the logo has already been broken apart into vector shapes. This text should all be fine. The only change Animate will make is to convert the text to CanvasFonts since HTML5 Canvas doesn't support anti-aliasing text.

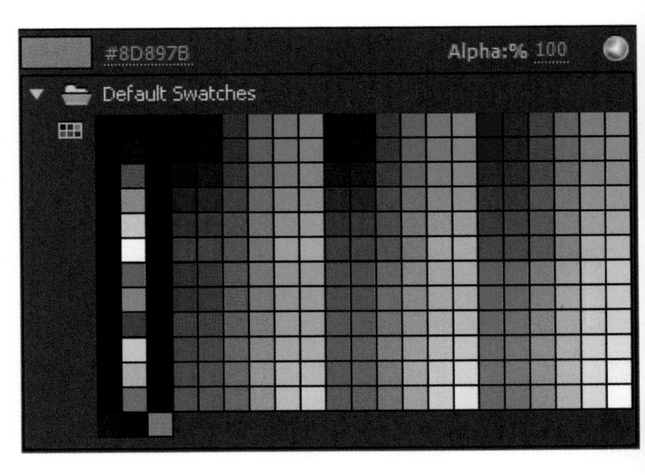

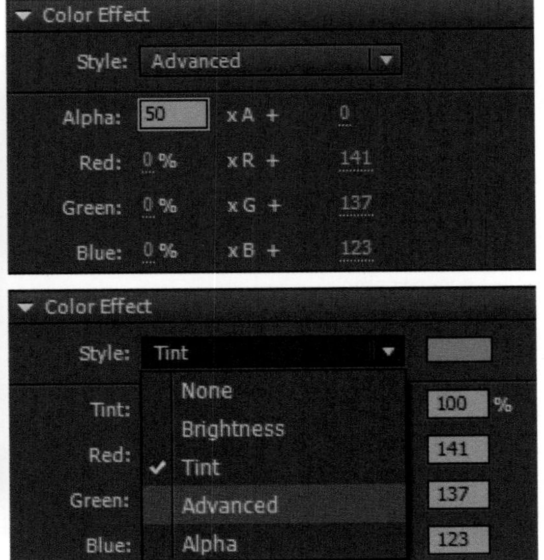

5 There are a lot of ways to make a drop shadow, so let's remove the filter and use a different method. One way is to duplicate the layer and apply a Tint in the Properties panel to the Movie Clip with a color of #8D897B. Change Tint to Advanced and set the Alpha to 50%.

Converting Your Document to HTML5 Canvas (cont.)

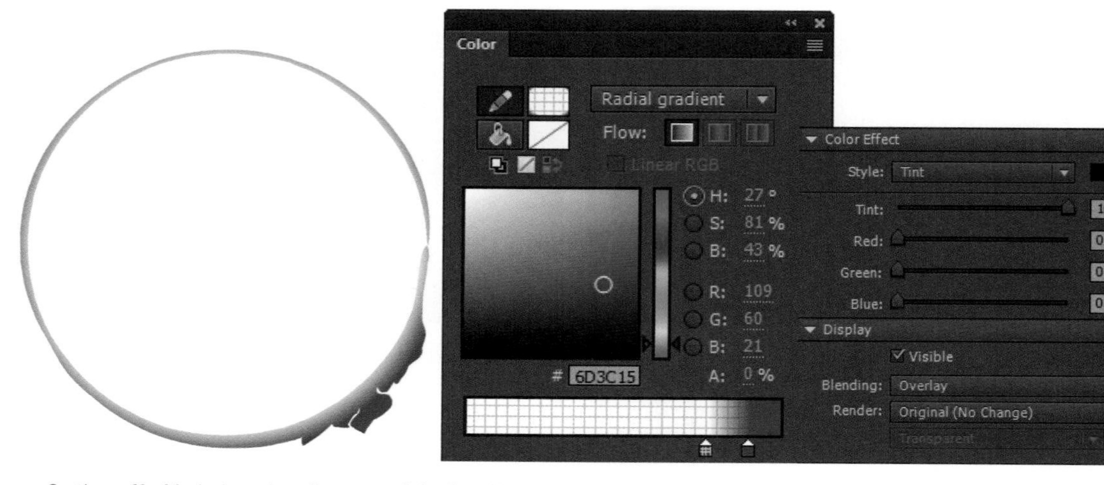

6 On the coffeeMarks layer is an instance of the Graphic symbol ringsAndDrip. That symbol contains an animation of the coffee rings made of circles with no fill and vector art brush strokes applied. These use Floral brushes from the Decorative > Elegant Curl and Floral Brush Set. The stroke color is a radial gradient of brown with an alpha of 0% at one stop and 100% on the other. The drip is filled with a linear gradient. All of the coffee rings and the drip are Movie Clips with a Blend Mode of Overlay applied. They also have a black tint applied, which makes them show up better against the background.

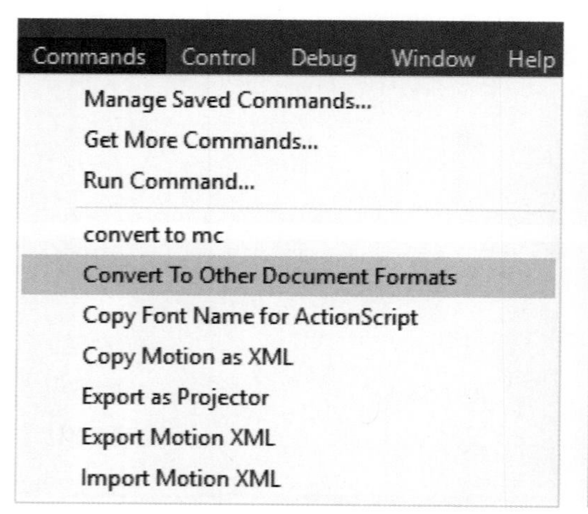

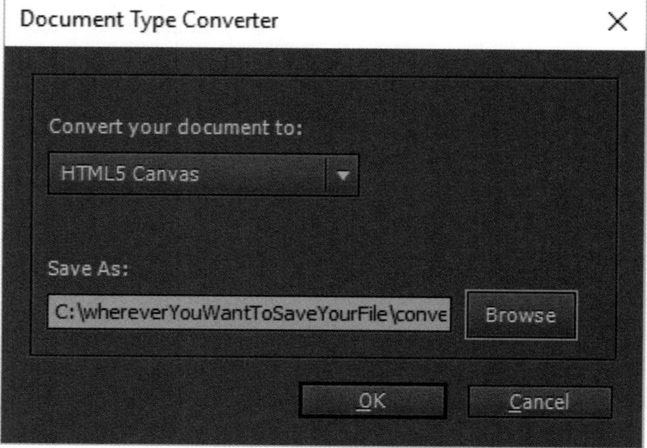

9 Test your animation before converting it. Does it still look about the same? Now go to Commands > Convert to Other Document Formats. The Document Type Converter dialog appears. In the drop-down menu, HTML5 Canvas is selected by default. You'll also see a path where your converted file will be saved. If you want to save it somewhere else, navigate to that location by clicking Browse. Click OK.

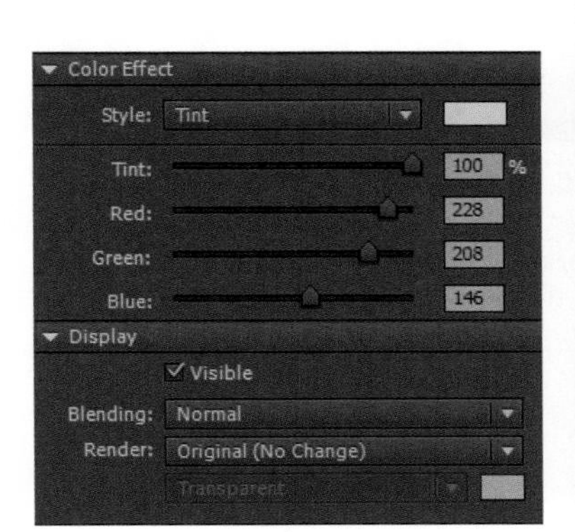

7 HTML5 Canvas won't support the Blend Mode, so let's remove the Blend Mode and change the Tint to #E4D092, which approximates the effect.

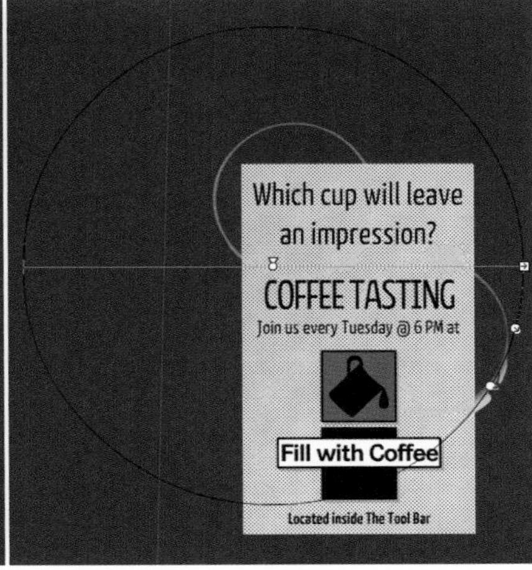

8 Finally, the background is a subtle radial gradient that has been scaled to an oval shape. HTML5 Canvas will support radial gradients but only circular ones. So let's change the shape of the radial gradient and scale it so that the effect is similar.

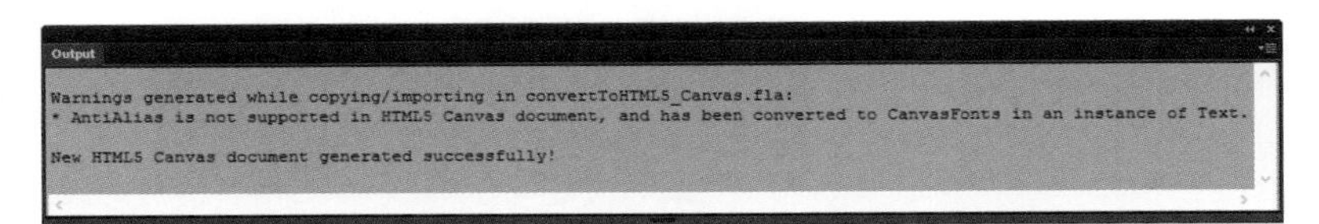

10 Review the messages in the Output panel to see if there's anything you need to address.

11 Test your movie ⌘ ctrl Enter. Your test will open in your default browser. Make any other changes as needed.

HOT TIP

Supported features for HTML5 Canvas are bound to improve. To keep track of them you can use this table from Adobe helpx.adobe.com/animate/kb/unsupported-features-html5-canvas1.html to let you know which features are supported and how. When you convert your document, Animate will generate a warning in the Output panel to let you know what was changed and any information related to the document conversion.

Document Setup

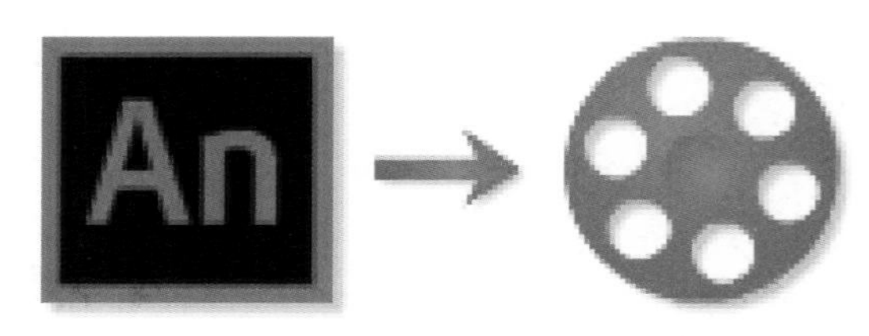

IF YOU'RE NEW TO EXPORTING AN ANIMATE project to video, it can seem like the complexity quickly escalates. I'll explain how to set your Stage size, know what format to use, and decide what other details you need to know (or can ignore) when making a video from your Animate project.

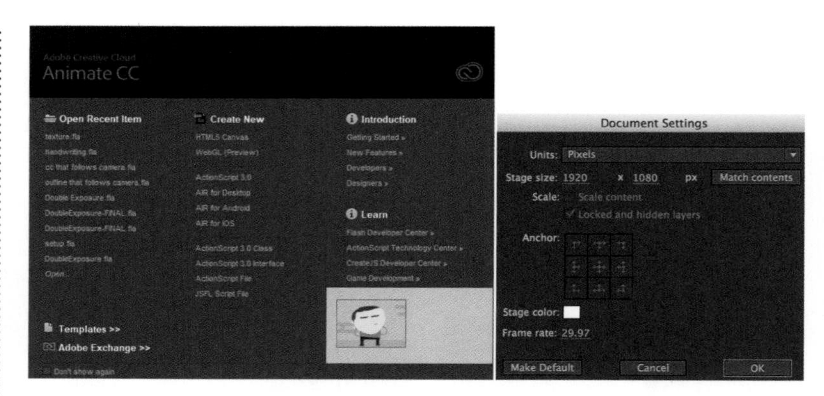

1 Let's start with the basics and open a new Animate document. Open the Document Settings panel using ⌘/ctrl J or click the Advanced Settings button in the Properties panel. Here you can determine the width and height of the movie and its frame rate. But before we change anything, we need to decide the aspect ratio we're using.

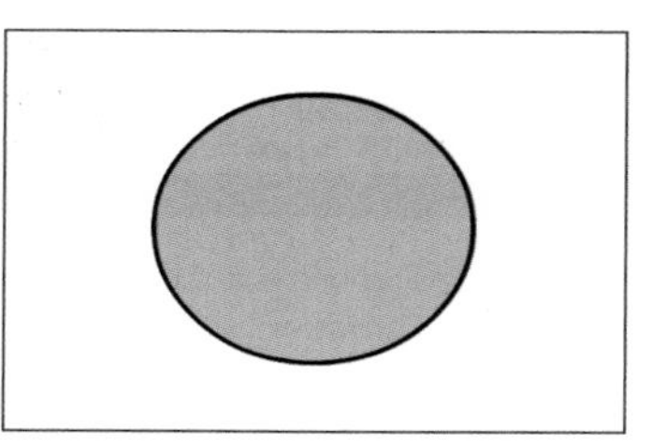

720 x 486

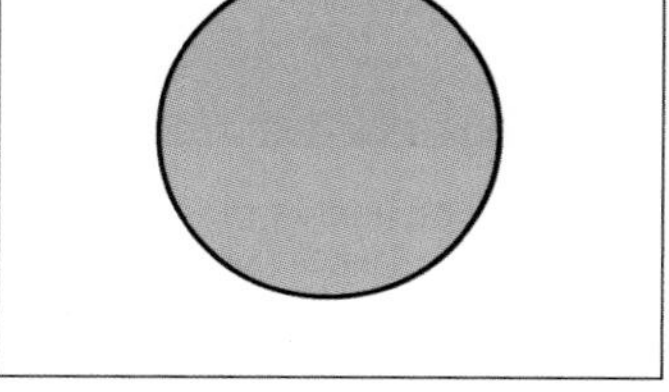

720 x 540

3 NTSC doesn't use square pixels; they are rectangular. A problem arises when you develop content for video on your computer because you are creating square pixels to be displayed as rectangular pixels. The problem is your video will look slightly stretched. To compensate for change in pixel shape, adjust the width of the movie so that the aspect ratio is 720 × 540.

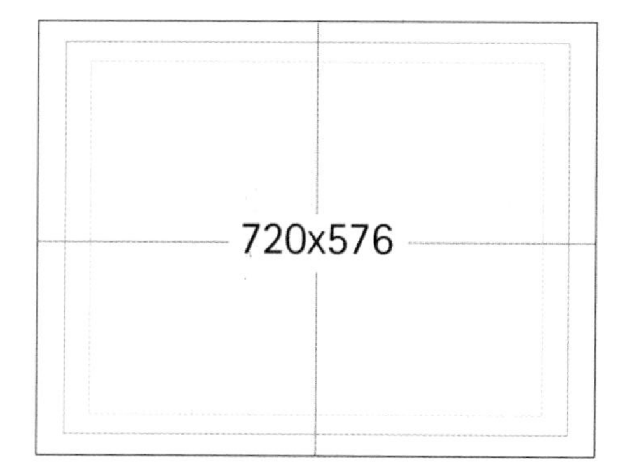

5 PAL (Phase Alternating Line), the predominant video standard outside the Americas, also uses the 4:3 aspect ratio but uses a 720 × 576 pixel aspect ratio. The frame rate is 25 fps. PAL has a greater resolution than NTSC and therefore has a better picture quality. Its higher color gamut level produces higher contrast levels as well. But the lower frame rate, compared to NTSC's frame rate, will not be as smooth.

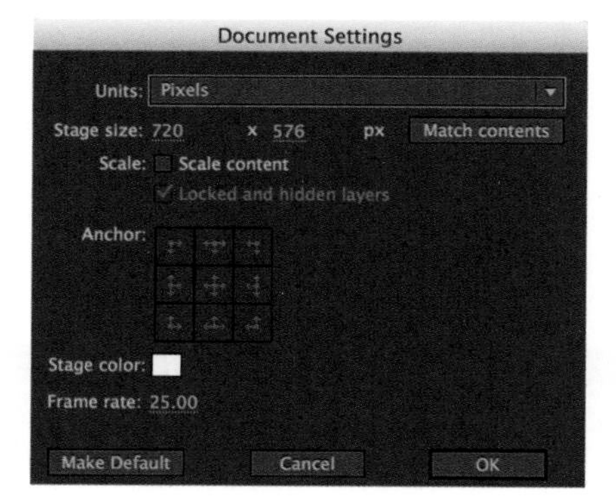

6 Film uses 24 fps, which is also a popular frame rate among animators. Although you can use 24 fps in your Animate project, when you export it to video, you will need to convert the frame rate as well. This conversion is easily done during the export process by specifying the appropriate frame rate.

Standard Television
4:3

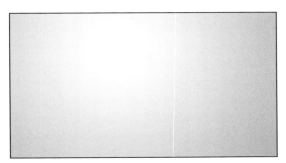

Widescreen Television
16:9

2 In 2009 the switch was made from analog broadcasts to digital ones, from the NTSC (National Television Standards Commission—or "Never the Same Color" depending on who you ask) to the ATSC (Advanced Television Systems Committee), and from the previous 4:3 aspect ratio to the new 16:9 standard. If you're not sure what aspect ratio to use, go with the current standard.

4 NTSC uses a frame rate of 29.97 fps. You can export Animate movies that have different frame rates such as 12, 15, or 24 fps and convert them to 30 with video editing software, although a movie converted from 12 to 30 fps will not look as smooth as a movie originally authored at 30 fps.

You can save your NTSC Animate document as a Template if you plan to create multiple files (File > Save as Template...). You can also create your own template categories by creating new folders in the "Templates" folder on your local hard drive where Animate CC is installed.

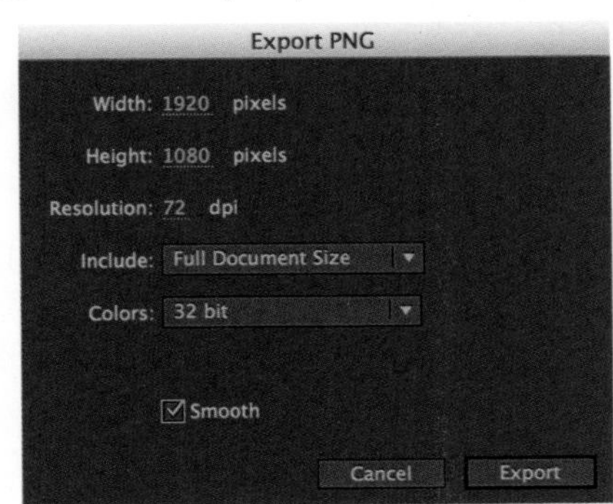

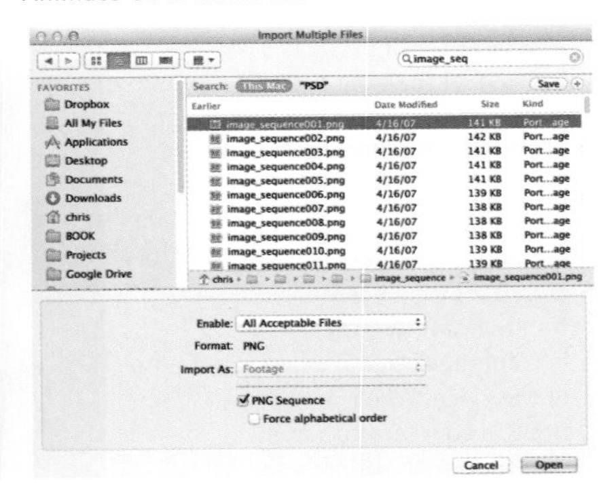

7 Exporting your movie as a PNG image sequence is often the best and most popular method. Go to File > Export Movie and select PNG Sequence as your format. I highly recommend creating a new folder where your image sequence can be saved since the number of images Animate creates is directly related to the number of frames in your animation (which can easily be hundreds or even thousands). A PNG sequence ensures your animation is frame accurate with lossless compression. If you are using After Effects to further refine or add effects to your animation, importing a PNG sequence is not only supported but is also treated as a single object, making it easy to manage.

HOT TIP

Using a video-based aspect ratio for the web is a good idea. You never know when the client might ask you to convert the web-based Animate movie into video format to be burned onto DVD and shown at their next big company summit meeting.

Title and Action Safety

TELEVISIONS DO NOT generally display the entire width and height of your movie. In almost all cases, televisions will show a smaller portion of the true display size. Using a visual guide that represents the potential Stage area in danger of being cropped will help guarantee that what you create in Animate shows up in its entirety on a variety of television sets.

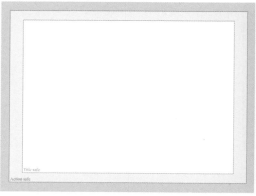

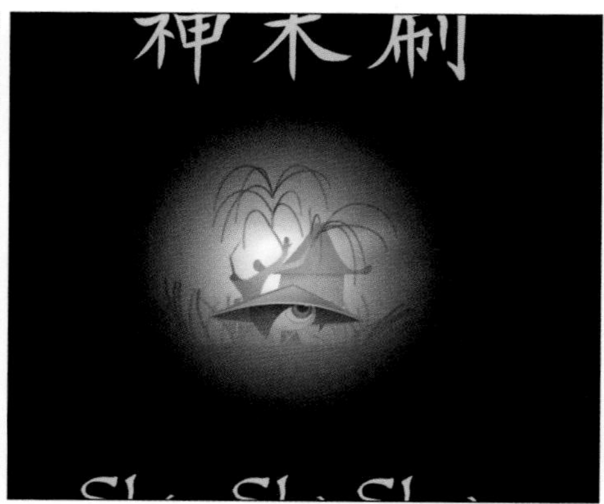

1 There's nothing worse than finding out too late that the title sequence you labored over for 10 hours appears on most televisions with several characters cropped, or is even completely invisible. To prevent this cropping, you need to define which area is considered the safe zone within the dimensions of your movie. There are two safe zones to consider: the action-safe zone and the title-safe zone.

2 To access the title-safe zone guides, go to File > New... and from the Templates tab select Media Playback from the Category list. The templates that appear include several document sizes with the corresponding Title Safe Area indicated on a guide layer. If you've already started your animation, you can open the new template and copy the guide layer and paste it in your current document.

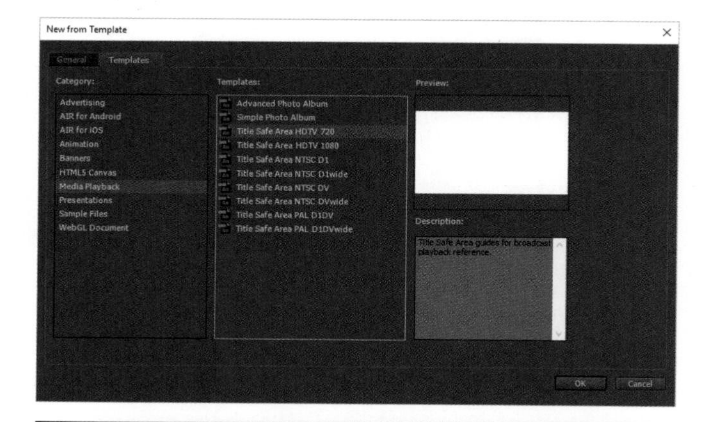

3 The title-safe zone is smaller than the action-safe zone because it is much more important to ensure that all titles are clearly legible without any chance of a single letter being cropped. For this reason, the title-safe zone lies 20% in from the absolute edge of the video. When you add titles to your movie, make sure they are positioned entirely within this safer title-safe zone to avoid being cropped.

4 The action-safe zone lies 10% inside the absolute edge of the video. You can assume that everything falling within this zone will appear on a television screen. Anything outside this zone can be potentially cropped and not visible. Compose your scenes based on the area within the action-safe zone, assuming this part will be the only area not cropped by the majority of televisions.

5 Keep the title-safe zone in your Animate project on its own layer above all other content. As long as it remains a guide layer, you won't need to delete it when you are ready to export to video. Guide layers are not included in your final export. Convert the layer containing the title-safe graphic to outline mode to reduce its visual impact and make it less noticeable. You can easily change the color of outline mode by clicking on the color swatch in the layer and selecting a different color in the swatch panel.

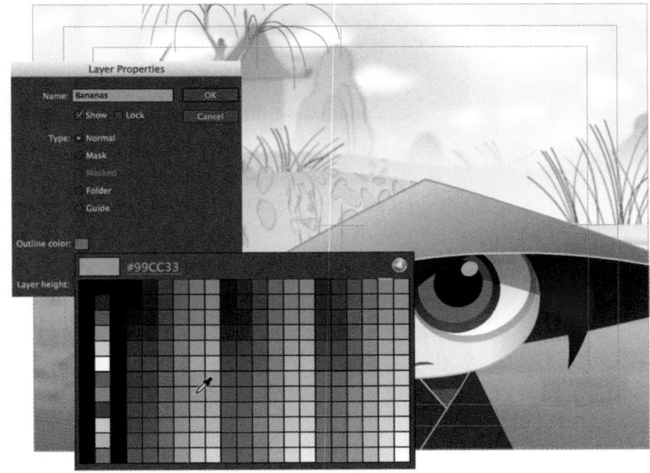

6 View > Pasteboard will allow you to see the work area beyond the Stage dimensions. This view is useful for working with graphics that extend beyond the width and height of the Stage. Having the title safety visible will indicate where the Stage is in relation to your artwork. Having the title-safe area visible is particularly useful for simulating camera moves such as panning and zooming.

HOT TIP

Animate CC supports the "Include Hidden Layers" option. Go to File > Publish Settings > Animate to locate this feature. When this feature is turned off, all layers with visibility turned off will not be exported. The advantage here is not having to delete the layer from your Timeline. You just need to remember to turn off its visibility before exporting.

CC Video Templates

ONE OF THE NICEST features of CC is actually more of a convenience. Adobe has provided us with an easy way to create Animate documents for video output in the form of templates. These template files provide everything you need to get started if you are producing content for video output. In some cases, it's actually a good idea to use these formats for web content as clients often will need to output their content to both the web and video formats.

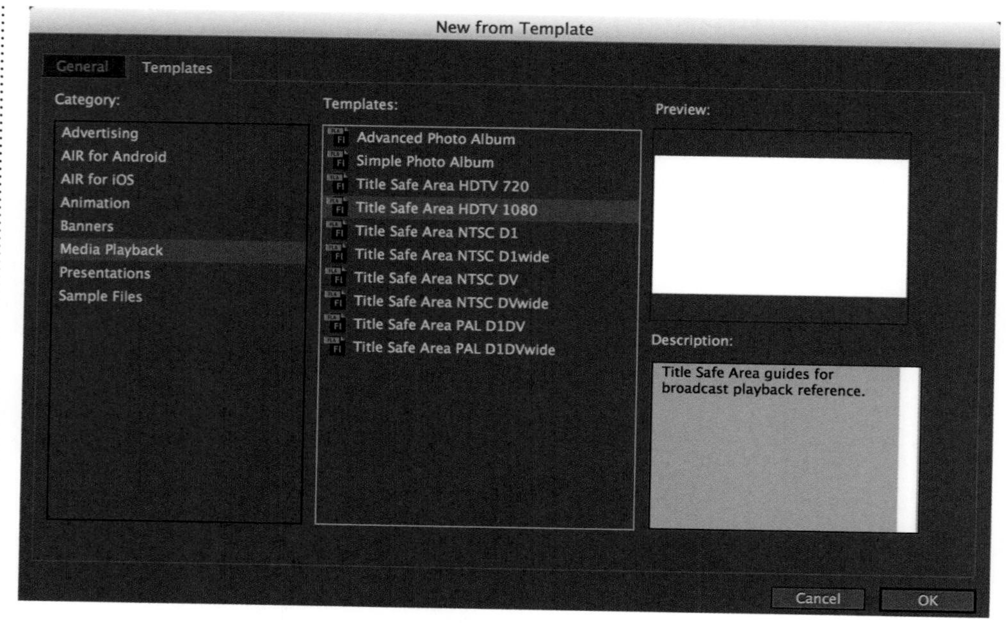

1 Go to File > New... and in the New Document panel click on the Templates button near the top. In the Category section select Media Playback. The Templates section will update with all of the various template files needed to produce content for video output. Select the template that best applies to your needs. The NTSC templates are for video output in America while PAL is used throughout Europe.

3 The title safety provides a clear defining boundary for text-based content as well as action-based content (everything other than text). The title safety region is indicated by guides that represent a 20% margin of the viewable area. The action-safe guides represent a 10% margin of the viewable area. To help discern between these two regions, the borders contain a fill color mixed with alpha transparency to allow for the content underneath to still be seen. Keeping within these guides ensures your content will not be cropped on older screens.

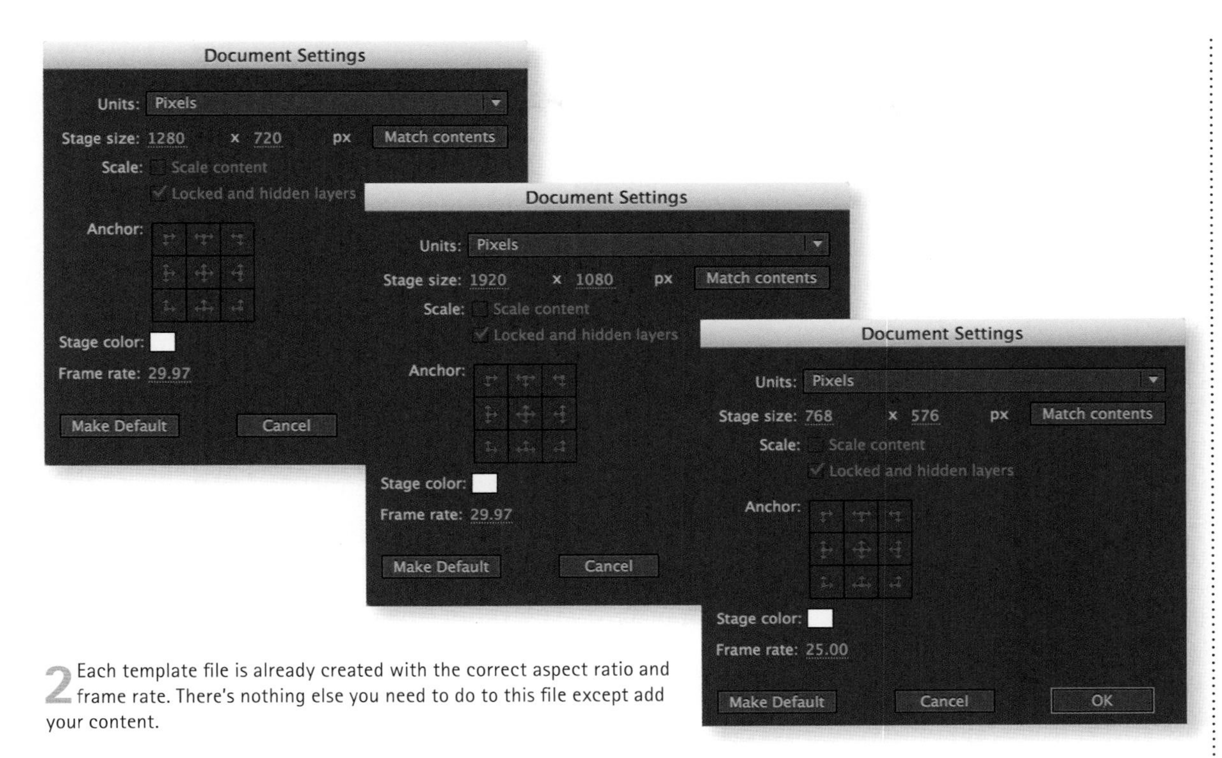

2 Each template file is already created with the correct aspect ratio and frame rate. There's nothing else you need to do to this file except add your content.

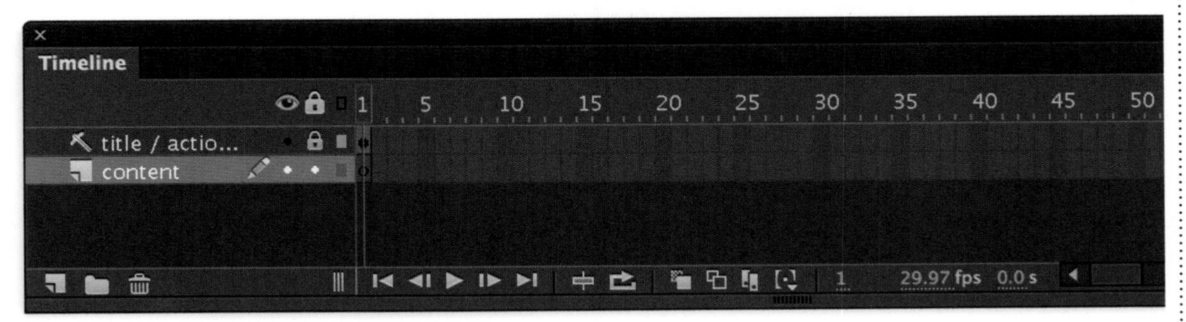

4 The Timeline consists of two layers: the action-safe layer and an empty layer for content. The action-safe layer is already converted to a guide layer so that it will not be included during export to SWF, to video or as an image sequence. There is only one layer for content, but depending on your needs you may need more. Feel free to add as many layers as you like.

HOT TIP

I highly recommend working with several smaller files rather than having a very long Timeline in a single document. The longer the Timeline and the more assets within a single FLA, the greater the risk of instability and possibly a corrupt file that can no longer be opened. Having several smaller files is simply more manageable and more stable.

Safe Colors

COLOR IS CRITICAL TO the success of your final file format. Since Animate is technically a web-based authoring tool, the range of colors far exceeds the color range a television can display. This example will show you how to mix colors while keeping them television-safe and also provide instructions for replacing the default color palette with a color-safe one (included in the downloadable assets).

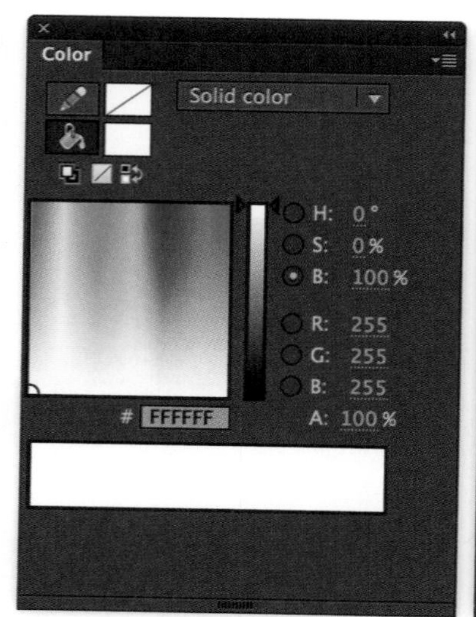

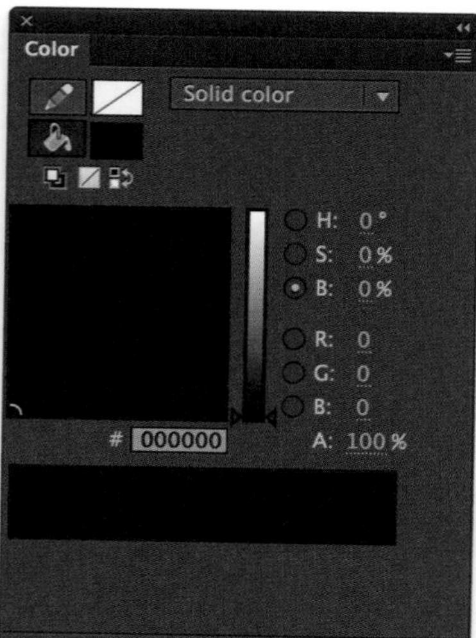

1 Your computer monitor is designed to display the full range of RGB color values (0–255). Television can only display a limited range of color values. There's a good chance you may be using colors in your Animate movie that fall outside the television value range, resulting in very noticeable color bleeding.

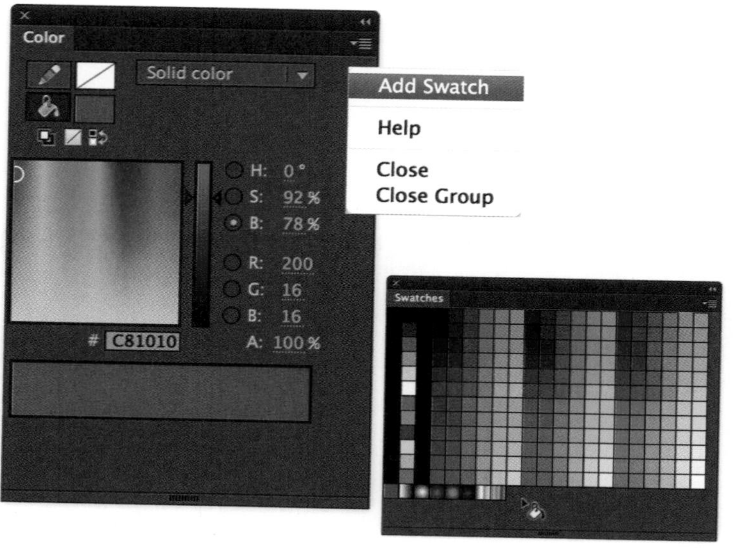

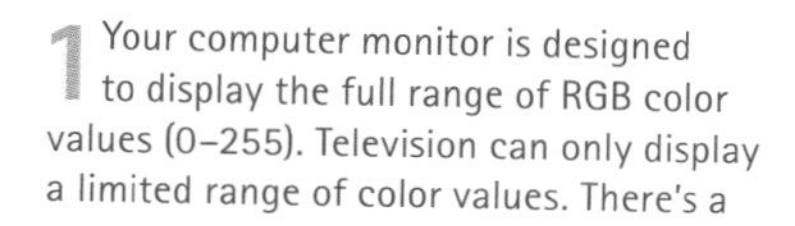

3 To add your new color as a swatch, use the drop-down menu in the upper right corner of the Color Mixer panel. An alternative method for adding colors to your Swatch panel is to hover over the empty area below the existing swatches. Your cursor automatically becomes a paint bucket, and when you click anywhere in this area, the current color will be added.

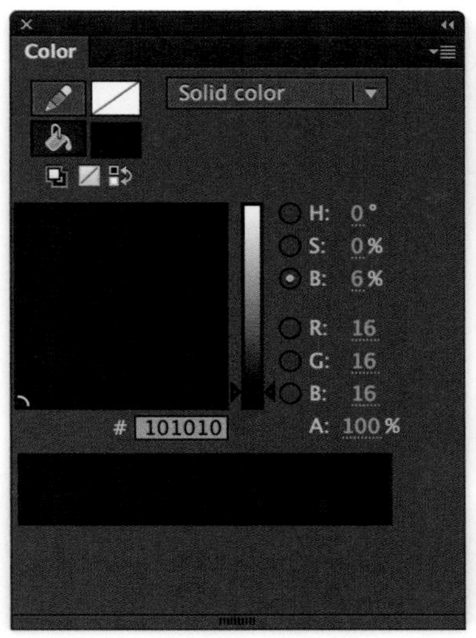

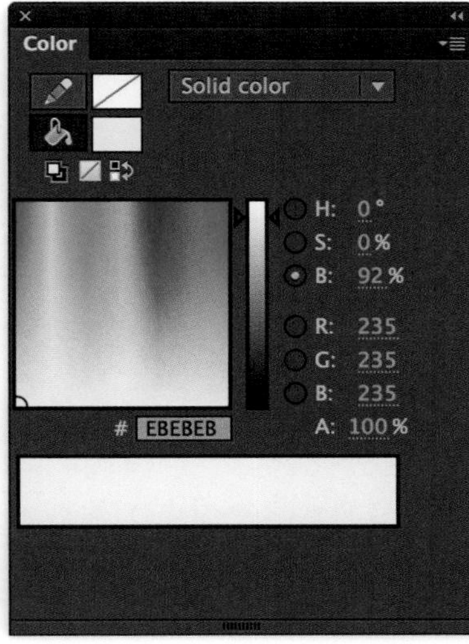

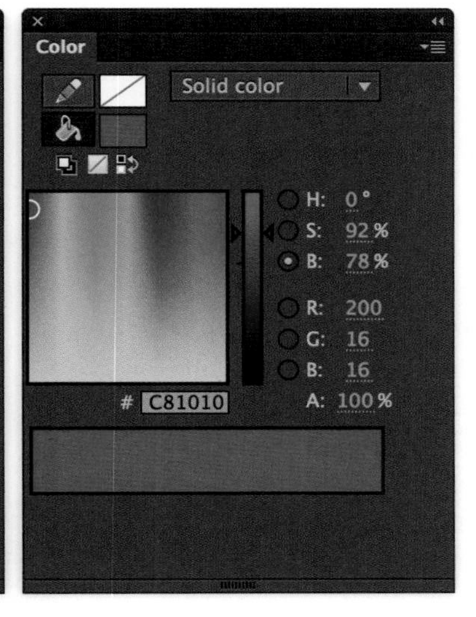

2 You will need to limit this range to between 16 and 235. The RGB color value of the darkest color (black) is 0-0-0. For television this value must be limited to 16-16-16. This setting should be your new black color for any project exported to video. The RGB value of the lightest color (white) is 255-255-255. This television white must be limited to 235-235-235 for export to video format. Since this will be the brightest color in your palette, it will appear to be stark white in comparison to all other colors. The color red has a tendency to bleed more than any other color, so it may be a good idea to compensate more than you need to by lowering the value to around 200-16-16.

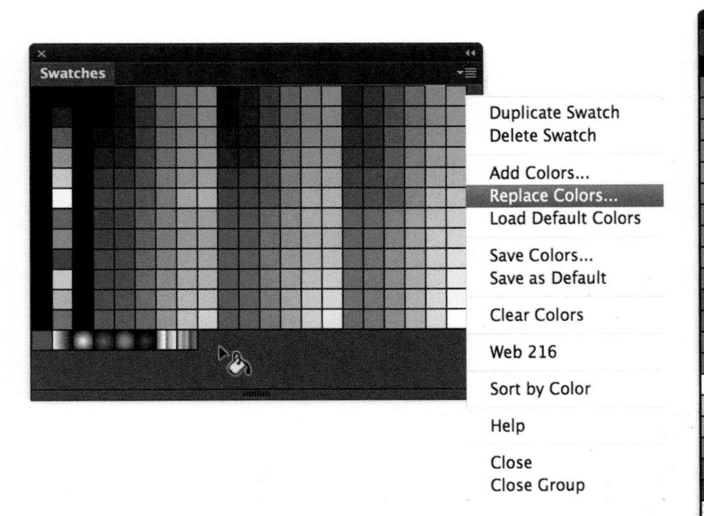

4 Sometimes the default color palette is not needed and simply gets in the way of your workflow. This is a good time to remove or replace the current swatches. You can start all over by mixing and adding new colors one at a time or by importing an existing color set, color table, or even a GIF file. From the drop-down menu choose Replace Colors and navigate to the *.clr, *.act, or *.gif file containing the colors you want to use. Here I have imported an NTSC safety color palette provided by Warren Fuller (animonger.com). This palette is included with the downloadable assets (NTSC.clr).

HOT TIP

Remember, Animate is resolution-independent. As long as you are working in the correct aspect ratio, you can always resize when exporting without a loss in quality. If you have imported bitmaps in your Animate movie, you'll want to use a width and height that is 100% of your final output to avoid having them scaled in Animate.

CLR

Ape Escape

APE ESCAPE IS BEST KNOWN AS A platform game for Sony's PlayStation gaming console. But it's also an animated series for television. Recently I was asked to help animate a few scenes and thought it would make for a great example of how a professional production creates animation with Animate as its primary tool for television broadcast. Many of the animators worked virtually, including myself. We shared files via FTP (File Transfer Protocol), and we were initially given storyboards in QuickTime format. The main characters were already set-up for us in Animate and each episode was broken down into several small chunks of time, specifically from 5 to 10 seconds in length. Breaking down the episodes created more files, but they were very small in size and easily shared via the web. All we had to do was upload the Animate source file so that the post-production crew could then export a PNG image sequence or QuickTime movie and edit all the scenes together using a video editing tool.

As you can see here, the duration of this scene is at 2.3 seconds. The entire duration of this shot is only about 5 seconds long. Each episode is a total 2 minutes in duration, made up of several 5- to 10-second shots. Each 2-minute episode could take anywhere from 10 to 20 different scenes.

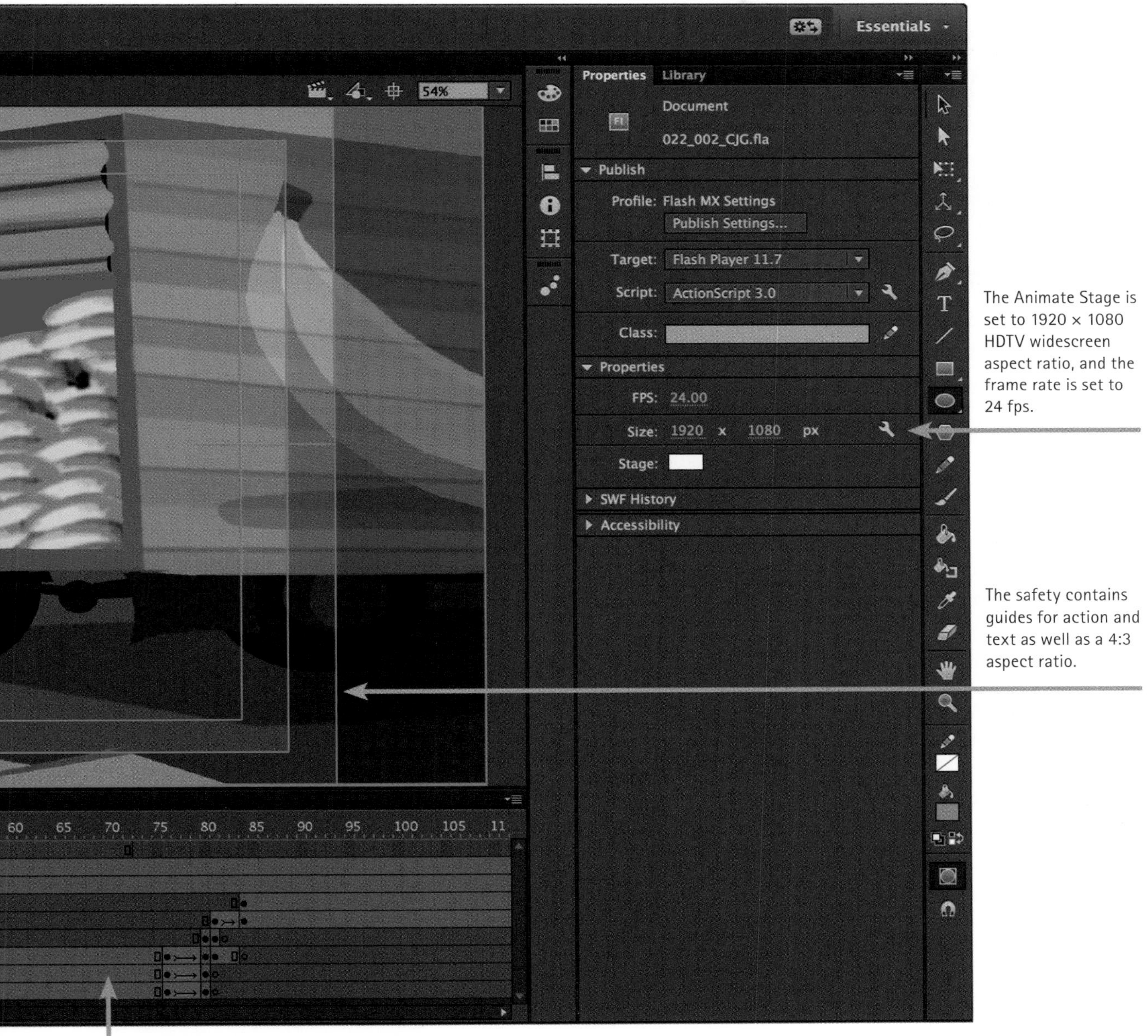

The Animate Stage is set to 1920 × 1080 HDTV widescreen aspect ratio, and the frame rate is set to 24 fps.

The safety contains guides for action and text as well as a 4:3 aspect ratio.

All animation is either on the main Timeline or nested in Graphic symbols, keeping them in sync with the main Timeline. The rule used to be, if it plays inside of the Animate authoring tool when you scrub the playhead or play your animation, it will export to video format successfully. With the latest QuickTime Exporter, dynamically generated content also exports to video as well.

Keeping It All in Sync

WE HAVE TWO OPTIONS FOR AUTHORING Animate for video output. The old-school method requires everything to be on the main Timeline. Movie Clip symbols must be avoided altogether since their Timelines are independent of the main Timeline and only render during runtime in the Animate Player. It's possible to add drop shadows, blurring, and other cool effects to Movie Clip symbols, but due to the dynamic nature of Movie Clips, they had to be avoided as well until the introduction of the QuickTime Exporter which solved this problem. We take a look at the enhanced QuickTime Exporter in Animate CC later in this chapter. For now, let's take a look at the old-school method of creating Animate animation for export to video. This example is analog Animate in its purest form: straight-ahead Timeline animation, streaming sound, and nested Graphic symbols.

1 If your Timeline contains Movie Clips, convert them to Graphic behavior so that they sync with the main Timeline. To convert a Movie Clip to a Graphic symbol, select the Movie Clip instance and change its behavior from Movie Clip to Graphic using the Properties panel. Then change its property from Single Frame to Loop or Play Once depending on your needs.

3 One of the disadvantages of using scenes is confusion during the editing process as it can be difficult to find assets within multiple scenes. Another disadvantage with multiple scenes is having more content in your FLA, which can result in a very large file size. This larger file size increases the chances of corruption and loss of work. It's usually better to work with several smaller files first, then edit the individual exported video files together in your video editor.

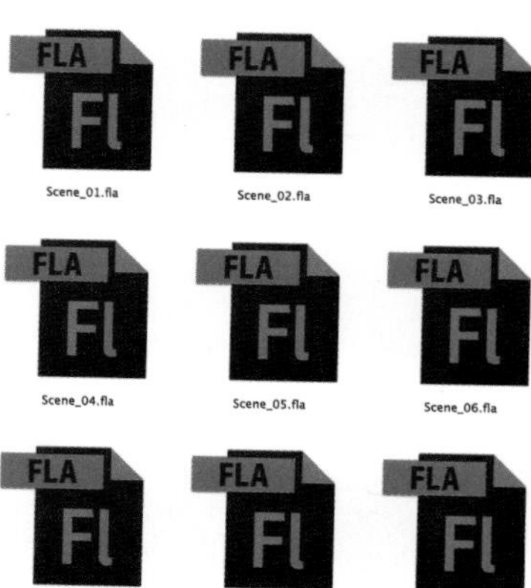

5 Layer folders are a great way to organize your Timeline, especially if your animation involves a great number of layers, which is often the case with animation. Layer folders combined with nesting animations can go a long way in making efficient Timelines. You can place all your character animations inside a Graphic symbol. One Graphic Symbol for each character makes it much easier to edit and control your entire scene from the main Timeline if you need to position, scale, pan, and zoom as if playing the role of a Director. Since the nested animations are inside Graphic symbols, you can still scrub the Timeline with the playhead to see the animations play.

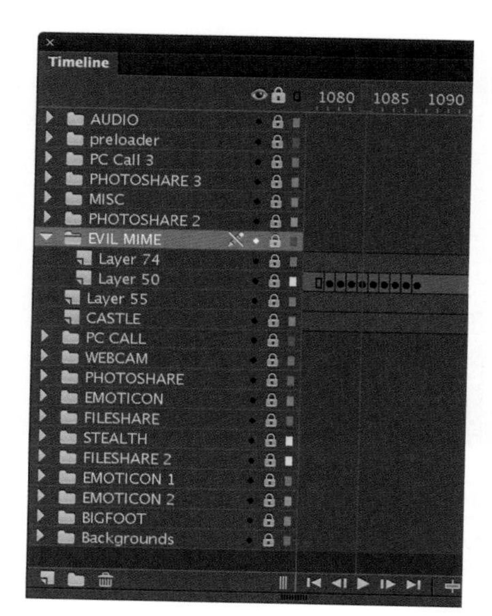

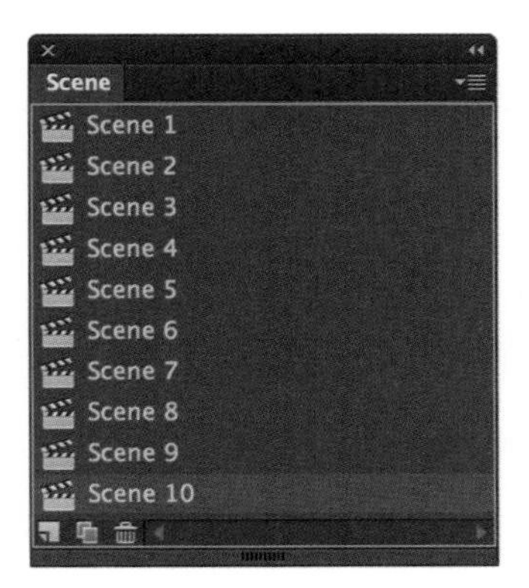

2 Scenes are a great way to manage long Timelines. For example, you could have your title sequence in Scene 1, your story in Scene 2, and ending credits in Scene 3. Using scenes is similar to multiple files chained together since each scene has its own Timeline. The Timeline of each scene combines into a single Timeline in the exported file. The advantage here is having the entire project in one FLA.

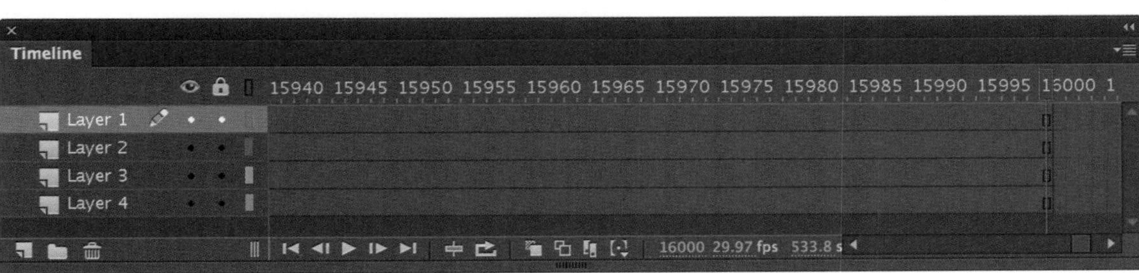

4 The Animate Timeline has its own limitations. Let's start with 16,000, the number that represents the maximum number of layers in a single Animate movie as well as the maximum number of symbol instances and frames. It is rare to see this number reached in any situation, but it is good to understand the limitations in order to avoid them. An Animate document that is 16,000 frames long at 30 fps is nearly 9 minutes long. A file that large will cause problems even in the best situations. The file will take longer to open as well as to save. It will exhaust your system's resources and make it harder to work with multiple Animate documents open at the same time. It will also take a very long time to export to video and will create an enormous file. If you export to AVI, you will very likely exceed the 2 GB limit that is placed on AVI files on most operating systems. Best practice is to break up your project into several smaller FLA files, typically between 30 and 60 seconds each. I often work with FLA files less than 20 seconds in length. It makes the entire process more manageable when animating, exporting, and editing.

6 You can quickly expand all layer folders by right-clicking over any one of your folders and selecting "Expand All Folders" from the context menu. Collapsing all folders is done the same way.

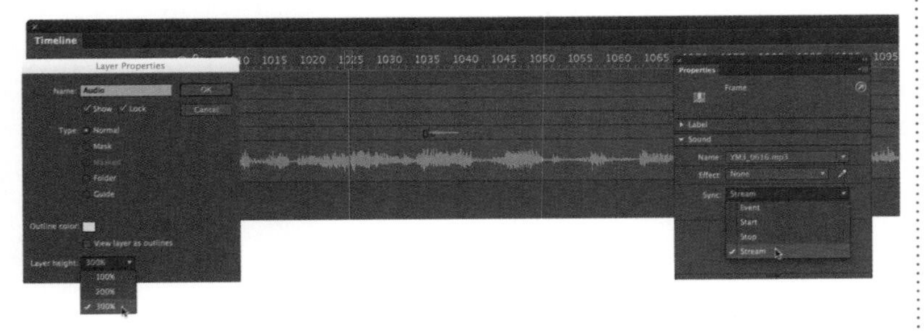

7 To sync your animations to a soundtrack, import your sound file and place it on the Timeline in its own layer. You can drag it from the Library to the Stage or use the Sound drop-down menu in the Properties panel to select the file. By default, the Sync setting will be Event and must be changed to Stream. The Stream behavior embeds the sound into the Timeline and will be in sync with any Timeline animation. You can adjust the height of a layer by right-clicking over the layer name and selecting Properties. In the Properties panel you can set the layer height to as much as 300%. This height can be useful if you want to see the waveform in as much detail as possible.

HOT TIP

To keep the file size of your FLA as small as possible, it is sometimes good practice to avoid importing high-quality stereo sound files. If you're planning on editing several exported video files together in your video editing program, then import a compressed MP3 audio file into Animate to use as a "scratch track." Place the sound file(s) on its own layer so that it can be easily deleted before export. You can simply turn off the visibility of this layer to exclude it from export. Use the high-quality stereo sound file in your video editing program instead.

SHORTCUTS
MAC WIN BOTH

QuickTime Exporter

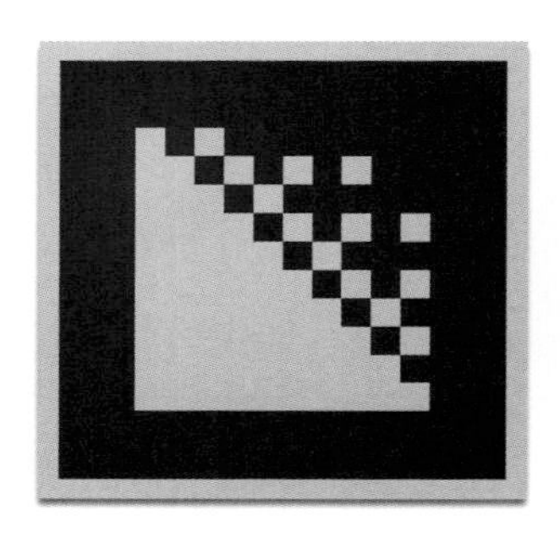

EXPORTING ANIMATE MOVIES TO VIDEO FORMAT USED to require that all animation be on the main Timeline. Dynamic content could not be exported to a fixed-frame video format. This content included Movie Clip animations, filters, ActionScript, and just about anything dynamically loaded into your SWF file. If it didn't play on the main Timeline, then it wasn't included in the exported video. Welcome the newly enhanced Animate CC QuickTime Exporter. With it you can export dynamically created Animate content including effects generated with ActionScript as well as effects created with Movie Clips and filters. The biggest enhancement to the QuickTime Exporter in Animate CC is the integration of the Adobe Media Encoder, providing a number of encoding presets for various devices and platforms. The next biggest enhancement to the exporter is performance. In previous versions of Animate, larger Stage sizes, higher frame rates, multiple filters, Blend Modes, animated effects, and lack of system resources could contribute to frames being dropped during the export process. As a result, the exported content would suffer from dropped frames or graphic anomalies. In Animate CC, these export issues are all in the past, which is great news for anyone wanting to export their dynamic or Timeline-generated Animate content to video format.

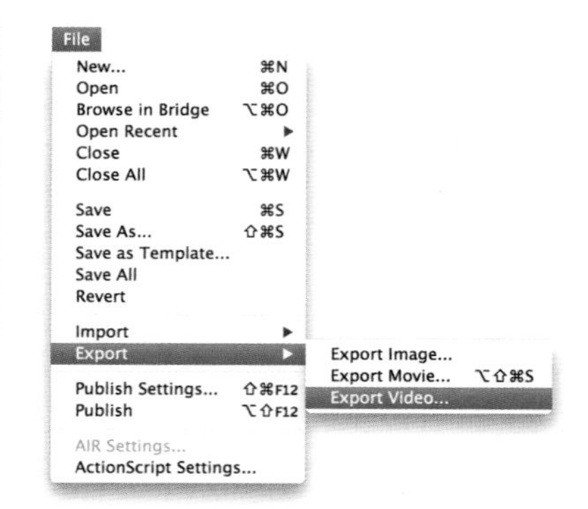

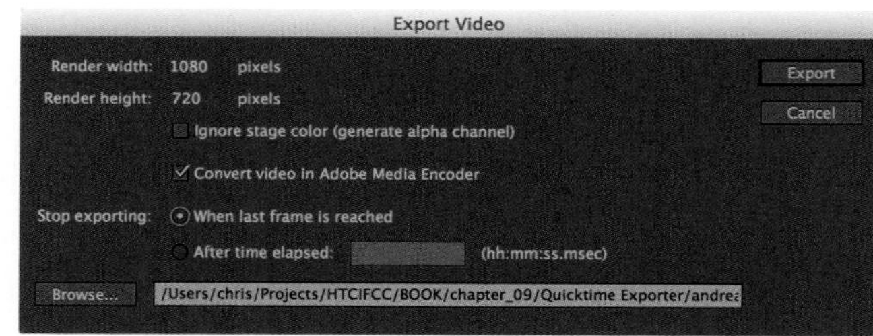

1 When you are ready to export your Animate movie to video format, go to File > Export > Export Video. In the Export Video window, the Convert video in Adobe Media Encoder is checked by default—leave it as is. Select When last frame is reached for Timeline-based animation. If your movie is dynamic, then select After time elapsed and then enter the desired duration in hh:mm:ss.msec format. Click Export when your settings are ready.

3 Preset categories offer several encoding formats to choose. Within the Web Video drop-down you will find a variety of formats within the Vimeo and YouTube sections. These formats will ensure your video will be encoded with the right compression for viewing on these types of web platforms.

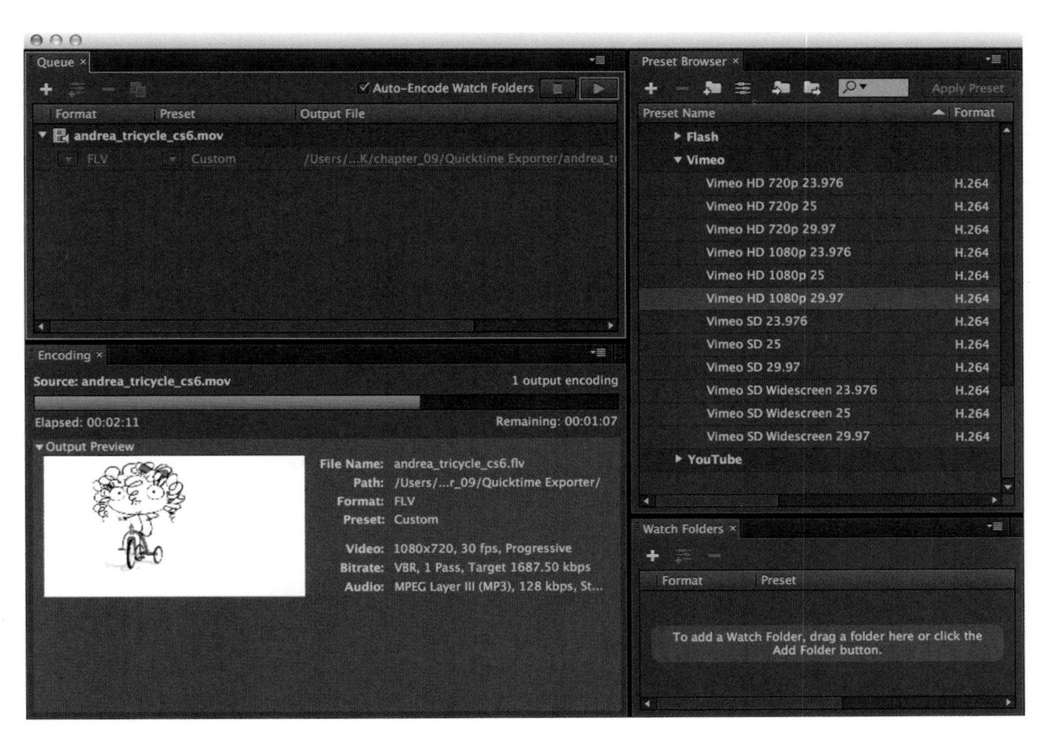

2 Once the export from Animate is complete, the Adobe Media Encoder will launch automatically. The exported MOV file will be automatically added to the queue as seen in the upper left panel. In the lower left corner is the Encoding panel where you can see a preview of the encoded movie along with data specific to the file itself. Along the right side is the Preset panel where you'll find a list of presets for just about any output you can imagine. From audio and broadcast output, to mobile devices and the web, the Adobe Media Encoder has just about every platform covered. With your preset selected, click the green arrow button in the top right corner of the Queue panel to start the encoding process. The Encoding panel progress bar will indicate the elapsed and remaining time encoding duration.

4 The encoded movie can be opened and played with the QuickTime Player before uploading to the web. The most notable enhancement besides the integration of the Adobe Media Encoder is the flawless export quality. No more dropped frames, and image quality is as expected: excellent.

HOT TIP

Knowing your intended output at the planning stage of your project can help smooth the production process. If you know you want to use a web-based platform such as Vimeo or YouTube, you can use the Adobe Media Encoder to check out the file format specifications and use that information when setting up your files. Do you want to develop for an Apple iPad? The Adobe Media Encoder lists multiple versions of the iPad from the newest to several previous versions. Use one of these settings when you create a new Animate document to ensure compatibility with the Apple iPad platform.

SWF & FLV Toolbox

THE SWF & FLV TOOLBOX IS A VERY HANDY third-party program that converts Adobe Animate files (SWF), Animate Video (FLV), and Projector (EXE) files to several different formats (AVI, JPEG, GIF, and BMP). You have complete control over the settings for each file format including codec control, keyframe rate, movie quality, bitrate, cropping, resizing, and more. I've been using this software quite a lot recently, and I really like its ease of use and no-frills interface.

Find out more by visiting www.eltima.com/wiki/user-guides/swf-flv-toolbox4.html. You can download the software at www.eltima.com/wiki/user-guides/swf-flv-toolbox4/install.html. SWF & FLV Toolbox is only supported for the Windows platform as of this writing.

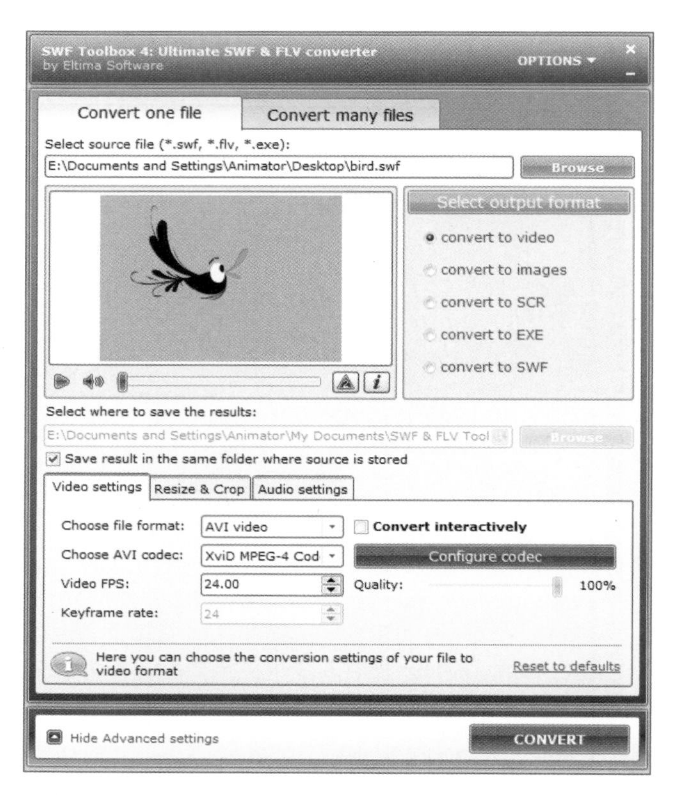

1 The first step is to publish your Animate document to generate a SWF file. Launch SWF & FLV Toolbox, click the Browse button, and select the SWF file. Select the output format and click Convert. That's basically all you need to do to convert your SWF files to a different format. Of course you have advanced settings to play with as well.

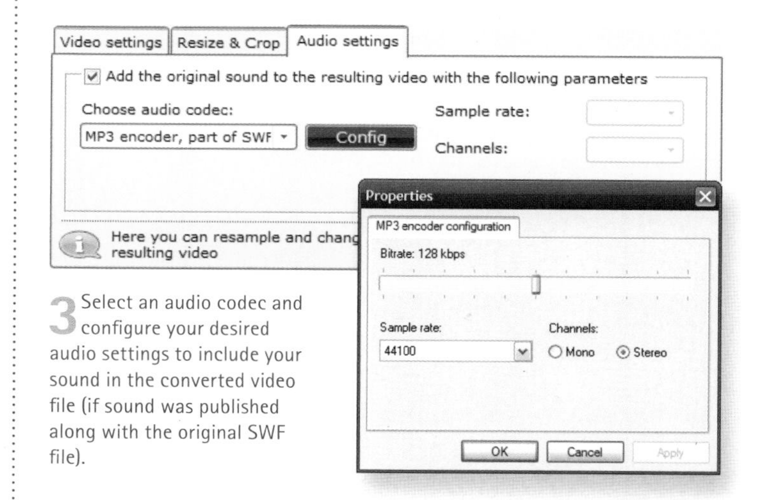

3 Select an audio codec and configure your desired audio settings to include your sound in the converted video file (if sound was published along with the original SWF file).

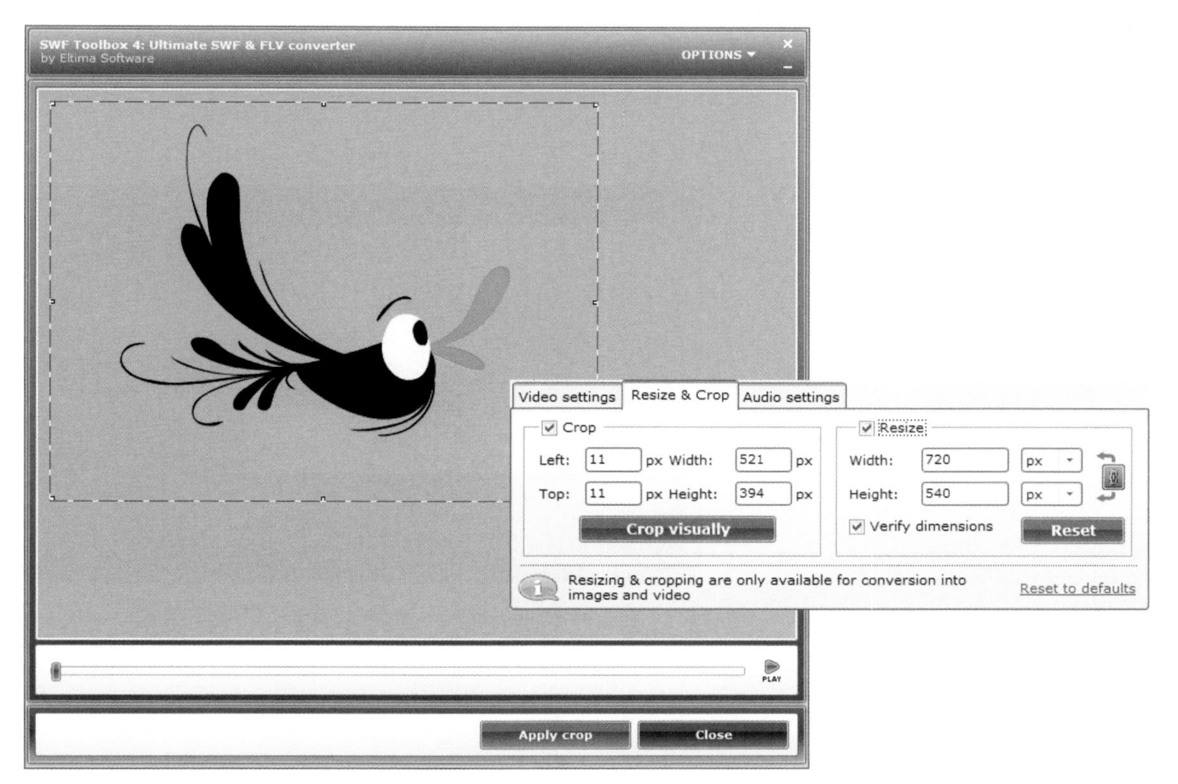

2 The advanced settings provide the option to crop your SWF file to any width and height by dragging the edges of the crop marquee or by typing in the numerical values. You can also resize the SWF by providing new values for the width and the height.

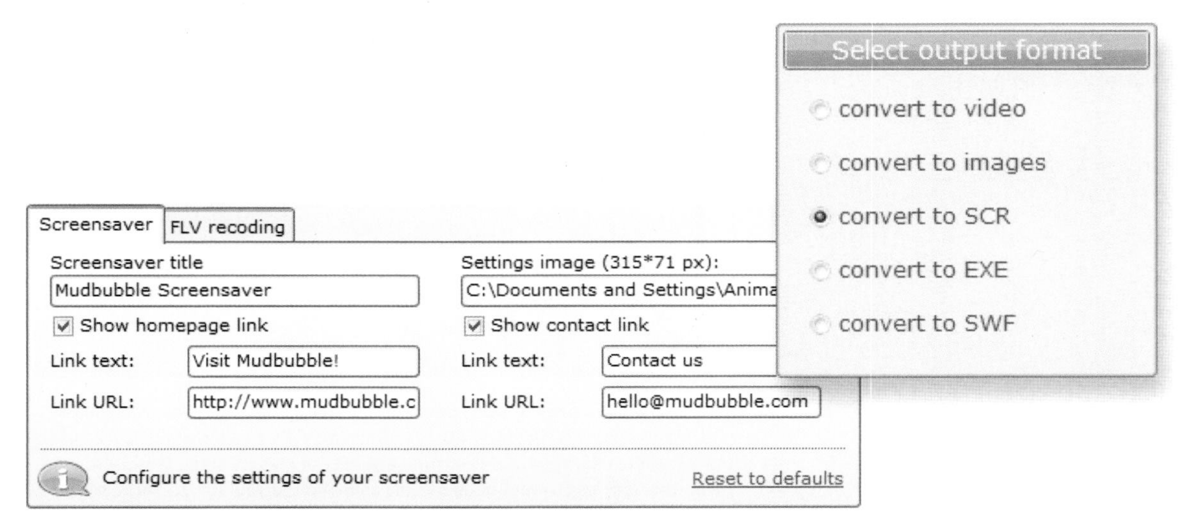

4 You can easily convert any SWF, FLV, or Projector EXE file to a Windows screensaver file. SWF & FLV Toolbox offers several options that allow you to customize your screensaver by adding a title, website URL, and email address.

HOT TIP

SWF & FLV Toolbox even allows you to batch convert several files at one time. Select the "Convert many files" tab in the main window and then click the "Add" button.

Exporting Video

THIS IMPROVEMENT MAY BE THE MOST exciting for animators! We've needed a reliable way to export our content directly from Animate to video format. In the past, we've experienced dropped frames or unexpected quality issues when exporting our animations due to an error-prone process that demanded large amounts of memory. The enhancements to the video exporter are the direct result of integrating the Adobe Media Encoder in Animate CC. This integration simplifies the video export workflow while providing many more encoding options for output to a variety of mediums.

1 The Animate document above contains a Timeline-based animation using nested Graphic symbols. The entire Timeline is about 15 seconds in duration. The Stage size is 1920 × 1080 at 24 fps.

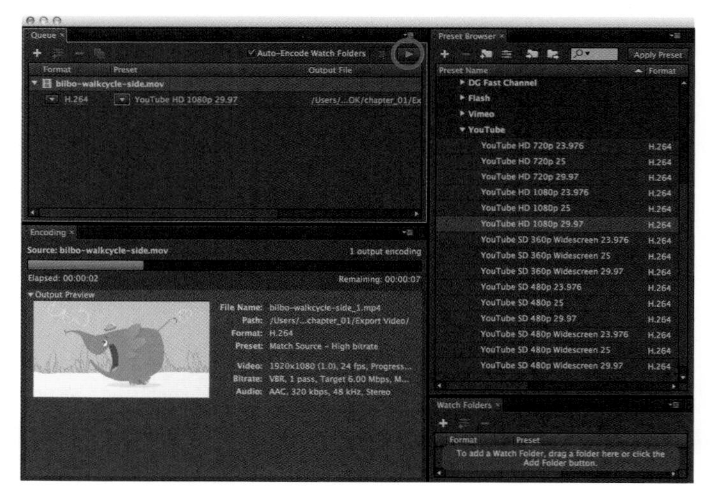

4 Once the video has been exported, the Adobe Media Encoder will launch automatically. The MOV file from Animate will be added to the Queue panel. Using the AME, you can select from a variety of presets in the Preset Browser on the right side. I want to upload my animation to YouTube, so I have selected the H.264 format, specifically the YouTube HD 1080p 29.97 preset in the Preset Browser. When you are ready to export, click the green arrow near the top of the AME to begin the encoding process.

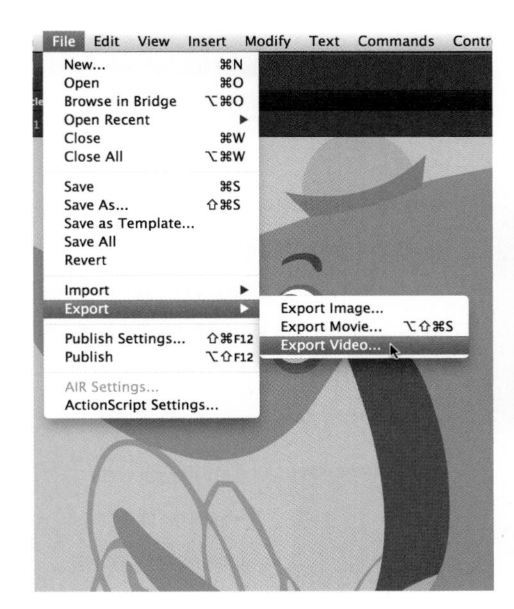

2 To begin the video export process go to File > Export Video...

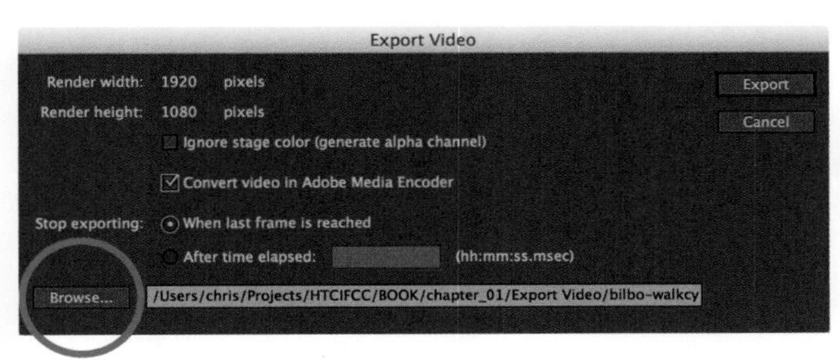

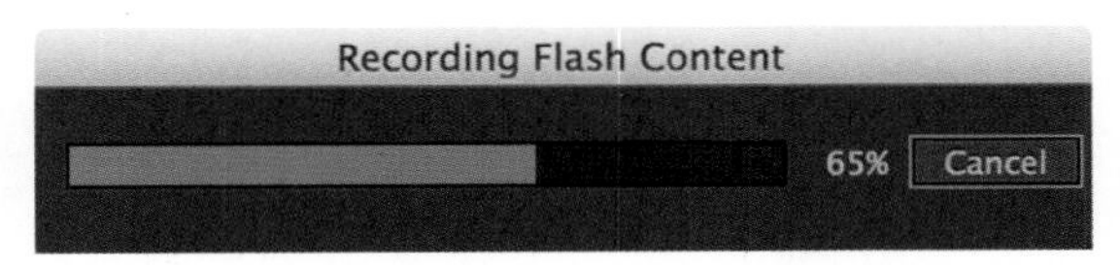

3 In the Export Video settings panel, make sure Convert video in Adobe Media Encoder is checked. Since my document contains Timeline animation, I have selected When last frame is reached as the stopping point of the export process. Click Browse to select the path where to save your video file and then click the Export button. The Recording Animate Content progress bar will display the export process.

5 With the encoding process complete, the video file can be opened and played in the QuickTime Player to verify the quality of the video is acceptable. In my experience with the new video exporter in Animate CC, each frame is flawless—even at 1920 × 1080 and with no dropped frames.

HOT TIP

Now Animate can scale your content and your Stage, so you can export to a wide variety of resolutions including 4K. Set the dimensions in the Properties panel and select Scale Content to simultaneously resize your artwork. Click Advanced Settings to set your anchor.

Prototyping

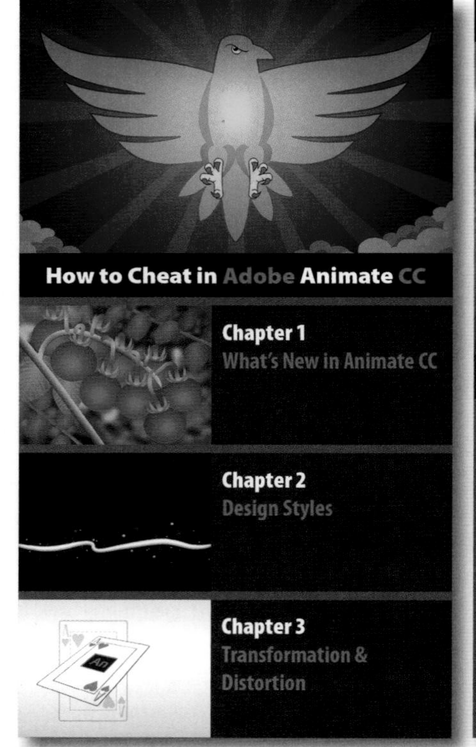

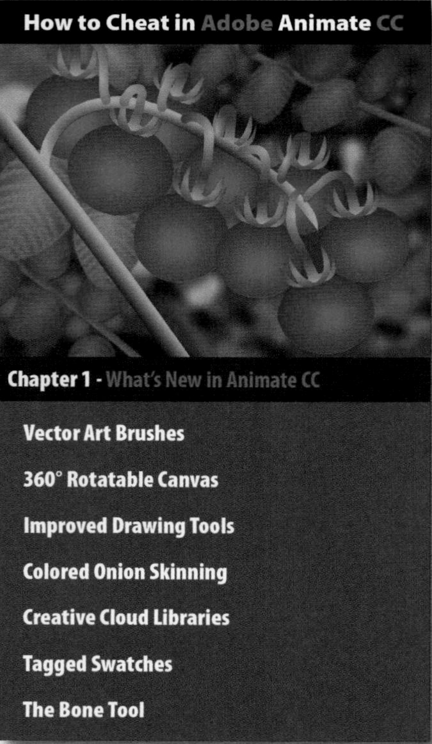

How to Cheat in Adobe Animate CC

Vector Art Brushes

Similar to Art Brushes in Illustrator, the new vector art brushes in Animate open up a world of creativity by applying a vector shape to a path. Use them to access specific shapes to be applied to a custom stroke, to recreate the appearance of various mediums, to generate banners or dividers, or to imagine your own creative uses.

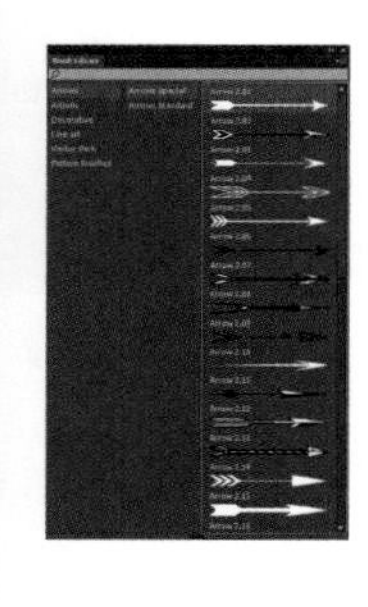

1. Animate comes with several styles of vector art brushes ready for use that include arrows, simulated artistic mediums, banners, and all sorts of shapes and patterns.

PROTOTYPING IS A QUICK WAY TO SHOW THE ANIMATION AND INTERACTIVITY YOU PLAN TO PUT in your app. It's like a working mock-up, but the idea is that it's a fast way to build a sample of interactions. It is not intended to be a final product, so you don't have to know how to code to make one. You just have to know how to cheat.

Of course, you can build a prototype with as much complexity as you want, but it's possible just showing the navigation will suffice. When that's the case, skip importing layers from the mock-ups, converting them to Movie Clips, managing all the assets, and writing perfect code. To make the building process as simple as possible, import flattened images of your screen designs. Use invisible buttons and add code snippets that Animate already has prepared for you. We'll use this approach to apply some navigation to a mock-up of this book if it were an app.

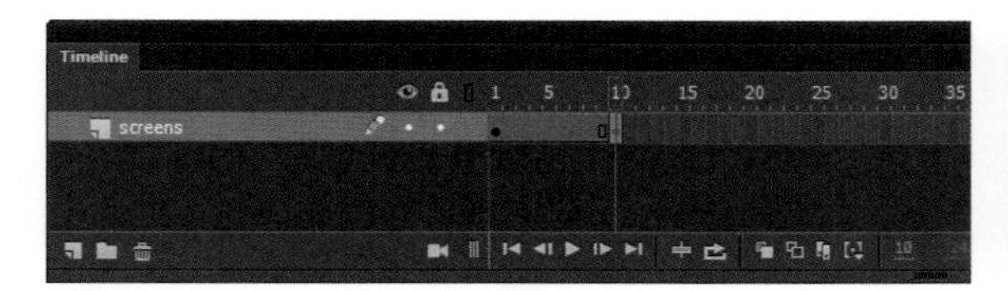

1 Import the three flattened sample screens to the Library. Drag the first one onto the Stage. Name this layer "screens."

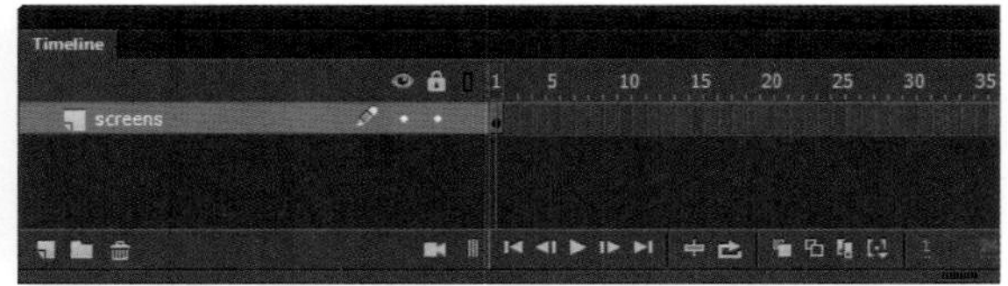

2 Add a keyframe at frame 10.

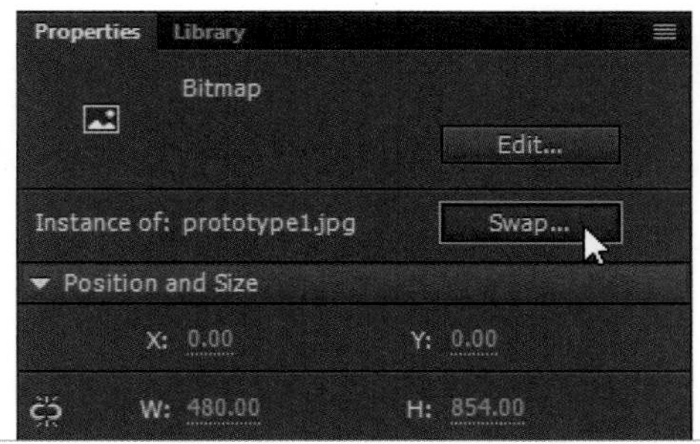

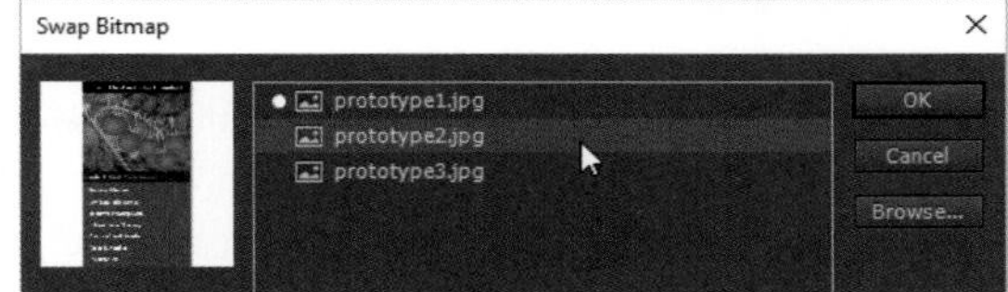

3 Swap the first image with the second screen image by going to the Properties panel, clicking Swap... and selecting the second image.

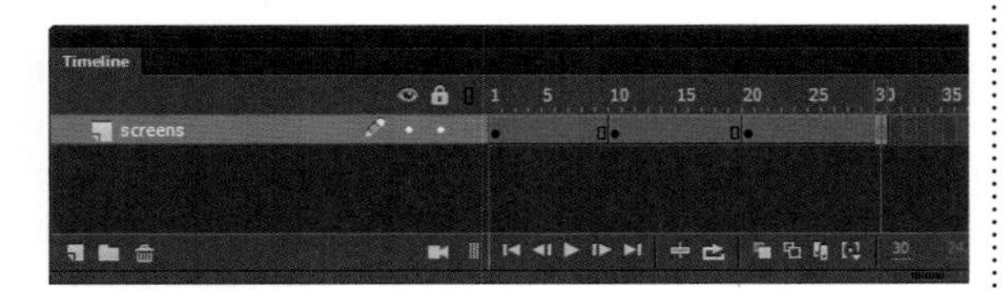

4 Make another keyframe at frame 20 and add frames to extend the Timeline to frame 30.

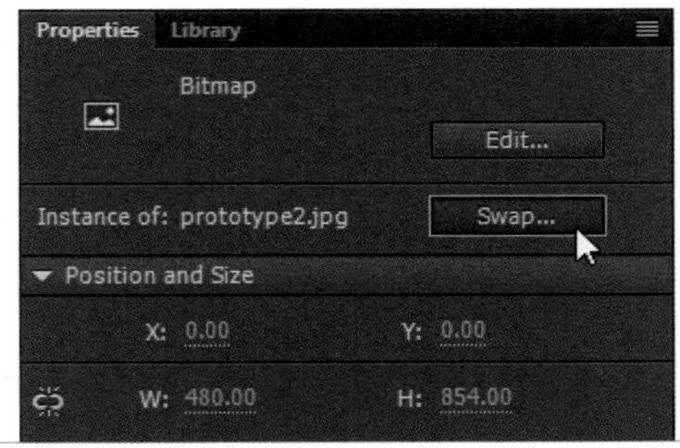

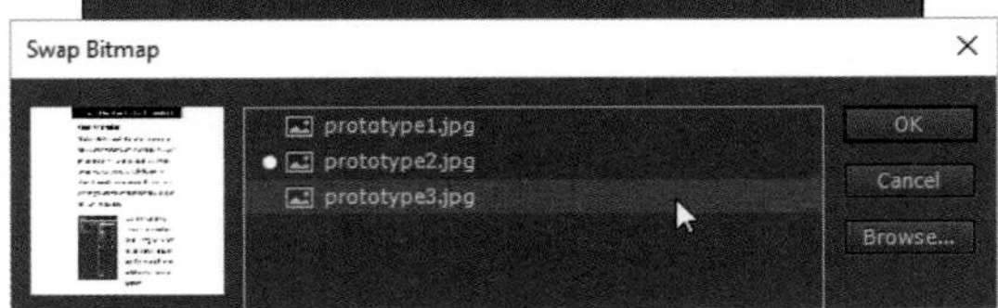

5 Swap the second image for the third.

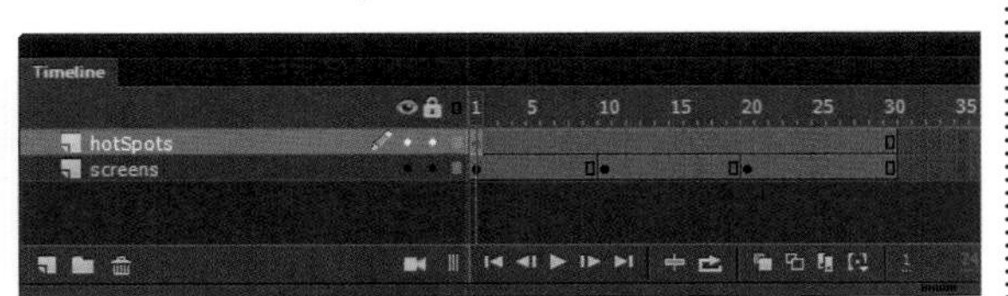

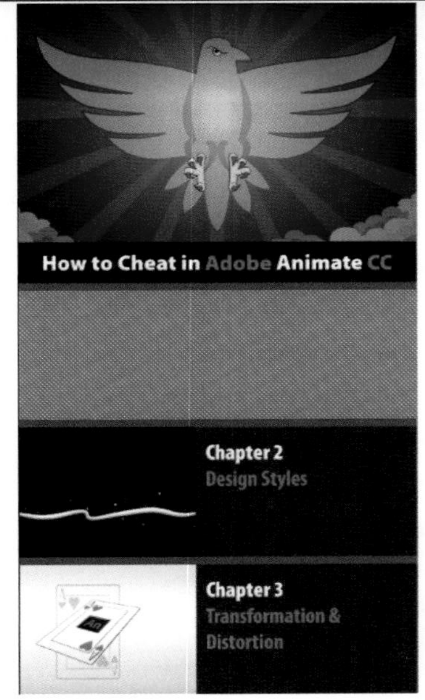

6 Make a new layer and name it "hotSpots" for our invisible buttons. On this layer, draw a solid rectangle 480 × 160 pixels with no stroke over the Chapter 1 section.

SHORTCUTS
MAC WIN BOTH

Prototyping (cont.)

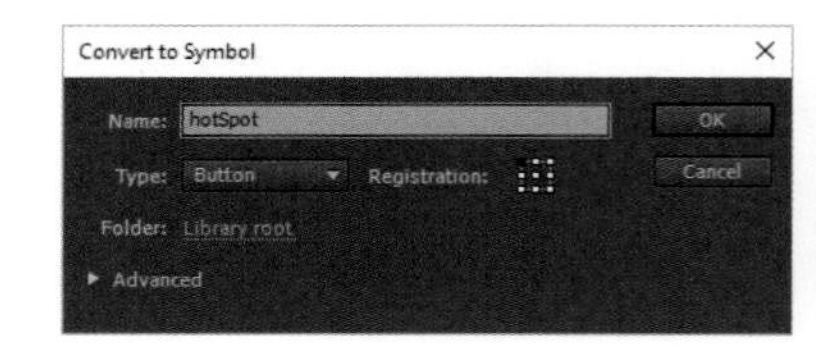

7 Convert the rectangle to a symbol F8 and set Type to Button.

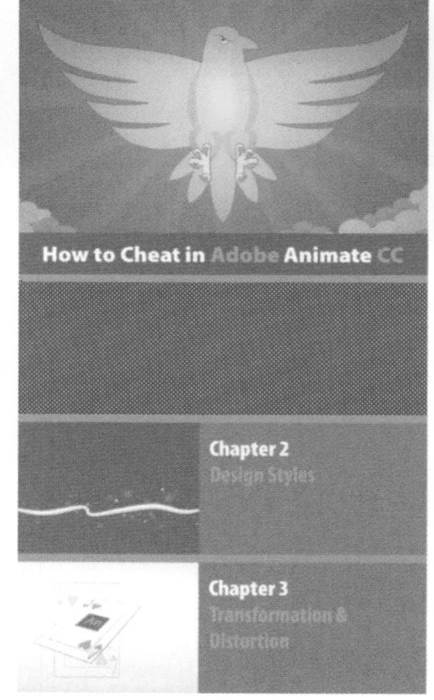

8 Double-click to open the Button symbol. If you're not familiar with buttons in Animate, you'll notice the Timeline is different. Instead of numbered frames, there are four states: Up, Over, Down, and Hit. We don't need the visual cues for the other states. All we really want is to activate a hotspot, so drag the keyframe in the Up state to the Hit state.

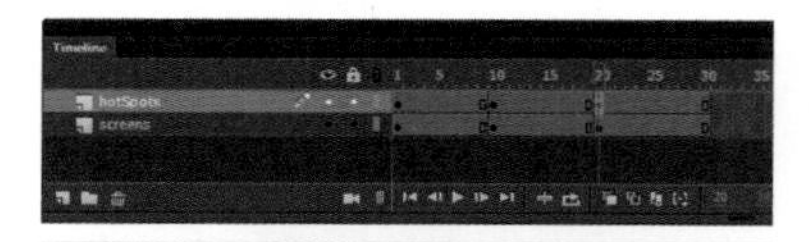

How to Cheat in Adobe Animate CC

Vector Art Brushes

Similar to Art Brushes in Illustrator, the new vector art brushes in Animate open up a world of creativity by applying a vector shape to a path. Use them to access specific shapes to be applied to a custom stroke, to recreate the appearance of various mediums, to generate banners or dividers, or to imagine your own creative uses.

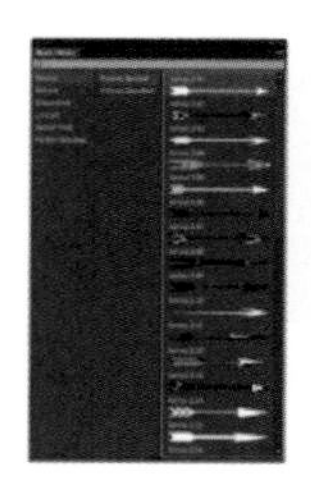

1. Animate comes with several styles of vector art brushes ready for use that include arrows, simulated artistic mediums, banners, and all sorts of shapes and patterns.

11 Insert a new keyframe on that layer at frame 20. Delete one of the buttons and drag the other to the title bar on the top.

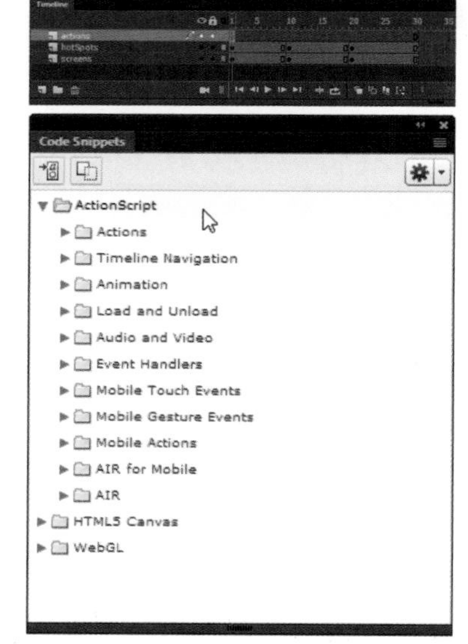

12 Make a new layer called "actions" and go to frame 1. Open the Code Snippets panel by going to Window > Code Snippets. Since we're using an ActionScript 3 document, open the ActionScript folder, otherwise you'd select the folder for whichever document type you were using.

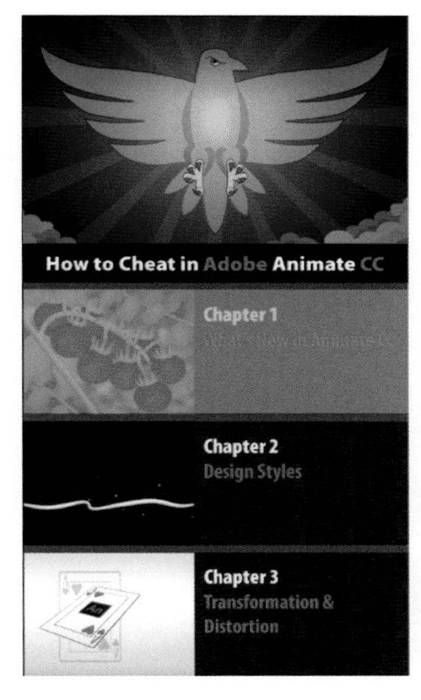

9 Without a shape in the other states, the button becomes invisible when it's published. For our benefit while we're working, Animate displays the invisible button as a transparent blue shape that represents the area covered in the Hit state.

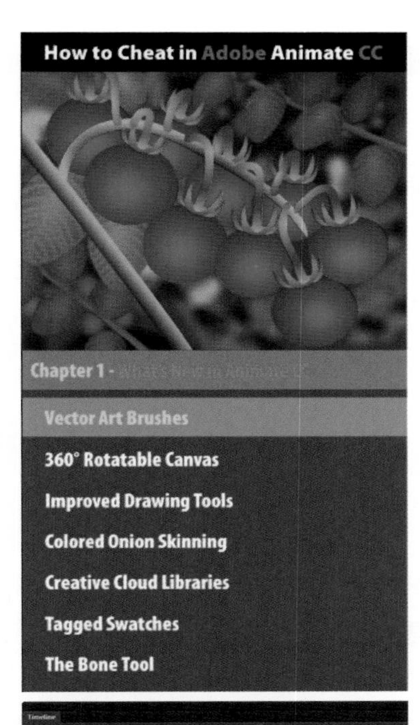

10 Since this is an example that illustrates only one path going from the Main screen to the Chapter 1 Table of Contents to the first content section and back to Main, you really don't need to copy and paste all the instances of the invisible button that you'd need if you were making a prototype that demonstrated the navigation of all the paths. Let's place the ones we do need by inserting a new keyframe on the hotSpots layer at frame 10. Resize the invisible button to go over the Chapter 1 heading. Copy and paste or ⌘/ctrl + drag the button to go over Vector Art Brushes section.

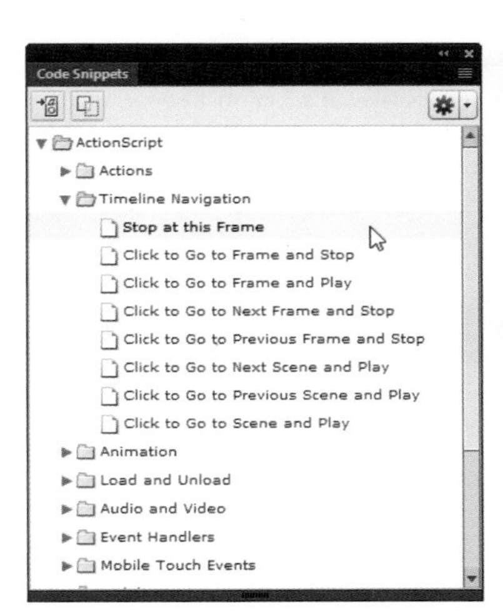

13 Open the Timeline Navigation folder. Animate will automatically play the Timeline unless we tell it to stop, so double-click Stop at this Frame to automatically have Animate add the code to the Actions panel.

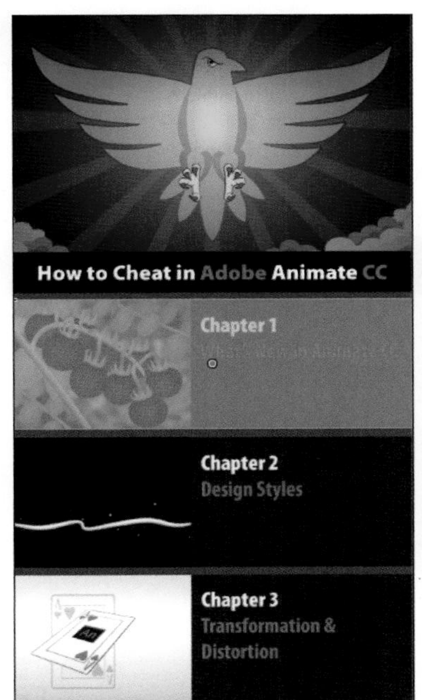

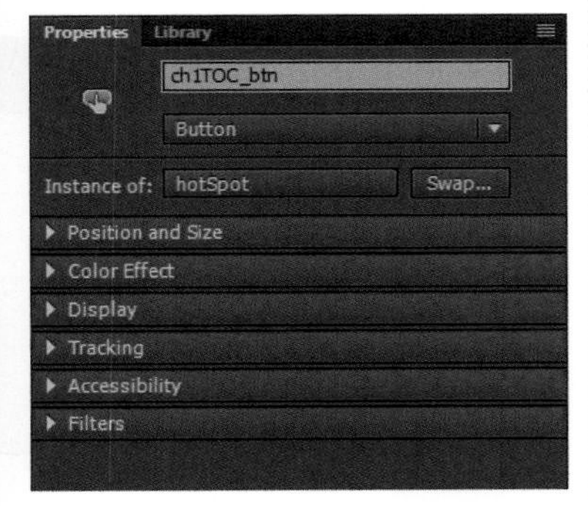

In frame 1 on the hotspots layer, select the invisible button over Chapter 1. Give it the instance name "ch1TOC_btn" in the Properties panel.

Prototyping (cont.)

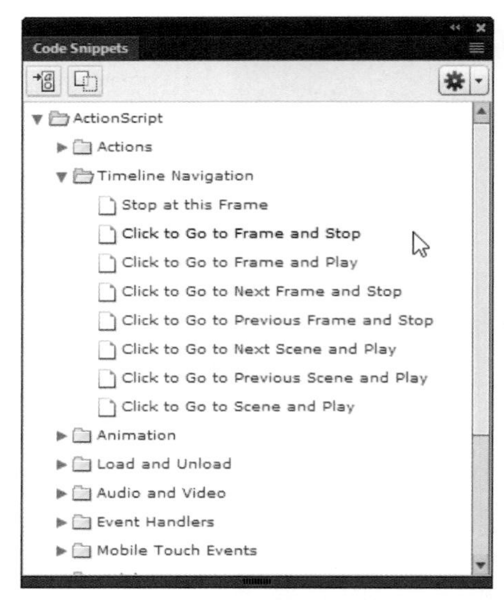

14 With the button instance selected, double-click Click to Go to Frame and Stop. Animate explains what the code does and instructs us to change the frame number to where the playhead should go. We want it to move to frame 10, so replace the 5 on line 21 with 10.

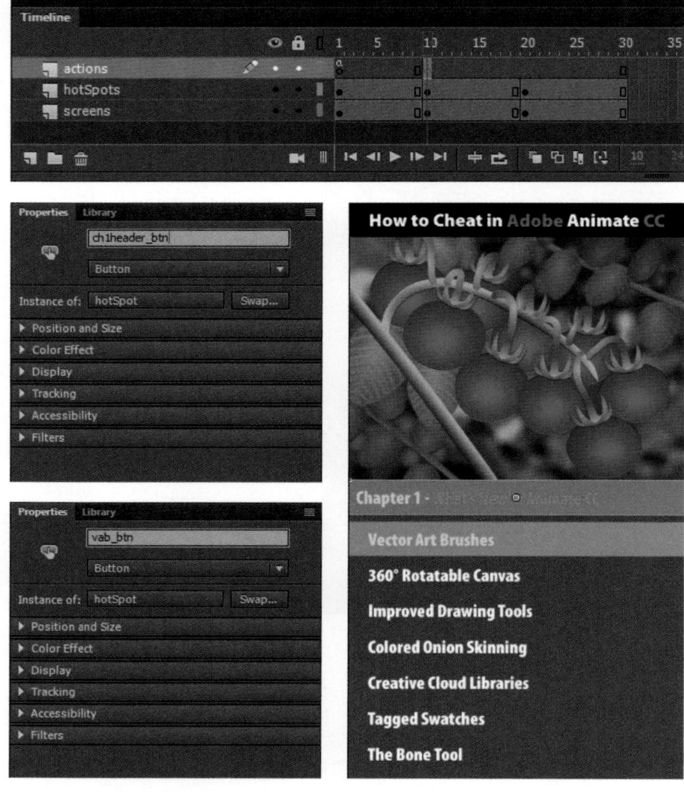

15 Insert a new keyframe on the actions layer at frame 10. Select the invisible button over the Chapter 1 header and enter "ch1header_btn" as its instance name. Select and name the other invisible button on this screen "vab_btn" in the Properties panel.

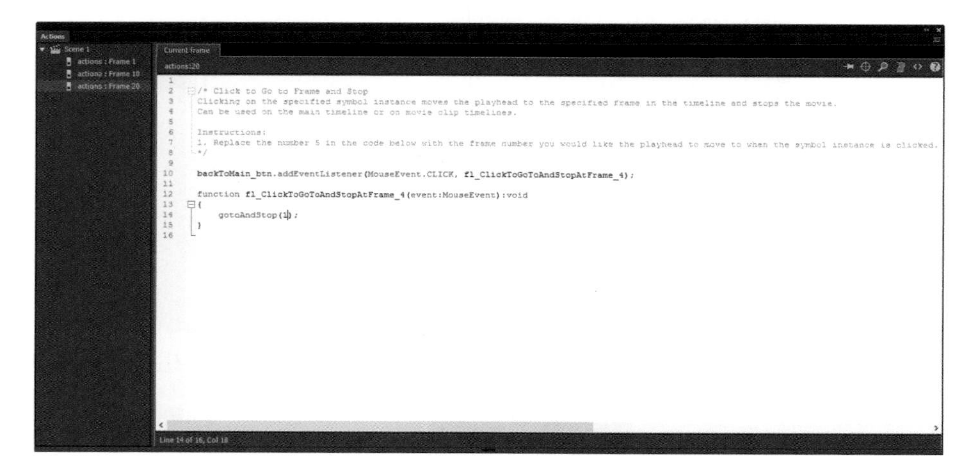

19 With backToMain_btn selected, double-click on Click to Go to Frame and Stop and change the frame number in line 14 to 1. Go to Control > Test or ⌘ ctrl Enter to test your prototype.

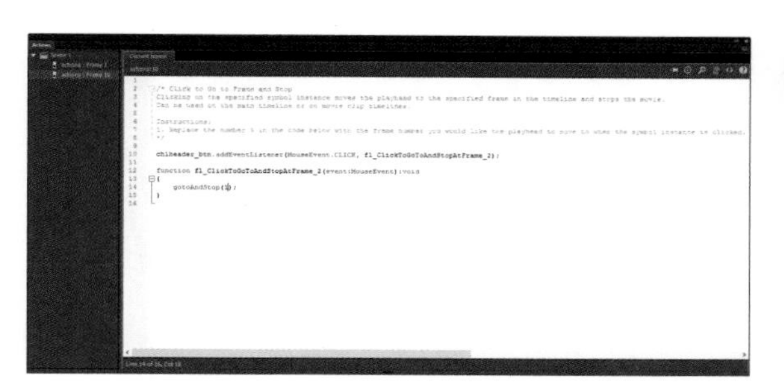

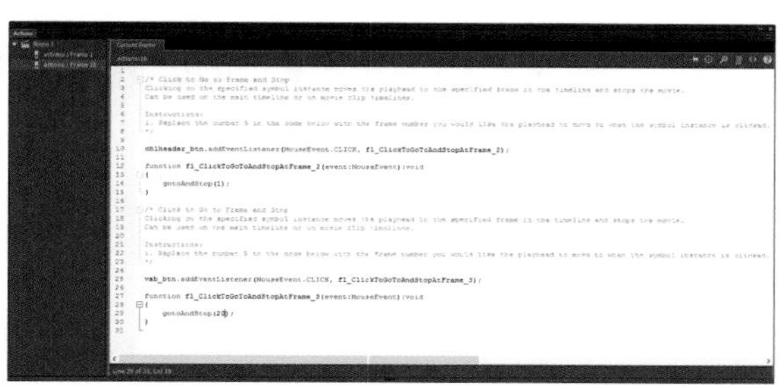

16 Select ch1header_btn and double-click Click to Go to Frame and Stop in the Code Snippets panel. Change the frame number in line 14 to 1 since clicking it should take you back to the beginning.

17 Select vab_btn and double-click Click to Go to Frame and Stop to add it. Change the frame number in line 29 from 5 to 20.

18 Add a new keyframe at frame 20 on the actions layer. Select the invisible button over the header and give it "backToMain_btn" as its instance name.

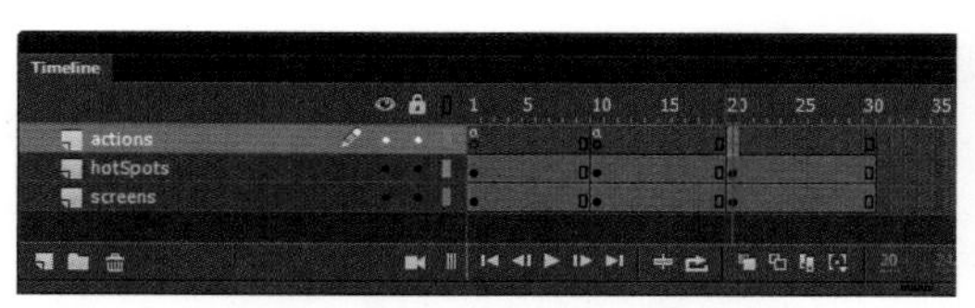

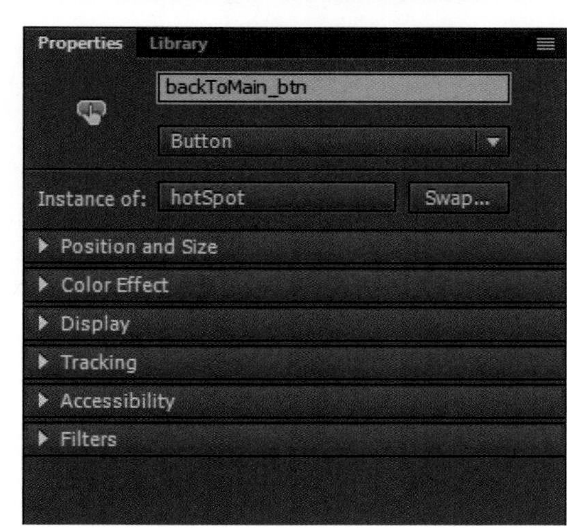

How to Cheat in Adobe Animate CC

Vector Art Brushes

Similar to Art Brushes in Illustrator, the new vector art brushes in Animate open up a world of creativity by applying a vector shape to a path. Use them to access specific shapes to be applied to a custom stroke, to recreate the appearance of various mediums, to generate banners or dividers, or to imagine your own creative uses.

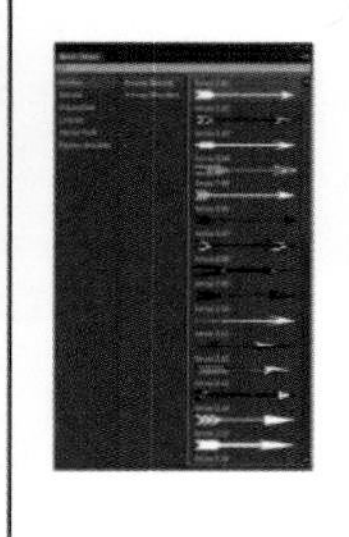

1. Animate comes with several styles of vector art brushes ready for use that include arrows, simulated artistic mediums, banners, and all sorts of shapes and patterns.

HOT TIP

Using Code Snippets not only automatically applies the code you need, but the commented descriptions can help you learn more about what the code does in case you want to learn to do the scripting yourself.

A Sweet Look Back on Trying Something New

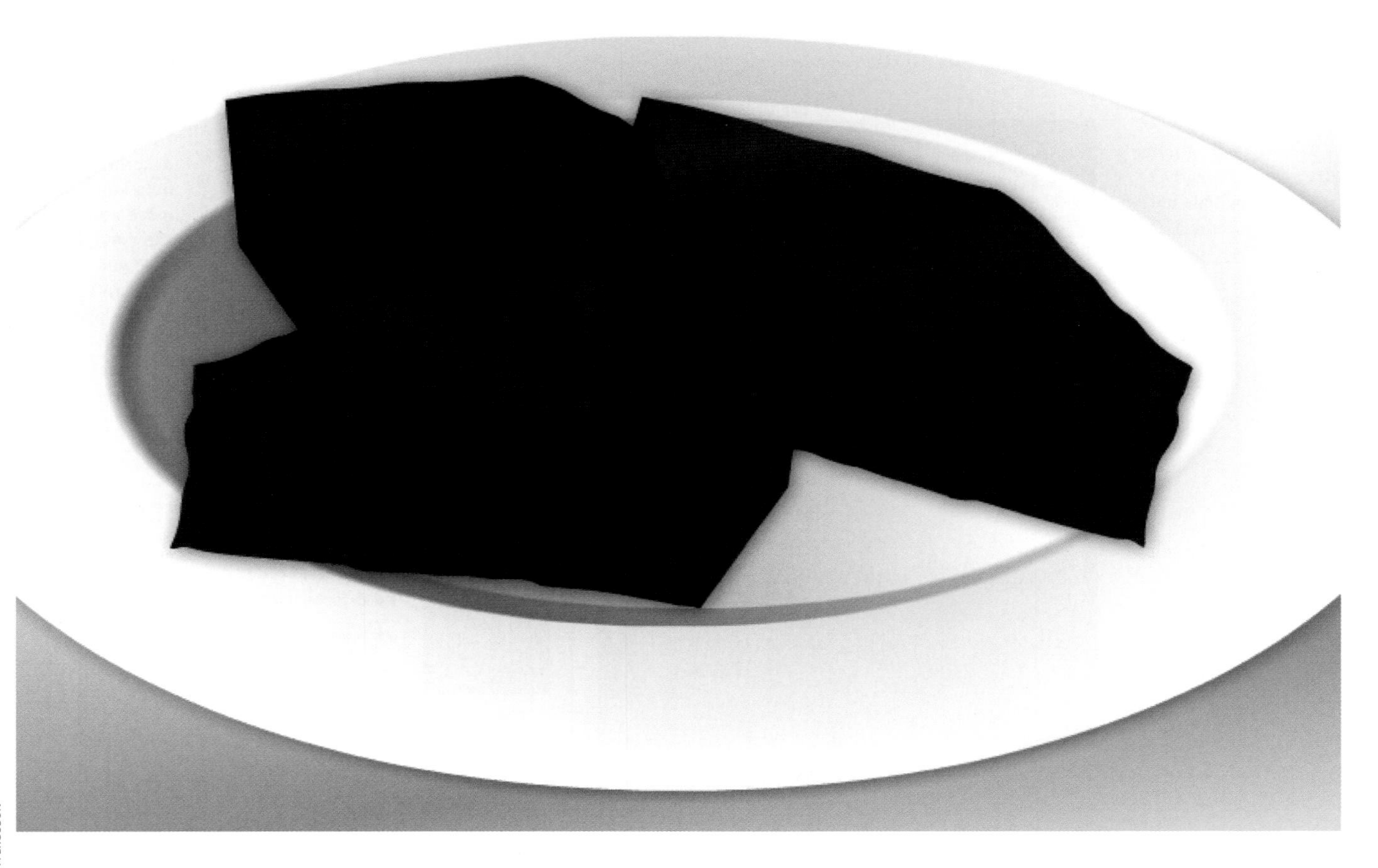

I MADE BROWNIES: VECTOR ILLUSTRATION: MYRA FERGUSON

I REMEMBER ONE DAY BACK IN GRADE SCHOOL COMING HOME AND DESPERATELY CRAVING brownies. This hunger for chewy, chocolatey goodness was, of course, of the after-school-desperation variety. In school we had been working on projects where we were learning that if we followed the instructions, we should eventually arrive at the desired result. Brownie mixes have instructions. I decided to go for it and make brownies! Did I mention I was a latchkey kid? So understand this activity was completely unsupervised.

I got out a box of brownie mix. I read what all the necessary ingredients were and made sure I had them before I started. Egg, water, vegetable oil. Check. Preheat the oven. Check. Mix ingredients. Check.

As I worked my way down the directions to the bottom of the box, I came across a step that stumped me: For high altitude add flour. High altitude? My young mind knew that altitude had something to do with height. Then I thought about where I lived—on a long street on an incline. Even though we were about halfway up the incline—or rather, large hill—I determined it was sufficiently elevated to qualify. Of course, that hill was in St. Louis, Missouri, an entire 465′ above sea level.

So I added the flour, poured the batter in the pan, put the pan in the heated oven, and waited.

When the timer buzzed, I excitedly opened the oven door! And then I'm sure a look of confusion and disappointment swept over my face. I pulled out a pan of fluffy chocolate cake. I made cake? The good news was I hadn't burnt it—that would be a cooking technique I'd unintentionally explore later. It turned out to be edible. It just wasn't ooey gooey chewy brownies.

Maybe the outcome of my endeavor wasn't what I had expected, but I believe there are several lessons to be learned from it that can be applied to any attempt at making something new:

1. Even when following someone else's steps, you always bring a part of yourself into the mix.
2. Sometimes when you intend to make one thing, you figure out—whether you mean to or not—a way to make something else.
3. Experiments don't always turn out the way you want, but even from mistakes there is something you can learn.

For sure after this experience, I learned what altitude meant and figured out that I did not live in an area considered to be high altitude—even despite our location on that hill. I learned not to add flour to a brownie mix unless I don't have a cake mix and actually intend to make cake. I also discovered it was possible to eat cake without frosting as I was not about to try my hand at a frosting recipe that required making it from scratch.

Whenever you're considering trying something new (especially with the exercises in this book), I hope you'll think about my cakey brownies and go for it. Don't expect perfection, but look forward to a sweet reward.

UPDATE: After our move to Colorado, I was reminded that I can now safely add the flour.

■ This chapter is divided into six stages. Stage 1 will show you how to dynamically create a character that can be controlled to run left, right, and jump. In subsequent stages, you will then add more characters, interactivity, parallax scrolling, particle effects, sound, and even touch controls for mobile devices.

10 Interactivity

ALL OF THIS DESIGN AND ANIMATION IS FUN, BUT THAT'S only one side of the Animate authoring experience. Interactivity is an entirely different, yet complementary side of Animate that when combined with design, makes for a compelling experience.

This chapter features a step-by-step process of how to design and code a game entirely within Animate CC. Thanks to the talented David Crawford, we will show you how to create a character that can be controlled in real time using keyboard shortcuts and ultimately how to build a complete interactive game.

David Crawford is the brain child behind PercyPea Ltd., a company that specializes in advanced online, single-player, multiplayer, Facebook, and iPhone game development, with games reaching hundreds of millions of players.

www.percypea.com

Stage 1

STAGE 1 WILL SHOW YOU HOW to set up a Movie Clip symbol with your animated character and how to include ActionScript to spawn multiple instances of this symbol. In addition, we will add ActionScript that provides the viewer the ability to control one of the Movie Clips with keyboard commands. Press the left arrow key, and the character will run to the left. Press the right arrow key, and the character will run to the right. Press the space bar, and the character will jump. You will create all of this interactivity using a single FLA file to keep things as simple as possible for nondevelopers. In later stages we will add more advanced features, but for now let's keep it simple.

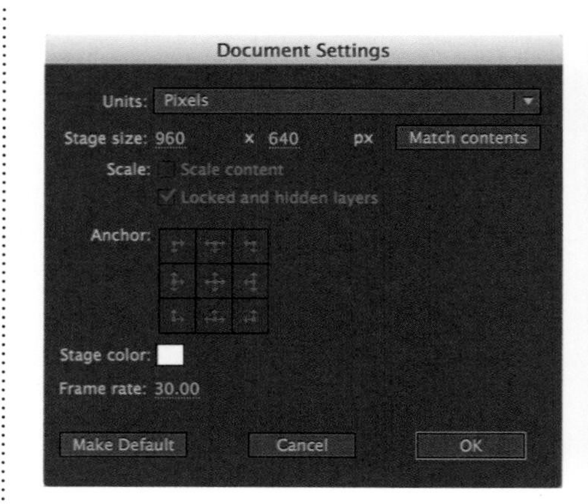

1 Start with creating new 960 × 640 FLA. This resolution is the native iPhone 4 screen size. It's also a reasonably good size for a web-based game (well maybe a bit too large, but not to worry, the game will scale nicely).

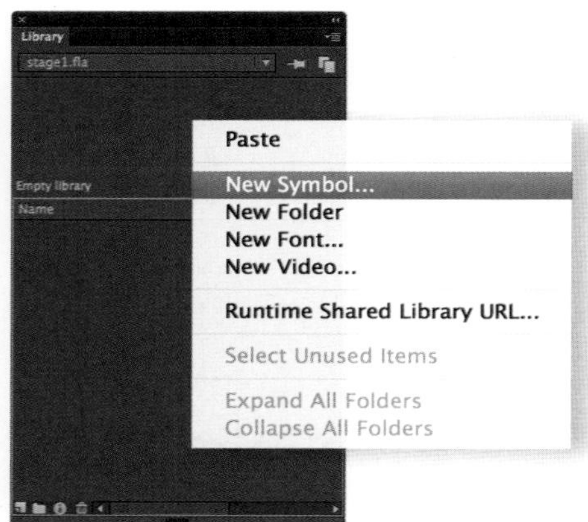

2 Create new Movie Clip for your character. For future coding ease, make the Movie Clip so that the 0,0 center point of the Movie Clip is at ground level and pretty much in the center of the symbol. If the center point is at the bottom and center, the character won't move too much when we flip him horizontally.

If you would prefer, included in the source files is **stage0.fla** which contains our preanimated Ninja. If you use this file rather than creating your own, simply jump to step 7.

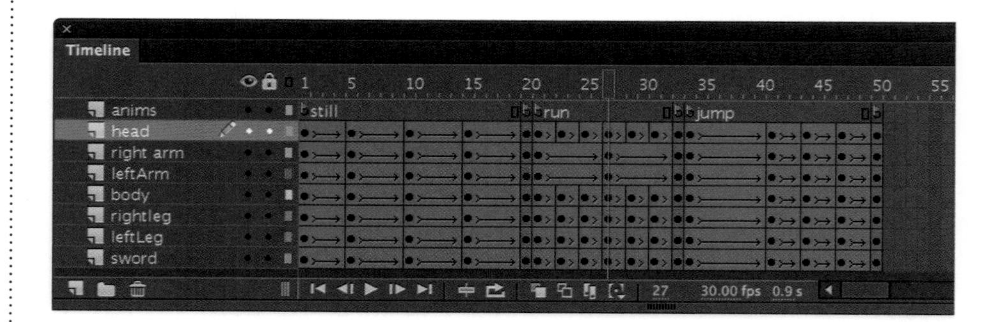

5 The Movie Clip Timeline contains three animations: still, run, and jump. Even though the first animation is still, there is some subtle motion of the character moving slightly back and forth. This state is often referred to as an idle animation and used for whenever the character is stationary. The subtle motion provides the illusion of breathing or resting, which looks more realistic, especially if your character is required to run a lot in what may be a side-scrolling game.

6 Create a new layer above all other layers and insert blank keyframes at the beginning and end of each animation cycle. In frame 1, add the label **still** and in the last frame of the still animation add the label **still_end**. Repeat these steps by adding labels to the other two animation cycles with descriptive names such as **run, run_ end, jump,** and **jump_end**. These labels will be used to control each animation dynamically when ActionScript is added later on.

3 Draw your character with each body part inside its own Movie Clip on its own layer. Before animating, give each body part an instance name in the Properties panel, **head**, **body**, **rightarm**, **leftarm**, **rightleg**, **leftleg**, and **sword**. Note the crosshairs that represent the center point of the symbol near the character's feet are located as instructed in the previous step.

4 Create three animations: a still, run, and jump. You can use tweens, keyframes, or a combination of both. Most importantly, make sure the start and end frames are the same for each animation that needs to loop.

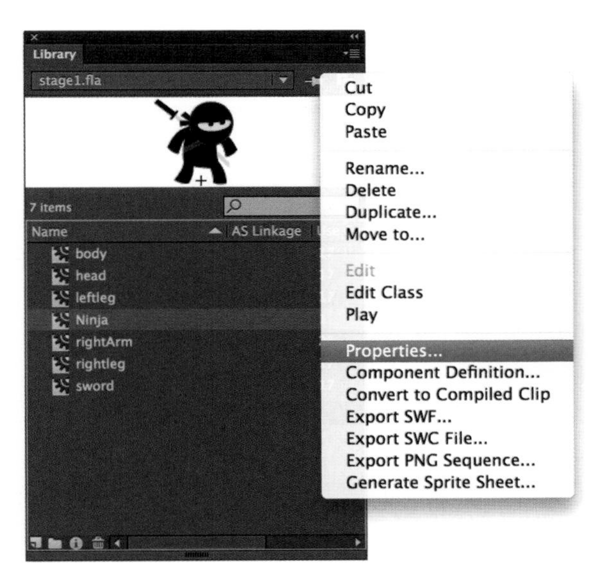

7 In the library is the **Ninja** Movie Clip. Right-click over it and select Properties from the context menu.

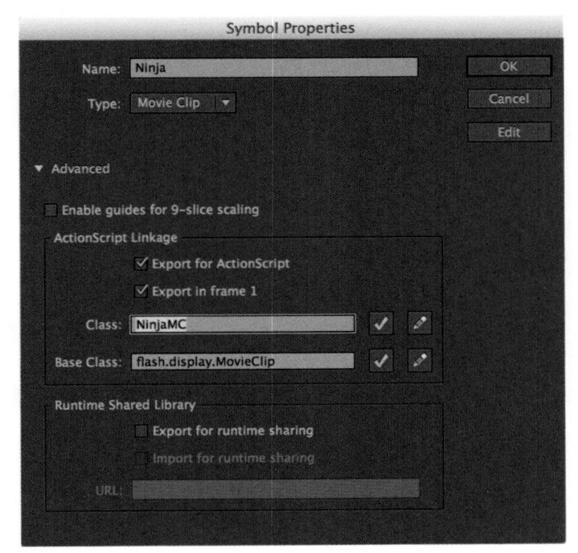

8 Open Advanced options and click the Export for ActionScript. By default the Class name will match the name of our Movie Clip; however, let's change that to **NinjaMC**. Assigning a Class name for ActionScript linkage automatically sets up the Properties of the Movie Clips so that we can access it via ActionScript and place as many instances of the ninja on screen as desired. Because we are now going to place the character on the screen programmatically, make sure you don't have your ninja already on screen in the main Timeline.

HOT TIP

Entering a Class name to a Movie Clip requires right-clicking over the Movie Clip in the library, clicking Advanced, and subsequently clicking the "Export for ActionScript" check box. A quicker way of assigning a Class name for export to ActionScript is to double-click in the empty space in the "AS Linkage" column next to the Movie Clip in the library. You can then immediately type in the Class name you want to use and the appropriate check boxes will have been checked automatically.

SHORTCUTS
MAC WIN BOTH

Stage 1 (cont.)

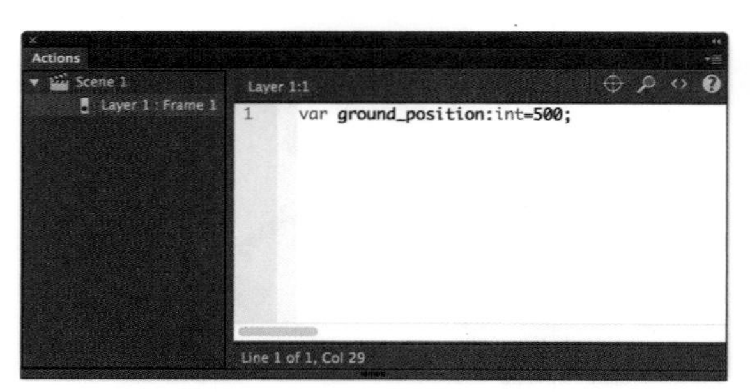

9 In your main scene, which should be a nice big empty Stage, add the first line of code into frame 1. Open the Actions panel by going to Window > Actions. Click on the empty keyframe in frame 1 in the Timeline and type the following code into the Actions panel:

```
var ground_position:int=500;
```

This code defines where the character will be placed on the Stage when the file is published to the SWF format and played in the Flash Player.

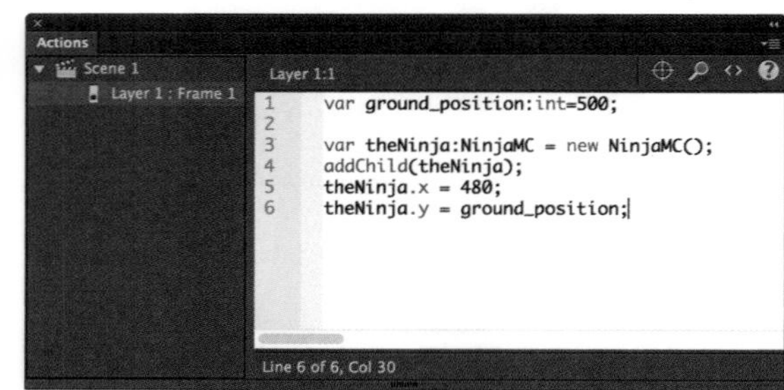

10 Let's add the code that will generate the character from the Movie Clip in the Library:

```
var theNinja:NinjaMC = new NinjaMC();
addChild(theNinja);
theNinja.x = 480;
theNinja.y = ground_position;
```

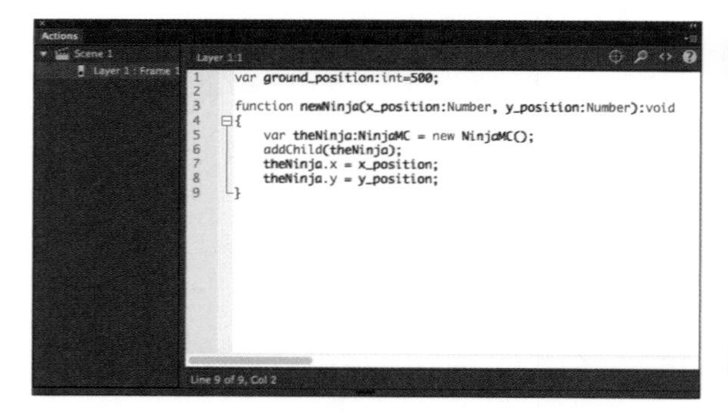

13 We will create a **newNinja** function that provides us with the ability to create an instance of our NinjaMC Class and then tell it where on the Stage it should be positioned. We will set up the function so that we can add some values to it.

```
function newNinja(x_position:Number,
y_ position:Number):void
{
var theNinja:NinjaMC = new NinjaMC();
addChild(theNinja);
theNinja.x = x_position;
theNinja.y = y_position;
}
```

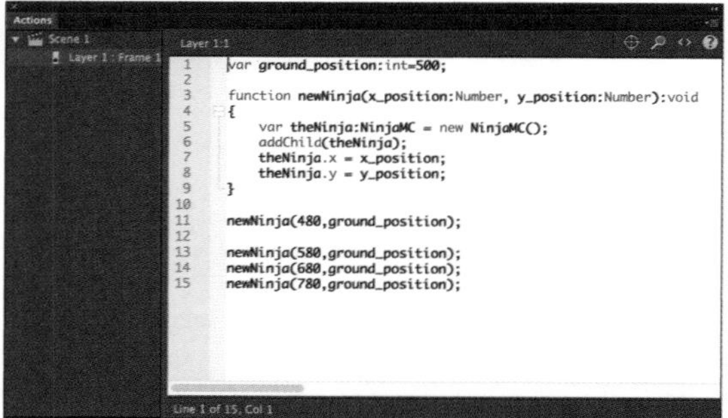

14 To call the function, we just need to write the line: **newNinja(480,ground_position);**

For every new ninja, we could then add:

```
newNinja(580,ground_position);
newNinja(680,ground_position);
newNinja(780,ground_position);
```

But once again, there's a more efficient way to add multiple instances of this Movie Clip in the next step.

11 Test the Animate movie by going to Control > Test Movie > In Animate. You should now see **theNinja** in the middle of the screen, playing through all of his animations. So far, so good. Let's add more ninjas!

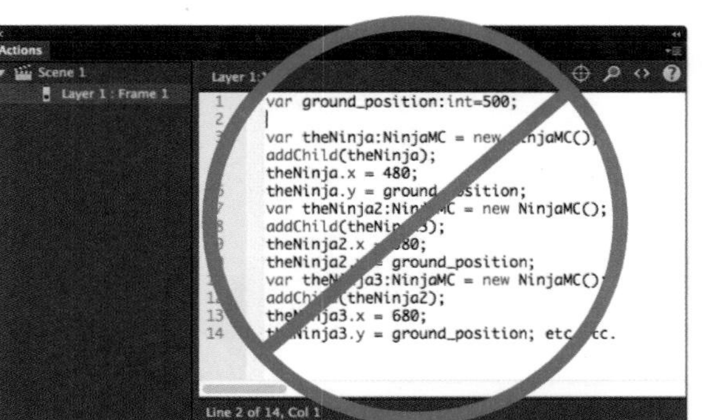

12 As intuitive as it may seem, instead of taking the previous code and duplicating it for each new ninja we want on the screen, let's make the code into a nice simple function that we only need to write once. The function will allow us to call upon it as many times as we want. The above image shows how not to write code that duplicates the character. It's not necessarily wrong. There are better and more efficient ways to use ActionScript.

```
var ground_position:int=500;

function newNinja(x_position:Number, y_position:Number):void
{
    var theNinja:NinjaMC = new NinjaMC();
    addChild(theNinja);
    theNinja.x = x_position;
    theNinja.y = y_position;
}

for(var a:int = 1; a <= 10; a++)
{
    var randomX_Position:Number = Math.random()*960;
    newNinja(randomX_Position, ground_position);
}
```

15 Add the following code that creates a convenient loop that will add 10 ninjas and place them at a random **x** position on the Stage.

```
for(var a:int = 1; a<=10; a++)
{
var randomX_Position:Number = Math.random()*960;
newNinja(randomX_Position, ground_position);
}
```

Test the movie to see the code spawn 10 instances of the Movie Clip containing the character playing through each of the animations inside its Timeline.

16 But we don't want the animations to loop like this! Let's continue by making the still animation simply loop by itself. To loop just the **still** animation, we will need to control the Movie Clips' Timeline—more specifically, the frames in between the **still** and **still_end** frame labels.

HOT TIP

When creating a function, we can set up values that get passed to it. In the case of our newNinja function we pass to it *x* and *y* position values for our ninjas.

The function itself calls them x_position and y_position and simply assigns them to our new ninja as *x* and *y* coordinates.

When we call the function we pass a random number for the x_position but the same ground_position value for the y_position. Changing only the x_position means all our ninjas will have the same *y* position, but it will be very unlikely that any share the same *x* position.

Stage 1 (cont.)

IN OUR NEWNINJA FUNCTION, WE NEED TO ADD SOME CODE to the Ninja itself to automatically loop its animation when it reaches the end of the Timeline inside the Ninja symbol. There is an undocumented feature in Animate where we can add function calls at certain frames. When using this method, frame numbers actually start from 0, rather than 1 as in the Timeline, so you need to remember to always subtract 1 from the frame number where you want to go to.

Furthermore, we actually want to go to the frame labeled still_end, so we can't very well say *goto "still_end"- 1*, as that will just confuse poor Animate.

Thankfully there is a quick fix. We simply tell our NinjaMC to go to the frame still_end then grab the real frame number for that frame, subtract 1 from it, and use the **addFrameScript** command with that number. The command addFrameScript unfortunately doesn't allow you to pass values into functions, so we can't directly call the **gotoAndPlay** command passing in still, but a simple fix is to give our ninja a new function, which doesn't need any values to be passed but then simply calls **gotoAndPlay("still");**.

Finally, we then add a bit of code to set the ninja back to playing its animation from the first frame.

17 So our **newNinja** function should look like this:

```
function newNinja(x_position:Number, y_position:Number):void
{
var theNinja:NinjaMC = new NinjaMC();
addChild(theNinja);
theNinja.x = x_position;
theNinja.y = y_position;
theNinja.loopStill = function()
{
theNinja.gotoAndPlay("still")
}
theNinja.gotoAndStop("still_end");
theNinja.addFrameScript(theNinja.currentFrame-1, theNinja.
loopStill); theNinja.gotoAndPlay(1);
}
```

20 We squeeze the above run and jump lines in before the **gotoAndPlay(1)** line, and at the bottom put in **theNinja.running=false;** as follows:

```
theNinja.jumpFinished = function()
{
if (theNinja.running)
{
theNinja.gotoAndPlay(theNinja,"run")
}
else
{
theNinja.gotoAndPlay(theNinja,"still")
}
}
theNinja.gotoAndStop("jump_end"); theNinja.
addFrameScript(theNinja.currentFrame-1, theNinja.jumpFinished);
theNinja.running=false;
```

18 But what about the run and jump parts of our animation? For the run, we simply do something similar to the still:

```
theNinja.loopRun = function()
{
theNinja. gotoAndPlay("run")
}
theNinja.gotoAndStop("run_end"); theNinja.
addFrameScript(theNinja.currentFrame-1, theNinja.loopRun);
```

19 For the jump, though, this isn't a looping animation, and when it's finished, we need to go back to either still or run animations. We will give our ninja a new property called running which later we will set to be either true or false, and jump will simply check that value.

```
theNinja.jumpFinished = function()
{
if (theNinja.running)
{
theNinja.gotoAndPlay("run")
}
else
{
theNinja.gotoAndPlay("still")
}
}
theNinja.gotoAndStop("jump_end"); theNinja.
addFrameScript(theNinja.currentFrame-1, theNinja.jumpFinished);
```

21 So now we have 10 ninjas on screen all looping their still animations and also set up to loop their run animations and return to either still or run from their jump animation. But what good is it if we don't know which of the 10 ninjas is you, the player! No good at all. Back where we created our newNinja function, you will see the word **:void** at the end of the first line. This first line tells Animate that when the function is called not to bother returning any information. We can easily change it so that instead we actually return that particular ninja we have just created.

```
function newNinja(x_position:Number,
y_position:Number):NinjaMC
{
var theNinja:NinjaMC = new NinjaMC();
addChild(theNinja);
theNinja.x = x_position;
theNinja.y = y_position;
theNinja.loopStill = function()
{
theNinja.gotoAndPlay("still")
}
theNinja.gotoAndStop("still_end");
theNinja.addFrameScript(theNinja.currentFrame-1, theNinja.
loopStill);
theNinja.loopRun = function()
{
theNinja.gotoAndPlay("run")
}
theNinja.gotoAndStop("run_end");
theNinja.addFrameScript(theNinja.currentFrame-1, theNinja.
loopRun);
theNinja.jumpFinished = function()
{
if (theNinja.running)
{
theNinja.gotoAndPlay("run")
}
else
{
theNinja.gotoAndPlay("still")
}
}
theNinja.gotoAndStop("jump_end");
theNinja.addFrameScript(theNinja.currentFrame-1, theNinja.
jumpFinished);
theNinja.gotoAndPlay(1);
theNinja.running=false;
return theNinja;
}
```

HOT TIP

Not only can functions be used to perform a little section of code over and over again, they can also be set up to return bits of information we may want.

On this page we are setting up our newNinja function to simply return the reference to the new ninja we have just created.

We next see how we can use this reference to pick out our own personal ninja from the crowd.

Stage 1 (cont.)

22 Now, after the loop of 10 ninjas, we can have an extra line where we create our 11th ninja, **player**. From this point forward our ninja will always be known as **player** to the rest of the code.

```
var player:NinjaMC = newNinja(480,ground_position);
```

23 Now let's make our ninja move! Each key on your keyboard has its own unique **keyCode**, for example, the **left** cursor key's code is **37**. We don't need to know these codes, as we can look them up in Animate's built-in Keyboard Class. The left cursor key is **Keyboard.LEFT**. There are lots of ways to assign key press actions to each key. I like to use a simple Array:

```
var keyPressedActions:Array = new Array();
```

26 We now need to create our functions that we've already started to assign to key presses. For now, in our move left and move right functions we'll simply subtract 20 pixels from the player's Ninjas *x* position when moving left, and add 20 when moving right. We'll also remember to set the **running** property to true, so when it comes to jumping we'll know if it's a run, jump, or still jump. You'll see that we also tell our Ninja Movie Clip to go to (and play) the run animation. We only tell it to run if the ninja previously wasn't running; otherwise the code would always go to the first frame of the run animation and not loop.

```
function moveLeft():void
{
    player.x -= 20;
    if(!player.running)
    {
        player.running=true;
        player.gotoAndPlay("run");
    }
}
function moveRight():void
{
    player.x += 20;
    if(!player.running)
    {
        player.running=true; player.
        gotoAndPlay("run");
    }
}
```

27 Our stopMoving function simply sets our ninja to go back to the **still** animation and also marks that it is no longer running.

```
function stopMoving():void
{
    player.running=false;
    player.gotoAndPlay("still");
}
```

30 Typically, when a user presses a key, the user expects to start doing something. While the key is held down, continue doing that something. Then when the key is released, stop doing that something. For example, pressing and holding the right arrow key, you would expect your ninja to move right and continue to do so until you release the right arrow. So how can we make the ninja start, continue to stop with just the above **press** and **release** functions, when we don't have a **hold** function, too? We can't! We now create possibly the most important piece of code for our game—what we will call the **gameLoop**. We will listen for a special event called ENTER_FRAME, which actually gets dispatched every single frame—so many, many times per second (depending on your swf frame rate, of course!).

```
stage.addEventListener(Event.ENTER_FRAME, gameLoop);
function gameLoop(e:Event):void
{
//check if key is continued being pressed and then do stuff
}
```

24 We then map function calls to the keys:

```
keyPressedActions[Keyboard.LEFT] = moveLeft;
keyPressedActions[Keyboard.RIGHT] = moveRight;
```

25 We also need an array for when our keys are released:

```
var keyReleasedActions:Array = new Array();
keyReleasedActions[Keyboard.LEFT] = stopMoving;
keyReleasedActions[Keyboard.RIGHT]= stopMoving;
```

28 We need to tell Animate to listen for key presses. Then depending on the key that is pressed, get the ninja to do something. We also need Animate to listen for when that key is then released to then stop the ninja from whatever it was doing. So... we add two listeners!

```
stage.addEventListener(KeyboardEvent.KEY_DOWN,
keyPressed);
stage.addEventListener(KeyboardEvent.KEY_UP,
keyReleased);
```

29 We then need to make the keyPressed and keyReleased functions; we will populate them shortly.

```
function keyPressed(theKey:KeyboardEvent):void
{
    //Do stuff
}
function keyReleased(theKey:KeyboardEvent):void
{
    //Stop doing that stuff
}
```

31 So we have our three listeners that will handle the keyboard: **pressed**, **continued being pressed** (our game loop), and **released**. For simplicity, we are going to actually deal with pressed and released. We will simply record which key was pressed and then **delete** that recording when we release. To keep track of which key is pressed, we make another new array to **record** or **store** that information. Place this line of code up above your keyPressed function.

```
var keys:Array = new Array();
```

32 We then modify our keyPressed function as follows:

```
function keyPressed(theKey:KeyboardEvent):void
{
keys[theKey.keyCode] = true;
}
```

and keyReleased function to this:

```
function keyReleased(theKey:KeyboardEvent):void
{
delete keys[theKey.keyCode];
if(keyReleasedActions[theKey.keyCode])
keyReleasedActions[theKey.keyCode]();
}
```

HOT TIP

The ENTER_ FRAME event is a powerful event to use.

Each and every frame of your 12, 24, 60, or even 120 fps that you set your swf to publish will dispatch this event.

By listening to it you can then run code to move and animate things just as if you had animated them using keyframes on the Timeline.

It's possible to create just one listener for this event to handle all possible looping code in your game.

Stage 1 (cont.)

33 You will notice the keyReleased function has an extra line which is needed to call our keyReleasedAction immediately. We don't have to call the keyPressedAction when we press the key, as our gameLoop handles that. In our gameLoop code, we examine our keys array to see if any of the values are true (i.e., a key has been recorded that it is pressed and still down) and then trigger the corresponding **keyPressedActions**. Because we are storing function references in our keyPressedActions Array, we can trigger these functions by simply putting () at the end.

```
function gameLoop(e:Event):void
{
for(var key:String in keys)
{
if(keyPressedActions[key]) keyPressedActions[key]();
}
}
```

34 You should now be able to test your game and move your ninja! So what's the first problem we see when moving our ninja left and right? That's right, he doesn't face left (assuming we drew him facing right by default). Thankfully the fix is simple. We flip the ninja horizontally via code when moving left and back again when moving right. To flip him, we adjust the Ninja's **scaleX property:** -1 means flip it, 1 means default. Our **moveRight** and **moveLeft** functions become:

```
function moveLeft():void
{
    player.x -= 20;
    if(!player.running)
    {
        player.running=true;
        player.gotoAndPlay("run");
    }
    player.scaleX = -1;
}
function moveRight():void
{
    player.x += 20;
    if(!player.running)
    {
        player.running=true;
        player.gotoAndPlay("run");
    }
    player.scaleX = 1;
}
```

37 Now, the trouble is because we already get our player to start off at our ground_position of 500. If we test the game, we see our player fall off into oblivion. We therefore add another bit of code to make sure that our player ninja never can go lower than the ground. We also will tell our player ninja that it is not jumping (because we know it is on the ground).

```
function gameLoop(e:Event):void
{
    for(var key:String in keys)
    {
    if(keyPressedActions[key]) keyPressedActions[key]();
    }
    player.y += player.gravity;
    if(player.y > ground_position)
    {
    player.y = ground_position;
    player.jumping=false;
    }
}
```

38 Of course now when we test the game, it looks like nothing has happened now as our ninja starts at ground level anyway. Let's add our jump function! First, let's assign a key to perform the jump command. Let's use the A key.

```
keyPressedActions[Keyboard.A] = jump;
```

Now the function:

```
function jump():void
{
    if(!player.jumping)
    {
    player.gotoAndPlay("jump");
    player.gravity = -8;
    player.jumping = true;
    }
}
```

To help keep the code organized, we add this block up near the moveleft and moveright functions, and also set the keyPressedAction for A with our two left and right settings.

35 Let's add jumping! First we need to understand what a "jump" really is. In the real world, we are constantly pulled down by gravity. By jumping, we are exerting a force from the floor and fighting with the pull of gravity. Once our feet have left the floor, we have no ability to continue to fight gravity, so eventually it wins and pulls us back down. Currently in our game, we have no concept of gravity. Our ninjas all look like they are on the ground simply because we've positioned them all at the same *y* value, using our ground_position variable. So the first thing first, let's actually emulate gravity! Don't worry if physics isn't your favorite subject; we're going to keep things very simple and not accurately simulate real-world gravity. Back in our newNinja function, we are going to add a new variable to our ninjas:

```
theNinja.gravity = 10;
```

36 We now go to our gameLoop function and code it so that this gravity value is constantly added to our player's *y* position (e.g., the player is always pulled down screen by the gravity, each frame/loop).

```
function gameLoop(e:Event):void
{
    for(var key:String in keys)
    {
    if(keyPressedActions[key]) keyPressedActions[key]();
    }
    player.y += player.gravity;
}
```

a "+=" bit of code is a quick way of writing **player.y = player. y + player.gravity;**

39 Finally, you see that we are setting our ninja's gravity from the default 10 to −8. We come to this value because it's half the number of frames in our jump animation (more on this below). There's one extra thing we now need to do. Setting the ninja's gravity to −8 means that in each game loop 8 is subtracted from the player's *y* position, therefore causing the ninja to float upward. To correct the floating, we simply add an extra line at the end of the game loop:

```
player.gravity += 1;
```

This single line of code means that for each loop, the gravity value gets greater by 1 and eventually becomes a positive number, which therefore will start moving the ninja back down to earth. Increasing the gravity value by 1 and starting the gravity setting at −8 when we jump means that gravity will be 8 by the time the ninja is back on the ground. The gravity setting will have changed a total of 16 times, which matches our frame count of the jump animation.

40 If we test the game, we will see now the ninja does jump; however, it is a puny and weak jump. To give our ninja more vigor, we just need to play around with the 1 value at the end of player.gravity+=1 and the −8 value that is set when we press jump. The rule is if we double the −8 value, then also double the 1 value. However, you will also find that you may want to change these values independently if you find that your ninja's jump animation is actually over too soon or carries on after he's landed. Alternatively, here is when you can adjust your ninja jump animation so that it fits better. For our ninja with a 16-frame jump animation, let's try the following:

```
player.gravity =- 40;
```

and

```
player.gravity += 5;
```

Perfect! :)

HOT TIP

In the jump function in steps 37 and 38 we use a new property of our player, "jumping." This property is added so that when we press our key to jump, the jump only happens once, rather than constantly while the key is held down. We just need to set player.jumping back to false when the ninja has landed, as only then do we want him to be able to jump again.

Stage 1 (cont.)

41 The full code for Stage 1 looks like this:

```
var ground_position:int = 500;

function newNinja(x_position:Number, y_position:Number):NinjaMC
{
            var theNinja:NinjaMC = new NinjaMC();
            addChild(theNinja);
            theNinja.x = x_position;
            theNinja.y = y_position;
            theNinja.loopStill = function()
            {
            theNinja.gotoAndPlay("still")
            }
            theNinja.gotoAndStop("still_end");
            theNinja.addFrameScript(theNinja.currentFrame - 1, theNinja.loopStill);
            theNinja.loopRun = function()
            {
            theNinja.gotoAndPlay("run")
            }
            theNinja.gotoAndStop("run_end");
            theNinja.addFrameScript(theNinja.currentFrame - 1, theNinja.loopRun);
            theNinja.jumpFinished = function()
            {
            if (theNinja.running)
            {
            theNinja.gotoAndPlay("run")
            }
            else
            {
            theNinja.gotoAndPlay("still")
            }
            }
            theNinja.gotoAndStop("jump_end");
            theNinja.addFrameScript(theNinja.currentFrame - 1, theNinja.jumpFinished);
            theNinja.gotoAndPlay(1);
            theNinja.running=false;
            theNinja.gravity = 10; return theNinja;
}
for(var a:int = 1; a <= 10; a++)
{
            var randomX_Position:Number = Math.random()*960;
            newNinja(randomX_Position, ground_position);
}

var player:NinjaMC = newNinja(480,ground_position);
var keyPressedActions:Array = new Array();
keyPressedActions[Keyboard.LEFT] = moveLeft;
keyPressedActions[Keyboard.RIGHT] = moveRight; keyPressedActions[Keyboard.A] = jump;

var keyReleasedActions:Array = new Array();
keyReleasedActions[Keyboard.LEFT] = stopMoving;
keyReleasedActions[Keyboard.RIGHT]= stopMoving;

function moveLeft():void
{
            player.x-=20;
            if(!player.running)
            {
                        player.running = true;
                        if(!player.jumping) player.gotoAndPlay("run");
            }
```

```
        player.scaleX = -1;
}

function moveRight():void
{
        player.x+=20;
        if(!player.running)
        {
                player.running = true;
                if(!player.jumping) player.gotoAndPlay("run");
        }
        player.scaleX = 1;
}

function jump():void
{
        if(!player.jumping)
        {
                player.gotoAndPlay("jump");
                player.gravity=-40;
                player.jumping=true;
        }
}

function stopMoving():void
{
        player.running=false;
        if(!player.jumping) player.gotoAndPlay("still");
}

stage.addEventListener(KeyboardEvent.KEY_DOWN, keyPressed);
stage.addEventListener(KeyboardEvent.KEY_UP, keyReleased);
var keys:Array = []
function keyPressed(theKey:KeyboardEvent):void
{
        keys[theKey.keyCode]=true;
}

function keyReleased(theKey:KeyboardEvent):void
{
        delete keys[theKey.keyCode];
        if(keyReleasedActions[theKey.keyCode]) keyReleasedActions[theKey.keyCode]();
}
stage.addEventListener(Event.ENTER_FRAME, gameLoop);
function gameLoop(e:Event):void
{
        for(var key:String in keys)
        {
                if(keyPressedActions[key]) keyPressedActions[key]();
        }
        player.y += player.gravity;
        if(player.y>ground_position)
        {
                player.y = ground_position;
                player.jumping=false;
        }
        player.gravity += 5;
}
```

Stage 1 is now complete!

HOT TIP

One final change that we make as shown in the code on this page is that we modify our moveRight and moveLeft functions so that our player ninja only does gotoAndPlay to run our animation if it's not actually jumping.

Stage 2

SO! WE'VE COMPLETED STAGE 1. WE KNOW HOW TO TAKE OUR ANIMATED CHARACTER, ATTACH MULTIPLE copies of it to the Stage via code, add basic code to control its animations, reference one in particular, and make it a playable character.

But we're still a long way off making a full game, and there are some things we'll have to do first to our existing code before continuing in our quest.

Right now, we stand at around 120 lines of code, give or take a few empty line spaces. We have a system set up to listen for keystrokes and an easy way to assign different functions and commands to those keys. We also have a nice GameLoop that is set up to manage everything. If we continue down this path, we are going to end up with many more lines of code, which will become harder and harder to manage. So, we are going to separate out our code into different files, files which are known as Classes.

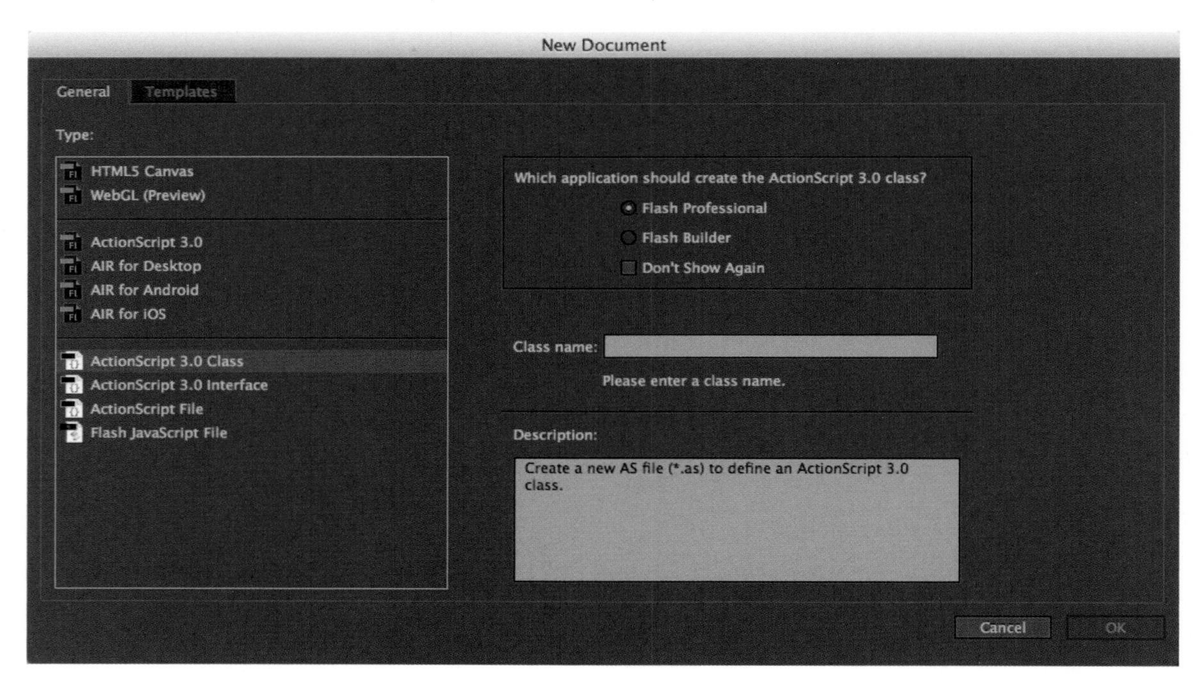

1 Our first Class! Go to File > New > ActionScript 3.0 Class, name it **Ninja** and save it in the same directory as the FLA file we created in Stage 1.

2 Now for the Ninja Class equivalent of our new Ninja function. It's similar, however a few places are changed over the function method in Stage 1. Put this code into our new Class:

```
package
{
        import flash.display.Sprite;
        public class Ninja extends Sprite
        {
                public var theNinja:NinjaMC
                public var running:Boolean;
                public var jumping:Boolean;
                public var gravity:Number;

                public function Ninja(x_position:Number, y_position:Number)
                {
                        theNinja = new NinjaMC(); addChild(theNinja);
                        x = x_position;
                        y = y_position;
                        theNinja.gotoAndStop("still_end");
                        theNinja.addFrameScript(theNinja.currentFrame - 1, loopStill);
                        theNinja.gotoAndStop("run_end");
                        theNinja.addFrameScript(theNinja.currentFrame - 1, loopRun);
                        theNinja.gotoAndStop("jump_end");
                        theNinja.addFrameScript(theNinja.currentFrame - 1, jumpFinished);
                        theNinja.gotoAndPlay(1);
                        running = false;
                        jumping = false;
                        gravity = 10;
                }
                public function loopStill():void
                {
                        theNinja.gotoAndPlay("still");
                }
                public function loopRun():void
                {
                        theNinja.gotoAndPlay("run");
                }
                public function jumpFinished():void
                {
                        if (running)
                        {
                                theNinja.gotoAndPlay("run");
                        }
                        else
                        {
                                theNinja.gotoAndPlay("still");
                        }
                }
        }
}
```

HOT TIP

You will notice that in front of all our variables and functions inside our Class, we have a new word "public." This word which means that the variable or function can be reached from any part of our code, such as our gameLoop, for example.

Although we won't be doing it in the course of making this game, it's also possible to use the word private instead of public. Making a variable or function private prevents other parts of code outside of the Class from accessing our values and more importantly changing them when perhaps we don't want them changed.

Stage 2 (cont.)

3 In Stage 1, in the main FLA Timeline code we have the following line:

```
var player:NinjaMC = newNinja(480, ground_position);
```

With our new Class, let's change this line to be these two lines:

```
var player:Ninja = new Ninja(480, ground_position);
addChild(player);
```

Let's also change our code that creates the 10 other ninjas to this:

```
for(var a:int = 1; a <= 10; a++)
{
	var randomX_Position:Number = Math.random()*960;
	var enemy:Ninja = new Ninja(randomX_Position, ground_position);
	addChild(enemy);
}
```

4 What we will do now, is move our **moveLeft**, **moveRight**, **stopMoving**, and **jump** functions to the new Ninja Class. We can cut them from the Timeline as they will be no longer needed there and paste them into our Ninja Class beneath the **jumpFinished** function. We need to add **public** before each **function** and remove most of the **player.** references. The ones which are **player.gotoAndPlay** however, we will replace with **theNinja.gotoAndPlay**.

```
package
{
	import flash.display.Sprite;
	public class Ninja extends Sprite
	{
		public var theNinja:NinjaMC
		public var running:Boolean;
		public var jumping:Boolean;
		public var gravity:Number;
		public function Ninja(x_position:Number, y_position:Number)
		{
			theNinja = new NinjaMC();
			addChild(theNinja);
			x = x_position;
			y = y_position;
			theNinja.gotoAndStop("still_end");
			theNinja.addFrameScript(theNinja.currentFrame - 1, loopStill);
			theNinja.gotoAndStop("run_end");
			theNinja.addFrameScript(theNinja.currentFrame - 1, loopRun);
			theNinja.gotoAndStop("jump_end");
			theNinja.addFrameScript(theNinja.currentFrame - 1, jumpFinished);
			theNinja.gotoAndPlay(1);
			running = false;
			jumping = false;
			gravity = 10;
		}
		public function loopStill():void
		{
			theNinja.gotoAndPlay("still");
		}
```

With these functions inside our Ninja Class, we need to make some minor modifications to our **keyPressedActions** and **keyReleasedActions** arrays.

Simply stick **player.** in front of all the function names as in the following:

```
keyPressedActions[Keyboard.LEFT] = moveLeft;
```

becomes

```
keyPressedActions[Keyboard.LEFT] = player.moveLeft;
```

```
public function loopRun():void
{
	theNinja.gotoAndPlay("run");
}

public function jumpFinished():void
{
	if (running)
	{
		theNinja.gotoAndPlay("run");
	}
	else
	{
		theNinja.gotoAndPlay("still");
	}
}

public function moveLeft():void
{
	x -= 20;
	if(!running)
	{
		running = true;
		if(!jumping)theNinja.gotoAndPlay("run");
	}
	scaleX=-1;
}

public function moveRight():void
{
	x+=20;
	if(!running)
	{
		running = true;
		if(!jumping)theNinja.gotoAndPlay("run");
	}
	scaleX = 1;
}

public function jump():void
{
	if(!jumping)
	{
		theNinja.gotoAndPlay("jump");
		gravity=-40;
		jumping=true;
	}
}

public function stopMoving():void
{
	running = false;
	if(!jumping) theNinja.gotoAndPlay("still");
}
	}
}
```

HOT TIP

In Stage 1, although we weren't directly using Classes, our NinjaMC in the library is actually a Class. Those eagle eyed will have spotted in the Symbol Properties panel that it uses a Base Class of "Movie Clip."

The MovieClip Class is known as a Dynamic Class, which means you don't have to declare the variables and functions that you want to add to it.

With our new Ninja Class, we do have to declare these values. Declaring them actually gives a nice performance boost though, as well as makes our code easier to manage and test, so it's a good thing.

SHORTCUTS
MAC WIN BOTH

Stage 2 (cont.)

SO, THAT WAS A CLASS EXAMPLE. However, because we want our ninja to exist in a 3D world, the Class is going to be a little bit different. Our Ninja Class isn't actually finished and won't work currently, but we will leave it for now because first of all we're going to set up our pseudo 3D engine. The first thing to create for any self-respecting 3D engine is a Camera! For our game and engine, we just need a very simple camera with just three properties: an **X**, a **Y**, and a **perspective.variable**. Despite having a 3D engine, we won't need a **Z** property as our Camera will never move into or away from our game (although for those brave enough, feel free to add this value and we'll drop some hints along the way as to how you could use it).

5 We create a new Camera Class. Note: we call our x and y properties **x3D** and **y3D** for reasons to be explained later.

```
package
{
	public class Camera
	{
		public static var x3D:Number = 480;
		public static var y3D:Number = 300;
		public static var perspective:int = 1000;
		public function Camera()
		{
		}
	}
}
```

As with our new Ninja Class, save this Camera Class into the same folder as our FLA.

Note that there is an important term "static" used when declaring our three properties/variables. In simple terms, what doesn't change about a static property or variable is its memory location, which makes it easier for the rest of our code to access these values.

This book isn't about coding ethics, so that explanation is all you need to know for now.

By default, we set our *x* value to 480 because this is half of our Animate game's width. For the *y* value, we use 300 because our **ground_position** is still 500. If we use 500 for the camera too, it will be as if the camera is actually sitting right on the ground and mean we're actually looking at our ninja's feet, which is fine from a distance but not when the ninja comes up close. At 300 we're just above our ninja's head. Perspective is a magical 1000. Why? Because 1000 works well.

In Stage 1, we just allowed left and right movement of our ninja, along the **X** axis, and jumping, using the **Y** axis. However, in the full game, we want to move our ninja into and out of the environment along the **Z** axis, using the up and down keys. As our ninja moves into the environment, he gets smaller giving a 3D effect.

It's not just our ninja that will have this 3D effect, but pretty much all of the characters and objects in the game will. Therefore, we want to code this 3D effect just once and allow all Classes to be able to use it if needed. We create a new Class which will be used as a base for all our other Classes: ninjas, blood splats, bunnies, etc.

Because we are now using a 3D world, we need to add the *z* coordinate. What's more, because our ninja will appear to be moving slower across the screen when he is far off in the distance, we no longer directly move the *x* and *y* values of our ninja. So we need some new *x* and *y* variables along with our *z*. We will use **x3D**, **y3D**, and **z3D**.

So let's create our new Class that all (or at least most of) our in-game objects will use as their Base. For this reason, we will call the Class **Base3D**.

We extend **Sprite** so that we can incorporate the native features for the Sprite object (i.e., its *x* and *y* values, the ability to scale it, add it to Stage, etc.).

6 Because in our 3D world, our objects will be scaled (using **scaleX** and **scaleY** properties) when they move in and out of the background, we can no longer set **scaleX** to be **1** or **-1** depending on if we want our ninja to face right or left. Therefore, we will create a new variable called **direction**.

In the **convert3D** function of this Class, those brave could try and combine their **Camera z3D** with the three **z3D** values if they felt up to the challenge.

```
package
{
	import flash.display.Sprite;
	import flash.display.MovieClip;

	public class Base3D extends Sprite
	{
		public var x3D:Number;
		public var y3D:Number;
		public var z3D:Number;
		public var direction:int;
		public var timeline:MovieClip;

		public function Base3D(x:Number, y:Number, z:Number = 1000)
		{
			x3D = x;
			y3D = y;
			z3D = z;
			direction = 1;
		}
		public function convert3D():void
		{
			x = (x3D - Camera.x3D)*(Camera.perspective/z3D)+480;
			y = (y3D - Camera.y3D)*(Camera.perspective/z3D)+320;
			scaleX=scaleY = (Camera.perspective/z3D);
			scaleX*=direction;
		}
	}
}
```

Again we will save this Class in the same folder as our FLA.

The **convert3D** function is where the magic happens. This function takes the *x*, *y*, and *z* 3D values of our object (in this case the Ninja) and converts them to on-screen *x* and *y* coordinates, as well as scaling the Ninja to give the illusion of depth. See how our new value **direction** is used right at the end to affect the **scaleX** value, which in turn will "flip" the ninja horizontally if needed. Finally, there's a Timeline variable, defined as a Movie Clip. We will want our Ninjas (and other Classes that extend **Base3D**) to be able to easily reference variables we still store in the Timeline. This Timeline variable will become our Timeline reference to be able to look up variables such as **ground_position** in our main FLA's Timeline.

Now that we have our **Base3D** Class, let's go back to our **Ninja Class** and modify it to make use of **Base3D**.

In our **Ninja Class**, change the line toward the top:
public class Ninja extends Sprite

to be
public class Ninja extends Base3D

Because **Base3D** manages our *x* and *y* coordinates, we can delete these lines from the Ninja Class. We also modify the default Ninja function to include **z_position;** we can even set it by default to be the **Camera.perspective** value, **1000**. By setting it to 1000, it means our Ninja will be the same size as if we weren't using 3D at all. I know that sounds a bit pointless, but bear with me to find out why. Finally, because the code in **Base3D** needs to do something too, we add this line at the end of the Ninja function:

super(x_position, y_position, z_position);

HOT TIP

Every Class that we will make must be saved with the same filename that the Class is called. It also must contain a function that matches the Class name, too.

You will see our Ninja.as file is our Ninja Class with a Ninja function. Our Base3D.as file is our Base3D Class with a Base3D function.

This Class name function is the first bit of code that will get run when you create a new instance of the Class.

As you will see with Camera though, the function doesn't necessarily have to do anything.

Stage 2 (cont.)

7 So the Ninja function of our Ninja Class now looks like this:

```
public function Ninja(x_position:Number, y_position:Number, z_position:Number = 1000)
{
	theNinja = new NinjaMC();
	addChild(theNinja);
	theNinja.gotoAndStop("still_end");
	theNinja.addFrameScript(theNinja.currentFrame 1, loopStill);
	theNinja.gotoAndStop("run_end");
	theNinja.addFrameScript(theNinja.currentFrame 1, loopRun);
	theNinja.gotoAndStop("jump_end");
	theNinja.addFrameScript(theNinja.currentFrame 1, jumpFinished);
	theNinja.gotoAndPlay(1);
	running = false;
	jumping = false;
	gravity = 10;
	super(x_position, y_position, z_position);
}
```

10 Next we need to modify our gravity code to affect **y3D** of player, instead of **.y**.

```
player.y3D += player.gravity;
if(player.y3D>ground_position)
{
	player.y3D = ground_position;
	player.jumping=false;
}
player.gravity += 5;
```

11 However, now that we have our Ninja Class extending **Base3D**, which in turn has the Timeline reference, we no longer need step 10's bit of code to happen in the main **gameLoop**. We need to create a new **loop** function inside our Ninja Class, and move the gravity stuff from our main **gameLoop** to our Ninja's internal loop. So actually, let's replace all that code in step 10 with this single line:

```
player.loop();
```

Then inside our Ninja Class, add the code:

```
public function loop():void
{
	y3D += gravity;
	if(y3D >= timeline.ground_position)
	{
		y3D = timeline.ground_position;
		jumping = false;
	}
	gravity += 5;
}
```

8 We also need to swap out our adjustments to **x** in the **moveLeft** and **moveRight** functions to be the new **x3D**. Remember we also have the new direction variable in **Base3D**, so we will swap the **scaleX = 1** and **scaleX = -1** lines to be **direction = 1** and **direction = -1**. Now we add **moveDown** and **moveUp** functions to our Ninja Class, which are similar to the **moveLeft** and **moveRight**, but instead of adjusting **x3D** we adjust **z3D**. Don't worry about direction as no horizontal flipping needs to happen here.

```
public function moveUp():void
{
	z3D+=20;
	if(!running)
	{
		running = true;
		if(!jumping) theNinja.gotoAndPlay("run");
	}
}
public function moveDown():void
{
	z3D-=20;
	if(!running)
	{
		running = true;
		if(!jumping) theNinja.gotoAndPlay("run");
	}
}
```

9 We've finished changing our Ninja Class for now. Make sure you have saved it, and then let's go back to the main code in our Timeline of our FLA and add some keyboard actions to call our new **moveUp** and **moveDown** functions.

```
var keyPressedActions:Array = new Array();
keyPressedActions[Keyboard.LEFT] = player.moveLeft;
keyPressedActions[Keyboard.RIGHT] = player.moveRight;
keyPressedActions[Keyboard.UP] = player.moveUp;
keyPressedActions[Keyboard.DOWN] = player.moveDown;
keyPressedActions[Keyboard.A] = player.jump;

var keyReleasedActions:Array = new Array();
keyReleasedActions[Keyboard.LEFT] = player.stopMoving;
keyReleasedActions[Keyboard.RIGHT] = player.stopMoving;
keyReleasedActions[Keyboard.UP] = player.stopMoving;
keyReleasedActions[Keyboard.DOWN] = player.stopMoving;
```

12 The last thing we need to do now, is when we create our player in the Timeline, we just add:

```
player.timeline = this;
```

Finally, to test our 3D effect we actually need to call our **convert3D** function on our ninja. We also need to call convert3D on our 10 **enemy** ninjas too, which is currently very hard, because in our **for loop** where we create the 10 ninjas, we don't actually store any easy reference to them, so that we can later call their **convert3D** function in the same way as we could call **player.convert3D** for our player. So we will come up with a solution. Due to the way our engine works, we know we need to call convert3D to all of our on-screen 3D objects (ninjas). Therefore, we will create a new **Array** to store these objects. We will call our array **Objects3D** as unfortunately we can't name an array starting with a number.

Right at the top of our Timeline code, add

```
var objects3D:Array = new Array();
```

13 Then we modify our for loop for adding our enemies:

```
for(var a:int = 1; a <= 10; a++)
{
   var randomX_Position:Number = Math.random()*960;
   var enemy:Ninja =
   new Ninja(randomX_Position, ground_position);
   addChild(enemy);
   enemy.timeline = this;
   objects3D.push(enemy);
}
```

As with our player, we pass the enemy a reference to our main Timeline, so they, too, can look up variables.

The final addition to our Timeline code, after we create player, is

```
objects3D.push(player);
```

Stage 2 (cont.)

14 At the bottom of the gameLoop function after the **player.loop()** line, add the following four lines of code:

```
var a:int;
for(a = 0; a < objects3D.length; a++)
{
        objects3D[a].convert3D();
}
```

Now test your game, and after all this extra code we've done you should see everything looks pretty much exactly like Stage 1.... um... OK... so what's the point of all this extra code? Don't worry, we haven't been wasting time. Try using the down arrow key ⬇ to control your ninja. You will see you can now move him closer to the camera. Use the up arrow key ⬆ and he'll move farther away. There is of course one problem. As you move your ninja farther away from the camera, he doesn't visually move behind the enemy ninjas, rather he just gets smaller.

16 Let's add the ability of the camera to track our Player if he runs off screen. In the Camera Class, underneath the empty **Camera** function, add

```
public static function track(player:Ninja):void
{
    var scaleValue:Number = perspective/player.z3D;
    var edgeDistance:Number = (280-100*
    scaleValue)/scaleValue;
    if(x3D < player.x3D-edgeDistance)
       x3D = player.x3D-edgeDistance
    if(x3D>player.x3D+edgeDistance)
       x3D=player.x3D+edgeDistance
}
```

Then in our **gameLoop** just after the **player.loop()** line and before the **objects3D.sortOn** line put

```
Camera.track(player);
```

17 The second to last thing we need to sort with our ninja is that we need to limit how close to the camera he can come and also how far off into the distance he can run. You may have spotted that if you keep down pressed, your ninja will not only run straight to the camera, but then somehow do a magic trick and start running on an invisible ceiling away from the camera. Not good. Let's fix it! In the Ninja Class, in the **moveUp** function where we have **z3D+=20** we add a little "if" statement beforehand:

```
if(z3D<5000)
        z3D+=20;
```

and in moveDown:

```
if(z3D>500)
    z3D-=20;
```

15 We need to now add some depth management. The method we will use isn't the most optimized, but it is the most simple and does the job well. In the gameLoop function before our for loop from step 14, where we call **convert3D()**, we need to sort all our **3D Objects** by their depth, which just happens to be their *z* value (**z3D**). The **z3D** value is a Numeric value, and we want to sort it from highest to lowest (descending), so we add the single line of code:

```
objects3D.sortOn("z3D", Array.NUMERIC | Array.DESCENDING);
```

Now, inside our new for loop from step 14, immediately underneath the **objects3D[a].convert3D();** line, we add

```
setChildIndex(objects3D[a],a)
```

This line sets the display ordering of our ninjas to the Stage so that the ones in the distance are drawn first and the rest on top. Test the movie now, and you will see you can run in front and behind the ninjas. Yay. But uh oh! You may notice that some of our ninjas flicker. This flickering happens because they all have the same z3D value at the moment, so when we do our array sort sometimes ninja 1 will be in front of ninja 2, and other times ninja 2 will be in front of ninja 1. Don't worry. We will fix this later by giving our ninjas their own z3D position. In the final game, it's very unlikely two ninjas will share the same z3D position and be close enough to overlap, so it won't be a problem.

18 To complete this stage, we are going to position our enemy ninjas at different depths. In our Timeline code, in the **for** loop where we create our 10 ninjas, let's change and add the new **randomZ_Position** line and modify the line that creates the ninjas so that the complete **for** loop looks like this:

```
for(var a:int = 1; a <= 10; a++)
{
        var randomX_Position:Number = Math.random()*960;
        var randomZ_Position:Number = Math.random()*1000+1000;
        var enemy:Ninja = new Ninja(randomX_Position, ground_position, randomZ_Position);
        addChild(enemy);
        enemy.timeline = this;
        objects3D.push(enemy);
}
```

Stage 2 is now complete!

Stage 3

CURRENTLY BOTH OUR ENEMY and player Ninjas use the same **Ninja.as Class**. Up until this point, using the same Class has worked fine. However, we now are going to add some differences to our **Ninjas**, both visually and code-wise. In the same way as our **Ninja Class** extends **Base3D** but adds lots of extra functionality, we can make two new Classes, one **Player** and one **Enemy**, which both extend our **Ninja Class** but then add even more functionality.

1 Let's start Stage 3 by making two new identical Classes, the only difference being their Class names. As always, save these in the same folder as your FLA:

Player.as

```
package
{
    public class Player extends Ninja
    {
        public function Player(x_position:Number, y_position:Number, z_position:Number=1000)
        {
            Super(x_position, y_position, z_position);
        }
    }
}
```

Enemy.as

```
package
{
    public class Enemy extends Ninja
    {
        public function Enemy(x_position:Number, y_position:Number, z_position:Number=1000)
        {
        super(x_position, y_position, z_position);
        }
    }
}
```

4 Next, inside our main Player function in the new Player.as Class, we add the line:

```
setColor(1);
```

In our Enemy Class, in our main Enemy function simply put

```
setColor(2);
```

5 We need to now make use of our new Player and Ninja **sub-Classes**. Let's go back to the Timeline and change our code a little to make new Player and new Enemy Instances instead of just new Ninjas.

Change our line where we create our player to the following:

```
var player:Player = new Player(480, ground_
position);
```

2 Let's differentiate the enemies from the hero ninja visually. We will keep our hero ninja in black but make our enemy ninjas red. The easiest way to assign different colors is to use two keyframes inside each of our ninja body parts. In the second keyframe we will fill the body parts in with red.

6 We also need to change our for loop that creates our 10 Enemy Ninjas:

```
for(var a:int = 1; a <= 10; a++)
{
    var randomX_Position:Number = Math.random()*960;
    var randomZ_Position:Number = Math.random()*1000+1000;
    var enemy:Enemy = new Enemy(randomX_Position,
    ground_ position,randomZ_Position);
    addChild(enemy);
    enemy.timeline = this;
    objects3D.push(enemy);
    enemies.push(enemy);
}
```

Also note, we've added an additional line of code. We now store a reference to our enemy in a new array called **enemies**, which of course needs creating first. So add the code to create this array just above our for loop. You should know how to create an Array on your own now. The reason we will create this new enemies array is so that when it comes to attacking, we just look in this array, rather than our complete **objects3D** array, to determine which (if any) enemies we will face.

3 Now, when we test the game all our ninjas, including our player, will flash rapidly between colors. So, let's go to our main Ninja Class and add the function below. Because both our new layer and Enemy Classes extend our Ninja Class, they will be able to have access to this function:

```
public function setColor(frame:int):void
{
        theNinja.rightarm.gotoAndStop(frame);
        theNinja.leftarm.gotoAndStop(frame);
        theNinja.leftleg.gotoAndStop(frame);
        theNinja.rightleg.gotoAndStop(frame);
        theNinja.head.gotoAndStop(frame);
        theNinja.body.gotoAndStop(frame);
}
```

7 Now, we actually have some bits of code still in our **Ninja Class** that our **Enemy Class** doesn't need to worry about, so these should really be moved to just our **Player Class**. These are the movement functions. Cut and Paste these functions and their code from the **Ninja Class** into our **Player Class**:

moveLeft
moveRight
moveUp
moveDown
stopMoving

Having fun yet? In the next step we'll start adding ninjas that will attack our hero ninja!

HOT TIP

If you have been using the Ninja Movie Clip provided in the stage0.fla, you will notice that there is no leftarm symbol in the library.

Instead the Ninja's left arm is actually the same Movie Clip as the rightarm but mirrored horizontally.

By giving it the instance name of leftarm it means that as far as our code is concerned, it's a completely separate object from the rightarm.

Stage 3 (cont.)

8 Currently our Ninja Movie Clip has three animation states: Still, Run, and Jump. In each of these states, we want it to be possible to perform an attack. One option could be to make three new animations, using the originals as a basis: **StillAttack**, **RunAttack**, and **JumpAttack**. However... what if we start an attack while still and then start running while the attack is still happening? Or what if we are running and press attack when the ninja steps onto his right foot, and then the next time, we want to start the attack when he's stepped onto his left foot? To think about and then make animations for all the possible combinations will take a lot of time. What's more, there would be a lot of code to correctly display the animation. So, we come up with a trick! We give our Ninja a third arm! This arm is complete with sword and contains a 20-frame animation of the arm reaching for the sword, swinging it, and then putting the sword away with extra blur for effect.

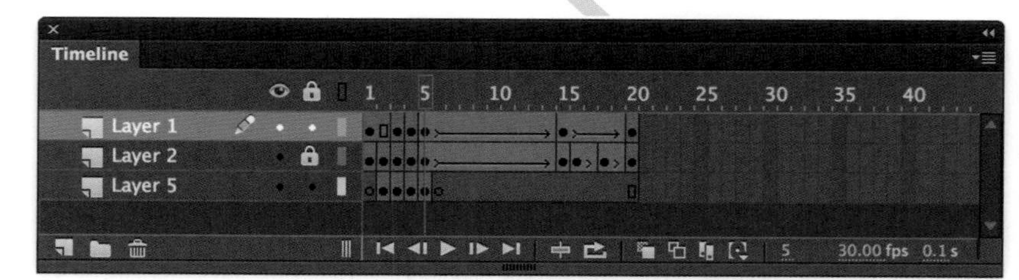

10 When our ninja jumps, we can see that if we keep our **A** key down, our ninja will constantly jump, which is perfectly fine.

However, with attacking we want the player to work for that attack and not have the ninja constantly swinging his sword if you just keep the **S** key down. Therefore, we will only trigger the next sword swing if the game has detected that the player has released the attack key after the previous sword swing.

Because this code is only related to our **Player** and not **Enemies** (they won't be controlled via the keyboard), we add a new variable to our **Player** Class, **attackKeyReleased**, and then set it to be true. So our Player Class will now look like this:

```
package
{
    public class Player extends Ninja
    {
        public var attackKeyReleased:Boolean;
        public function Player(x_position:Number, y_position:Number, z_position:Number=1000)
        {
            super(x_position, y_position, z_position);
            setColor(1);
            attackKeyReleased=true;
        }
        public function moveLeft():void
        {
            x3D -= 20;
            if (!running)
            {
                running = true;
                if (!jumping) theNinja.gotoAndPlay("run");
            }
            direction = -1;
        }
        public function moveRight():void
        {
            x3D += 20; if (!running)
            {
                running = true;
                if (!jumping) theNinja.gotoAndPlay("run");
            }
        direction = 1;
        }
}
```

9 We place this third **Arm** Movie Clip, which we will give the instance name **swordarm**, in roughly the same place inside our **Ninja** Movie Clip as the **rightarm**. With code, we now make sure that we only show either the **rightarm** or **swordarm** and never both (thus never making our ninja appear to have three arms). Also, we need to hide the sword on our ninja's back when the **swordarm** is in swing. In our main Ninja Class inside the Ninja function, let's add the following line of code:

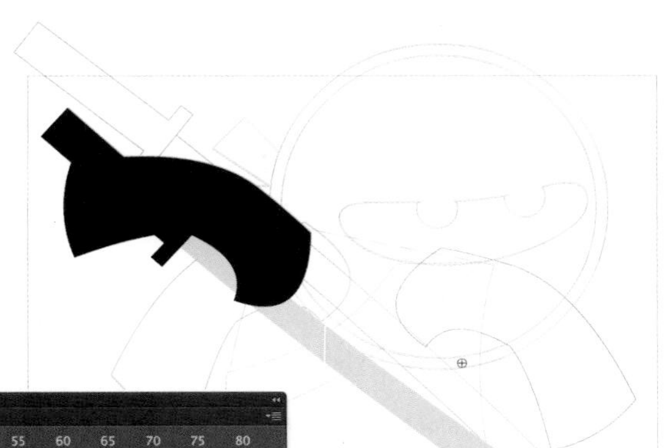

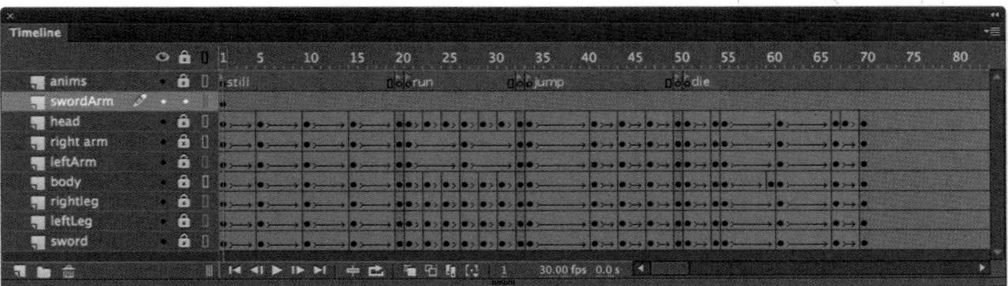


```
theNinja.swordarm.visible = false;

public function moveUp():void
    {
        if(z3D<5000)
            z3D += 20;
        if (!running)
        {
            running = true;
            if (!jumping) theNinja.gotoAndPlay("run");
        }
    }

    public function moveDown():void
    {
        if(z3D>500)
            z3D -= 20;
        if (!running)
        {
            running = true;
            if (!jumping) theNinja.gotoAndPlay("run");
        }
    }

    public function stopMoving():void
    {
        running = false;
        if (!jumping) theNinja.gotoAndPlay("still");
    }
}
```

Stage 3 (cont.)

11 In the next two steps we are going to modify our Ninja Class to add support for attacking.

When our Ninja performs an attack, we need to remember to hide the normal **rightarm** and show the new **swordarm**. Likewise, when the attack animation is over, we need to hide the **swordarm** and show the **rightarm** again. We also need to hide and show the sword on the Ninja's back appropriately.

So we add **addFrameScript**, a function call to the last keyframe of our **swordarm** animation so that we can change the visibilities. We make a new **attackfinished** function that makes the **swordarm** invisible and the **rightarm** and **sword** visible.

Currently our complete Ninja Class should look like the following:

```
package
{
	public class Ninja extends Base3D
	{
		public var theNinja:NinjaMC;
		public var running:Boolean;
		public var jumping:Boolean;
		public var gravity:Number;

		public function Ninja(x_position:Number, y_position:Number, z_position:Number = 1000)
		{
			theNinja = new NinjaMC();
			addChild(theNinja);
			theNinja.gotoAndStop("still_end");
			theNinja.addFrameScript(theNinja.currentFrame - 1, loopStill);
			theNinja.gotoAndStop("run_end");
			theNinja.addFrameScript(theNinja.currentFrame - 1, loopRun);
			theNinja.gotoAndStop("jump_end");
			theNinja.addFrameScript(theNinja.currentFrame - 1, jumpFinished);
			theNinja.swordarm.visible = false;
			theNinja.swordarm.addFrameScript(theNinja.swordarm.totalFrames-1, attackFinished);
			theNinja.gotoAndPlay(1);
			running = false;
			jumping = false;
			gravity = 10;
			theNinja.swordarm.visible = false;
			super(x_position, y_position, z_position);
		}

		public function setColor(frame:int):void
		{
			theNinja.rightarm.gotoAndStop(frame);
			theNinja.leftarm.gotoAndStop(frame);
			theNinja.swordarm.rightarm.gotoAndStop(frame);
			theNinja.leftleg.gotoAndStop(frame);
			theNinja.rightleg.gotoAndStop(frame);
			theNinja.head.gotoAndStop(frame);
			theNinja.body.gotoAndStop(frame);
		}

		public function loopStill():void
		{
			theNinja.gotoAndPlay("still");
		}
```

```
        public function loopRun():void
        {
                theNinja.gotoAndPlay("run");
        }

        public function jumpFinished():void
        {
                if (running)
                {
                        theNinja.gotoAndPlay("run");
                }
                else
                {
                        theNinja.gotoAndPlay("still");
                }
        }

        public function attackFinished():void
        {
                theNinja.swordarm.visible=false;
                theNinja.rightarm.visible=true;
                theNinja.sword.visible=true;
        }

        public function jump():void
        {
                if (!jumping)
                {
                        theNinja.gotoAndPlay("jump");
                        gravity = -40;
                        jumping = true;
                }
        }

        public function loop():void
        {
                y3D += gravity; if (y3D >= timeline.ground_position)
                {
                        y3D = timeline.ground_position;
                        jumping = false;
                }
                gravity += 5;
        }
    }
}
```

Stage 3 (cont.)

12 Because we will want both our Player and Enemies to be able to attack, we add our attack function to the Ninja Class. In this function, because the first five frames of the **swordarm** animation are the actual attack part and the remaining frames are a much slower animation of the ninja putting the sword away, we actually want our ninja to be able to reattack after frame 5. So we check to see if the **swordarm** animation is currently either on the first frame or on a frame after frame 5, before animating the sword attack. In the same way that our **attackFinished** function hides our **swordarm** and shows our normal **rightarm** and **sword**, the attack function hides the **rightarm** and sword and shows the **swordarm**. We also tell the **swordarm** to play the animation from frame 1.

```
public function attack():void
{
        if(theNinja.swordarm.currentFrame == 1 || theNinja.swordarm.currentFrame > 5)
        {
                theNinja.swordarm.gotoAndPlay(1);
                theNinja.swordarm.visible=true;
                theNinja.rightarm.visible=false;
                theNinja.sword.visible=false;
        }
}
```

15 Now let's start working with the enemy! Currently we are only calling **loop** on our ninja player. We now want to get all the enemy ninjas doing new things too, so we need to start calling **loop** for them. We already have a bit of code that loops through all of our Objects and runs a command on them **convert3D**, so we can delete our **player.loop** line and add **objects3D[a].loop();** in our for loop, like so:

```
for(a = 0; a < objects3D.length; a++)
{
        objects3D[a].loop();
        objects3D[a].convert3D();
        setChildIndex(objects3D[a],a)
}
```

16 Give the enemy a brain! We know that Enemy extends Ninja and that Ninja has a function in it called loop, which gets called every frame. Currently this function just handles gravity. However, we can add extra features to this function, features just for our Enemies, just like we did with our Player attack function in step 13. So in our Enemy Class, add this:

```
override public function loop():void
{
        super.loop();
}
```

19 But what about movement!? We need our enemy to **decide** on where he wants to run to and then make **steps** toward getting there. First of all, we need to add three new variables to the top of our Enemy Class:

```
public var steps:int;
public var xStep:Number;
public var zStep:Number;
```

20 Let's make a new **runTo** function inside our Enemy Class.

```
public function runTo(x:Number, z:Number):void
{

}
```

Note that we pass **x** and **z** (not **y**, as **y** is for jumping) to our **runTo** function.

13 So both our enemies and player now can attack, but we actually need some extra code for our **Player** to check if they are allowed to attack (have they let go of the attack key). Instead of rewriting a complete **attack** function in our Player Class, we can use the special keyword **override**, which means we can then add some extra code to the function that already exists in our Ninja Class. The other special keyword used is **super**, which means that we then perform all the code that exists in the Ninja Class attack function. Add this code to your Player Class:

```
override public function attack():void
{
	if(attackKeyReleased)
	{
		super.attack();
	}
	attackKeyReleased=false;
}
```

14 Finally we need to add to our Player Class a **stopAttacking** function. This function sets our **attackKeyReleased** Boolean to true, which means that our code will allow us to attack again.

```
public function stopAttacking():void
{
	attackKeyReleased = true;
}
```

Of course, what good are **attack** and **stopAttacking** functions if we have no keyboard command to trigger them? In our main Timeline code, we add **keyPressedAction** and **keyReleasedAction**. You should know where to place these:

```
keyPressedActions[Keyboard.S] = player.attack;

keyReleasedActions[Keyboard.S]= player.stopAttacking;
```

17 The **super.loop** means that we keep running our loop function with gravity-related code in our Ninja Class, rather than getting rid of it all together. But let's add some new code that will be unique to our enemies.

```
override public function loop():void
{
	if(int(Math.random() * 100) == 1) jump();
	super.loop();
}
```

18 The code in the previous step is basically saying that there is a 1 in 100 chance the enemy will **decide** to jump. Let's add this line in, too:

```
if(int(Math.random() * 100) == 1) attack();
```

If we test our game we'll see that we have red, random sword-swinging, jumping enemy ninjas. Yay.

21 Let's say our enemy ninja is currently standing at 100,100 in *x,z* coordinates. And we want to tell him to **runTo(500,200)**, possibly because that's where our player is. First, we have to work out the distance from where our enemy currently is to where he wants to go. We need a bit of Pythagorean Theorem. Inside our new **runTo** function, we add

```
var distanceX:Number = x-x3D;
var distanceZ:Number = z-z3D;
var totalDistance:Number = Math.sqrt(distanceX * distanceX + distanceZ * distanceZ);
```

HOT TIP

In the code in step 12, you will notice || in the line. This symbol is not the number eleven, instead it represents the word "or." In our attack function we are telling Animate to perform the commands if the swordarm is on frame 1, "or" the "swordarm" is on a frame greater than 5.

Sometimes you will see && instead of || which means "and."

Stage 3 (cont.)

22 Now that we know the **totalDistance** our enemy has to run, we can work out how many steps it will take him to get there. For now we are going to use a speed value of 20 (literally, moving **20** pixels per **gameLoop**), which is the same as our player Ninja. Continue putting this code inside our **runTo** function:

```
steps = totalDistance / 20;
```

We know how many steps our ninja will need to take to get from 100,100 to 500,200, so we then use that to work out each step (or distance) in *x* and *z* he will need to make per **gameLoop**:

```
xStep = distanceX / steps;
zStep = distanceZ / steps;
```

23 Finally, we need to work out which direction our enemy should be facing when moving:

```
direction = 1;
if(distanceX < 0) direction = -1;
```

and then set his animation to running:

```
running=true;
if(!jumping)theNinja.gotoAndPlay("run");
```

25 Since our enemy can **runTo** somewhere, let's actually tell him where to run. Make a function called **runToRandomPosition**. We always want our ninjas to be close to the player, so we make sure the random position the enemy runs includes our player's **x3D** and **z3D** coordinates. We then make sure our Enemy won't run too close or far from the camera. Finally we call the **runTo** function.

```
public function runToRandomPosition():void
{
	var x:Number = Math.random()*600-300 + timeline.player.x3D;
	var z:Number = Math.random()*400-200 + timeline.player.z3D;
	if(z > 5000) z = 5000;
	if(z < 300 ) z = 300;
	runTo(x,z);
}
```

26 Just like the jump and attack, we add the line to our loop function. Note this time we just use **50**, instead of 100 giving a 1 in 50 chance our Enemy will choose to run somewhere. We also want to only choose a new position to run to, if our Ninja isn't mid-jump.

```
if(int(Math.random() * 50) == 1 && !jumping) runToRandomPosition();
```

24 So our complete runTo function:

```
public function runTo(x:Number, z:Number):void
{
        var distanceX:Number = x-x3D;
        var distanceZ:Number = z-z3D;
        var totalDistance:Number = Math.sqrt(distanceX * distanceX + distanceZ * distanceZ);
        steps = totalDistance / 20;
        xStep = distanceX / steps;
        zStep = distanceZ / steps;
        direction = 1;
        if(distanceX < 0) direction = -1;
        running=true;
        if(!jumping)theNinja.gotoAndPlay("run");
}
```

27 We need to continue modifying our loop function to get our Enemy to take these new steps we have. We also need to tell our enemy ninja to go back to its **still** animation if it has taken all its steps and arrived at its goal. We only go to **still** if the enemy isn't also jumping. Our loop function is now

```
override public function loop():void
{
    if(int(Math.random() * 100) == 1) jump();
    if(int(Math.random() * 100) == 1) attack();
    if(int(Math.random() * 50) == 1) runToRandomPosition();
    if(steps > 0)
    {
        steps--;
        x3D += xStep;
        z3D += zStep;
    }
    else
    {
        if(running)
        {
            running=false;
            if(!jumping)theNinja.gotoAndPlay("still");
        }
    }
    super.loop();
}
```

28 Currently all our attack function does is handle the sword swinging. We don't yet see if the swing will hit an enemy or if the enemy's swing will hit the player. Before we can check for a hit, we are going to add some extra variables to our Ninja Class to simulate some very basic physics, namely, when a Ninja is attacked, we want it to be pushed away by the force of the sword swing. At the top of our Ninja Class, add these two lines:

```
public var forceX:Number = 0;
public var forceZ:Number = 0;
```

Then at the bottom of our loop function, we put

```
x3D += forceX;
z3D += forceZ;
forceX *= .8;
forceZ *= .8;
```

HOT TIP

Creating a force variable and then using the multiplication assignment operator means that whatever the force was, is now reduced to 80%.

Stage 3 (cont.)

29 Let's apply these forces to our enemies if our player successfully hits them. We loop through our enemies' array in the Timeline and test for all ninjas within a certain distance from the player. The ones that are close enough, we then affect their force. Place this code in our Player Class.

```
public function checkEnemies():void
{
    var attackReachX:int = 280;
    var attackReachZ:int = 150;
    var attackForce:int = 80;
    for each(var enemy:Enemy in timeline.enemies)
    {
        var distanceX:Number = enemy.x3D- x3D;
        var distanceZ:Number = enemy.z3D - z3D;
        if(distanceX * direction > 0 && Math.abs(distanceZ) < attackReachZ && Math.abs(distanceX) <attackReachX)
        {
            var angle:Number = Math.atan2(distanceZ,distanceX);
            enemy.forceX = attackForce * Math.cos(angle);
            enemy.forceZ = attackForce * Math.sin(angle);
        }
    }
}
```

*The distanceX * direction > 0 check in our if statement means we only look for ninjas our player is facing (not those close behind).*

31 We now modify the attack function in the Player Class again:

```
override public function attack():Boolean
{
        if(attackKeyReleased)
        {
                if(super.attack())
                        checkEnemies();
        }
        attackKeyReleased = false;
        return true;
}
```

32 Remember where we limited the Ninjas z3D value so that it couldn't go less than 300 or more than 500? Since we are now using **forceZ**, it's possible that the ninjas could exceed these values. We need to add some more code to our **loop** function of the Ninja Class so that the Ninjas appear to bounce off of this boundary. Note we shall also only reduce our force variables if our ninja is on the ground.

```
public function loop():void
{
        y3D += gravity; if(y3D >= timeline.ground_position)
        {
                y3D = timeline.ground_position;
                jumping = false;
        }
        gravity += 5;
        x3D += forceX;
        z3D += forceZ;
        if(z3D < 300 || z3D > 5000)
        {
                forceZ =-forceZ;
                z3D += forceZ;
        }
        if(y3D == timeline.ground_position)
        {
                forceX *= .8; forceZ *= .8;
        }
}
```

30 We need to **checkEnemies** when we know an attack has been performed. In our Ninja Class, we need to modify our attack function slightly so that it will return a true or false value depending on if the attack (sword swing) was made successfully.

```
public function attack():Boolean
{
	if(theNinja.swordarm.currentFrame == 1 || theNinja.swordarm.currentFrame > 5)
	{
		theNinja.swordarm.gotoAndPlay(1);
		theNinja.swordarm.visible=true;
		theNinja.rightarm.visible=false;
		theNinja.sword.visible=false;
		return true;
	}
	return false;
}
```

33 We can physically hit the enemy ninjas, but they never die. To be able to die you first need to live. Let's give the Ninja Class "life." We will also stun our Ninjas for a short time when we hit them so that ultimately they can't immediately hit us back as that would be mean! Make a second new variable **stunned**:

```
public var life:int;
public var stunned:int;
```

While we are in the Ninja Class in our loop function, add

```
stunned--;
```

Now in Enemy Class in the main Enemy function add

```
life = 3;
```

We'll give our Player life, too. A higher value makes him tougher, so in the Player Class in the main function add

```
life = 20;
```

In the **checkEnemies** function of the player, let's add a function call just below our **enemy.force** lines:

```
enemy.hurt();
```

34 Go back to the Ninja Class, and we will add our new **hurt** function:

```
public function hurt():void
{
		stunned = 15;
		life--;
		if(life ==0)
		{
				dead();
		}
}
```

Now add the "dead" function. In case our ninja was attacking when it died, we hide the swordarm and make the rightarm and separate sword visible.

```
public function dead():void
{
	theNinja.swordarm.visible=false;
	theNinja.rightarm.visible=true;
	theNinja.sword.visible=true;
	theNinja.gotoAndPlay("die");
}
```

Stage 3 (cont.)

35 We don't have a death animation, so we'll need to make one. Just a simple animation of our ninja falling over will suffice. If you make the animation fade out at the end, your ninja will disappear nicely. This fade can be handled via code, but a Classic Tween works just as well. The death animation was created using keyframes poses and Classic Tweens. No new assets for the ninja were necessary as the death animation uses the same body parts. Just animate the ninja collapsing to his knees first before keeling over and eventually lying flat against the ground. You may find the use of keyframes may work better than Classic Tweens or a combination of both. There's no right or wrong way to create this animation. Use your imagination and come up with something unique if you'd prefer.

36 As with the other animations, we need the frame labels **die** at the beginning of the death animation and then **die_end** in the final frame of the animation. As shown, a new layer was created just for Frame Labels to reside. Having a dedicated layer for labels is just for file management purposes.

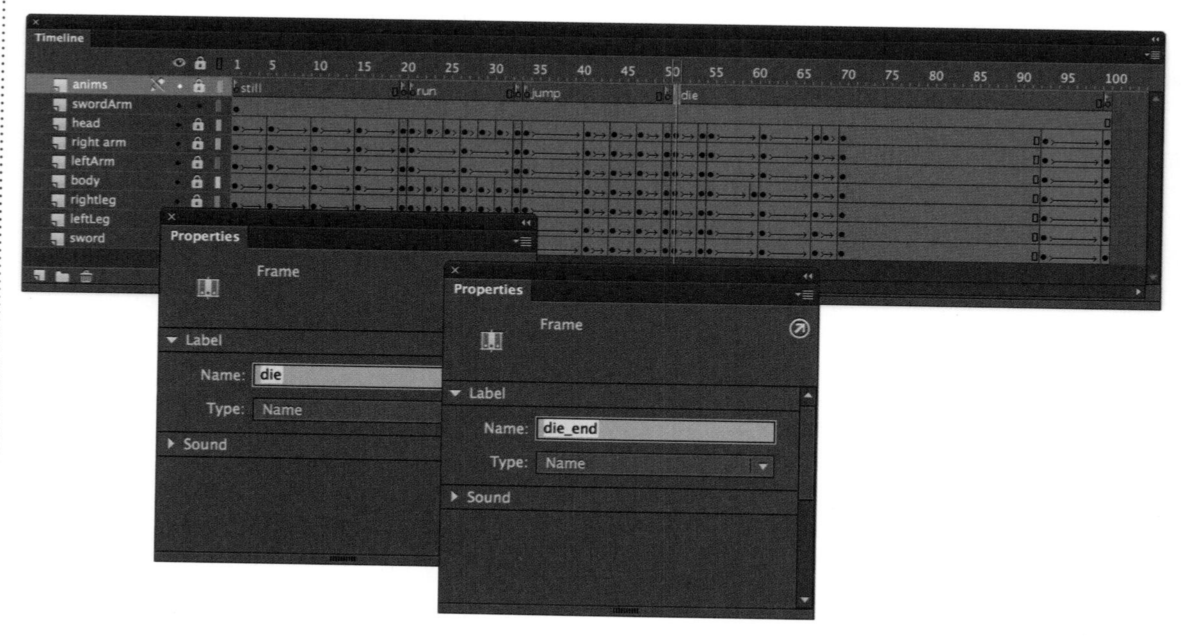

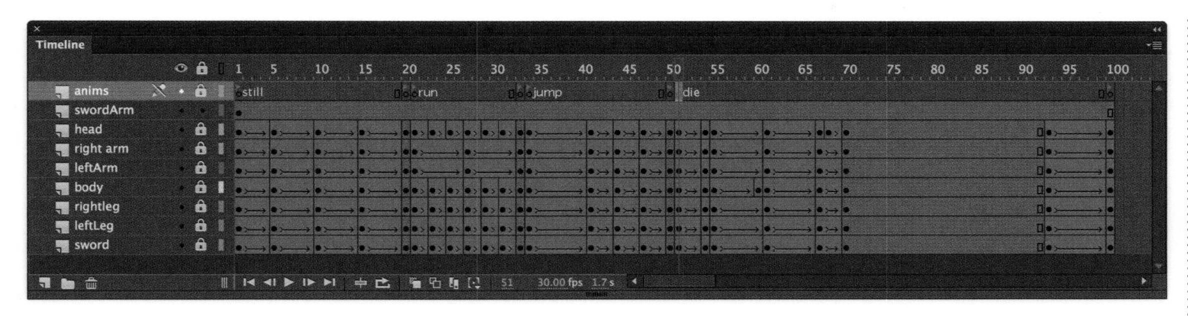

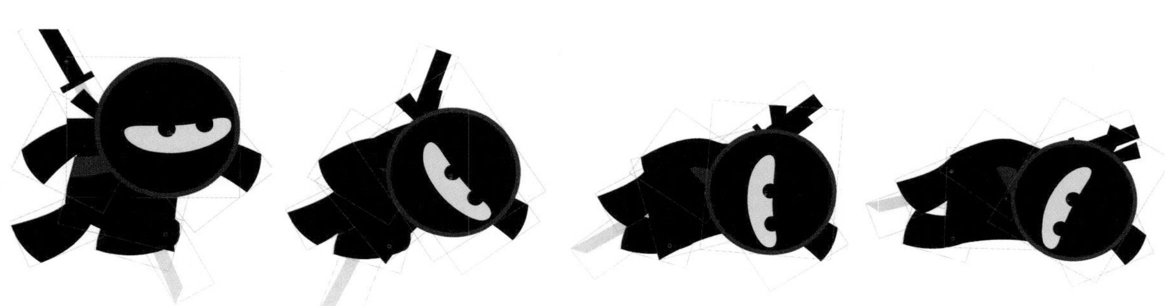

37 Because we have a new animation sequence in our ninja, we need to add the following two lines of code to our Ninja Class, place them just below the other **addFrameScript** lines in our main function:

```
theNinja.gotoAndStop("die_end");
theNinja.addFrameScript(theNinja.currentFrame-1, dieFinished);
```

Then add the following function:

```
public function dieFinished():void
{
        removeChild(theNinja);
        markForRemoval = true;
}
```

The function **removeChild** removes the Movie Clip from wherever it is sitting. We remove **theNinja** Movie Clip but not the actual Ninja Class just yet. Instead we mark it for removal. The **markForRemoval** is a new variable we haven't used before and want to define in our Base3D Class:

```
public var markForRemoval:Boolean;
```

38 Rather than removing Class instances straight away when we no longer need them, it's often good practice to do a "tidy up" of your instances right at the end of the main game loop. There should be no other code running associated with those Class instances, and therefore you are less likely to get any bugs when removing them. To remove everything that has **markForRemoval** set to "true," we add a new for loop right at the bottom of our **gameLoop** in the Timeline:

```
for(a = 0; a < objects3D.length; a++)
{
        if(objects3D[a].markForRemoval)
        {
                removeChild(objects3D[a]);
                objects3D.splice(a, 1);
                a--;
        }
}
```

When the ninja dies, not only does he visually disappear from the Stage, but he gets removed from the **objects3D** array, which means there is no longer any loop or **convert3D** code running for this Ninja. Because we have now removed all references to this Ninja, Animate will free-up some of the memory used, and your game will continue to perform well.

HOT TIP

If you make the animation fade out at the end where the ninja is in his last frame of dying, your ninja will disappear nicely. This fade can be handled via code, but we aren't going to do that as it's just as easy to apply a Classic Tween and some alpha to make him disappear.

Stage 3 (cont.)

39 When our Enemy has no life or when he is stunned, we don't want him to still randomly decide if he wants to jump, run, attack, etc. In the Enemy Class we add two **if** statements around this code in the **loop** function:

```
if(life > 0)
{
	if(stunned <= 0)
	{
		if(int(Math.random() * 100) == 1) jump();
		if(int(Math.random() * 100) == 1) attack();
		if(int(Math.random() * 50) == 1)runToRandomPosition();
		if(steps > 0)
		{
			steps--; x3D+= xStep;
			z3D += zStep;
		}
		else
		{
			if(running)
			{
				running=false;
				if(!jumping)theNinja.gotoAndPlay("still");
			}
		}
	}
}
```

40 When our Enemy has died, we need to remove it from the **enemies** array so that our player can no longer hit/attack it. To remove it, in the Enemy Class we add a new variable:

```
public var removedFromEnemies:Boolean;
```

In our loop function where we already have the **if(life>0)** statement, add the following after it:

```
else
{
	if(!removedFromEnemies)
	{
		removedFromEnemies = true;
		for (var a:int = 0;
		 a < timeline.enemies.length; a++)
		{
			if(timeline.enemies[a] == this)
			{
				timeline.enemies.splice(a,1);
				break;
			}
		}
	}
}
```

43 We also need to put an **if** statement in the Players **stopMoving** function:

```
public function stopMoving():void
{
	if(life>0)
	{
		running = false;
		if(!jumping)theNinja.gotoAndPlay("still");
	}
}
```

44 To be fair to our enemies, let's allow our player to get hurt. Similar to how our Player hits an Enemy, we can get our Enemy to hit our Player. In our Enemy Class, we override the attack function just like in the Player Class but call a **checkPlayer** function instead. We only call this function if we know our player still has life left:

```
override public function attack():Boolean
{
	if(super.attack() && timeline.player.life > 0)checkPlayer();
	return true;
}
```

41 If you kill an enemy when he is jumping, we don't want the run or still animation to be played when he falls to the ground. So we put the if statement in our Ninja Class, too:

```
public function jumpFinished():void
{
	if(life > 0)
	{
		if (running)
		{
			theNinja.gotoAndPlay("run");
		}
		else
		{
			theNinja.gotoAndPlay("still");
		}
	}
}
```

42 Although our Player can't get hurt yet, let's make sure that if he has no life or if he is stunned, he no longer can be controlled. It's best if we actually go to where the keys are pressed in our main Timeline's **gameLoop**:

```
if(player.life > 0 && player.stunned <=0)
{
    for(var key:String in keys)
    {
        if(keyPressedActions[key]) keyPressedActions[key]();
    }
}
```

45 Our **checkPlayer** function will be similar to check Enemies. The only difference is that we don't do the **for** loop as there's only one player to check:

```
public function checkPlayer():void
{
	var attackReachX:int = 280;
	var attackReachZ:int = 150;
	var attackForce:int = 80;
	var distanceX:Number = timeline.player.x3D - x3D;
	var distanceZ:Number = timeline.player.z3D - z3D;
	if(distanceX * direction > 0 && Math.abs(distanceZ) < attackReachZ && Math.abs(distanceX) <attackReachX)
	{
		var angle:Number = Math.atan2(distanceZ,distanceX);
		timeline.player.forceX = attackForce * Math.cos(angle);
		timeline.player.forceZ = attackForce * Math.sin(angle);
		timeline.player.hurt();
	}
}
```

Stage 3 (cont.)

46 Having 10 enemies all running around at the start of a game is a bit excessive. Let's ease the Player into the game by starting with just one Enemy. Back in our main Timeline, we are going to delete all our code for adding the 10 enemies (the entire **for** loop). Then, after we create our player, put in this code:

```
function addEnemy()
{
        var randomX_Position:Number = Math.random()*2000 + player.x3D - 1000;
        var randomZ_Position:Number = 2000+Math.random()*1000;
        var enemy:Enemy = new Enemy(randomX_Position, -500, randomZ_Position);
        enemy.jumping = true;
        addChild(enemy);
        enemy.timeline = this;
        objects3D.push(enemy);
        enemies.push(enemy)
}
addEnemy();
var totalEnemies:int = 10;
```

48 Not to be insulting but the enemy Ninjas are a bit dumb. They currently attack randomly regardless of their location on screen, and they don't make any extra effort to aim their attacks at your player. Currently they operate on a 1 in 100 chance of **deciding** to attack. We'll leave the decision making up to them but code it so that when they get closer to the player the chance of attack increases. In the **loop** function in the Enemy Class we work out the distance the enemy is from the player. If that distance is less than 1000, we will divide that distance by 10 (that way we never get above our 1 in 100 chance). Then we'll use that value **attackChance**, when determining if the enemy should attack. We'll do a quick check to make sure that chance is never less than one in three:

```
override public function loop():void
{
        if(life > 0)
        {
                if(int(Math.random() * 100) == 1) jump();
                var attackChance:int = 100;
                var distanceX:Number = timeline.player.x3D x3D;
                var distanceZ:Number = timeline.player.z3D z3D;
                var totalDistance:Number = Math.sqrt(distanceX * distanceX + distanceZ * distanceZ);
                if(totalDistance<1000) attackChance = totalDistance/10;
                if(attackChance < 3) attackChance = 3;
                if(int(Math.random() * attackChance) == 1) attack();
        }
}
```

47 Notice how we've changed the code a little? Enemies will now start far away in the background as well as in the air, which is why we set jumping to be "true." Creating enemies this way gives them the nice effect of "dropping in" to give the player a little warning. We also now have a **totalEnemies** variable. In our main **gameLoop** we can check if we have less enemies on screen than the total allowed (**totalEnemies**). If the number of enemies starts to drop off, we can randomly add new enemies as needed. Add this code right at the top of the **gameLoop**:

```
if(int(Math.random()*50) == 1 && enemies.length < totalEnemies)
{
        addEnemy();
}
```

49 It would be a good idea to make sure the enemy is facing our player when they attack:

```
override public function attack():Boolean
{
        if(super.attack() && timeline.player.life > 0)
        {
                checkPlayer();
                direction = 1;
                if(timeline.player.x3D < x3D) direction = -1;
        }
        return true;
}
```

Stage 3 is now complete!

Stage 4

SO WE HAVE THE BASICS OF A GAME! YOU CAN attack and die as can your enemies attack and die. Let's keep going and add some UI elements!

But we have a slight problem. In our code we do some depth sorting on our ninjas so that when they are in the foreground they are above the ninjas in the background. This depth sorting uses the **setChildIndex** command to put each ninja in the correct order, typically putting them on top of everything else in the game.

If we start to put our UI elements on the Stage, when we run the game our ninjas will be placed on top of them. What we really want is for the UI elements to always be on top of the ninjas. We could run some code in our **gameLoop** to always call **setChildIndex** on each of our UI elements after the depth sorting for the ninjas. However, this method is a little messy, and there is an easy trick for better separation of the game from the UI. We can make two Movie Clips, one called "game" and one called "ui." From this point forward we make sure that all of our game objects (our ninjas) are initially added to our game Movie Clip via **addChild** and all our UI objects are inside "ui." We then place "game" on our Stage first and then "ui" on top. We no longer have to worry about having to change the **childIndex** of our UI elements.

1 Because we will visually want to edit our UI, let's create the instance of the Movie Clip the normal Animate way by using the Library panel's drop-down menu. Create a new empty Movie Clip called **ui** and place it in a new Layer on the Stage at **0,0** in **x** and **y** coordinates. Give it the instance name **ui**.

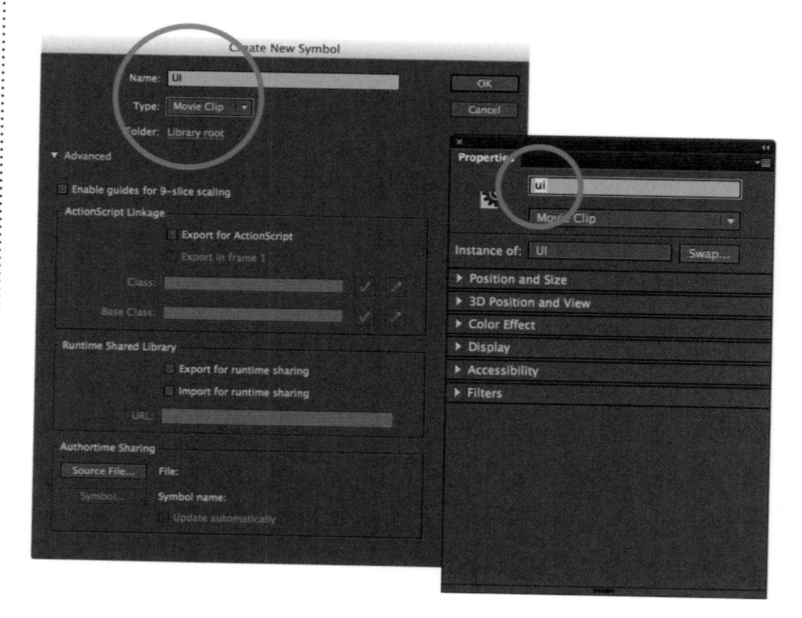

4 Let's now add the UI. The first thing we need to do is add a text field to our ui Movie Clip to show the score. "Edit in Place" the ui Movie Clip and create a new dynamic text field in the top left of screen. Select a large font and add the instance name **scoreTF** (which stands for score Text Field). If you type **0123456789** into the text field, we can be sure the font will be embedded easily.

2 In the Timeline code above everything else, add these three lines of code:

```
var game:MovieClip = new MovieClip();
addChild(game);
addChild(ui);
```

Because our ui is already created and on Stage, we call the **addChild** command to make sure it's on top of our game Movie Clip.

3 There are four places where we need to reference our new **game** Movie Clip: in our two **addChild** lines for the player and the enemy, then where we call **setChildIndex(objects3D[a],a);** and finally where we call **removeChild**.

Find those four lines in our main Timeline code and change them to the following:

```
game.addChild(player);

game.addChild(enemy);

game.setChildIndex(objects3D[a],a);

game.removeChild(objects3D[a]);
```

5 In your Timeline code add the following:

```
var score:int = 0;
ui.scoreTF.text="00000";
```

And then we add a new updateScore function:

```
function updateScore():void
{
	score++;
	var fullScore:String = String(score);
	while(fullScore.length<5)
	fullScore="0"+fullScore;
	ui.scoreTF.text = fullScore;
}
```

6 In our **Player.as Class** let's call **updateScore** after our **enemy.hurt** line in the **checkEnemies** function. Remember we need "timeline" first:

```
timeline.updateScore();
```

Whenever we hit an enemy, our score increases by 1. But let's make it more fun. Let's add a basic combo scoring system where if we hit enemies in quick succession, we get more points for each new hit. Back in the main Timeline, we add three new variables:

```
var comboCounter:int = 0;
var lastHitTime:int = 0;
var maxCombo:int = 0;
```

HOT TIP

Entering a Class name to a Movie Clip requires right-clicking over the Movie Clip in the Library, clicking Advanced, and subsequently clicking the "Export for ActionScript" check box. A quicker way of adding a Class is to double-click in the empty space in the "AS Linkage" column next to the Movie Clip in the library. You can then immediately type in the Class name you want to use, and the appropriate check boxes will have been checked automatically.

Stage 4 (cont.)

7 Let's now modify our **updateScore** function:

```
function updateScore():void
{
    if(getTimer() - lastHitTime < 500)
    {
        comboCounter++;
    }
    else
    {
        comboCounter = 1;
    }
    lastHitTime = getTimer();
    score+= comboCounter
    var fullScore:String = String(score);
    while(fullScore.length<5)
        fullScore="0"+fullScore;
    ui.scoreTF.text = fullScore;
}
```

8 Let's add two more text fields to our **ui** Movie Clip using the same font as the score: one text field to show our last combo and a second to show our maximum combo. Give these two text fields instance names of **lastComboTF** and **maxComboTF** and type into them "Max Combo: 0" and "Last Combo: 0." We don't need to include numerals 1 through 9 as they are already embedded in the score text field. Let's modify the **updateScore** function again. This time where we have **comboCounter = 1** we add these lines before it:

```
else
{
        if(comboCounter > 1)
        {
                if(maxCombo < comboCounter) maxCombo = comboCounter;
                ui.maxComboTF.text = "Max Combo: " + maxCombo;
                ui.lastComboTF.text = "Last Combo: "+comboCounter;
        }
        comboCounter = 1;
}
```

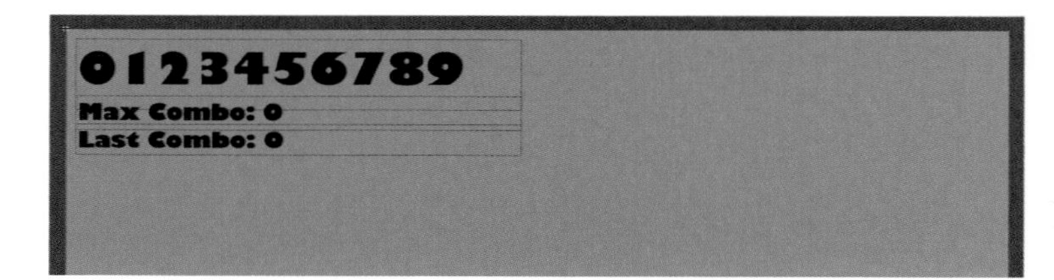

11 In **gameLoop** we'll add an extra line of code:

```
ui.healthBar.scaleX = 1/20*player.life;
```

We use **20** because that is our player's maximum life.

12 Finally we're going to add a timer countdown. In the top right of the **ui** Movie Clip, add a final text field and name it **countdownTF**.

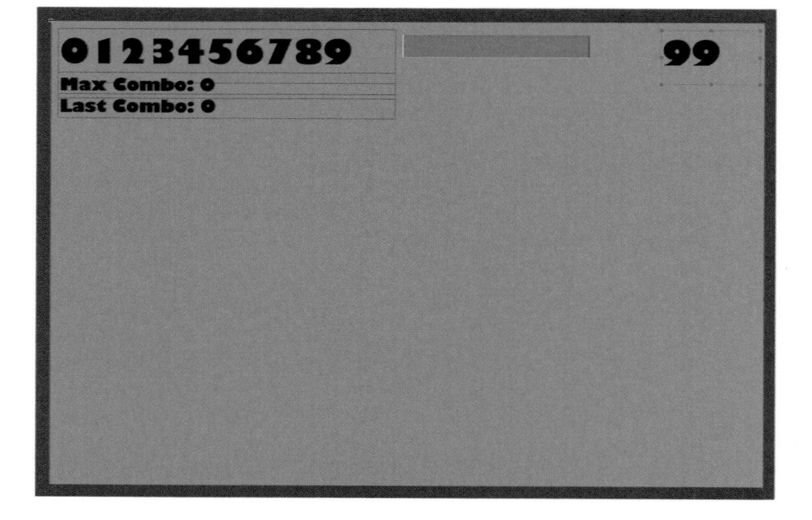

9 Let's add a health bar for our player. Inside our **UI** Movie Clip make a new Movie Clip with a red rectangle and place it along the top of the screen. Name the Movie Clip **healthBar** and make sure the anchor point is on the left somewhere (top, bottom, or center).

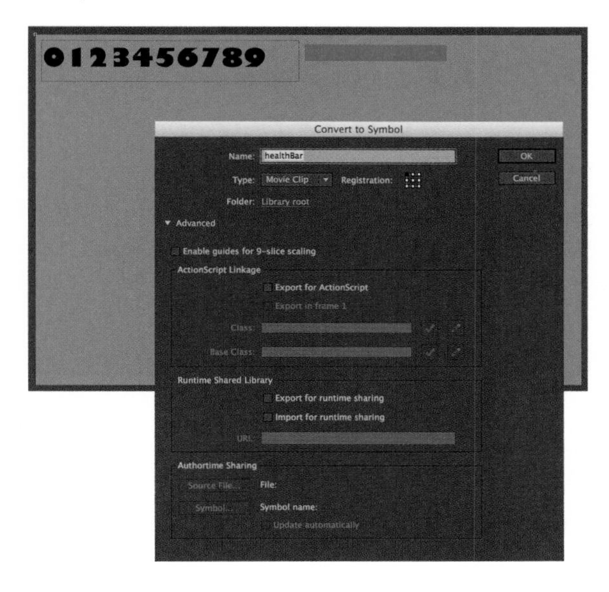

10 Select the **healthBar** Movie Clip and give it the instance name **healthBar**.

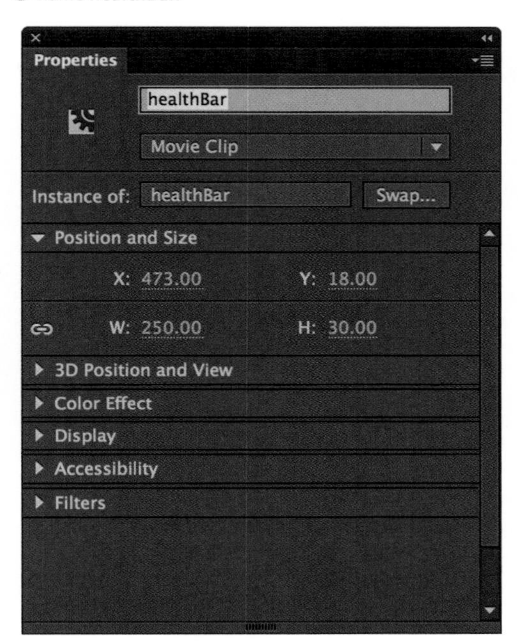

13 In our Timeline add a new variable:

```
var timer:Number=99;
```

and in our game loop add:

```
timer -= 1/30;
ui.countdownTF.text = String(Math.ceil(timer));
```

Our game will run at 30 fps. For each frame we subtract a 30th of the time. So what happens when time runs out or we run out of health? Yes, game over!

14 Make a new Movie Clip inside our ui called "**gameover**." Give it an instance name **gameoverMC** and place three text fields inside it. The first and third can be static text fields, while the second will be dynamic for showing the score. Give this dynamic text field an instance name of **scoreTF**.

Stage 4 (cont.)

15 The first text field can say something like "Game Over, You scored" and be placed above or next to your dynamic text field.

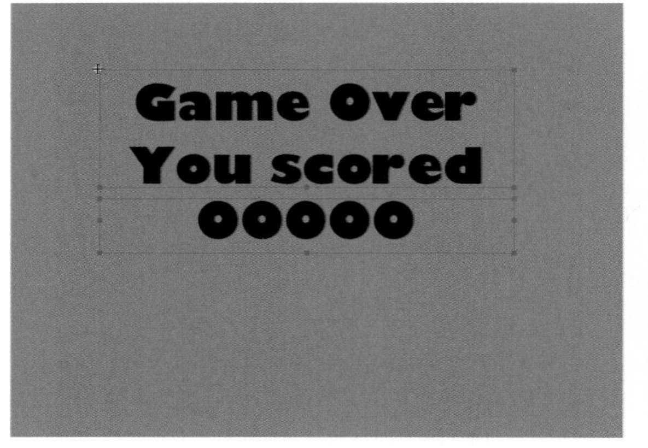

16 Then underneath the score, the third text field can say "click anywhere to play again" or something similar. Note, I've put a large blue rectangle containing 80% alpha behind my text so that you can read the black font easily (otherwise it will clash with our player ninja).

18 Let's create our **gameover** function, which we can add to the bottom of our main Timeline code:

```
function gameover():void
{
    if(!gameIsOver)
    {
        ui.gameoverMC.visible=true;
        ui.gameoverMC.scoreTF.text=ui.scoreTF.text;
        gameIsOver = true;
        player.stopMoving();
        addEventListener(MouseEvent.CLICK, resetGame)
    }
}
```

19 We need to call that function when our player dies and when the time runs out. For a timer in our game loop after we have the line **timer-= 1/30**, we add these lines:

```
if(timer < 0)
{
        gameover();
        timer = 0;
}
```

For a **gameover** when our player dies, we're going to be a little clever. In our Player Class, we're going to override our **dieFinished** function from Ninja but not **super()** it, meaning all the code will be ignored. We will just call **timeline.gameover()**. This cheat means that our Player instance is never actually removed from the game. Instead, we will be reusing it when the user clicks to start a new game. If we don't remove the Player instance, then we don't have to reassign all the **keyboardActions**. In the Player Class let's add the following code:

```
override public function dieFinished():void
{
        theNinja.stop();
        timeline.gameover();
}
```

17 Back in our Timeline code, we want to make sure this **gameover** Movie Clip isn't visible when the game starts.

```
ui.gameoverMC.visible = false;
```

We also want a new variable to tell the code whether or not the game is over. For example, we don't want the player to be able to continue to attack once **gameover()** has been called.

```
var gameIsOver:Boolean = false;
```

All we then need to do is adjust our **if** statement in the game loop to also check to see if **gameIsOver** is not true:

```
if(player.life > 0 && player.stunned<=0 && !gameIsOver)
```

20 Back to the Timeline you'll notice our gameover function calls **resetGame** when you click the mouse, but we don't have a **resetGame** function! Basically this function needs to reset everything back to the first time you start the game: 20 health, 99 seconds, 0 points, 0 enemies, etc. It's kind of a cleanup function. The only thing we don't clean up is **Player** as we reposition him and revive him:

```
function resetGame(e:MouseEvent):void
{
	removeEventListener(MouseEvent.CLICK, resetGame);
	gameIsOver = false;
	ui.gameoverMC.visible=false;
	timer=99;
	score=0;
	ui.scoreTF.text="00000";
	comboCounter=0;
	lastHitTime=0;
	maxCombo = 0;
	ui.maxComboTF.text = "Max Combo: "+maxCombo;
	ui.lastComboTF.text = "Last Combo: "+comboCounter;
	player.stopMoving();
	for(var a:int=0; a<objects3D.length; a++)
	{
		if(objects3D[a]!=player)
		{
			game.removeChild(objects3D[a])
		}
	}
	objects3D = [player];
	enemies = [];
	player.theNinja.gotoAndPlay("still");
	player.life = 20;
	player.x3D = Camera.x3D;
	player.z3D = 1000;
}
```

Stage 4 (Preloading)

THERE ARE SEVERAL WAYS TO HANDLE the preloading of Animate files, and countless tutorials exist on the web as to how to create them. Given that preloading plays a relatively small part of our game, let's not get too complicated with animated bars and percentages. For this example we'll just show a little bit of text to inform the player that the game is indeed loading. You can always come back to this preloader and add a looping animation if you prefer, but it's not necessary.

1 In our main Timeline, currently we have placed everything in frame 1. Our code, our UI, and even our Classes in the library are set up to be exported on frame 1. To make room on our Timeline for a preloader, select the two keyframes on our layers, and drag them to frame 2. Frame 1 should now be empty.

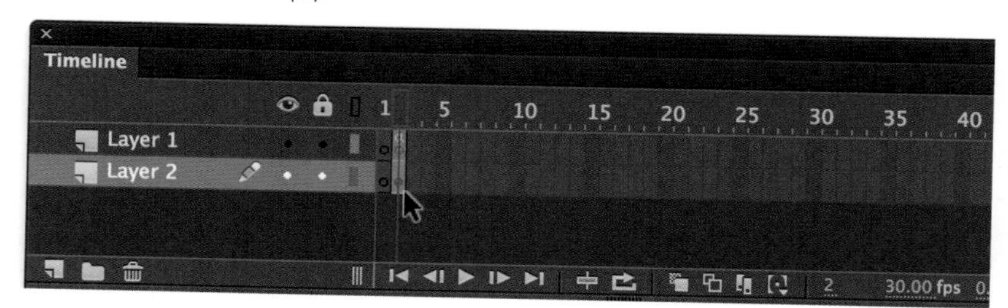

4 Finally, go to File > ActionScript Settings, and change the 1 in "Export Classes" input field to the value of 2. Now when a user starts the game, frame 1 will load quickly, showing the user that the rest of the game is loading. When the load is complete, frame 2, and therefore the game, will start automatically.

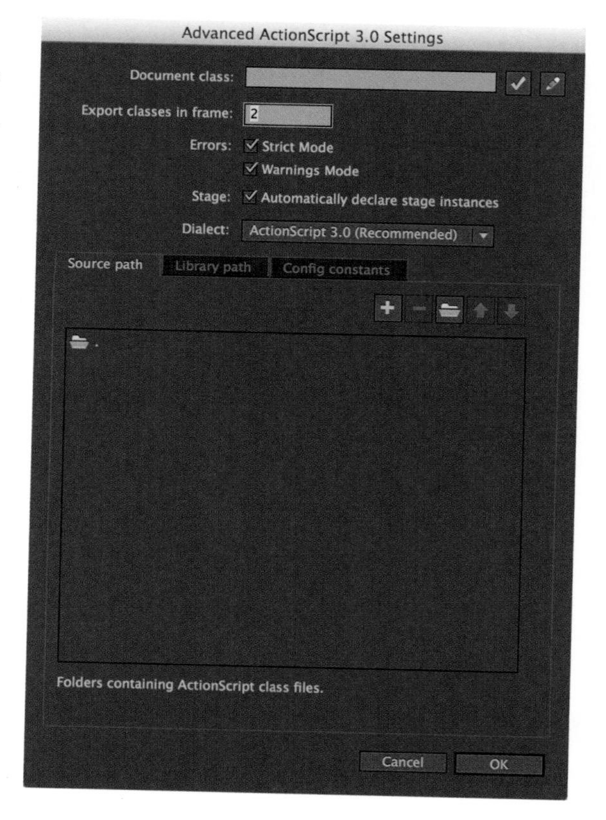

2 Add a text field to the Stage in frame 1 and type the text "loading..." into it.

Loading...

There's nothing preventing you from creating a looping animation in a Movie Clip instead of or alongside the text field above. Often we see preloaders with various spinning graphics to indicate something is being loaded. Whatever you decide to create should be as small as possible as not to bloat the file size and defeat the purpose of the preloader.

3 In our code layer, which is in frame 2, just add at the top a **stop();** command.

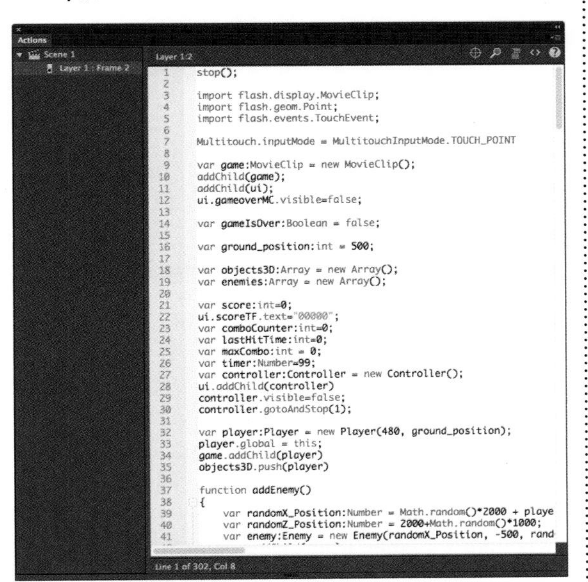

Actions
Scene 1
Layer 1 : Frame 2
Layer 1:2
1 stop();
2
3 import flash.display.MovieClip;
4 import flash.geom.Point;
5 import flash.events.TouchEvent;
6
7 Multitouch.inputMode = MultitouchInputMode.TOUCH_POINT
8
9 var game:MovieClip = new MovieClip();
10 addChild(game);
11 addChild(ui);
12 ui.gameoverMC.visible=false;
13
14 var gameIsOver:Boolean = false;
15
16 var ground_position:int = 500;
17
18 var objects3D:Array = new Array();
19 var enemies:Array = new Array();
20
21 var score:int=0;
22 ui.scoreTF.text="00000";
23 var comboCounter:int=0;
24 var lastHitTime:int=0;
25 var maxCombo:int = 0;
26 var timer:Number=99;
27 var controller:Controller = new Controller();
28 ui.addChild(controller)
29 controller.visible=false;
30 controller.gotoAndStop(1);
31
32 var player:Player = new Player(480, ground_position);
33 player.global = this;
34 game.addChild(player)
35 objects3D.push(player)
36
37 function addEnemy()
38 {
39 var randomX_Position:Number = Math.random()*2000 + playe
40 var randomZ_Position:Number = 2000+Math.random()*1000;
41 var enemy:Enemy = new Enemy(randomX_Position, -500, rand
Line 1 of 302, Col 8

5 Stage 4 is complete. At this point you have a pretty cool game built entirely in Adobe Animate. In Stage 5 we will add support for touch controls, so the game will work on mobile devices (Android and iOS). Finally, in Stage 6 we will add sounds, a background, and a cool Particle System.

Stage 4 is now complete!

Stage 5

ANDROID AND IOS! THE INITIAL CHUNK OF CODE we need to add when dealing with both iOS and Android apps is support for when the app is in the background. By default AIR apps slow down to 4 fps when minimized, which means that slowly but surely the player will get beaten up if you suddenly have to answer a phone call mid-play. We need to get the game to listen out for when it has been minimized and maximized, in other words deactivated and activated. We then pause it or unpause it appropriately.

1 First, let's add the ability to pause the game. In our main Timeline code create a new variable:

```
var paused:Boolean = false;
```

4 We're going to cover three different types of touch controls here: a simple "tap" for attacking, a "drag" for moving, and a "swipe" for jumping. We are going to add three new listeners to handle each of these, but first we need to enable **MultiTouch** control. Add this line into the Timeline code:

```
Multitouch.inputMode = MultitouchInputMode.TOUCH_POINT;
```

6 We are going to use two new Arrays to store data on each touch that is made. The first Array will store the time that the touch was made. The second Array will record the **Y** coordinate of the touch. Both of these arrays will be used when working out whether an upward swipe has been made, in which case we'll make our ninja jump.

```
var timeTouched:Array = new Array();
var touchPointsY:Array = new Array();
```

2 Because we know that everything that happens is executed or triggered from within the main **gameLoop**, we add an if statement around everything:

```
function gameLoop(e:Event):void
{
        if(!paused)
        {
        .......
        all game loop code
        .......
        }
}
```

3 We add our listeners (a good place would be to put them with the other listeners):

```
stage.addEventListener(Event.DEACTIVATE, deactivate)
stage.addEventListener(Event.ACTIVATE, activate)
```

and their functions:

```
function deactivate(e:Event):void
{
    paused = true;
}
function activate(e:Event):void
{
    paused = false;
}
```

5 Next let's add your listeners. For code neatness and organization, add these near to our existing **keyPressed/keyReleased** listeners:

```
stage.addEventListener(TouchEvent.TOUCH_BEGIN, touchDown);
stage.addEventListener(TouchEvent.TOUCH_MOVE, touchMoving);
stage.addEventListener(TouchEvent.TOUCH_END, touchUp);
```

7 For movement we will need three things: two "point" objects that store *x* and *y* coordinates of our initial touch and where we move that to. Because we can make multiple touches at once, we add a new variable that keeps track of which touch is our movement touch.

```
var touchPoint:Point = new Point();
var movePoint:Point = new Point();
var movingTouch:int = -1;
```

8 For jumping we first add our **touchDown**, which records the time and *y* value (**stageY**) of our touch:

```
function touchDown(e:TouchEvent):void
{
    timeTouched[e.touchPointID] = getTimer();
    touchPointsY[e.touchPointID] = e.stageY;
}
```

SHORTCUTS
MAC WIN BOTH

Stage 5 (cont.)

9 Then we create our **touchUp** function. We check to see if the touch has been released within 500 ms (half of a second) of it first being made and if it's released at a *y* position of more than 40 pixels higher than it was started. A quick vertical swipe would achieve this, and when triggered, we make our **Player** jump. We need to reuse our if statement found in the **gameLoop** to make sure we only allow this jump to happen if our Player is still alive, isn't stunned, or if the time hasn't run out.

```
function touchUp(e:TouchEvent):void
{
        if(player.life > 0 && player.stunned<=0 && !gameIsOver)
        {
                if(getTimer()-500< timeTouched[e.touchPointID])
                {
                        if(e.stageY < touchPointsY[e.touchPointID] -40)
                        {
                                player.jump();
                        }
                }
        }
}
```

11 On to moving. In this game we do something unusual. Rather than having set controls on the screen, we allow movement control to happen from any touchpoint on the screen. If our gamer places their finger or thumb anywhere on the touchscreen and then starts to move it around, our on-screen game pad appears and our gamer can make the player move up, down, left, or right. Of course while we play the game, we will make multiple touches to the screen for attacking, jumping, and moving. So we only want one of these touches to create the Directional pad (dpad) that allows thumb-operated control of player movement. We therefore find the first touch that seems to be treated as a movement and assign the id value for this touch to our **movingTouch** variable. To work out if a touch appears to be a movement-type touch, we measure the distance from where the touch was started to where it is now. If it's more than 10 pixels, it's likely the player wants to use this touch as the controller. We add our **touchMoving** function:

```
function touchMoving(e:TouchEvent):void
{
    if(movingTouch == -1 || movingTouch == e.touchPointID)
    {
        movePoint.x = e.stageX;
        movePoint.y = e.stageY;
        var dx:Number = e.stageX-touchPoint.x;
        var dy:Number = e.stageY-touchPoint.y;
        var dz:Number = Math.sqrt(dx*dx+dy*dy);
        if(dz>10)
        {
            if(movingTouch == -1)
            {
                touchPoint.x = e.stageX;
                touchPoint.y = e.stageY;
            }
            movingTouch = e.touchPointID;
        }
    }
}
```

10 We also want to handle our attack in the **touchUp** event. If we handle it in **touchDown**, then we wouldn't actually know if the touch was the start of a swipe for jumping or an attack. In the **touchUp** function, we add a temporary variable to record if the touch was for jumping or not. We set this to true at the same point of telling our Player to jump. We only then call **player.attack()** if **touchIsJump** is not true. Note: we also call **player.stopAttacking()**—if you remember, stopAttacking is normally called to make sure that the gamer has released the attack key when playing on a computer. As a **touchUp** is the same as releasing a key, we call it here as well.

```
function touchUp(e:TouchEvent):void
{
	if(player.life > 0 && player.stunned<=0 && !gameIsOver)
	{
		var touchIsJump:Boolean;
		if(getTimer()-500< timeTouched[e.touchPointID])
		{
			if(e.stageY < touchPointsY[e.touchPointID]-40)
			{
				touchIsJump = true;
				player.jump();
			}
		}
		player.stopAttacking();
		if(!touchIsJump) player.attack();
	}
}
```

12 We need to update our **touchUp** function so that movement is stopped. Note that if the movement is being stopped, we don't do the attack:

```
function touchUp(e:TouchEvent):void
{
	if(player.life > 0 && player.stunned<=0 && !gameIsOver)
	{
		var touchIsJump:Boolean;
		if(getTimer()-500< timeTouched[e.touchPointID])
		{
			if(e.stageY < touchPointsY[e.touchPointID]-40)
			{
				touchIsJump = true;
				player.jump();
			}
		}
		player.stopAttacking();
		if(!touchIsJump && movingTouch != e.touchPointID) player.attack();
	}
	if(movingTouch==e.touchPointID)
	{
		player.stopMoving();
		movingTouch = -1;
	}
}
```

Stage 5 (cont.)

13 Finally, inside our **gameLoop** we need to handle the player movement, so just before our for loop for checking the **keyPressedActions** add these new lines:

```
if(player.life > 0 && player.stunned<=0 && !gameIsOver)
{
        if(movingTouch != -1)
        {
                var dx:Number = movePoint.x-touchPoint.x;
                var dy:Number = movePoint.y-touchPoint.y;
                if(dx > 20) {player.moveRight();}
                if(dx < -20){player.moveLeft();}
                if(dy > 20) {player.moveDown();}
                if(dy < -20){player.moveUp();}
                if(Math.abs(dx) < 20 && Math.abs(dy) < 20) {player.stopMoving();}
        }
        for(var key:String in keys)
        {
                if(keyPressedActions[key]) keyPressedActions[key]();
        }
}
```

16 In our **touchMoving** function where we set our **touchPoint** *x* and *y* values, we add three lines:

```
if(movingTouch == -1)
{
        touchPoint.x = e.stageX;
        touchPoint.y = e.stageY;
        controller.x = touchPoint.x;
        controller.y = touchPoint.y;
        controller.visible = true;
}
```

17 Then to make the controller invisible again, we modify the **touchUp** function:

```
if(movingTouch==e.touchPointID)
{
        player.stopMoving();
        movingTouch = -1;
        controller.visible = false;
}
else .........
```

14 We currently have movement, attacking, and jumping all handled by the touchscreen. The last thing to do is to add our visual control pad. Make a new Movie Clip and draw a classic Nintendo Entertainment System-style cross control pad in it. Make sure the center of the cross is the center of the Movie Clip. Give it an AS Linkage name "Controller." Give the Movie Clip nine different frames. The first frame will be still (no direction pressed), then the subsequent frames need to be as follows:

Frame 2 = down
Frame 3 = up
Frame 4 = down right
Frame 5 = up right
Frame 6 = right
Frame 7 = down left
Frame 8 = up left
Frame 9 = left

15 The frame numbers have a slightly random ordering as opposed to creating frames of the dpad being pressed in a clockwise-type motion. Assigning directions to different frames means we can more easily choose which frame to show with code, which we shall come to in a bit.

First though, we need to add our controller Movie Clip to our UI. We add it at the start of our Timeline code, but we make the Movie Clip invisible as we only want to show it when the gamer is touching the screen.

```
var controller:Controller = new Controller();
ui.addChild(controller)
controller.visible = false;
controller.gotoAndStop(1);
```

18 Finally, to set the correct frame (direction) for the controller, we modify **gameLoop** again:

```
if(movingTouch!=-1)
{
        var dx:Number = movePoint.xtouchPoint.x;
        var dy:Number = movePoint.ytouchPoint.y;
        var controllerFrame:int = 4;
        if(dx > 20)
        {
                player.moveRight();
                controllerFrame += 2;
        }
        if(dx < -20)
        {
                player.moveLeft();
                controllerFrame += 5;
        }
        if(dy > 20)
        {
                player.moveDown();
                controllerFrame -=2;
        }
        if(dy < -20)
        {
                player.moveUp();
                controllerFrame - =1;
        }
        if(Math.abs(dx) < 20 && Math.abs(dy) < 20)
        {
                player.stopMoving();
                controllerFrame = 1;
        }
        controller.gotoAndStop(controllerFrame);
}
```

Stage 5 (cont.)

19 Let's test our game on a touch device! This section doesn't go into creating your icons or submitting the compiled game to an app store. We're going to keep it simple and test locally, meaning on your own computer. You can choose between testing on an iOS or Android device. Android testing is the easier option because Animate CC compiles much quicker for Android than it does for iOS, and it's free and easier to set up. Apple iOS development has a $99 annual charge from Apple, whereas Google Play requires only a one-time $25 registration fee. But it's still free to test your app with the Android OS by simply connecting your Android device to your computer.

Up until now we've been testing our game for the default Flash Player. Let's change the default testing platform by going to **File > Publish Settings** and change the target drop-down to **AIR 3.6 for Android**.

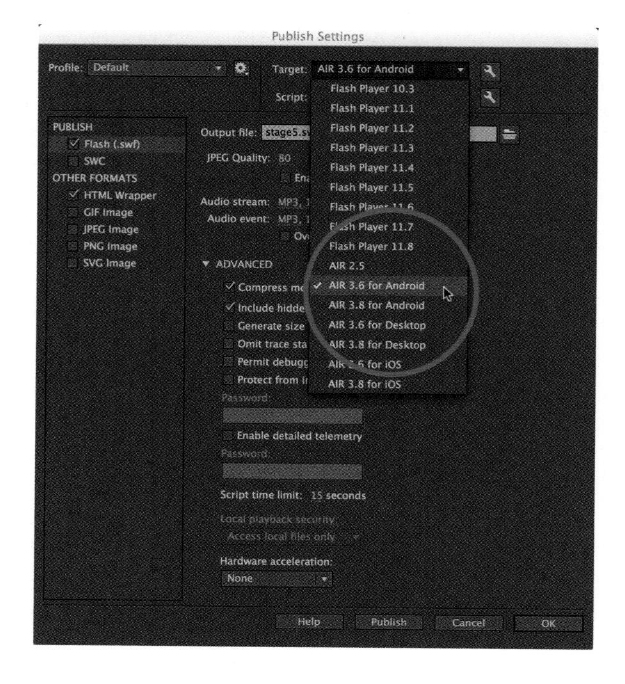

21 You can choose between **Portrait**, **Landscape**, or **Auto** from the **Aspect ratio** drop-down menu. You can select **Full screen** as well as **Auto orientation** using the check boxes. We've selected **Auto** in the drop-down menu and checked **Auto orientation** for our game. This setting means the user can choose to play in landscape or portrait, and due to the nature of our game, either works well. The most important thing here is to set **Render mode** to **GPU**. Because we use vectors in our game and no fancy filter effects or features not supported by **GPU** mode, this render mode gets us the best performance/frame rate out of our **Android** device. This render mode is also the best choice for **iOS**. If you were to use **Starling** or another **Stage3D** engine, you would use **direct** instead here. CPU mode would be used if you found some of your visuals don't look correct in **GPU**. Thankfully, all of ours do.

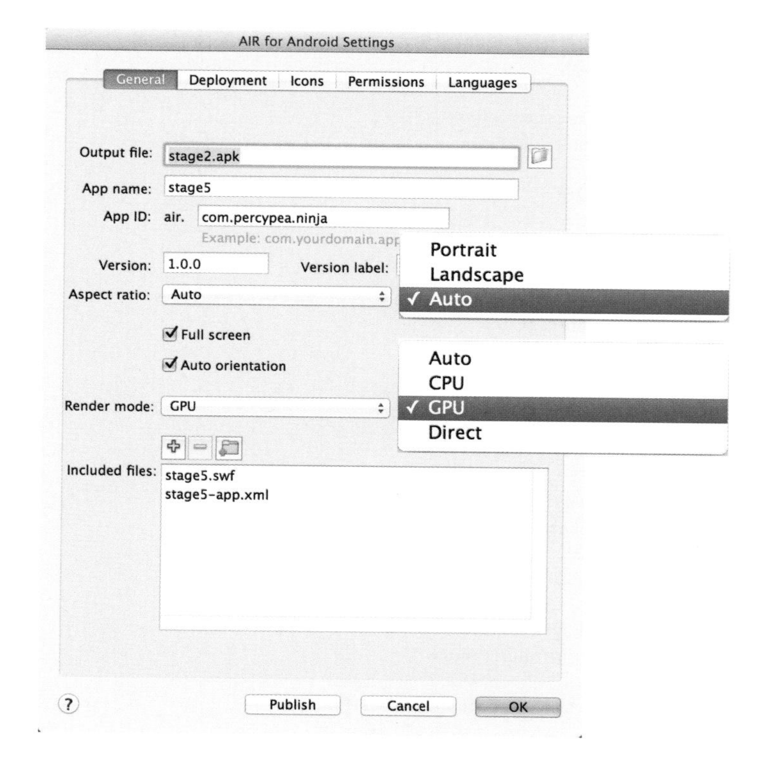

20 Click the little settings button next to the Target drop-down menu represented by the little wrench icon. In the General tab you can leave the default Output file and App name as they are. In the App ID field enter: **com.mydomainname.ninja**. (I used com.percypea.ninja.)

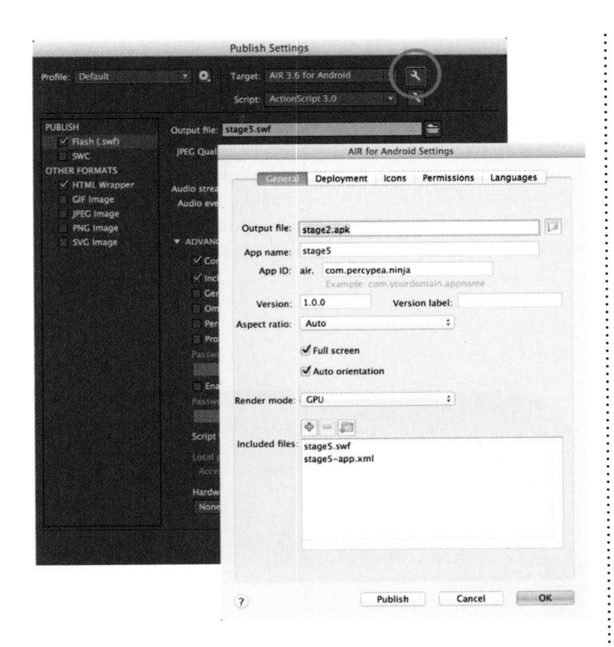

22 The **Deployment** tab is the most important tab for testing. Click the **Create** button, fill out the fields, and add a password in the Password field. Specify a location where you want to save your file to and then click OK. Whatever password you used when creating the certificate, just type it into the password box back in the Deployment tab. Leaving deployment type as **Device release** is fine as we aren't going to be doing any real debugging.

Stage 5 (cont.)

23 Embedding the **AIR runtime** with the application adds 9.4 MB to the file size of the app. Our app would only be around 60 KB without the AIR runtime, so this file size is comparatively huge and makes it very tempting not to Embed it. If it's not embedded and the user doesn't have AIR already, they should automatically be taken to the Google Play store and given the option to download AIR. We are going to embed it in our game so that the end user won't have to worry about this step. Also, not all Android devices have access to the Google Play store.

AIR for Android Settings

General | Deployment | Icons | Permissions | Languages

Certificate: [ ] Create...
Password:
Remember password for this session
Android deployment type
Device release
Emulator release
Debug
Network interface for remote debugging
Default
AIR runtime
Embed AIR runtime with application
Get AIR runtime from: Google Play
After publishing
Install application on selected Android devices
Launch application on selected Android devices
Select | Device Serial No.
Refresh
? Publish Cancel OK

24 Back to our **Deployment** panel, if you have your Android device connected to your computer, you can select to install and launch it directly after it has compiled. Select **Publish** and you should have your game running on your Android device with touch controls fully integrated!

Testing devices on iOS works the same way, but you'll need a P12 Certificate for iOS distribution which is harder to get. You'll need to be registered with Apple as a developer, get the UDID for your iDevice, and add it to your Apple developer account. We won't provide details as to how to become an iOS developer as that information can be found by going to apple.com. We also don't want you to spend $99 just to test your game on an iOS device since you can test for free on an Android device. If you want to learn more about becoming an iOS developer you can visit the following links.

developer.apple.com

developer.apple.com/support/technical/certificates

www.adobe.com/devnet/air/articles/packaging-air-apps-ios.html

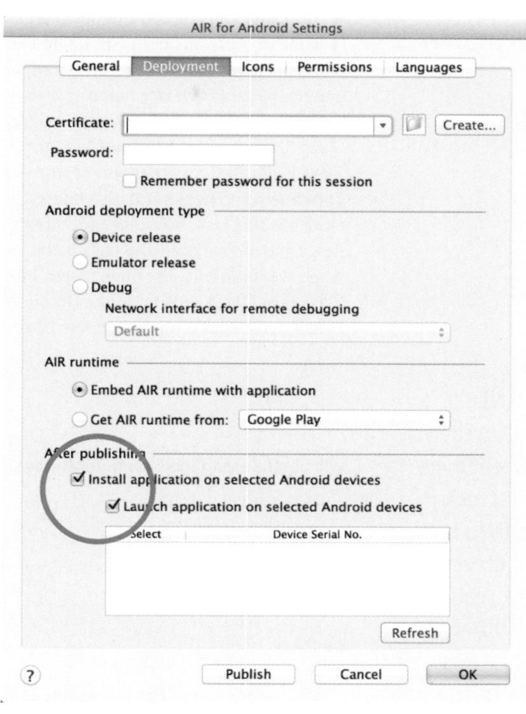

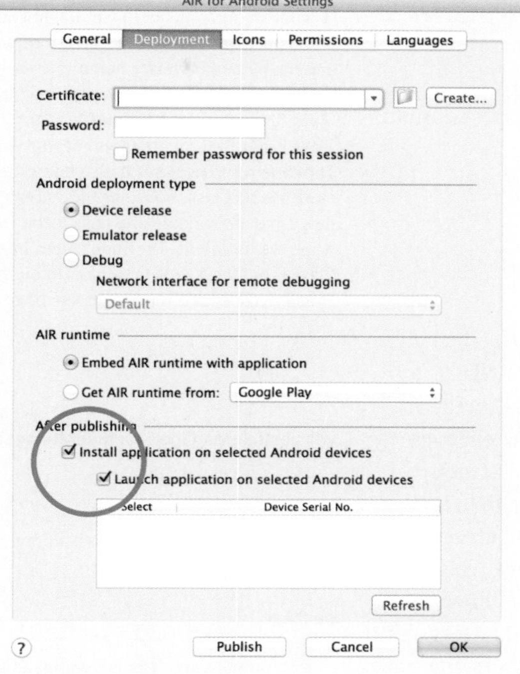

Stage 5 is now complete!

Stage 6

MUSIC, SOUND, AND visual effects! Currently our player can attack enemies and our enemies can attack the player, but other than that there's no visual effect to enhance the attack. This section will show you how to add some blood splatters as well as sound effects and music. A huge special thanks goes out to Tom McCaren of **www.tommccaren.co.uk** for graciously designing the awesome sound effects and music for this game. Tom is a talented UK-based sound designer and composer working primarily in the gaming industry.

1 Let's add some blood! Rather than have code in our Timeline to set up and add our blood particles, in the same way that we add our enemy ninjas we are going to create a manager Class. Make a new ActionScript 3.0 Class file and call it **ParticleManager**. This Class is our first one that will need to have a **Timeline** reference, but it also doesn't extend our **Base3D** Class. So we need to create a new Timeline variable and pass it the Timeline when we initiate it. The code to put into this Class is in step 2, but first, back in our main Timeline code, add this single line of code:

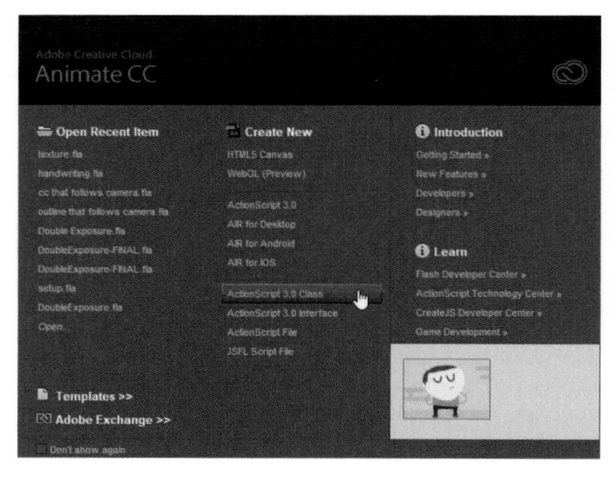


```
var particleManager:ParticleManager = new ParticleManager(this);
```

3 Let's create our Blood Class (Blood.as). This Class will extend Base3D as we want our particle to be in our 3D world:

```
package
{
	public class Blood extends Base3D
	{
		public var blood:BloodMC;
		public function Blood(x_position=0, y_position=0, z_position=0)
		{
			blood = new BloodMC();
			blood.stop();
			addChild(blood);
			super(x_position, y_position, z_position);
		}
	}
}
```

2 In our new ParticleManager Class file add the following code:

```
package
{
	import flash.display.MovieClip;
	public class ParticleManager
	{
		public var timeline:MovieClip;
		public function ParticleManager(timeline)
		{
			this.timeline = timeline;
		}
	}
}
```

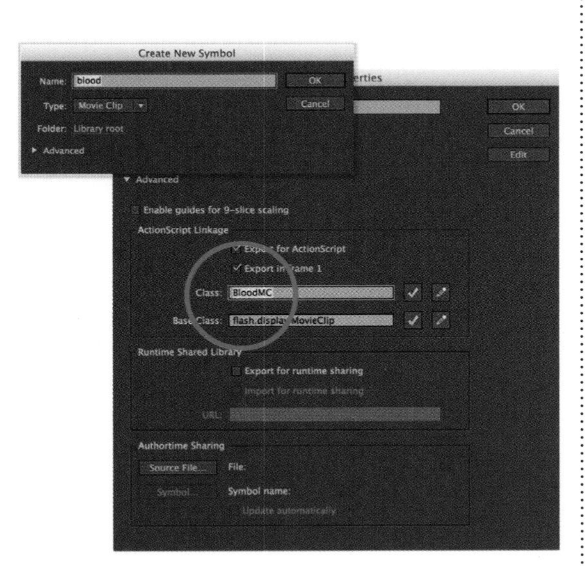

4 Finally we need to create our Blood Movie Clip (BloodMC) in our library. In the FLA make a new Movie Clip and inside it create an animated blob of blood. This blob should be just a looping animation that doesn't move except for some kind of oscillating effect. In the **Stage6.fla** included with the downloaded example files, you can find this symbol in the file's Library panel. Open the blood symbol and play the Timeline animation to see the animated effect. The overall movement of the blood during game play will be handled via code. Make sure it has the AS Linkage name BloodMC by right-clicking over the symbol in the Library panel and selecting Properties. In the Advanced section type BloodMC in the Class input field.

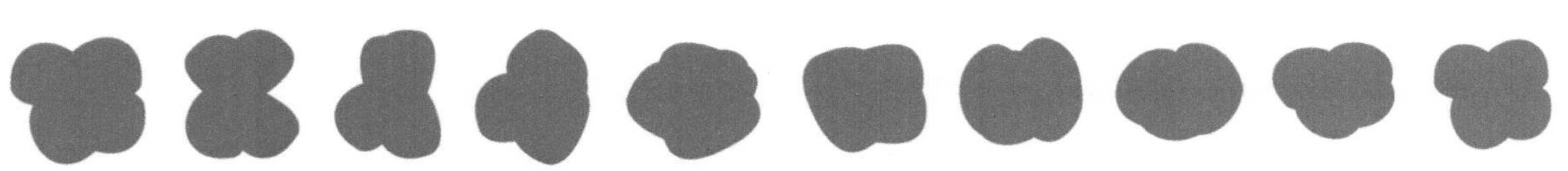

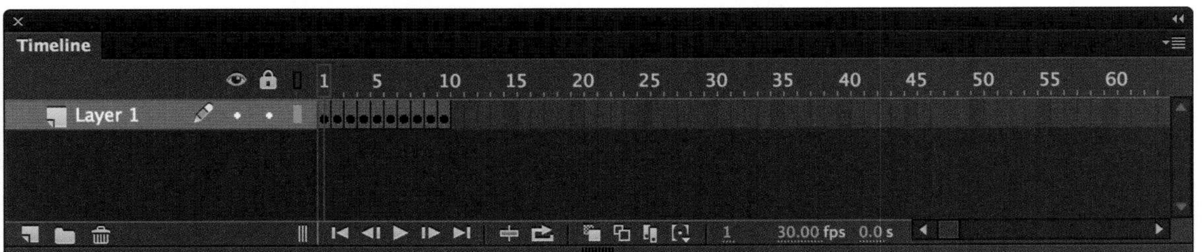

Stage 6 (cont.)

5 Why are we using a **ParticleManager** rather than adding our blood to the game area in the same way as we add our Ninjas? With our blood we want to be able to add several blood drops at a time and possibly end up having close to 50 particles on screen at once. At the same time we want to manage the number of particles on screen for performance reasons. Finally, initiating a Class and an **addChild** function to the Stage can cause performance issues if we do it a lot at once. So this **ParticleManager** will work around these performance issues. First, we do what is termed as **Object Pooling**. Let's decide that the maximum blood particles we want on the screen at any time is 50. We can now create all 50 blood instances right at the start of the game and then store them in our "pool" to easily grab and show them via code when needed. In our **ParticleManager** add this code:

```
package
{
        import flash.display.MovieClip;
        public class ParticleManager
        {
                public var timeline:MovieClip;
                public var bloodPool:Array;
                public function ParticleManager(timeline)
                {
                        this.timeline = timeline;
                        bloodPool = new Array();
                        for(var a:int=0;a<50;a++)
                        {
                                var blood:Blood = new Blood();
                                blood.timeline = timeline;
                                bloodPool.push(blood);
                        }
                }
        }
}
```

7 The **removeParticle** function is a little simpler. It marks our blood particle for removal so that our main code loop knows to remove it from screen and then pushes it back into the pool. Although in this tutorial we won't add any more particles to the game, the **ParticleManager** is actually coded to handle more than just our blood particles, so we look up which **particlePool** is the one where we push our particle back into.

```
public function removeParticle(particle)
{
        particle.markForRemoval = true;
        this[particle.particlePool].push(particle);
}
```

8 Let's update our **Blood Class** now. First add some new variables to the Class. The three velocity variables are going to be our speed in each direction for the blood particle. The **y_velocity** is actually the same as our "gravity" value for the ninjas. The **particlePool** is the reference our **particleManager** uses to know which pool is where the particle is in. The **fadeOut** Boolean is used to determine if the blood particle should be fading out or not, and the **waitForFade** is a value we use as a little timer before the fade out happens.

```
public var x_velocity:Number;
public var y_velocity:Number;
public var z_velocity:Number;
public var particlePool:String = "bloodPool";
public var fadeOut:Boolean;
public var waitForFade:int;
```

6 We now want to add two functions: one to take the blood particles from our **bloodPool** and display them on screen and the other to remove them again and put them back into our **bloodPool** to be able to be reused. The first function **addBlood** will be created so that we can tell the **particleManager** how many blood particles to add along with where to add them in our 3D world. The **shift()** command means we "shift" the first item (in this case a Blood drop) out of the **bloodPool**. We then call a function called **init** which we have yet to create in our **Blood Class**. Finally, we check to see if we are already using that blood particle, and if not, we push that blood particle into our main **objects3D** array so that its loop function (also not yet created) can be called and so that it will be positioned in our world:

```
public function addBlood(totalBlood:int, x_position:Number, y_position:Number, z_position:Number)
{
        for(var a:int=0; a<totalBlood;a++)
        {
                if(bloodPool.length>0)
                {
                        var blood:Blood = bloodPool.shift();
                        blood.init(x_position, y_position, z_position);
                        var alreadyInObjects3D:Boolean = false;
                        for(var b:int=0;b<timeline.objects3D.length;b++)
                        {
                                if(timeline.objects3D[b]==blood) alreadyInObjects3D = true;
                        }
                        if(!alreadyInObjects3D)
                        {
                                timeline.objects3D.push(blood);
                                timeline.game.addChild(blood);
                        }
                }
        }
}
```

9 We then add our **init** function to the **Blood Class**, the init function is also like a reset function. Because this blood instance gets reused from our **bloodPool**, properties like its alpha and animation need to be reset:

```
public function init(x_position, y_position, z_position)
{
        x3D = x_position;
        y3D = y_position;
        z3D = z_position;
        x_velocity = Math.random()*40-20;
        z_velocity = Math.random()*40-20;
        y_velocity = -Math.random()*40-30;
        fadeOut=false;
        this.alpha = 1;
        waitForFade = 30; blood.play();
        markForRemoval=false;
}
```

Stage 6 (cont.)

10 Finally, our main loop code gets added to the **Blood Class**. While the blood particle is still in the air, we adjust its *x*, *y*, and *z* position by the velocities. (We also adjust the **y_velocity** in the same way as we adjust the gravity value in our Ninja Class.) Then if the blood particle hits the floor, we make its animation stop and tell it to **fadeOut**. The **fadeOut** part of the code first of all reduces our **waitForFade** timer. When it is less than 0 it reduces the alpha of our blood until it is less than 0.1 (10%). Then we call the **removeParticle** function from the **particleManager**.

```
public function loop()
{
    if(!fadeOut)
    {
        y_velocity += 5;
        x3D += x_velocity;
        y3D += y_velocity;
        z3D += z_velocity;
        if(y3D >= timeline.ground_position)
        {
            y3D = timeline.ground_position;
            fadeOut=true;
            blood.stop();
        }
    }
    else
    {
        waitForFade--;
        if(waitForFade<0)
        {
            this.alpha-=.1;
            if(this.alpha<.1)
            {
                timeline.particleManager.removeParticle(this);
            }
        }
    }
}
```

12 In our game we'll just have one background which will repeat as you move left to right (and right to left). Make a Graphic symbol (not a Movie Clip) called **backgroundImage** in your main fla and create a lovely background. Make sure this background is wider than your screen area (ideally by at least 30%). Making it wider is necessary because not all mobile handsets/tablets are created equal, and some will have wider screens than others. Remember we're currently working on a screen that matches the iPhone 4 which certainly isn't even the widest iPhone screen, let alone handset screen.

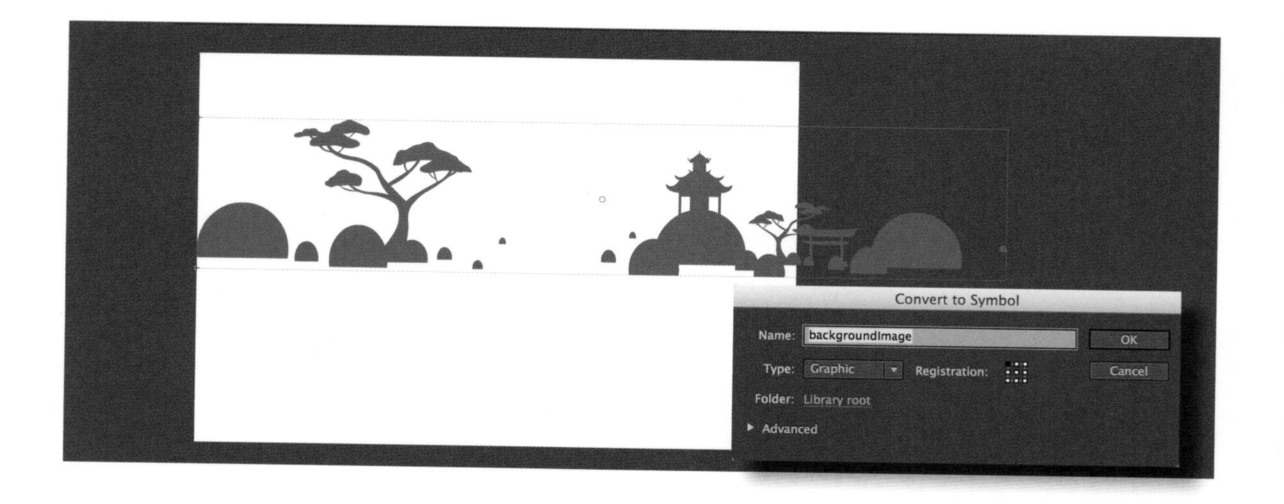

11 We have our **particleManger** and blood particle complete, so let's create some blood! Remember that our **Ninja Class** contains a **hurt** function. Let's add these two lines inside that function:

```
var totalBlood:int=Math.random()*3+3;
timeline.particleManager.addBlood(totalBlood, x3D, y3D-100, z3D);
```

So we determine that we want between three and five Blood particles (**Math.random()*3** will be 0, 1, or 2 when made into an int). And we position them at our ninja's x3d, y3d, and z3D values. Note we actually subtract 100 from the y3D value because y3D is at the ninja's feet. Blood Complete! Feel free to increase the **totalBlood** value for more gore. If you increase it too much though, you will notice that some attacks give no (or very little) blood. This result is because you've got all the particles from your **Blood Pool** on screen already and have to wait until they've gone back in for reuse. A solution is to start with more than 50 particles but beware of the performance impact!

13 Make a new empty Movie Clip called "background" and place two copies of your **backgroundImage** in it side by side. Make sure that these two copies are aligned to the left edge and bottom edge of the Movie Clip. The reason we place two copies next to each other is because if we only had one **backgroundImage**, eventually we would get to the end of it when we keep scrolling it to the left (or right). By having two copies, the second **backgroundImage** looks like it's the start (or repeat) of the first **backgroundImage**. We then use some clever code to make sure we never go past this second copy. Rather we jump back enough pixels so the camera shows the first background again and our player never notices. Magic!

Stage 6 (cont.)

14 We have our two **backgroundImage** Graphic symbols inside our **background** Movie Clip. Manually place our background into the game by dragging an instance of it from the Library panel to the Stage. Make a new layer for it below the **UI** and put it in the second keyframe. Give it the instance name **background**.

16 Let's make a function in our main Timeline code. Feel free to place it anywhere, though I have it directly beneath the **gameLoop** function:

```
function moveBackground()
{
}
```

17 Inside our **gameLoop** itself just after we call the **Camera.track(player)** command and before **objects3D.sortOn** is where to call our new function:

```
Camera.track(player);
moveBackground();
objects3D.sortOn(["z3D","uniqueID"], Array.NUMERIC | Array.DESCENDING);
```

20 If you actually test your game now, you should see your background move at the correct speed and fit nicely in our 3D world. However, it won't loop/repeat. The fix is to keep moving the background by half its width (remember you have two background images next to each other, so half the width is one complete image) in the correct direction. So we add these two lines:

```
function moveBackground()
{
	background.x =-Camera.x3D*(Camera.perspective/6000);
	while(background.x<-background.width/2) background.x+=background.width/2
	while(background.x>0) background.x-=background.width/2;
}
```

15 Set the *x* value of the Movie Clip to 0, although this isn't really that important. What is important is the *y* value which we need to set to 353.3. "Why this strange value?" I hear you ask. Well our background won't be controlled by our 3D code that controls all other movement; however, it does need to look like part of our 3D scene. So to get the 353.3 value, we pretend that our background has a z3D value of 6000 (remember our Ninjas can't go beyond 5000). We also know that it sits on the **ground_position** of 500. Finally, we know that all our other 3D objects have their *y* coordinate worked out with this line:

```
y = (y3D Camera. y3D)*(Camera.perspective/z3D)+320;
```

If we plug in our background values to that equation, we'll get

```
y = (500 Camera. y3D)*(Camera.perspective/6000)+320
```

Which after reminding ourselves what our Camera.y3D and Camera.perspective values are gives 353.3. Now in fairness, we could quite easily get away with just 353 or even 354, but there's no harm in using 353.3. So *y* is worked out. In our game we don't ever adjust Camera.y3D (tilting the camera up and down), so we won't have to worry about moving the background up and down either. However, *x* we do want to move.

18 Let's have a quick reminder of our equation for all our other 3D objects starting with *x*:

```
x = (x3D-Camera.x3D)*(Camera.perspective/z3D)+480;
```

19 We've put our background at 0 currently, so we can remove **x3D** from the equation. We also don't need to worry about that +480 at the end really, as we know we want our background to loop as we move and are not really that worried about where it starts in relation to the game. So we simplify it a little and create this:

```
function moveBackground()
{
    background.x = -Camera.x3D*(Camera.perspective/6000);
}
```

21 If you test now, your background should loop seamlessly. And to the untrained eye, it all looks perfect. Sadly, it's not quite as simple as that. On your computer, on an iPhone 4 which has the resolution of 960 × 640, or on any device which has the same screen ratio the background will look correct. However, on an iPhone 5 where we have a wider screen we will actually see a gap occasionally on the left-hand side where the background hasn't correctly wrapped itself. This gap is because our Animate game scales itself so that it fits onto any size screen. Scaling is a very handy feature as it means our UI and enemies will always show, no matter the screen size or orientation. On wider screens users get to see more of the game, so they have the benefit of possibly seeing more attacking ninjas that would perhaps be off screen on an iPhone 4. It is because they can see more of the sides that they then see the missing piece of the background because the coordinate 0,0 is no longer right on the left-hand side of the screen. Rather extra space has been added there, so the coordinates go into negative numbers. For example, on an iPhone 4 with a screen size of 960 × 640 the coordinate 0,0 will be the top left. This is because our game is also 960 × 640 in Animate and therefore no scaling has to be done. The iPhone 5's screen is 1136 × 640. Our game automatically gets centered on the screen, which means there are an extra 88 pixels to both the left and the right. We'll call these our **leftMargin** and our **rightMargin** although we won't mention the right again. However, because of the 88 pixel **leftMargin**, the coordinate −88,0 is actually the top left of the screen on an iPhone 5 in landscape mode.

Stage 6 (cont.)

22 We need to modify our **moveBackground** function to account for whether the screen is more widescreen than an iPhone 4. We work out what our **leftMargin** is. There are many, many different screen ratios, so it's no good just knowing what each screen is. We need a way to work it out. First we work out the screen ratio of our phone/handset.

```
var screenRatio = stage.fullScreenWidth/stage.fullScreenHeight;
```

23 We know our default screen ratio is 1.5 (960/640). We only need to worry about whether the **leftMargin** ratio is bigger than 1.5:

```
var leftMargin:int = 0;
if(screenRatio>1.5) leftMargin = 640*(1.5-screenRatio)/2;
```

25 Almost there! There is one other slight issue. We want the web version of our game to be able to be distributed to gaming portals, but not all of them will embed it in their site at the correct ratio. However, because the web game won't be fullscreen, we can't use the **fullScreenWidth** and **fullScreenHeight** properties to work out our **screenRatio**. Instead we have to use the **stageWidth** and **stageHeight** properties. We look at our Stage **displayState** property to see if the game is running in fullscreen (on a device) or not (web). The bad news is because our game is created using scaling (so that it will scale to fit any device nicely and the UI stays centered, etc.), **stageWidth** and **stageHeight** always return 960 and 640, our default width and height, no matter what size the portal has made the game on their website. However, there is an easy solution. We sneakily tell Animate that we don't want to have scaling any more, which then cheats Animate into working correctly and being able to accurately get **stageWidth** and **stageHeight**. We then quickly work out the **screenRatio** and then tell Animate, "Sorry, we actually do want scaling after all." So finally, our **moveBackground** function becomes:

```
function moveBackground()
{
	var screenRatio:Number;
	if(stage.displayState == StageDisplayState.NORMAL)
	{
		stage.scaleMode = StageScaleMode.NO_SCALE;
		screenRatio = stage.stageWidth/stage.stageHeight;
		stage.scaleMode = StageScaleMode.SHOW_ALL;
	}
	else
	{
		screenRatio = stage.fullScreenWidth/stage.fullScreenHeight;
	}
	var leftMargin:int = 0;
	if(screenRatio>1.5) leftMargin = 640*(1.5-screenRatio)/2;
	background.x = -Camera.x3D*(Camera.perspective/6000);
	while(background.x<-background.width/2+leftMargin) background.x+=background.width/2;
	while(background.x>leftMargin) background.x-=background.width/2;
}
```

24 We can use the leftMargin in our while loops:

```
while(background.x<-background.width/2+leftMargin) background.x += background.width/2;
while(background.x>leftMargin) background.x =background.width/2;
```

Music and Sound Effects

26 Download the ZIP file containing all of the example files for this book. In the Chapter 10 folder you will find all of the sound effects and music for this game courtesy of talented sound designer Tom McCaren of **www.tommccaren.co.uk**.

Import all of the sound effects and music into the library and give them AS Linkage names. We will use Linkage names that start with SFX (even for the music) so that it's easy to remember they are Sound Classes.

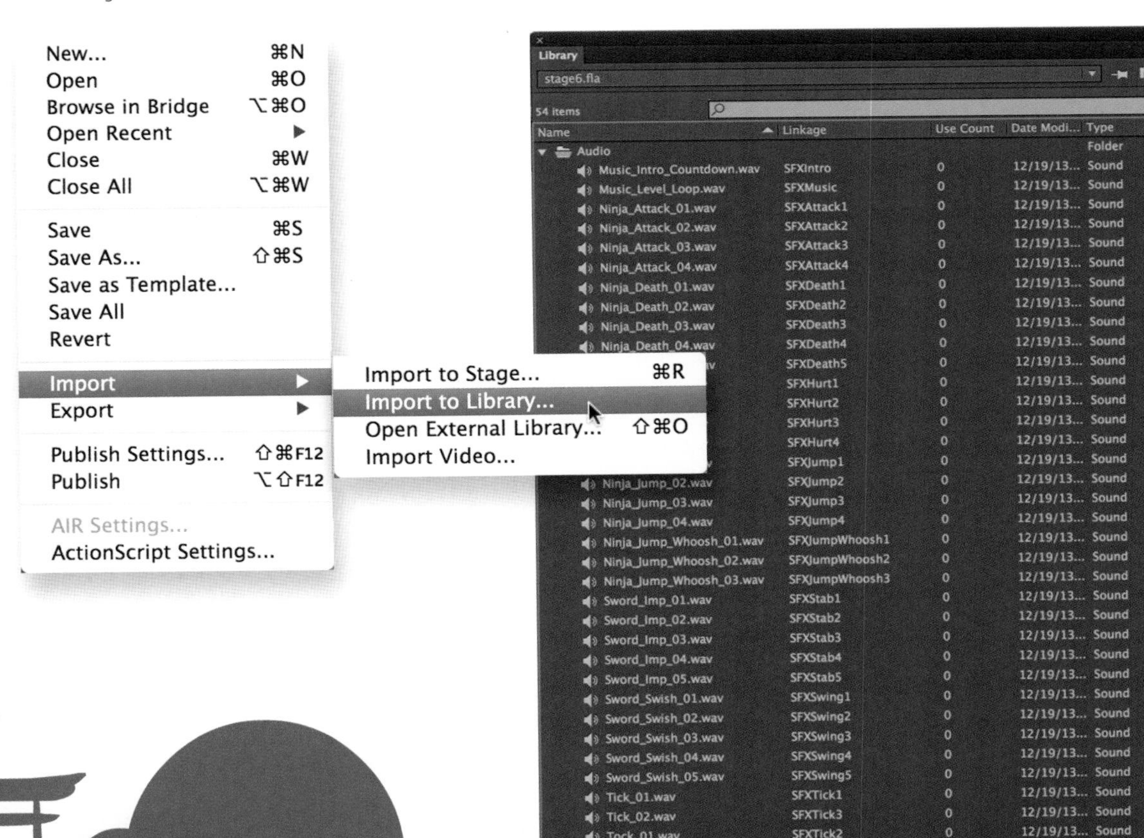

HOT TIP

For organization purposes, create a new folder within your Library (using the upper right corner drop-down menu) for all imported audio files. As seen in step 25, all imported sound files are in a folder named "Audio." Organizing files using folders helps keep your Library clean and organized.

Stage 6 (cont.)

27 By default, when we publish a. swf file, Animate will use relatively poor audio quality settings. You can change these in **File > Publish Settings**. For web games I find that **MP3, 64 kbps, Mono** gives a good balance between quality and file size.

If publishing for mobile though, particularly on older devices, it's actually best to select **Disable** from the Compression option in Sound Settings. Disabling this option will drastically increase your app file size but will give the best performance in terms of playing audio.

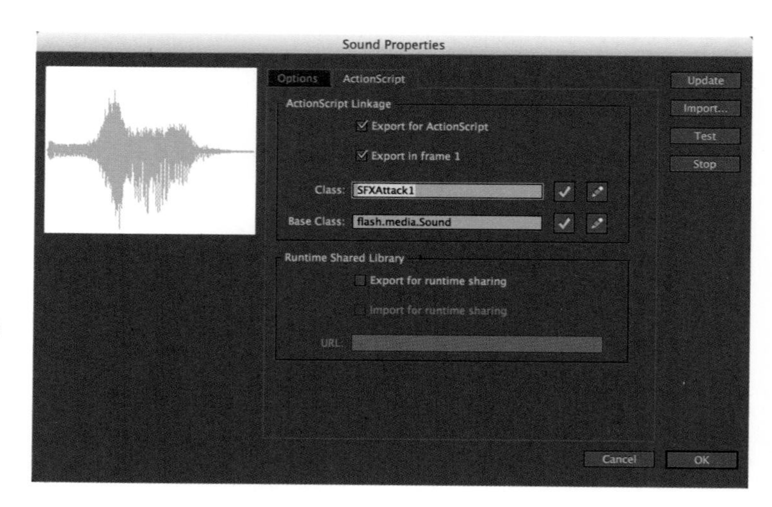

30 In AS3 whenever a sound is played, a new sound channel is created. Once **SoundChannel** is created, we have more control over the sound. We can monitor it, stop it, check it to see if the sound has finished, or adjust the volume of the sound as it is playing. In Chapter 8 we didn't need to worry about these sound channels, and on the whole we won't here either apart from a little trick we will use to get the music to start. As soon as the **introSFX** has finished and also on Android devices if the game is minimized, we need to make sure the music stops. So let's start the audio!

```
function startAudio():void
{
        if(!musicChannel)
        {
                musicChannel = intro.play();
                musicChannel.addEventListener(Event.SOUND_COMPLETE, playMusic)
        }
}

startAudio();
```

28 Give or take a few empty lines, we're getting close to 300 lines of code in our Timeline now. This amount of code is over double what we had at the start of Stage 2 when we decided to use Classes. What we're going to do now will be very frowned upon by most developers. In fact they will already be gnashing their teeth at our use of the Timeline to house code. But for simplicity sake, we're going to add a new layer in our Timeline, name it **Audio Code** and add more code into it.

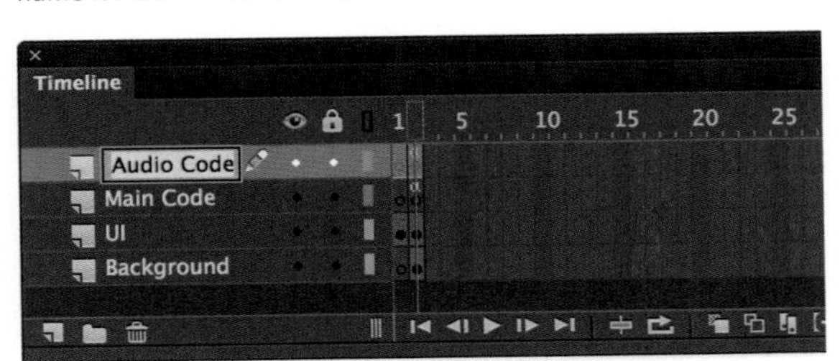

29 You may have noticed that for a lot of the sounds, there are multiple versions, four to five of each sound. We use multiple versions to give a slight variation on each sound effect so that the audio doesn't become too repetitive to the player. Let's start with the simple sounds though, the ones with only one version. In the new **Audio Code** layer, add the code:

```
var intro:SFXIntro = new SFXIntro();
var fight:SFXFight = new SFXFight();
var gameoverSFX:SFXGameover = new SFXGameover();
var music:SFXMusic = new SFXMusic();
var musicChannel:SoundChannel;
```

This initial block of code has initiated but won't start playing four sounds, three sound effects, and one music track. The last line sets up a **SoundChannel**.

31 We create a **startAudio** function that starts playing our 3, 2, 1 countdown intro sound effect, but then also adds a listener to that sound channel to see when it is complete. When that happens it will call the **playMusic** function which we need to write:

```
function playMusic(e:Event):void
{
        musicChannel.removeEventListener(Event.SOUND_COMPLETE,playMusic);
        musicChannel = music.play(0,9999);
        playSound(fight);
}
```

This function tells the **musicChannel** we don't need to worry about listening for when the sound has completed playing. Notice the 9999, in the **music.play()** command. This number tells the sound to repeat 9999 times before stopping. This setting is potentially a bug as it will eventually mean our music will stop playing if someone plays the game long enough, but as our music track is almost a minute long that's over 150 hours of looping music—pretty much a week. So it's not something we need to worry about, especially as we'll restart the music after our 99-second **gameplay** time anyway.

Stage 6 (cont.)

32 Note the last line of our **playMusic** function is a call to a new function **playSound**. Let's add to that:

```
function playSound(sound):void
{
        sound.play();
}
```

We should be able to test our game, hear the intro countdown with music start, and have the intro followed seamlessly by the full music track and the fight sound effect.

33 Let's get more complicated. Underneath our line **var musicChannel:SoundChannel;** add

```
var swordSounds:Array = new Array();
swordSounds.push(new SFXSwing1());
swordSounds.push(new SFXSwing2());
swordSounds.push(new SFXSwing3());
swordSounds.push(new SFXSwing4());
swordSounds.push(new SFXSwing5());
```

What we have done is made a small Array containing five Sword Swinging sound effects. Let's add a function that will play one of them:

```
function swordSFX():void
{
        playSound(swordSounds);
}
```

35 Finally, we need to call our **swordSFX** function from somewhere. Let's open up our **Player.as** Class. In our **checkEnemies** function at the bottom before the closing } add

```
timeline.swordSFX();
```

A sword sound should be played whenever you swing your sword.

36 But why do we call the **swordSFX** from **Player.as** and not from **Ninja.as** in our attack function? Surely that would then mean that both the player and the enemy ninjas make use of our lovely sword swing sound effect. Well, we want our **swordSFX** to only play if the sword does not hit an enemy. If it hits an enemy we want a different set of sound effects to play.

There are three different types of sounds we will want to play depending on what happens when we swing our sword: the normal swish which we'll call type 0, an impact when we hit an enemy which we'll call type 1, and a death sound if that hit is the final blow which we'll call type 2. In our **Player Class**, at the top of our **checkEnemies** function before the "for each" line add

```
var swordSFXType:int = 0;
```

34 Our **playSound** function is expecting a normal sound to **play()**, but we are passing it an Array of five sounds. So let's modify our **playSound** function:

```
function playSound(sound):void
{
        if(sound is Array) sound = sound[int(Math.random()*sound.length)];
        sound.play();
}
```

What we have done is checked to see if what is being passed is an Array, and if it is, then it selects one of the sounds at random from within the Array to play.

37 Then after our **enemy.hurt()** line inside the **for** loop and before the **timeline.updateScore()**, insert the following code:

```
enemy.hurt();
if(enemy.life>0) swordSFXType = 1;
else swordSFXType = 2;
timeline.updateScore();
```

38 We then modify our **timeline.swordSFX()** line to become

```
timeline.swordSFX(swordSFXType,this);
```

Not only do we pass our **swordSFX** function the type of effect to play, but we also pass it "this" which is our Player character. Why? Find out in Step 40!

Stage 6 (cont.)

39 Back to our Audio Loop layer in the main Timeline. First let's add our stab, hurt, and death sounds:

```
var stabSounds:Array = new Array();
stabSounds.push(new SFXStab1());
stabSounds.push(new SFXStab2());
stabSounds.push(new SFXStab3());
stabSounds.push(new SFXStab4());
stabSounds.push(new SFXStab5());

var hurtSounds:Array = new Array();
hurtSounds.push(new SFXHurt1());
hurtSounds.push(new SFXHurt2());
hurtSounds.push(new SFXHurt3());
hurtSounds.push(new SFXHurt4());

var deathSounds:Array = new Array();
deathSounds.push(new SFXDeath1());
deathSounds.push(new SFXDeath2());
deathSounds.push(new SFXDeath3());
deathSounds.push(new SFXDeath4());
deathSounds.push(new SFXDeath5());
```

40 Then let's modify our **swordSFX** function:

```
function swordSFX(type:int, from:Base3D):void
{
        if(type == 0)
        {
                playSound(swordSounds, from);
        }
        else if(type == 1)
        {
                playSound(stabSounds, from);
                playSound(hurtSounds, from);
        }
        else if(type == 2)
        {
                playSound(deathSounds, from);
        }
}
```

Notice that if the sound effect type is 1, meaning that your sword has connected to an enemy but not killed them, we play two different sounds: the sword stab sound as well as a hurt ouch sound.

42 If you test it now, one thing you will notice is that the death sounds aren't quite so loud compared to the other sounds. We could take these audio files into some audio editing software to increase their volume and then reimport into Animate, but let's give them a volume boost from within Animate itself. Modify the **playSound** function yet again to be

```
function playSound(sound:*, from:Base3D = null, volumeMultiplier:Number = 1):void
{
        if(sound is Array) sound = sound[int(Math.random()*sound.length)];
        if(!from) volumeController.volume=1;
        else volumeController.volume=.125+400/from.z3D; volumeController.volume*=volumeMultiplier;
        sound.play(0,0,volumeController);
}
```

Then go up to our **swordSFX** function and change the **deathSounds** line to be

```
playSound(deathSounds,from,3);
```

This code will make **deathSounds** play three times their volume, which should certainly be loud enough to be heard above any other sounds.

41 We need to modify our **playSound** function again to handle this new **from** object, which if you remember is our Player. But first, why do we actually want to know where the sound is being triggered? Because, as our player moves away from the **camera** we want the sound effect to be quieter. So the **playSound** function needs to know how far an object is from the camera and adjust the volume of the sound accordingly. First we need to create a volume controller from a **SoundTransform** Object as we use it to transform sound. At the top of your **Audio Code**, place

```
var volumeController:SoundTransform = new SoundTransform();
```

Let's modify **playSound** to make use of it:

```
function playSound(sound, from:Base3D = null):void
{
        if(sound is Array) sound = sound[int(Math.random()*sound.length)];
        if(!from) volumeController.volume=1;
        else volumeController.volume=.125+400/from.z3D;
        sound.play(0,0,volumeController);
}
```

Because **playSound** is also called with our **Fight** SFX which isn't associated with a Ninja, we need to allow for our **from** variable to be nonexistent (or null). Our new line checks whether the sound comes from **from**. If so, it sets the volume to be default which is 1. If the sound has come from a Ninja, we use the z3D value of that Ninja to work out the volume.

43 We have sound effects associated with our player, but what about the enemies? Open **Enemy.as** and find the **checkPlayer** function, and we mirror what we have done to **Player.as**:

```
public function checkPlayer():void
{
        var attackReachX:int = 280;
        var attackReachZ:int = 150;
        var attackForce:int = 80;
        var swordSFXType:int = 0;
        var distanceX:Number = timeline.player.x3D - x3D;
        var distanceZ:Number = timeline.player.z3D - z3D;
        if(distanceX * direction > 0 && Math.abs(distanceZ) < attackReachZ && Math.abs(distanceX) < attackReachX)
        {
                var angle:Number = Math.atan2(distanceZ,distanceX);
                timeline.player.forceX = attackForce * Math.cos(angle);
                timeline.player.forceZ = attackForce * Math.sin(angle);
                timeline.player.hurt();
                if(timeline.player.life>0) swordSFXType = 1; else swordSFXType = 2;
        }
        timeline.swordSFX(swordSFXType, this);
}
```

Stage 6 (cont.)

44 There are two final things we need to do for the **swordSFX**. You may notice that if you run away from the enemies, you still hear them loud and clear. So we make a new function to determine if the sound effects for the enemies are allowed. Add this code to the bottom of the **Audio Code** layer:

```
function allowSFX(from):Boolean
{
	if(from.x<-100 || from.x>1060) return false;
	return true;
}
```

47 Now we need one more type of sound for both our player and enemy ninjas: a jump sound. As with the sword sound, we have a one in three chance for a jump-type grunt sound to play, too. Unlike sword though, we don't need to have a type. Because our whoosh sounds are quite loud, we actually use a value of 0.4 for the volumeMultiplier to reduce the sound. This reduces the sound volume to 40% for the jump whoosh sounds.

```
var jumpSounds:Array = new Array();
jumpSounds.push(new SFXJump1());
jumpSounds.push(new SFXJump2());
jumpSounds.push(new SFXJump3());
jumpSounds.push(new SFXJump4());

var jumpWhooshSounds:Array = new Array();
jumpWhooshSounds.push(new SFXJumpWhoosh1());
jumpWhooshSounds.push(new SFXJumpWhoosh2());
jumpWhooshSounds.push(new SFXJumpWhoosh3());

function jumpSFX(from:Base3D):void
{
	if(allowSFX(from))
	{
		if(int(Math.random()*3)==1)playSound(jumpSounds,from);
		playSound(jumpWhooshSounds,from,.4);
	}
}
```

45 And finally, let's add a bit of extra random sound to the attack, a nice occasional grunt from a Ninja as he swings his sword. The below code shows both the check to see if a SFX is allowed and the new line which gives a one in three chance to add a grunt (attack sound):

```
function swordSFX(type:int, from:Base3D):void
{
    if(allowSFX(from))
    {
        if(int(Math.random()*3)==1) playSound(attackSounds, from);
        if(type == 0)
        {
            playSound(swordSounds,from);
        }
        else if(type ==1)
        {
            playSound(stabSounds,from);
            playSound(hurtSounds,from);
        }
        else if(type == 2)
        {
            playSound(deathSounds,from,3);
        }
    }
}
```

46 For **attackSounds**, we have a new array:

```
var attackSounds:Array = new Array()
attackSounds.push(new SFXAttack1());
attackSounds.push(new SFXAttack2());
attackSounds.push(new SFXAttack3());
attackSounds.push(new SFXAttack4());
```

48 Because we don't need to work out the type of jump sound as we did the sword sound, we can put the trigger for the **jumpSFX** in our main **Ninja.as** Class so both the Player and Enemy can trigger it. Open up Ninja.as, and in the **jump()** function above the **Ninja.gotoAndPlay("jump");** line add

```
timeline.jumpSFX(this);
```

49 There are two more types of sounds we want to include, a game over and ticking clock noises for the last 10 seconds remaining. We already have our **gameoverSFX** sound initiated, and we already have a function in our main code layer that gets called when **gameover** happens, so we modify this function to include two lines:

```
function gameover():void
{
    if(!gameIsOver)
    {
        ui.gameoverMC.visible=true;
        ui.gameoverMC.scoreTF.text=ui.scoreTF.text;
        gameIsOver = true;
        player.stopMoving();
        stage.addEventListener(MouseEvent.CLICK, resetGame)
        musicChannel.stop();
        playSound(gameoverSFX);
    }
}
```

Note that the first line will stop our music from playing as we don't want that to continue. The second line plays our **gameoverSFX**.

Stage 6 (cont.)

50 We then need to make sure we start the music again when the user hits "try again." At the end of our **resetGame** function, add these two lines:

```
musicChannel=null
startAudio();
```

51 The Tick sounds are a little more complicated. Back in our **Audio Code** layer, add the following to initiate the four tick sound effects and a little counter that we will use to determine which of the four ticks to play for each of the remaining 10 seconds:

```
var tick1:SFXTick1 = new SFXTick1();
var tick2:SFXTick2 = new SFXTick2();
var tick3:SFXTick3 = new SFXTick3();
var tick4:SFXTick4 = new SFXTick4();
var tickCounter:int = 1;
```

Then add a **tickSound** function:

```
function tickSound()
{
        playSound(this["tick"+tickCounter])
        tickCounter++
        if(tickCounter>4) tickCounter=1
}
```

54 In our Main Code Layer, add to the existing **deactivate** function:

```
function deactivate(e:Event):void
{
        paused = true;
        stopAudio();
}
```

55 And then add to our **activate** function:

```
function activate(e:Event):void
{
paused = false;
startAudio();
}
```

52 To trigger the **tickSound** on each second, in the Main Code Layer we go down to the line **timer-=1/30;** and sandwich it between these lines:

```
var oldTimer:int=timer;
timer-=1/30;
if(Math.ceil(timer)<10 && int(timer)!=oldTimer)
tickSound();
```

If we didn't use **oldTimer** then we would get a tick sound happening on every single frame which would be 30 times for every 1 second.

53 There's one last tweak for sounds. As previously mentioned on Android devices when the game is minimized, the music still plays which we don't want. So add this function to our **Audio Code** Layer:

```
function stopAudio():void
{
        if(musicChannel) musicChannel.stop();
        musicChannel = null;
}
```

Congratulations! If all went well, you were able to build an interactive game complete with animation, particle effects, sound effects, and music using Adobe Animate CC! Feel free to use this game example as a template and get creative! By changing the graphics and code, you could easily expand upon what we've already started.

This chapter would not have been possible if not for the amazing work and dedication from David Crawford himself. Not only did he write the code and set up the Animate files, he painstakingly documented each step for this book. Without his talent and efforts, this example may not have been possible.

Special thanks goes out to Tom McCaren as well for his awesome sound effects and music. Tom brought this fun little game to a whole new level with his sound design, and I can't thank him enough.

As for the ninja, we have our own plans to continue working on this game by adding exploding bunnies, more animations, effects, and maybe even levels.

SHORTCUTS
MAC WIN BOTH

I'd Like to Thank...

VECTOR ILLUSTRATION: MYRA FERGUSON

I HAVE SEVERAL FRIENDS WHO HAVE WRITTEN INSTRUCTIONAL BOOKS OVER THE YEARS. I remember early in my career being asked if I'd be interested in writing one. Yes, of course! But I didn't feel qualified—despite my education and experience. I was under the misconception that I needed to be proficient in every aspect of a piece of software to truly be qualified to write about it, so I shied away from pursuing the idea. I'm not sure what gave me that impression. I couldn't have been more wrong.

Although I do know much more about a number of applications and have a lot more experience now, it wasn't any single accomplishment that led to my contributions to this book. It was the support and encouragement of my family and friends and the enjoyment I get from sharing the techniques I've discovered.

I am indebted to Chris Georgenes for not only being a great friend but also a mentor as he brought me along to help with technical editing on *Pushing Pixels* and previous editions of *How to Cheat in Adobe Flash*. Now that he's having me take the helm on this series, I am even more grateful to him for this opportunity.

And thank you, readers, for your interest in Adobe Animate and trying out some new techniques. I hope that you found them useful, fun, and relevant to your projects. If you have questions about this book, please let me know on the Facebook page at www.facebook.com/htcianimate. It's my hope that I can continue to bring you innovative tips and attainable results.

Index

D

E

F

N

O